# Computer Applications in Production and Engineering

## IFIP – The International Federation for Information Processing

IFIP was founded in 1960 under the auspices of UNESCO, following the First World Computer Congress held in Paris the previous year. An umbrella organization for societies working in information processing, IFIP's aim is two-fold: to support information processing within its member countries and to encourage technology transfer to developing nations. As its mission statement clearly states,

> IFIP's mission is to be the leading, truly international, apolitical organization which encourages and assists in the development, exploitation and application of information technology for the benefit of all people.

IFIP is a non-profitmaking organization, run almost solely by 2500 volunteers. It operates through a number of technical committees, which organize events and publications. IFIP's events range from an international congress to local seminars, but the most important are:

- the IFIP World Computer Congress, held every second year;
- open conferences;
- working conferences.

The flagship event is the IFIP World Computer Congress, at which both invited and contributed papers are presented. Contributed papers are rigorously refereed and the rejection rate is high.

As with the Congress, participation in the open conferences is open to all and papers may be invited or submitted. Again, submitted papers are stringently refereed.

The working conferences are structured differently. They are usually run by a working group and attendance is small and by invitation only. Their purpose is to create an atmosphere conducive to innovation and development. Refereeing is less rigorous and papers are subjected to extensive group discussion.

Publications arising from IFIP events vary. The papers presented at the IFIP World Computer Congress and at open conferences are published as conference proceedings, while the results of the working conferences are often published as collections of selected and edited papers.

Any national society whose primary activity is in information may apply to become a full member of IFIP, although full membership is restricted to one society per country. Full members are entitled to vote at the annual General Assembly, National societies preferring a less committed involvement may apply for associate or corresponding membership. Associate members enjoy the same benefits as full members, but without voting rights. Corresponding members are not represented in IFIP bodies. Affiliated membership is open to non-national societies, and individual and honorary membership schemes are also offered.

# Computer Applications in Production and Engineering

## IFIP TC5 International Conference on Computer Applications in Production and Engineering (CAPE '97)
## 5–7 November 1997, Detroit, Michigan, USA


Edited by

**Frank Plonka**
*Wayne State University*
*Michigan*
*USA*

and

**Gustav Olling**
*Chrysler Corporation*
*Michigan*
*USA*



SPRINGER-SCIENCE+BUSINESS MEDIA, B.V.

First edition 1997


Originally published by Chapman & Hall in 1997
MyCopy version of the original edition 1997

DOI 10.1007/978-0-387-35291-6



A catalogue record for this book is available from the British Library

Printed on permanent acid-free text paper, manufactured in accordance with ANSI/NISO Z39.48-1992 and ANSI/NISO Z39.48-1984 (Permanence of Paper).
www.springer.com/mycopy

# CONTENTS

## Preface

In the latter half of the 20th century, forces have conspired to make the human community, at last, global. The easing of tensions between major nations, the expansion of trade to worldwide markets, widespread travel and cultural exchange, pervasive high-speed communications and automation, the explosion of knowledge, the streamlining of business, and the adoption of flexible methods have changed the face of manufacturing itself, and of research and education in manufacturing. The acceptance of the continuous improvement process as a means for organizations to respond quickly and effectively to swings in the global market has led to the demand for individuals educated in a broad range of cultural, organizational, and technical fields and capable of absorbing and adapting required knowledge and training throughout their careers. No longer will manufacturing research and education focus on an industrial sector or follow a national trend, but rather will aim at enabling international teams of companies to cooperate in rapidly designing, prototyping, and manufacturing products.

The successful enterprise of the 21st century will be characterized by an organizational structure that efficiently responds to customer demands and changing global circumstances, a corporate culture that empowers employees at all levels and encourages constant communication among related groups, and a technological infrastructure that fully supports process improvement and integration. In changing itself to keep abreast of the broader transformation in manufacturing, the enterprise must look first at its organization and culture, and thereafter at supporting technologies.

The Sixth International Conference for Worldwide "Computer Applications in Production and Engineering," CAPE '97, was organized by the International Federation for Information Processing (IFIP) Technical Committee 5 (Computer Applications in Technology), co-sponsored by the Computer and Automation Systems Association of the Society of Manufacturing Engineers in cooperation with the North American Manufacturing Research Institution, and held in conjunction with AUTOFACT '97, Cobo Center, Detroit, Michigan, U.S.A.

The sessions were organized into 12 tracks: Production Definition and Data Management, Worldwide Supply Chain, Manufacturing Engineering Processes, Business Process Modeling, Process Planning, Manufacturing

Computer Applications in Production and Engineering. F. Plonka and G. Olling (Eds.)

System Design & Simulation, Process Control, Manufacturing Planning and Control, Technology 2 Methodologies Needed for Worldwide Production and Engineering, Knowledge Based Simulation and Planning, Technology 1 Enterprise Modeling and People Practices. The last day hosted the International Program Reports along with a Tools and Techniques for Collaborative Works session.

The conference brought together leading thinkers from industry, research and academia to discuss innovative concepts and methods for improving the competitive position of the manufacturing industry given the present cultural, economic, and technological environments.

On the whole, the conference opened a dialog between representatives of industry, research, and academia to collectively seek strategies that will make manufacturing successful in the year 2000 and to identify the kinds of talent and training that people will need to excel in their professions.

Improved quality, responsiveness to customers, process control and flexibility, and development of a suitably skilled workforce have become a determinant of global competitiveness in manufacturing. The integration necessary for excellence in these areas involves not just a reconciliation of the technical environments of CAD, CAE, CAM, and MIS, but also the integration and harmonious interaction between manufacturers, suppliers, and educators. The introduction of advanced manufacturing technology will seldom yield anticipated gains in flexibility and productivity without changes in the organization itself. Changes must be made in the attitudes and practices of managers and engineers to establish new relationships between manufacturers, suppliers, and educational institutions working toward a common goal.

Hopefully, this conference will serve as an encouragement for future TC5 activities focusing on fostering the dialog between practitioners, educators, and researchers.

On behalf of the International Organizing Committee, we thank all the people who contributed to the success of this conference.

Frank Plonka
Gustav Olling

# 1
# Towards Computer-Aided Rapid Product Realization

*G. J. Olling*
*Chrysler Corporation*
*800 Chrysler Drive CIMS: 483-05-01*
*Auburn Hills, MI 48326 USA*
*Tel: (248) 576-2788 Fax: (248) 576-2029*

**Extended Abstract**

During the closing of the twentieth century, U.S. based manufacturers are contending with an increasing number of international competitors. In pursuit of world-class manufacturing status, U.S. firms have come to realize that corporate commitment to quality and responsiveness to customers' demands are now the benchmarks of outstanding enterprises. Industry leaders distinguish themselves from competitors by the rapidity of their product introductions, striving for the highest possible quality at the lowest possible price. World-class manufacturing has become a continual improvement process focusing on the need to reduce lead time dramatically while continuing to innovate and assure quality.

In this climate of intensified global competition, the computer technology of manufacturing has flourished. Designers and engineers now use Computer-Aided Design and Engineering (CAD/CAE) tools to create three-dimensional images that can be shaded, analyzed, and optimized to refine the product design. Manufacturing engineers use Computer-Aided Manufacturing (CAM) systems for process planning, tool design, and machine programming. Administrators draw upon Management Information Systems (MIS) in production planning, production and inventory control, sales, research, and forecasting.

Computer-Integrated Manufacturing (CIM) is the ultimate goal in integrating CAD/CAE, CAM, and MIS technologies. However, the rapid development of these technologies has stretched and distorted the meaning of CIM. Today, the concept has elements of Group Technology (GT), Materials Requirements or Resource Planning (MRP), and Computer-Assisted Process Planning (CAPP). It also draws upon the fields of product design, production planning, and production control. In its implementation, CIM has been expressed in a tremendous number of specialized software packages developed by vendors with divergent perceptions of manufacturing and no great desire to integrate with on another.

Computer Applications in Production and Engineering. F. Plonka and G. Olling (Eds.)

The need to stay abreast of product and process innovation worldwide and to build a world-class manufacturing operation will require the creation of industrial systems that convey the states of markets, competition, technology and the ensemble of techniques and technologies that automate, integrate, and optimize the process of manufacturing, from innovation to customer response.

Since prevailing need will be for rapid adjustment to changing demand, the systems approach requires an organizational framework that is flexible and adaptive, employees at all levels that are knowledgeable about human relations, methods, tools, and the effective use of existing technologies.

The successful enterprise of the 21st century will be characterized by an organizational structure that efficiently responds to customer demands and changing global circumstances, a corporate culture that empowers employees at all levels and encourages constant communication among related groups, and a technological infrastructure that fully supports process improvement and integration. In changing itself to keep abreast of the broader transformation in manufacturing, the enterprise must look first at its organization and culture, and thereafter at supporting technologies. Too often, today, companies look for a quick fix of technology, throwing vast capital at its problems, only to find that its organization is still adhering to the same attitudes, methods, and schedules that caused the problems in the first place.

In the effort to achieve end-to-end integration, from the beginning of design to the completion of manufacturing, CAD data represents a critical resource. The ideal system would assure the integrity of CAD data by having everyone use the same integrated set of CAD/CAE/CAM tools, communicate over a single network, share a common database, and adhere to standard design practices.

The chief advantages of this uniform system would be to prevent the loss of design intent through the imperfect translation of data between systems, to eliminate the preparation of data before translation and the cleanup afterwards, and facilitate the implementation of concurrent engineering in product development and manufacturing divisions.

At Chrysler Corporation for example, we are pushing for a core-system solution to tighten the integration within the company and its many suppliers. A major concern is to minimize translation. Since competing CAD/CAM systems usually have differing approaches to data representation, translations between systems make arbitrary interpretations and compromises. In sensitive areas, such as the design of outer skins in automotive applications, translations do not preserve the original design intent and integrity well enough to produce a satisfactory product. Ultimately, the company would like to eliminate all intermediate forms, -- not only models from other CAD systems and the IGES files used to translate them, but physical bucks and mock-ups, clay models and background CAD models. Experience has shown that intermediate forms add delay and cost, create synchronization problems and confusion and lead to quality shortcomings.

A video is presented to illustrate the application of CAE/CAD/CAM technology throughout the entire vehicle development process, starting with Conceptual Design, spanning Body Engineering, Digital Model Assembly, Powertrain Design, Rapid Prototyping, and finishing with Stamping and Assembly.

With a CAD/CAM foundation in place, Chrysler's next challenge is to incorporate business, engineering, manufacturing and suppliers know-how into a single integrated system. A "next-generation" CAD/CAM system will be based on precise solids with a feature-based structure that stores information related to all the steps in the product development and manufacturing processes. The system will have parametric associativity so that design changes in one aspect of the product are automatically reflected in all other aspects of the product. Finally, the system will be generative. Through built-in intelligence, engineering analysis models, manufacturing process models, business cost models, and purchasing materials models will all be generated from the base product design model. This kind of generation will be possible because the product model will no longer be geometry represented in the computer but rather a section of the on-line product database.

Although Chrysler has made steady progress in the evolution of its products and process development technology, it has much work planned for future development. The goal is to achieve barrier-free, real-time access to shared, associative product development information throughout the enterprise. Perhaps the most important lesson Chrysler has learned in its transformation is that corporate-wide integration and simultaneous engineering are not objectives that a single company, even a large one, can accomplish alone. Such profound changes require broad cooperation among the company, its design and component suppliers, its software and services vendors, educators and researchers in nearby communities and at-large, its customer groups and related professional organizations.

**Key Words**

CAE, CAD, CAM, CIM, Product Realization

# 2

# Enhancing life-cycle integration through the application of Case-Based Reasoning to Quality Function Deployment

*D.A. Adams[1], C. Irgens[1], E. MacArthur[2] and B. Lees[3].*
*[1]Faculty of Engineering, The University of the West of England, Bristol, BS16 1QY*
*[2]Department of Mathematics and Statistics.*
*[3]Department of Computing and Information Systems.*
*[2,3] University of Paisley, High Street, Paisley, PA1 2BE, UK.*
*[1]Contact: David Adams, Email: adam-mm0@wpmail.paisley.ac.uk,*
*Phone: ++44 141 848 3553, Fax: ++44 141 848 3555.*

**Abstract**

Quality Function Deployment (QFD) is a product development methodology that is primarily aimed at increasing customer focus throughout the product development process. One benefit of this approach is a more structured and visible decision making process which spans a number of life-cycle activities. In this way QFD is often regarded as a facilitator of life-cycle engineering techniques such as Concurrent Engineering.

One of the problems of QFD, however, is the scalability of the methodology: it is often impractical to remain true to the principles of the methodology when developing anything but the simplest of products. This suggests that some form of computational support for the QFD methodology, which leads to a more effective application of the principles advocated by the methodology, could be beneficial. If this is achieved, the effectiveness of life-cycle engineering activities within the organization should be increased.

The paper describes a prototype system that applies an artificial intelligence technique known as Case-Based Reasoning (CBR) to the QFD methodology.

[1] D. A. Adams will remain at his Paisley (Dept. of Mechanical Engineering) address until Sept. 1997 despite being affiliated to The University of the West of England.

Computer Applications in Production and Engineering. F. Plonka and G. Olling (Eds.)

Through this approach it is possible to evaluate decisions made at an early stage of the product life cycle in terms of other life cycle activities based on previous experience.

The prototype builds upon previous work which has resulted in practical experience of the contribution to life cycle engineering activities offered by the approach. This is reported upon in the paper.

**Keywords**
Concurrent Engineering, Life-cycle integration, Case-Based Reasoning, Quality Function Deployment

## 1 INTRODUCTION

Quality Function Deployment (QFD) is a market driven design and development methodology for products and services to meet or exceed customers' needs and expectations (Prasad, 1996). The methodology was developed in 1966 in Japan by Yoji Akao. Akao defined QFD as being "a method for developing a design quality aimed at satisfying the consumer and then translating the consumers' demands into design targets and major quality assurance points to be used throughout the production stage." (Akao, 1990).

The first industrial application of QFD methodology occurred at Mitsubishi's Kobe shipyard in Japan in 1972. Motivation for use of QFD at Kobe arose from a necessity of the company's products (ocean transportation vessels) to meet the market's requirements of high quality products coupled with stringent government regulations (Prasad 1996). Since this initial use of QFD, the methodology has grown in popularity (if only recently) in the western world. For example, Ford, General Motors, Chrysler, AT&T, Proctor and Gamble, Hewlett-Packard, and Digital Equipment, have been reported (Prasad, 1996) to have used the methodology to some extent.

When successful, the benefits obtained from QFD practices have been reported as:

- increasing the level of team working including providing a communication platform for concurrent engineering (Prasad 1996, Sanchez et al 1993, Cohen 1995),
- reducing the time to market (ASQC/ASI 1992, Sanchez et al 1993),
- reducing the amount of re-work (Wilson and Greaves 1990), and
- increasing the quality of the product (Wilson and Greaves 1990, Aako 1990, Sullivan 1986, Hauser and Clausing 1988).

However, these benefits - or indeed successful adoption of QFD - are far from universal. Problems with QFD have arisen due to the subjectivity of decisions that are required in the process. This has been particularly evident at the first stage of the process where it is necessary to translate subjective customer statements into objective engineering measures (Sanchez et al 1993). Decisions taken at this stage are often found to be "arbitrary" and subject to the "whims" of the designer or design team (Franceschini and Rossetto 1995). Because of this, QFD can be a time consuming process (Cohen 1995) which can lead to a lack of the necessary (Akao 1990, Sullivan 1986) management and team buy-in. A further problem with QFD lies in the QFD paradox: although QFD is advocated as providing a platform for team working and concurrent engineering, the methodology is by definition a sequential stepwise process (see next section). Concurrent engineering, therefore, is not supported by the process of QFD itself but rather by the multifunctional team based activity that is required in the initial stages of the process. It is our experience that some organizations either fail to realize this, or realize this but do not have the necessary skills, expertise, or information infrastructure to apply the methodology successfully.

These issues have lead to the development of a computer-based approach primarily aimed at alleviating these difficulties in the QFD process. The approach utilizes Case-Based Reasoning techniques and is based upon the hypothesis that, if experience from QFD developments can be captured in some useful form, then this experience can be reused in future QFD developments that are in some way similar to previous developments. This will reduce the severity of some of the above problems by giving QFD decision makers a starting point from which to base their decisions based on what was done in similar situations. Therefore, when presented with a set of customer requirements to be satisfied, the QFD team will have available to them an easily accessible body of experience which may provide direction and advice based upon the solution steps, i.e. the QFD matrices, and rationale that were taken to achieve similar requirements in the past.

It would be unwise, however, to blindly use previous solution steps without some form of evaluation. The approach, therefore, utilizes feedback information as an evaluation of the solution based upon the solution's use. As will be discussed in the next section, this feedback information can come from a number of life-cycle stages with the final feedback coming from the customer. By utilizing feedback at the early stages of QFD, the approach effectively promotes and enhances life-cycle integration within the product development life-cycle.

# 2 QUALITY FUNCTION DEPLOYMENT

## 2.1 QFD process

In general, the process of QFD comprises four stages: Product Planning, Design Deployment, Process Planning, and Production Planning (Sullivan 1986, Ranky 1994, Sanchez 1993). Each of these stages consists of a translation process between the input to the stage and the output from the stage. The output from one stage is the input to the following stage. The initial input is the customer requirements with the final output being a set of production plans. These production plans should result in a manufactured product that reflects the customer's voice. The process is shown in Figure 1.

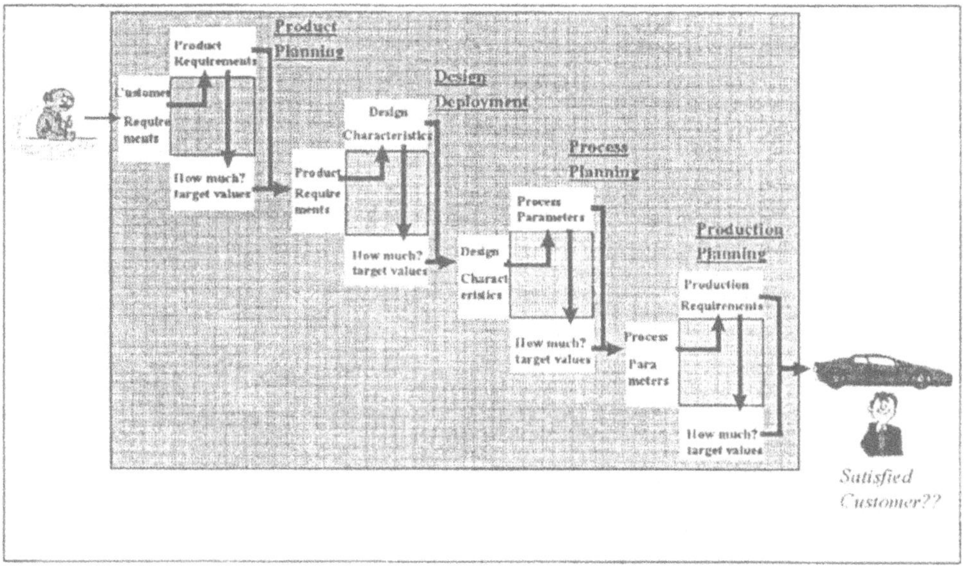


**Figure 1** The QFD Process.

This process should be conducted by a multidisciplinary team with the assistance of a number of matrix-based charts. These charts serve as the means by which the customers' wants and needs are propagated though the product life-cycle and also as a focus for team activities. A matrix typically used at the first stage of the process, although applicable to each stage, is the House of Quality (Hauser and Clausing 1988, Sullivan 1986, Cohen 1995, Prasad 1996). This is shown in Figure 2. Use of the House of Quality (HoQ) is as follows (Adams et al 1996):

1. Obtain Customer Requirements and their degree of importance. ('Whats')
2. Determine any trade-offs between the customer requirements. (Requirements matrix)
3. Determine the required product characteristics. ('Hows')
4. Determine the relationships between the 'Whats' and the 'Hows'. This is called the *Relationship Matrix*.
5. Determine any trade-offs that may exist between product characteristics. This is done in the 'roof' of the HoQ and is known as the *Correlations Matrix*.

6. Determine product goals or 'How Much'. In this area two values are derived. The first of these is a goal value for the particular product characteristic and the second is an importance weighting illustrating how important the achievement of the product characteristic is to achieving the customer requirements

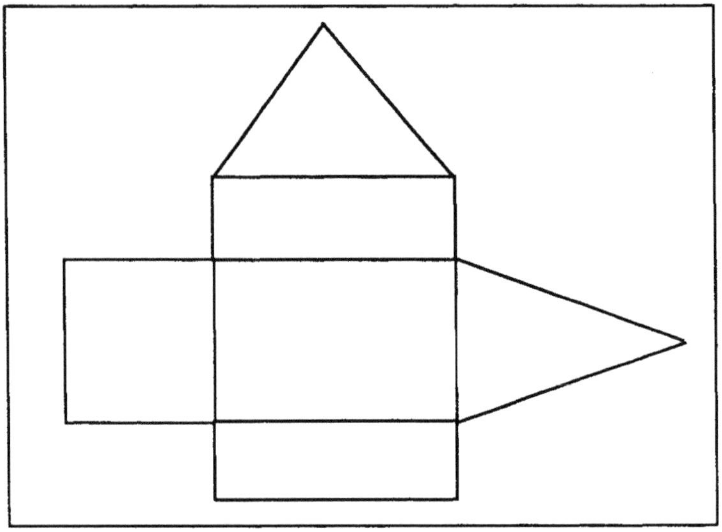

**Figure 2** The House of Quality

The output from the HoQ, therefore, is a set of product characteristics with their target values and importance weightings. If the first stage has been conducted properly and thoroughly, by a multifunctional team, who understand both the customer and the capabilities of the organization, then the set of product characteristics should reflect the customer requirements and have all potential engineering bottleneck areas identified (Akao 1990). If this is the case, then the remainder of the development should incur no unforeseen difficulties. This, however, seldom occurs which results either in 'bad' decisions being taken downstream because of inappropriate product characteristics being assigned or back-tracking to previous stages to make changes. This process results in a body of feedback information - the flow of which is not modeled by the traditional QFD process shown in Figure 1 - which could be used beneficially in future QFD processes if captured and utilized.

## 2.2 Life-cycle integration in QFD

As mentioned above, there is normally a significant amount of feedback information which occurs informally within the QFD process. Possible feedback routes are shown in Figure 3.

As indicated in Figure 3, each stage of QFD - apart from the first one - could have feedback concerning any or all of the preceding stages. For example, problems discovered in the process planning stage may be due to decisions made in the design deployment stage. However, the decisions made in the design deployment stage are linked to the output from the first stage of the process which means that the decisions undertaken in this stage may be affected. The further the development progresses, the more possibilities for feedback occurs, until the product is eventually released onto the market. At this point the possibilities for feedback come from all internal sources as well as the external source of the customer. This feedback will be concerned with a deviation between what was expected and what was delivered. For the customer this will be a deviation from the expectations of the product and what was delivered, whilst internal sources of feedback will be concerned with a deviation with the expected output from the preceding stage and what was presented.

Each stage of the QFD process has as its customers all downstream activities as well as the consumer of the product. Making this more formal, (Prasad 1996) considers "voice of the customer" data ($D_{voc}$) to be a function of "internal customers" ($D_{ic}$), "external customers" ($D_{ec}$), and "past and future customers" ($D_{p\&f}$). Prasad expresses this as:

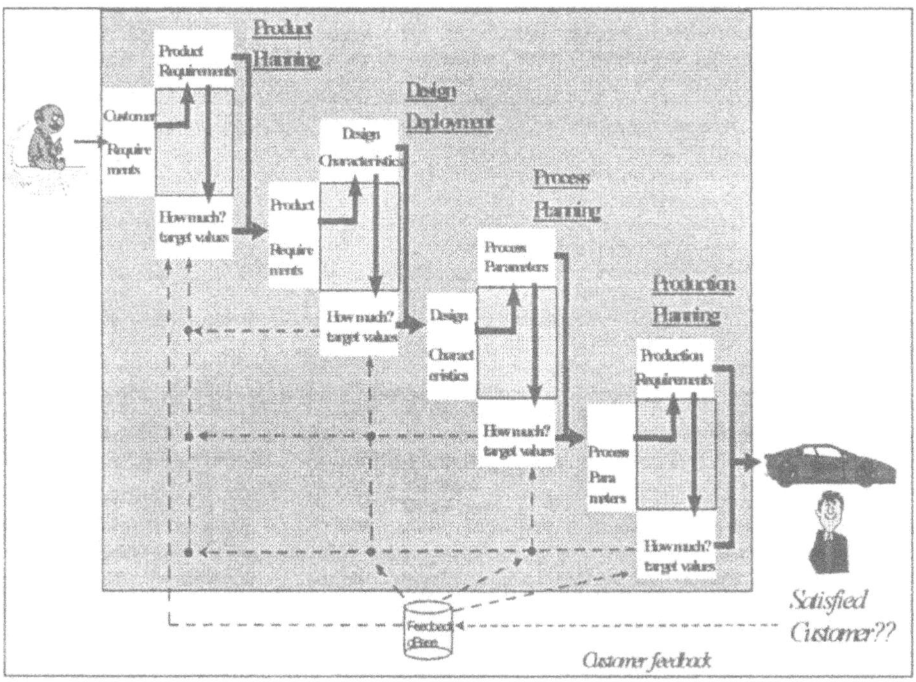


**Figure 3 QFD with Feedback**

$$D_{voo} \equiv f[D_{ic}, D_{ec}, D_{p\&f}]. \quad (1)$$

We extend this formalism by decomposing the internal and external customer data as follows:

$$D_{ic}, D_{ec} \equiv f[D_{pr}, D_{ps}], \quad (2)$$

where $D_{pr}$ relates to present customer (both internal and external) data, and $D_{ps}$ relates to past customer data. The past customer data can then be further decomposed to:

$$D_{ps} \equiv f[D_r, D_s, D_f], \quad (3)$$

where $D_r$ relates to past requirements, $D_s$ relates to past solutions, and $D_f$ relates to past feedback.

By storing the past information, comprising the past requirements, past solutions and associated feedback, it is possible to use this information in making decisions about present requirements and their solutions. In this way downstream activities can be incorporated effectively into decision making at the initial stages of the product development life-cycle based on experience. In theory, therefore, this helps the QFD team take account of all life-cycle stages. The problem, however, is establishing similarities between past and present customer (internal and external) requirements. A computational technique known as Case-Based Reasoning offers significant potential to this approach.

## 3 CASE-BASED REASONING

### 3.1 Background

Case-based reasoning (CBR) is an artificial intelligence technique that has its roots in cognitive science research and the role of "remindings" in human reasoning (Schank 1982). The technique concentrates on the use of specific problem solving experiences in the solution of new - but similar - problems. Basically, CBR utilizes the characteristics of a problem situation to facilitate a "reminding" to a previous problem situation, or experience, that has similar characteristics. The solution to the previous problem is then reused either as a complete solution to the new problem or as a starting point to a new solution. For an general introduction to CBR see (Aamodt 1995, Kolodner 1993, Leake 1996, Watson 1995).

As an approach to computational reasoning, CBR has many advantages (Leake 1996, Watson 1995) which make it attractive. More interesting, however, are the benefits that successful implementation of CBR can offer the host organization. Althoff et al (Althoff et al 1995) have identified the following potential benefits of utilizing CBR within an organizational setting:

- delivering more consistent decisions throughout the organization (assuming the system is used universally);
- preserving the know-how of specialists by capturing their experience;
- transferring experience from the skilled specialist to the novice;
- building a form of corporate memory by sharing individual experience.

These benefits make CBR an ideal instrument for implementing the approach to QFD and, in turn, the integration of the life-cycle that has been discussed. A more detailed overview of how CBR is conducted is now given.

## 3.2 The CBR Process

The process of CBR is described in (Aamodt and Plaza 1994) as the CBR cycle. This is shown in Figure 4 and involves the following steps:

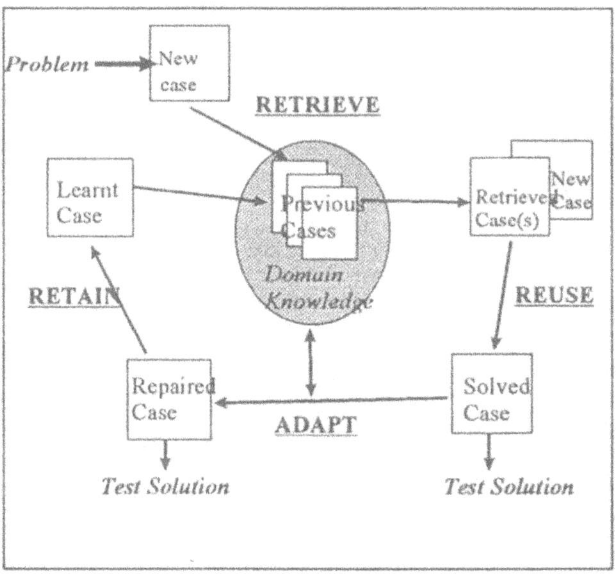


**Figure 4 - The CBR Cycle (Aamodt & Plaza)**

1. **Retrieve** the most similar case(s) by using some form of similarity assessment measure.
2. **Reuse** the solution(s) in the retrieved case(s) as a starting point for solving the new problem. Test the solution at this point to evaluate the solutions worth.
3. **Adapt** the proposed solution in order to solve the new problem. Continually test and adapt the solution until a satisfactory solution is achieved. This may be aided by a body of domain knowledge.
4. **Retain** the significant parts of this experience for use in future problem solving.

Any implementation of Case-Based Reasoning must take into consideration the above aspects. Each of these has attracted significant amounts of research activity from the computer science and cognitive science research communities. Discussion of these issues is out with the scope of this paper, however, the interested reader is directed to (Kolodner 1993).

A fundamental consideration in CBR, is the composition of the "case". Although this is application specific, the general composition of a case is described below.

## 3.3 Case content

A useful definition of a case is given in (Kolodner 1993):

"A case is a contextualised piece of knowledge representing an experience that teaches a lesson fundamental to achieving the goals of the reasoner." (Kolodner 1993)

A case is considered to be a specific experience which is internally representable by a computational machine. A case-base or case library is a collection of cases. It is from this library of cases, and in turn the specific cases themselves, that the reasoning in the process is facilitated. A critical factor, therefore, in the effectiveness of a CBR system, is the contents of each case which makes up the library.

In order to remain true to the definition given above, it is suggested (Kolodner 1993) that each case should consist of three major parts: (i) **Problem/Situation description** - this is the description of the problem needing solved and essentially defines the context of the experience or case, (ii) **Solution** - this is a description of the solution used to solve the problem and can include rationale and use domain knowledge (Aamodt and Plaza 1994). (iii) **Outcome** - this is the success or otherwise of the solution after it was applied to the problem and is the means by which the technique avoids repeating unsuccessful solutions.

Deciding the contents of each of the above parts is a major concern in the development of case-based systems.

## 3.4 Some example CBR systems

Case-Based Reasoning has found employment in a broad range and diversity of applications ranging from the very popular help-desk systems (e.g. Acorn and Walden 1992) to the more unique application of using CBR to simulate biological neural networks (Wendel 1993). The technique has also broken out of the confines of the research community and found many industrial applications. The first of these was by Lockheed Aerospace in Palo Alto, California in 1990 (development began in 1987) (Hennessy and Hinkle 1992) with another notable application occuring within General Dynamics' Electric Boat Division (Simoudis 1992).

An area that has received a substantial amount of attention by the CBR research community is that of the design task. This has resulted in a sub-area of CBR being established called Case-Based Design (CBD). For an overview of this area consult (Maher et al 1995). Examples of interesting CBD systems are CYCLOPS (Navinchandra 1988), Kritik-2 (Goel 1989), CADET (Sycara et al 1991), MIDAS (Domeshel et al 1994), and CADRE (Hua et al 1993).

# 4 LIFE-CYCLE INTEGRATION USING CBR

## 4.1 Previous work: RA-IQSE

The Revision Advisor - Integrated Quality Support Environment (RA-IQSE) (Irgens 1995), is a prototype system which uses CBR techniques to supply the early stages of the design process with experience-based information from previous developments. The system has a front-end and a back-end. The front-end provides the designers interface to the system and allows the designer to conduct design activities and request advice about the suitability or 'fitness-for-purpose' of the proposed design. The 'fitness-for-purpose' of the design is based on information entered via the back-end of the system. Here, data from testing, manufacturing, and warranty forms, are input for completed/in-service products. If advice is requested by the user, then the CBR mechanism locates a "similar" past design and uses the feedback information associated with the past design to provide advice in the creation of the new design.

The RA-IQSE project enforced the idea that ultimate quality is largely determined at the design stage and attempted to improve quality by making designers more aware of past product successes and failures. The prototype was implemented at an automotive parts manufacturer with positive results, the most significant of which was the acceptance by the part designers of the CBR technique.

## 4.2 Proposed approach: applying CBR to QFD to enhance life-cycle integration

For RA-IQSE, the front and back ends of the system were purposely built to achieve the system's goals. Similarly the underlying data structures and case representations were fixed and permitted no opportunities for receiving pertinent life-cycle information from sources other than the system feedback interface. Furthermore, at the front end of the system only tightly specified 'customer requirements' could be entered which were more akin to product characteristics within the QFD process. The designer then created a design based on these product characteristics and received advice of the proposed design. RA-IQSE, therefore, supported the second stage of the QFD process and avoided the first stage which is recognized as being the most crucial and difficult to complete (Sanchez et al 1993).

These factors contributed to the motivation for developing a new approach which continued the philosophy initiated with RA-ISQE but that attacks the problem with an extended set of goals. The ultimate goal of utilizing feedback information more effectively still remains. However, by adopting the full QFD process as a framework, the approach can achieve a greater focus upon the customer and encompass a greater span of the life-cycle more effectively. The greater focus on the external customer is achieved by making use of the approach at the first stage of the QFD process and is compounded by taking account of actual customer feedback once the product is in use. Through achieving this, the system provides the host organization with a customer responsive mechanism (Davis and Manrodt 1996).

In terms of internal customers, the new approach makes it far easier for feedback to be collated. In RA-IQSE, as mentioned above, the 'Quality Observations' had to be entered via the feedback interface regardless of their origin. This is not as convenient as the developed approach whereby the case is used to integrate information residing in independent databases dealing with the various stages of the life-cycle. In this way, the CBR component of the system may be seen as an integrating mechanism.

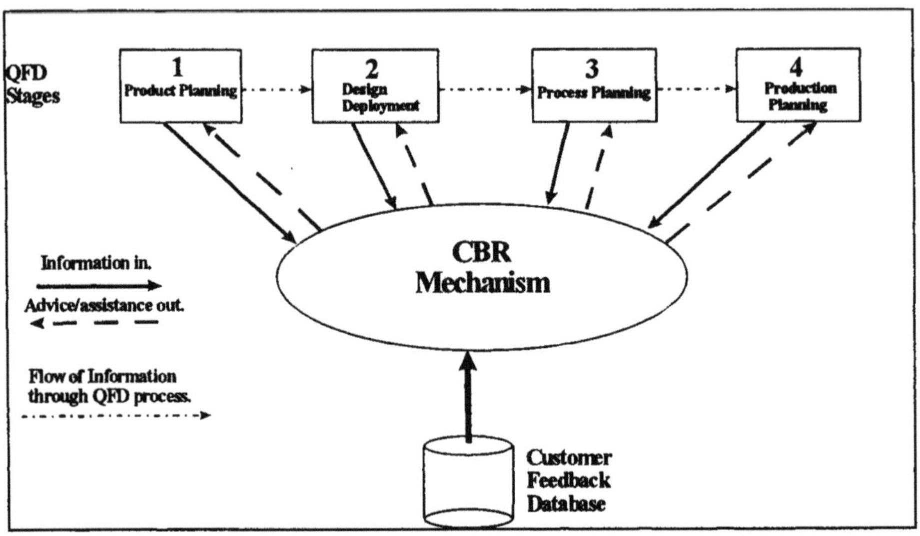


**Figure 5** General Approach

The approach is illustrated in Figure 5 focusing in particular on the use of the CBR mechanism as a life-cycle information integrator.

# 5 PROTOTYPE IMPLEMENTATION

## 5.1 Prototype delineation

A prototype implementation of the described approach is currently being constructed with the imposed limitations of only utilizing customer feedback information and relating this feedback to the initial stage of the QFD process. The rationale for utilizing customer feedback information is that such information reinforces the philosophical slant of QFD (i.e. getting 'close' to the customer) and therefore potentially offers the greatest benefit to the organization in general and the QFD process in particular. Furthermore, this information is frequently recorded by manufacturing organizations but is seldom utilized fully (Goodman et al 1996). The described approach makes significant utilization of this information.

The reason for only relating the customer feedback data to the first stage of the QFD process is two-fold. Firstly, this stage is the most subjective (Franceschini and Rossetto 1995) of all the QFD stages and as such has no underlying model against which to evaluate decisions. Therefore, specific feedback about a product - after appropriate interpretation - may prove useful in evaluating decisions at the first stage. Secondly, the first stage of the QFD process effectively defines the product the customer will receive and thus is the most important of all the stages. Therefore supporting the first stage offers most leverage in terms of final product quality.

Despite these limitations life-cycle integration is still being achieved and - as argued - possibly being achieved over the life-cycle activities which lead to greatest customer satisfaction.

## 5.2 Architecture

The basic architecture of the prototype system is illustrated in Figure 6. The current implementation of the system utilizes a House of Quality database at the start of the life-cycle and a customer feedback database in the later stages of the life-cycle. A knowledge-base is also used by the CBR mechanism. It is important to note that these databases are independent and have a purpose on their own. It is the CBR mechanism which acts as a collector and correlator of information through a case which is independent of both systems.

The architecture (Figure 6) greatly simplifies many of the issues relating to the case-based aspects of the approach. For a more detailed examination of how the CBR mechanism works see (Adams et al 1997).

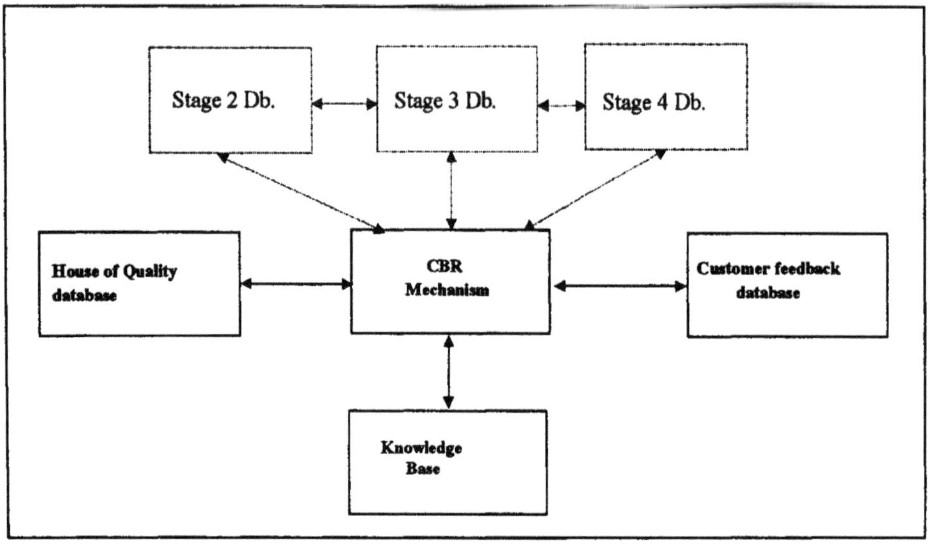


**Figure 6** System Architecture

## 5.3 System use

Although the flexible nature of the system means that the user can interact with the system in many ways, a typical example of the system would operate as shown in Figure 7 and is described below:

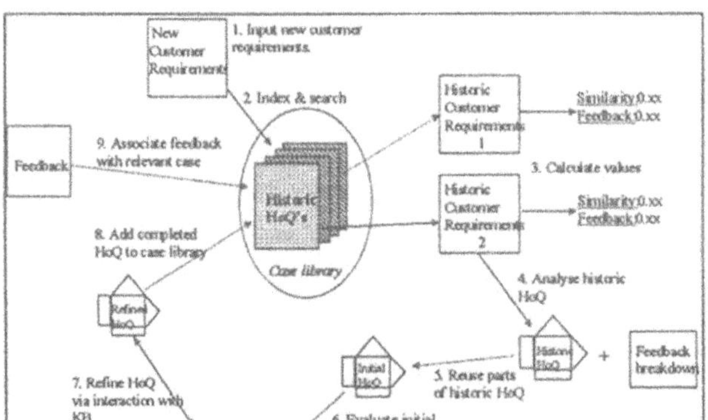


**Figure 7** Typical user interaction

1. The contents of the case are described as the situation for which advice is to be given - this may be range from an almost empty HoQ through to a completed HoQ.
2. Case identifying indices are assigned to the new case and a retrieval operation is performed on the case library.
3. For each retrieved

case two values are calculated: the similarity measure and the feedback assessment measure.
4. The retrieved cases are analysed and the parts of the cases which can be reused for the new case transferred.
5. An initial attempt at constructing the new HoQ is performed.
6. The result of 5 is evaluated for any constraint violations in the requirements, relations and correlation's matrices.
7. The new case is completed by providing solutions to the customer requirements that remain unsolved. This is achieved by allowing the user to select product characteristics that provide the functionality required. During this process continual evaluation is performed therefore allowing the user to see the effects of his/her decisions immediately.
8. The completed HoQ is then stored in the case library for future use.
9. Any feedback information that is received is interpreted and associated with the relevant case.

For an illustrative example of the system see (Adams et al 1996).

## 6.0 SUMMARY AND FUTURE WORK

It is anticipated that the approach described in this paper will offer significant benefits in the areas of continuous improvement of products and life-cycle integration. The first of these benefits being achieved essentially through the provision of the later. The approach follows the philosophical direction of our previous work on RA-IQSE but aims to extend and enhance the RA-IQSE work as has been described in the paper.

The prototype system that has been described is due for industrial evaluation in the Autumn of 1997. Based on the results achieved from the evaluation, the direction for future work on the approach will be established. This will be reported upon at the appropriate time.

## 7.0 REFERENCES

Aamodt, A., (1994) "Case-based Reasoning in Context: The Technology and its Impacts.", *in Case-Based Reasoning: A new force in Advanced Systems Development*, UNICOM Seminars, pp. 9-23, 27.
Aamodt, A., Plaza, E., (1994) "Case-Based Reasoning: Foundational Issues, Methodological Variations, and System Approaches.", AICOM, vol. 7, no. 1.
Acorn, T. L., Walden S. H., (1992), "SMART: Support Management Automated Reasoning Technology for Compaq Customer Service", Proc. 4th Innovative Applications of Artificial Intelligence Conference, CA.

Adams, D. A., Irgens, C., Lees, B., MacArthur, E., (1996) "A case-based reasoning approach to QFD and product life-cycle information navigation -the potential of case outcome", VDI Berichte 1289, München.

Adams, D. A., Irgens, C., Lees, B., MacArthur, E., (1997) "Using case outcome to integrate customer feedback into the Quality Function Deployment process", 5th German Workshop on Case-Based Reasoning, Bad Honnef, March 1997.

Althoff, K-D., Auriol, E., Barletta, R., Manago, M., (1995), "A Review of Industrial Case-Based Reasoning Tools", AI Intelligence.

Akao, Y. (Ed.), (1990), *Quality Function Deployment: Integrating Customer Requirements into Product Design*, Productivity Press.

ASQC/ASI, (1992), Transactions from the 4th symposium on QFD, June 15-16, Nov., MI.

Cohen, L., (1995), *Quality Function Deployment*, Addison-Wesley Publishing.

Davis, F. W., Manrodt, K. B., (1996), "Customer-Responsive Management: The Flexible Advantage", Blackwell Publishers, Inc.

Domeshek, E. A., Herndon, M. F., Bennett, A. W., Kolodner, J. L., (1994), "A Case-Based Design Aid for Conceptual Design of Aircraft Subsystems", in *Proc. of 10th IEEE conference on Artificial Intelligence for Applications*, Washington, 1994.

Franceschini, F., Rossetto, S., (1995), "QFD: The problem of comparing Technical/Engineering Design requirements", *Research in Engineering Design*, vol. 7, pp. 270-278.

Goel, A., (1989), *Integration of case-based reasoning and model-based reasoning for adaptive design problem solving.* PhD, Dept. of Computer and Information Science, Ohio State University.

Goodman, J., DePalma, D., Broetzmann, S., (1996) "Maximizing the Value of Customer Feedback", *Quality Progress*, December 1996.

Hauser, J., Clausing, D., (1988), "The House of Quality", *Harvard Business Review*, vol. 66, no. 3, pp. 63-73.

Hennessy, D., Hinkle, D., (1992), "Applying Case-Based Reasoning to Autoclave loading", *IEEE Expert*, vol. 7, pp. 21-26.

Hua, K., Faltings, B., (1993), "Exploring Case-Based Building Design - CADRE", AI EDAM, vol. 7, no. 2, pp. 135-143.

Irgens, C. I., (1995) "Design support based on projection of information across the product-development life cycle by means of case-based reasoning", *IEE Proc.-Sci. Meas. Technol.*, vol. 142, No. 5.

Kolonder, J. L., (1993), *Case-Based Reasoning*, Morgan Kaufmann.

Leake, D. B., (1996) "CBR in Context: The Present and Future", in, *Case-Based Reasoning: Experiences, Lessons, and Future Directions,* ed. Leake, D. B., AAAI Press.

Maher, M., L., Balachandran, M., B., Zhang, D., M., (1995), *Case-Based Reasoning in Design*, Lawrence Erlbaum Associates, Inc..

Navinchandra, D., (1988), "Case-based reasoning in CYCLOPS, a design problem solver", in *Proceedings: Workshop on case-based reasoning (DARPA), Clearwater, Florida.*

Prasad, B., (1996), *Concurrent Engineering Fundamentals: Volume 1*, Prentice Hall.
Ranky, P. G., (1994), *Concurrent/Simultaneous Engineering*, CIMware Ltd., 1994.
Sanchez, S. M., Ramberg, J. S., Fiero, J., Pignatiello, J. J., (1993), "Quality by Design", in *Concurrent Engineering: Automation, Tools, and Techniques*, ed. Kusiak, A., John Wiley & Sons.
Schank, R., (1982), *Dynamic Memory: A theory of Learning in Computers and People*, Cambridge University Press.
.Simoudis, E., (1992), "Using Case-Based Retrieval for Customer Technical Support", *IEEE Expert*, vol. 7, pp. 7-13.
Sullivan, L. P., (1986), "Quality Function Deployment", *Quality Progress*, June 1986.
Syncara, K., Navin Chandra, D., Guttal, R., Koning, J., Narasimhan, S., (1991), "CADET: A Case-Based Synthesis Tool for Engineering Design.", *Int. Journal of Expert Systems*, vol. 4, pt. 2.
Watson, I., (1995), "An introduction to Case-Based Reasoning", *1st UK Workshop on Case-Based Reasoning*, BCS Specialist Group on Expert Systems, University of Salford, 12 January 1995.
Wendel, O., (1993), "Case-Based Reasoning in a Simulation Environment for Biological Neural Networks.", First European Workshop, EWCBR-93, Kaiserslautern, November 1-5.
Wilson, P. M., Greaves, J. G., (1990), "Forward Engineering - A strategic link between design and profit.", *Mechatronic Systems Engineering*, Vol. 1, No. 1.

# 3

# A Case Study on CAD/CAM data transfer in CIM Environment

*K. P. Mahadevan*
*J. Mou*
*M. R. Henderson*
*D. L. Shunk*
*Department of I&MSE*
*Arizona State University*
*Tempe, AZ 85287*
*U.S.A.*

**Abstract**

This case study enumerates the steps involved in testing the data exchange among dissimilar CAD systems using a standard exchange mechanism and discusses the level of inter-operability that can be achieved to facilitate successful transfer of CAD data among three CAD software's namely Pro/E version 17, I-DEAS Master series version 3.1 and AutoCAD release 13 in a CIM environment. First the Initial Graphics Exchange Specification (IGES) is used as the data exchange mechanism to test these software's using a standard test procedure. The same test procedure is then used to find out the effectiveness of the data exchange between Pro/E and I-DEAS using a different exchange standard called the Standard For Exchange Of Product Model Data (STEP). AutoCAD does not support STEP. Experimental results show that Pro/E and I-DEAS have the capability to share complete CAD information but AutoCAD has some limitations in transferring information on surfaces and solids using IGES. By using the STEP translator, we are able to translate CAD data efficiently one way from Pro/E to I-DEAS and vice versa but have some difficulty carrying out back and forth data transfer between them.

Computer Applications in Production and Engineering. F. Plonka and G. Olling (Eds.)

**Keywords**

Computer Aided Design (CAD), Computer Aided Manufacturing (CAM), Computer Integrated Manufacturing (CIM), Inter-operability, Initial Graphics Exchange Specification (IGES), Standard For Exchange Of Product Model Data (STEP).

## 1 INTRODUCTION

Traditionally CAD systems have competed on ease and speed with which the geometry is created, but there is an increasing need for these systems to have the capability to integrate seamlessly with other systems in a CIM environment. The present day manufacturers are working concurrently with a wider range of dedicated suppliers, each having their own legacy systems with varying levels of technical sophistication. In addition to this these manufacturers and suppliers have access to more product information and a variety of CAD/CAM products to choose from. So it is very important for these suppliers to be able to effectively communicate vital product data with the manufacturers, quickly and effectively regardless of the system they have [1]. If this is achieved the manufacturers can obtain quick feedback from the suppliers on new designs, existing designs can be modified faster and product variations can be minimized by utilizing the existing standard components from the product database thereby reducing product development costs. To obtain these benefits of seamless integration we have to evaluate the effectiveness of the CAD data exchange among the systems available using a standard exchange mechanism. The effectiveness depends on the extent to which the data exchange satisfies the user's specific requirement working under a particular environment. Data is exchanged from the base system to the target system by first translating into a neutral file format and then to the data structure of the target system. Data exchange between any two dissimilar CAD systems can either be a simple data transfer involving simple geometry, or a complex model having a variety of entity types. So in order to get the desired results, it is important for one to understand the CAD application, how it is used, the operating system requirements, the hardware requirements, the mode of communication, knowledge of files and file transfer protocols.

The objective of this paper is to find out the compatibility of the three dissimilar CAD systems, namely AutoCAD 13 [2], I-DEAS 3.1 [3], and Pro/E 17 [4] using Initial Graphics Exchange Specification (IGES) as the standard for exchange of CAD data. IGES is the specification for the structure and syntax of the neutral file in binary or ASCII format. Here AutoCAD (supporting IGES 5.1) was operated in a Windows NT environment having a 64MB RAM with Pentium processor, I-DEAS and Pro/E both supporting IGES 5.1, in a Silicon Graphics workstation with 64MB RAM, 2GB hard drive and MIPS R4600 (134 MHz) CPU. We see that the hardware requirements of Pro/E and I-DEAS are greater than AutoCAD. All the three softwares were on different servers.

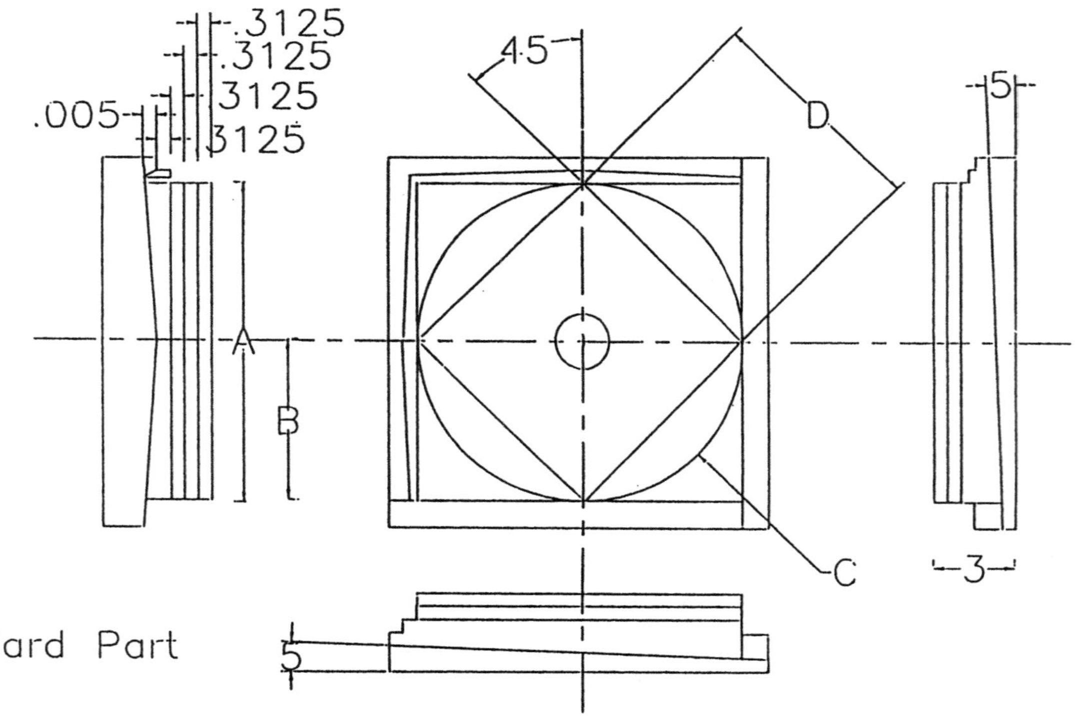


Fig 1.Standard Part

All dimensions in inches

| DIM | A | B | C | D |
|---|---|---|---|---|
| TY1 | 12 | 6.0 | 12 | 8.4 |
| TY2 | 6.0 | 3.0 | 6.0 | 4.2 |

## 2 TESTING PROCEDURE

A standard drawing of the part, as shown in Figure 1, is created in each of the three softwares. This provides a common ground for comparison. The following steps have been carried out for each of the software to evaluate their compatibility.

*Step One*

Create a CAD file in the base system, generate the IGES file for the same using the export option (igesout). Check the .log file for any errors or warning message and identify the causes in the pre-processor. Then import it (igesin) into the same base system. Again check .log file for any error messages by the post-processor. Check whether the plots look the same and the geometry is correct. This method uses the pre-processor and post processor (translator) of the same CAD system. See Figure 2.

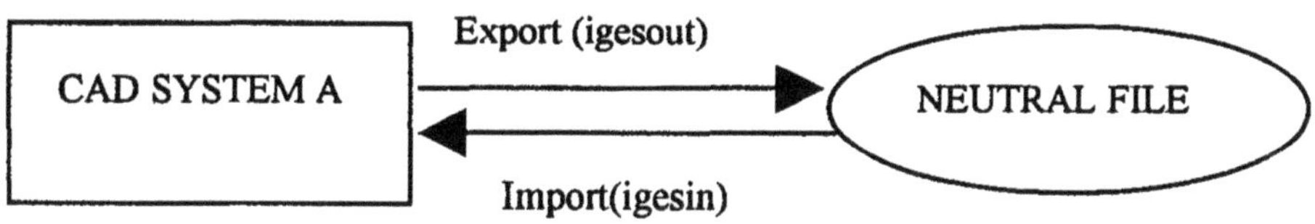


**Figure 2** Step one of testing procedure

*Step Two*

Create a CAD file in system A, generate the IGES file and transfer this file to another CAD system say system B using File Transfer Protocol (FTP), see Figure 3. Before creating the IGES file in the base system A using the export option check the requirements of the receiving system B, like acceptable tolerances, type of representation of the model, so that the file created can be easily transferred to the receiving system. For example if the receiving system easily recognizes surfaces, then represent the solid model as a set of surfaces using the available IGES configurations or options in the base system.

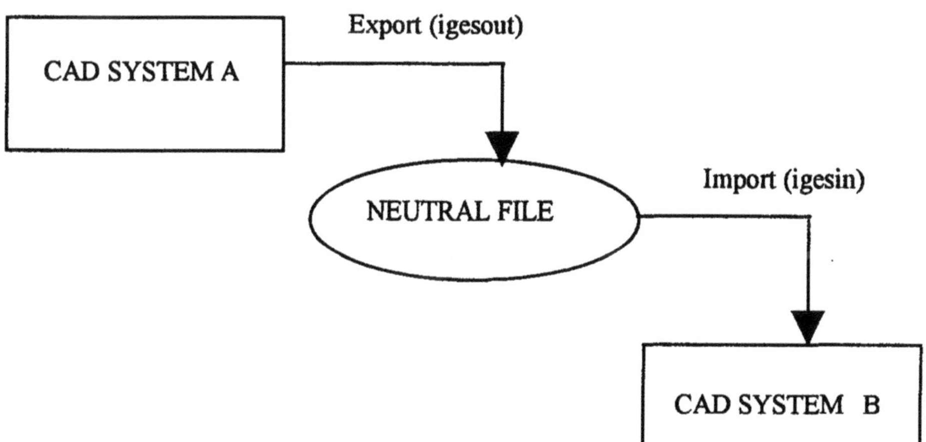

This facilitates easier transfer of data into the receiving system satisfying its requirements. Then recreate the solid in the receiving system by merging or stitching the set of surfaces into a solid. For the IGES file created in the base system, check the .log file for any errors and repeat the same for the receiving system. Check whether the plots look the same in both the systems. Look for any inconsistencies in the geometry and text. Also ensure that the units of the CAD file in both the systems are the same. One way to ensure that the units are the same is to check the mass properties like density, volume, surface area, etc. If the file is transferred completely without changing the form and function the mass properties will be the same. For example if the base system sends a solid, and the receiving system receives it as a wireframe or a set of surfaces, the resulting model will have no mass.

*Step Three*
Create a CAD file in system A, generate the IGES file and transfer this file to system B using FTP, create an IGES file of this transferred file in system B and transfer it back to system A using FTP. It should be noted that we do not recreate the model in system B. Thus this step involves repeating the *Step Two* twice, once from A to B and once from B back to A, see Figure 4.

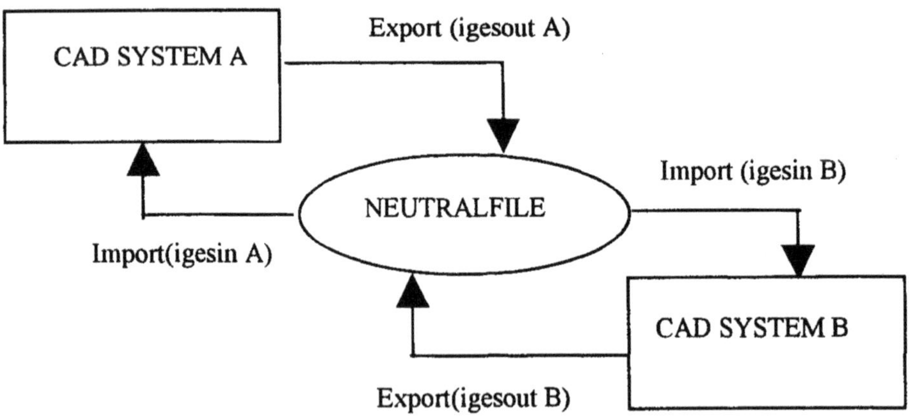


**Figure 4** Step three of testing procedure

## 3 OBSERVATIONS

### (i) IGES

*Pro/Engineer 17*
A solid model of the part is created in the Part mode. Choose Interface from Part mode and Export from the Interface menu to create an igesout file. Pro/E creates a .prt file for all the parts created. This file lists the sequence of operations carried out in making the model in numerical form. This raw data is compiled into a

relevant .inf (information) file. This .inf file gives information like filename, units used (mm or inch), the features created, internal feature number, feature id, dimensions involved, the type of operations performed (Extrusion, Protrusion), etc. Pro/E also creates a .log file for all files that are imported and gives information about the IGES entities. It gives information about the IGES number associated with each entity (e.g. circular arc is represented by 100), entity name, the number of occurrences of that particular entity, whether all the entities present have been converted into IGES entity. It also gives the total number of curves, surfaces, trimmed surfaces it has identified as present in the model and total processing time. In order to accomplish the first step the exported file was imported back to Pro/E. The geometry and the plot looked the same. The .log files were checked for any error messages. It did not show any error messages, also the total number of entities remained the same. Thus we can see that the pre and post processors of Pro/E are consistent in translating the IGES files.

*Pro/E ----> I-DEAS*

The model of the part created in Pro/E is exported to I-DEAS. To accomplish this we use the Part - Interface - Export menu options and then use the binary mode in file transfer protocol to transfer the .igs file of the model to the server where I-DEAS resides. To open the file in I-DEAS we create a new model file and use the File - Import - IGES (view independent) menu. The model is imported as a set of open surfaces, using the default tolerance available in I-DEAS (3.94E-4 inches or 0.01 mm). Thus I-DEAS recreates the geometry based on the geometric definition, the topology and the required tolerance. If there are any errors during the transfer process, I-DEAS detects and lists the ill-defined or missing surfaces needed to be merged to form a solid. The .log file lists all the errors, this .log file is stored as a .ipr (information processing report) file in the directory. In order to merge these open surfaces we open the file in the master surface module and use the autostitch menu to stitch all the individual surfaces and form a single solid. If this does not work we have to try doing the same using tighter tolerances so that the gaps in the open surfaces are reduced. This model imported from Pro/E as a set of surfaces is autostitched at a tolerance of 5.94E-4, even though it was imported using a tolerance of 3.94E-4. The part now looks identical to the original part; its mass properties like volume and density are the same. Also the size of the .igs file is same in both systems, ensuring completeness in the data transfer.

Although the size of the files and the overall geometry is same there is no one to one correspondence in the way the individual entities are identified and defined (as seen in the .log files of the individual systems, which gives the number, type and the IGES number of each entity) by the pre-processor (IGES translator in Pro/E) and the post-processor (IGES translator in I-DEAS). This means that some differences exist in the way the IGES translator, in each of the system interprets the individual entities that comprise the model, even though the overall geometry remains the same after the transfer. Thus the configuration of the IGES translator varies from system to system.

*(Pro/E ---->) I-DEAS ----> Pro/E*

The third step in the procedure is carried out by exporting the I-DEAS solid (created in Pro/E) back to Pro/E. I-DEAS creates a .ipr file, which is checked for any error messages. The .igs file is transferred to Pro/E by representing the I-DEAS solid in the form of surfaces using the Surfaces Curves and Points option. This is because Pro/E prefers to import solids in the form of surfaces, as it has the capability to construct the solid from the imported data. Pro/E automatically creates a solid when sufficient data is available during import to create a solid, otherwise we can use Redefine - Fix Boundaries options or Merge quilts option to form a solid. Upon observation, this transferred model looks almost like the original with the mass properties, but the number of entities that make up the model (as seen in the new .log file) are more than that was originally transferred to I-DEAS. This is probably because of the autostitching performed on the model in I-DEAS.

Thus we see that for a part created in Pro/E we are able to move back and forth between Pro/E and I-DEAS using a standard exchange mechanism.

*Pro/E ----> AutoCAD*

In order to check the compatibility between Pro/E and AutoCAD we have to follow the steps two and three of the test procedure as the first step has already been performed. First model the part in Pro/E, and then export it using the Part - Interface - Export option. Here we have an option of either exporting it as a solid model or a drawing containing the different views generated from the model. If we want to export it as a drawing we need to use Drawing - Interface - Export option. There are several configuration options available that support the export of Pro/E parts and drawings to IGES. This helps in tailoring the IGES files to the receiving system's requirement. The iges_out_spl_crvs_as_126 configuration option sets all part geometry spline curves to IGES entity 126 (B-SPLINE) when creating an IGES file. With these options available the .igs file of the part is exported to AutoCAD (residing on a different server) using FTP. This file is viewed in AutoCAD using the Import option. As before we check the .igs file of the part for any error messages or warnings during the data transfer. The .igs file gives only the numerical values of the entities that are transferred. The plan view of the solid model is seen in 2 dimensions. To view the 3D wireframe of the part we have to go to Views - Viewpoint and select the desired angle to view.

Thus AutoCAD does not have the capability to convert this into a solid or a surface model. So it is preferable to import the .igs file created from the drawing file containing the different views of the model.

*(Pro/E ---->) AutoCAD ----> Pro/E*

The .igs file of the part imported into AutoCAD from Pro/E is created using the Export - Igs option. This file is transferred back to Pro/E using FTP. We observe that Pro/E is able to get back only the wireframe of the original solid model. We see from the .log file that the AutoCAD translator has defined the whole model in the form of wireframe entities like lines and circular arcs. Thus much of the information about the surfaces that was sent originally from Pro/E are lost in AutoCAD during translation. So AutoCAD is able to send only wireframe information back to Pro/E. Thus we see that the configuration and capabilities of the IGES translator of each of these systems are different. Pro/E has the capability to create a solid model of the part by using wireframe as the reference. For this we have to create datum planes for sketching and use the through option to construct the solid feature in the geometric tools menu. But this is a tedious process when bigger models are present.

Thus for a part created in Pro/E it is advisable to transfer 2D drawings into AutoCAD. It is not desirable to move the solid model back and forth between these two systems as much of the information on the surfaces and solids are lost in between due to the capabilities of the translators.

*I-DEAS 3.1*

A Solid model of the standard part is created in I-DEAS master series 3.1. For each model created two model files are generated by I-DEAS. This model file is exported using the File - Export - IGES option. I-DEAS has a variety of options for export depending on the receiving system called flavors. We can either use a standard flavor or a specific flavor depending on receiving system like AutoCAD, CADAM, CATIA, CAMAND, UNIGRAPHICS, VDA, INTERGR0APH, Ford-PDGS, GM-CGS. For the curves and surfaces the default flavor is B-spline, represented as Non Uniform Rational B-splines (NURBS). Solids can be exported as a set of surfaces, curves, points or model, space curves or model, space parameter space curves depending on the requirements of the receiving system. To perform the first step the model is exported using IGES and standard flavor as the option. Then this file is imported back to the system. In both cases the .ipr file which gives the information processing report is checked for any errors.

There was no error and the geometry of the model was the same in both cases, indicating that the IGES processor of I-DEAS is able to transfer CAD data completely without change of content and functionality.

*I-DEAS ----> Pro/E*

The standard part is created in I-DEAS using the Master Modeler and Design menus. This part is exported using the File - Export - IGES option. Since I-DEAS does not have a specific flavor for Pro/E as such we use the IGES option. Here we use the option of representing the I-DEAS solid as a set of surfaces, curves and points in IGES. Use the default tolerance of 3.94E-4. The .log file is checked for errors or warning messages. There were no errors recorded by the pre-processor in reading the IGES entities. This file is run in Pro/E, and again the .log file is checked for any errors. There were no error messages. The plots look the same, the geometry is correct.

Thus indicating that the post-processor (Pro/E translator) is able to read the IGES entities sent by the pre-processor (I-DEAS translator).

*(I-DEAS ---->) Pro/E ----> I-DEAS*

The above file in Pro/E (Originally modeled in I-DEAS), has to be sent back to I-DEAS. The Interface - Export option is used in Pro/E to create the igesout file for the part. There were no errors recorded. This is then sent back to I-DEAS using FTP. The size of the .igs file is the same in both the systems, thus indicating that the completeness of the data transfer. The part, which is transferred as a set of surfaces, has to be stitched using the Master surface module to form a solid. The resulting solid is compared to the original solid that was modeled. It has the same geometry, mass properties are also the same. This shows that there was no loss of information during the transfer and also that the translator is able to identify the entities created by the IGES processor of Pro/E. Thus a model created in I-DEAS can be sent back and forth to Pro/E effectively.

*I-DEAS ----> AutoCAD*

The solid model created in I-DEAS is exported to AutoCAD (in a different server) using the AutoCAD flavor option. The .log files are checked for any errors. The file is then read in AutoCAD using the Import - igsin menu. The 2D view of the model appears in AutoCAD. The 3D wireframe of the solid created in I-DEAS is viewed in AutoCAD using the Views - Viewpoint menus. If the AutoCAD flavor option in I-DEAS is not used we see a distorted image of the geometry when transferred to AutoCAD. This is because the AutoCAD is not able to recognize the surface information sent by I-DEAS processor. This is evident upon checking the mass properties (which says that the part volume is zero). I-DEAS also has the capability to convert the solid model created in the Master modular to 2D drawings. To do this we have to open the same model in the Drafting Setup module then use the Create Layout icon to enter the information to create the drawing of the parts already modeled, then use the Move icon to reposition any dimensions or make sections, and add annotations to the drawing and go to the Drafting Detailing module. From here the drawing can be exported to AutoCAD using the AutoCAD flavor. These drawings can be viewed in AutoCAD without any changes.

*(I-DEAS ---->) AutoCAD ----> I-DEAS*

Using the export menu in AutoCAD the part is transferred back (using FTP) to I-DEAS. We get the wireframe of the original model, but the .log file shows that the AutoCAD processor has interpreted the entire model as a collection of only two entity types namely lines and circular arcs. There are many open edges in the part that cannot be modified because I-DEAS does not have enough information to generate a solid model from this IGES file from AutoCAD. Although I-DEAS transferred information about the curves (B-splines), and surfaces to the AutoCAD processor, much of the information about the model is lost when a .igs file (of the same part) created in AutoCAD is transferred back to I-DEAS.

Thus indicating that the IGES translator of AutoCAD has the capability to transfer only 2D and 3D wireframe information but not about surfaces and solids.

*AutoCAD*
The standard part is drawn in AutoCAD. This file is exported using File - Export - Igesout option. AutoCAD 13 supports IGES 4.0 and it requires the files to be exchanged in fixed length ASCII format. The AutoCAD translator (Version 3.04) creates the .igs file. This is then imported back to AutoCAD using the File - Import - Igesin option. The drawings appear exactly the same, the size of the .igs file is the same, and there are no changes in the text and annotations.

Thus Igesin and Igesout options of AutoCAD support the translation of drawings and preserve the geometry and functionality of the entities.

*AutoCAD ----> Pro/E*
The drawing created in AutoCAD is exported to Pro/E, the drawing is regenerated by the translator of Pro/E, with all the text, dimensions and annotations, without any errors. Pro/E also regenerates the 3D wireframe created in AutoCAD.

*(AutoCAD ---->) Pro/E ----> AutoCAD*
The above part in Pro/E (from AutoCAD) is exported using the Interface - Export option and transferred to AutoCAD using FTP (ASCII mode). The file is viewed in AutoCAD using the Igesin. All dimensions and annotations are visible, but AutoCAD is not able to define the drawing extents. Thus the wireframe originally created in AutoCAD, when transferred back from Pro/E is regenerated without any errors. We see that the translators of AutoCAD and Pro/E are able to recognize and interpret the IGES files created by one another correctly.

*AutoCAD ----> I-DEAS*
The part created in AutoCAD is exported to I-DEAS. We first transfer the drawing and then the wireframe geometry of the part to I-DEAS. Text and annotations are lost when we transfer drawings.

*(AutoCAD ---->) I-DEAS ----> AutoCAD*
The file is transferred back to AutoCAD, from I-DEAS. Here again there are no annotations and text. But the overall file transfer is smooth and we get whatever information that was sent originally from AutoCAD back.

## (ii) STEP

The same testing procedure is used to test the interoperability of Pro/E and I-DEAS, by using the Standard For Exchange Of Product Model Data (STEP) standard as the data exchange mechanism. Both Pro/E and I-DEAS support the AP 203IS of the ISO 10303 STEP format. This format provides file exchange for Configuration Controlled three-dimensional designs of mechanical parts and assemblies with advanced B-Rep solids, Non-Topological surface and Wireframe.

*Pro/Engineer 17*
The solid model of the part is created in part mode and then exported to STEP format using Interface - Export option. This procedure is same as IGES except

that we select the STEP menu from the Export option. Here we have the choice of exporting the part as a wireframe, surfaces, solid, shells, and datum curves. We select the solid option. Pro/E creates a .stp file and a .log file, which contains the list of STEP entity types used in creating the exported file.

To carry out the *Step One* of the testing procedure this .stp file is imported back to Pro/E. This is done by choosing Interface - Import option and then select STEP menu. Then create a Co-ordinate system to locate the STEP data. The system starts processing the STEP data. On checking the .log file the number of entity types that make up the part remains the same, the solid model and its properties like mass, density, etc. remain the same. Thus we see that the STEP translator is consistent in parsing the input data created by itself.

*Pro/E ----> I-DEAS*

The *Step Two* of the testing procedure is then carried out by transferring the exported STEP file (.stp) to I-DEAS using the file transfer protocol. The exported solid model from Pro/E is imported by I-DEAS using the geometry translators menu. We observe that the solid model is transferred in its entirety with the mass properties remaining the same. Thus the STEP translator of I-DEAS is able to transfer the CAD data without losing much information.

*(Pro/E ---->) I-DEAS ----> Pro/E*

This follows the *Step Three* of the testing procedure, wherein the part created in Pro/E is transferred back to Pro/E from I-DEAS. Here we use the Interface - Import option to import the STEP data from I-DEAS after selecting the Co-ordinate system. Pro/E gives out an error message saying "could not construct feature geometry" as the translator is not able to process some entities that help in finalizing the topology.

*I-DEAS*

The solid model of the standard part is created first and then the *Step One* of the testing procedures is performed. For this we switch to geometry translators, open the model file that contains the part then use the Export option. Complete translation is possible using the default option for export. When we export the part a relationship is created between the exported part and the resulting STEP file. All user attributes will be mapped to the Configuration management data which gives information on the part, part number, name descriptor, etc. The configuration management data keeps pertinent information about the part even as the part moves from different suppliers and vendors. When we export two files are created namely the .step and .opr (output processing report) files. The .opr file gives the list of parameters that are set and the list of STEP entities.

This file is imported back by I-DEAS. For this we switch back to geometry translators, open the model file that contains the part and use the Import option. It should be noted that only single parts can be imported into I-DEAS from STEP translator. The system automatically creates a .ipr (input processing report) file. We see that the model remains the same in form and has the same mass properties.

Thus indicating that the STEP translator is consistent in translating data created by itself.

*I-DEAS ----> Pro/E*
The STEP file that was exported by I-DEAS is imported by Pro/E after creating the co-ordinate system. We observe that the part is translated without any change in the shape, mass properties, etc. Thus indicating that the STEP translators of Pro/E and I-DEAS are able to communicate effectively. By this we have completed the *Step Two* of the testing procedure successfully.

*(I-DEAS ---->) Pro/E ----> I-DEAS*
This is the *Step Three* of the testing procedure. The STEP file of the part from I-DEAS is created in Pro/E using the Export option. This is then transferred back to I-DEAS using the geometry translators and import option. I-DEAS gives out a message saying that the system has encountered errors parsing the input file. It also says that mapping of a particular entity to and from STEP is not supported by the STEP translator.

Thus we observe that both Pro/E and I-DEAS are able to transfer the STEP file to itself (*Step One* of testing procedure) and to the other system (*Step Two* of testing procedure) successfully. But is not able to translate the data back to the native system from another system.

## 4 CONCLUSION

We see that Pro/E is compatible with both I-DEAS and AutoCAD, with regard to back and forth transfer of CAD data using IGES. But AutoCAD is not efficient in transferring data on surfaces and solids. This could be due to the inherent differences in the capabilities of the individual CAD software or due to the way the part is modeled as there are no modeling standards available. STEP translators are efficient in one way transfer of data between I-DEAS and Pro/E, but are not able to aid in back and forth transfer of CAD data between these software. Thus there exists some differences in the interpretations of the STEP standard by different CAD/CAM software vendors.

## 5 REFRENCES


1. Elwood, G. P. (1993) Interoperability acceptance testing methodology version 1.01
2. AutoDesk Inc. (1996) AutoCAD Release 13 guide, AutoDesk Inc. Publications, California.
3. Lawry, M.H (1995) I-DEAS Master series guide, OnWard Press, New Mexico.
4. Parametric Technology Corporation. (1996) Pro/Engineer Fundamentals, Massachusetts

5. National Aerospace Standard, (1969), " Uniform cutting tests-NAS series metal cutting equipment specification," Aerospace association of America Inc., Washington D.C.

# 4
# The object-oriented modeling for product data management (PDM)

*Sunn-Ho Kim • Tae-Hoon Oh*
*Department of Industrial Engineering*
*Myong-Ji University*
*San38-2, Nam-dong, Yongin-si, Kyunggi-do 449-728, Korea*
*Phone: +82-335-30-6451 FAX: +82-335-35-9998*
*Email: shk@wh.myongji.ac.kr*

*Joo-Young Park*
*Hyundai Information Technology Co., Ltd.*
*12Fl. Woorim Bldg., 136-6 Seocho-dong*
*Seocho-gu, Seoul 137-070, Korea*

**Abstract**

Current commercialized PDM tools have drawbacks in representing a variety of data types such as CAD data, images, audio, long text, etc. by relational data modeling. For this reason, object-oriented approaches have been suggested as an alternative. In this paper, using the object-oriented paradigm, an object-oriented data model for the PDM system is proposed. The scope of the modeling is limited to management information for drawings, parts, and product structure. Rumbaugh's OMT (Object Modeling Technique) has been adopted for the system design. In the modeling, classes of data vault and workspace are taken into account for the review or approval of drawings and parts data based on the concurrent engineering concept. For parts and corresponding product structure, classes of phantoms, options, substitutes, etc. are added to the model. In addition, state transition and data flow diagrams are suggested based on the analysis of work and data flows of drawings and parts.

**Keywords**

PDM, object-oriented modeling, OMT, concurrent engineering,

Computer Applications in Production and Engineering. F. Plonka and G. Olling (Eds.)

# 1. INTRODUCTION

In recent years, the interest of industry begins to change from cost reduction and quality improvement to reduction of the time-to-market of new products. In other words, in order for the industry to strengthen a competitive position in markets and pursue a continuous improvement, new strategies are required so that the industry can respond quickly to customer's needs placing emphasis on diversification, high quality, and differentiation of products (Kim, 1994).

As one of the strategies, a Concurrent Engineering (CE) concept has been applied to product design processes. CE takes into account most of engineering and manufacturing information related throughout a product's life cycle period, based on harmonious communications among product development teams, sharing of information, and simultaneous processes.

PDM (Product Data Management) is one of the systematic approaches for the implementation of CE. PDM makes concurrent processes possible by managing comprehensively design and drawing tools, engineering data bases, shared electronic documents, etc. In other words, it provides users with all the information needed at desired places in adequate formats at an appropriate point of time (HP1993, CIMdata 1994, Lee 1996, Choi 1995).

In general, PDM deals with data such as drawings, documents, product structure, engineering data, workflow and processes, project management, etc. concerned with product development. However, as this data consists of complex structured data, image or vectored files, voice, audio, etc., it is not convenient to treat the data with current PDM tools oriented to relational databases.

Relational DBMSs have been developed to fit applications which need static or simple data used in business areas with data represented in a table format. For this reason, traditional RDBMSs have a drawback for not adequately serving certain applications. These include CAD/CAM, CASE, multimedia, and systems with very complex objects (Samsung HP 1993, Lee 1996, Kim 1994, Shin 1995, Kim 1994). There has been continual effort in developing PDM systems for several years. However, the PDM systems have the same problems of RDBMS.

To overcome this problem, researchers (Kim1992, Chung 1994) proposed a data modeling based on an object-oriented approach. Even in STEP (STandard for the Exchange of Product model data), data models are represented by the object-oriented modeling language, EXPRESS (Yoo, 1995). With ODBMSs, it is easy to treat long transactions in CAD, versioning, unstructured objects, and complex objects (McHenry, 1993). In addition, it is possible to represent semantic concepts such as generalization and aggregation and to handle engineering data which has a hierarchical structure of composite objects (Chung,1994).

For these reasons, in this research we analyze product data from the viewpoint of "objects" and propose a data model for PDM systems using an object-oriented paradigm. In the model, classes of workspaces and vaults are taken into account for concurrent information sharing of documents such as drawings, parts. etc. In the modeling of product structures, the concepts of phantom (or virtual) parts, optional parts, and substitutes are included. In addition, based on the analysis of the processes and data flows, state transition and data flow diagrams for drawings and parts are also proposed. As a modeling methodology, Rumbaugh's OMT (Object Modeling Technique) is used (Rumbaugh,1991).

## 2. CONCURRENT ENGINEERING IN PDM

For simultaneous processes of data, reviewer's opinions must be gathered concurrently through the network. Figure 1 shows this concept (CIMLINK, 1991). A document is generated by the integration of drawings and parts data and this is sent in parallel to all members of a designated group simultaneously for the review or approval. They attach their comments to the drawings by redlining and markup or by electronic mail through terminals. Reviewer's annotations are collected and combined with the original document for consideration by its creator. Through this process of review, annotation and feedback, CE-based engineering changes, approvals and notifications are carried out (Kim, 1996).

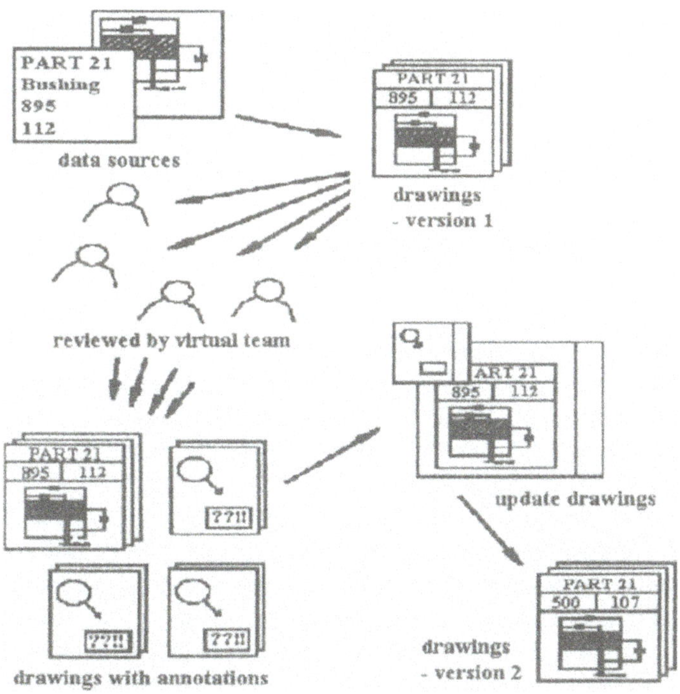


Figure 1. The concurrent engineering control for drawings (CIMLINK,1991)

As shown in Figure 2, all data concerned with product development is managed through the processes of generation, change, release, and disposal based on the CE concept, and stored in an electronic vault or workspaces. In the workspaces, the data under progress by designers or other users is stored. In case the needs for data share occur after the completion of these processes, the data moves to the vault by a scenario of workflow (Lee, 1996).

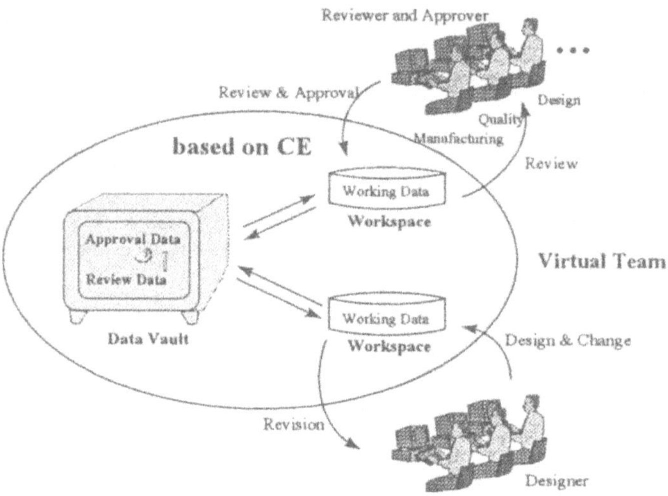


Figure 2. Data flow based on CE.

## 3. OBJECT-ORIENTED MODELING FOR PDM

### 3.1 Introduction

Most of the object-oriented methods are based on object-oriented paradigms and approach world models from two related viewpoints: the static relation and the dynamic behavior. In Rumbaugh's object-modeling technique (OMT), three views of modeling systems are used: 1) object modeling, 2) dynamic modeling, and 3) functional modeling (Choi 1996, Rumbaugh 1991).

The object modeling represents the structure of objects or classes in a system - their identity, their relationships to other objects, their attributes, and their operations. These remain unchanged regardless of the time flow or sequencing of operations. Associations, generalization and inheritances, aggregations, etc. are included in the static relation. An association is a special case of inheritances and aggregations and describes a group of links with common structure and common semantics. In addition, although they are modeled as bi-directional they do not have to be implemented in both directions. They can be implemented as pointers if it is only traversed in a single direction. Generalization and inheritance are powerful abstractions for sharing similarities among classes while preserving their differences. Inheritance means that a subclass inherits attributes and methods from one or more superclasses. In this concept, the subclass can have its own attributes and methods regardless of attributes and methods of its superclasses. Aggregation is the "part-whole" or "a-part-of" relationship in which objects representing the components of something are associated with an object representing the entire assembly (Taylor,1990).

Dynamic modeling describes that aspect of a system concerned with time and the sequencing of operations - events that mark changes, sequences of events, states that define the context for events, and the organization of events and states. This model is represented graphically with state diagrams. Each state diagram shows the state and event sequence permitted in a system for one class of objects.

The functional modeling describes those aspects of a system concerned with transformations of values-functions, mappings, constraints, and functional dependencies. The functional model captures what a system does without regard for how or when it is done. It is represented with data flow diagrams. Data flow diagrams show the dependencies between values and the computation of output values from input values and functions, without regard for when or if the functions are executed (Rumbaugh 1991, Choi 1995).

### 3.2 Identification of Object Classes and Object Modeling

For the construction of object models for PDM, objects and their classes have to be identified in advance and their relations defined such as associations, generalization and inheritance, aggregations, etc. In this stage, attributes and methods, which describe characteristics of the classes, may be included in static diagrams. The PDM system proposed in this research consists of three modules, i.e., drawing data management, part data management, and product structure management modules. Object classes identified for these modules are summarized in Table 1. The association diagram among the classes is shown in Figure 3.

**Table 1.** Objects identified in PDM

| Module | Objects |
|---|---|
| drawing data management | drawing, drawing history, edition history, check history, approval history, disposal history, release history, version |
| part data management | part, part information, GT-code, supplier, alternate, product, assembly, component |
| product structure management | product, BOM information, family information, phantom, common module, option module, kit |
| data share management | vault, vault location, workspace, work location, user, user's role, authority |

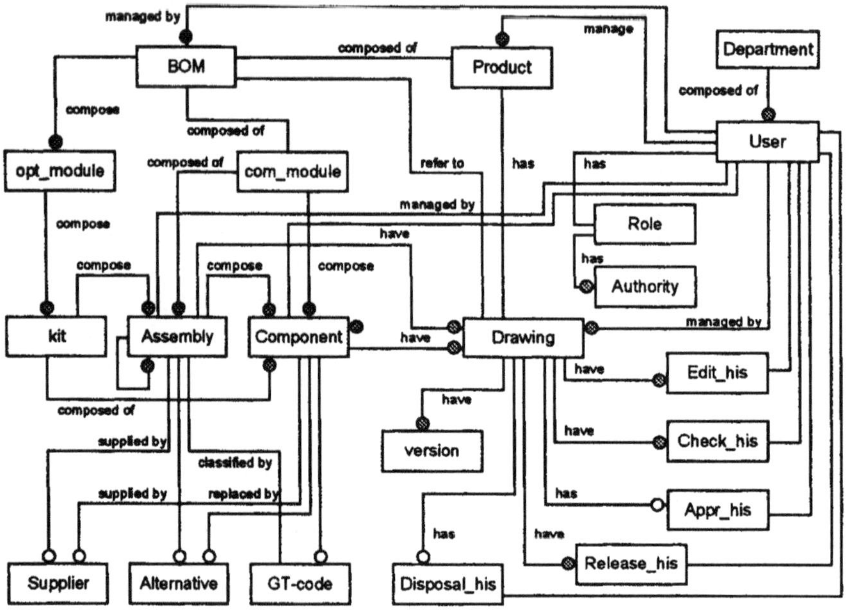


Figure 3. A class association diagram

### 3.3 Object Modeling for Drawing Data Management

Documents concerned with a product design include drawings, specifications, instructions, standards, 3D models, technical documents, etc. Each document can have common attributes of document number, author, written date, etc. Figure 4 represents the relations of generalization and inheritance by generating a superclass named "document" and inheriting its attributes to subclasses named "Drawing", "Standard", "Instruction", and "Spec.". A new document class can be created by inheritance of attributes of its abstract class and addition of its own attributes. Figure 4 also shows the object model of the drawing data management module. A drawing generates history data of edition, check, approval, release, disposal, version, etc. through the workflow and life cycle period of time. These history classes create an abstract class of "Drawing_his" and keep the relation of generalization. On the other hand, the drawing history class becomes a composite object of the drawing class, "Drawing", and history classes under the drawing history class become component objects. This represents an aggregation which have the relation of "a_part_of". When such document objects related to a drawing are treated as composite objects, corresponding data can be kept consistently by class dependency.

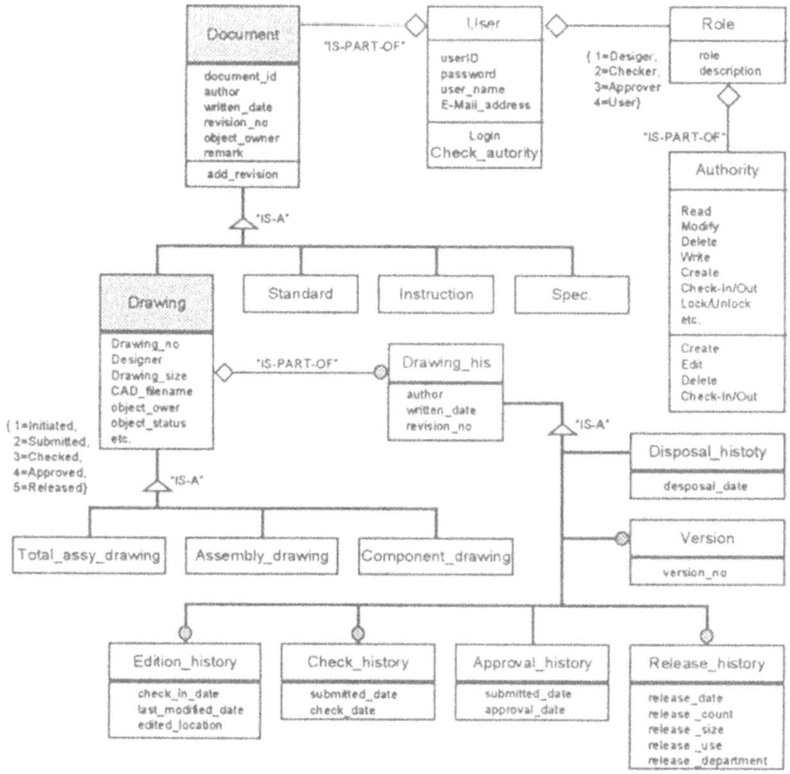


Figure 4. The object model for drawing data management

## 3.4 Object Modeling for Part Data Management

An object model for the part data management is shown in Figure 5. In the figure, classes "Assembly" and "Component" have common attributes of part number, part name, parent part number, GT code, etc., and common methods of creation, revision, query, deletion, print, etc. These two classes can be generalized by creating an abstract class named "Part". In this object model, "Component" implies objects which consist of raw materials and unit parts and "Assembly" objects which consist of component parts and subassemblies. The class "Alternate" means alternate parts replaced when standard parts can not be used and have attributes of effective date and effective quantity for alternate control. In addition, classes of "Supplier", "Alternate", "GT-code", and "Drawing" are dependent on the part information class "Part_Info" and construct a relation of aggregation. Here, "Part-Info" becomes a dependent object of the class "Part".

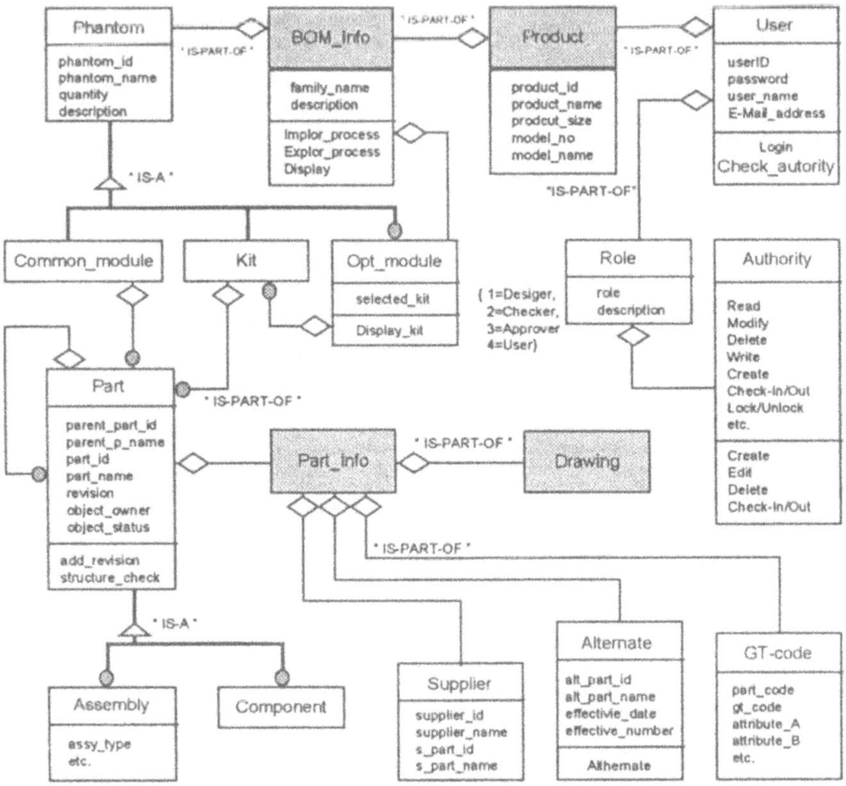


Figure 5. The object model for part data management

### 3.5 Object Modeling for BOM

Under the environment where a variety of options for a product exists, BOM data must be managed in terms of options. For this reason, in this research, the product structure is modeled based on the concept of family BOM. Family BOM is a data structure where products of similar characteristics are grouped into family and the product structures of the family are represented by modularized common and optional parts. In this method, common and optional parts have their own product structures and a BOM is generated by the selection of the common and optional parts.

In the object model proposed in Figure 5, a BOM is created with classes of "Common_module", "Option_module", and "Kit". Above these three classes is the superclass "Phantom" which means a virtual part. Virtual parts are not included in the parts list for manufacturing or assembly, but used as group names of common, optional, and kit parts for the convenience of design or planning. Common modules, the one which classify parts commonly used in a product group, consist of assembly parts and component parts. Kits, i.e., virtual parts which represent optional specifications, also consist of assembly parts and component parts. Optional modules are the kits classified by grouping optional specifications within a product group.

### 3.6 Object Modeling for Data Share

As shown in Figures 2 and 6, in order for users to create, change, review, and approve objects concerned with a product such as drawings, parts, documents, etc., these objects have to be transferred from workspaces where data is not shared to vaults where data is shared. This function is called "check-in" and reverse the function, which gets data from the vaults is called "check-out". Document information consists of meta data which includes location or index data, and corresponding documents such as CAD files, image files, text files, audio data, video data, etc. These two types of data must be stored separately in vaults or workspaces. Figure 7 represents the object model for the whole system including the object model for data share.

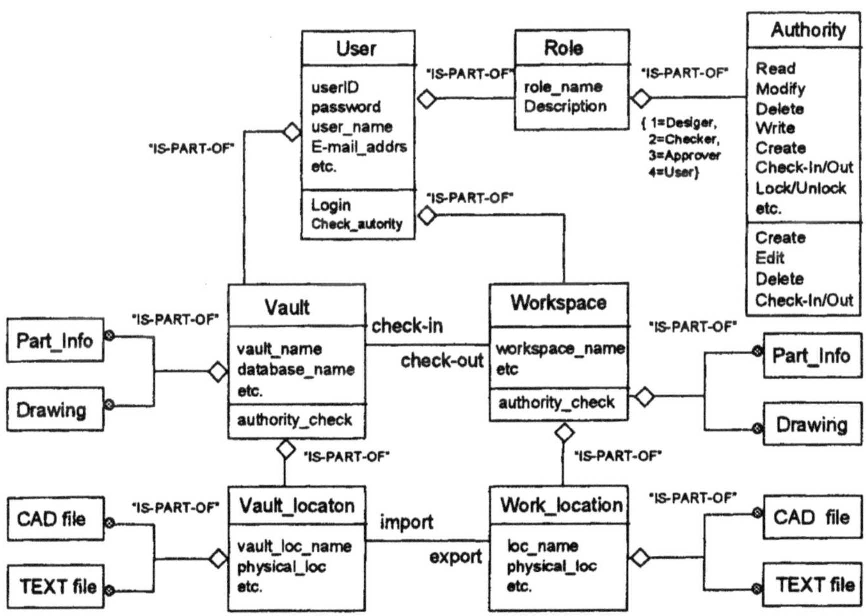


Figure 6. The object model for data share

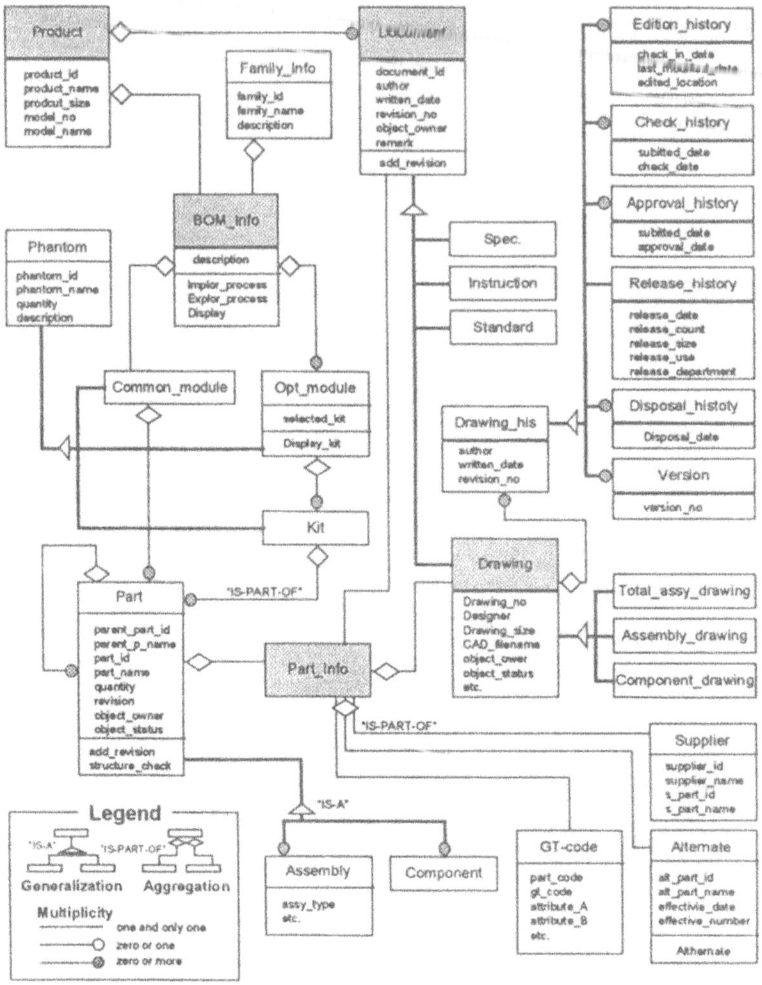


Figure 7. Object model for PDM

### 3.7 Dynamic Modeling for Drawings

Dynamic modeling is to define object states which change according to activities of the object, and to analyze the object life-cycle on how state transition flows precede as time goes by or events break out.

These flows are closely related to the workflow, a set of activities performed by specific events of parts, drawings, documents, etc. As an example, a state transition diagram for drawings is shown in Figure 8. The drawings can be divided into four states of on-progress, approval, release, and disposal. The on-progress state is again divided into sub-states of create, check, and edit. A designer creates a new drawing and requests a review to review groups. The reviewers attach their annotations to the drawing. By this time, the drawing keeps the state of on-progress. When an approval is requested, the state of the drawing changes to approval and the decision maker determines approval or rejection. If it is rejected the state of the drawing again changes to on-progress. The printing and release of the drawing is followed by the decision maker's release approval. When he or she determines a disposal, the state changes to disposal.

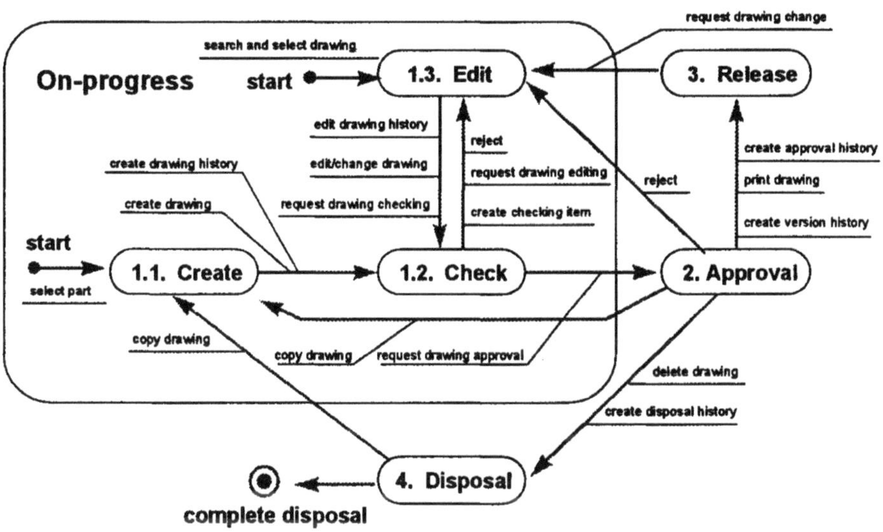


Figure 8. The state transition diagram for drawings

### 3.8 Functional Modeling for Drawings and Parts

The functional model consists of multiple data flow diagrams which specify the meaning of operations and constraints. A data flow diagram (DFD) shows the functional relationships of the values computed by the system, including input values, output values, and internal data stores. The DFD usually contains processes that transform data, data flows that move data, actor objects that produce and consume data, and data store objects that store data passively. The DFDs for drawings and parts are shown in Figures 9 and 10, respectively. In the DFD for drawings, processes for drawings only are included. However, in the DFD for parts, processes for parts, BOM, and GT-codes are all represented.

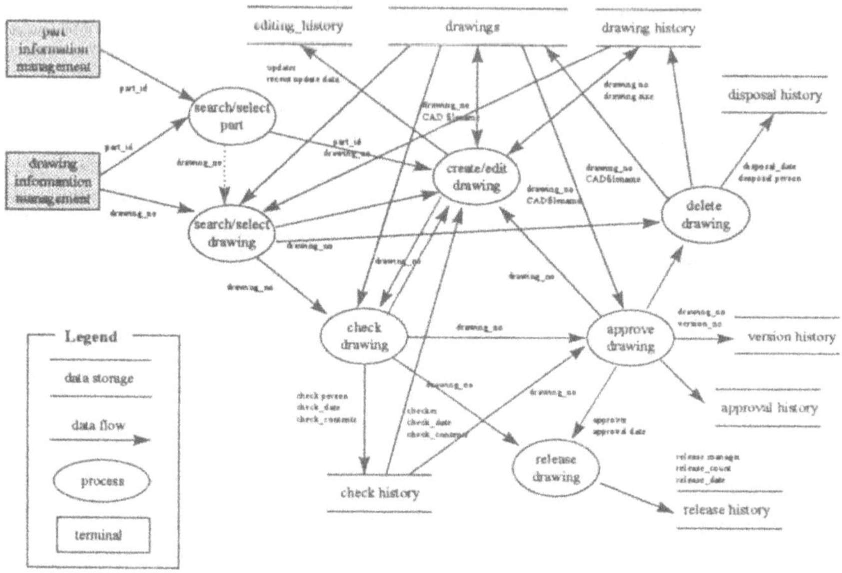


Figure 9. The data flow diagram for drawings

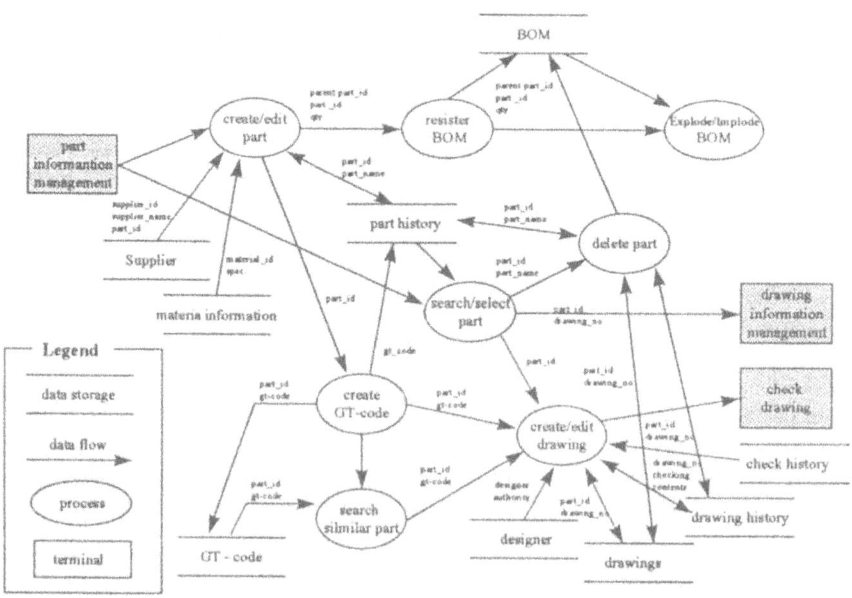


Figure 10. The data flow diagram for parts

## 4. CONCLUSION AND FUTURE RESERCH

In this research, we have analyzed elements of PDM from the viewpoint of objects and proposed object-oriented models for PDM systems using Rumbough's Object-Modeling Technique (OMT). In the object model for the data share, classes of vaults and workspaces for drawings, parts, documents, etc. have been taken into account. In the object model for the product structure, the concept of a family BOM has been reflected with virtual parts (phantom), options, alternates, etc. In addition, through the analysis of work and data flows for drawings and parts, state transition and data flow diagrams have been proposed. Through the further study for workflow and configuration management modules, we plan to develop an object-oriented prototype for PDM systems.

Acknowledgment: This work was developed with a grant from Korea Research Foundation(01-E-0717).

## REFERENCES

Choi, S.U., Dho, H.S., Kye, W.K., (1996) Trends of Object-Oriented Software Development Methodology, *Journal of Information Science*, Vol.14, No.10., 4-11.

Choi, Y.H., (1995) The PDM System for CE Implementation, December, *Computer World*, 162-167.

Choi, Y.K., Huh, K.B., (1995) *Object-Oriented Software Engineering*, Korea Silicon.

Chung, Y., Fischer, G.W., (1994) A Concept and Issues for an Object-Oriented Bill of Materials(BOM) Data Model, *Computers & Industrial Engineering*, Vol.26, No.2, 321-339.

CIMdata, (1994) Product Data Management : A Technology Guide.

CIMLINK, (1991) *Linkage-Automated Manufacturing Information Flow*, CIMLINK.

HP, (1993) *Product Data Management : Understanding the Fundamental Technology and Business Concepts*, Hewlett-Packard Co.

Kim, C.H., Lim C.K., Chung, W.Y., Kim, W.S., (1994) A Study on the Structure of the EDB System for Engineering Data Integration, *Interfaces : Industrial Engineering*, Vol.7, No.3, 137-145.

Kim, K.S., Kim, C.H., (1992) A Modeling Methodology for Manufacturing Information Systems based on Object-Oriented Approach, *Proceedings of the '92 Conference, KIIE*, 192-201.

Kim, S.H., Yoon, H.C., (1994) The Development of the Drawing Information Management System for Technical Document Management, *Interfaces : Industrial Engineering*, Vol.7, No.3, 213-225.

Kim, S.H., Shin, Y.H., Moon, H.S., (1996) The Development of the CE-Based Drawing Information Management System, *Interfaces : Industrial Engineering*, Vol.9, No.1, 41-52.

Kim, W., (1990) *Introduction to Object-Oriented Databases*, MIT Press.

Lee, C.H., (1996) A Case Study on the Development of the R&D Integration System Using CALS/PDM. *IE Magazine*, Vol.3, No.1, 58-62.

Lee, C.H., et al. (1996) The Development of K-CE for Product Development Process Improvement, *Interfaces : Industrial Engineering*, Vol.8, No.3, 25-37.

McHenry, S., (1993) RDBMS vs. ODBMS for Product Information Management Systems, *Proceedings of AUTOFACT '93 Conference*, 28/13-30.

Rumbaugh, J., Blaha, M., Premerlani, W., Eddy, F., Lorensen, W., (1991) *Object-Oriented Modeling and Design*, Prentice-Hall International, Inc.

Samsung HP, (1993) *Implementation Guides for CIM(I,II)*, Computer Reengineering, Inc.

Shin, Y.K., et al. (1995) An Efficient Structure of the Integration Solution for Technical Information Management, *Interfaces : Industrial Engineering*, Vol.8, No.3, 197-203.

Taylor, D.A., (1990) *Object-Oriented Technology : A Manager's Guide*, Addison-Wesley Publishing Co.

Yoo, S.B., Seo, H.Y., Ko, K.W., (1995) Product Data Exchange in Production Systems by Use of STEP, *Interfaces : Industrial Engineering*, Vol.8, No.3, 75-95.

# 5

# Definition of numerical models for rapid product development

*A. Bernard, M. Véron*
*Research Center for Automatic Control of Nancy*
*BP 239 - 54506 - Vandoeuvre Cedex - France*
*Tel : + 33 (0) 3 83 91 27 29 ; Fax : + 33 (0) 3 83 91 23 90 ; e-mail : bernard@cran.u-nancy.fr*

**Abstract**

The initial stage of design needs CAD software for direct numerical and virtual definition, or requires a man-made model for direct experimental validation on a 3D physical model (ergonomics, aesthetics). After this validation phase the physical model is digitized and a numerical model is obtained from point clouds using sensors and special reverse engineering software. Most often, these two complementary techniques (CAD and scanning) are both used for the design of the complete object. After the complete definition of a numerical model the next step is the manufacturing of functional prototypes, whose characteristics are very close to those of the final industrial product (material, color, manufacturing process,). This demands the obtention of temporary tools (molds) which are used for small batch production (five to twenty parts), and the production of parts using layer manufacturing machines which are integrated as lost models during processes like investment casting. These different stages, from the idea to the functional prototypes, highlight the necessity of data integration, not only for part models and simulation results, but also for intermediate parts and tools definition. The final numerical reference model has to be coherent with the different intermediate numerical models (point clouds, STL files, tool models, etc.). In order to assume such objectives, we propose some first basic elements of a representation model for prototypes and temporary tools. This aspect corresponds to different tasks of the IMS-RPD project. The parametric aspect is discussed and its interest is shown for families of parts (tiles, jewels, etc.). The different links and types of elements of the models are proposed and illustrated by an industrial example.

**Key words**

Rapid product development, data integration, rapid prototyping, reverse engineering

Computer Applications in Production and Engineering. F. Plonka and G. Olling (Eds.)

# 1 INTRODUCTION

One of the main factors in achieving primacy in a continuously changing market is the ability to rapidly introduce new products.
The time is past when it was enough to have the best product at the lowest cost and with the best quality/price ratio. If an industrial firm is to satisfy the requirements of its customers and overcome the competition, it must be able to control delivery times (increasingly short), quality (increasingly high) and costs (increasingly low).
Mastering these three aspects with their apparently contradictory constraints involves introducing approaches of the "concurrent engineering" type. One of the advantages of this kind of approach is that several design alternatives can be tested and simulated within an acceptable time.
Against this background, where the processes of designing and industrializing a new product take place in parallel, the use of physical models to validate an overall product design or an industrialization process takes on increased importance. The virtual model used in CAD is no longer enough and most often does not permit complete or adequate evaluation. As far as certain products are concerned, there is no substitute for the ability to touch, manipulate, validate or operate a prototype (design or feasibility model).
It is possible today, by additional treatment of physical models produced through a rapid prototyping process, to go further, indeed to design the process for producing standard parts (models or intermediate parts that can be used in industrialization such as EDM electrodes or mold cavities).
Rapid prototyping (Binstock, 1994) (Bernard, 1995) makes it possible to directly create the physical model from the digital CAD model within twenty-four hours, or at the most a few days. The economic advantage is obvious. Moreover, rapid prototyping provides guidance for design choices (modification, alternatives. etc.) by making a model available much earlier in the project planning stage.
After a short description of rapid prototyping ways and means, we propose some parametric models and present some methodological results on mechanical and jewelry applications.

# 2 RAPID PROTOTYPING: WAYS AND MEANS

The aim of rapid prototyping is to produce a physical model in record time, at the least possible cost and using a minimum of tooling. With this method it is possible at any time, to try out different alternatives in parallel with a view to choosing the best, to validate the chosen approaches as quickly as possible to minimize the number of iterations, to acquire physical and experimental data as a basis for moving the project forward and to have a concrete basis for discussion for the concurrent engineering project teams.
During the past years rapid prototyping has been used mainly to produce form prototypes (needed for validating shapes and as a basis for communication (aesthetic design, part geometry, mechanical design, etc.), functional prototypes (in

a material close to the real product, any type of process, needed for validating the required functions and assemblies) and industrialization prototypes (needed for validating and determining the feasibility of the production processes, in the real material (or similar) and process similar to the final one).
Rapid prototyping means are well known as techniques based on layer-by-layer manufacturing in order to produce any shape without tooling.The main layer-by-layer processes available in industry account for over 2100 installations around the world including about 80 in France (mainly 3D Systems, EOS, Helisys, Stratasys, DTM, Cubital, Sanders, BPM, Soligen and Stratoconception processes). We shall not go into the detail of each process here since these were covered in many publications (AFPR, 1996).

The essential need in the field of rapid prototyping is always a numerical definition of parts, from CAD modeling or reverse engineering.This approach applies to digitizing and duplicating single objects produced by hand, to comparing and tracing modifications made to a physical model, to designing, developing and producing tooling, to duplicating or even generating a range of parts directly from the file of points (STL file, CLFile), and to following up all the iterations in the design cycle.
Some CAD software packages now offer modules for dealing with point clouds to assist the draughtsman in creating surfaces (Bernard, 1997).

Rapid prototyping also includes post-treatments (for plastic and metallic parts) (Yeung, 1996).Plastic parts can be obtained either directly on layer manufacturing machines (stereolithography, SLS, BPM, FDM), or using vacuum casting in silicone rubber molds, or through the use of metallized prototype molds which are used for the injection of a small batch production. Metallization processes can also be used for EDM electrodes obtention.Prototype metallic parts are mainly produced or raw formed by foundry (Shell, block, and sand casting) or by rapid prototyping processes.One can notice the ability of direct manufacturing of Croning type cores, using SLS process (EOSSint, 1996).
Globally, the development of such processes illustrates the industrial demand for rapid tooling. The ability of rapid tool manufacturing implies particular functions and models which have to be generated and managed, when taking into account the specific technological rules of each technology and the capability to interact between parts and tools (PROD, 1997)

## 3 PARAMETRIC MODELLING IN RAPID PRODUCT DEVELOPMENT

As shown before, the development of a mechanical object widely uses CAD, reverse engineering and rapid tooling techniques. The first example below illustrates the interactivity between the different data models, point clouds, reference models, parametric models, etc. (Dionigi, 1996).

The objective of this work was to define a parametric model of a tile and to undertake the acquisition of points belonging to its basic shapes (Figure 1) to modify some kinds of tiles and to compare them to a reference model in order to avoid a drift of geometry at one time. It is indispensable to have CAD models of all kinds of produced tiles, and to decrease the stocking of pattern models.
Positive results were obtained on both the modeling and the methodology level. A complementary constraint concerned the imposed CAD platform, Pro/Engineer (PTC_PE, 1996).

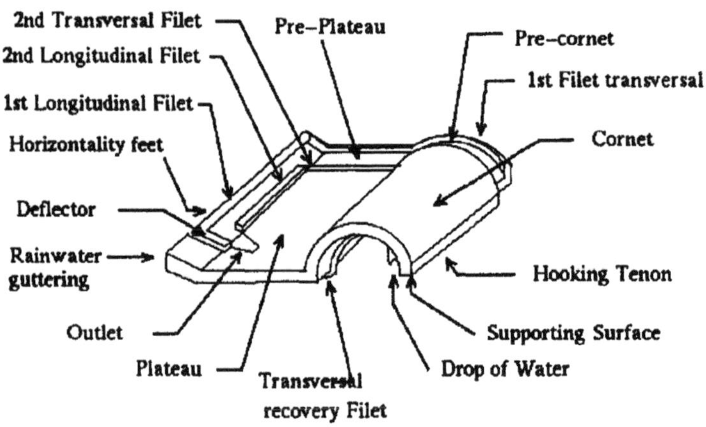


**Figure 1** Schema of a roofing tile

## 3.1 Functional parametric approach

Research work related to a functional approach of object modeling are mainly relative to kinematic connections (Rieu et al., 1994) and mechanical components (Chambolle, 1995).
In our approach, we do not design a part from its external forms, but re-build it from its trade-parameters.
The tile is a complex technical object related to a particular context both in elaboration and in utilization. The norms about tiles are solely relative to the process of tile manufacturing; we cannot use them for tile definition. So, it was indispensable to work with professionals of this trade in order to analyze with them the functional forms and constraints.
Fortunately, the part is well known and it can be modeled from its trade-parameters. The expertise gives us the functional surface decomposition.
The first question for parametric model elaboration is the choice of parameters, which means defining tile surfaces and constraints between the surfaces.
In the following paragraphs, each step of our approach to obtain the parametric design model and process of tile is explained in detail.

*Research of parameters*

We applied a functional analysis in order to determine forms of tiles and their constraints as the consequence of functional product needs.

We are not going to stress on the methodology used and the same is available in (Dionigi, 1996). The relationships of the tile had to be defined together with its external context, its functions, and the interactions between functions and the constraint sub-functions they imply. The consequence of these functions and sub-functions is the definition of functional constraints of forms constituting the tile. For example, in addition to classic functions of inclemency and aggression protection, tiles have to be piled up in order to allow their transportation and their manipulation. One understands the interest to constrain the definition of some external and internal forms. So, applying this analysis on our functional surface decomposition, we are able to determine all the constraints for each functional surface (complementary forms, distances, etc.).

Thus, in order to reach our aim of determining the tile parameters, we had to define for every functional surface, the parameters needed to create it, and the constraints it has to respect. Then, we are able to propose a functional generic parametric model of the tile.

*Functional parametric model*

The proposed model is based on an object-oriented representation.

Each functional form of the tile is described by:

- its name as identifier (eg. : cornet)
- its physical description (eg. : rounded shape constituting a major element of the morphology of the tile)
- its site on the tile, in reference to a predefined orientation of the tile (ex : right part of the tile)
- its functions (eg. : piping of water; recovery right/left; recovery over/under; horizontality of piling)
- a parametric construction with dimensions accessible or allowable from the external forms of the tile (in fact, accessible by digitizing)
- a design process, here in the environment of Pro/Engineer (eg. : definition of plan profiles and construction of the general form of the cornet by the function "smooth protrusion" with respect to limit constraints)
- its relationships with the other functional forms like constraints of form, dimensions, etc. (e.g., condition of compatibility between external and internal profiles for piling; condition of connection with the plateau; limitation along length direction). In general manner, these relationships show trade as well as the next following constraints : identical to; extremity of; parallel to; defined by; pasting to; confuse with.

Complementary relationships, that we have called "option of forms", were introduced at the global level of the tile model (cornet more longer than the plateau, tile squared, etc.). The update of the library of global options allows for the integration of new tile models.

*Implementation of the model*

The model was implemented under Pro/Engineer. The design process is directly dependent on parametric possibilities and functions of creation of available forms under Pro/Engineer. Especially, basic forms (cornet, plateau) are most often built using a protrusion function, and filets and tenons are constructed by the deformation of basic forms.

The user can choose and modify each parameter, directly on the screen with the mouse or using the software interface that makes elementary parameters and relationship tables (external and internal parameters) accessible.

Thus, from the basic model and from the specification of the "option of forms", the designer has directly a model that will be completed and finished according to final specifications and additional local details. This last phase is essentially relative to the fine definition of internal forms that, in case they exist, are specific to each model.

In the environment of Pro/Engineer one can undertake a rapid simulation of jointing (installation on roofing) and of piling (stocking). One can thus pilot some global dimensions by a constraint of the number of tiles to the squared meter.

In conclusion, we propose a parametric CAD model and apply it to a roofing tile. First we undertake a functional approach of the tile and build a parametric model of the tile, sufficiently generic for defining a great number of its forms solely from functional specifications (dimensions, relationships, sections, etc.), the general topology being automatically managed by Pro/Engineer.

Finally, the parametric model allows us to produce different prototypes of tiles, using stereolithography, and different prototypes of dies for tile forming using three axis NC machines.

The introduction of parametric data can be undertaken by the user directly on the CAD workstation, or via Pro/ScanTools module (PTC_PST, 1996), by digitizing of forms on the physical model (Figure 2).

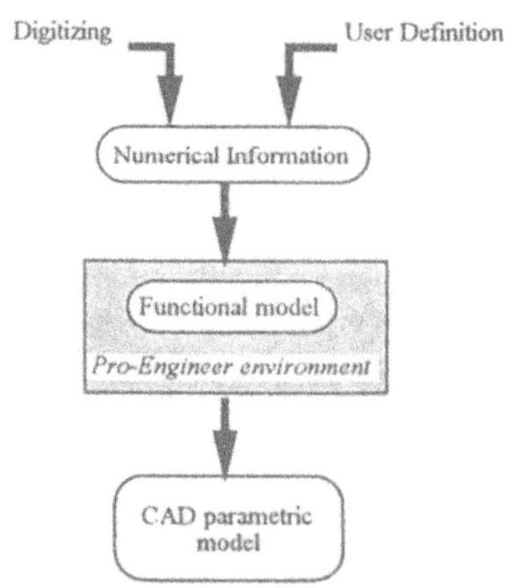


**Figure 2** Two ways for parametric model definition

## 3.2 Integration of digitizing entry in the design phase

The introduction of parametric data is undertaken by the user directly on CAD workstation, or via the Pro/ScanTools module, by the digitizing of parametric curvilinear elements on the physical model. The main difficulty is to determinate these curves from the point clouds obtained by digitizing. For the scanning, we have used a line laser sensor (Kréon, 1996) on CREATE platform (CREATE, 1993) (European Rapid prototyping Center for Assistance, Transfer and Experiments.
The different steps of reverse engineering process are described on Figure 3.

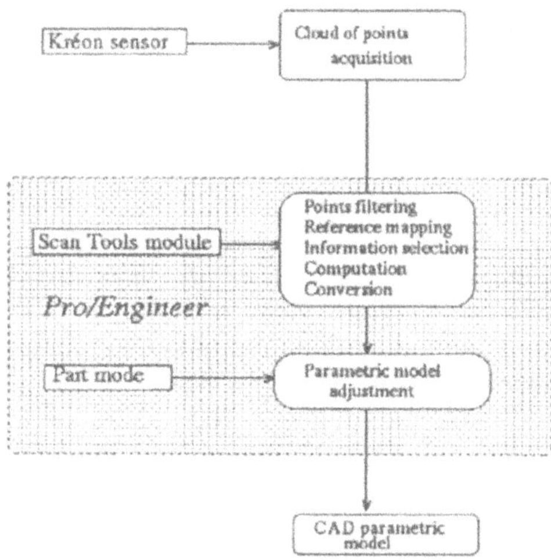


**Figure 3** Different steps of reverse engineering integration for tile

One of the main problems was to fit the reference systems of the physical part with those of Pro/Engineer. Then, we were able to introduce scanned parametric curvilinear elements into the generic parametric model of tile.

# 4 INTEREST OF PARAMETRIC MODELLING FOR JEWEL DESIGN

More generally, today the field of artistic creation is directly concerned by the evolution of the design methods and rapid manufacture of new objects. Many artists and creators use computers to program geometrical forms referring to complex combination criteria and generation (Becker, 1995) (Lavigne, 1995). If the shading of results is easily available, the unique solution for the manufacturing of volumic objects is layer-manufacturing.
Concerned by the creation of aesthetic and artistic objects, several companies that create jewels have requested case studies for digitizing, layer-manufacturing of prototypes and validation in the foundry (Suret, 1996).

In the following paragraphs we are going to present several examples that, completely or partly, have been realized by the CREATE platform during the last years.

## 4.1 Creation of normalized finger diameter rings from a unique master

In this study the goal is to decline all normalized finger diameter rings from a master created in the traditional manner by the jewel designer from the view of its manufacture in a gold foundry.
After an analysis of the shapes (identical motives connected by round blendings of imposed value), we operated the 3D scanning of the master on a Surveyor LD 500 integrated digitizing environment by using a laser point sensor (Laser Design, 1995). As the acquisition of a motive cannot be undertaken in one position, a setting was realized. First we accessed in polar to external forms, thanks to the fourth axis of the Surveyor, then, we recaptured in cartesian scanning the lateral forms rejoining the interior of the two sides. Then it was necessary to adjust the three point clouds with respect one another. In order to do that, the elements of reference (cylinders and planes) were machined on the used setting and scanned at the same time as the forms of the master for each position of the setting on the digitizing machine.
Then one identified the parameters of repositioning (rotations and translations) from the elements of reference and one applied them to the complete point clouds. Then it was classically necessary to filter noises coming from the machine of acquisition and to preserve only significant points for the external surface construction of the ring in the CAD environment. In the present case the next phase was undertaken on the Strim-RDS module (Strim-RDS, 1996).
The first step was to construct elementary surfaces of the ring from the point clouds, while already thinking of the future declination corresponding to normalized diameters of fingers. Indeed, the designer required that the width not vary in the same manner as the two other dimensions, while being able to preserve the same number of motives and the same weight of the jewel.
Parting from the surfaces of the external form one determined those that will limit the material thickness. Thanks to this thickness parameter, one could postpone the variation of the mass of the ring until the moment of the creation of the offset form constituting the interior. The global difficulty was to integrate the totality of constraints fixed by the designer to the chosen final solution.
The complexity of this phase of construction of the complete surface model of a ring depends mainly on the judicious choice of the parametric decomposition used and the methodology used with Strim-RDS tool.
It is difficult for the designer to appreciate the numerical result displayed on the screen of the workstation, we validated using a stereolithography manufacturing in order to have an object to compare to the basic master. Some modifications were necessary on the CAD model, essentially on the curve of the motive constituting the periphery of the ring.

After validating the created numerical representation made on a new part in stereolithography, the phase of diameter declination of fingers was undertaken. At this level the pertinence of the choice of the initial topology of surfaces and the methodology of construction of the first model had considerably facilitated the work.
After the construction of the ten models, STL files were created via the corresponding interface and prototypes manufactured in stereolithography on the SLA250 3D Systems machine of the CREATE.
These prototypes were then exploited during the final foundry phase, to create industrial tools necessary for the gold foundry.
The whole process brought about a gain in terms of cost and time (about 40%) compared to traditional methods used until then, despite the prospective character of this study.

### 4.2 Towards an efficient declination of a range of jewels in the field of figurines

The problem of family declination of jewels concerns basic composite figurines that are either porters of stones or inserted on rings with known diameters and thickness. In this case, one undertakes the scanning of a master corresponding to a particular model (stone diameter or characteristics of a well-known ring) and in most of the cases one can apply a direct homothety to the scanned model. Subsequently, the transition to a CAD surface model is not indispensable. Indeed, we have a direct interface for STL format from point clouds.
In the future, the declination of a line of jewels based on figurines (celebrities, animals, objects, etc.) is oriented to a parametric definition of a CAD model reconstructed from point clouds. In order to do that, one works on a functional analysis of forms, with the placement in obviousness of definition parameters intrinsic of forms, variables of positioning and laws governing the global topology of the family of jewels that has to be elaborated.
One can thus construct a library of objects of parametric parameters, offering the possibility to preserve the coherence of the model in the case where, for example, the position of an arm, a leg, the chest or that of the head changes.
The main difficulty of this approach comes from the appropriate definition of the parameters for the reconstruction of the models.
This parametric way is explored in parallel of works relative to the automatic line determination characteristic of clouds of scanned points, in order to be able to make the quasi-automatic definition of a division of constructed surfaces, and the parameter definition.

## 5 CONCLUSION

Rapid prototyping is a set of tools for computer aided design and industrialization of a new product. Nowadays, it is widely used for the concurrent engineering approach.In this paper, we have exposed applications in the field of product integrated design.

A functional parametric model was presented using functional analysis of a technical object (tile). This model, exploited in the environment of Pro/Engineer, is a real aided-design system for tile definition for the designer, also using the reverse engineering "closing loop" through the acquisition of significant elements by 3D scanning of a physical part. The model remains open and can be personalized thanks to an object structure, relationships between internal parameters (dimensions) and external ones, and constraints of forms.
We also presented applications of parametric modeling for jewel design.The re-engineering and the evolution of models are greatly favored, due to the fact that the parametric model and conditions of existence of each form.
The rapid product development implies the installation of relevant and coherent data structures, directly driven from some relevant functional parameters.
Some particular efforts on global data modeling and integration of all the described functions are ongoing today, mainly based on the STEP Standard (Mony, 1996) (IMS-RPD, 1997).

## 6 REFERENCES

AFPR (1996), 5th European Conference on Rapid Prototyping, French Rapid Prototyping Association, Paris

Becker, A., Bernard, A. (1995), Numerical design of art objects and jewels, 4th European Conference on Rapid Prototyping, Paris

Bernard, A. (1995), Rapid prototyping, International ISTA Conference, Barcelone

Bernard, A. (1997), State of the art of reverse engineering, MICAD 97, Paris

Binstock, L. (1994), Rapid Prototyping Systems : Fast Track to Product Realization, Society of Manufacturing Engineers

Chambolle, F. (1995), Functional design of cutting tools, Graduate report, DEA Production Automatisée, ENS Cachan, France

CREATE (1993), Official inauguration of the European Rapid prototyping Center for Assistance, Transfer and Experiments, École Centrale Paris, France

Dionigi, O. (1996), Modelization of functional shapes of mechanical parts for reverse engineering application on a tile, Graduate report, DEA GSI, Ecole Centrale Paris, France

EOSSint (1996), Selective laser sintering process of Croning type sand, Technical documentation, EOS, Germany

IMS-RPD (1997), European and International proposals on Rapid Product Development

Jacobs, P.F. (1992), Rapid Prototyping and Manufacturing ; Fundamentals of Stereolithography, SME

Kréon, (1996) Reverse engineering demonstrations and applications, Kréon Industries, France

Laser Design (1995), Surveyor LD 500 and DataSculpt user manuals, Laser Design Inc, USA

Lavigne, C. (1995), For a new approach, the meeting of artist and engineer, 4th European Conference on Rapid Prototyping, Paris

Mony, C. (1996), Integration of Rapid Product Development Technologies information models using STEP, Rapid Product Development Technologies, Proceedings of SPIE International Conference, Boston, volume 2910, 156-165

PROD project (1997), Rapid Production of Consommable Tools, project proposal, Ecole Centrale Paris, France

PTC_PE (1996) Generalities - Pro/Engineer Release 17.0, Parametric Technology Corporation, USA

PTC_PST (1996) Pro/ScanTools User's Guide Release 17.0, Parametric Technology Corporation, USA

Rieu, D., Constant, D., Nguyen, G.T. and Tollenaere, M. (1994) Integrated design of kinematic connections, IFIP conference, Valenciennes, France

Strim-RDS (1996), Technical documentation, MatraDataVision, France

Suret, S., Bernard, A., Bocquet, J.C. (1996), Using rapid prototyping for new products development : application to jewellery design, Rapid Product Development Technologies, Proceedings of SPIE International Conference, Boston, volume 2910, 216-225

Yeung, M.K. (1996), Rapid tooling : a step change in mold manufacturing, Rapid Product Development Technologies, Proceedings of SPIE International Conference, Boston, volume 2910, 176-186

## 7 BIOGRAPHY

A. Bernard was graduated in 1982 at ENS Cachan. He contributed to LURPA laboratory, with Prof. Bourdet, since 1983 and obtained his PhD in 1989, on 3D feature-based manufacturing of forging dies. As an assistant professor, he worked from 1990, for six years, with Prof. Bocquet in Ecole Centrale Paris on product, technology and process modeling. He also created, in 1993, the rapid prototyping and reverse engineering platform of Ecole Centrale Paris, the CREATE. He is the vice-president of AFPR (French Rapid Prototyping Association). Since September 1996, he is Professor in CRAN laboratory in Nancy.

M. Véron is professor and has been the chairman of CRAN laboratory (Research Center for Automatic Control of Nancy) during the last six years. He also manages an integrated CAD/CAM and production engineering platform (AIPL) used by the students of the university. He is also the general secretary - treasurer of CIRP (International Institution for Production Engineering Research).

6

# Impacts of data mining technology on product design and process planning

*Cihan H Dagli and Hsi-Chieh Lee*
*Smart Engineering Systems Laboratory*
*Department of Engineering Management, University of Missouri-Rolla*
*Rolla Missouri 65409-0370*
*dagli@umr.edu*
*Phone: 573 341-4374*
*Fax: 573 341-6567*

**Abstract**

Recent advances in computers and networking technologies and a fast-growing internet community created immense distributed data bases located miles away and having a capability to be updated continuously without the knowledge of the possible and prospective users. The ability to collect and store all kinds of data have outpaced the capabilities of individuals to analyze, summarize, and extract "knowledge" from them. Traditional methods of data analysis, based mainly on the analysts dealing directly with the data, is no longer the best alternative to be used. Although the database technology provided the basic tools for efficient storage and lookup for large data sets, the issues of how to enable engineers to understand large bodies of data remains a difficult problem. Recently, data mining approaches based on artificial neural networks, fuzzy logic, machine learning, statistics, expert systems, and data visualization are creating new intelligent tools for automated data mining and knowledge discovery.

All these changes will have a profound impact on current practices used in manufacturing. The way bills of materials are created, products designed and process plans generated will be definitely different with the availability of this new technology. In this paper the nature of these changes and their implication on current practices will be discussed in reference to an intelligent data mining system being developed in the smart engineering system design laboratory.

Computer Applications in Production and Engineering. F. Plonka and G. Olling (Eds.)

## 1 INTRODUCTION

The advances of computer and networking technologies and fast-growing Internet community have brought a data glut problem to the world of science, business and government. The capabilities for collecting and storing data of all kinds have far outpaced the abilities to analyze, summarize, and extract "knowledge" from this data. The Manufacturing sector is not immune to this change.

Traditional methods of data analysis, based mainly on the individual dealing directly with the data are becoming obsolete. While database technology has provided us with the basic tools for the efficient storage and lookup of large data sets, the issue of how to help humans understand and analyze large bodies of data remains a difficult and unsolved problem. To deal with the problem, a new generation of intelligent tools for automated data mining and knowledge discovery is needed. This need has been recognized by researchers in different areas, including machine learning, statistics, intelligent databases, neural networks, fuzzy systems, expert systems, and data visualization. In this paper the impact of these new technologies on manufacturing practices, namely, product design and process planning is discussed.

The Internet is basically a network of networks. It currently connects millions of networks to allow users to globally share information and computer resources. With the existence of the Internet, an user can share virtually anything that can be stored in a file. Internet communication is possible among networks on different platforms and in different environments. This capability of exchanging data dynamically is in part due to the development of communication protocols. Protocols are agreed-upon standards for exchanging data, and enable computing devices to communicate among various networks.

The Transmission Control Protocol and the Internet Protocol (TCP/IP) were developed in the 1960s to provide a communication link, even if some of the connecting links between the devices were to fail. In 1969, the Department of Defense began using ARPANET, the first network based on the protocol technology. ARPANET initially connected four supercomputers. In the 1970s, educational and research institutions began to connect to ARPANET to create a community of networks. In the late 1970s, TCP/IP became the official protocol to use on the Internet. During the 1980s, the U.S. National Science Foundation replaced ARPANET with a high-speed network. This is the network that now serves as the backbone for the Internet today. When ARPANET was first used in 1969, it consisted of only 213 registered hosts. By 1986, there were over 2300 host computers. In the early 1990s, the U.S. National Science Foundation transferred the maintenance and funding of the Internet to private foundations and corporations. Today, the Internet has several million host computers worldwide. The development of other protocols and other technologies, such as the World Wide Web, has contributed to this growth.

The World Wide Web (WWW) is a distributed hypermedia system for information discovery, retrieval, and collaboration. It was created by scientists at CERN who wanted to share and gain access to research information through a common interface. By using a common interface, researchers no longer had to perform the many steps necessary to gain access to the different available Internet services. More and more people who use the Internet have seen the value of using a common interface (i.e. web browser). In just three years since it was introduced, the Web has grown to include users from all ages and vocations. It has proven its usefulness for browsing large, distributed document structures. However, as the amount of information available through the World Wide Web increases, it becomes more and more important to provide additional tools and techniques for finding servers of documents which contain relevant information on one's special interest. The main difference between a hypertext network and conventional linear text is that in a hypertext system, navigation is up to the user. The HyperText Transfer Protocol [1] is used by web servers to communicate with each other and a variety of client applications, such as, FTP, Gopher, and WAIS.[2,3].

Manufacturing systems of the twenty-first century need to be able to use this dynamic distributed data base environment, and change their product design and process planning practices in time. Hence, there is a need to design "smart" systems for this purpose that can interact with their environment, namely, continuously changing distributed manufacturing information base residing on the interconnected computers of the world and adapt to the changes in time and space by their ability to manipulate the environment through self-awareness and perceived models of the world based on both quantitative and qualitative information. This need will integrated base functions of manufacturing, product design, process planning and control even further to be able to respond to global customer's changing requirements. The emerging technologies of artificial neural networks, fuzzy logic, evolutionary programming and data mining will provide essential tools for designing these smart manufacturing systems. In the following section a brief description of these technologies is given.

## 2 EMERGING TECHNOLOGIES

### 2.1 Neural Networks

Neural Network models have been studied and used extensively in the last decade in order to achieve human-like intelligence. The earlier works by McCulloch and Pitts [4], Hebb [5], Rosenblatt [6], and Widrow [7] as well as the more recent works by Feldman [8], Grossberg [9], Hopfield [10, 11, 12], Rumelhart and McClelland [13], Sjnowski [14], and others [15- 20] have brought the world many useful applications. Typical applications include: classification, decision making, financial analysis, medical diagnostics, optimization, pattern recognition, process control, robotics and automation, signal processing, and targeted marketing, time series prediction.

Artificial Neural Networks are the mathematical models, which represent the biological process of the human brain. In an Artificial Neural Network, there are three main components: neurons, interconnections, and learning rules.

### *Neurons*

The neuron is a simple device which approximates the function of the fundamental unit of the biological nervous systems. It receives and processes signals from either other neurons or the outside environment, then continually passes its output to the next level neurons. Each neuron can receive many input signals simultaneously, but there is only one output signal which depends on the input signals, weights of connections, threshold, and the activation function.

Neurons can be classified into three types based on their inputs and outputs: input, output and hidden neurons. Input neurons are the ones that actually receive input from the environment. Output neurons are those that send the signals out of the system, and neurons, which have inputs and outputs within the system, are called hidden neurons.

The purpose for including the activation function in the neuron is to confine the neuron's output to a pre-specified range.

### *Interconnections*

The interconnection is a part of the network architecture, which propagates signals in a single direction from one neuron to the others, or even to itself. There is a weight value assigned to each connection.

There are three different kinds of connections that link neurons in a network.

- Intrafield connections: Connect neuron in the same layer.
- Interfield connections: Connect neuron in different layers.
- Recurrent connections: Connect neuron to its self.

### *Learning Rules*

Learning in an artificial network is considered to as a change in the weight matrix. It can be categorized into two groups: supervised and unsupervised learning.

Supervised learning uses the data set that contains input vectors and corresponding output vectors to train the network. The weight matrix of the network is updated as long as the total network error is greater than $\varepsilon$ (acceptable range of error). Such updating techniques as error-correction learning, reinforcement learning and stochastic learning are always included in this type of learning. *Error-correction learning* adjusts the whole weight matrix in proportion to the difference between the desired and the actual values of the output neuron. *Reinforcement learning* is a technique in which weights are reinforced for properly performed actions and punished for inappropriate ones. *Stochastic learning* makes a random change in the weight matrix then determines resultant energy of the network. If the resultant energy is lower than the previous one, the change is accepted, otherwise the change is considered under a pre-chosen probability distribution.

Unsupervised learning does not incorporate external teacher. It relies only on local information and internal control.

## 2.2 Fuzzy Logic

Multivalued logic was first introduced in the 1920s and 1930s as a result of logical paradoxes. In 1965, Lofti Zadeh [21] published the paper "Fuzzy Sets" which formally developed multivalued set theory. This was thought of as the first time that the term "fuzzy" was introduced into the technical literature, and which inaugurated a second wave of interest in multivalued logic system. The recent new theory and application in fuzzy logic led to the current third wave of interest in fuzzy systems. Fuzziness measures the degree that an event may occur or the degree that an entity may be classified as something. Fuzzy logic systems permit variables to belong to more than one set of class. [22]. The fuzzy set concept used in intelligent data mining system described in this paper was introduced by Zadeh [21, 23] and summarized by Kosko [24].

## 2.3 Data Mining

Data mining (also known as Knowledge Discovery in Databases- KDD) has been defined as "The nontrivial extraction of implicit, previously unknown, and potentially useful information from data" [25]. It uses machine learning, statistical and visualization techniques to discovery and present knowledge in a form which is easily comprehensible to humans. There might be valuable information in your data, but you simply cannot see it. It could not be as profound as a new law of nature. But no human who has looked at your data has seen this hidden information which might be important. How can people find it? Data mining lets the power of computers do the work of sifting through the vast data stores.

In recent years, data mining has attracted the interest of many researchers due to its importance of finding knowledge in growing size of databases [26-36]. Data mining deploys a variety of algorithms. Generally, the more algorithms in use, the higher the likelihood of accurate results. There are no certain rules and tools. As a result, current data mining researchers are fielding architectures that combine these techniques: neural networks, induction, association, fuzzy logic, statistical, and visualization.

Gerber [37] summarized the commonly used approaches into the following four categories:

- Predictive modeling: In OLAP (On-Line Analytical Processing), it uses deductive reasoning; in data mining, it uses inductive reasoning. Predictive modeling can be implemented in a variety of ways, including neural networks or induction algorithms.
- Database segmentation: The automatic partitioning of a database into clusters. It generally uses statistical clustering in its implementation.
- Link analysis: Identifying connections between records, based on association discovery and sequence discovery.

- Deviation detection: The detection of an explanation for why records cannot be put into segments. This can be implemented via different kinds of statistics.

Generally, data-mining process includes the following sub-tasks:

- Preprocess data: It includes the data collection, data cleaning, and data storing.
- Search for patterns: This is usually the most crucial part of the data-mining process. A number of tools are being used for this purpose such as queries, rules, neural networks, machine learning, and statistics.
- Analyst reviews output: The output of the previous sub-task is investigated here to decide whether to report the findings or to perform a revised pattern search.
- Report findings: The findings will be further interpreted and response accordingly.

All of these new technologies are incorporated into the intelligent data mining system that is under development.

## 3 IMPACTS ON MANUFACTURING PRACTICES

Availability of adaptive data mining system can have profound impact on product design and process planning. These can be summarized briefly as described in the following paragraphs

### 3.1 Impact on Product Design

Engineering design is essentially the process of converting the desires and needs of the customer into detailed specifications for a useable end product. It is a highly knowledge intensive and time-consuming activity which requires a great many decisions and judgments on the part of the human designer. It is also an imprecise art, since each designer differs in background, experience, preferences, and formal training. The more knowledge and experience the designers have, the better the chances for generating creative designs. Final product design impacts sixty to eighty-five percent of the total manufacturing cost. Hence, through analysis of design alternatives is essential prior to the finalization of the product design process. This is not an easy task as the number of possible design solutions increases exponentially as new functional requirements and manufacturing constraints are introduced. The NP-complete (non polynomial in time characteristic of the design problem necessitates different search strategies in selecting the final design creating a wide variety of approaches adopted by researchers. How does an artifact get designed? How do fuzzy mental images and abstract concepts get converted to the crisp design: The process is not well understood at this time. Each researcher approaches the problem in a different way in an effort to generate the best design satisfy functional requirements.

Suh defines design as the culmination of synthesized solutions in the form of products, software, processes, or systems by the appropriate selection of design parameters that satisfy perceived needs through the mapping from functional requirements in the function domain to design parameters in the structure domain. This mapping process is not unique, and more than one design may result from the generation of design parameters that satisfy the functional requirements. Therefore, there can be an infinite number of feasible design solutions and mapping techniques. Suh's design axioms provide the principles the mapping technique must satisfy in regard to input requirements in order to produce a good design and provide a framework for comparing and selecting designs. The axioms are independence and information. The independence axiom states that in an acceptable design, the design parameters and the functional requirements are related in such a way that a specified design parameters can be adjusted to satisfy its corresponding functional requirements without affecting other functional requirements. The information axiom states that the best design is a functionally uncoupled design that has a minimum information content.

Many researchers have been trying to develop a scientific theory or at least a mode of design. Their perspectives and views on the nature of design can be visualized as a feed-back loop of synthesis, evaluation, and analysis. The general model of the design process is inherently iterative and requires improvements until requirements are satisfied.

Product design goes through all the above stages. Intelligent data mining system can provide valuable information to the designer in all stages as it has the capability to predict the need of the designer and receive relevant information from the interconnected computers of the global village. This capability will impact four basic distinct aspects of product design:

- Problem definition from fuzzy sets of facts and myths into a coherent statement of the question
- Creative process of devising a proposed physical embodiment of solutions
- Analytical process of devising a proposed physical embodiment of solutions
- Ultimate check of the fidelity of the design product to the original perceived needs

## 3.2 Impact on Product Design

Manufacturing planning, process planning, material processing, process engineering and machine routing are some of the names given to the topic referred to here as process planning.

Process planning is the act of preparing detailed operation instructions to transform an engineering design to a final part. It is the critical bridge between design and manufacture. Design information can only be translated through process planning into manufacturing language. The detailed plan contains the route, processes, process parameters, machines, and tools required for production. The process plan provides the instructions for production of the part. These instructions dictate the cost, quality and rate of production. Therefore process planning is of utmost importance to the production system. In general, a process plan is prepared using the available design data, and manufacturing knowledge.

Process planning is a data intensive activity that requires extensive search. Intelligent data mining system due to its ability to predict the need of the process planner and locate the source of information and knowledge to restrict the search can provide an important input in generating process plans. It is very difficult to envision the impact of this capability in manufacturing practices.

# 4 INTELLIGENT DATA MINING SYSTEM

## 4.2 The Model

The term "Cyberspace" has existed for decades, while the term "World Wide Web" had not been known until recently. Cyberspace is a unified conceptualization of space spanning the entire Internet. It is a spatial equivalent of the World Wide Web. There is only one Cyberspace, just on an irregular network topology. It has brought the information from a distributed environment into a global information universe. As the number of web servers increases, surfing the Web is increasingly difficult. The proposed model, Cyber Agent, is seeking a computational model which can efficiently implement high-level intelligent processes instead of seeking to model the detailed biological aspect of the human brain.

The Cyber Agent (Fig. 1) is a smart engineering system built to help users search and organize the information. It contains two major subsystems, namely, WebTracer and WebOrganizer. They adapt behavior dynamically according to the environment and the special requirements of each individual. WebTracer is the wavefront of the CyberAgent while WebOrganizer is the brain of the CyberAgent. They are implemented using PERL and Common Gateway Interface (CGI) [38].

Figure 1: The CyberAgent Model

## 4.2 WebTracer

WebTracer (see Fig. 2) is the wavefront of the Cyber Agent which obtains the information from Cyberspace. While there are a number of search engines available which hold a tremendous amount of data, WebTracer is not meant to be another database-base search engine. Instead, it resides on top of the existing search engines, web robots, web spiders, and web wanderers [39]. This speeds up the searching process and eliminates the requirement for huge storage locally. It incorporates WAIS's [3] ability which answers Z39.50 information requests to search several databases at once and lets the users select those databases. A hybrid system consisting of neural networks and fuzzy associative memory is used for conceptual search and approximate string matching. It improves queries based on the user's feedback. It creates links dynamically to the user's particular interests using HyperText Markup Language (HTML) [40].

The beauty of the World Wide Web is the wide availability of resources. To utilize the resources in Cyberspace, WebTracer first consults the online libraries which contain dictionaries, thesauruses, and encyclopedias for the keywords that the user provided and then launches the existing search engine to search the related information obtained from the online libraries.

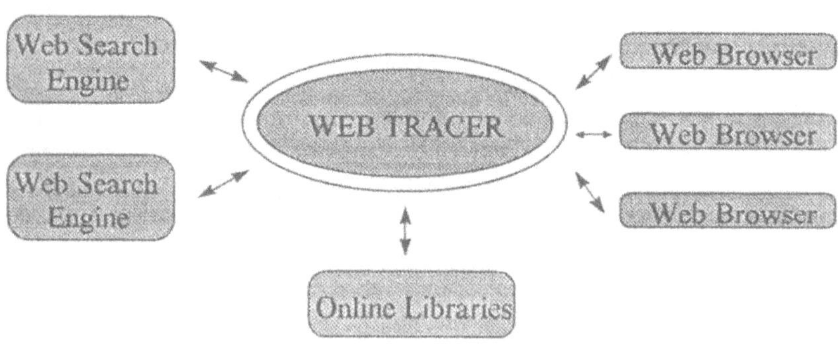


Figure 2: The WebTracer Diagram

## 4.3 WebOrganizer

The popularity of web servers and web browsers has brought the information from a distributed environment into a global information universe which is available at one's fingertips. As more information is available in Cyberspace, the users will find more information interesting to them. As the user surfs the web and adds bookmarks, it is increasingly difficult for them to find their desired information from their bookmarks.

The WebOrganizer (see Fig. 3) is the brain of the CyberAgent. It serves as a housekeeper of the web pages and bookmarks. Since the information in Cyberspace and the distributed network environment is maintained by many people, documents may be moved or deleted, referenced information may change, and the hyper-links (Uniform Resource Locators, URL[41]) may be broken. Like

MOMspider [42], WebOrganizer maintains the hyper-links by transversing in Cyberspace. It checks the existence of hyper-links, moved documents, and recent modification dates. Besides, WebOrganizer can also expand the bookmarks by referring to the existing hyper-links in it. It also has the capability to organize the bookmarks in a variety of ways specified by the user. WebOrganizer consults WebTracer for the validity of hyper-links, and recent modification dates of hyper-links.

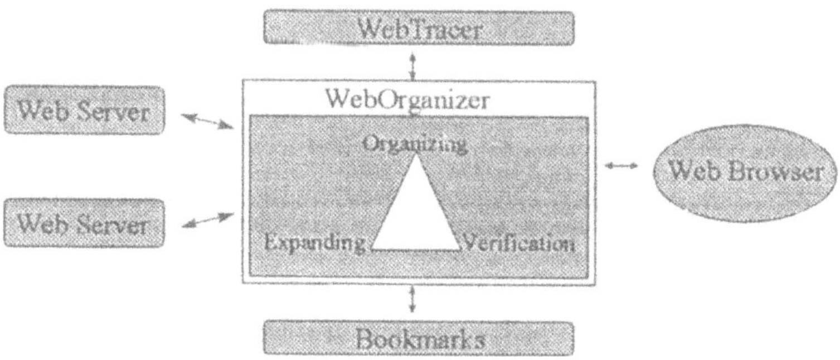


Figure 3: The WebOrganizer Diagram

## 5 REMARKS

Manufacturing engineers of the future need to understand and use large bodies of manufacturing data distributed globally and should be able to make sound product design and process planning decisions. This is possible through smart data base systems that can interact with their environment and adapt to changes both in space and time. Emerging technologies of artificial neural networks, fuzzy logic and evolutionary programming are providing the necessary foundation to design such systems as described by the intelligent data mining system.

## 6 REFERENCES

[1]"Hypertext transfer protocol," *URL:http://www.info.cern.ch/hypertext/WWW/Protocols/HTTP/HTTP2.html.*

[2] Kahle, B. (1991) *An information System for Corporate Users*, WAIS. Thinking Machines Corporation.

[3] "Wide-area information system," *URL:http://www.wais.com/z3950.html*

[4] McCulloh, W. S. and Pitts W. (1943) "A logical calculus of the ideas imminent in nervous activity", *Bulletin of Mathematical Biophysics*, **5**, 115-132.

[5] Hebb, D. O. (1949) *The Organization of Behavior.* Jan Wiley & Sons, New York.

[6] Rosenblatt, R. (1959) *Principles of Neurodynamics.* Spartan Books, New York.

[7] Widrow, B. and Hoff M. E. (1996) "Adaptive Switching Circuits," *1960 IRE WECON* **Conv. Record Prt. 4**, 96-104.

[8] Feldman, J. A. and Ballard D. H. (1982) "Connectionist models and their properties," *Cognitive Science*, **6**, 205-254.

[9] Grossberg, S. (1996) The Adaptive Brain I: *Cognition, Learning, Reinforcement, and Rhythm*, and The Adaptive II: *Vision, Speech, Language, and Motor Control*. Elsevier/Nth-Holland, Amsterdam.

[10] Hopfield, J. J. (1982) "Neural networks and physic systems with emergent collective computational abilities," *Proc. Natl. Acad. Sci. USA*, **79**, 2554-2558.

[11] Hopfield, J. J. (1984) "Neurons with graded response have collective computational properties like those of two-state neurons," *Proc. Natl. Acad. Sci. USA*, **81**, 3088-3092.

[12] Hopfield, J. J. and Tank, D. W. (1986) "Computing with neural circuits: A model," *Science*, **233**, 625-633.

[13] Rumelhart, D. E., Hinton, G. E. and Williams, R. J. (1986) "Learning internal representations by error propagation," *Parallel Distributed Processing: Explorations in the Microstructure of Cognition*, **1**

[14] Sejnowski, T. and Rosenberg, C. R. (1986) "Nettalk: A parallel network that learns to read aloud," *Johns Hopkins Univ. Technical Report*, **JHU/EECS-86/01**.

[15] Lippmann, R. P. (1987) "An introduction to computing with neural nets," *IEEE ASSP Mag.*, **4(2),** 4-22.

[16] Kohohen, T. (1989) *Self-Organization and Associative Memory.* Springer-Verlag, 3rd ed.

[17] Carpenter, G. A. and Grossberg, S. (1987) "A massively parallel architecture for a self-organization neural pattern recognition machine," *Computer Vision, Graphics and Image Processing*, **37**, 54-115.

[18] Carpenter, G. A., Grossberg, S. and Rosen, D. B. (1991) "Fuzzy art: Fast stable learning and categorization of analog patterns by an adaptive resonance system," *Neural Networks*, **4**, 759-771.

[19] Smith, M. (1993) *Neural Networks for Statistical Modeling*. Van Nostrand Reinhold.

[20] Lee, H. C., Dagli, C. H. and Ercal, F. (1994) "Neuro-fuzzy approach for data clustering: A prototype architecture," *Submitted to Artificial Neural Networks In Engineering*.

[21] Zadeh, L. A. (1965) "Fuzzy sets," *Information and Control*, **8**, 338-353.

[22] Lawrence, J. (1992) *Introduction to Neural Networks and Expert Systems*. California Scientific Software.

[23] Zadeh, L. A. (1983) "A computational approach to fuzzy quantifiers in natural languages," *Computers and mathematics*, **9(1)**, 149-184.

[24] Kosko, B. (1992) *Neural Networks and Fuzzy Systems; A dynamical Systems Approach To Machine Intelligence*. Prentice-Hall.

[25] Frawley, W., Piatetsky-Shapiro, G. and Matheus, C. (1991) "Knowledge discovery in databases: An overview," *AI Mag.*, 213-228, Fall(Autumn) 1992. Reprint of the introductory chapter of Knowledge Discovery in Databases collection, AAI/MIT Press.

[26] Agrawal, R., Imielinski, T. and Swami, A. (1993) "Database mining: A performance perspective," *IEEE Transactions on Knowledge and Data Engineering*, **5**, 914-925.

[27] Kaufman, K. A., Michalski, R. S. and Kerschberg, L. (1991) *"Mining for knowledge in databases: Goals and general description of the inlen system,"* in Knowledge Discovery in Databases (G. Piatetsky-Shapiro and W. J. Frawley, eds.), Menlo Park, California: AAAI Press / The MIT Press, 1st ed.

[28] Michalski, R., Kerschberg, L. and Kaufman, K. (1992) "Mining for knowledge in databases: The inlen architecture, initial implementation and first results," *Journal of Intelligent Information Systems*, 85-113.

[29] "Data mining: Intelligent technology gets down to business," *PC AI*, Nov-Dec 1993

[30] Agrawal, R., Imielinski, T. and Swami, A. (1993) "Database mining: A performance perspective," *IEEE transactions on knowledge and data engineering*, **5(6)**, 914-925.

[31] Michalski, R. S., Kerschberg, L. and Kaufman, K. A. (1992) "Mining for knowledge in databases: the INLEN architecture, initial implementation and first results," *Journal of Intelligent Information Systems*, **1**, 85-113.

[32] Al-naemi, S. (1992/3) "*Temporal aspects in data mining*," tech. Rep., Computer Science Department, Univ. of Birmingham.

[33] "Getting to grips with arrears: 'data mining' systems at the Leeds," *Expert Systems*, **11**, 122-124, 1994.

[34] Holsheimer, M. and Siebes, A. P. (1994) "*Data mining: the search for knowledge in databases*," Tech Rep. CS-R9406, CWI.

[35] Zytkow, J. M. and Baker, J. (1991) "*Interactive mining for regularities in databases*," 31-35, Menlo Park, California: AAAI Press.

[36] Holsheimer, M. and Siebes, A. P. (1994) "*Data mining: the search for knowledge in databases*," Tech. Rep. CS-R9406, CWI.

[37] Gerber, C. (1996) "Excavate your data," *Datamation*, **42(9)**.

[38] McCool, R. (1993-1994) "*The Common Gateway Interface*," National Center for Supercomputer Applications, Univ. of Illinois at Urbana-Champaign.

[39] Koster, M. "World Wide Web Robots, Wanderers, and Spiders" *URL:http://www.infor.webcrawler.com/mak/projects/robots/robots.html*

[40] Berners-Lee, T. (ed.), "Hypertext Mark-up Language," CERN *URL:http://www.infor.cern.ch/hypertext/WWW/MarkUp/MarkUp.html*

[41] Berners-Lee, T. (1993) "Uniform Resource Locators," *Internet Engineering Task Force Draft*, CERN, Geneva, Switzerland.

[42] Fielding, R. T. (1994) "Maintaining Distributed Hypertext Infostructures: Welcome to MOMspider's Web," University of California at Irvine, *URL:http:///www.ncsa.uiuc.edu/demonweb/html-primer.html*

# 7
# On the implementation of product model interfaces in CIME

*T. Sørensen*
*Department of Control- and Engineering Design,*
*Building 421, Technical University of Denmark*
*DK-2800 Lyngby*
*Phone: +45 45 25 45 32*
*Fax: +45 45 88 40 24*
*E-mail: torben.soerensen@iks.dtu.dk*

**Abstract**

This paper address how neutral product model interfaces can be identified, specified, and implemented to provide intelligent and flexible means for information management in manufacturing of discrete mechanical products.

The use of advanced computer based systems, such as CAD, CAE, CNC, and robotics, offers a potential for significant cost-savings and quality improvements in manufacturing of discrete mechanical products.

However, these systems are introduced into production as 'islands of automation' or 'islands of information', and to benefit from the said potential, the systems must be integrated into an integrated manufacturing unit. Such units are known as Computer Integrated Manufacturing and Engineering (CIME) systems.

The basic concept in CIME is to share and reuse information between the different computer based subsystems. Consequently, for the integration purposes, the CIME systems are highly dependent on reliable product model interfaces to bridge the information islands together.

The neutral product model interfaces addressed in this paper are used to facilitate an integration strategy know as 'the open systems CIME architecture'. This architecture is basically based upon three different domains; the CA(X) systems are placed in two different domains for design and planning, respectively. A third domain within the CIME architecture comprises the automated equipment on the shop floor.

Computer Applications in Production and Engineering. F. Plonka and G. Olling (Eds.)

**Keywords**
Neutral product model interface, STEP, CIME, information modeling, function modeling, schema-driven processors.

# 1 INTRODUCTION

The success of a manufacturing process is determined by the degree to which the manufacturing system masters the essential constituents of a product: Matter, energy, and *information*, (Schlechtendahl, 1989).

For the manufacturing of discrete mechanical products three different types of information are relevant. 1) *Product definition data*, that defines product properties such as geometric and kinetic features, and 2) *process definition data*, that define the process parameters such as welding speed, -current, and -voltage, and 3) *production definition data*, such as bill of materials, logistics and production management data.

The history of the manufacturing of discrete products is characterized by a continuous expansion of emphasis from matter via energy towards information, leading to the domain of *information technology*. One main reason for this is the fact that information technology and manufacturing automation have proven to be important instruments to reduce costs, increase product quality and to accelerate the process within an enterprise, especially within product development and preparation for manufacturing. Today, manufacturing of e.g., automobiles, airplanes, and ships is no longer cost-effective and competitive without modern information technology and automation.

The information technology domain has two important sub-areas: Information *processing*, and information *communication*, (Schlechtendahl, 1989).

Computer aided information processing systems, CA(X), such as CAD for design, CAR for robotics, CAQ for quality assurance etc., are prerequisites for the automated manufacturing of discrete products based upon programmable, general purpose, automatic shop-floor machines, such as robotic systems and NC machines. However, these information processing systems are inherently stand-alone systems and act inevitable as ‘islands of information’, or ‘islands of automation’ when they are introduced into production. What is needed is the other aspect of information technology, namely free communication of information for integrating or ‘bridging’ these ‘islands’ together by information exchange.

This development led to new manufacturing concepts such as Computer Integrated Manufacturing and Engineering (CIME). The main objective of a CIME system is to provide a reliable and rational manufacture of products. A CIME system integrates the information flow of product data that is communicated between the various CA(X) systems, or CIME subsystems, that feature the functional ‘building blocks’ of a computer based manufacturing system. The CIME area encompasses the whole range of computer integrated activities with CA(X) systems.

The basic concept in CIME systems is to *share* and *reuse* information between the different subsystems. In modern manufacturing technology a huge amount of product information must be created, identified, stored and transferred. The CIME concept therefore needs intelligent communication of product data back and forth between the sub-systems, inside the CIME system in question, as well as between sub-systems of other CIME systems, e.g., those at a sub-contractors site.

Often the individual subsystems are purchased from different vendors and have been developed over many years. The systems tend to use non-standard ways to represent product definition data which leads to integration problems due to the lack of inter-system communication and data exchange possibilities. The growing number of diverse sub-systems that appear on the CIME market place further amplifies this interconnection problem.

One problem in CIME is therefore to define an *integration strategy* sufficient to solve these inter-communication and data exchange problems between the various CA(X) systems.

Another problem is that the CIME architecture must provide an *infrastructure* for building individually tailored CIME sub-systems. This way, the CIME sub-systems can later be updated, expanded, added or excluded in accordance to the users needs and opportunities, in an evolutionary and progressive way, without ruining the overall architecture, (Trostmann, 1987).

A promising concept, used to solve these problems, is known as the *open systems'* architecture. Open systems CIME architecture can appropriately be implemented based upon *neutral interfaces.* In this context the term 'neutral' denotes that the data and program formats have been universal accepted as a carrier of data and programs, irrespective of native data and program formats used by the sending or receiving CIME sub-system.

## 2. THE OPEN SYSTEMS' CIME ARCHITECTURE

An open system CIME architecture is conceptually based upon three different domains as shown in Table 1; the CA(X) subsystems are placed in two different domains for design and planning, respectively. A third domain within the CIME architecture comprises the automated equipment for real-time execution of the manufacturing tasks on the shop floor. Neutral interfaces are defined between each domain to assure the free exchange of product definition data and programs, both between CIME-subsystems in different domains and between CIME-subsystems in the same domain. The product model interfaces are implemented as physical files, as databases, or as application programming interfaces by use of processor programs.

**Table 1** An open CIME system kernel (Kroszynski, 1991)

| *Function* | *CIME sub-system* | *Neutral Interface* |
|---|---|---|
| Domain 1:<br>Product design, analysis and evaluation. | CAD / CAE | |
| | | Product model description |
| Domain 2:<br>Manufacturing and process planning, simulation, and programming. | CAM / CAP / CAR | |
| | | EMC description (data & programs) |
| Domain 3:<br>Explicit Machine Control (EMC) of automated manufacturing equipment, for real-time shop-floor manufacturing. | NC / CNC / DNC<br>Robots/FMS/AGV | |

*The first neutral interface* in Table 1 refers to the product model description interface, which should include all the relevant characteristics of the object to be produced i.e., the product-, the process-, and the production definition data mentioned above.

CAD/CAE systems usually generate a description of the product definition data, i.e. geometrical characteristics such as shape, dimensions, and topology, of each single component, subassembly, and entire machine part.

CAD/CAE/CAP application modules, or dedicated software packages and systems supplement the product definition data with, e.g., the kinematics that governs the moving parts of the product, as well as process-, and production definition data. The first neutral interface is associated to the acronyms IGES (IGES, 1991), SET (SET, 1989), VDA-FS (VDA-FS, 1987), CAD*I (CAD*I, 1989), and the international standard STEP (ISO 10303-1, 1993). STEP is the working title for 'ISO10303-STandard for the Exchange of Product model data' for communication and storage of information models represented as *neutral product definition data*, and *neutral program* formats.

*The second neutral interface* in Table 1 refers to the actual programs that drive the computer controlled manufacturing equipment on the shop floor. These programs, generated at the CAM/CAP/CAR level of the CIME system, can range from instructions to perform a drilling cycle to produce a pattern of holes, to a complex program for the assembly of a mechanism by a robot system. Explicit Machine Control (EMC) descriptions for numerically controlled machine tools are realized with the standardized programming language 'NC-processor' (ISO 4342), which is based on the well-known APT language. The NC-processor languages produce two standardized output formats 'CL-data and structure' (ISO 3592), and 'CL-data for post-processing' (ISO 4343). For robotics, no robot programming languages have matured enough, politically and/or technically, to become an international accepted standard yet. Today, robot programming languages are at best, national standards such as the two German DIN standards IRDATA, (IRDATA, 1986), and IRL, (IRL, 1992).

Having shortly discussed the open systems' architecture, we now turn our attention to the development of the product model interface, which is addressed above as the 'first' neutral interface to implement this architecture.

## 2 DEVELOPMENT OF NEUTRAL PRODUCT MODEL INTERFACES

The development of a product description interface for exchange of advanced, discrete product models introduces some new and interesting challenges to be met.

Some of these challenges are to find appropriate *interface design-* and *implementation* methodologies, as well as *tools* for increasing the inter-system communication capabilities, and accordingly contribute with solutions to the above-mentioned integration problem in an intelligent fashion.

A proper solution of these interrelated challenges is a prerequisite for raising the integration level and thereby increasing the degree of *interoperability* in CIME. Interoperability in CIME reflects the capability of diverse CIME sub-systems to work together for the benefit of the total CIME system to achieve a desired goal.

The design phase, in Table 1 Domain 1, is distributed over 'traditional' computer Aided Design (CAD) and Computer Aided Engineering (CAE) systems such as Computer Aided Control Systems Design (CACSD) systems. This distributed design phase gives raise to *interoperability problems* because two different designs are often transferred concurrently as a compound model in order to fulfill primarily specific functional needs of the receiving CAM/CAP/CAR system in Table 1, Domain 2.

Therefore, the generic, enhanced product description interface has to be designed with the said open architecture and by use of proper methodologies to provide mechanisms to administer and integrate these distributed designs, reliably and efficiently.

Three 'classic' phases of work are used for interface development, i.e. the identification phase, the specification phase, and the implementation phase. Each of these phases has its own associated methodologies; the identification phase utilizes function modeling, the specification phase is based upon information models, and the implementation phase is based upon a computer programming language.

The choices of methodologies for interface development affects the scope (or capabilities) of the interface and consequently the application of the interface. It is therefore important to choose the best possible framework for the interface development.

It is, of course possible to develop dedicated processors by use of arbitrary processor development principles and home-made interface formats, but the scope and application of such processors and interfaces are quite limited.

A more appropriate approach is to base the open systems' CIME architecture upon neutral interfaces and corresponding neutral processor programs as mentioned above.

Today, the international STEP initiative (ISO-10303-1, 1993) provides a promising infrastructure to cope with function modeling and information modeling of product definition data for the development of neutral product model description interfaces, and it provides a common, universally accepted data and program format for information transfer.

The STEP methodology allows (among other) us to use the IDEF0, (IDEF0, 1981) function modeling technique for identification, and EXPRESS/EXPRESS-G (ISO-10303-11, 1994), information modeling techniques for specification as shown in Figure 1. For the interface implementation purposes one is free to use whatever programming language preferred (e.g., C++ is quite suitable for use with STEP).

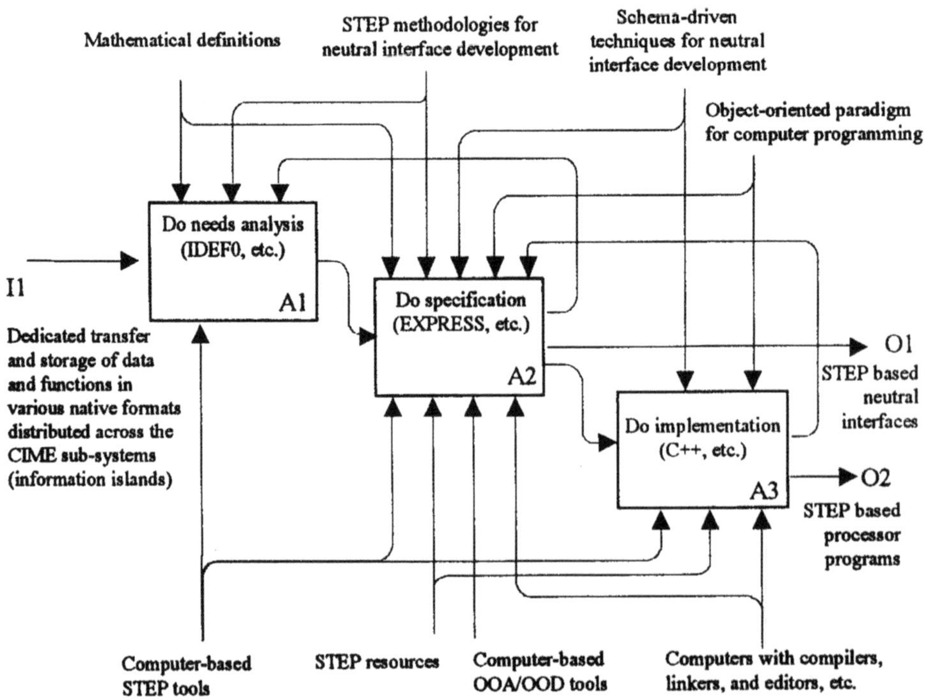


**Figure 1** IDEF0 diagram showing the different phases of the iterative interface developments by use of the ISO-STEP methodology (Sørensen, 1996).

Generally speaking, the purpose of such initiatives as STEP is to enable *sharing of product model information between different computer applications.* For information to be shared between two systems, an agreement on the contents and the semantics must be made. In STEP this is accomplished by defining information models in EXPRESS, a formal information modeling language (based upon data identified by use of e.g. IDEF0 as shown in Figure 1). EXPRESS has been developed specifically to describe product information for exchange between engineering applications, and the semantics of an information model is determined partly by the EXPRESS text (schema), and partly through natural language annotations.

The role of a product information model for the definition of interfaces is shown in Figure 2.

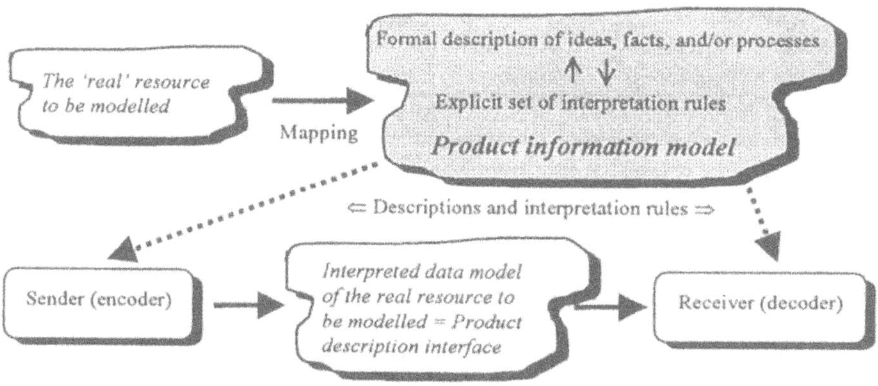


**Figure 2** The role of an information model for interface definition for transfer and storage of information (Sørensen, 1996).

An information model represents the structure and semantics of information within the modeled system or subject area.

Information models for interface definition (Figure 2) 'maps' ideas, facts, and processes, related to the 'real' resources to be modeled, into formal interface descriptions defining the scope and constraints of the information resources. Moreover, information models utilize explicit sets of rules defining how data, which are subject to transfer via the interface, should be interpreted.

An information model can be defined as (Schenck, 1994):

*An information model is a formal description of types of ideas, facts, and processes which together form a model of a portion of interest of the real world, and which provides an explicit set of interpretation rules. (If an information model is written in EXPRESS or any other computer sensible representation, it has the additional quality of being computer processible).*

An information model requires three interconnected concepts: *scope*, *perspective* and *purpose*. Scope means what is included and what is excluded from the model; in other words it defines the boundaries of the model. Perspective represents the viewpoints that are incorporated into the model. The model will be affected by the objectives of the modeller's perspectives, and thus the purpose of the model is also important; what is the model intended for?

## 3 IMPLEMENTATION OF PRODUCT MODEL INTERFACES

The last stage in the iterative development process of a neutral product model interface, addressed above, and shown in Figure 2, is the *physical implementation* of the interface. The neutral interface is implemented by use of *processors*. Processors, or translators, are computer programs that facilitate transfer, access, and storage of data within a neutral interface defined by the information model.

The implementation of the STEP based product model interface implies the selection of proper processor development techniques, implementation paradigm, CASE tools, and exchange scenario for processor implementation and tests.

A product model interface implementation has been done at the Technical University of Denmark (DTU) facilitating the exchange of dynamic control models between general purpose Computer Aided Control Systems Design (CACSD) Systems and Computer Aided Robotics (CAR) systems for dynamics simulation of robot control systems. This test set-up is using the so-called schema-driven processor development technique, the object-oriented implementation paradigm, and a fourth generation STEP based CASE tool.

Such STEP based processor development is an iterative modeling and programming process with functional modeling in IDEF0, information modeling in EXPRESS-G and EXPRESS (or NIAM or IDEF1X), and implementation specification with e.g. OOA/OOD, and implementation with OOP as show in Figure 3. The chronological modeling and development order goes from IDEF0 modeling to EXPRESS-G and EXPRESS, and further on to OOA/OOD followed by OOP.

One advantage with the interface implementation chosen at DTU is that the link between the EXPRESS schema and the data structure of the processor program is facilitated by a compiler (CASE tool) that translates the EXPRESS language into an intermediate data structure of the implementation language (typically C++). This feature promotes interoperability between the CIME sub-systems by allowing easy adoptions of new information models and easy modifications of the existing information models and thereby allowing distributed sub-designs to act together in the interface as a virtual complex design.

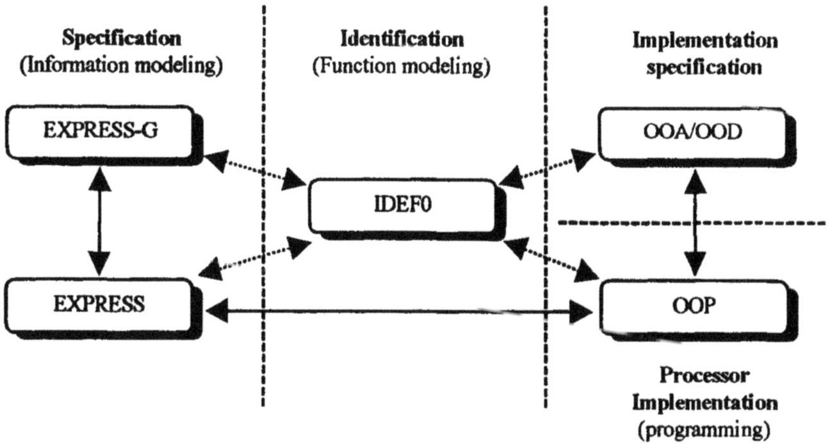


**Figure 3:** The iterative modeling process between lexical and graphical representations. Dotted arrows indicate manual model data transfer and full arrows indicate automatic conversion between data representation formats (Sørensen, 1996).

Note that for 'non-schema-driven' processors the EXPRESS schema is interpreted and translated *manually* into the intermediate data structure. This also implies that, for every change in the EXPRESS schema the intermediate data structure has to be exposed to a slow, error-prone, and tedious manual updating process.

Another advantage with the chosen approach is that it uses a 'modular' architecture for developing interfaces that reduces the overheads in creating neutral interfaces, such as those based upon STEP. Only the so-called pre-processor 'front-end', and the post processor 'back-end' are specific to a given CA(X) system, and the intermediate data structure is derived directly from the information model (represented here by the EXPRESS schema). In addition to this, the use of the modular architecture together with computer aided software engineering (CASE) tools, allow for the data to be manipulated and checked as a part of the translation process.

The creation of pre- and post processor programs for another system therefore requires development of only the 'front-end' and the 'back-end' elements. Advanced architectures for data exchange (here STEP based exchange) include not only the ability to create and maintain the internal data structures directly from the information model (here the EXPRESS schema), but also the creation and mappings between different (EXPRESS) data models.

# 4 CONCLUDING REMARKS

In this paper we have seen how neutral product model interfaces can be identified, specified, and implemented to provide intelligent and flexible means for information management in manufacturing of discrete mechanical products.

The international STEP initiative provides an infrastructure for the identification, specification, and implementation of neutral interfaces based upon the open systems' CIME architecture.

The generality and flexibility of the open systems' architecture, based upon neutral interfaces and implemented by processor programs, is strongly affected by the choice of the processor development techniques, the implementation paradigm, the CASE tools, and the exchange scenario for processor implementation and tests.

A product model interface implementation has been done at The Technical University of Denmark (DTU) facilitating the exchange of dynamic control models between general purpose CACSD Systems and CAR systems for dynamics simulation of robot control systems. This test set-up is successfully using the schema-driven processor development technique, the object-oriented implementation paradigm, and a fourth generation STEP based CASE tool. The set-up is very flexible and general in the sense that it is easy to update with new product model features directly based upon EXPRESS specifications, modular, and relatively easy to maintain.

# 5 REFERENCES

(CAD*I, 1989) 'CAD Data Transfer for Solid Models', E. G. Schlechtendahl (ed.), ESPRIT Research Reports, Vol. 3, CAD Interfaces (CAD*I), Springer Verlag, Heidelberg, D, 1989.

(ISO 10303-11, 1994) 'ISO IS 10303-11: Product Data Representation and Exchange: Description Methods: The EXPRESS Language Manual', ISO IS, 19 August 1994.

(IDEF0, 1981) 'ICAM Architecture, Part II, Volume IV - Function Modeling Manual (IDEF0),' Report number AFAWL-TR-81-4023 (U.S. Air Force Wright Aeronautical Laboratories, Wright-Patterson Air Force Base, OH, June 1981).

(IGES, 1991) 'The Initial Graphics Exchange Specification (IGES) Version 5.1' Iges/Pdes Organization, NIST, Gaithersburg. MD 20899, USA.

(IRDATA, 1986) 'IRDATA, VDI 2863, Blatt 1, Entwurf', VDI - Verlag GmbH, Dusseldorf, 1986.

(IRL, 1992) 'Industrial Robot Language (IRL)', DIN 66312 Teil 1, Deutsches Institut für Normung, Beuth Verlag, Berlin, 1992.

(ISO 10303-1, 1993) 'Part 1: Overview and Fundamental Principles', Industrial Automation Systems - Product Data Representation and Exchange, ISO/TC 184/SC4, 1993.

(Kroszynski, 1991) 'Driving Robots via Neutral Interfaces', U. Kroszynski, T. Sørensen, T. G. Clausen and E. Trostmann, Proceedings of the Annual ESPRIT Conference, Brussels, 25-29 November 1991, pp. 646-660.

(Schenck, 1994) 'Information modeling the EXPRESS way', Schenck, D., Wilson, P., Oxford University Press, New York, Oxford, 1994.
(Schlechtendahl, 1989) 'Intelligent communication of product definition data', E. G. Schlechtendahl, 11th World Computer Congress, IFIP '89, San Francisco. Pre-print pp. 1-5.
(Sørensen, 1996) 'Interoperability of CAD Standards and Robotics in CIME', T. Sørensen, Ph.D. Dissertation. Department of Control and Engineering Design, Technical University of Denmark. June 1996. ISBN 87-90130-08-1.
(Trostmann, 1987) 'Cad Data Interfaces for Robot Control', E. Trostmann, Paper for the 2. Duisburger Kolloquium, Automation und Robotik, 15 - 17 July 1987, Universität Duisburg.
(VDA-FS, 1987) 'VDA Surface Interface Version 2.0', Verband der Automobilindustrie e.V (VDA), W-6000 Frankfurt am Main, Westendstrasse 61, Germany, 1987.

## 6 BIOGRAPHY

*Assistant professor, Ph.D. Torben Sørensen*
received his M.Sc. degree in electrical engineering from the Technical University of Denmark (DTU) in 1986, and his Ph.D. degree in Mechanical Engineering from DTU in 1996. In 1986 he joined the Control Engineering Institute of DTU where he was appointed as a research fellow, and later as a senior engineer in the CAD and Robotics areas. Since 1996 he has been an assistant professor at the Department of Control and Engineering Design of DTU.

Dr. Sørensen has been supervisor, co-supervisor, and external reviewer for several M.Sc. students in the CAD and Robotics areas during the last seven-eight years. Currently, he teaches CAD, Robotics, and basic Control Engineering at Masters' level.

He has participated as Senior Researcher and Group Leader in large international projects, and is currently engaged with research in the areas of robot control and CAD.

He has published several papers and co-authored two books in the above fields of interest.

# 8

# A Long-term Planning Approach for Small-medium Enterprise Networks

*F. Bonfatti, P. D. Monari, R. Montanari, A. Morini*
*Department of Engineering Sciences - University of Modena*
*Via Campi 213/B - 41100 Modena (Italy)*
*tel +39 59 378514, fax +39 59 378515*
*e-mail bonfatti@unimo.it*

**Abstract**

The paper presents the long-term planning approach which has been studied to support small-medium enterprise networks of competing nodes in evaluating their capability to meet the foreseen customer demand. The network as a whole uses long-term planning to identify possible resource lacks in some productive phases and to plan critical materials purchase. The participating nodes use long-term planning to decide the most convenient amount of productive capacity they make available to the network. The planning functions keep demand uncertainty in due consideration and adopt a proper family-based network process model.

**Keywords**

Enterprise Network Strategies, Long-term Planning, SME Network, Distributed Manufacturing.

## 1 INTRODUCTION

Long-term (strategic) planning is a very important support tool for manufacturing enterprises. The effects of foreseen demand configurations are simulated to derive timely estimates of purchasing volumes and times, and of resources workloads (Gessner, 1986). A good long-term plan gives hints to arrange convenient open contracts with suppliers, deferring to medium-term planning the details on product types and volumes. Moreover, it identifies the needs of internal and external productive resources and helps deciding on investments to undertake for improving the enterprise productive capacity.

Unfortunately, small-medium sized enterprises (SMEs) are seldom in condition to employ long-term planning techniques. The reasons are many, in particular:

Computer Applications in Production and Engineering. F. Plonka and G. Olling (Eds.)

- Strategic planning functions, often named Master Production Schedulers (IBM, 1985), are included in costly and burdensome MRP II packages.
- SMEs adopt a lean work organization which cannot afford diverting human resources from directly productive activities to planning activities.
- SMEs frequently apply subcontracting for the execution of process phases, hence these phases are objectively withdrawn from planning.

New organizational paradigms, leading to the constitution of SME networks, are gaining increasing relevance. One of them, addressed to discrete production, is studied within the project EP20723 - PLENT (Planning Small-medium Enterprise Networks) of the European Esprit R&D program (Bonfatti, 1995).

According to this model: (i) every node can participate in more than one network and maintain its own direct customers; (ii) network nodes have equal rights, although their roles are affected by the declared capacity and the proven reliability; (iii) every node is free in declaring the phases it can perform and the amount of productive capacity it makes available to the network for every phase; (iv) the network takes advantage of the competition of different nodes on the same productive phase; (v) workload distribution among competitor nodes is made on the basis of objective rules that represent the network management policy; (vi) every node is autonomous in deciding investments to improve its own position with respect to competitors within the network.

This organization calls for the introduction of a network coordinating unit (Bonfatti, 1996, 1997). Its capability of applying neutrally the decision and evaluation policy agreed upon by the network nodes, without assuming independent decision powers, is a necessary condition for overcoming the historical distrusts between enterprises, often belonging to the same industrial district, traditionally in competition with each other.

Co-ordinating unit functions are: (i) manage the network process representation in terms of the macro-phases which can be carried out by the different nodes; (ii) manage the representation of work capacities, current states and past performances of the different nodes, with respect to each macro-phase; (iii) manage customer orders, and decide their subdivision into balanced orders to the network nodes so as to pursue node satisfaction and network efficiency; (iv) send orders to the respective nodes, informing them on their position in that specific productive chain (for each node, which are the supplier and the client nodes); (v) arrange new workload distributions in case of problems that cannot be damped down within the network, taking into account node counter-proposals.

With this organization the network can afford design and production of complex products which are out of reach of the single enterprise. Moreover, the network can accept large volume orders thus accessing market segments which otherwise would be precluded. Last but not least, the network can invest in advanced planning techniques, including strategic planning packages. The information coming from long-term planning is relevant for both the network as a whole and the single nodes, as it regards the evaluation of their respective capabilities of meeting the expected customer demand:

- For the network, long-term planning is used to identify possible lacks of resources on some phases, so as to ask in time the existing nodes to increase their productive capacity, or even to involve new nodes.
- For the single node, long-term planning gives hints to decide on the benefits that could come from modifying its involvement in the network in terms of the subset of phases it performs and the relative declared capacity.

These peculiar goals make the traditional strategic planning techniques unsuitable for enterprise networks. In fact, they adopt process models which are not conceived to represent distributed manufacturing. Moreover, they are focused on estimating material requirements (Volkens, 1995) while for an SME network it is more important to evaluate the overall workload and the effects of different workload distribution policies among nodes. In other words, the specific relationships within an SME network and the particular answers of the involved entities call for the definition of an indeed new approach to long-term planning.

It is the aim of this paper to describe the solution which is studied within the PLENT project. The proposed technique is split into an initial demand definition step and two following planning functions, namely the network plan generation and the nodes plan generation:

- The network plan generation function computes network workloads per phase, and possible critical materials requirements, with respect to the hypothesized external demand, starting from a proper representation of the manufacturing phases which realize the network processes.
- The nodes plan generation function is instead aimed at simulating alternative distributions of the nodes workloads, taking into account their declared productive capacities and according to different network policies.

Either function can be executed autonomously and repeatedly to study different hypothesized scenarios: essentially, demand scenarios for the former and node capacity scenarios for the latter. The intrinsic demand uncertainty is expressed according to a family-based process representation which includes alternative productive paths and the corresponding variations of times and workloads.

The paper presents four main sections. Section 2 introduces the process model supporting the planning functions. Section 3 describes the external demand definition. Finally, Section 4 and Section 5 present and discuss the network plan generation function and the nodes plan generation function, respectively.

## 2 THE PROCESS MODEL

Long-term planning requires to model the network manufacturing processes and the activities that each node can carry out. Considering the planning goals, a high level of detail is not useful. The most natural choice is decomposing every manufacturing process into phases obtained by intersection of the nodes declared activities. The manufacturing process of all the variants of a product family can conveniently be described as a unified direct acyclic graph (DAG), called network *operational scheme*, which includes alternative production phases and paths. The operational scheme syntax is based on the graphical primitives shown in Figure 1.

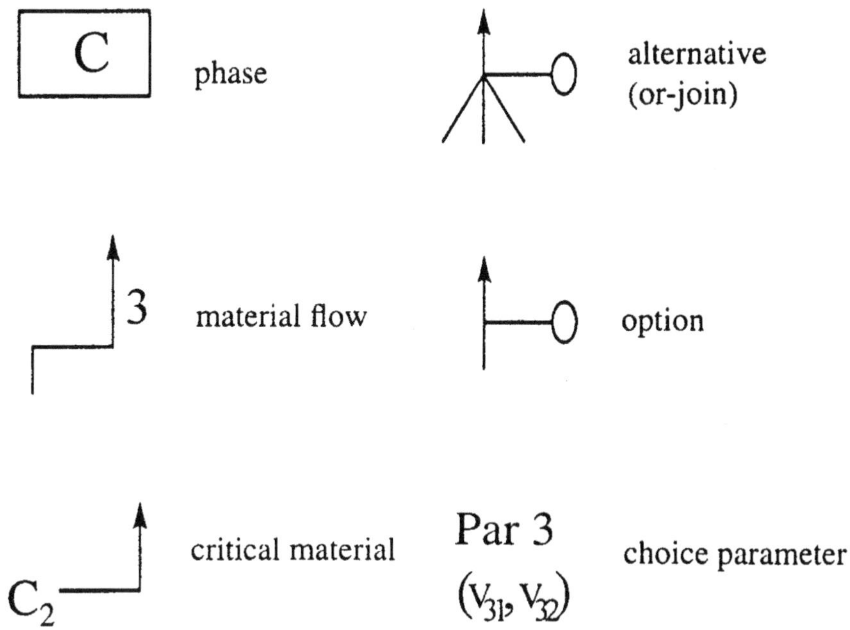


**Figure 1** Primitives of the network operational scheme.

*Phase*

We define network process phase every sequence of manufacturing operations, no matter how complex, which can be executed by one or more network nodes without interruptions. If node N1 can execute a given sequence of operations and node N2 can execute only a part of it, the N1 activity must be split into three phases, one of which is executed by either nodes. Nodes performances with respect to a given phase differ in execution time and productive capacity.

*Material flow*

Oriented arcs represent the flows of materials between the phases which produce them and those which use them. When more than one phase uses the same material, as many flow lines leave the phase producing it. Every arc has associated the corresponding multiplying factor, a positive integer number expressing the quantity of input material required to realize a unit of output material. The absence of this number means that a unitary factor is applied.

*Critical material*

This primitive represents the raw material or component whose purchasing is in charge of the network as a whole (components purchased by the single node are not considered to preserve the autonomy of its behavior). The represented critical materials are visible to the network planning function so as to properly estimate their requirements over time. Also critical materials are characterized by quantity multiplying factors.

*Alternative*

Each product variant has its own operational scheme, but often it shares most phases with other products of the same family. Moreover, a given component may be obtained following alternative, interchangeable production paths which, leading to the same result, do not impact on the subsequent phases. The alternative primitive represents either situations (Bonfatti, 1998) and avoids the redundancy which could result from writing a different scheme for every variant of the network final product.

*Option*

A particular case of alternative is given by the possibility of choosing between executing or skipping a certain phase. These phases correspond to manufacturing activities of optional components or auxiliary tasks required under particular circumstances. For instance, the request of a customized product sometimes involves the execution of a design phase which is otherwise unnecessary.

*Choice parameter*

Both the above alternative types have associated choice parameters with as many values as the number of options. The same parameter can be associated to more than one operational scheme alternatives, provided that they present the same number of options, to denote that those alternatives are subject to the same choice criterion. A particular combination of parameter values identifies a sub-family or a single variant. This mechanism is used in external demand definition.

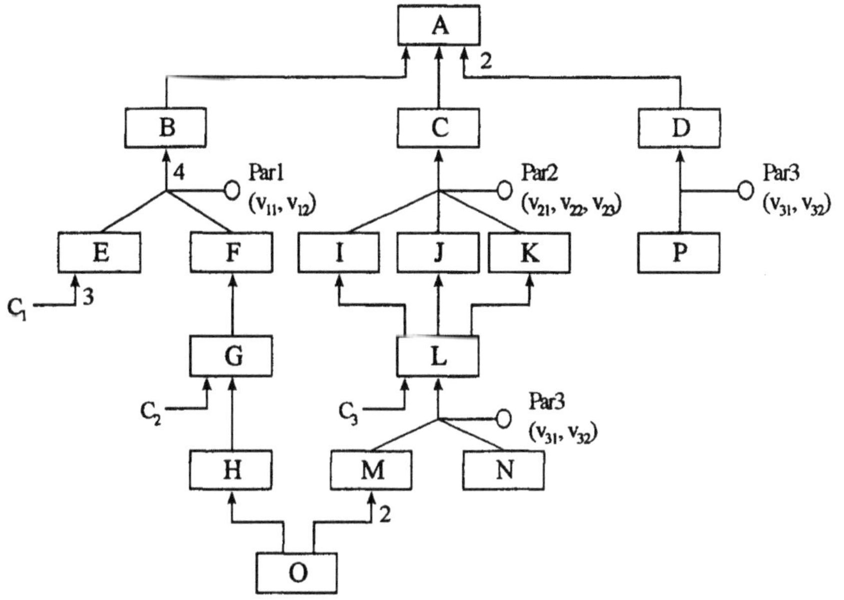


**Figure 2** Example of network operational scheme.

Figure 2 reports an example of operational scheme. In case of discrete production, the graph root (phase A in the example) is unique and corresponds to the last process phase, for instance final assembly or packaging and delivery. Leaves (phases E, O, N and P) are many and indicate the initial manufacturing phases which realize the simplest semi-finished products.

The operational scheme in Figure 2 shows situations that can be recognized as typical cases of workflow management, as they are defined in the WfMC reference model (Hollingsworth, 1995). A case of *and-split* corresponds to the flows leaving phase O to feed in parallel two successive independent phases. The flow leaving phase L is an *or-split* as it implies, when executing a given order instance, the choice of one of the possibilities leading to phase I, J or K, alternatively. An *and-join* case is constituted by the material flows entering phase A and expresses the simultaneous use of three input materials (two particular and-join occurrences are also given by the flows entering phases G and L). Finally, three *or-join* cases realize the convergence of the alternative paths leading to phases B, C and L.

Observe that, in the example of Figure 1, parameter Par3 is associated to both the alternative leading to phase L and the option leading to phase D. This means that the values assigned to the choice parameter options affect both manufacturing paths although they belong to independent branches of the operational scheme.

*Node capacity per phase*

The process model is completed by the declaration of the productive capacities that each node makes available to the network with respect to the phases it can execute. Taking into account the long time horizon of strategic planning, we assume the day as time unit. Then, every pair (node, phase) has associated the *daily capacity*, $C_d$, expressing the average number of output material units produced every day. We suppose that the productive capacities of the node are not concurrent, i.e., they are independent from each other.

## 3 DEMAND REPRESENTATION

The first step of the planning procedure is aimed at declaring the demand configuration that represents the long-term production budget. Starting from the sales forecasts provided by the marketing function, a set of external demand items, properly distributed along the planning horizon, are issued. Each item represents the total requirement on a given period for a certain family or sub-family of products. We consider sufficient to express the requirement temporal granularity on a weekly basis. The demand item presents the following structure:

| *Year* | *Week* | *Family* | *Quantity* | *Configuration* |
|---|---|---|---|---|
| 1997 | 11 | F1 | 200 | Par1 ($v_{11}$=40, $v_{12}$=60) |
| | | | | Par2 ($v_{21}$=0, $v_{22}$=100, $v_{23}$=0) |
| | | | | Par3 ($v_{31}$=25, $v_{32}$=75) |

- Year and Week express the due date of the requirement instance.
- Family and Quantity indicate, respectively, the type of product to plan and the number of pieces of the requirement instance.
- Configuration is made of as many expressions as the family choice parameters: it is aimed at representing the distribution of product variants within the considered family. Every parameter must be instantiated, each option must receive a value and the sum of these values must always be 100.

It is worth observing how this representation of the requirement instance configuration can characterize every possible type of demand. If one or more parameters have specified just one option with value 100 (as for parameter Par2) then the demand item refers to a sub-family where the choices corresponding to the zero value options are excluded. Moreover, if all the family parameters present the 100 choice, the demand item refers to a single family variant.

## 4 NETWORK PLAN GENERATION

We call *network planning* the computation of phases workloads and critical materials requirements as they results with respect to the hypothesized external demand. The planning algorithm works at infinite capacity, hence it can process one demand item at a time. The operational scheme of the single demand item is examined backward (from root to leaves) to calculate quantities of output materials and duration of each phase. In correspondence of the alternatives the computation considers the different paths and the rates associated to each of them. Figure 3 shows the requirements of output and critical materials resulting for the operational scheme of Figure 2 in case of a demand item of 100 pieces, and according to the parameter values reported in legend.

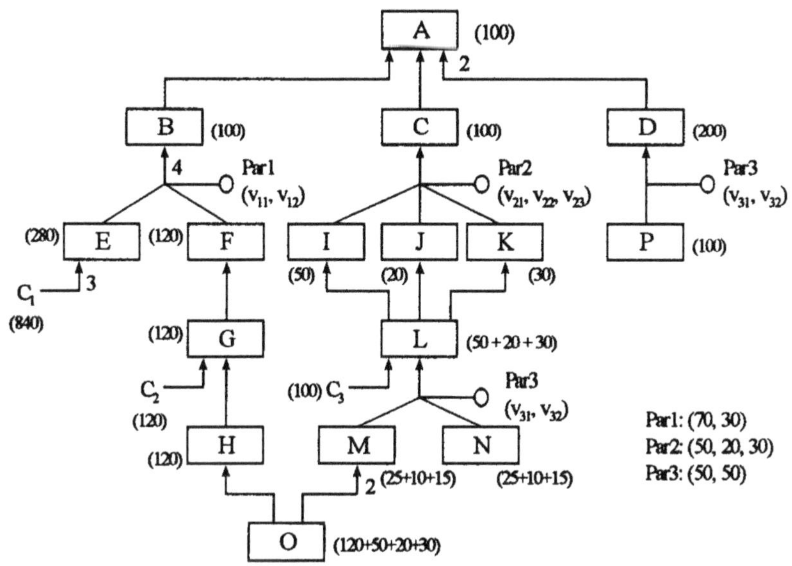


**Figure** 3Materials requirements per phase.

For the execution of the network planning function we choose the most efficient workload distribution among the network nodes, i.e., the distribution which minimizes the lead-times. The main aim we pursue with network planning is in fact determining the minimal execution time to adopt as a reference datum for evaluating the criticality of the network behavior. Since every phase can be carried out by a number of competing nodes, its duration may change considerably depending on the actual workload distribution.

In order to determine the distribution which minimizes the phase execution time, let us denote with $BS_j$ the output batch size of the j-th phase ($BS_j$ is a function of the quantities consumed by the following phases) and suppose it can be executed by n nodes. The distribution is obtained by solving the following system of (n+1) linear equations:

$$T_j = \frac{x_{ij}}{c_{ij}} \qquad i = 1..n$$

$$\sum_{i=1}^{n} x_{ij} = BS_j$$

where $x_{1j}$, $x_{2j}$, ... $x_{nj}$ express the number of pieces produced by each of the n nodes, $c_{ij}$ the capacity of node i on phase j, $T_j$ the minimal execution time.

For example, suppose that three enterprises declare to perform the j-th phase with a productive capacity of 10, 40 and 100 pieces per day, respectively. If it is $BS_j = 400$, the solutions are $x_{j1} = 26.66$, $x_{j2} = 106.66$, $x_{j3} = 266.6$ with $T_j = 2.66$. Since workloads must be expressed by integer numbers, the three nodes will have assigned 26, 107 and 267 pieces, respectively. The actual phase duration coincides with the time spent by the slowest node: $T_{j2} = 107/40 = 2.75$ days (here, the second T index identifies the node). It means that the phase lasts for three days: in two of them the nodes work at their maximum capacity while in the third day only a fraction of the capacity is actually spent.

The start date of the j-th phase is finally computed by subtracting the $T_j$ duration from the phase due date. Whenever a phase must feed two or more following phases, these issue independent requirements which are managed autonomously. In the example of Figure 3 this situation is represented by lists of batches associated to phases L and O (and phases M and N as they precede L).

Once the network planning function has been applied to all the demand items, resource profiles such as that reported in Figure 4 give a measure of the global capacity and the capacity peaks the network must for every phase.

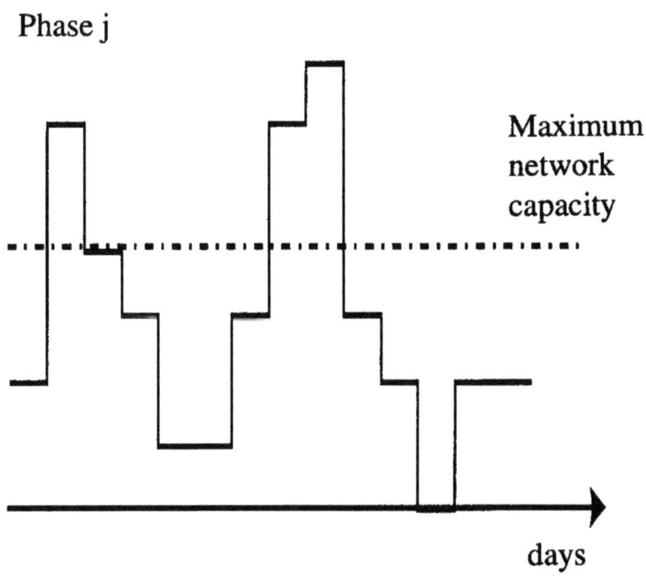


**Figure 4**Resource profile for the j-th phase.

## 5 NODES PLAN GENERATION

The *node workloads planning* function is executed to evaluate which task assignments every node may expect to receive with reference to the hypothesized demand. The computation is carried out at finite capacity so as to take into account the concurrence of demand items on the productive capacities. The planning algorithm realizes a simplified simulation of the network policy: it tries to balance the ratio between the tasks assigned to the different nodes and their declared capacities by taking also into account the rank attributed to each node.

The planning algorithm examines one demand item at a time. The demand items are examined from the nearest week to the most distant future. Within a week, the examination order is decided by the planner. Assignment of demand item phases to nodes is carried out according to a backward approach and each phase is assigned to a single node, without introducing batch splittings. For each phase, workload assignment to nodes is executed on a daily basis: starting from the phase due date the algorithm determines the node that is more entitled to receive the assignment. If the daily available capacity is not sufficient to run out the batch size, the selected node is charged for the needed number of days. The node daily capacity is decreased according to each received assignment.

Whenever two or more nodes are able to perform a phase, a dynamic node priority is used to decide which node has the right to obtain the assignment. The priority of the i-th node on the j-th phase is given by the expression:

if $a_i > 0$

if $a_i = 0$

where:

- Ri is a coefficient ranging between 0.0 and 1.0 which expresses the node rank (this coefficient expresses node reliability as it results from the evaluation of its past performances);
- $x_{ijk}$ represents the number of pieces assigned to node i on phase j for the k-th day (d is the due date of the demand item under examination);
- $c_{ij}$ represents the productive capacity declared by node i for phase j
- $a_j = \text{card}\,\{k \mid \exists\, i : x_{ijk} \neq 0\}$ counts the number of days where at least one node has received an assignment for phase j.

As an example, consider three nodes α, β and γ which declare respectively a capacity of 40, 20 and 60 pieces per day for phase j. Suppose that the requirements for phase j are: (i) 50 pieces on day 96, (ii) 200 pieces on day 98 and (iii) 100 pieces on day 99 and that the following plan constitutes the situation as it results from the previous assignments:

| | $c_{ij}$ | days | 92 | 93 | 94 | 95 | 96 | 97 | 98 | 99 |
|---|---|---|---|---|---|---|---|---|---|---|
| α | 40 | ... | | | | | | | | |
| β | 20 | ... | 10 | 20 | | | | | | |
| γ | 60 | ... | | | 30 | | | | | |

Assuming $R_i = 1$ for every node, the priorities result: $P_{\alpha j} = 1$, $P_{\beta i} = 0.5$, $P_{\gamma j} = 0.83$. Then the (i) batch is assigned to node α, more precisely 40 pieces on day 95 and the remaining 10 pieces on day 94. The new priorities become: $P_{\alpha j} = 0.69$, $P_{\beta i} = 0.62$, $P_{\gamma j} = 0.88$. Thus the (ii) batch is assigned to node γ on days 97 to 94. Finally, the priorities change again: $P_{\alpha j} = 0.79$, $P_{\beta i} = 0.75$, $P_{\gamma j} = 0.36$ and the (iii) batch is assigned to node α, on days 98 to 96. The resulting plan is now:

| | $c_{ij}$ | days | 92 | 93 | 94 | 95 | 96 | 97 | 98 | 99 |
|---|---|---|---|---|---|---|---|---|---|---|
| α | 40 | ... | | | 10 | 40 | 20 | 40 | 40 | |
| β | 20 | ... | 10 | 20 | | | | | | |
| γ | 60 | ... | | | 50 | 60 | 60 | 60 | | |

and the corresponding priorities are $P_{\alpha j} = 0.46$, $P_{\beta i} = 0.79$, $P_{\gamma j} = 0.45$. It means that the next batch (if any) will be assigned to node $\beta$.

In conclusion, observe that this finite capacity workload distribution can be executed many times changing the node priorities (i.e. their rank and declared capacities) to evaluate different planning scenarios. These results, together with the network resource profiles, are made available to the network nodes to support them in deciding their own strategy and the network general policy.

This approach is currently under validation at four enterprises networks: (i) an Italian network manufacturing a family of wheel-motors; (ii) a Spanish network manufacturing complex transfer machines; (iii) a Greek network producing garments; (iv) an Hungarian network producing oil for food industry.

# 6 REFERENCES

Bonfatti, F. and Monari, P.D. (1995) Planning small-medium enterprise networks. *Proc. of the Int. Conf. IMPDE '95 on Improving Manufacturing Performance in a Distributed Enterprise*, Edinburgh.

Bonfatti, F., Monari, P.D. and Paganelli, P. (1996) Co-ordination functions in SME networks, in *Balanced Automation Systems II* (ed. L.M. Camarinha-Matos, H. Afsarmanesh), Chapman & Hall, London.

Bonfatti, F., Monari, P.D. and Montanari, R. (1997) Information flows and processes in a SME network. *Proc. of the OE/IEEE/IFIP Int. Conf. ISIP '97 on Integrated and Sustainable Industrial Production*, Lisbon.

Bonfatti, F., Monari, P.D. and Paganelli, P. (1998) Resource-free and resource-dependent aspects of process modeling: a rule-based conceptual approach. *Int. Journal of Computer Integrated Manufacturing (IJCIM)*, Taylor & Francis, London.

Gessner, R.A. (1986) *Master Production Schedule Planning*. John Wiley & Sons, New York.

IBM (1985) *Master Production Schedule Planning Reference Manual*. Atlanta.

Hollingsworth, D (1995) *The Workflow Reference Model*. The Workflow Management Coalition, Brussels.

Volkens, B. (1985) Planning bills for master production scheduling. *Proc. of the APICS 28th Int. Conf.*, Toronto.

## 7 BIOGRAPHY

Fluvio Bonfatti. Graduated in Electronics Engineering. Associated professor of Fundamentals of Computer Science and lecturer of Software Engineering. Scientific responsible of a number of national and international research projects.

Paola Daniela Monari. Graduated in Mathematics. Consultant in manufacturing information systems and industrial applications and lecturer of Industrial Informatics. Involved in several national and international research projects.

Roberto Montanari. Graduated in Informatics Engineering. PhD student in software engineering for industrial applications.

Andrea Morini. Graduated in Informatics Engineering. Researcher in product modeling and production planning. Involved in international research projects.

# 9
# Global supply chain integration

*Prof. Dr.-Ing. F.-L. Krause*
*Fraunhofer-IPK, Pascalstr. 8-9, 10587 Berlin, Germany*
*phone: +49–30–39 00 62 43, fax: +49–30–393 02 46*
*email: Frank-L.Krause@ipk.fhg.de*

*Dipl.-Ing. M. Doblies*
*IWF / TUB, Pascalstr. 8-9, 10587 Berlin, Germany*
*phone: +49–30–39 00 62 65, fax: +49–30–393 02 46*
*email: Matthias.Doblies@ipk.fhg.de*

**Abstract**

The migration to a global economy is accompanied by a rapid change in communication technologies. The WebProM collaborative environment (WCE) supports communication along the supply chain. The WCE consists of Internet-based product library, multimedia email and conferencing system. The main focus is the product library which is used for information distribution to a broad audience and for data exchange in virtual teams with members of different companies. The overall goal of this product library application is to enable easy integration of as many companies as needed into one digital information exchange network. Therefore the application addresses issues like common data formats, data security, heterogeneous platforms, and simple maintenance of contents, users and access rights.

**Keywords**

Global Product Management, EDM, Internet

Computer Applications in Production and Engineering. F. Plonka and G. Olling (Eds.)

# 1 INTRODUCTION

Migration to a global economy is taking place everywhere. The technologies accompanying this process are changing rapidly and keeping up with them is expensive in terms of money and time. Especially small enterprises do not have the resources needed to accomplish this challenge. As with every commercially viable technology the relation between costs and benefits has to be right. This means the technology used must not be too expensive, and it has to be easy to implement in business.

Therefore several industrial and governmental research projects concentrated on developing technologies for a global and cost effective supply chain integration. This leads towards Virtual Product Development, a technology that all companies will be confronted with in the near future (Spur 1997). It goes along with the establishment of several regional centers across Europe where small companies receive support for the introduction and operation of relevant technologies.

The multimedia working environment consists of a product library, multimedia email and a conferencing system including components for video/audio conference, shared whiteboard and application sharing. The main focus is the product library. The product library serves two purposes. It is used for information distribution to a broad audience as is associated with the term *product library*. Furthermore it is used for data exchange in virtual teams with members of different companies.

The network infrastructure is scaleable from analog modems to bundled ISDN lines and up to ATM to allow the network connections to be as powerful as required and as inexpensive as possible.

# 2 COMMUNICATION ALONG THE SUPPLY CHAIN

The players in today's manufacturing business become more and more global. Looking for example at Fiat (Vio 1997), a remarkable increase in globalization can be seen, where in five years the amount of components delivered from outside Italy has risen from 17% to 38%. The absolute value of components delivered from Italy has decreased slightly, so the growth has taken place only outside the OEM's country.

This shows the trend towards global project teams devoted to creating a product. Since these teams are working together while being physically dispersed across different nations and even across different continents they are called virtual teams. Fast and reliable communication in these virtual teams is crucial to success but proven techniques like phone, fax and personal visits fail to deliver. They are simply incapable to distribute the amount of required information fast enough to all communication partners and in useable data formats.

*Information gathering*

The first problem being addressed by the WCE is the time required to gather all relevant information for the business process. The task of information gathering is only one of the five basic activities of product development processes (Krause 1995a) but it is very time consuming (figure 2). Engineers spend a lot of their time with information gathering, figures vary between 30% (Noble 1986) and 70% (SMAC 1994). The exploitation of modern communication technologies like video conferencing or Intranet information systems can reduce this time drastically.

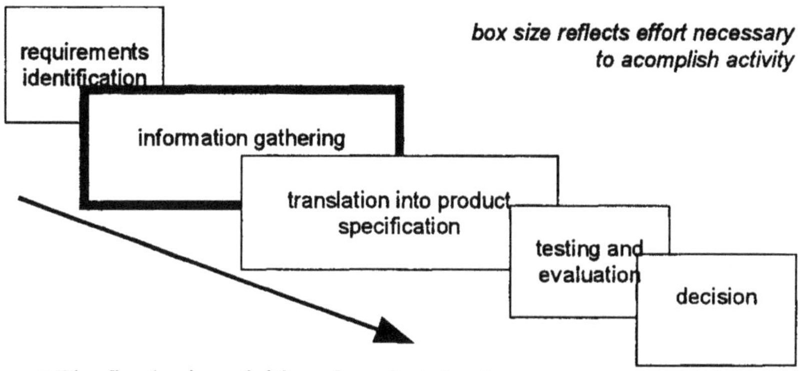


**Figure 1** The five basic activities of product development processes.

Another common problem is the status of information, i.e. whether the information is up-to-date or obsolete. At least partially this problem can be solved when all users access the same data on-line via one common data pool. Having on-line access to the data is not enough, the use of this facility must be ensured to maximize its value.

Even when the user knows where the data he is looking for resides, it can take him a week to exchange it via a tape. Furthermore many companies are unwilling to release emerging drawings and other project documents. So a central networked repository for all these data would be very important.

Table 1 gives an overview of the requirements for an environment to distribute and exchange information (TEAM 1996).

**Table 1** List of requirements for application addressing information gathering

- simple to use, especially no special knowledge like HTML necessary;
- low cost;
- availability, i.e. data must be available to all authorized users all the time;
- fast access to data, i.e. minutes instead of days;
- data formats that can be viewed and processes by all users;
- documents organized in net-like structure;
- revision control for documents;

- gateways to existing databases and engineering data management systems;
- high security, that includes access control, secure storage, and secure transmission;
- directory services for all virtual team members, i.e. directory services across multiple companies;
- workflow support to ensure the right person performs the appropriate action;
- support for multiple languages.

---

*Problem solving*

Another problem is the amount of time being devoted to problem solving. Especially the delay between problem detection and actual problem solving can be reduced. This delay consists mostly of the time

- to identify the people who have to be involved in the problem solving process,
- to find a common time slot for a meeting, and
- to travel to the meeting pace.

The travel time vanishes if it is possible to set-up a virtual meeting. Without the necessity to travel the common time slot necessary for the meeting is reduced and therefore easier to find. Identification of the important people can be facilitated by directory services and by the right composition of virtual teams. The latter increases chances that all necessary people are already in the relevant virtual team.

The functionality required to solve or at least ease the problems mentioned above should fulfill the requirements listed in Table 2 (SMAC 1984).

**Table 2** List of requirements for application addressing problem solving

---

- simple to use;
- low cost;
- directory services for all virtual team members, i.e. directory services across multiple companies;
- scheduling of conferences;
- invitation of users or virtual teams to conferences;
- ability to join and leave a conference without restarting or terminating the conference;

- multi-point conferences, i.e. conferences between more than two persons;
- whiteboard for general discussions, preferably with multiple pages and the ability to save these to disk as minutes;
- sharing of CAD applications, spreadsheets, word processors.

---

The sharing especially of CAD applications requires fast connections. It is not really a necessity, an acceptable alternative is (1) to capture the view describing the problem, (2) put it onto a whiteboard, and (3) to discuss the problem using the whiteboard.

*Heterogeneous Environment*
The lack of interoperability of software applications in heterogeneous environments is a common but nevertheless important problem. And in a supply chain a heterogeneous environment is rather normal because companies who supply more than just one manufacturer will have their own software and hardware environment.

Therefore a general requirement is the availability of the connecting software application in a variety of software and hardware environments (see table 3).

**Table 3** List of general requirements

- support for all major operating systems,
- support for all major types of computers, i.e. workstations and personal computers, and
- support for all important types of networks, like Ethernet, Token Ring, ATM etc.

---

## 3 WEBPROM COLLABORATIVE ENVRIONMENT

Two problem areas have been identified in the previous section, i.e. information gathering and problem solving. The WebProM Collaborative Environment (WCE) addresses the former by a Web-based Product data Management (WebProM) system (Krause 1995) and the latter by a conferencing environment including audio/video conferencing and application sharing. The technical problem of interoperability is addressed by the overall architecture of WCE, which relies on standards and de-facto-standards as far as possible.

*The conferencing environment*

The conferencing environment is made up of *MBONE* conferencing tools and application sharing is performed using Team Solution's Team Conference. Interoperability between different conferencing systems is achieved by relying on the ITU-T recommendation H.320 (ITU 1996). But interoperability of application sharing systems is currently hard to achieve because the ITU-T recommendation T.120 (ITU 1996a) provides not enough functionality for full-fledged application sharing.

*Web-based Product data Management*

WebProM meets two major requirements. On one hand, WebProM gives enterprises the ability to publish up-to-date product catalogues and to grant public or restricted access to these data. On the other hand project partners from different companies can store, retrieve and maintain required information in the project library.

(1) Public static data, which is available to a broad audience, e.g. all potential customers. This information group includes e.g. national and international standards, design relevant regulations and laws, but as well product catalogues or service information for garages, etc. Furthermore always up-to-date company profiles and other general information can be made available.

(2) Company related static data, which is accessible by customers and sub-contractors. This includes engineering and design standards, company standards, company's interpretations of national and international laws and standards, or even phone directories.

(3) Project related dynamic data, which is available to a small group, usually the project team. This group includes product specifications, 3-d CAD models, 2-D design drawings, timing plans, old designs, test results, material specifications, data on human resources, standard parts, minutes of meetings or decisions. Some of the users may as well have write access and update this information.

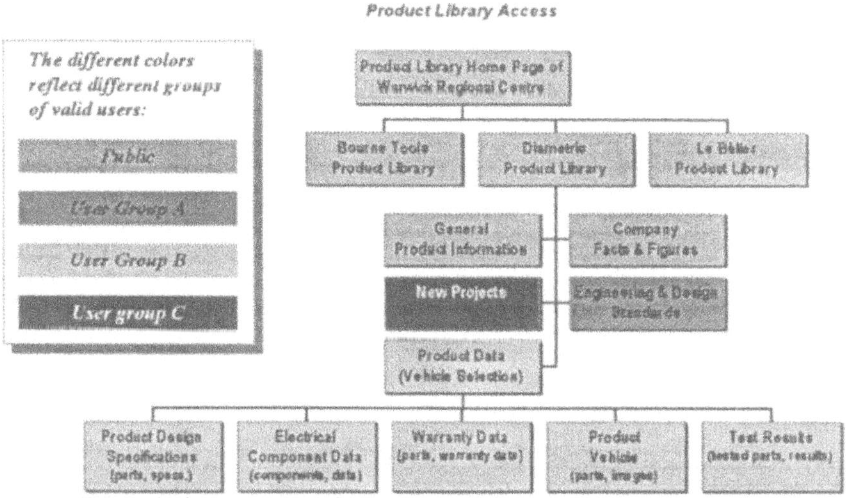


**Figure 2** Example for structure of product library.

An information source like that not only gives external project partners access to current project data, but as well enables internal staff to access up-to-date information like engineering and design standards, where at the moment it is not always possible to guarantee access to the latest revision of a standards document. Figure 3 gives an example for a product library.

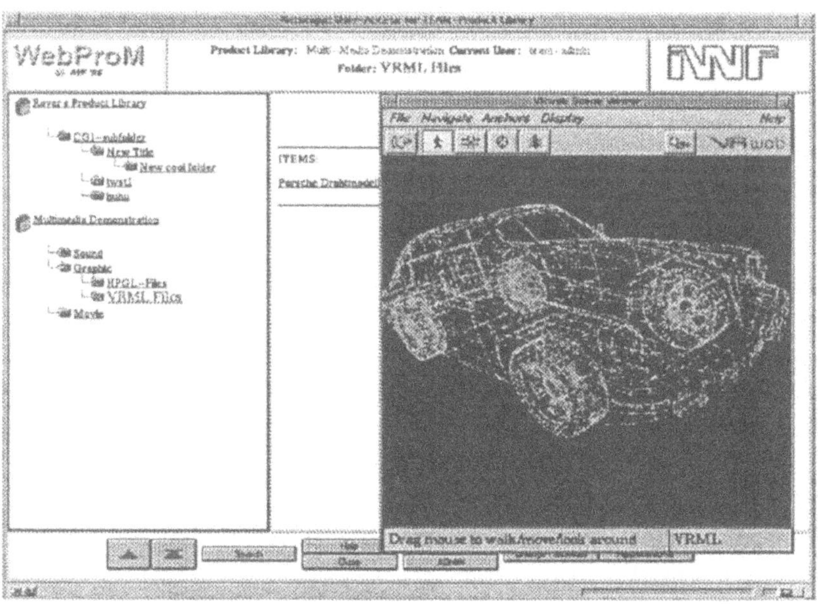


**Figure 3** Navigation and viewing in WebProM. (Porsche by [ORC 1996])

An important aspect in the development of WebProM was the ease-of-use of the user interface, thus reducing training times to a minimum. So common user interface elements are used wherever appropriate. However the underlying technology poses limits to the interface design. For example drag-and-drop functionality is difficult to implement while retaining web-browser behavior. The user interface is split in three operating modes, one for browsing (Figure 3), one for contents editing (Figure 4) and one for administration of users and groups ( Figure 5).

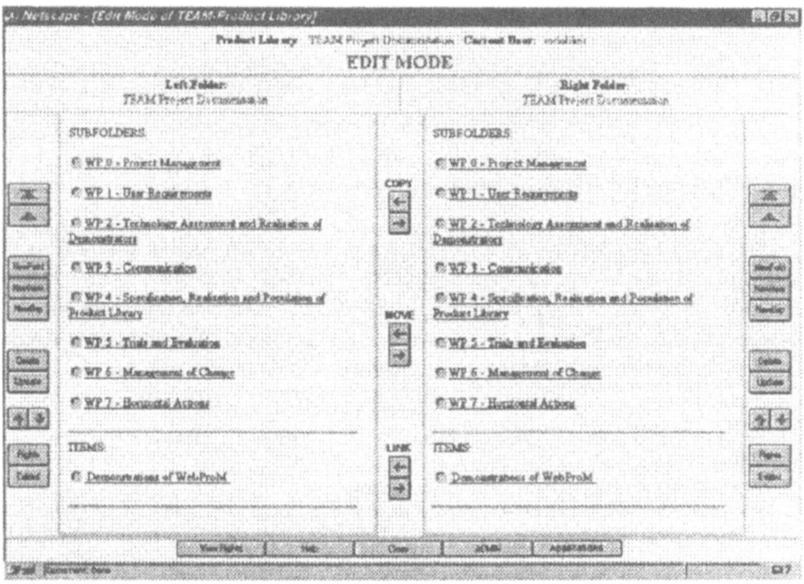


**Figure 4** Maintenance of the information stored within WebProM.

## *Organization of information*

Files are the smallest unit of information supported directly by WebProM. They can be combined to groups. Items, groups and folders can be combined into folders. Groups are helpful for example to build a product catalogue where information for one product may consist of several items like general description, data sheet, drawing and CAD model. If these items are grouped together they will be displayed accordingly in a grouped form. Furthermore there are references to items and folders. These are updated automatically when the object being referenced is moved.

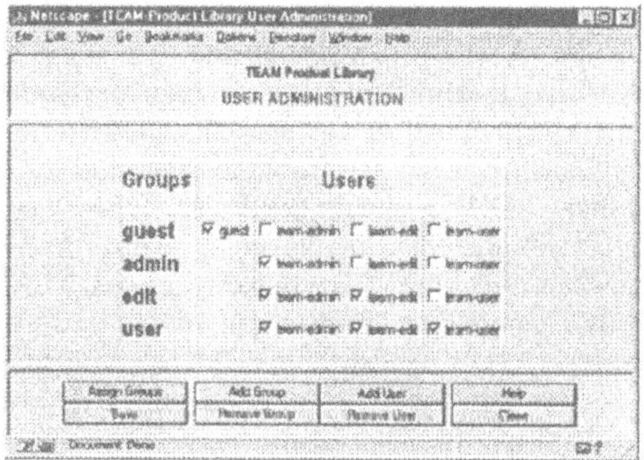


**Figure 5** Administration of users and virtual teams.

### *Data Formats*

By using widely available web technology to implement WebProM it is very simple to integrate new data formats. The following list gives the main criterias for selection of appropriate data formats for publishing.

(1) Information availability: The information must be available in the data format, either native or by means of converting. If a conversion is necessary, it has to be easy, preferably automatic.

(2) Viewer availability: The user has to be able to display the information. Therefore a viewer for that format must be available. For standard formats there are a lot of viewers available on various platforms. Viewers for CAD data are not that common, but even these are beginning to evolve because of increased demand and increased computing power available to the user.

(3) Convenience: Users must be able to use the environment without much effort. So selecting the native data to be published, converting it to the appropriate format and then publishing it must be effortless. Even structuring the data and setting appropriate access rights has to be easy. Last but not least the handling of the viewer must be quick and simple.

Using web browsers opens a new opportunity called plug-ins. Plug-ins are browser extensions that are capable to display one or more special data formats the browser normally does not support. They come from third-party vendors and are easily installed. They integrate so tightly with the web browser that the user does not notice them other than by the browser's sudden ability to display additional data formats like e.g. DXF files. Currently plug-ins are available only on Personal Computers but their availability on UNIX workstations can be expected soon.

(4) Processing ability: Often simple viewing of the data is not sufficient especially when accessing data of a current development project. There is the need to work on that data and maybe even upload the changed data back into

the library. Most plug-ins and viewers do not allow this. Because there is more functionality necessary to work on the data being downloaded many users are only willing to work using their standard applications.

This imposes severe limits to the use of standard formats because in a business environment it is not applicable to download for example an IGES file, import it into CADDS 5, change the design, export it as IGES and upload it back into the library. This works on a regular basis only in special environments where only limited functionality is used (TEAM 1996).

Publishing data in multiple formats can be an interesting option. CAD models for example can be published in VRML because conversion to VRML is easy and viewer are widely propagated and additionally they can be published in at least one standard format like STEP where viewers are not as common as for VRML but the „value" of the transmitted data is much higher than with VRML.

All these requirements make the selection of appropriate data formats very difficult. Therefore two different strategies are proposed: For public information like product catalogues where the audience is not well defined only standard data formats should be used because otherwise the viewer availability is unknown. But for the exchange of project related information the audience is known and therefore the users' preferences in terms of applications and their native data formats is known. Here the environment becomes more productive when as many of the users' day-to-day applications are used thereby minimizing the learning curve. In such an environment the use of proprietary data formats is a viable option, because there is simply no point in distributing for example text documents in Rich Text Format (RTF) when all users are using the same word processor. Furthermore for many proprietary formats there is no alternate standard format.

### *Security*

Access restrictions are based on virtual teams (user-groups) as well as folder structures for read and write access. Selected users can access the user administration and create new users or virtual teams.

Furthermore the use of so called security proxy servers allows a secure transmission of data through a 1024-bit SSL encryption 9 (Krause 1996). This is a very secure encryption in comparison to the usual 40-bit SSL encryption (Netscape 1995) used in commercial software packages. To provide maximum security this security proxy server has to be combined with a firewall (Antoine 1996).

### *Gateways to existing information*

Gateways to Engineering Data Management Systems (EDMS) and Database systems are important to reduce redundancy by enabling the direct embedding of information held in private company systems.

### *Networks of WebProM servers*

References allow the linkage of several WebProM servers. So users do not even notice which server they access.

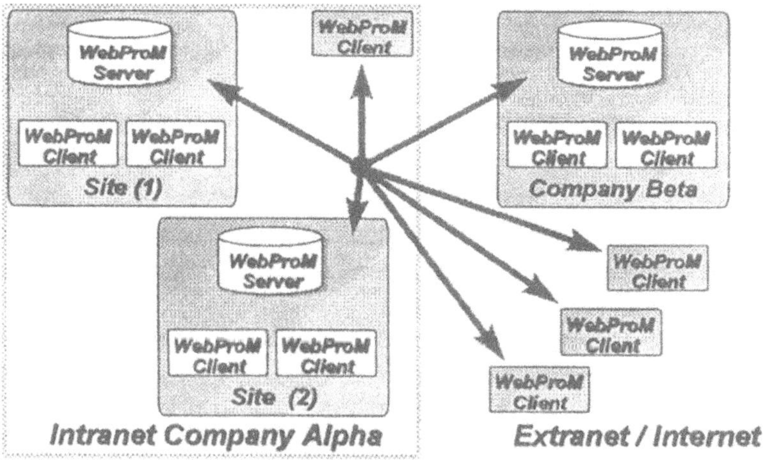


**Figure 6** An Intranet / Extranet WebProM-Installation.

*Architecture*

WebProM is based on TCP/IP-networks and can therefore be used on the public Internet as well as on private TCP-IP-based Intranets. This ensures broad availability from the network point of view since TCP/IP network traffic can run on almost any network architecture.

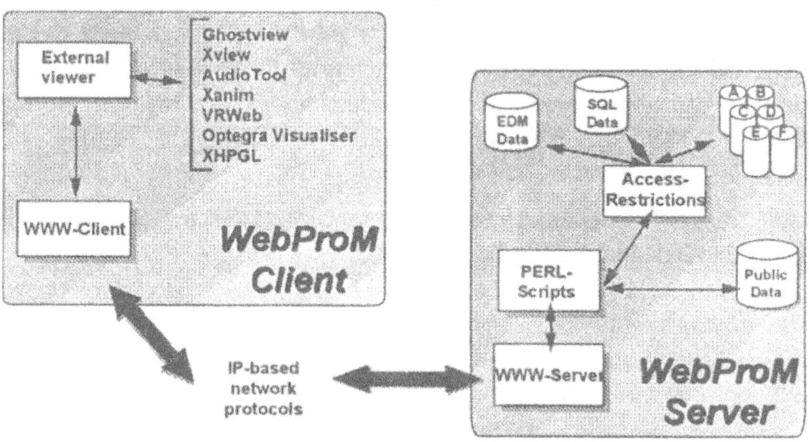


**Figure 7** Software architecture of WebProM.

The user accesses WebProM through a Java and JavaScript enabled WWW-browser like the Netscape Navigator or the Microsoft Internet Explorer. Data are enhanced by Perl-scripts and Java-applications and then published by a WWW-server.

*Use in industrial environment*

A supplier can use WebProM to publish his product catalogue. Interested users can access the public part of the catalogue through a guest account. OEMs can access more sensible information like CAD-models or individual price lists through a dedicated account. This flexible and cost effective way of providing up-to-date manufacturing information to every customer makes the information exchange by ordinary paper catalogues nearly obsolete. The same advantages are gained when company internal best-practice-, standard-, or similar documents are published in WebProM.

Project data can be managed, distributed and stored by WebProM. Dedicated user groups like external project partners and project managers can be granted specific read and, if needed, write access in different parts of the data structure. This structure can for example contain directories for test reports, milestones, inspection protocols, etc.

To implement a clearance mechanism, an *incoming* directory can be created, in which all project partners can write and store their data files. Project managers or dedicated supervisors can then move this data to an appropriated level of the project data structure.

## 4 REGIONAL CENTERS

For many small enterprises it is too costly to buy technology like the WCE because it is very time consuming to decide which applications and equipment to buy and to install and maintain it. So it is of huge interest for SMEs to have regional centers where they can get in touch with the technology. These regional centers can support the SMEs with expertise, workshops, demonstrators, consulting services, training and even the option of renting equipment to test the profitability. For example in the European TEAM project three regional centers have been established in Ireland, Great Britain and Italy.

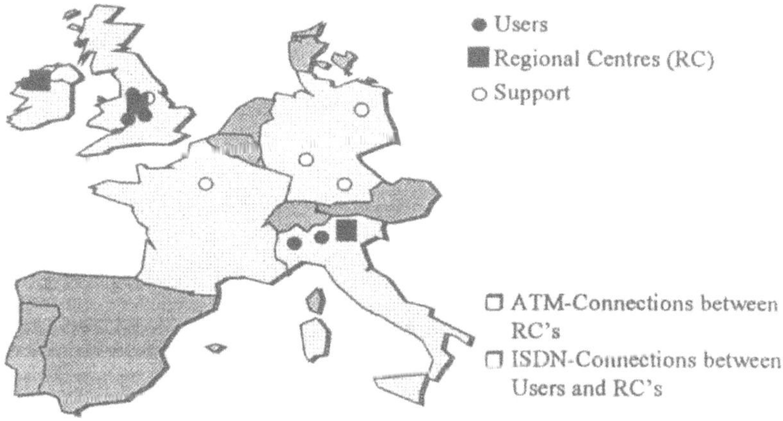


**Figure 8** Regional Centers in the European TEAM project (ACTS 070).

## 4 REQUIREMENTS BEYOND TEAM

During the work done in several research projects and the extensive use of WCE in different companies several other important topics have been identified where more work is needed.

There is currently no ultimate standard format available, i.e. a format capable of replacing all proprietary formats and all other standard formats. An approach clearly requiring more research is automatic format conversion. Conversion between complex formats requires manual work; this includes formats for CAD data but as well formats for text documents.

There is a clear need of supporting more EDM systems across different companies to show companies the benefits of networked environments.

When a product is described by a product structure this product structure currently has to be replicated in several applications throughout the product development process. There is yet no way of accessing one unified master product structure.

During research on intranet applications at Siemens Automotive (Wartelle 1997) four major deficits have been identified:

- Virtual private networks are still difficult to set-up and maintain; but there is a real need to create secure Intranets in a cost-aware way.
- Security must be improved, especially the limitation of firewalls to IP traffic is a drawback in a network environment where ATM is gaining momentum.
- Network support for multimedia data streams like the ATM Adaptation Layers [N.N. 1996] has to be supported in other network environments as well. An approach to this problem is contained in IPv6 (Deering 1996) which will slowly substitute IPv4, the current Internet Protocol, during the next years.

- Support for the existing flow of information must become better by providing more inter-application gateways and broadening the use of standard data formats and protocols.

These comments should not lessen the fact that the technology is already very beneficial to real users; and the development is progressing rapidly.

## 5 REFERENCES


Antoine, P. (1995) Creating a Secure Firewall. [http://softway.com.au/softway/firewalls/parta.html]. Sydney.

Deering, S. and Hinden, R. (1996) Internet Protocol, Version 6 (IPv6) Specification. RFC 1883, 01-04-1996

ITU (1996) [H.320] Recommendation H.320 (03/96) - Narrow-band visual telephone systems and terminal equipment. http://www.itu.int/itudoc/itu-t/rec/h/h320_23397.html

ITU (1996a) [T.120] Recommendation T.120 (07/96) - Data protocols for multimedia conferencing. http://www.itu.int/itudoc/itu-t/rec/t/t120_35511.html

Krause, F.-L.; Doblies, M. (1995) An Open Architecture for Distributed Product Libraries. Proceedings of *Second International SMAC/TEAM Workshop on Integrated Broadband Communications and Collaborative Work in the Automotive Industry*. TIRAC, Sligo Regional College.

Krause, F.-L.; Golm, F.; Loske, B.; Raupach, C. (1995a) Simulation von produktentwicklungsprozessen. In ZWF 90 (1995) 3. Carl Hanser Verlag München.

Krause, F.-L.; Doblies, M. (1996) Verteilte Konstruktion mittels Internet-basierter Informationssysteme. In: VDI Berichte Nr. 1289. VDI-Verlag Düsseldorf.

Netscape Communications (1995) Netscape SSLRef 2.0. [http://home.netscape.com/newsref/std/sslref.html]

N.N. (1996) AAL - ATM Adaptation Layer. http://cell-relay.indiana.edu/cell-relay/FAQ/dictionary/A/AAL.html

Noble, C. E. I.; Cave, P. R. (1986) Engineering Design Data Management. Proceedings EMTA '86, University of Swansea, UK.

ORC – Ocnus' Rope Company Inc. (1996) VRML model of Porsche 911. http://www.ocnus.com/models/Vehicles/82_porsche_911sc.wrl.gz

SMAC (1994) Refined User Needs. R2112/REN/DIO/DS/R/004. University of Loughborough, UK, 1994.

Spur, G. (1997) Auf dem Weg zur virtuellen Produktentwicklung. In: ZWF 92 (1997) 3. Carl Hanser Verlag München.

TEAM (1996) Deliverable DRR003 – User and Organisational Requirements. University of Loughborough.

Vio, Roberto (1997) Managing the virtual enterprise. In: *Proceedings of Workshop „Towards the Virtual Enterprise: Tools, Technologies and Models“* on 03-24-1997. University of Trento.

Wartelle, Dominique (1997) Internet and Intranet: new ways of managing enterprise communication. In: *Proceedings of Workshop „Towards the Virtual Enterprise: Tools, Technologies and Models“* on 03-24-1997. University of Trento.

## 6 BIOGRAPHY

Prof. Dr.-Ing. Frank-Lothar Krause, born in 1942, studied mechanical engineering at the Technical University of Berlin. In 1976 he was awarded Ph.D. for his thesis: "Methods for the design of CAD systems". He has been head of the department of Design Technology at the Institute of Production Systems and Design Technology of the Fraunhofer Association since 1977. As a member of the Technical University of Berlin he has been professor for Computer Aided Design and Technological Planning since 1983. In addition to his position at the Fraunhofer-Institute he became professor at TU Berlin for Industrial Information Technologies in 1990. He is responsible for fundamental research as well as for performing projects in this area. He is member of VDI, GI, IFIP-WG 5.2, WG 5.3. Furthermore he is chair of the working group of VDI and GI concerning artificial intelligence for CAD. International activities are the associated membership in CIRP and the CIM-Europe planning team of the EC.

Dipl.-Ing. Matthias Doblies, born in 1965, studied aerospace engineering at the Technical University of Berlin. In 1994 he joined the department of Industrial Information Technologies at the Institute of Machine Tools and Manufacturing Technology of the Technical University of Berlin.

# 10

# A platform to support production planning and management in a virtual enterprise

*Luis M. Camarinha-Matos*
*New University of Lisbon - Faculty of Sciences and Technology*
*Quinta da Torre - 2825 Monte Caparica - Portugal*
*Email:* cam@uninova.pt

**Abstract**

The materialization of the paradigm of virtual enterprise, although enabled by recent developments in communication technologies and computer networks, requires the definition of a reference architecture and the design and development of a supporting platform and appropriate protocols and mechanisms. This paper describes the approach being developed by the European Esprit project PRODNET, which aims at designing and developing an open platform to support industrial virtual enterprises with special focus on the needs of small and medium enterprises.

**Keywords**

Virtual enterprise, supply chain management, production management, federated systems

## 1 INTRODUCTION

Recent developments on communications and computer networking infrastructures represent enabling factors to support more effective cooperation forms among companies which face the challenge of continuous market scenario changes. The formation of a temporary consortium or alliance of companies that share skills and resources to explore fast-changing market opportunities (NIIIP 96, Walton and Whickers 96), i.e., a Virtual Enterprise (VE), may give small and medium enterprises (SMEs) the opportunity to reach world class level and some degree of independence. The manufacturing process is not carried on by a single enterprise anymore. In a networked organization, every enterprise is just a node that adds some value to the process (a step in the manufacturing / supply chain). Although most classic examples of networked organizations can be found in some particular business domains such as the automotive industry, this tendency is spreading to many other areas including the food and agribusiness industry (Camarinha 97b). A number of projects, worldwide, are nowadays

Computer Applications in Production and Engineering. F. Plonka and G. Olling (Eds.)

addressing different aspects of the virtual enterprises. Some of the most representative ones are the North-American NIIIP and the European VEGA, X.CITTIC, PLENT, LogSME, MARVEL OUS and PRODNET.

This paper describes the current approach and preliminary results being developed by the Esprit project PRODNET, which aims at designing and developing a reference architecture and an open platform to support industrial virtual enterprises with special focus on the needs of small and medium enterprises. PRODNET involves 10 partners from Portugal (CSIN, Miralago, Estec, New University of Lisbon, Uninova), Netherlands (University of Amsterdam), France (Lichen Informatique), UK (CIMIO), and Brazil (Fred Jung and Federal University of Santa Catarina).

## 2 CLASSES OF VIRTUAL ENTERPRISES

The virtual enterprise research is a growing multidisciplinary area still lacking unified definitions and terminology. A number of "competing" terms, such as extended enterprise, supply chain management, electronic commerce, etc., representing related concepts or partial views, are sometimes mistakenly used as synonymous of virtual enterprise. In fact different forms of virtual enterprises can be found nowadays. As a consequence there is clearly a need to classify different perspectives of the VE paradigm before it can be properly addressed and modeled. In a first attempt in the direction of this classification, a number of characteristics can be identified (Camarinha 97a), among which the duration, topology, and co-ordination are described in this section.

***Duration.*** There are alliances made for a single business opportunity and which are dissolved at the end of such process, and long term alliances that last for an indefinite number of business processes or for a specified time span. Typical examples of single business alliances can be found in large scale engineering systems, such as, for instance, building a bridge. In the case of food industry it is more typical to find long-term alliances.
***Topology.*** Another way of characterizing a VE, with major impact on requirements specification for a supporting infrastructure, is to look for the topology of the network. The most demanding case is the one that shows a variable / dynamic nature, in which enterprises (non strategic partners) can dynamically join or leave the alliance according to the phases of the business process or other market factors. But in many sectors there are supply chains with an almost fixed structure (little variation in terms of suppliers or clients). Another facet related to the 'geometry' is the possibility of an enterprise participating simultaneously in various networks or being committed to a single alliance (exclusivity). It is also important to analyze whether the VE operates in a situation of monopoly or under open market conditions.
***Co-ordination.*** In terms of network co-ordination various models can be found. In some sectors, as typified by the automobile industry, there is a dominant company "surrounded" by a relatively fixed network of suppliers (star-like structure). The dominant company defines "the rules of the game" and imposes its own standards, namely in terms of information exchange. Similar examples can be found in the agribusiness sector. A different organization could be found in some supply chains without a dominant company (democratic alliance) in which all nodes cooperate on an equal basis, keeping their autonomy, but joining their core competencies. Once a successful alliance is formed, companies may realize the mutual benefits of having some common management of resources and skills and they may tend to create a kind of common co-

ordination structure (federation). There are less real life examples of federated structures, but it will not be surprising if the market dynamics forces SMEs to embark in such deeper co-ordination alliances. Both related to topology and coordination is the aspect of visibility scope, i.e., "how far", along the network, can one node "see". In many cases a node only sees its direct neighbors (suppliers, clients). That is the case of most supply chains. In more advanced coordination situations, a node might have some visibility over other (non direct) levels.

## 3 REQUIRED FUNCTIONALITIES

Let us now have a closer look on the basic functionalities required to support an industrial VE (Camarinha97a, Afsarmanesh97).

### 3.1 Information related functionalities

The following aspects have to be considered:

-Information flows and types: frequency, amount, actors, which takes the initiative, classes (commercial, technical, quality-related etc.), broadcast or point to point flows, etc.

-Shared information: catalogues update and access rights, market information etc.

Interactive electronic catalogues and multimedia based shopping vehicles are becoming more and more important and are likely to become a fundamental component of a VE infrastructure. As the number of end consumers with access to computer networks increases, besides the members of the network, the access to such catalogues will be granted to an undetermined number of "visitors" / clients (home-initiated electronic transactions), with different rights than the VE members. Another example of shared information can be market data. For instance, in the agribusiness sector it is important to have access to worldwide statistics and forecasts on crops production.

-Electronic Trading Posts. Some experiments are already available in terms of using Internet-based "blackboards" for post product offers / buyers notices. More recently some more "active" marketing mechanisms ("push technology"), that take the initiative to forward the information to potential clients, are being experimented. On the other hand, the electronic links also create an opportunity for a much more responsive channel for end user registration and feedback, service and post-sale support than the traditional mail and phone systems.

-Security Some of the most obvious problems requiring a solution are: Access rights and firewalls, privacy and encryption, authentication, validation and auditability.

-Other information related services: browsers, monitoring orders etc.

Fax or other non-electronic media lead to a non-effective monitoring of the orders' status. Delays in orders processing, temporary incapacity of a supplier, changes in not completed orders, the need to re-adjust delivery times, etc., are some factors that point to the need for a more flexible and reliable interchange of information. The implementation of a truly Just-In-Time philosophy requires an infrastructure that supports stronger clients - suppliers interactions.

-Formats and protocols. The extensive use of EDI standards, instead of fax, is becoming a reality for the interchange of commercial documents, like orders. A major difficulty comes, however, from the existence of various versions of an EDI standard. The adoption of STEP for the exchange of electronic product model data throughout the product life-cycle is essential for flow of technical data between nodes. For other types of information a standardization effort is necessary. Inter-operability between the various standards employed is also a requirement.

## 3.2 Materials related functionalities

A second class of functional requirements is related to materials flows. It is important not to confuse the flow of information across the network with the flow of products and services through the supply chain, although the two aspects might be inter-related. Some required functionalities include:

-Logistics Transportation, inventory and warehousing planning This includes route planning, vehicles / crew assignment, distribution sequencing, etc., i.e. all activities which provoke materials flow between a point of origin and a point of consumption (Pfohl 96), including the subsets supply logistics, production logistics, distribution logistics and waste logistics.

-Materials flow management Identification, representation and monitoring (according to orders flow and status) of all materials flows within the network.

-Forecasting The use of electronic links to transmit information from points of sale to production units and suppliers, combined with historic data, will allow the implementation of forecasting functions.

-Specific information flows related to product (bar coding, Point of Sale - POS information) In particular it is important to understand and coordinate the interactions between materials flows and information flows.

## 3.3 Advanced functionalities and requirements

Once an effective electronic interlinking infrastructure is established, it is natural to expect a growth in the number and level of associated services. As the process of alliances (federation) formation among enterprises is a very competition-sensitive one, a step by step creation approach and trust building is the most adequate one. Building confidence and reliability requires experience of co-operation and a clear demonstration of the existence of benefits for all parties. Some early experiments and recent proposals suggest a number of future functional improvements in the VE architectures. Let us consider some examples (Camarinha97a):

Co-ordination. A joint coordination of activities and resources for a more global optimization may be an important step towards a federation-style of network coordination. This will include topics such as: Workflow related services; Distributed scheduling; Definition of roles / assignment of responsibilities; and Collaborative engineering (concurrent engineering over the network).

-Creation / Configuration. Functions to help the formation of a VE, including partners search, decision support tools to help the negotiation process and all the dynamics associated to the joining / leaving of enterprises (definition of roles, duties, rights).

-Characterization by "area" of the network (i.e., position in the value chain). The behavioral patterns of sub-networks may vary depending on their position along the value chain or even their geographical location. There are "areas" that are relatively stable and share some crucial information (strategic partners in the network) and other "peripheral zones" that are much more volatile and involving lower levels of interaction.

-Re-organization and training. Tools to support the internal re-organization / business processes (BP) re-engineering and training of people.
-Configuration tools. Configurability is a must for any supporting platform as we may face many different organizational structures and not a single VE profile.

Also, as some levels of trust, based on personal relationships, may dynamically change (based on reputation), configuration tools must support this dynamism. Figure 1 tries to organize the identified functionalities by levels. At the bottom level there are the most basic ones.

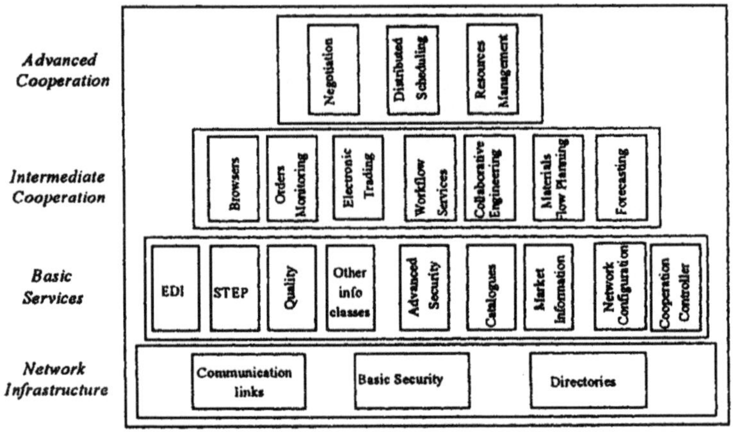


**Figure 1** - Some of the basic and advanced VE supporting functionalities

# 4 PRODNET'S APPROACH

## 4.1 General aspects

As a basic requirement for an infrastructure to support VEs, it can be pointed out that the companies must be able to inter-operate and exchange information in real time so that they can work as a single integrated unit although keeping their independence / autonomy. It also has to be taken into account that legacy systems were not designed with the idea of directly connecting to corresponding systems in other enterprises. Typically, enterprises pre-exist before they decide to join in an information sharing and exchange network. Consequently, every enterprise is autonomous, developed independently of other enterprises and uses distinct information management and control strategies that serves its purposes best. The situation is thus one of great heterogeneity and requiring adaptation of existing production planning and control systems (PPC) to electronic linking. However, for these enterprises to cooperate, on one hand they need to share and exchange a part of their information with the others, and on the other hand every company would like to preserve its local autonomy. Furthermore, distinct enterprises have distinct and often contradictory views and semantics associated with the information they store.

To support this environment the PRODNET infrastructure will include two main modules for each node (enterprise) in the network: Internal Module and Cooperation Layer (Fig. 2). The Internal Module represents the autonomous unit of a particular company. It includes the complete structure of the company's information (databases, information systems, etc.) and all the internal decision making processes / enterprise activities (internal PPC and engineering systems). The Cooperation Layer (Fig. 3) contains the functionalities for the inter-connection between the company and the whole net. It represents the communication and coordination role and works as the interlocutor of the company within the net. As a first approach, this module functions as a buffer of information input / output (represented by EDI, STEP, Coordination Information, etc. sub modules) between the enterprise and the network.

Our aim is that "nodes" exchange information, but at the same time, there is a guarantee that existing systems may run independent from the network. Namely, although there will be joint cooperative information exchange within the network, each node can keep its privacy and independence.

One of the necessary components is a kind of Cooperation Controller (PCL) that coordinates the interactions with other nodes in the network. Some of the advanced functionalities are strongly dependent on several non-technical factors. For instance, global VE coordination functionalities depend on the level of cooperation and trust achieved or desired by the enterprises. For some other functionalities there are already some tools on the market or solutions are being developed in various projects. That is the case, for instance, of logistics planning, forecasting or collaborative engineering tools. Therefore, and taking into account the available resources, the PRODNET consortium is not addressing all these topics. Instead, a subset of functionalities are being developed, including:

- Exchange of commercial data (EDIFACT).
- Exchange of technical product data (STEP).
- Orders status monitoring.
- Quality related information exchange.
- Common information system supporting, not only administrative information about the VE, but also all the information a node (enterprise) decides to make available to the network.
- Coordination module that handles all cooperation related events (execution of a local work flow).
- Configurator, allowing the definition and parametrization of the VE and the behavior of the particular node.
- Extended PPC system, adapted to interact with a VE environment and including the management of incompletely and imprecisely specified orders (along their life cycle).

Additionally, the usefulness and implementation feasibility of some more experimental modules on advanced coordination functionalities will be investigated:

- DRP - Distributed Resources Planning.
- Negotiation support system to facilitate partners search and the contractual processes during the formation of a VE.
- Management of a contracts data base.
- Electronic catalogue and its supporting services.

In terms of software organization (Figures 2e,3), some of the mentioned functionalities (EDI, STEP, Cooperation Information, network directories, etc.) deal with basic cooperation services and will be included in the PRODNET Cooperation Layer. Other functionalities, like orders management, are intrinsically associated to the PPC system and will be included in the Internal Module. Finally, the more advanced coordination functionalities will be considered as separate modules, out of the Cooperation Layer, but in strong interaction with it. It shall be noticed that not all enterprises will be interested in all functionalities. Moreover, the various functionalities can be enabled or disabled according to a set of configuration parameters.

## 4.2 PRODNET Cooperation Layer

As mentioned before, the PRODNET Cooperation Layer (PCL) contains the basic functionalities for the inter-connection between the company and the whole net. It represents the communication role and works as the interlocutor of the company within the net.

The main components of this module are: EDI component, STEP component, Distributed Information Management System (DIMS), Communications component, Authentication and safety modules, External Messages class identifier, Configuration component (CONFIG), Local coordination component, and Human Interface (HI).

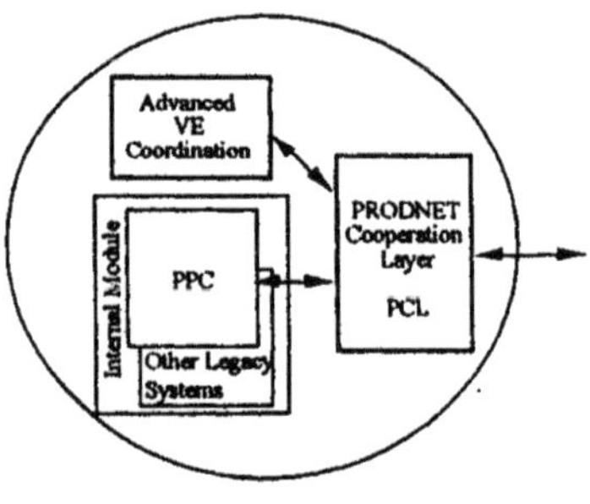


**Figure 2** General structure of a PRODNET node

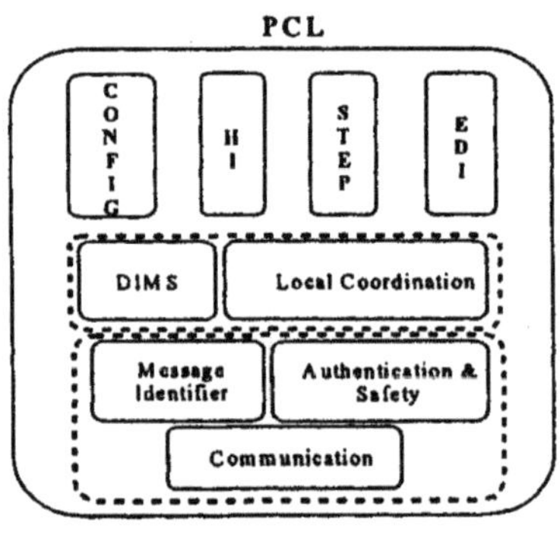


**Figure 3** - Main components of PCL

***EDI Component.*** This module is responsible for receiving and formatting orders-related messages in EDIFACT format. Among its functionalities, it will check / parse EDIFACT syntax (for various versions of the standard), check for completeness of messages contents, and generate appropriate formats for sending out EDI messages. It will also detect and extract EDI messages embedding information represented in other formats, such as a STEP specifications associated to an order.

***STEP Component.*** The STEP module's function is to handle the technical product data used within PRODNET. Ideally all product data should be exchanged in STEP format. The STEP services provided to PRODNET will allow for the transmission and reception of STEP files that have been clear text encoded according to a defined schema; as described in Part 21 of the STEP standard. It should also be possible to query that STEP data held within PRODNET by the usage of the Standard Data Access Interface, SDAI, defined as part 22 of ISO 10303.

***DIMS - Distributed Information Management System.*** The Distributed Information Management Subsystem in the PRODNET Cooperation Layer is responsible to model and manage all cooperation support information (Afsarmanesh97), such as:

-*Node Self Information*: information which is controlled and managed by the node itself, e.g. enterprise profile, information which the node wants to make available to the network, local information such as part of a workflow plan, etc.. Any part of this information can only be accessed by authorized users. The Self Information also contains a part of the local information at PPC, that PPC decides to move into the PCL partly for being used within the local PCL and partly for sharing with other nodes.

-*Node Acquaintance Information*: information that needs to be accessible from other enterprises for this node's internal purposes. For example, general profile of other enterprises which can become potential partners in a VE, or information which can be specifically acquired from a close sister enterprise.

-*Virtual Enterprise Information*: this category refers to all the information which is associated with a VE, such as VE configuration information, control and status information for the VE coordinator, information to support the cooperation between the enterprises in a VE, etc..

The implementation of DIMS follows the federated database paradigm.

***Communications.*** This module is responsible for handling all communications with the other nodes in the network. It includes functionalities such as: Selection of communications protocol and channels; Basic communications management; Privacy mechanisms (cryptography); and Tight interactions (direct channels) between nodes.

***Authentication and safety.*** This module is responsible for the implementation of safety and authentication mechanisms, at the VE level. It has to check access rights, handle keys management, etc.

***External Messages class identifier.*** As different classes of messages, coming from the network, can arrive at the PCL, this module will try to identify them in order to facilitate its internal assignment. Examples of such classes are: EDI messages, STEP messages, general PRODNET messages, DIMS queries, etc.

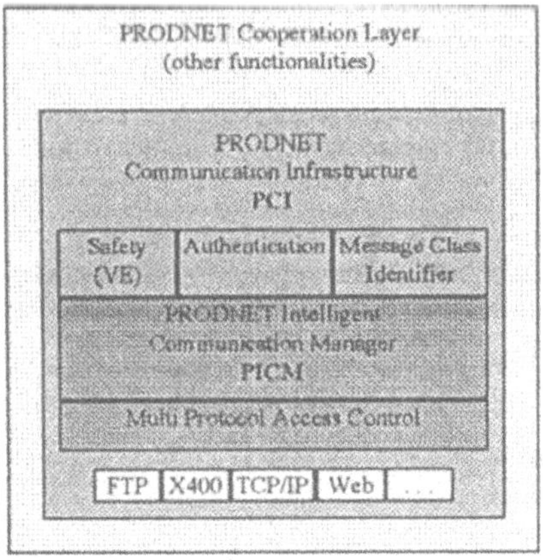


**Figure 4** Communications infrastructure

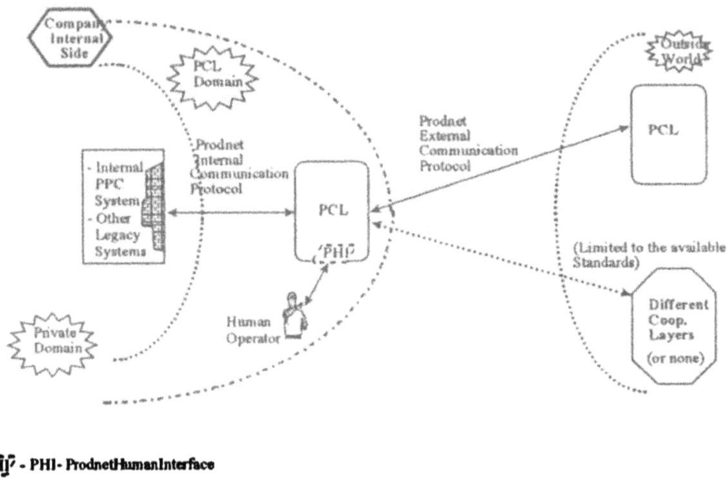


**Figure 5** Interactions with the PCL

It shall also be noted (Fig. 5) that PCL has to interact not only with nodes having a similar PCL but also with foreign cooperation layers. At the moment, for foreign cooperation layers, only standardized information messages (EDIFACT and STEP) are considered.

***Configuration Component.*** The PRODNET platform is intended to support a large diversity of enterprises and interconnection modes. This means a large heterogeneity in terms of available / installed services and desired management procedures. For instance, some companies may want to use all communication functionalities and standards, whilst others may be interested in using mainly EDI. Some companies may want a strong human-based control of the interactions process, whilst others may prefer a more direct channel to the PPC system. Therefore it is necessary to specify the desired cooperation behavior in an explicit plan (each enterprise has to define its particular activity flow plan) that will be "executed"/controlled by the Local Coordination Module. Additionally, the Configuration Component will allow a manual specification of the structure of the VE and the access rights of all its members.

***Local Coordination Module.*** This component is the "executor"/controller of the activity flow plan defined by the Configuration Component (a kind of workflow engine). In other words, it is responsible for the behavior of the PCL and interacts with all the other modules. It handles all Cooperation Events according to the specified rules for the particular enterprise. These events have an asynchronous nature and are provoked by other nodes of the VE, by the Internal Module of the enterprise or by the Human Interface.

***Human Interface.*** This component assures an interface between the human operator (responsible for the interactions with the VE) and the PCL. As mentioned before, the level of human intervention in this process will depend on the policy of each company and will be specified at the configuration phase (configuration and workflow plan).

## 4.3 Main PPC functionalities

According to PRODNET the main functionalities required from a PPC system suited for the needs of a SME are: Industrial Logistics Management: i) Orders flow management, Product data management, Sales Forecasts handling, Actual Requirements Planning; ii) Master Production Scheduling; iii) Production Control; iv) Quality Control / Tracking; v) Industrial Costing. The "gray boxes" in Fig. 6 represent extensions or components of the PPC system that need major re-engineering in order to integrate it into a VE environment.

***Mappings.*** This module is responsible for the interface between the PPC system and the PCL, using the PRODNET Internal Communication Protocol. Such kind of interface has to be developed for each legacy system the company wants to connect to PCL.

***Orders management.*** Orders management is one of the most important functionalities of the Virtual Enterprise. This component is mainly influenced by EDI connections and the possibility of receiving direct inquiries about orders status from other nodes (clients). An explicit state transition diagram has to be kept for each order, however this information cannot be kept in the PCL DIMS. Therefore, the PPC system must be prepared to answer queries about the orders states coming from PCL. Additionally, technical product specifications may be associated to an order and received also electronically.

On the other hand, it is PRODNET's intention to handle orders that, at a given stage, might be incompletely or imprecisely specified. All the dynamics associated

to an order, namely the process of receiving further information to complete it, needs to be defined in a good interaction with the PCL system. Let us consider an example of an order for a car model X, where it is possible to specify particular features (optional characteristics), like the type of engine, the color, etc. An **incomplete order** is one which does not include all required product details. An order could, for instance, simply specify a car model X. If an order like that is received then it is possible to start immediately the production of the chassis, the doors, etc., independently of the missing information about complementary attributes. This process continues until all details about the required product are specified. An **imprecise order** is an order in which the value of some attribute is not missing but it is specified in a vague way. For instance, in the car example, the attribute color, in the initial specification, could say "dark color" or "one of blue, black, green". Only later on this attribute would get a specific (precise) value. Another example of vagueness could be on the quantity. An order could specify a tentative amount of between 100 and 120 units (to be confirmed later). New "orders" (or messages) are supposed to arrive in the future complementing the missing attributes in the "original" order (these orders are not really new orders but additions to the original one). Thus they should be associated to the original one (logically merged).
Besides the exchange of the order itself, using an EDI standard, the order has to be followed up in order to cope with, for example, delays in orders processing, temporary incapacity of a supplier, changes in not completed orders, the need to re-adjust delivery times, and so on. A client node might even want to know details about the manufacturing state of the ordered products in order to prevent any difficulties for itself. This requires an infrastructure that supports a stronger clients - suppliers interaction. One important aid to orders management is the order's state transition diagram (Fig. 7). Such diagram can be used to obtain a "snapshot" of the life cycle of any order circulating inside a company. This diagram could also facilitate the follow up of an order during its execution.

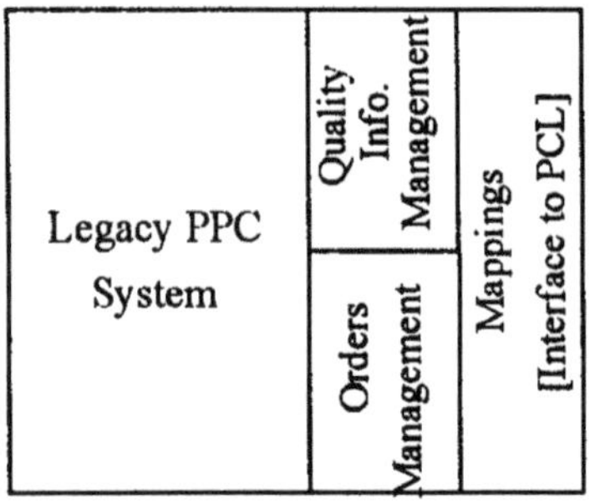


**Figure 6** Major changes to a PPC system

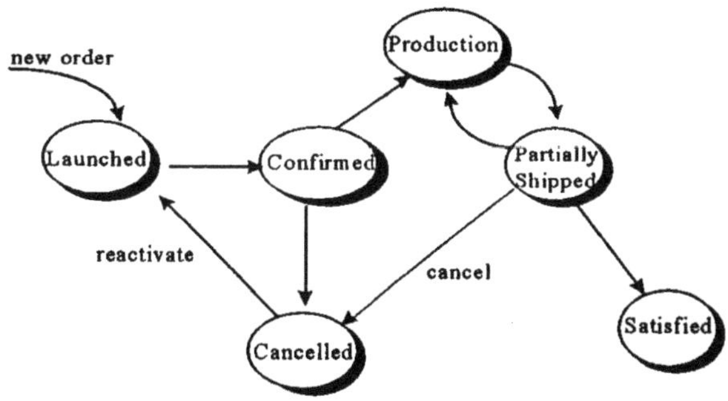


**Figure 7** Order's state transition diagram

***Quality information management.*** The extended PPC system will include functionalities to manage the basic information needs for a standard (ISO 9000) quality system (inside the company). At network level, the situation is more ambiguous as there is no standard yet. Nevertheless, new legislation regarding responsibilities for components included in a product will provoke an increasing demand for such information to be exchanged at network level.
In the absence of standard definition of the contents and structure of quality related information to be exchanged between nodes in the VE, the following principles are proposed:
-The report will have a free format [to be agreed between interacting nodes].
-Two levels of reports are foreseen:
i) One related to the value added by the particular enterprise. Examples of information: Who has supplied the raw materials / components; Quality certification information; Identification of production batch, production history; Rejected parts in this production batch; Other production statistics; etc.
ii) Another level with "tracing" information related to components used by the enterprise but supplied by other nodes.
-The access to quality information will be provided on request.
It doesn't make sense to have this information stored on DIMS: it might be a huge amount; it can even be stored on historical backups [not on-line]. Therefore, only a "log" of requests and trace of answers will be stored in DIMS.

***PPC imitator.*** In some industry sectors, some enterprises interact with dozens of very small suppliers (subcontractors) that don't even have a PPC system. It would be however very convenient to integrate these suppliers in the VE supporting infrastructure. This would mean install in such small companies a PC with the PCL module. But in this case, due to the lack of an installed PPC system, it will be necessary to develop a small software module (PPC imitator) that supports manual introduction of the information requests coming from the network via PCL.

### 4.4 Advanced Co-ordination Functionalities

As mentioned before, the co-ordination aspects of a Virtual Enterprise, although important, still face many open questions, some of them of a non-technological nature. For instance, the legal barriers and the need for re-organizational changes implying retraining of people and new roles assignment (new power structures i) take time to implement and require a very careful approach. On the other hand, the development of advanced inter-network co-ordination mechanisms and safety procedures has to be accompanied by trust building actions, an area whose exact evolutionary shape is hard to anticipate at current stage. These uncertainty factors recommend a step-by-step approach instead of an ambitious general infrastructure development approach as followed by some other projects. Therefore, PRODNET will follow two complementary approaches:

1. A minimal coordination level, mostly based on human decision making, is included in the PCL.
2. A set of experimental components on advanced coordination mechanisms will be investigated:

***Decision support system for VE partners search and negotiation.*** Including: Public announcements (over a network), Use of electronic commerce services, Industrial associations as directories of suppliers, Negotiation, Legal consortia formation.

***Management of contracts data base:*** Contracts with suppliers, Derivation of parameters for the local controller.

***Electronic Catalogues:*** Link to the bidding process, link to WWW / visualisation and browsing.

***Distributed Resources Planning (DRP):*** Abstraction level higher than MRP activity to be done at network-wide level.

## 5 CONCLUSIONS

This paper presented an attempt to classify virtual enterprises according to the duration, topology and coordination perspectives and to identify the required functionalities for a supporting platform. The structure of the platform being developed by the Esprit project PRODNET was described and a characterization of its main blocks were made. Major open questions, requiring further investigation, are related to the advanced coordination functionalities which depend on the level of integration / federation the companies participating in a virtual enterprise decide to achieve. On the other hand, it is important to note that the concept of VE raises new requirements in terms of methods and contents of work and the skills of the human resources involved. Therefore, the social and re-organizational aspects have to be analyzed together with the technological developments.

## ACKNOWLEDGMENTS

This worked was funded in part by the European Commission (PRODNET project). The author also thanks the contributions of the partners of the mentioned project.

## REFERENCES

H. Afsarmanesh, L.M. Camarinha-Matos - **Federated Information Management for Cooperative Virtual Organizations**, Proceedings of DEXA'97, Springer-Verlag, Toulouse, Sep 97.

Browne, P. Sackett, H. Wortmann - **Future manufacturing systems - Towards the extended enterprise.** J. Computers in Industry 25 (1995), pp. 235-254.

L.M. Camarinha-Matos, H. Afsarmanesh, C. Garita, C. Lima - **Towards an Architecture for Virtual Enterprises**, Proceedings of the 2nd World Congress on Intelligent Manufacturing Processes & Systems, Budapest, Hungary, June 10-13, 1997.

L.M. Camarinha-Matos, Ricardo Carelli, J. Pellicer, M. Martín - **Towards the virtual enterprise in food industry,** Proceedings of the ISIP'97 OE/IFIP/IEEE Int. Conf. on Integrated and Sustainable Industrial Production, Lisboa, Portugal, 14-16 May 1997, Chapman & Hall, ISBN 0 412 79950 2.

Ingrid Hunt , Alexandra Pereira Klen, Jiangang Zhang- **Cross Border Enterprises: Virtual or Extended !,** Proceedings of the ISIP'97 OE/IFIP/IEEE Int. Conference on Integrated and Sustainable Industrial Production, Lisboa, Portugal, 14-16 May 1997, Chapman&Hall, ISBN 0 412 79950 2.

The NIIIP Reference Architecture, 1996, www. niiip.org

Ricardo Rabelo, L.M. Camarinha-Matos - **Towards Agile Scheduling in Extended Enterprise,** Proceedings of BASYS'96: Balanced Automation Systems II - Implementation Challenges for Anthropocentric Manufacturing, Chapman & Hall, Jun 1996, ISBN 0-412-78890-X.

# 11
# A Fuzzy approach for the globalization of production activities

*A. Portioli*
*Dipartimento di Economia e Produzione, Politecnico di Milano*
*Piazza L. da Vinci 32, I-20133 Milano, ITALY*
*Tel. ++39 2 2399.2733*
*Fax ++39 2 2399.2700*
*e_mail portioli@mail.ecopro.polimi.it*

**Abstract**

Globalization is one of the most important and dynamic changes in the last decades. Companies can globalize in different ways, such as: exporting, licensing, starting a production activity abroad. During the last few years, there has been an increasing number of companies choosing to globalize by starting a new plant abroad. Moreover, most models presented in literature are difficult to implement in real situations, mainly due to the following reasons: (1) many models do not manage both quantitative and non quantitative information together; (2) in globalization decisions a large number of elements are involved and their relationships are complex and difficult to model mathematically; (3) some models are crispy: they divide alternatives into good and bad, giving no idea about their degree of "goodness". In this paper a Fuzzy Logic based Decision Support System that avoids these drawbacks is presented, and an implementation of the system in an European company that was undertaking a decision process for transferring abroad some production activities is described.

Results show the usefulness and effectiveness of the proposed tool.

**Keywords**

Fuzzy logic, globalization, production systems

Computer Applications in Production and Engineering. F. Plonka and G. Olling (Eds.)

## 1 INTRODUCTION

Over the past 15-20 years globalizations increased tremendously: richest markets attract competitors from all over the world and this caused an intensification of the competitive pressure. In order to cope with this situation, many companies adopted a combination of the following two approaches (Fawcett, 1993): (1) to improve their internal manufacturing competence through the adoption of JIT and TQM principles; (2) to develop coordinated global manufacturing networks to take greater advantage of available worldwide resources.

Despite the tremendous relevance of the globalization of production activities, very little research work has been carried out on this subject, compared with JIT, TQM and other approaches to improve internal competitiveness of the company (Portioli and Sianesi, 1993).

Globalization is such a complex process that it cannot be addressed as a whole, but rather has to be approached hierarchically. In Iskra et al. (1994) a literature review of globalization models is presented, and a decision process is proposed that utilizes different models at different hierarchical levels. In particular three hierarchical levels can be identified: at the first level the main issue is about what area of the company to globalize (Purchasing, Manufacturing, R&D, Distribution), and De Toni et al. (1992) proposed a model to support such a decision. If it has been chosen to globalize part (or all) of the production activities, models such as those proposed by Fawcett (1993), McGrath and Bequillard (1989), and Ferdows (1989) help in identifying the strategic role of the overseas activities. Finally, the third level concerns the location of the production activities, and Van de Ven (1993), Vos (1991) and Haug (1992), proposed decision models to help companies in identifying the best location, minimizing such costs as production cost, transportation cost, investment cost, etc., taking into consideration also issues as the transportation system of the target country, its political stability, etc.

As for this third level, most of the models presented in literature are difficult to implement in practice because of three main drawbacks:

1. many models have difficulties in managing quantitative and non quantitative information at the same time;
2. globalization decisions involve many different elements, linked by complex relationships, that are difficult to model mathematically in a satisfactory way;
3. some models (e.g. all those based on LP) present a black and white solution, where the optimal alternative is selected (white) and all the others are black, giving no information if, for example, the second one is a very close one, or a much worse one. On the contrary managers for their decisions would appreciate better a tool that indicates the degree of goodness and badness of alternative solutions, so they can improve the solution by taking into consideration other elements also.

Moreover, most of the models presented in literature do not explicitly help to identify what part of the production system to transfer, but they rather take as given that information.

Therefore, in this paper a Fuzzy Logic (FL) based Decision Support System (DSS) that captures qualitative aspects, allows to easily and quickly model relationships, and supplies information about the goodness of the alternative solutions, is proposed. Besides, this DSS explicitly addresses the issue of which products, and which steps of their production process to transfer abroad showing the usefulness of this tool.

The proposed DSS has been implemented in a European middle sized company and the results have been compared with the ones yielded by their traditional decisional process.

The reminder of the paper is organized as follows: in Section 2 the proposed DSS is presented, in Section 3 its implementation in a real case is described and in Section 4 the results of the proposed DSS are analyzed. In Section 5 conclusions are given.

## 2 THE PROPOSED DSS

The decisional model proposed is characterized by the following steps:

1. analysis of the products and of the processes;
2. ordering of alternatives;
3. identification of alternative worth in further investigation;
4. quantitative evaluation of alternatives and final choice.

In the following sections each step will be described.

### 2.1 Analysis of products and processes

At this step products are analyzed in order to identify the ones that can give more advantages if their production is transferred abroad. For this analysis three classes of elements are taken into consideration: market issues (e.g. evolution in the demand, position in the product life cycle, distribution and selling characteristics, etc.), cost issues (e.g. cost distribution among manpower, raw material, etc.), and physical characteristics (weight, dimensions, number of components, etc.).

Besides the analysis of the products, an analysis of the production processes is necessary. All the processes carried out by the company are broken down into activities (steps of the production process), that are then classified on the basis of a portfolio analysis along two dimensions: effectiveness and efficiency (Figure 1)

A **competence activity** is an activity that the company carries out efficiently thanks to its competence.

A **core activity** is an activity that is cardinal for the market performances of the company (thanks to this activity the company is more effective on the market).

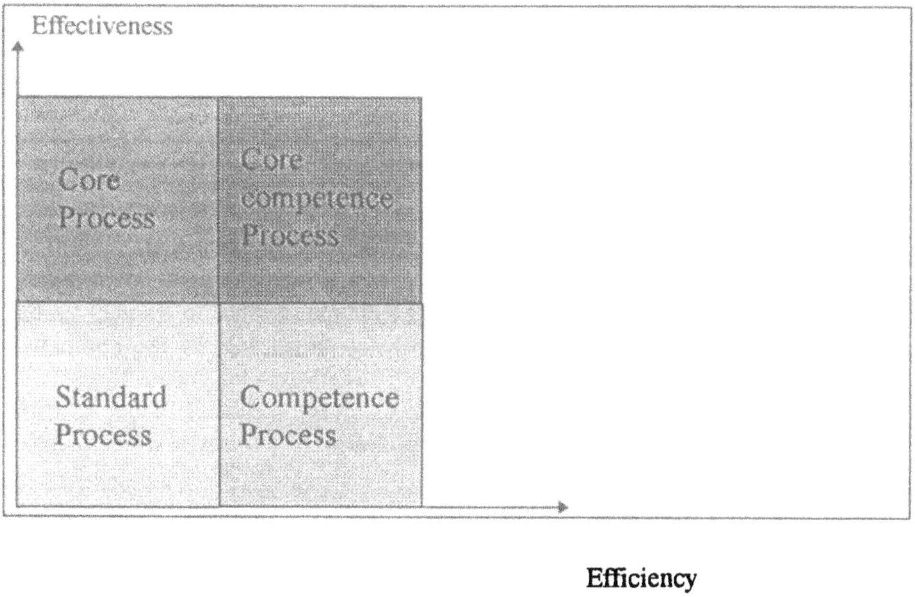


**Figure 1**: portfolio analysis

A **core competence activity** is an activity that is both cardinal for the market performances of the company, and is carried out efficiently.

A **standard process** is a process that is neither peculiar to neither the company, nor it is carried out more efficiently than by the competitors.

Non core activities can easily be transferred abroad, or even given to other companies (suppliers or subcontractors) that are more efficient in carrying them out. On the contrary, core activities are the one that the company has to concentrate on and to tightly control.

This kind of portfolio analysis is well known and it is always included in the decision models for globalization. What it is often overlooked is an analysis about links and interactions among activities. In fact, besides a portfolio analysis a cluster analysis is necessary. Sets of activities are considered to identify technological constraints (for example two activities that are to be performed in close sequence because of the high temperature of the material) and organizational constraints, in order to identify clusters of independent activities (independent clusters). In fact, it is necessary to take into consideration for transfer, not the single activity, but an independent cluster.

Transferable clusters are, therefore, independent clusters (i.e. do not have any core activity), that the products analysis has shown to be potentially profitable to transfer abroad.

Once the set of transferable clusters, and the set of alternative countries, are identified, the next step is to order the combinations of clusters and countries, according to their "goodness".

## 2.2 Ordering of alternatives

As it has been stated above, for the managers it is much better to have all alternatives ranked on a scale, than just having the best one identified.

The problem is to choose the right scale.

Two main factors affect the goodness of the choice of what to transfer abroad and where: (1) adequacy to the transfer, and (2) fulfillment of the company's objectives.

Adequacy to the transfer is very difficult to estimate, because it is due to many different aspects, most of which are not quantifiable. In particular we have taken into consideration:

- technical complexity;
- affinity with non transferable functions;
- additional costs;
- distance from the market.

Each of these categories is further detailed in subcategories. For example the technical complexity is divided into product complexity, process complexity and environmental conditions. Each transferable cluster is given an evaluation on each one of the subcategories, for each alternative country (or location, if more than one alternative is considered for each country). In fact, such evaluation is strongly location dependent. For example, a production process can be evaluated with a high process complexity, if the location under consideration is China, but with a medium process complexity if the location under consideration is the Czech Republic, because of the different technology development and average manpower training of the two countries.

All these subcategories are difficult to quantify and are linked one another by a complex relationship that is impossible to represent mathematically. A lexical description is much easier, much faster, and even closer to reality. Therefore, a FL model has been developed to capture this capital aspect (managers can easily describe these relationships by means of IF.... THEN... statements).

On the contrary, as for the fulfillment of the company's objectives, a multi objective function has been preferred, because it allows a straightforward understanding and more transparency.

The objectives of a company when transferring part of the production abroad can be one or more of the following (Ferdows, 1989):

- access to low cost production input factors;
- proximity to the market;
- use of local technological resources;

- control and amortization of technological assets;
- pre-emption of competition.

Each one of these objective has been further detailed (e.g. low cost production input factors are: raw material, energy, money, manpower) to help in better estimate the value, for each transferable cluster and each alternative country. Each company sets the weights for the objectives so to get a customized overall objective function.

## 2.3 identification of alternative worthing further investigation;

By means of step 1 and step 2 we obtain the position of the different alternative on the scale of the adequacy to the transfer, and on the scale of the fulfillment of the company's objectives, for each country. It is therefore possible to chart the transferable clusters on a two dimensional diagram (Figure 2)

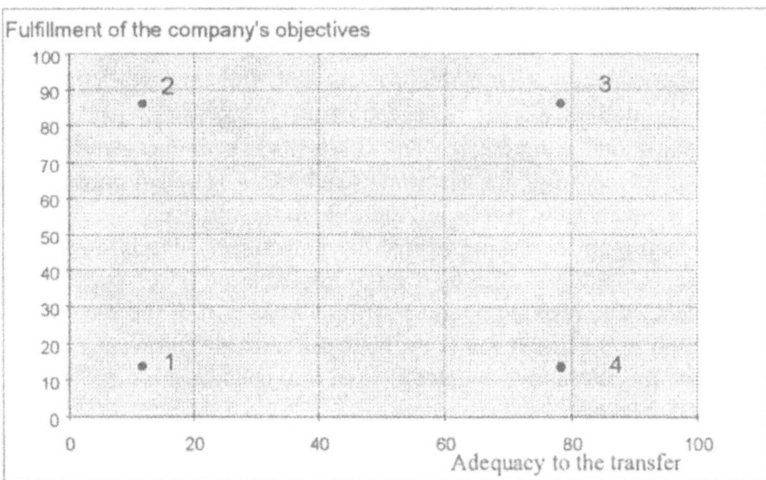


**Figure 2**: Example of the valuation chart for alternative transferable clusters for a certain country.

Alternatives in position 3 present a high value for both fulfillment of the company's objectives and for the adequacy to transfer, and so deserve further analysis. On the contrary, alternatives in position 1 can be disregarded because are difficult to transfer and give a low contribution to the fulfillment of company's objectives. Also, alternatives in position 4 have low interest. Finally, alternatives in position 2 could cause difficulties if transferred, but could yield a large advantage to the company if the transfer is correctly implemented: they can be seen as opportunities that require particular attention and need a deeper analysis.

## 2.4 quantitative evaluation of alternatives and final choice.

For the alternative that the previous step has shown worth further consideration, an investment analysis is carried out in order to have monetary data also. The amount of the investment necessary is evaluated, the cash flows are estimated and a financial plan is formulated to decide which alternative to actually implement, and when. This is a standard analysis, and therefore it will not be further described.

The proposed DSS has been first tested for internal consistency by applying the model to different benchmark situations (cases with well defined characteristics, for which the good solutions were known and clear). Then, it has been implemented in a real case, that is described in the next section.

# 3 THE GLASS-WORKER COMPANY CASE

The Glass-worker company (for confidential reasons we use a fictional name) is a middlesized European company, that employs about 800 workers, with a turnover of about 140 million dollars a year. The industries it works for are: Glass, Optoelectronics, Quartz and Automotive. The Glass-worker produces some 15% of the world market of capsules for electronics devices (e.g. electronic airbag sensors), and some products show a relevant increase in the turnover.

The market was facing an increasing degree of competition, mainly due to the entry of new Asian competitors offering similar products at lower costs. The management had decided to respond by transferring abroad part of the production, so they started to analyze the problem and evaluate different alternatives.

After a first analysis, the alternative countries taken into consideration are: China, Czech Republic, and Malaya.

After 8 months the decision process was almost at the end, so we thought it a good opportunity to undertake a parallel process with other managers of the company, adopting the proposed tool, in order to prove its practical feasibility and its advantages over the traditional one.

The products analysis and the process analysis have allowed as to identify the products that could get considerable advantages if transferred abroad, and the clusters that do not contain any core activity. A further constraint set by the management is that a transferable cluster must contain all activities necessary to complete an end product, or a component that is sellable (i.e. that is not only for internal production, but that has its own market). Therefore, in this case a transferable cluster is also identified by the item it realizes (Table 1 presents the items corresponding to the transferable clusters).

Then a manager of the Glass-worker was asked to use the FL based software for determining the adequacy to transfer of the transferable clusters, for each one of

the 3 alternative countries, indicating a value of very low, low, medium, high, very high, for each of the subcategories building up the adequacy.
As for the fulfillment of the company's objectives, management gave the weights shown in Table 2.

**Table 1**: Transferable clusters/items

| Number | Description | Code |
|---|---|---|
| 1 | Glassdust | AZ851 |
| 2 | PR for Reed | WQ882 |
| 3 | Transistor TO 5/ TO39 | ZA854 |
| 4 | DIP-Socket | KW850 |
| 5 | SQ-Floor | WF870 |
| 6 | Top of Actuator for CFZ | XS863 |
| 7 | Top of Actuator for Sensors | KB866 |

**Table 2**: Objectives' weight for the Glass-worker case.

| Objective | Weight |
|---|---|
| access to low cost production input factors | 0.8 |
| proximity to the market | 0.2 |
| use of local technological resources | 0 |
| control and amortization of technological assets | 0 |
| pre-emption of competition | 0 |

All transferable clusters have been taken into consideration according with this overall objective function and an evaluation chart has been derived for each country. In Figure 4 the Czech Republic's evaluation chart is reported.

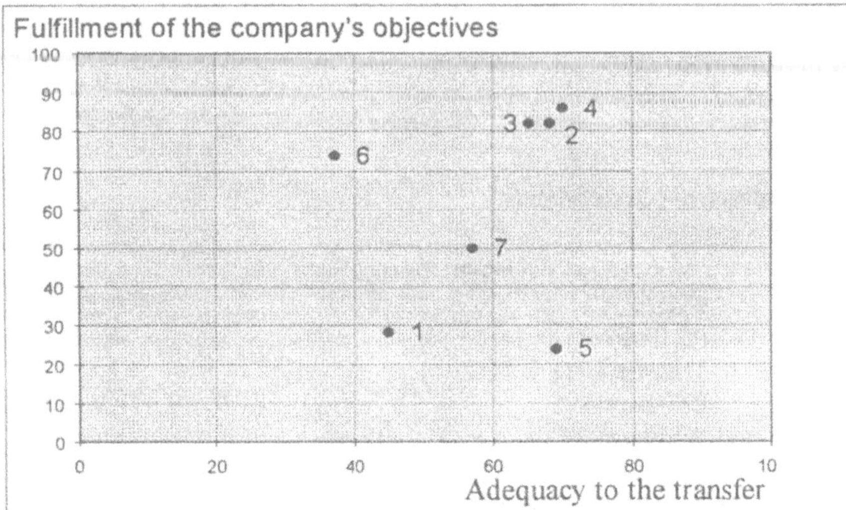


**Figure 3**: the valuation chart for alternative transferable clusters for the Czech Republic

From the chart it can be seen that items 2, 3 and 4 should be transferred, item 5 has a lower priority (it fulfills less the company's objectives), but it is interesting also, and should give little problem if transferred. Item 6 would give a great advantage if transferred, but has also a low adequacy to transfer, this is due to its high affinity with non transferable functions (in particular frequent and intense information exchange with the R&D).

Comparing the evaluation charts for the different countries it can be seen that the Czech Republic is the one that yields the best values. The main reasons can be found in that, on the one hand China has higher transportation costs, low quality standard for raw materials and does not have an internal market for the items considered. On the other hand, Malaya has a heavier fiscal policy, and a harsh environmental regulation, that would require costly additional investments.

At this point results have been compared with the one achieved by means of the traditional decision process.

## 4 ANALYSIS OF RESULTS

The Glass-worker company's traditional decision process had selected for transferring items 3, 4 and 6. A deeper analysis has been carried out together with the Glass-worker company's management, in order to understand the reasons for the differences:

1. the proposed DSS suggests item 2 as a good one to transfer, but the Glass-worker's management notices that it is an item that in the near future will be replaced by a new one, adopting a different technology. This aspect would have been captured in the quantitative analysis, when estimating the cash flows;
2. items 7 and 5 had not been selected for transfer by the Glass-worker's management because improvement in performances was mainly pursued by cutting production costs (0.8), while proximity to the market and the opportunity to increase sales was not considered very important (0.2). Therefore, in meeting after meeting all choices discussed, focused more and more on costs ("it is not possible to keep in mind always everything: you have to focus on main points"). Nevertheless, particularly item 7, showed a great selling potential, thus increasing significantly the fulfillment of the company's objectives (the weight of the objective is low, but the selling potential of 7 is very high). The proposed DSS, unlike the traditional process, had no problems in considering also low priority objectives, thus allowing the capture of more opportunities. The Glass-worker company's management accepted the suggestion of the FL tool and added item 7 to the pool of items to be further considered for transferring.
3. item 6 has been selected for transferring by the Glass-worker's management, but the proposed DSS highlights a low adequacy to transfer (because of its affinity with non transferable functions). The management agreed with the results of the DSS. They decided to confirm transfer of item 6, but to launch a study to activate all possible actions so to guarantee the intense information transfer that the proposed DSS highlighted to be necessary (e.g. electronic connections with the new site, video conferencing , pc networks, etc.).

When compared with the traditional Glass-worker company's decision process, the proposed DSS shows to be more structured and allows making explicit relationships among characteristics that otherwise could remain unexpressed and could: on the one hand increase the degree of subjectiveness (not all terms are clear to everybody), on the other hand delay the decision process (a good part of the meetings is lost in focusing the discussion and in clarifying, or reminding, the interrelations among the considered elements). Therefore, the Glass-worker company's management appreciated the ability of the tool to shorten the decision process (the traditional one took 10 months, using the FL tool 2 months were enough), and to reduce the degree of subjectiveness. This last point has been further proven by undertaking the decision process with different persons (sharing similar knowledge about the company's products, processes and objectives) and showing that the results were quite similar.

## 5 CONCLUSIONS

In this paper a new system for supporting the decision process of companies that want to globalize their production system has been presented, and its application to a real case has been described.

Managers of the company where it has been implemented appreciated very much this method, because it is able to:

- manage both quantitative and non quantitative data;
- manage uncertain and subjective information;
- cope with a high number of interrelations among parameters, that are not easy to model mathematically (if not impossible), but, on the contrary, can be easily treated in the proposed DSS by means of IF, THEN statements;
- present the degree of "goodness" of each alternative, and not just to point out the best one.

Moreover, the managers involved in the test appreciated particularly the ability of the tool to consider at the same time more than one objective, thus not forgeting low priority objectives also. Finally, reduction in the time to perform the decision process and in its degree of subjectiveness were also considered major advantages of the proposed tool.

## 6 REFERENCES


De Toni A., Filippini R., Forza C. (1992) Manufacturing strategy in global markets: an operations management model. *International Journal of Operations and Production Management*, **12**, 4, 7-18.

Fawcett, S.E. (1993) Conversion system cost characteristics in global manufacturing: the maquiladora example. *International Journal of Production Research*, **31**, 3, 647-664.

Ferdows K. (1989) Mapping international factory networks, in *Managing international manufacturing* (ed. K. Ferdows), North-Holland, Amsterdam.

Haug P. (1992) An international location and production transfer model for high technology multinational enterprises. *International Journal of Production Research*, **30**, 3, 559-572.

Iskra R., Marinoni A., Portioli A., Sianesi A. (1993) Analysis of internationalization models. *Advanced topics on production systems design and management*. Varenna (Lecco), ITALY, June 1-4 (in Italian).

Mc Grath M.E., Bequillard R.B. (1989) International manufacturing strategies and infrastructural considerations in the electronics industry, in *Managing international manufacturing* (ed. K. Ferdows), North-Holland, Amsterdam.

Portioli A. and Sianesi A. (1993) Globalization of the companies and of their production systems.To be an Industrial Engineer today... and tomorrow? ANIMP XX national conference, Capri (Naples) 14-16 October (in Italian).

Van de Ven A.D.M. and Ribbers A.M.A. (1993) International logistics: a diagnostic method for the allocation of production and distribution facilities. *International Journal of Logistics Management*, 4, 1, 67-83.

Vos G.C.J.M. (19921 A production-allocation for international manufacturing strategy. *International Journal of Operation and Production Management*, 11, 3, 125-134.

## 7 BIOGRAPHY

Alberto Portioli carries out his research activity at the Dipartimento di Economia e Produzione of the Politecnico di Milano in Italy. His research interests are in the areas of production systems design, operations management, manufacturing strategy and quality. On these subjects he published papers on international journals as International Journal of Production Research, Production Planning and Control, and others. Alberto Portioli also teaches Operations Management in an undergraduate course and in a MBA course of the Politecnico di Milano.

# 12
# Modeling to support a food industry in the extended enterprise

*I. Hunt, Dip. B.Sc. M.Sc.*
*CIMRU (Computer Integrated Manufacturing Research Unit)*
*University College Galway, Ireland.*
*Tel. +353-91-750414, Fax No. +353-91-562894*
*E-mail: Ingrid.Hunt@UCG.IE*

*Prof. Dr. R. Carelli, & Eng. Jorge Pellicer,*
*Institute of Automation,*
*University of San Juan,*
*San Juan, Argentina*
*Tel. +54-64-213303 Fax No. +54- 64-213672*
*E-mail: rcarelli@inaut.edu.ar*
*pellicer@inaut.unsj.edu.ar*

*Prof. I. Mazon Gonzalez, & Prof. V.H. Chacón*
*University of Costa Rica,*
*San Jose, Costa Rica.*
*Tel. +506-3836094 Fax No. +506 2242619*
*E-mail: imazon@pacuare.eie.ucr.ac.cr*

**Abstract**

This paper highlights research carried out in the Food Industry in Latin America today. The paper discusses the food industry and the role of the supply chain in an extended enterprise concept. It also looks at two ways of modeling a supply chain and a brief description of both is given.

**Keywords**

Extended Enterprise, Supply Chain Management, Food Industry, Business Process Modeling, $IDEF_0$, Petri Net.

## 1 INTRODUCTION

Enterprises within an extended enterprise concept are always looking for ways to improve their business efficiency. Many approaches are taken, from implementing a total quality management system to redesigning the business processes. All approaches require a real understanding of the business enterprise. One question

Computer Applications in Production and Engineering. F. Plonka and G. Olling (Eds.)

that should be asked when identifying an enterprise is what is the organization trying to achieve with its processes, i.e. its business goals and objectives. Every organization has a number of business processes that it carries out in order to achieve its business objectives; for example processing orders, customer complaints and designing new products, for many organizations the list is endless.

With companies around the world involving themselves in extended enterprise structures many researchers and academics are focusing on business processes and how they can be modeled within this network of enterprises. Before we go on any further we should define what the Extended Enterprise is and also what a business process is. Browne et al. tell us that the manufacturing system can no longer be seen in isolation, it must be seen in the context of the total business and the linkages of the business back through the supplier chain and forward into the customer chain. The challenge for the future is to consider the extended enterprise and facilitate inter-enterprise networking across the value chain. This concept of inter-enterprise networking is called the extended enterprise for short, (Browne, 1995). The extended enterprise extends beyond traditional organizational boundaries. It includes the relationships that an enterprise has with its customers, suppliers, business partners etc. The extended enterprise reflects the high interdependence that exists between organizations as they conduct business.

A business process can be defined as a collection of activities that takes one or more kinds of input and creates an output that is of value to the customer, (Hammer, M., Champy, J., 1995). A business process then is a specific ordering or arranging of work activities across time and place, including the beginning of the process and the end of the process and clearly identifying the inputs and outputs of the business process being modeled. In order to model the supply chain process of an enterprise the model must clearly identify its inputs and outputs.

The most effective way to identify the needed information of the enterprises and obtain access to the enterprises information is through modeling the extended enterprise operation. This should not only cover the business processes involved in the enterprises but also it should identify both their internal and external relationships. Kosanke et al. state that to achieve sufficient flexibility for maintaining the models and keeping them really up-to-date, modeling has to become a tool not only for planning but for operational support as well, (Kosanke et al., 1995).

Business Process Modeling of the supply chain allows the extended enterprise to build a model of its current supply chain process ("as-is") or its proposed supply chain process ("to-be"). The model allows for the supply chain performance to be analyzed. Modeling the supply chain process of any enterprise is an important step in building a more efficient supply chain.

New tools, methods and knowledge for the supply chain of a food industry in the extended enterprise are necessary and they can only be developed by increased co-operation between research institutions, academics, the agribusiness and food industries.

Modeling tools are new for the extended enterprise, therefore when enterprises want to model the business processes of their organization; the tools they use are "borrowed tools".

## 2. THE FOOD INDUSTRY

The Food Industry was once seen as a low tech and high labor intensive industry. Things are rapidly changing and for once this industry is becoming the focus of many research projects, for example SCM+[1] and LOGSME[2].

Both projects have industrial partners that are in the food industry and the research concentrates on the integration of their supply chain.

The food industry is now beginning to realize that integration of their supply chain is an area that will lead to the success of their organization. The creation of supply chain management functions have pulled together disparate parts of this industry and turned them now into cohesive operating units, (Lamey, 1996). The food industry supply chain is defined by Folkerts and Koehorst as a set of interdependent companies that work closely together to manage the flow of goods and services along the value-added chain of agricultural and food products, in order to realize superior customer value at the lowest possible costs, (Folkerts and Koehorst 1997).

Intense competition in the food industry has led to innovative distribution techniques and increased efficiencies, such as enterprise integration all of that benefit the customers.

According to Lamey, the need to provide customers simultaneously with higher service levels at a lower cost whilst building customer loyalty has provided a difficult working environment for the food industry. Part of the solution for success in this industry can be found in re-engineering the supply chain, (Lamey, 1996). Re-engineering the supply chain entails rethinking and redesigning the business processes that make up the supply chain in order to achieve improvements. These improvements include cost, quality, and service improvements. Enterprises within the food industry are becoming more adept at making their supply chains responsive to each other. Integration of information is becoming a vital ingredient for the success of these enterprises. In order for an enterprise to be considered as an extended enterprise then information integration throughout the enterprises is critical. For the food industry this includes information regarding stock levels, customer orders, process orders etc.

## 3. THE FOOD INDUSTRY IN LATIN AMERICA

The food industry is a very important activity now in Latin American countries. This activity primary involves small and medium size enterprises that tend to function independently on a weak capital base. However, the speed of change in both the local and the global market parameters and the complexity of its element forces these enterprises to take bigger and faster steps toward lean, agile, and cost-effective production. Furthermore, the constant changes in product and process technologies and the increasing pressure for healthier, more nutritious and organic products, and the environment benign production systems with emphasis on waste reduction and energy management enhances this challenge. Additionally, emerging international legislation, particularly relevant in the commercial relationships between other countries, has to be considered.

[1] SCM+ Beyond Supply Chain Management in Food Industry, INCO-DC Project: 950880

[2] LOGSME, Logistics to Support Continuous Improvement for SME's in the Virtual Enterprise, Esprit No. 22633.

In general for many developing sectors i.e. coffee, milk, bananas, tomatoes etc., enterprises seek to work in an extended enterprise concept. This includes wholesalers and retailers, producers and their supply chain, food processors and packers, farmers, transportation and delivery services, working together. Emerging now is the concept of agribusiness, defined as the set of all operations involved in the processing and distribution of the agropecuary products, the production operations within the farm and the storing, processing and distribution of all agropecuary products and their derivatives.

A major facilitator for the coordinating function of an extended enterprise is through Information Technology. Inter-enterprise and inter-enterprise networking across the value chain can be supported by today's advances in computing and telecommunication technologies and they're emerging integration into the Information Superhighway.

For small and medium enterprises the real competitive advantage can only be achieved and sustained through the creation of relationships and strong information links and honest co-working among the enterprises involved in the various steps of the supply chain. These concepts are definitely needed for enterprises, in order for them to efficiently utilize their relevant human, organizational, and business resources and also for them to be able to facilitate the necessary interdependencies between their suppliers (farmers and other materials and services suppliers), manufacturers, distributors, sellers and ultimately customers.

Figure 1 shows a typical supply chain for the food industries in the SCM+ project.

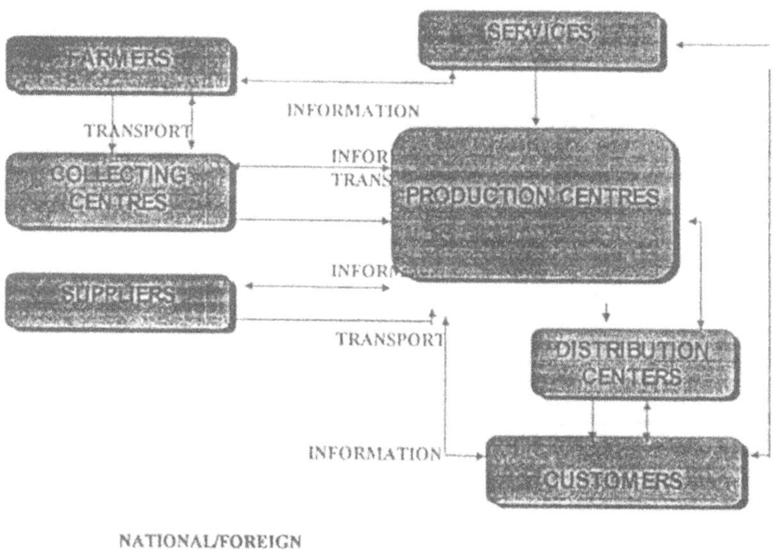


**Figure 1** Supply Chain, for the Food Industry.

From the point of view of communications and, in general, the information interchange, the big enterprises have a high rate of interactions with suppliers and clients. However, they are similar to the small enterprises as they link their information through classical channels, i.e. person to person, telephone or fax.

Many enterprises are involved strongly now in Internet applications with their suppliers and are building relationships for electronic data interchange with their big clients (the supermarkets for example). Active sectors in this area for example: coffee and milk suppliers are beginning to commercialize products through the Internet. In the supply chain channel in the food industry it is clear that there are some links stronger and more critical than other links. Customers can be seen as very important links of the chain, they demand final products with high quality and as fast as possible; therefore, the communication with them is critical for maintaining them as good customers. For farmers the communication is also important, they need to have information regarding the production plants and commercialization of the products. Many enterprises are interested in increasing their communications with farmers, as this has been found to be the weakest link of the supply chain.

To implement a data communication infrastructure to support an extended enterprise there are several difficulties depending on the links of the supply chain. In order to study the feasibility for applying the extended enterprise concept, it is of critical importance to know the current social aspects of the enterprises who are involved, considering them as reference case of the agricultural processed food companies of their region. For the industries investigated in the SCM+ project it was found that many managers in developing countries have very little information regarding the extended enterprise. Similarly, the training and the courses planned in-house in enterprises do not include a strong program for information system technologies In general technical personnel are not prepared for extended enterprise operations.

For large clients and critical suppliers it can be easy to implement good information channels. For many members of the extended enterprise the information transmitted to and from each other is very different. In any case, it is very important to have an inner data communications infrastructure that may support each enterprises communications need. For many food industries voice infrastructure communication between the enterprises is acceptable and is in accordance with the normal requirements of any enterprise.

## 4. THE SUPPLYCHAIN MODEL

The supply chain used as an example for this writing could be seen as a complex web of interrelated processes and systems - sometimes the very complexity of an enterprise defeats any attempt to improve or transform it. Production, processing, supply and distribution all used to be regarded as individual processes; nowadays the food supply chain is rapidly becoming an integrated system with each of these links in the chain having interconnected systems.

Modeling the supply chain process therefore simplifies the way we see the complex business process, making the supply chain a real process allowing us to understand and communicate the activities within the supply chain. The food supply chains can vary considerably as they can be seen to be highly dependent on historical and cultural aspects as well as regulatory environments. Government legislation plays a major role in the food supply chain also.

$IDEF_0$ (Integration Definition for Function Modelling) and Petri Net are the modeling tools used to support the food industries involved in the SCM+ project. The model focuses on the different links in the chain, which are required to manage the supply chain process.

$IDEF_0$ comprises of a set of methods that can assist in understanding a complex subject. It uses top-down decomposition to break-up complex topics into small pieces which can be more readily understood and which are set in their proper context with respect to system elements. $IDEF_0$ provides the ability to show what is being done within a process, what connects the activities and what constrains the activities. It uses a structured set of guidelines based around hierarchical decomposition, with excellent guidance on abstraction at higher levels. This $IDEF_0$ model shows a systemic perspective of the supply chain of this food enterprise. Figure 2 shows the top level of the supply chain process, which has been modelled.

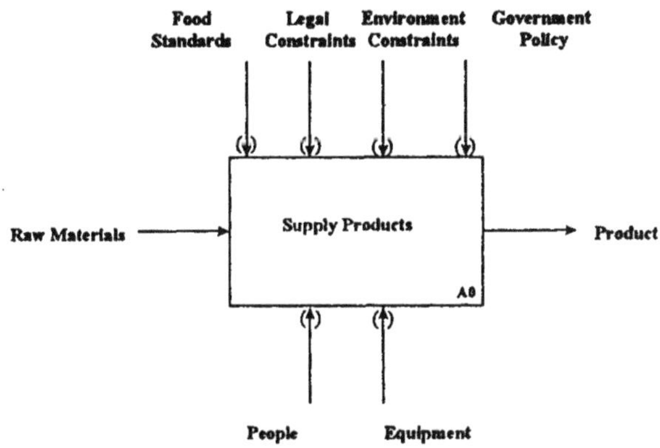


**Figure 2** Supply chain model for a food industry in the extended enterprise.

The supply chain model was built on the functional activities of the supply chain process of the food industries and it identifies the products and information that flow between these activities. This level is broken down further to give a clear identification of the inputs, mechanisms, controls and outputs identified for each area of the supply chain process. Using $IDEF_0$ as a modeling technique ensures that the content for any part of a process model under analysis in relation to the whole of the process model is always known, (CAM-1, 1980). Therefore the food organization can focus on the part of a process model it is interested in and develop further levels of detail without losing its context within the whole process. The development of the supply chain process model once again helps this enterprise understand how the processes work within its extended enterprise identifying the links it has with other enterprises. In order to be able to use the information from the model the activities in the process, the process boundaries and the resources used in the supply chain modeling process all need to be understood by those involved in making decisions, within that enterprise. The modeling of the "as-is" situation of the supply chain process gives the enterprise the opportunity to model their enterprise towards a "to-be" situation. It also allows for the process model to be simulated if necessary and then its performance to be analyzed. This process may have to be carried out many times in order for the enterprise to obtain its optimum "to-be" process.

The building of this supply chain process model aids understanding of the actual processes involved in supplying goods to the end customer. It is beyond the scope of this paper to show the complete $IDEF_0$ model of the supply chain under investigation in this research.

## 5. APPROACH TO MODELLING THE SUPPLY CHAIN USING PETRI NETS

The interrelationship between the enterprises participating in the supply chain, is mainly governed by events which represent the forwarding or reception of relevant information - data, orders, receipt acknowledgments, etc.-, as well as the physical interchange of products. Therefore, the main focus in searching adequate dynamic modeling methodologies and tools should be set on the representation of discrete-event systems. Additionally, continuous system representation could complement the models, when trying to refine the model in order to realistically represent the time lapses involved in some events (Bernhardt et. al., 1994), (Carelli et. al., 1995). The model should be able to capture the dynamic nature of the interactions as well as an adequate representation of the dynamics of each component of the value chain.

In recent years, many techniques for modeling discrete-event systems have been developed. Among them, the following ones can be mentioned: Markov processes and their imbedded Markov chains, Petri Nets, queuing networks, automata and finite-state machines, finitely recursive processes, min-max algebra models, and discrete event simulation and generalized semi-Markov processes (Cao and Ho, 1990), (Ho, 1989). Petri nets represent a tool for modeling systems with interacting and concurrent components. It represents an analytic and graphical approach useful for modeling, analyzing and simulating discrete event dynamic systems.

The next section presents an approach based in Petri nets for dynamically modeling the supply chain in the context of the extended enterprise concept. The model is a simplified version of a real supply chain described in some detail by the SCM+ partners in their research of the food industries supply chains. Different elements of the chain have been considered, including the model of the supplier of raw material, the supplier of supplies and commodities for production, the factory, the clients and the relationships between them.

## 6. A CASE STUDY - THE SUPPLIERS-FACTORY-CLIENTS RELATIONSHIP MODEL.

*Characteristics of the chain.* Producers of tomatoes from San Juan, Argentina (production: 23,500 Tn) offer their production to the factory in San Juan. The factory places an order (in the model each order is for 500 Tn tomato or 20 trailers) when its warehouses are ready for receiving this load. Mendoza producers (26,500 Tn) offer their production. The factory also places orders to Mendoza producers when its warehouses are ready for receiving this load. Orders for 69 Tn tin sheet (totaling 3 trailers) are placed when the warehouse is ready to receive this material. With all this raw material, the factory plans to elaborate 50,000 Tn tomato sauce. The Petri net model is presented in Figure 3. The supplier sends these 3 trailers provided he has the material available in stock. The Buenos Aires Distribution Centre (hCenterer BA DC) places an order for seven 27.4 Tn trailers of finished products provided its warehouse has free capacity. Provided this processed volume is available at the factory in San Juan, the cargo is sent right away to Buenos Aires. A similar procedure is followed for the Cordoba Distribution Center (hereafter Córdoba DC). The DC-client relationship is described in a similar way. A simplified suppliers-factory-clients relationship model is presented below.

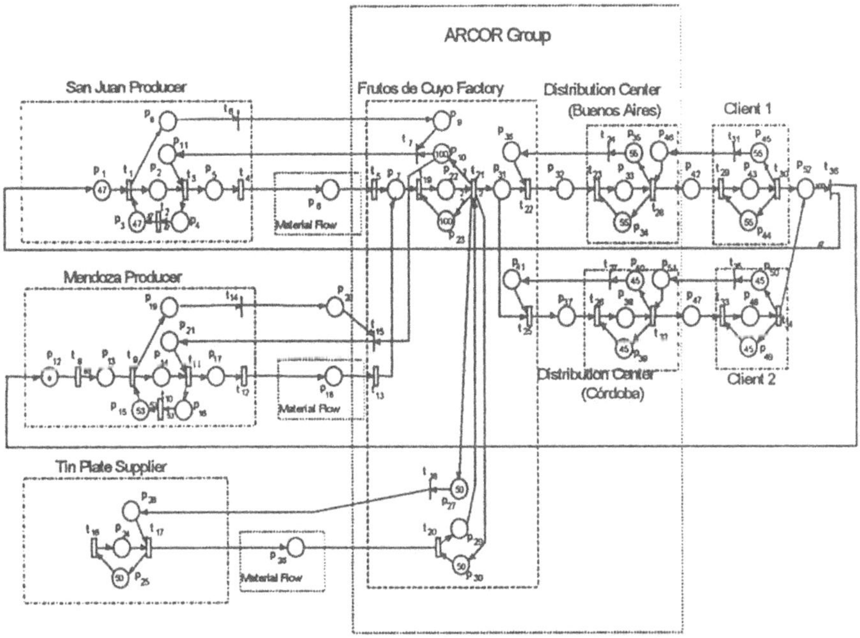


**Figure 3** Petri net model of the Tomato Production Chain.

*PN elements description.* The interpretation of places and transitions of the Petri net model is shown as follows:

**Places**

p1: Initial condition for San Juan producers.
p2: Tomatoes ready to be cropped (SJ producer).
p3: Total tomato volume to produce (SJ producer).
p4: Monitor of tomatoes already cropped (SJ producer)
p5: Tomatoes cropped ready to be shipped (SJ producer).
p6: A cargo of 500 metric tons (Tn) of tomato (20 trailers) has been sent by the SJ producer to the factory in San Juan.
p7: Tomato trailers in queue at the factory.
p8: An offer from the SJ producer has been placed.
p9: An offer from the SJ producer has been received at the factory.
p10: Monitor of tomato orders.
p11: An order for 500 Tn tomato (20 trailers) has been delivered to the SJ producer.
p12: Initial condition for Mendoza producers.
p13: Production enabling.
p14: Tomatoes ready to be cropped (M producer).
p15: Total tomato volume to produce (M producer).
p16: Monitor of tomatoes already cropped (M producer).
p17: Tomatoes cropped ready to be shipped (M producer).

p18: A cargo of 500 Tn of tomato (20 trailers) has been sent by the M producer to the factory in San Juan.
p19: An offer from the M producer is issued.
p20: An offer from the M producer has been received at the factory.
p21: An order for 500 Tn tomato (20 trailers) has been delivered to the M producer.
p22: Tomatoes in stock in the factory, ready to be processed.
p23: Quantity of tomato to be processed.
p24: Tin sheet ready to be sent by the supplier.
p25: Tin sheet to be manufactured by the supplier.
p26: A cargo of 69 Tn tin sheet (3 trailers) has been sent by the supplier to the San Juan factory.
p27: Monitor of tin sheet orders.
p28: An order for 69 Tn tin sheet has been delivered to the supplier.
p29: Tin sheet in stock at the San Juan factory.
p30: Quantity of tin sheet to be processed.
p31: Tomatoes already processed in the factory.
p32: 191.8 Tn of finished product (7 trailers) has been sent from the factory to the BA DC.
p33: Final product in stock at BA DC.
p34: Free capacity of finished products in warehouse at BA DC.
p35: Monitor of finished product orders at BA DC.
p36: An order for 191.8 of finished product is placed by the BA DC.
p37: A cargo of 191.8 of finished product (7 trailers) has been sent from SJ to the Córdoba DC.
p38: Finished product in stock at Córdoba DC.
p39: Total capacity of finished products in warehouse at Córdoba DC.
p40: Monitor of finished product orders at Córdoba DC.
p41: An order for 191.8 Tn of finished product is placed by the Córdoba DC.
p42: A finished product trailer has been sent from the BA DC to Client 1.
p43: Finished product in stock at warehouses of Client 1.
p44: Total capacity of finished products in warehouse of Client 1.
p45: Monitor of finished product orders at Client 1.
p46: An order from Client 1 for finished products has been delivered to the BA DC.
p47: A finished product trailer has been sent by Córdoba DC to Client 2.
p48: Finished product in stock in warehouses of Client 2.
p49: Total capacity of finished products in warehouse of Client 2.
p50: Monitor of finished product orders at Client 2.
p51: An order from Client 2 for finished products has been delivered to the Córdoba DC.
p52: Condition for re-starting.

**Transitions**
t1: A San Juan farmer produces 500 Tn of tomatoes
t2: A new plantation is prepared by San Juan producer.
t3: 500 Tn tomato is cropped by San Juan farmer.
t4: 500 Tn tomato (20 trailers) is sent to the factory.
t5: Trailers from SJ producer arrive at the factory in San Juan.
t6: San Juan producer notices the factory that he has 500 Tn tomatoes available.
t7: The factory accepts and places an order for this 500 Tn tomato offers.
t8: Enabling for starting production of Mendoza producer.
t9: A Mendoza farmer produces 500 Tn of tomatoes.
t10: A new plantation is prepared by M P.

t11: 500 Tn tomato is cropped by M P.
t12: 500 Tn tomato (20 trailers) is sent by MP to the factory in San Juan.
t13: Trailers from Mendoza arrives at the factory.
t14: A MP gives notice to the factory that he has 500 Tn tomato available.
t15: The factory accepts and places an order for this 500 Tn tomato offers.
t16: The tin sheet supplier produces 69 Tn tin sheet.
t17: A cargo of 69 Tn tin sheet (3 trailers) is sent by the supplier to the factory.
t18: The factory issues an order for 69 Tn tin sheet.
t19: Tomato trailers are unloaded at the factory's warehouse.
t20: Tin sheet trailers from supplier are unloaded at the factory's warehouse.
t21: Tomatoes are processed.
t22: Seven 27.4 Tn trailers with finished product are sent by the factory to the BA DC.
t23: Final product trailers are unloaded at the warehouses of BA DC.
t24: The BA DC places an order for seven 27.4 Tn trailers have finished product.
t25: Seven 27.4 Tn trailers of finished product are sent by the factory to the Córdoba DC.
t26: Finished product trailers are unloaded at the warehouses of the Córdoba DC.
t27: The Córdoba DC places an order for seven 27.4 Tn trailers have finished product.
t28: Finished product trailers are sent by the BA DC to Client 1.
t29: Finished product trailers are unloaded at warehouses of Client 1.
t30: Client 1 sells the finished products.
t31: Client 1 places an order for seven 27.4 T trailers of finished product to the BA DC.
t32: Final product trailers are sent by the Córdoba DC to Client 2.
t33: Final product trailers are unloaded at the warehouses of Client 2.
t34: Client 2 sells the final products.
t35: Client 2 places an order for seven 27.4 T trailers of finished product to the Córdoba DC.
t36: Re-Starting the cycle.

*Conflict Resolution.* A typical conflict arises when the factory receives offers from a larger number of producers than needed for the planned industrialized production. Therefore, the factory has to decide which producers are to fill the needs. In the Petri net model, this conflict is evidenced by a conflict in transitions t1 to Tn respecting place p1, see Figure 4. A supervisory model becomes imperative, and this is inserted at a higher Petri net layer.

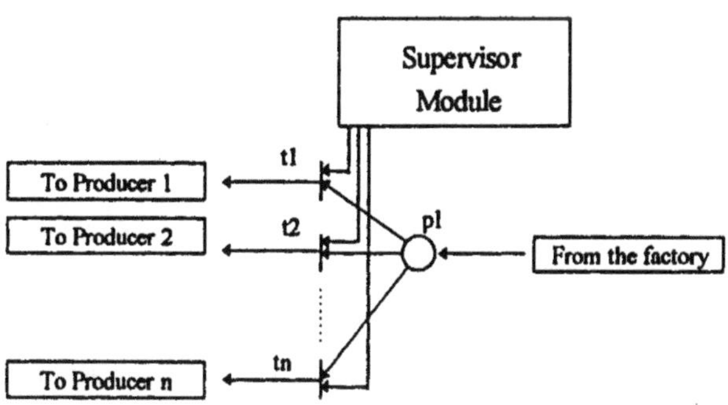


**Figure 4** Supervisor Module for solving conflicts.

In the model of extended enterprise concept, certain decision-making mechanisms are necessary in order to modify or fit the model's configuration to any given situation. A proposal for solving this, though still under elaboration, consists in supervisor module for modifying the Petri net models for each producer and their interrelationships with the factory.

## 7. CONCLUSION

Up until recently there has been very little food industry research. The food industry never really demanded research in this area before, as they felt it wasn't necessary. Now with the introduction of the extended and virtual enterprise concepts and information technology, many industries including the food industry are looking for ways to adopt these concepts and in doing so improving their supply chain activities.

This paper has highlighted what research has found in the food industry in Latin America. The paper has also tried to show how one industry supply chain was modeled using $IDEF_0$ modeling and Petri Net modeling. A first approach for modeling the food supply chain was presented in this paper using $IDEF_0$ and Petri Nets. Petri nets have been proposed as a promising tool for modeling and analyzing the supply chain producer-factory within the extended enterprise concept. Petri nets provide useful models that capture the precedence relationships and structural interactions of stochastic, concurrent and asynchronous events. Conflicts can be modeled and deadlock situations in the system can be detected. Petri nets are mathematical and graphical tools with a well-developed mathematical and practical foundation. Timed Petri nets allow for the quantitative analysis of the supply chain models. As the paper is just highlighting research in this field, the full $IDEF_0$ model is beyond the scope of the paper.

The development of the supply chain process models once again helps this enterprise under investigation and others like it to understand how the processes work within their extended enterprise and importantly identifying the links it has with other enterprises.

## 8. ACKNOWLEDGEMENTS

The authors wish to thank all the members of the SCM+ project, INCO-DC 950880 for giving them the opportunity to write this paper.

## 9. REFERENCES

Bernhardt R., Schreck G., Colombo W., Carelli R. (1994) *Integrated Discrete Event and Motion Oriented Simulation for Flexible Manufacturing Systems,* Studies in Information and Control, Vol. 3, Nos. 2-3, pp. 209-217.

Browne, J., Sackett, P.J. and Wortmann, J.C. (1995) Future Manufacturing Systems-Towards the Extended Enterprise, *Computers in Industry*, 25, 235-254.

CAM-1, (1980) *Architect's Manual ICAM Definition Method "IDEF-0",* Arlington, Texas.

Cao X.-R. and Ho Y-C. (1990) *Models of discrete event dynamic systems*, IEEE Control Systems Magazine, Vol.10, No.4.

Carelli R., Colombo W., Bernhardt R., Schreck G. (1995) *Discrete Event and Motion - Oriented Simulation for FMS*, BASYS '95, Balanced Automation Systems. Architectures and Design Methods, Chapman and Hall, pp. 363-372.

Folkerts, H., Koehorst H., (1997): *Challenges in international food supply chains: vertical co-ordination in the European agribusiness and food industries*, Supply Chain Management, An International Journal, Vol.2, No.1.

Hammer M., Champy J., (1995) *Reengineering the Corporation - A Manifesto for Business Revolution*, Nicholas Brealey Publishing.

Kosanke, K., Mollo, M., Naccari, F., Reyneri, C., (1995) *Enterprise Engineering with CIMOSA-Application at Fiat*, Integrated Manufacturing Systems Engineering, Chapman & Hall.

Lamey, J., (1996) *Supply Chain Management-Best practice and the impact of new partnerships*, Financial Times, Management Reports, Pearson Professional.

## 10. BIOGRAPHY

**Ingrid Hunt** graduated from Sligo Regional Technical College in 1994 with a B.Sc. in Quality Assurance after also completing a Diploma in Electronic Engineering. She graduated from the University of Ulster in 1995 with an M.Sc. in Manufacturing Management. She has worked as a Vendor Engineer and also worked as a Quality Manager in a medical device-manufacturing organization. She joined CIMRU in May 1996 and is currently Project Manager for Esprit and INCO-DC projects in the area of Logistics and Supply Chain Management. She is currently working on her Ph.D. at CIMRU, in the area of Supply Chain Management.

**Ricardo Carelli** received his Electrical Engineering degree (with honors) from the National University of San Juan (Argentina) in 1976 and the Ph.D. degree in Electrical Engineering from the National University of Mexico (UNAM) in 1989. He is presently Professor of Automatic Control at the National University of San Juan and research-worker of the National Council for Scientific and Technical Research (CONICET). His current research interests are in the fields of robot control, manufacturing systems and artificial intelligence applied to systems control. Dr. Carelli is a member of IEEE and AADECA, the Argentine NMO of IFAC.

**Jorge Eduardo Pellicer,** received his Electronic Engineering degree (with honors) from the National University of San Juan (Argentina). He is currently pursuing his Master Degree in Control Engineering on Coordination Control of Discrete Event Systems. He is holding a grant from the National Council for Scientific and Technical Research (CONICET) in the subject "Supervisory Control of Discrete Event System". His current research interests are in the fields of Petri Nets, Discrete Event Systems Control and Manufacturing Systems. Ing. Jorge Eduardo Pellicer is a student member of Institute Electrical and Electronics Engineers (IEEE).

**Ismael Mazon** graduated from the University of Costa Rica in 1976 in Electrical Engineering and 1982 from University Santa Maria, Chile in Automatic Control. He is presently Cathedratic at the University of Costa Rica, Electrical Engineering School. His current research interest is in the fields of intelligent control systems, automatic control of energy systems, and real time control systems.

**Victor H. Chacon** graduated from the University of Costa Rica in 1974 in Electrical Engineering and 19790 from CINVESTAV, Mexico in Communications Systems. He is presently Cathedratic at the University of Costa Rica, Electrical Engineering School. His current research interest is in the fields of telematics, data communication systems and local area networks.

13

# Utilizing real-time market demand information in the integration of the supply chain in the food industry

*J.Slotte, M.Sc.(Eng.)*
*E-mail: Jonas.Slotte@hut.fi*

*H.Nyman, M.Sc.(Eng.), M.Sc.(Econ.)*
*E-mail: Hannu.Nyman@hut.fi*

*J.Holmström, Ph.D.(Eng.)*

*Helsinki University of Technology, TAI Research Center*
*P.O.BOX 9500, FIN-02150 HUT, Finland*
*Tel. +358-9-4511, Fax +358-9-4513665*

**Abstract**

This paper outlines exploitation of the existing communication infrastructure to improve the interaction between various echelons of the logistic chain in the food processing industry, right from the mill to the table of the consumer. It is commonly known that step-wise delivery chains tend to accumulate the true demand at the upstream of the chain, i.e. rather stable demand pattern is amplified along the chain resulting a significant demand variation at the factory. Key issues are related on how to collect reliable real-time information of the end consumption and on how to distribute it to all players of the logistic network. Other important facets of the research concern electronic communication and how to establish an information integrated supply chain.

**Keywords**

Diverging logistic network, demand amplification, electronic communication, information integrated supply chain, food-processing industry

Computer Applications in Production and Engineering. F. Plonka and G. Olling (Eds.)

# 1 INTRODUCTION

A modern production control system requires input not only from production and material requirements planning, but also from various points in the whole supply chain. The customer point of view was introduced in manufacturing with the Just-In-Time philosophy. In a competitive customer oriented manufacturing environment the questions of customer responsiveness is the main focus. Increasingly market surveys find that customers see the delivery performance and accuracy as the most important feature of the supplier. For example, A.T. Kearney (1993) found in a survey commissioned by the European Logistics association a wide gap between supplier delivery service and the service levels required by customers.

In the traditional MRP literature, focus is put on production lead-time in the search for a fast reacting and lean operation. If the total production lead-time, including the planning lead-time of the products is longer than the required delivery time to customer the operation has to rely on demand forecasts (Stalk and Hout 1990). The more production is dependent on forecasts the more customer service has to rely on goods in stock.

In a modern operation, Quick Response Capability and Efficient Consumer Response (ECR) are the focus in supply chain and supplier management. Quick response capability is the ability to deliver the full product range within the customer acceptable delivery time. In the evaluation of the quick response capability of a production and distribution system, the focus must be put simultaneously on time and quantity. The lead time to produce the full product range is compared to the customer acceptable delivery time. At the same time customer demand is compared to capacity within the customer acceptable delivery time.

ECR on the other hand is a new philosophy in product range management and co-operation between supplier and wholesaler in the commodities market.

# 2 SUPPLY CHAIN DYNAMICS AND CONTROL

The control practices of industrial firms directly affect how the operational situation is perceived and how effectively resources are allocated.

Uncertainty of the operational situation and the controllability of the operation are emergent properties of the operational practices of the firm and the industries it is engaged in. This view is based on the observations that:

- demand changes are easily distorted and amplified in supply chains (Forrester, 1961)
- unsynchronized planning and control practices induce load surges (Burbidge, 1989 and 1994)

Thus, operational uncertainty and inefficiency is to a large extent a consequence of demand distortion in supply chains, self-induced uncertainty caused by unsynchronized planning. Demand distortion was first described by Forrester in his classic supply chain model, but it is only recently that the full extent of the problem has been recognized (Towill, 1996). Congestion caused by quality problems and rework, and complexity imposed by product designs and processes are other important contributing factors. Towill (1992) presents an example of how the combined effect of demand amplification in supply chains and load surges caused by unsynchronized control procedures results in high uncertainty of the operational situation.

The basic principle proposed to reduce self-inflicted operational uncertainty and to enable a more efficient use of resources is to focus efforts on speed and accuracy of communication and control of the information available in the supply chain.

The accumulation of needs in supply chains is discussed as a basic cause for operational uncertainty and low controllability. The purpose is to demonstrate that high operational uncertainty and low controllability are partly self-induced and may be avoided by implementing improved communication and control practices in the management of the supply chain. The discussion is based on experiences from development projects in the food industry.

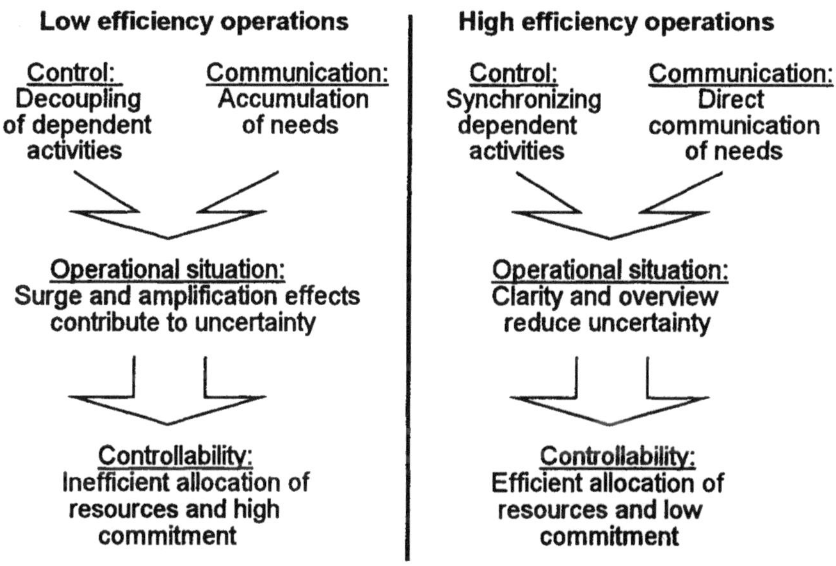


**Figure 1** Interdependency of communication, uncertainty, and controllability.

## 2.1 The effect of demand amplification in the supply chain

The effect of accumulation is clearly evident in the operation of the sweet manufacturer case. The sweets manufacturer has both manufacturing and distribution operations in all of the Scandinavian countries and Finland.

The manufacturer perceives that demand for its products are highly volatile and unpredictable. The deliveries from the largest factory of a selection of key products were analyzed. The analyzed products are high volume products representing roughly 50% of the total output of the factory. In the delivery volumes significant medium-term fluctuations were present. For example, over a half year period there was first a dramatic surge followed by a sharp decline of demand. In the short-term the manufacturer experienced delivery problems due to great demand variations from week to week. However, over the long term consumption had been rising but only slowly. From week to week the consumption of sweets was stable, hence, this is an example of amplification caused by an accumulation of needs in the distribution chain.

The conclusion of the analysis was that the sweets manufacturer supplies an oscillating distribution chain. Pipeline inventory accumulation alternates with the distribution chain living off accumulated inventory buffers. This oscillation was clearly visible when comparing the delivery and consumption of the main product (Figure 2). Deliveries were first lower than consumption, then higher than consumption, and finally below consumption again.

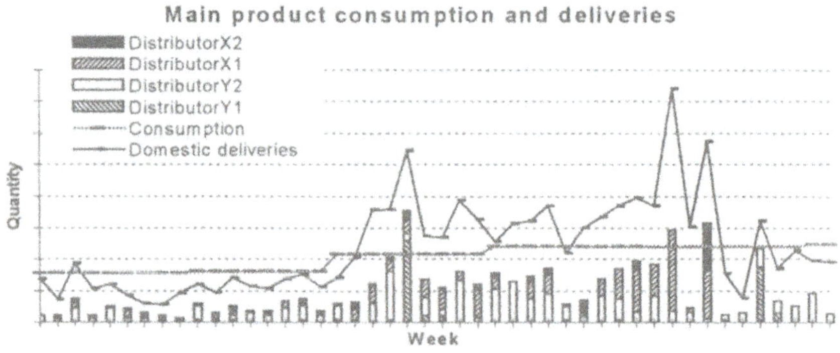


**Figure 2** Example of amplification caused by accumulation of needs

The unpredictable delivery peaks caused havoc for the sweets manufacturer because the distribution network responded to signs of weakening delivery capabilities by increasing buffers. The perceived radical rise in demand prompted investment in more production capacity for the manufacture of the main product. Additionally, resources were wasted on training new employees who later proved unnecessary. Overtime and extra shifts were also necessary to meet the peak demand. In the subsequent quiet periods it was necessary to close production lines for a week on several occasions.

In the sweets manufacturer case it is obviously extremely difficult to run the operation efficiently over a longer period of time as long as the oscillating supply chain distorts demand.

## 2.2 Required delivery time

In the consumer goods market a special feature is the required delivery time to the wholesalers. In Finland and Scandinavia it is from four to 48 hours. In an industry where the manufacturers product range can be up to 500, the whole product range cannot be manufactured in the required delivery time. The solution to this is delivery from stock. In an operation there are three possibilities to control the deliveries of manufactured goods:

- The full product range can be planned, produced and transported within the customer acceptable delivery time.
- The delivery time requirements from customers are shorter than the time to plan and produce the full product range and to transport it to the customers.
- An intermediate point in the production process can be found from which onwards the full product range can be planned, produced and transported within the customer acceptable delivery time.

The demand of consumer goods and especially food products are quite stable in all the examples analyzed. The case examples cover meat, confectionery, dairies and brewery industries. The only exceptional demand pattern is in the brewery industry, where warm periods in the summer time affect demand dramatically.

## 2.3 Market demand and Efficient Consumer Response

The industry's answer to the need of more effective management practices is to improve its operating efficiency and service (Pontin et al. 1995). This effort is known as Efficient Consumer Response ( e.g. Robins, 1994, Yohalem, 1995). The goal is to eliminate waste and increase service by building up a demand driven supply chain. The focus of both suppliers and retail chains is to improve profitability and market share by responding better and quicker to consumer demand. In the retail trade the roles of product brands and product line extensions are diminishing and the importance of strategic product categories is rising (Quelch and Kenny, 1994). The essence of this shift of focus is to align service with consumer needs.

# 3 UTILIZING REAL-TIME DEMAND INFORMATION

The existing operations in the food industry can be improved by using real-time demand information. This information can be used in the production planning to shorten the delay between actual selling of the goods and the arrival of the order to the supplier. If the supplier gets accurate information about sales earlier he can plan his production more optimally.

The use of this technology is based on the assumption that the supermarkets belong to a chain controlled by a wholesaler, like K-Mart in the USA. If several such chains make up a significant part of the consumer market, their combined demand information is good enough to be used as an estimate for the whole market.

### 3.1 Using product sales information

The key in this process is the utilization of information provided by bar codes in the actual products. The bar codes enable us to collect information about sales of each product. The sales information is collected by the cash registers in the shops. The information collected by cash registers in a shop is first combined on the shop level and then transmitted into the wholesaler. In the test cases in the Finnish consumer goods market this process is done daily. Thus the wholesaler gets accurate sales information from the shops and gets a clear picture of each product's actual sales almost in real-time.

This is already part of the normal daily operations. But this sales information has value also to the other parties in the logistics chain. The suppliers could use it for their production planning and their material suppliers could use the production schedules based on the acquired sales information. The main idea is to shorten the delay between the actual sale and the moment when the supplier gets the order to refill wholesalers storage.

The wholesaler, who is the customer of the product supplier, accumulates the combined sales figures for those products that belong to their product range. This information can be processed so that the weekly demand of products of a supplier is calculated and transmitted to the supplier.

The wholesaler can also give information about his product inventory. The supplier could use also this information to enhance production planning. The production planning can be based on this ideology only in those cases where the wholesaler tries to keep the inventory levels constant on the long term. If the wholesaler's inventory has no clear correlation to the sales, the inventory information does not provide any new information of use.

### 3.2 The benefits of the information exchange

This exchange of sales information is not meant to replace the normal ordering process. The main idea is to use sales information as an early warning of forthcoming orders.

*Wholesaler and suppliers*

Accurate sales information can increase the delivery performance since the supplier gets information about product consumption earlier. He can then plan his production based on the assumption that the shops will refill their inventory from the wholesalers who in turn then will refill their own storage by ordering the products from the supplier. The time between the actual sales and the arrival of the responding order is usually several weeks. On the other hand the allowed delivery time is currently very short, only 24 to 48 hours. Because the production lead times are remarkably longer the suppliers are forced to keep large inventories in order to be able to fulfill the orders in time. If the supplier gets the sales information shortly after the sales, e.g. on weekly basis, he can plan his production based on this information and be better prepared to fulfill the arriving orders.

So, the idea is to give supplier more time to plan his production. He does not need to wait for the actual order but he can start the production planning shortly after the actual sales based on reliable information. The delivery performance should increase since obtaining information earlier diminishes the effects of long lead times.

Another aspect to be considered is the quality of the information. The aggregate weekly consumption figure does not suffer from the Forrester effect or Burbidge effect. This figure is not biased in any direction and the different order periods and ordering strategies do not effect the figures. So, this is a much better data to be used for production planning than the figure obtained from arriving orders.

This holds true in the long term. In long term this will enable the supplier to fulfill the orders and to keep the product inventories on a reasonable level. In the short term, the supplier's inventory will fluctuate since the arriving orders do not equal the actual consumption since the ordered product volumes are distorted by Forrester and Burbidge effects.

*Supplier and raw material suppliers*

If the supplier has a tight relationship with his key material suppliers, the supplier can provide this sales information further to the material suppliers. That makes it easier for them to be able to deliver all required raw materials in time. In order to be able to benefit from the sales figures the material suppliers have to know roughly the raw material requirements of products.

Another way to deliver quality information to the material suppliers is to keep them aware of the planned production. If they know the material requirements and the production schedules they can calculate the actual material requirements.

Both methods give a qualified material requirements estimate to the material supplier. This estimate can be used in the production scheduling process before the formal order from the client arrives.

## 3.3 Requirements for the co-operation

The previously explained co-operative communication sets many requirements for the participants. The co-operation can only be realized in a stable and continuous business relationship. The participating companies must be willing to share traditionally "private" information like production schedules and product structures. The participating companies must agree about the extent of their partnering.

Partnering in this context means an agreement between two or more companies to do business together on a long-term basis. The partners will share information and work together in order to create business benefits. Partnering is possible only in those cases where the business between partners makes up a significant part of the company's business.

Partnering requires also discussion about business ethics and rules. In order to be as effective and efficient as possible the partners should be open towards each other. This means that they should tell each other about future sales promotion campaigns and other significant events. The main problem of this kind of information is the confidentiality of the information and more exactly the information that is left out or not delivered. In a case example when a wholesaler does not have a promotion activity within a time frame of the partner supplier's products the supplier could figure out possible promotion activity with competitors products. This could then lead to hostile activities trying to minimize effects of the competitors possible promotion, and the outcome would be a difficult situation in the partnership between the initial supplier and the wholesaler.

*Communication technology*

The co-operation should be built using open systems technology. The idea is that the same communication system can be used by many different partners. A closed system for bilateral communication is not profitable in the long run since it would require a separate system for each partner. The system should use TCP/IP technology, the internet, to be modern. The actual communication can be realized as EDI (Electronic Data Interchange) messaging, but internet is the current de facto standard for open communication.

Heard (1994) points out that the initial goal to improve the performance of the distribution chain is easily corrupted by a strong technical focus. The quick response movement in the US has not been able to improve the performance of suppliers despite the widespread introduction of communications technologies with potential to enhance the speed and accuracy of communication. The reason for failure is that the speed and accuracy of communication has not been utilised to synchronize production with demand. The operating practices of the distribution chain have remained the same.

## 4 CONCLUSIONS AND FURTHER ACTIONS

The consequences of industrial dynamics in demand amplification can not be exaggerated (Schonberger 1990). It has been even reported in fast growing industries that component factories have been established to supply the biased demand. It has become one of the key competitive advantages to have reliable and up-to-date information on the real market situation. This is one reason why the grocery stores and other consumer product retailers are implementing sophisticated technological means to transmit on-line information of front-line consumption, i.e. by linking the cash registers directly with the inventory system, which in turn is connected to the wholesalers information system. Yet, this is not enough as the overall efficiency stems from collaboration not only in information sharing, but also on the physical material flow level. These two flows must be incorporated into one operational system throughout the supply chain.

As the supply chain integration evolves to an operational system, every part of the system is aware of the materials flow and how this will affect their future operation. This requires changes in both the technical and organizational structure of the actors in the supply chain. Especially the relationship between supplier and wholesaler requires a new approach. ECR and the category management view addresses into this problem. The customer will in the future dictate how the supply chain will run its whole operation, from category management to efficient replenishment of goods to the retail stores. Category management takes the viewpoint of the retailer and retail chain. The objective is to create distinct manageable groups of products that consumers perceive as interrelated or substitutable and to define the strategic role of the category in the retail echelon (ECR Best Practices Operating Committee, 1995).

The sales information acquired through cash registers offers the food industry a practical way of collecting a base for efficient management of the operation. One elementary requirement is that the retail stores in the target market have a high level of automation. Also the scanned stores have to represent an extensive part of the target market. This is possible in the Finnish market where the market place of five million inhabitants is dominated by three nation-wide wholesalers and over 90% of the retail stores are equipped with bar code readers connected to the cash registers. The use of sales information requires ways to integrate the information into existing operation control systems.

Using the sales information as a planning base of production and delivery control gives an opportunity to decrease the effects of supply chain dynamics caused by Forrester and Burbidge effects. An accurate information flow enables flexible production control and therefore better delivery performance and lower inventory levels throughout the chain.

## 5 REFERENCES

A.T Kearney (1993) Logistics Excellence in Europe, *Study prepared by A.T. Kearney on behalf of the European Logistics Association*

Burbidge, J.L. (1989) Production Flow Analysis - For planning Group Technology, Clarendon Press, Oxford

Burbidge, J.L. (1994) The use of period batch control (PBC) in the implosive industries, *Production Planning & Control*, **5**, No 1, 97-102

ECR Best Practices Operating Committee, (1995) Category Management Report - Enhancing Consumer Value in the Grocery Industry, *Joint Industry Project on Efficient Consumer Response*, USA,

Forrester, J. (1961) Industrial Dynamics, MIT Press Cambridge, Ma

Heard, E. (1994) Quick response: Technology or knowledge?, *Industrial Engineering*, August, 28-30

Pontin, M. & Hutter, L. (1995) Colgate-Palmolive: Meeting our customers' needs, *Logistics Focus*, **3**, No 7, 2-5

Quelch, J. & Kenny, D. (1994) Extend Profits, Not Product Lines, *Harvard Business Review*, Sep-Oct

Robins, G. (1994) Sailing into ECR's uncharted waters, *Stores*, **76**, No 10, 43-44

Schonberger, R.J. (1990) Building a Chain of Customers: Linking Business Functions to Create the World Class Company, Free Press, New York,.

Stalk Jr. G., Hout T.M. (1990) Competing Against Time, The Free Press, New York, USA

Towill, D. (1992) Supply Chain Dynamics - the change engincering challenge of the mid 1990s, *Proc. Instn. Mech Engrs*, No 206, 233-245,

Towill, D. (1996) Time compression and the supply chain - a guided tour, *Supply Chain Management*, **1**, No 1, 15-27

Yohalem, K. (1995) Is the consumer your CEO?, *Sporting Goods Business*, **28**, No2, 30

## 6 BIOGRAPHY

Jonas Slotte is a project manager at the TAI Research Center at Helsinki University of Technology (HUT). He has been involved in several research projects concerning the logistics management and supply chain control in different industries. His special interest is in the management of the extended supply chain in food industry. He has received his Masters exam at HUT and is a Ph.D. student at the Department of Industrial management at HUT.

Hannu Nyman is a project manager at TAI Research Center at HUT. His previous research has involved IT-tools in the control of the logistics chain. The research work has been in both construction and food industry. He received his Masters diploma (Engineering) from HUT and Masters (Economics) from Helsinki School of Economics and Business Administration and is currently a Ph.D. student at the Department of Industrial management at HUT. He is involved in a major project developing the control practices if information in the Finnish food industry.

Jan Holmström is a Docent at the Department of Industrial Management at HUT. He has been involved in various research projects: Developing support systems for Purchasing Logistics in the automotive industry (Saab-Valmet, Adam Opel AG). Developing Purchasing Logistics concept for a manufacturer of circuit boards. Definition of Production Planning and Control requirements in integrated garments manufacture. Development of efficient logistics practices in the Nordic food industry. He has received his Masters degree at the Department of Computing Sciences and the Licentiate and Ph.D. at the Department of Industrial Management at HUT.

14

# Multi-axis machining with additional-axis NC system

*S.H. Suh, J.J. Lee, S.K. Kim*
*Computer Automated Manufacturing Lab*
*Department of Industrial Engineering*
*POSTECH, P. 0. Box 125, Pohang, orea, 7@784*
*Tel: +82-562-279-2196, Fax: +82-562-279-5998*
*E-mail: shs@gvision.postech.ac.kr, http://camlab.postech.ac.kr*

**Abstract**

While multi-axis machining is an advanced technology for dealing with complex shaped parts with a four or five-axis CNC machine, its application is very limited due to the large amount of investment in practice. The Additional-axis method, typically obtained by attaching rotary/tilt table to the existing three-axis machine, is a powerful alternative to the problem while achieving multi-axis machining. In this research, we attempt to establish a theoretical background and implementation methodology for achieving the genuine multi-axis NC system. The research is composed of : a) the hardware setup for implementing the additional-axis NC system, b) an interface study for implementing multi-axis machining with the hardware configuration, c) versatile CL-data generation algorithms for NC machining, and d) implementation of the algorithms to develop multi-axis CAM system for the additional-axis NC system. Together with a detailed presentation on the above enabling the additional-axis machining system, we will show that the additional-axis system can be effectively used for five-axis machining through two specific application examples.

**Keywords**

Multi-axis machining, Five-axis machining, Rotary/tilt table application, Additional-axis NC system, CL-data decomposition

Computer Applications in Production and Engineering. F. Plonka and G. Olling (Eds.)

# 1. INTRODUCTION

With the development of NC technologies, the five-axis machine has been recently introduced to improve the overall efficiency (reducing machining time and enhancing machining accuracy) of machining sculptured surfaces such as automobile bodies, aircraft, and ship hulls [1-2]. Traditional methods for machining sculptured surfaces have been implemented on the three-axis machine with ball-end cutters, requiring long machining time and a hand-finishing process to remove cusps. For more complex surfaces, multiple setup changes (time consuming and a source of inaccuracy). On the other hand there are several aspects limiting the practical application of contemporary five-axis machining technology. First, it requires a large investment to purchase the machine tools (the typical five-axis machining center cost over US$ 1 Million (3). Another limiting factor has been due to the complexity of part programming, requiring supporting software together with programming skills. Thus, for practical propagation of the sophisticated method, an economically feasible method has to be sought. In this paper, we investigate a new method called additional-axis machining technology, utilizing the three-axis CNC machine tools by attaching an additional apparatus, such as an indexing table and a rotary/tilt table (RT table).

# 2. ADDITIONAL-AXIS NC SYSTEM

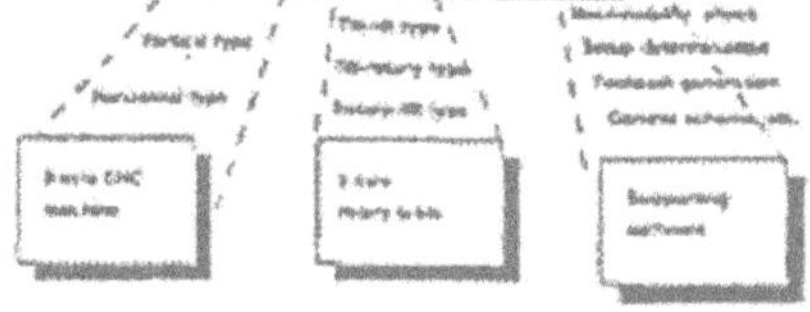


Figure 1. A typical additional-axis machining system.

The additional-axis machining system can be constructed by interfacing manual or servo controlled rotary table to the three-axis machine tools together with supporting software. The typical system shown in Figure 1 is a practical alternative to the problem while achieving five-axis machining. The attachment (manual indexing table or servo controlled rotary/tilt table) has been used practically in the machine shop, as a means for changing part orientation. Note, however, that due to insufficient study on the additional axis machining (specifically on the supporting software), its application has been limited, to simple operations, such as multi-face machining and multiface drilling by the indexing mechanism. In fact, no contemporary CAD/CAM system supports the additional-axis machining methods enabling the five-axis surface machining operations. To extend it for achieving the five-axis machining of free surfaces, various research including: a) hardware interfacing and its control, together with b) supporting software for tool path planning and execution have to be carried out, which has been the theme of our research.

## 2.1 Configuration code

Five-axis machines, in general, have three linear and two rotational axes. Depending on the arrangement of the five axes, there are a variety of configurations for the 'genuine" five-axis machine (For the details, see [4]).

Theoretically, the additional-axis machine takes a variety of configurations depending on its mechanical structure and controller capability. Table 1 shows various configurations by the following code:

$[D_m, C_m, S_m, D_a, S_a]$

$D_m$ : # of axis in the machine,
$C_m$ : # of controllable axis by the machine controller,
$S_m$ : # of simultaneous control axis by the machine controller,
$D_a$ : # of axis in the rotary table,
$S_a$ : # of simultaneous control axis for the rotary table.

Table 1. Configurations of the Additional-axis machine

| | | |
|---|---|---|
| [illegible] | [illegible] | [illegible] |
| [illegible] | [illegible] | [illegible] |
| [illegible] | [illegible] | [illegible] |
| * [illegible] | [illegible] | [illegible] |
| * [illegible] | [illegible] | [illegible] |
| * [illegible] | [illegible] | [illegible] |
| [illegible] | [illegible] | [illegible] |
| [illegible] | * [illegible] | [illegible] |
| [illegible] | [illegible] | [illegible] |
| [illegible] | [illegible] | [illegible] |
| [illegible] | [illegible] | [illegible] |
| [illegible] | [illegible] | [illegible] |
| [illegible] | [illegible] | [illegible] |
| [illegible] | * [illegible] | [illegible] |
| [illegible] | [illegible] | [illegible] |
| [illegible] | [illegible] | * [illegible] |
| [illegible] | [illegible] | [illegible] |
| [illegible] | [illegible] | [illegible] |

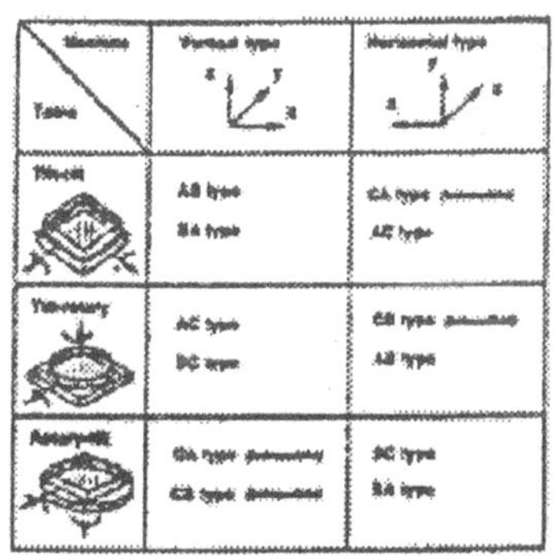

Figure 2. Feasible structure configuration.

Table 1 shows all the configurations for D. = 3. The typical configurations often found in the practice are marked by (*). For example, [3,3,3, 0, 0] means the conventional three-axis machine without an additional-axis, and [3, 3, 3, 2, 0] the three-axis machine tools equipped two-axis manual indexing table. On the other hand, [4,4,3, 1, 1] means the four-axis machine, whose three axes are controlled simultaneously, interfaced with a one-axis servo controlled rotary table. It is worth pointing out that: a) the number of controllable axes should be greater than or equal to the number of simultaneously controlled axes, and b) the number of simultaneous controls is less than or equal to the number of mechanical axes;

$$Cr, \geq S_{,,}, \text{ and } D. + D, \geq Sm + S,. \qquad (2)$$

In the following Sections, the detailed characteristics for the [3,3,3,2,*] will be discussed for a) structure configuration, b) control scheme of rotary axes, and c) feasible tool orientation.

### 2.2 Kinematic structure

Based on the structure of the three-axis machine (horizontal and vertical) and the additional two-axis rotary table (tilt/tilt, tilt/rotary, and rotary/tilt), there are 12 types of structure for the additional-axis machine of [3, 3, 3, 2 *] as shown in Figure 2. The AB type means that the A axis is nearer to the machine bed than the B axis. The four structures marked as 'infeasible" do not give two degrees of freedom but one. In this case, the tool does not have five degrees-of-freedom but four. It is interesting to note that these occur when the nearest rotational axis to the machine bed is the C axis. The above analysis shows that the [3, 3, 3, 2, *] should be constructed based on the eight feasible structures.

### 2.3 Interface scheme of rotary axes

Depending on how the rotary axes are interfaced with the main (three-axis) controller, the control of the rotary axes can be classified into three schemes: a) directly synchronized (DS); where the rotary axes are directly controlled by the main controller, b) indirectly synchronized (IS); where the rotary axes and the machine are controlled independently by two control units, and c) sequential; where the motion of the rotary axes are sequentially executed before or after the machine motion. The genuine DS scheme is only obtained by the originally (not by additionally) five-axis controller. Thus, this scheme can be implemented for the configurations, where Sm, $\geq$ Dm + Da and Sa = 0, marked by ⊕ED in Table 1. In the DS scheme, the main and an additional controller can communicate directly, and hence it is basically the same as the genuine five-axis controller machine tool. Thus, the five-axis CL-data prepared for [5, 5, 5, 0, 0] can be executed by [3, 5, 5, 2, 2]. Note, however, that DS scheme is not common in practice.

In the IS scheme, the rotary axes are controlled by another controller. Thus, the synchronization of the two control units (one for the linear motions and the other for the rotational motions) and the execution method of the CL-data via the two controllers are two issues in the IS scheme. For the configurations (S. $<$ *D@* + D,, and S,, $\geq$ 1), (e.g., [3, 3, 3, 2, 1] and [3, 3, 3,2, 21 fail into this group), IS scheme should be employed for five-axis machining. In the sequential scheme, the rotary axes are not controlled simultaneously with the machine. Thus, in order to manufacture the five-axis part with this scheme axis-reduction method" (to be discussed later) should be employed. Sm, = *Cm,* = *Dm, Sm* = 0 fall into this group, and [3, 3, 3, 2, 0] is an example.

## 2.4 Feasible tool orientation

The feasible tool orientation of the additional-axis machine is determined based on the structure configurations and the number of simultaneous controls for rotary table as well as the rotational limits of rotary axes. Depending on the structure configurations, the feasible tool orientation of the additional axis machine can be classified into three types: a) AC (or BC), b) AB, and c)BA type. Defining the tool orientation as the direction vector on the unit sphere, the feasible tool orientation for the three types can be represented as shown in Figure 3 where AB type is represented by a spherical cone, and AB and BA by spherical rectangles. In the figure, 'great arc" (resp. "Plane arc") represents the rotational motion of the nearest (farthest) rotation4xis he machine bed (i.e., great arc in AC type refers to the rotational motion of the A axis.), and the lengths of these arcs also represent the rotational limit of the rotary axes.

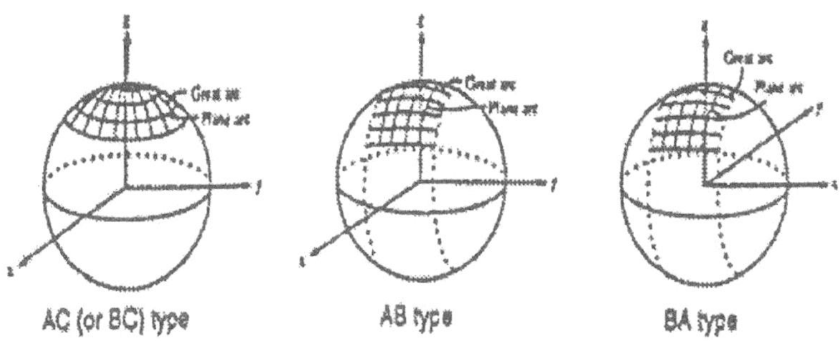


Figure 3. Feasible tool orientations of the three structure types.

Depending on the number of simultaneous controls of the rotary table) the additional-axis machine has three control modes: a) zero control, b) one control, and c) two control. Zero control means that the rotary table is an indexing table. [3,3,3,2, 0], one control means that only one of the two simultaneously controlled (e.g. [3, 3, 3, 2, 1]), and two control axes can be simultaneously controlled (e.g. [3, 3, 3, 2, 2]).

## 3 VERSATILE CAM (V-CAM) SYSTEM

The key to achieve multi-axis machining with the additional-axis system is the software algorithm for tool path planning and execution for the two systems machine tools and additional axes. Depending on the configuration of the additional-axis system, the issues to be addressed are varied. It should be pointed that the previous tool path planning algorithms for multi-axis NC machining (e.g., Reference [5-71]) cannot be applied to the additional-axis machining environment

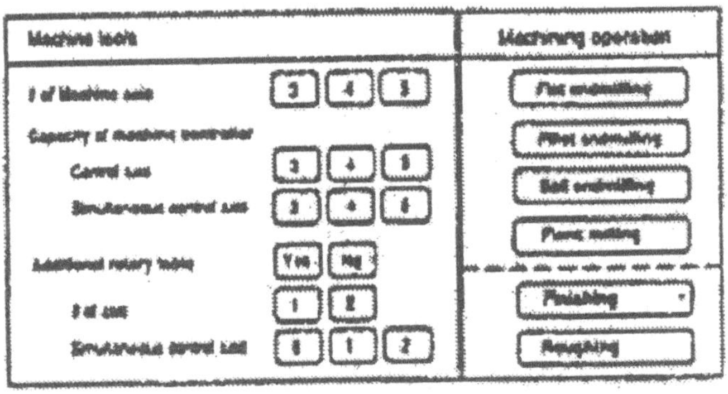

Figure 4. CAM function supported by VCAM.

as the previous methods are valid under the following assumptions: 1) All the axes are simultaneously controlled, 2) The dimension of CL-data is equal to the number of simultaneous controlled axes, and 3) The CL-data is executed by a single controller.

Taking into consideration of type of machining operations (e.g., rough/finish cut, tool shape) together with the hardware configuration, there are various combinations. Figure 4 shows the combination where a finish cut using a ball endmill cutter on a three-axis machine tool with a two-axis manual indexing

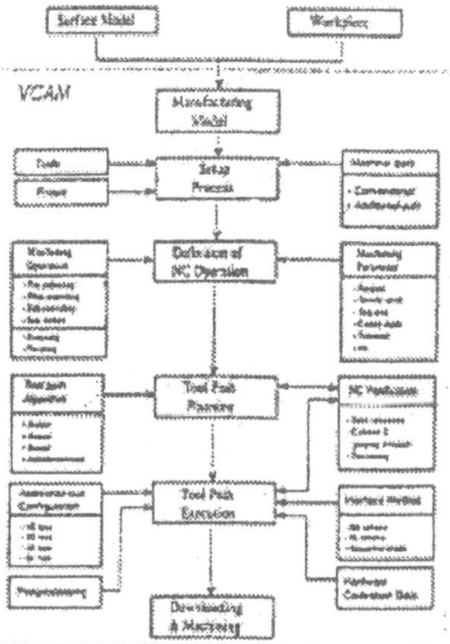


Figure 5. The schematic diagram of VCAM.

a comprehensive CAM system (called Versatile CAM System or V-CAM System). Figure 5 shows the architecture of the V-CAM system capable of generating the tool paths and execution data from the surface model of the part surface. Note that V-CAM system is able to perform conventional CAM functions for multi-axis machining. In particular, the V-CAM system is distinguished from the contemporary CAM system by the shaded and dotted boxes in Figure 5. In the following sections, we briefly describe the details of the algorithms and hardware interfaces implemented on the V-CAM system for two examples; 1) Finish cut ball endmilling with [3, 3,3,2,0], and 2) Finish cut flank milling with [3,3, 3,2,2].

(a) an impeller (b) a section between two blades

Figure 7. Test example.

## 4 ILLUSTRATIVE EXAMPLES AND DEVELOPMENT

### 4.1 Example 1: Five-axis ball endmilling with three-axis CNC machine tools and manual indexing table

In this section, we present a versatile CAM method by which the five axis machining can be effectively carried out with a three-axis CNC machine together with a rotary-tilt type indexing table, denoted by [3,3,3,2,0] (see the typical configuration shown in Figure 6). In this environment, the tool orientation is obtained by changing the part setup by the manual indexing table. Thus, to machine the five-axis free surface (free surfaces requiring full five-axis control, see Reference [8] for the details) with this configuration, multiple part setups are required. Note that this is 'fewer-axis machining" as where the number of the simultaneously controllable axes is fewer than required (in this case, the number of simultaneously controllable axes is 3, while the required is 5)To minimize this handicap, we have to seek a tool path planning method (called axis-reduction method") such that: a) The number of part setups (this is to minimize the manual setup change time) and b) The switching effect (this is to minimize the possible tool marks or ridges on the surface where multiple tool paths join).

Table 2: Optimal solutions minimizing part setups.

| | Tool axis in polar angle | | Indexing table angles | | Total number of switchings |
|---|---|---|---|---|---|
| | Setup 1 | Setup 2 | Setup 1 | Setup 2 | |
| Alternative 1 | (-15,90) | (15,90) | (90,-165) | (90, 165) | 31 |
| Alternative 2 | (-15,90) | (25,90) | (90,-165) | (90, 155) | 37 |

(a) machinable surface area (b) non-machinable area (c) index table orientation

Figure 8. Minimum setup configuration.

For the test, an impeller shape shown in Figure 7(a) was taken. The impeller is made up of eight blades. It is sufficient to show the developed procedure for the surface between the blades (Figure 7(b)) as the results can be rotated and applied to the rest of the blades. Applying the solution procedure (Note that the details were not given in this paper due to page limitations. See reference [9] for the details), the, minimum number of setups be two, with the setup combinations shown in Table 2, where alternative 1 with 31 switchings (fourth column of Table 2) turned out to be the optimal. See Figure 8 for the comparison of the two setups. Finally, Figure 9 shows the actually machined part.

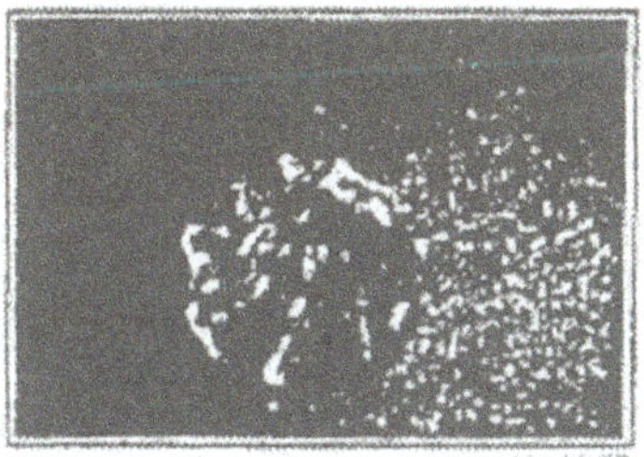

**Figure 9. Results of machining experiment.**

### 4.2 Example 2: 5-Axis flank milling with servo con-trolled rotary/tilt table

Since ruled surfaces are represented by a one-parameter family of straight ruling lines (e.g., a conic surface), they are particularly well suited for five-axis machining using flank milling which is one of the crucial features that the five-axis NC machine offers. Compared with bottom-edge based machining, flank milling can increase productivity significantly as well as improve surface finish. Thus, we developed flank milling method for NC machining of ruled surfaces with the additional-axis machine, the three-axis CNC machine interfaced with a two-axis controlled tilt/rotary table, denoted by [3,3,3,2,2].

In this example, we took the system consisting of a vertical three-axis CNC machine, a servo controlled rotary-tilt table, and a host control system coordinating the machine tool and the rotary table controllers. To achieve five-axis flank milling of the ruled surface with this system, algorithms for tool path planning and execution including CL-data composition and the synchronization method were developed. Due to page limitations, however, we do not describe it here (the details can be found in Reference [10], but we show the results of implementation, calibration and cutting experiment.

#### 4.2.1 Implementation

The presented AFA scheme was implement for Bridgeport 3-axis CNC milling machine run on the three-axis controller (Heidinhain TNC 151 model). A rotary/tilt table (manufactured by Troyke Manufacturing Co.) was interfaced with a two-axis controller (DSP board). The two controllers were coordinated via a host controller, a rotary/tilt table and a host computer where a DSP board is installed together with the V-CAM system.

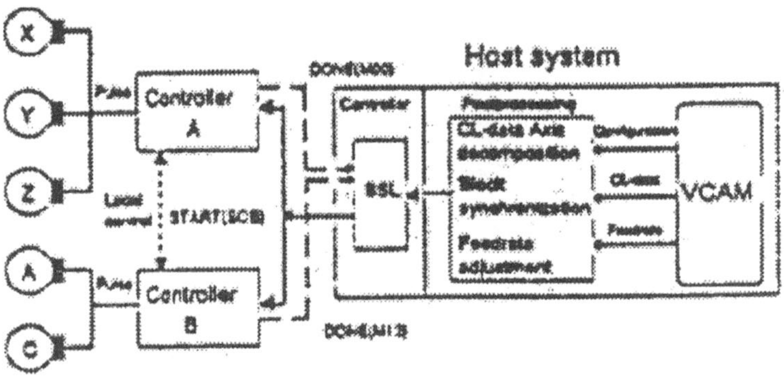


Figure 10. IS control scheme of AFA.

#### 4.2.2 Calibration of the controllers

The practical validity of the above synchronization method is determined based on the difference of the execution time. Without calibration, there exists a time difference in almost all the cases, even if the computed execution time was the same. This is due to the difference in the control logic of the two controllers. Also, it was found that the time difference is dependent on the values of the feed rate and moving distance as shown in Figure 11 9a) (called characteristic map or CM), showing the time difference under various feed rates and distances.

Applying the hardware calibration method, we obtained the characteristic map shown in Figure 11 (b) indicating the maximum of 30 ms throughout the entire range of the moving distance and fee rate. In practice, 30 ms are allowable for most of the precision. Further, as the time difference is constant over the entire range, its effect can be virtually eliminated by compensating the time lag in the

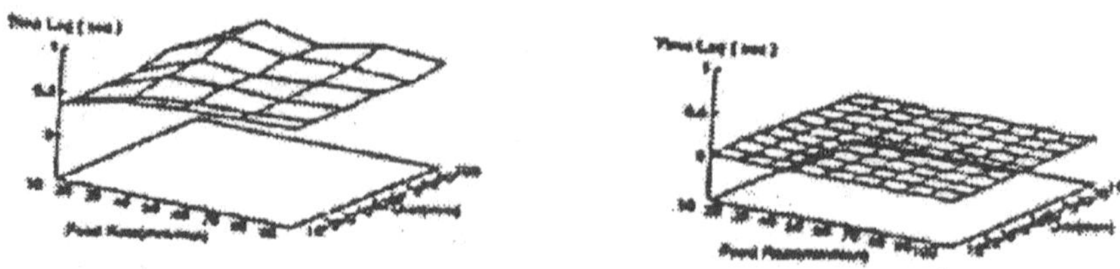

(a) Before calibration (b) After calibration

postprocessing procedure.

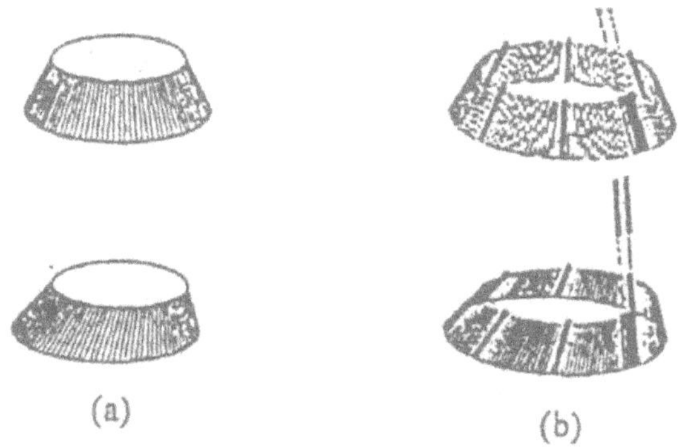

Figure 12. Two cone ruled surfaces

#### 4.2.3 Cutting experiment

Two examples shown in Figure 12 (a) are a ruled surfaces with the circle diameter of 60 mm and 80 mm for the upper and lower base curves. Applying the tool path algorithm, the CL-paths including tool approach and departure were obtained as shown in Figure 12 (b). Applying the procedures of tool path planning followed by path execution, the two parts of G-codes were obtained. By executing the G-codes for the two controllers, parts shown in Figure 13 (c) was obtained. Note that Figure 12 includes the results of rough cut (a) and semifinish cut (b). The finished part showed dimensional accuracy and good surface finish.

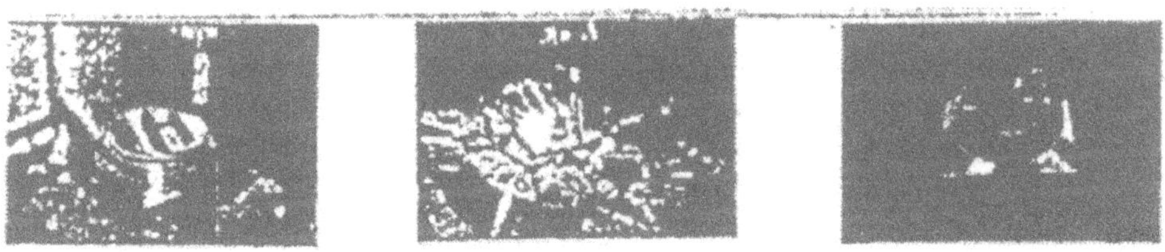

(a) rough cut (b) semifinish cut (c) final shape

Figure 13. Cone cutting experiment.

## 5 CONCLUDING REMARKS

In this paper, the additional-axis machining method was presented with the enabling theories and hardware implementation methods for achieving five-axis machining with three-axis machine tools and an additional attachment. Investegating the characteristic of the additional-axis system, we established the architecture of a comprehensive software (called V-CAM) system, supporting various configurations and machining operations.

To show its validity and provide a detailed illustration, we took two application, we took two application examples: [3,3,3,2,0] and [3,3,3,2,2]. In the first example, using the manual indexing table, the tool orientation is obtained by changing the part setup manually. Since this method is very simple and economical (the indexing table cost a few thousand dollars), it can be effectively applied in the medium to small industry where capital investment for the five-axis system is a burden. With the continuously controlled motion of the rotary/tilt table [3,3,3,2,2] taken in the second example, the additional-axis system performs like a generic five-axis system. We showed that the flank milling operation requiring simultaneous five-axis controls can be effectively carried out by developing tool path planning and execution algorithms together with hardware implementation and the calibration method.

## ACKNOWLEDGEMENTS

This research was supported by KOSEF (Korea Science and Engineering Foundation) research fund (Contract Number: 961-1007-060-2).

## REFERENCES

[1] Mason, F. (1991) 5x5 for high-productivity airfoil milling, American Machinist, 37-39.

[2] Schultz, D. (1993) Why five-a@?, Modern Machs'ne *Shop, 50-59.*

[3] Cover story: Machining Centers, American Machz'nt'st, Sept. 1991.

[4] Sakamoto, S. and Inasaki, I. (1993) Analysis of generating motion for five-axis machining centers, Transactz'on *of NAMRI/SME,* XXI, 287-293.

[5] Hansen, A., Arbab, F. (1988) Fixed-axis tool positioning with built-in global interference checking for NC path generation, *IEEE J. Robotics* and Automation, 4, 610-621.

[6] Li, S. and Jerad, R. (1994) 5-axis machining of sculptured surfaces with a flat endmill cutter, Computer-Aided Design, 26, 3, 165-178.

[7] Loney, G. and Ozsoy, T. (1987) NC machining of free form surfaces, Computer-Aided *Design, 19,* 2, 85-90.

[8] Suh, S. and Kang, J. (1995) Process planning for multi-@ NC machining of free surfaces, Int. *J. Prod. Res., 33,* 10, 2723-2738.

[9] Suh, S. and Lee, J. (1997) Five-axis part machining with three-axis CNC machine tools, *ASME Trans.* J. Manufacturing Science and Engineering, to appear.

[10] Lee, J. and Suh, S. (1996) Flank milling of ruled surface with additionally-five-@ CNC machine, *Proc. First Intl Conf.: IDMME'96,* April 1996, Nantes, France, pp. 375-384.

# 15

# The validity of Z-map model for mold and die machining

*Park, J. W. and Choi, B. K.**
*School of Mechanical Engineering, Yeungnam University*
*214-1 Dae-Dong, Kyoungsan*
*Kyoungbuk, 712-749 Korea*
*Tel: +82-53-810-3524,*
*Fax: +82-53-813-3703,*
*E-mail: jwpark@ynucc.yeungnam.ac.kr*

** IE Dept., KAIST*
*373-1 Kusong-dong Yusong-gu*
*Taejon, 305-701 Korea*
*Tel: +82-42-869-3115,*
*Fax: +82-42-869-3110,*
*E-mail: bkchoi@bezier.kaist.ac.kr*

**Abstract**

Z-map is a special form of discrete nonparametric representation in which the height values at grid points on the xy-plane are stored as a 2D array z[i,j]. While Z-map is the simplest form of representing sculptured surfaces and it is the most versatile scheme for modeling nonparametric objects, the application of Z-map to die machining (eg, finish cutting, clean-up cutting) aroused much controversy over its weaknesses: accuracy, singularities (e.g., vertical walls), and some excessive storage needs.

Although it has such limitations, much research on the application of Z-map can be found in various articles. However, research involving systematic analysis of Z-map to represent sculptured surfaces or CL (cutter location) surfaces for mold and die machining is rather rare.

Presented in this paper are the following: evaluation of the height value of a point which is not a pre-defined grid point, exact (within machining tolerance) Z-map representation of sculptured surfaces containing vertical walls and sharp edge lines (i.e., the common edges of adjoining faces which violate tangential

Computer Applications in Production and Engineering. F. Plonka and G. Olling (Eds.)

continuity) by adopting a Core Z-map or EZ-map (Extended Z-map) model, and several methodologies of computing CL surface in a Z-map form. Also presented are examples of die machining in industry.

**Keywords**
Surface modeling, Z-map model, CL Z-map, mold and die machining

# 1 INTRODUCTION

Surface modeling for CAD/CAM has been developed mainly based on parametric (polynomial) representations such as NURBS (Non-Uniform Rational B-Spline surface). The parametric surface model is very powerful and flexible, but it also has some limitations or difficulties in handling certain geometrical problems (Choi 95).

In a nonparametric representation, a surface is defined by its height values at given points on the xy-plane, and it has the functional form

$$z = f(x,y) \quad (1)$$

when the surface is defined in Cartesian coordinates. Z-map is a special form of discrete nonparametric representation in which the height values at grid points on the xy-plane (domain) are stored as a 2D array z[i,j] of the form (see figure 1)

$$z[i,j] \text{ with } x = x_o + d_x*i \text{ and } y = y_o + d_y*j. \quad (2)$$

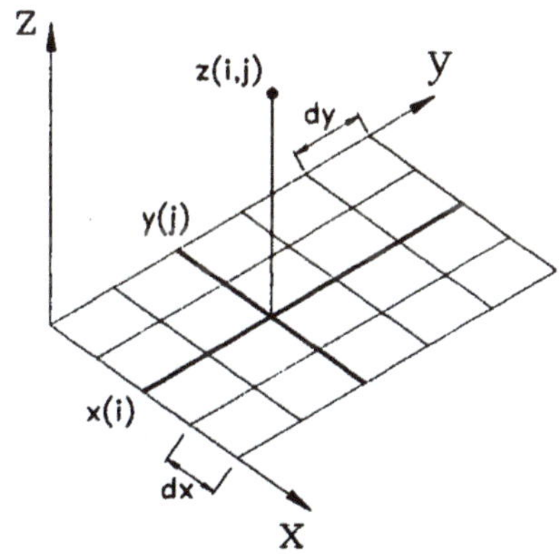


**Figure 1** Z-map model

When a domain point (x,y) is a grid point, the values of the index variables i,j are determined from

$$i = (x-x_o)/d_x \text{ and } j = (y-y_o)/d_y \quad (3)$$

and then its z-value is accessed from the array. If a point (x,y) is not a grid point, its z-value can be estimated by some interpolating schemes.

The Z-map model has limitations of representing general 3-dimensional shapes including vertical walls, multi-leveled z-values (ie, more than one z-value is defined at a domain point), and sharp edges. For representing multi-leveled z-values, a multi-level Z-map model which is known as dexel in the literature (Hook 1986, Kim 94) may be adopted.

Much research on Z-map applications can be found in various articles, including NC toolpaths verification (Andersen 78, Choi 94, Hsu 93, Kim 94, Takata 89), computer-aided process planning (CAPP) and die cavity machining (Choi 94). Also various research efforts in cutter path generation from the Z-map model (Choi 88, Takeuchi 89, Saito 91, Choi 93, Choi 94) can be found.

Section 2 shows a representation of vertical walls and sharp edges in a Z-map form by the use of some extended methods while retaining the simple (see figure 1) Z-map structure. Several methods to get an accurate (within a tolerance value) CL surface in a Z-map form are shown in the following section, and finally some examples are presented.

## 2 Z-MAP REPRESENTATION OF SURFACE

### 2.1 Computation of a z-value at a pre-defined grid point

Given a set of parametric surfaces, a Z-map z[i,j] whose xy-domain bounds that of the surfaces can be obtained by evaluating the z-value(s) at each pre-defined grid point [i,j] (see figure 2).

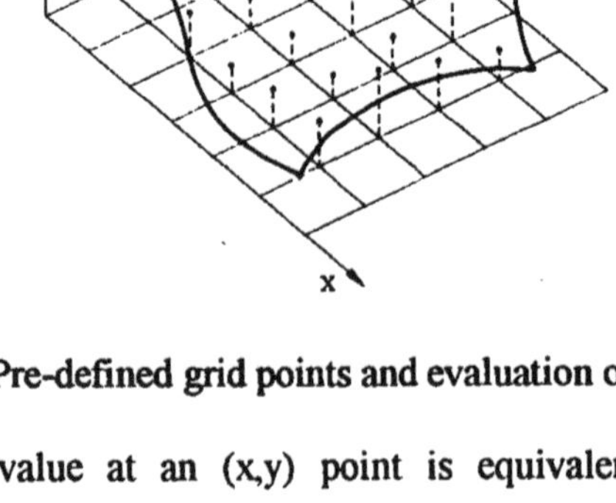


**Figure 2** Pre-defined grid points and evaluation of z-values

Computing a z-value at an (x,y) point is equivalent to evaluating the

intersection point (x,y,z) between a surface and an infinite vertical line at (x,y). This algorithm is called "2D Jacobian Inversion" (Choi 91), and efficiently computes the z-value within a given tolerance value. When multiple z-values are obtained, the highest one is chosen to avoid gouging.
Using differential geometry, the algorithm happens to fail to converge (ie, to evaluate an intersecting point). In that case, through a surface tessellation (e.g., triangulation) the z-values can be evaluated.

## 2.2 Interpolation of a z-value for a domain point

As shown in the previous section, all the z-values of pre-defined grid points can be obtained, and they can be accessed directly from z[i,j] by eqn. (3) as long as a domain point (x,y) is a grid point.

The problem now becomes the evaluation of a z-value at a domain point (x,y) which is not a pre-defined grid point. If a set of surfaces has neither a vertical wall nor a sharp edge, then we can assume without loss of generality that the overall surface is smooth enough to be well represented in a simple Z-map form such that the z-value at any arbitrary (x,y) can be estimated through interpolating z-values of neighboring pre-defined grid points. Methods for handling vertical walls and sharp edges will be developed in the following section.

The authors use a "nonparametric cubic Bezier curve interpolating" scheme to estimate a z-value by considering 12 z-values of neighboring grid points. A nonparametric Bezier curve construction can be found in the literature (Choi 91, Farin 97).

Figure 3 shows 12 grid points on the xy-domain, which constitute four sets of control vertices $\{V_i; i=0,..,3\}$ of nonparametric cubic Bezier curves (note that four grid points g1,g2,g5,g6 are used twice) such that

$\{V_i\}_1 = \{g0,g1,g2,g3\}$, $\{V_i\}_2 = \{g4,g5,g6,g7\}$,
$\{V_i\}_3 = \{g9,g5,g1,g8\}$, $\{V_i\}_4 = \{g11,g6,g2,g10\}$.

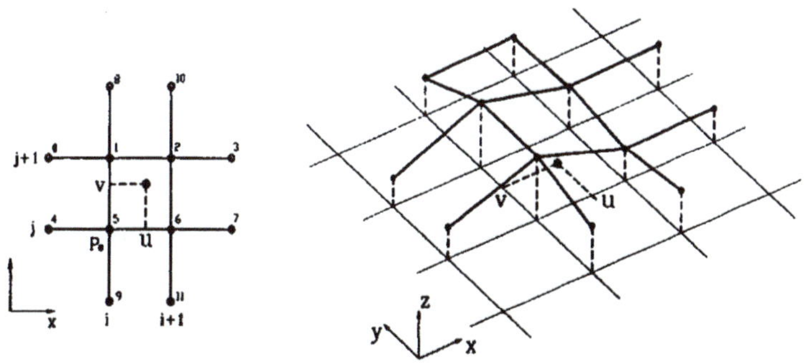


**Figure 3** Nonparametric Bezier interpolation

Then each $\{V_i\}$ makes a nonparametric Bezier curve, and four z-values can be evaluated from each curve equation with parameter domain values of u or v (ie, u for 2 horizontal curves, v for 2 vertical ones, respectively). The (u,v) pair is determined by considering local coordinate values of (x,y) within the local rectangular domain (g1,g2,g5,g6) with (u,v)=(0,0) at Po. Now the z-value at (u,v) can be estimated through a linear blending of the four z-values. If the domain point (x,y) falls into a grid point [i,j] within a tolerance, then z[i,j] becomes the estimated z-value.

For a domain point (x,y) where all 12 neighboring grid points cannot be defined (e.g., on the xy-domain boundary), linearly extended dummy grid points are added to construct a complete set of control vertices.

Comparing the estimated z-values with the exact ones on two typical smooth surfaces, we got the following results (ε=error value):

$\varepsilon_{max} = \pm 1.2 \times 10^{-4}$(□) for a bilinear surface: $z=100\sin(\pi x/180)$,

$\varepsilon_{max} = \pm 3.0 \times 10^{-5}$(□) for an upper hemisphere: $x^2+y^2+z^2=100^2$, $z>70$,

larger ε-values occur on near-boundary areas (as predicted),

with a grid step distance (interval) of $d_x=d_y=1$□ (usually 0.7□ for a real application). Considering that a typical machining tolerance value in finish-cut machining of mold and die is in the range of $10^{-3}$ to $10^{-2}$□, we can say that the simple Z-map representation works fine for practical mold & die machining as long as the overall surface is smooth. Figure 4 shows the scaled error patterns for those sample surfaces with $d_x=d_y=10$□ and $d_x=d_y=20$□, respectively.

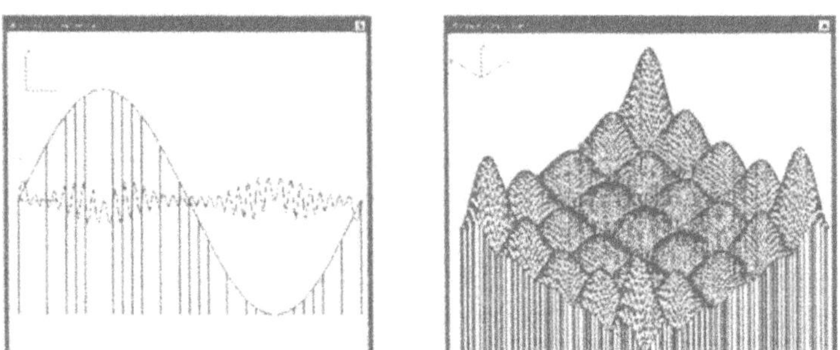

(a) $z=100\sin(\pi x/180)$ (b) $x^2+y^2+z^2=100^2$, $z > 70$

**Figure 4** Scaled error patterns when (a) $d_x=d_y=10$□, (b) $d_x=d_y=20$□

## 2.3 Extended models for handling vertical walls and sharp edges

Most mold die-surfaces contain such features as sharp edge-lines and vertical walls, and so does automobile press die-surfaces (e.g., sharp convex edge-lines on an outer hood surface). The simple Z-map model, however, has the power to represent the special features only with a very small grid interval value (see figure 5), which cannot always be applied to finish machining due to excessive memory storage needs. Accordingly, some other methods should be conceived to overcome such difficulties.

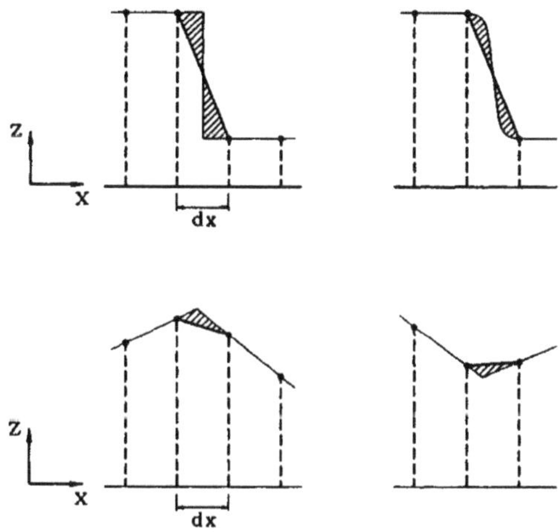


**Figure 5** Wrongly defined vertical walls and sharp edges in a simple Z-map form

In order to represent the local features accurately (within a tolerance), the authors adopted the following auxiliary models:

- ***Core Z-map model,***
- ***EZ-map (Extended Z-map) model.***

## • Core Z-map model

A core Z-map, with a much smaller $d_x$ and $d_y$ (equal to machining tolerance in a real application) than that of a simple Z-map, can be thought as a hard steel core embedded selectively (and locally) into a large die-surface area. In other words, it locally enhances the accuracy of the original Z-map on which it is located (see figure 6). Owing to selective localization much less memory storage is required, which, while preserving the accuracy and the Z-map form, makes it feasible to handle a large domain.

The "selective" locating of core maps is made possible by identifying areas of vertical wall and sharp edge lines (e.g., analyzing the Z-map and parametric surfaces). Then, a series of local domains of core Z-maps are defined and constructed along a sharp edge line or a vertical wall line (a series of domain points each with a local maximum gradient), as shown in figure 6. In general, different grid interval values for $d_x$, $d_y$ of a core Z-map are assigned to minimize the memory usage. Evaluating a z-value on a core map (when a domain point (x,y) falls within the core map's domain) is similar to that on a Z-map (section 2.2).

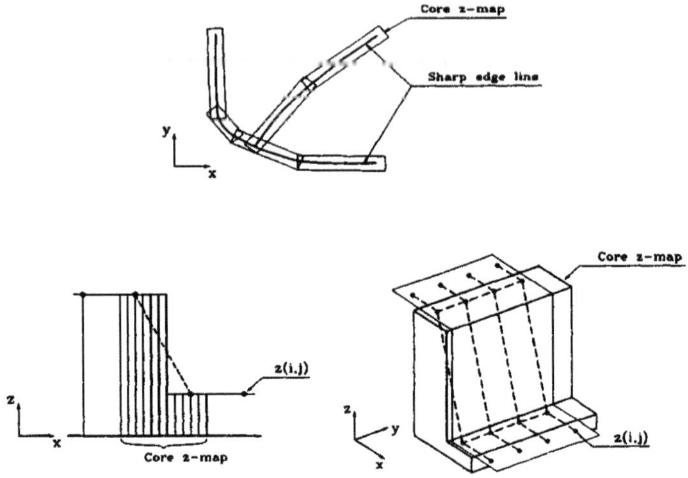


**Figure 6** Schematic model of Core Z-map

• EZ-map model

The EZ-map (Extended Z-map) model defines "edge grid points" on each selected grid-line of a Z-map to recover the accuracy, while preserving the "localization" property (see figure 7). A grid-line of a Z-map means a 3D line segment connecting two consecutive 3D grid points. Identifying a grid-line on which edge grid points should be added is similar to the core Z-map model, and the number of points is determined to satisfy the machining tolerance δ (i.e., a function of dx,dy,δ).

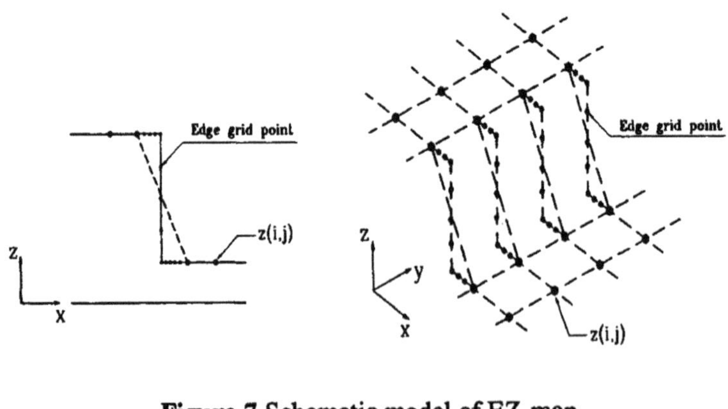


**Figure 7** Schematic model of EZ-map

Evaluating the z-value at an (x,y) domain point is similar to a Z-map, except that the edge grid points (if any) are additionally utilized and sharp edge lines can be considered.

# 3 Z-MAP REPRESENTATION OF CL-SURFACE

## 3.1 CL surface and the singularity

A parametric surface model can be represented as a vector valued function

$$\mathbf{r}(u,v) = (x(u,v), y(u,v), z(u,v)) \quad (4)$$

and it is in fact a regular mapping from the parameter domain (u,v) to the 3D cartesian space (x,y,z). The CL surface of $\mathbf{r}(u,v)$ for a general round-end milling cutter with a fixed cutter axis can be defined such that

$$\mathbf{r}^{o}(u,v) = \mathbf{r}(u,v) + \alpha(\mathbf{n} - \mathbf{u}) + (R - \alpha)(\mathbf{n} - \lambda\mathbf{u})/(1 - \lambda^2)^{1/2} \quad (5)$$

*where* $\lambda = \mathbf{n}\cdot\mathbf{u}$,
$\mathbf{n} = \mathbf{n}(u,v)$: *unit normal vector at (u,v),*
$\mathbf{u} = (0,0,1)$: *cutter axis,*
R: *cutter radius (half the diameter),*
$\alpha$: *cutter nose radius,*

and any CL point of the cutter (i.e., reference point) is located on $\mathbf{r}^{o}(u,v)$. Then, eqn. (5) can be reduced to CL surfaces for ball or flat-end milling cutters if $\alpha$ becomes R or zero, respectively. The CL surface $\mathbf{r}^{o}(u,v)$ is also a vector-valued function (x(u,v), y(u,v), z(u,v)), and it may be a regular mapping from (u,v) to (x,y,z).

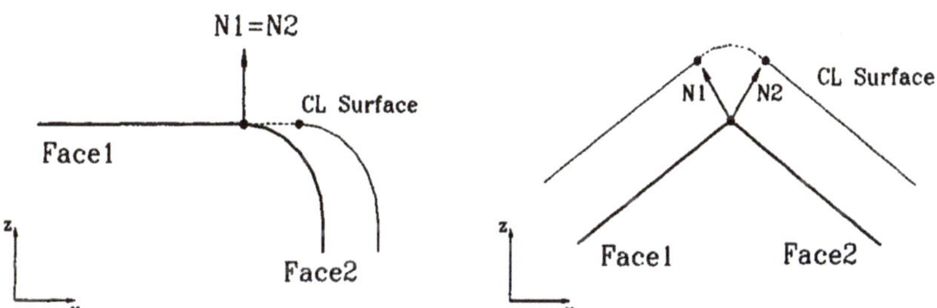


(a) For flat-end cutter (b) For all cutter types

**Figure 8** Singularity of a CL surface

There possibly exists, however, a CC (cutter contact) point $\mathbf{r}(u,v)$ at which a regular mapping is impossible due to a singularity (see figure 8), and a unique CL point cannot be determined. For example, figure 8-b shows a sectional view of two adjoining faces and a common edge, which is convex and tangentially discontinuous. In the case of a ball-end milling cutter, a point on the edge curve should be mapped into a curve (e.g., a circular arc for a ball-end milling cutter) rather than a point, and the edge curve into a surface (eg, a cylindrical surface for a ball-end milling cutter) to fill the gap on the CL surface (dotted line). Figure 8-a shows another type of singularity at which, for a round or flat-end milling cutter, a gap (dotted line for a flat end-milling cutter ) on the CL surface is inevitable without special treatment.

Some methods to construct a gouge-free CL surface are presented in the following sections.

## 3.2 CL surface construction

The computation of a CL surface has been a very important issue in cutter path generation, which should be accurate (i.e., avoiding overcut and undercut) and efficient in its computation time. A CL surface construction (i.e., offsetting) based on the simple Z-map model can be found in the literature (Saito 91, Takeuchi 89). However, hardly any enhancement in accuracy has been demonstrated.

The authors' research group developed the following algorithms to obtain an accurate (within machining tolerance) CL Z-map (EZ-map):

- ***Z-map-based inverse offset,***
- ***Surface-based inverse offset,***
- ***Surface-based offset-facet sampling & edge-based inverse offset,***

where "surface" means a parametric surface, and "Z-map" can be easily extended to an EZ-map form.

### • Z-map-based inverse offset

A Z-map obtained from parametric surfaces can be considered as a soft "master model", with all the grid points and edge grid points (if any) containing exact z-values. By applying the inverse offset method of a Z-map (Choi 91) to generate a CL surface, we can obtain a CL Z-map directly from the master model Z-map. Figure 9 shows the schematic view of this method for a ball-end milling cutter.

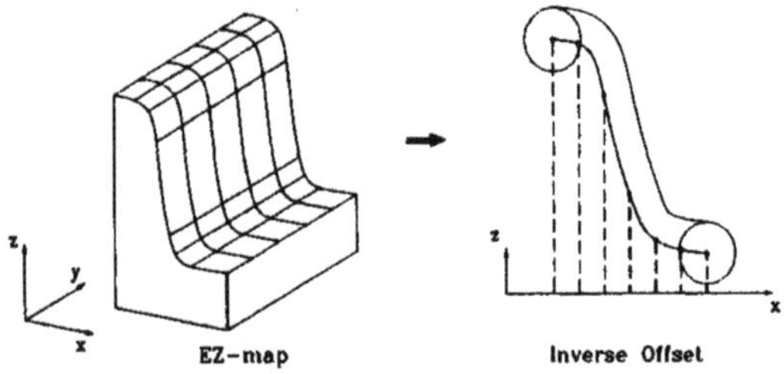


**Figure 9** Z-map-based inverse offset (ball-end milling case)

The main advantages of the method are speed (i.e., efficiency in computation time) and robustness, that is, in any case it is possible to obtain a CL Z-map regardless of the singularity problem.

• Surface-based inverse offset

While it is a Z-map that the previous method employs as a master model, this method utilizes the surface itself; sampled isoparametric curves and all the boundary edge curves (see figure 10). Each curve consists of a series of 3D points, and grid points on the xy-domain are updated so that a CL Z-map can be constructed by the inverse offset of 3D points sequence (i.e., inverse cutting simulation along the 3D points). The 3D step-over distance between consecutive isoparametric curves of a surface is determined from differential geometry so that it satisfies a given tolerance value. The singularity problem (figure 8) is resolved through the inverse offset of all boundary edge curves.

It takes much more computation time than the previous method, since the inverse offset should be applied to closely positioned 3D points from the curves. In addition, most points in the previous method are regularly spaced grid points (on the xy-domain), which makes it possible to utilize a more efficient optimizing process (i.e., minimizing the updating area on the domain).

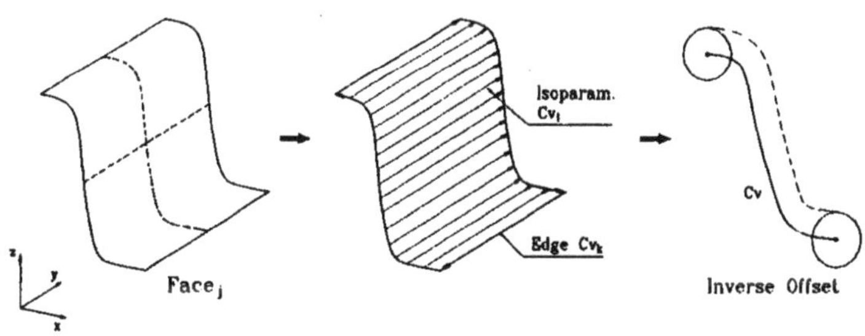


**Figure 10** Surface-based inverse offset (ball-end milling case)

• Surface-based offset-facet sampling & edge-based inverse offset

This can be said to be the most efficient method among the three, considering both accuracy and speed. We construct a CL Z-map by evaluating the 3D "offset triangles" of surfaces rather than doing the inverse offset of isoparametric curves. The triangular facet model of a surface can be obtained through tessellation of the surface, and each triangle is represented by three vertices located on the surface. Then, the "offset triangles" of a surface are constructed so that all vertices on the surface are moved to the corresponding CL points according to a given cutter type (Eqn.(5)) to become "offset vertices".

The same inverse offset algorithm is applied to all the boundary edge curves to resolve the singularity problems, as in the previous method (see figure 11).

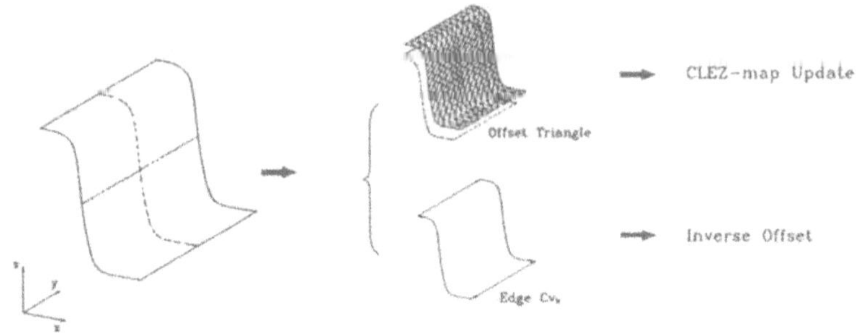


Figure 11 Surface-based offset-facet sampling and edge-based inverse offset

Finally, some error types are defined as follows:

- $\varepsilon_1$ = Z-map intrinsic error for representing CL surface ($\mathbf{r}^{o}(u,v)$),
- $\varepsilon_2$ = Z-map intrinsic error for representing CC surface ($\mathbf{r}(u,v)$),
- $\varepsilon_3$ = Discretization error of isoparametric curves,
- $\varepsilon_4$ = Triangulation error.

The second error value ($\varepsilon_2$) comes from the difference between parametric surfaces and the "master model" Z-map, the first ($\varepsilon_1$) from that between a CL Z-map and the ideal CL surface. The third one ($\varepsilon_3$) is actually a combination of the following two; error in discrete 3D points of an isoparametric curve on the given surface, and error caused by non-zero step-over distance between the isoparametric curves. The error in discrete 3D points of a boundary edge is neglected. The triangulation error ($\varepsilon_4$) comes from the difference between the ideal CL surface and an offset triangulated facet model. Roughly speaking, the relations between errors are; $\varepsilon_1 = \varepsilon_2 > \varepsilon_3 > \varepsilon_4$. Now, Table 1 summarizes the presented methods.

**Table 1** Summary: Z-map representation of CL surface

| Method | Error total | Speed* | Accuracy | Applicability |
|---|---|---|---|---|
| A | $\varepsilon_1+\varepsilon_2$ | 1** | 3 | 2 |
| B | $\varepsilon_1+\varepsilon_3$ | 3 | 1 | 3 |
| C | $\varepsilon_1+\varepsilon_4$ | 2 | 2 | 1 |

*A. Z-map-based inverse offset,*
*B. Surface-based inverse offset,*
*C. Surface-based offset-facet sampling & edge-based inverse offset.*
** Speed for construction of CL surface.*
*** Number denotes rank (the larger the worse)*

## 4 EXAMPLES

Figure 12 shows construction of a "master model" Z-map, its CL Z-map, and parallel-to-plane toolpaths for a very simple model surface (part of a connecting rod). The xy-domain of the Z-map is 110x120□, and the grid interval is 0.7□.

When the Z-map is represented in an EZ-map form with tolerance=0.02, about 400Kbytes memory storage is needed (about 7% of all grid lines contain edge grid points, with 40 points each). So for the CL Z-map, roughly.

Figure 13 shows another example with 1880 faces total. The xy-domain is 1200x900□ with a grid interval of 1□. The EZ-map requires about 10Mbytes memory storage, given the tolerance=0.02. In this case, about 3% of Z-map grid lines have edge grid points (with 50 points each).

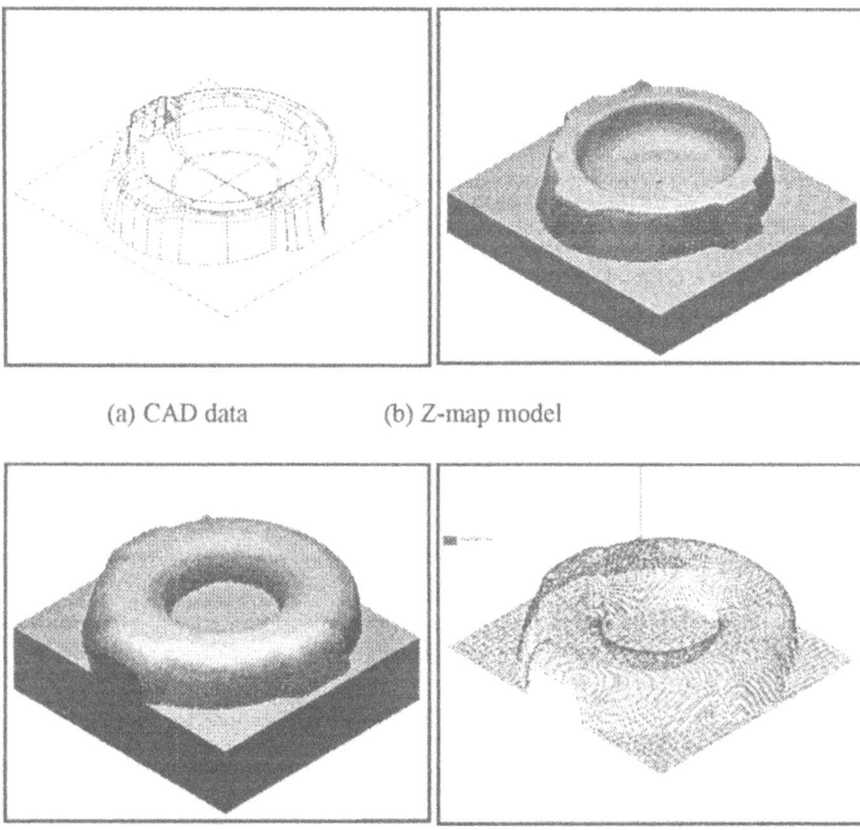

(a) CAD data (b) Z-map model

(c) CL Z-map (d) Parallel-to-plane toolpaths

**Figure 12** Application example: connecting rod (partial)

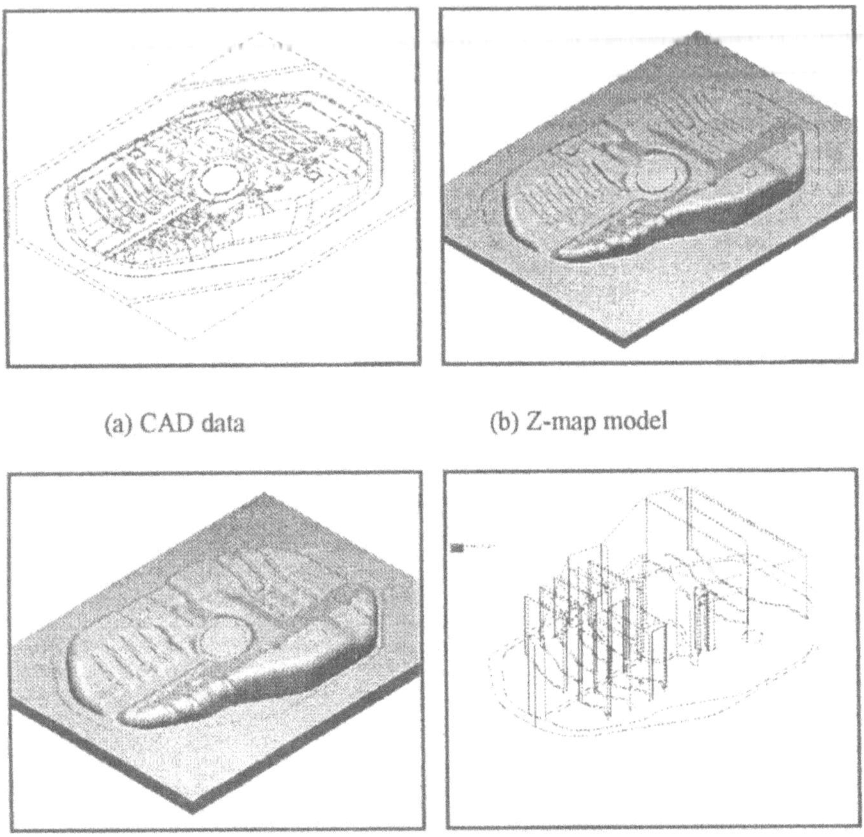

(a) CAD data (b) Z-map model

(c) CL Z-map (d) Pencil curve machining toolpaths

**Figure 13** Application example: fuel tank

## 5 CONCLUSIONS

It has been shown that the Z-map model and its extended models are powerful tools that can be successfully utilized in manufacturing. The main limitations of Z-map are the resolution problem in dealing with "vertical walls" and "real" sharp edges and the O(n) complexity problem (i.e., the memory and time complexity is proportional to the square of the resolution). Two approaches to handling these problems were illustrated; namely, core Z-map and EZ-map models. In addition, three methods for constructing a CL surface in a Z-map (or EZ-map) form were presented.

In fact, Z-map type models are utilized in many of the leading commercial CAM software systems (Cliks 91, Worknc 93), and in a few in-house systems for Chrysler Corporation (METD, MI, USA), Hyundai Motor Company (Korea), and other mold & die manufacturing companies. The commercial CAM software Z-MASTER (Zmaster 92) employed a Z-map type model equipped with the presented algorithms, and has been used for mold & die manufacturing.

# 6 REFERENCES

Andersen,R.O.(1978) Detecting and eliminating collisions in NC machining. *Computer-Aided Design*, V10 N4, 231-237.

Choi,B.K.(1991) *Surface modeling for CAD/CAM.* Elsevier, New York.

Choi,B.K., Park,J.W. and Jun,C.S.(1993) Cutter-location data optimization in 5-axis surface machining. *Computer-Aided Design*, V25 N6, 377-386.

Choi,B.K., Chung,Y.C., Park,J.W. and Kim,D.H.(1994) Unified CAM-system architecture for die and mould machining, *Computer-Aided Design*, V26 N3, 235-243.

Choi,B.K., Chung,Y.C. and Park,J.W.(1995) Application and extension of Z-map model, *Proc. of the Pacific Conference on Computer Graphics and Applications*, Seoul, Aug, 221-234.

Cliks(1991) *CLIKS user manual.* ARGO Technos 21, Japan.

Farin,G.(1997) *CAGD: a practical guide.* Academic Press, New York.

Hook,T.V.(1986) Real time shaded NC milling display. *Computer Graphics,* V20 N4, 15-20.

Hsu,P.L. and Yang,W.T.(1993) Realtime 3D simulation of 3-axis milling using isometric projection. *Computer-Aided Design*, V25 N4, 215-224.

Kim,C.B. and Yang,M.Y.(1994) A study on the verification of 5-axis CNC machining. *Journal of KSME*, V18 N1, 93-100 (in Korean).

Saito,T. and Takahashi,T.(1991) NC machining with G-buffer method. *Computer Graphics,* V25 N4, 207-216.

Takata,S. Tsai,M.D. and Inui,M.(1989) A cutting simulation system for machinability evaluation using a workpiece model. *Annals of the CIRP*, V38, 417-420.

Takeuchi,Y. Sakamoto,M. Abe,Y. and Orita,R.(1989) Development of a personal CAD/CAM system for mold manufacture based on solid modeling techniques. *Annals of the CIRP*, V40, 455-458.

Worknc(1993) *WORKNC user guide version 3.5.* Sescoi, France.

Zmaster(1992) *Z-Master reference manual.* Cubic Tech, Korea.

# 7 BIOGRAPHY

Jung W. Park is a full-time lecturer of mechanical engineering. He received a BS in physics from Seoul National University, Korea, in 1987, and an MS from the Korea Advanced Institute of Science and Technology in 1991, also a Ph.D. in 1995 from the same institute, all in industrial engineering. He has worked for Chrysler Corporation (Chrysler Technology Center), USA, from mid-1995 through early

1997 as a CAD/CAM software system developer. He joined Yeungnam University in early 1997. His research interests are in surface modeling, multiaxis NC machining, and off-line programming.
Byoung K. Choi is a professor of industrial engineering. He received a BS from Seoul National University, Korea, in 1973, an MS from the Korea Advanced Institute of Science and Technology in 1975, and a PhD from Purdue University, USA in 1982, all in industrial engineering. He joined KAIST in early 1983, and spent a year at Purdue in 1988, and half a year at UNH (University of New Hampshire) in 1996 through early 1997, as a visiting professor. His current research interests include surface modeling, CAD/CAM, CAPP, and discrete-event system modeling and simulation.

# 16
# Probabilistic Approaches for Estimating Surface Roughness in Multi-pass Horizontal Grinding Operations

H.G.Choi, M.K.Yeo, J.Y.Kim

*Sung Kyun Kwan University, Department of Indusrtrial Engineering Suwon Kyong Ki Do 440–746 S.Korea, Phone number:(nation code)-331-290-7616, Fax number:(nation code)-331-290-7610, E-mail address:hgchoi@yurim.skku.ac.kr.*

**Abstract**

**The grinding operation is one of the most popular finishing operations, which requires high costs and large machining times to achieve a given surface roughness. Although the operation has been used to produce better surfaces after several interim operations, a few theoretical and practical research about its operational characteristics has been presented. The surface roughness resulted by an abrasive wheel is the typical characteristic. This study presents mathematical models to estimate probabilistically surface roughness in multi-pass horizontal surface grinding operations from the initial surface roughness distributions of a workpiece, the distributions of the wheel radius , and the distributions of distances between active grains. As a result, we can show either the probability satisfying a given surface roughness or the range of surface roughness satisfying a given probability when grinding conditions are fixed. Also, we can establish the relationship between grinding conditions satisfying the range of surface roughness under a given probability.**

Keywords

Probabilistic Estimation , Surface Roughness , Multi-pass Grinding Operations

## 1 Introduction

The surface roughness in grinding operations is determined by a combined effects of irregular factors of a grinding wheel such as rotational speed, feed rate,

Computer Applications in Production and Engineering. F. Plonka and G. Olling (Eds.)

diameter, active grain size, and distance between active grains. Vibration, thermal effect, and friction between the wheel and a workpiece are another factors to affect the roughness. A lot of existing studies have reported the most recommendable roughness values to be obtained experimentally or empirically. Recently, however, the need of mathematical models for estimating the surface roughness has been exposed to reduce inaccurate estimation or ambiguous decisions in grinding areas.[1][4] Several features of grinding operations have been represented mathematically or statistically. Law and et.al[3] presented that the distance between neighboring active grains follows an exponential distribution and a sum of the wheel radius and the active grain size follows a Z distribution. Malkin[4] presented that the irregularities on a workpiece surface come from the wheel characteristics such as grain sizes, wheel radius, wheel material, etc. Also, he suggested uniform distributions for both the distance between neighboring active grains and the active grain sizes because the grain extraction and bonding methods have been evolved to make more uniform wheels.

In this study, a probabilistic modeling approach is used for estimating accurately surface roughness under mathematical characteristics of a wheel. A horizontal grinding machine is assumed to perform grinding operations. A worktable with a loaded workpiece moves back and forth to obtain a specified surface roughness while a wheel continuously rotates. It is hard to achieve a given roughness by one pass of the worktable, and so multiple number of passes are usually required. The following assumptions are adopted to estimate surface roughness in horizontal grinding operation:

1. The number of passes will not affect to the wheel characteristics.
2. The active grain size is smaller than the initial surface roughness of a workpiece in multi-pass cases.
3. The cutting fluids and wheel dressing are not applied.
4. The surface roughness is not affected by irregular factors such as vibration, thermal effect, friction, etc.

Assumptions 1., 2., and 4. describe that no factors related to the wheel wear are considered. The second assumption means that the initial surface roughness of a workpiece is ground repeatedly to obtain a desired roughness.

## 2 Ideal Surface Roughness in Horizontal Grinding Operations

In this study, the ideal surface roughness equation presented by Malkin[4] has been used for deriving a probability density function of surface roughness. The ideal surface roughness[4] depicted in Figure 1 is determined by Equation (1). Every pass of the grinding wheel over a workpiece creates a new roughness represented by Equation (1).

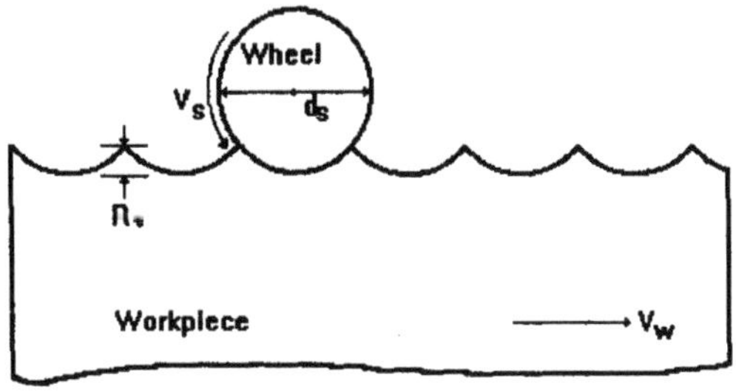


Figure 1: Ideal surface roughness[4].

$$R_t = \frac{1}{4}\left[\frac{V_w X}{\sqrt{2}V_s Y^{1/2}}\right]^2 = \frac{V_w^2}{8V_s^2}Z = \alpha Z \quad (\alpha = \frac{V_w^2}{8V_s^2}) \tag{1}$$

Where $R_t$=ideal surface roughness(peak-to-valley surface roughness), $V_s$=rotational speed of a spindle or a grinding wheel, $V_w$ =work table speed, $X$=distance between neighboring active grains, $Y$ = ds/2, $Z$ =$X^2/Y$, $d_s$ = wheel diameter.

$R_t$ is a function of $Z$ and is a random variable. When a statistical distribution is defined for the distance between the active grains or for the wheel radius, a probability density function of surface roughness $f_U(u)$ is defined for multi-pass cases.

# 3 Probabilistic Models

When a workpiece surface is ground several times to obtain a given roughness, the (n-1)th roughness is affect to the nth roughness where n is the number of travels required for a worktable. In this study, the initial surface roughness ($T$) is set as a uniform distribution. The highest roughness and the lowest roughness of the initial surface are h and g, respectively. Then, the roughness is reduced in every pass as much as the constant amount,$R_t$.

$$f_T(t) = \frac{1}{h-g}I_{(g,h)}(t), \quad R_t^{[n]} : \text{surface roughness after the } n\text{th pass}$$

where $I_{(g,h)}(t)$ is an indication function which is defined by either 1 in the range of $g \le t \le h$ or 0 in other ranges.

$$T - R_t = R_t^{[1]}.$$
$$R_t^{[1]} - R_t = R_t^{[2]}.$$
$$R_t^{[2]} - R_t = R_t^{[3]}.$$
$$\vdots$$
$$R_t^{[n-1]} - R_t = R_t^{[n]}.$$

Then, these equations are combined together and simplified as follows:

$$T - 2R_t = R_t^{[2]} \quad (T - R_t = R_t^{[1]}).$$
$$T - 3R_t = R_t^{[3]}.$$
$$\vdots$$
$$T - nR_t = R_t^{[n]}.$$
$$T - nR_t = T - \beta Z = U \quad (\beta = \tfrac{nV_w^2}{8V_s^2},\ U = R_t^{[n]}).$$

Both $T$ and $U$ are random variables. Then, the p.d.f of surface roughness is defined by $f_U(u)$ for multi-pass cases.

## 3.1 Uniform distance and uniform radius

Both the distance between neighboring active grains, $X$ and the wheel radius, $Y$ are defined as uniform distributions,

$$f_X(x) = \tfrac{1}{b-a} I_{(a,b)}(x),\ f_Y(y) = \tfrac{1}{d-c} I_{(c,d)}(y),\ K_2 = 3(b-a)(d-c)(h-g)$$

where $I_{(a,b)}(x)$ is an indication function that is defined by either 1 in the range of $a \le X \le b$ or 0 in other ranges. $I_{(c,d)}(y)$ is defined similarly. Then, two separated p.d.f must be defined as follows:

- CASE I ($\frac{b^2}{d} < \frac{a^2}{c}$)

$$f_U(u) = \tfrac{1}{K_2}\{-3bc + 2c\sqrt{c}\sqrt{\tfrac{g-u}{\beta}} + \tfrac{\beta b^3}{g-u}\} I_{(g-\frac{\beta b^2}{c},\, g-\frac{\beta a^2}{c})}(U)$$
$$+ \tfrac{1}{K_2}\{3ac - 3bc + \tfrac{\beta b^3}{g-u} - \tfrac{\beta a^3}{g-u}\} I_{(g-\frac{\beta a^2}{c},\, g-\frac{\beta b^2}{d})}(U)$$
$$+ \tfrac{1}{K_2}\{3ac + 3bd - 3bc - 2d\sqrt{d}\sqrt{\tfrac{g-u}{\beta}} - \tfrac{\beta a^3}{g-u}\} I_{(g-\frac{\beta b^2}{d},\, g-\frac{\beta a^2}{d})}(U)$$
$$+ \tfrac{1}{h-g} I_{(g-\frac{\beta a^2}{d},\, h-\frac{\beta b^2}{c})}(U)$$
$$+ \tfrac{1}{K_2}\{3ac + 3bd - 3ad - 2c\sqrt{c}\sqrt{\tfrac{h-u}{\beta}} - \tfrac{\beta b^3}{h-u}\} I_{(h-\frac{\beta b^2}{c},\, h-\frac{\beta a^2}{c})}(U)$$
$$+ \tfrac{1}{K_2}\{3bd - 3ad + \tfrac{\beta a^3}{h-u} - \tfrac{\beta b^3}{h-u}\} I_{(h-\frac{\beta a^2}{c},\, h-\frac{\beta b^2}{d})}(U)$$

$$+\frac{1}{K_2}\{-3ad+2d\sqrt{d}\sqrt{\frac{h-u}{\beta}}+\frac{\beta a^3}{h-u}\}I_{(h-\frac{\beta b^2}{d},h-\frac{\beta a^2}{d})}(U)$$

- CASE II ($\frac{a^2}{c}<\frac{b^2}{d}$)

$$f_U(u)=\frac{1}{K_2}\{-3bc+2c\sqrt{c}\sqrt{\frac{g-u}{\beta}}+\frac{\beta b^3}{g-u}\}I_{(g-\frac{\beta b^2}{c},g-\frac{\beta b^2}{d})}(U)$$
$$+\frac{1}{K_2}\{3bd-3bc+2(c\sqrt{c}-d\sqrt{d})\sqrt{\frac{g-u}{\beta}}\}I_{(g-\frac{\beta b^2}{d},g-\frac{\beta a^2}{c})}(U)$$
$$+\frac{1}{K_2}\{3ac+3bd-3bc-2d\sqrt{d}\sqrt{\frac{g-u}{\beta}}-\frac{\beta a^3}{g-u}\}I_{(g-\frac{\beta a^2}{c},g-\frac{\beta a^2}{d})}(U)$$
$$+\frac{1}{h-g}I_{(g-\frac{\beta a^2}{d},h-\frac{\beta b^2}{c})}(U)$$
$$+\frac{1}{K_2}\{3ac+3bd-3ad-2c\sqrt{c}\sqrt{\frac{h-u}{\beta}}-\frac{\beta b^3}{h-u}\}I_{(h-\frac{\beta b^2}{c},h-\frac{\beta b^2}{d})}(U)$$
$$+\frac{1}{K_2}\{3ac-3ad+2(d\sqrt{d}-c\sqrt{c})\sqrt{\frac{h-u}{\beta}}\}I_{(h-\frac{\beta b^2}{d},h-\frac{\beta a^2}{c})}(U)$$
$$+\frac{1}{K_2}\{-3ad+2d\sqrt{d}\sqrt{\frac{h-u}{\beta}}+\frac{\beta a^3}{h-u}\}I_{(h-\frac{\beta a^2}{c},h-\frac{\beta a^2}{d})}(U)$$

## 3.2 Exponential distance and uniform radius

When the p.d.f of the distance between neighboring active grains and the p.d.f of the wheel radius are given respectively as follows:

$$f_X(x)=\lambda e^{-\lambda x},\ f_Y(y)=\frac{1}{d-c}I_{(c,d)}(y),\ K_3=(e^{-\lambda a}-e^{-\lambda b})(d-c)(h-g)$$

the p.d.f of $f_U(u)$ for Case I and Case II are obtained.

- CASE I ($\frac{b^2}{d}<\frac{a^2}{c}$)

$$f_u(u)=\{\frac{\lambda b e^{-\lambda b}(20b^2+5b^3\lambda+b^4\lambda^2)}{60K_3}\frac{\beta}{g-u}+\frac{2\lambda c\sqrt{c}}{3K_3}\sqrt{\frac{g-u}{\beta}}e^{-\lambda\sqrt{c}\sqrt{\frac{g-u}{\beta}}}$$
$$+\frac{5\lambda a^2c^2}{12K_3}\frac{g-u}{\beta}e^{-\lambda\sqrt{c}\sqrt{\frac{g-u}{\beta}}}+\frac{3\lambda a^3c^2\sqrt{c}}{20K_3}\sqrt{\frac{g-u}{\beta}}\frac{g-u}{\beta}e^{-\lambda\sqrt{c}\sqrt{\frac{g-u}{\beta}}}$$
$$+\frac{7\lambda a^4c^2}{720K_3}(\frac{g-u}{\beta})^2e^{-\lambda\sqrt{c}\sqrt{\frac{g-u}{\beta}}}+\frac{\lambda a^5c^3\sqrt{c}}{1800K_3}\sqrt{\frac{g-u}{\beta}}(\frac{g-u}{\beta})^2e^{-\lambda\sqrt{c}\sqrt{\frac{g-u}{\beta}}}$$
$$-\frac{\lambda bce^{-\lambda b}}{K_3}-\frac{\lambda^2b^2ce^{-\lambda b}}{2K_3}-\frac{\lambda^3b^3ce^{-\lambda b}}{6K_3}-\frac{7\lambda^4b^4ce^{-\lambda b}}{720K_3}-\frac{\lambda^5b^5ce^{-\lambda b}}{1800K_3}\}I_{(g-\frac{\beta b^2}{c},g-\frac{\beta a^2}{c})}(u)$$
$$+\{\frac{\lambda be^{-\lambda b}(20b^2+5b^3\lambda+b^4\lambda^2)-\lambda ae^{-\lambda a}(20a^2+5a^3\lambda+a^4\lambda^2)}{60K_3}\frac{\beta}{g-u}$$
$$-\frac{\lambda bce^{-\lambda b}}{K_3}-\frac{\lambda^2b^2ce^{-\lambda b}}{2K_3}-\frac{\lambda^3b^3ce^{-\lambda b}}{6K_3}-\frac{7\lambda^4b^4ce^{-\lambda b}}{720K_3}-\frac{\lambda^5b^5ce^{-\lambda b}}{1800K_3}$$
$$+\frac{\lambda ace^{-\lambda a}}{K_3}+\frac{\lambda^2a^2ce^{-\lambda a}}{2K_3}+\frac{\lambda^3a^3ce^{-\lambda a}}{6K_3}+\frac{7\lambda^4a^4ce^{-\lambda a}}{720K_3}+\frac{\lambda^5a^5ce^{-\lambda a}}{1800K_3}\}I_{(g-\frac{\beta a^2}{c},g-\frac{\beta b^2}{d})}(u)$$
$$+\{-\frac{\lambda ae^{-\lambda a}(20a^2+5a^3\lambda+a^4\lambda^2)}{60K_3}\frac{\beta}{g-u}-\frac{2\lambda d\sqrt{d}}{3K_3}\sqrt{\frac{g-u}{\beta}}e^{-\lambda\sqrt{d}\sqrt{\frac{g-u}{\beta}}}$$
$$-\frac{5\lambda^2d^2}{12K_3}\frac{g-u}{\beta}e^{-\lambda\sqrt{d}\sqrt{\frac{g-u}{\beta}}}-\frac{3\lambda^3d^2\sqrt{d}}{20K_3}\sqrt{\frac{g-u}{\beta}}\frac{g-u}{\beta}e^{-\lambda\sqrt{d}\sqrt{\frac{g-u}{\beta}}}$$

$$-\frac{7\lambda^4 d^3}{720K_3}\left(\frac{g-u}{\beta}\right)^2 e^{-\lambda\sqrt{d}\sqrt{\frac{g-u}{\beta}}} - \frac{\lambda^5 d^3\sqrt{d}}{1800K_3}\sqrt{\frac{g-u}{\beta}}\left(\frac{g-u}{\beta}\right)^2 e^{-\lambda\sqrt{d}\sqrt{\frac{g-u}{\beta}}}$$

$$-\frac{\lambda bce^{-\lambda b}}{K_3} - \frac{\lambda^2 b^2 ce^{-\lambda b}}{2K_3} - \frac{\lambda^3 b^3 ce^{-\lambda b}}{6K_3} - \frac{7\lambda^4 b^4 ce^{-\lambda b}}{720K_3} - \frac{\lambda^5 b^5 ce^{-\lambda b}}{1800K_3}$$

$$+\frac{\lambda ace^{-\lambda a}}{K_3} + \frac{\lambda^2 a^2 ce^{-\lambda a}}{2K_3} + \frac{\lambda^3 a^3 ce^{-\lambda a}}{6K_3} + \frac{7\lambda^4 a^4 ce^{-\lambda a}}{720K_3} + \frac{\lambda^5 a^5 ce^{-\lambda a}}{1800K_3}$$

$$+\frac{\lambda bde^{-\lambda b}}{K_3} + \frac{\lambda^2 b^2 de^{-\lambda b}}{2K_3} + \frac{\lambda^3 b^3 de^{-\lambda b}}{6K_3} + \frac{7\lambda^4 b^4 de^{-\lambda b}}{720K_3} + \frac{\lambda^5 b^5 de^{-\lambda b}}{1800K_3}\Big\} I_{(g-\frac{\beta b^2}{d}, g-\frac{\beta a^2}{d})}(u)$$

$$+\Big\{\frac{1}{(e^{-\lambda a}-e^{-\lambda b})(h-g)}\Big(\lambda be^{-\lambda b} - \lambda ae^{-\lambda a} + \frac{\lambda^2 b^2 e^{-\lambda b}}{2} - \frac{\lambda^2 a^2 e^{-\lambda a}}{2} + \frac{\lambda^3 b^3 e^{-\lambda b}}{6} - \frac{\lambda^3 a^3 e^{-\lambda a}}{6}$$

$$+\frac{\lambda^4 b^4 e^{-\lambda b}}{720} - \frac{\lambda^4 a^4 e^{-\lambda a}}{720} + \frac{\lambda^5 b^5 e^{-\lambda b}}{1800} - \frac{\lambda^5 a^5 e^{-\lambda a}}{1800}\Big)\Big\} I_{(g-\frac{\beta a^2}{d}, h-\frac{\beta b^2}{c})}(u)$$

$$+\Big\{-\frac{\lambda be^{-\lambda b}(20b^2+5b^3\lambda+b^4\lambda^2)}{60K_3}\frac{\beta}{h-u} - \frac{2\lambda c\sqrt{c}}{3K_3}\sqrt{\frac{h-u}{\beta}}e^{-\lambda\sqrt{c}\sqrt{\frac{h-u}{\beta}}}$$

$$-\frac{5a^2c^2}{12K_3}\frac{h-u}{\beta}e^{-\lambda\sqrt{c}\sqrt{\frac{h-u}{\beta}}} - \frac{3\lambda^3 d^2\sqrt{c}}{20K_3}\sqrt{\frac{h-u}{\beta}}\frac{h-u}{\beta}e^{-\lambda\sqrt{c}\sqrt{\frac{h-u}{\beta}}}$$

$$-\frac{7a^4c^3}{720K_3}\left(\frac{h-u}{\beta}\right)^2 e^{-\lambda\sqrt{c}\sqrt{\frac{h-u}{\beta}}} - \frac{\lambda^5 c^3\sqrt{c}}{1800K_3}\sqrt{\frac{h-u}{\beta}}\left(\frac{h-u}{\beta}\right)^2 e^{-\lambda\sqrt{c}\sqrt{\frac{h-u}{\beta}}}$$

$$-\frac{\lambda ade^{-\lambda a}}{K_3} - \frac{\lambda^2 a^2 de^{-\lambda a}}{2K_3} - \frac{\lambda^3 a^3 de^{-\lambda a}}{6K_3} - \frac{7\lambda^4 a^4 de^{-\lambda a}}{720K_3} - \frac{\lambda^5 a^5 de^{-\lambda a}}{1800K_3}$$

$$+\frac{\lambda ace^{-\lambda a}}{K_3} + \frac{\lambda^2 a^2 ce^{-\lambda a}}{2K_3} + \frac{\lambda^3 a^3 ce^{-\lambda a}}{6K_3} + \frac{7\lambda^4 a^4 ce^{-\lambda a}}{720K_3} + \frac{\lambda^5 a^5 ce^{-\lambda a}}{1800K_3}$$

$$+\frac{\lambda bde^{-\lambda b}}{K_3} + \frac{\lambda^2 b^2 de^{-\lambda b}}{2K_3} + \frac{\lambda^3 b^3 de^{-\lambda b}}{6K_3} + \frac{7\lambda^4 b^4 de^{-\lambda b}}{720K_3} + \frac{\lambda^5 b^5 de^{-\lambda b}}{1800K_3}\Big\} I_{(h-\frac{\beta b^2}{c}, h-\frac{\beta a^2}{c})}(u)$$

$$+\Big\{\frac{\lambda ae^{-\lambda a}(20a^2+5a^3\lambda+a^4\lambda^2) - \lambda be^{-\lambda b}(20b^2+5b^3\lambda+b^4\lambda^2)}{60K_3}\frac{\beta}{h-u}$$

$$-\frac{\lambda ade^{-\lambda a}}{K_3} - \frac{\lambda^2 a^2 de^{-\lambda a}}{2K_3} - \frac{\lambda^3 a^3 de^{-\lambda a}}{6K_3} - \frac{7\lambda^4 a^4 de^{-\lambda a}}{720K_3} - \frac{\lambda^5 a^5 de^{-\lambda a}}{1800K_3}$$

$$+\frac{\lambda bde^{-\lambda b}}{K_3} + \frac{\lambda^2 b^2 de^{-\lambda b}}{2K_3} + \frac{\lambda^3 b^3 de^{-\lambda b}}{6K_3} + \frac{7\lambda^4 b^4 de^{-\lambda b}}{720K_3} + \frac{\lambda^5 b^5 de^{-\lambda b}}{1800K_3}\Big\} I_{(h-\frac{\beta a^2}{c}, h-\frac{\beta b^2}{d})}(u)$$

$$+\Big\{\frac{\lambda ae^{-\lambda a}(20a^2+5a^3\lambda+a^4\lambda^2)}{60K_3}\frac{\beta}{h-u} + \frac{2\lambda d\sqrt{d}}{3K_3}\sqrt{\frac{h-u}{\beta}}e^{-\lambda\sqrt{d}\sqrt{\frac{h-u}{\beta}}}$$

$$+\frac{5\lambda^2 d^2}{12K_3}\frac{h-u}{\beta}e^{-\lambda\sqrt{d}\sqrt{\frac{h-u}{\beta}}} + \frac{3\lambda^3 d^2\sqrt{d}}{20K_3}\sqrt{\frac{h-u}{\beta}}\frac{h-u}{\beta}e^{-\lambda\sqrt{d}\sqrt{\frac{h-u}{\beta}}}$$

$$+\frac{7\lambda^4 d^3}{720K_3}\left(\frac{h-u}{\beta}\right)^2 e^{-\lambda\sqrt{d}\sqrt{\frac{h-u}{\beta}}} + \frac{\lambda^5 d^3\sqrt{d}}{1800K_3}\sqrt{\frac{h-u}{\beta}}\left(\frac{h-u}{\beta}\right)^2 e^{-\lambda\sqrt{d}\sqrt{\frac{h-u}{\beta}}}$$

$$-\frac{\lambda ade^{-\lambda a}}{K_3} - \frac{\lambda^2 a^2 de^{-\lambda a}}{2K_3} - \frac{\lambda^3 a^3 de^{-\lambda a}}{6K_3} - \frac{7\lambda^4 a^4 de^{-\lambda a}}{720K_3} - \frac{\lambda^5 a^5 de^{-\lambda a}}{1800K_3}\Big\} I_{(h-\frac{\beta b^2}{d}, h-\frac{\beta a^2}{d})}(u)$$

- CASE II ($\frac{a^2}{c} < \frac{b^2}{d}$)

$$f_u(u) = \Big\{\frac{\lambda be^{-\lambda b}(20b^2+5b^3\lambda+b^4\lambda^2)}{60K_3}\frac{\beta}{g-u} + \frac{2\lambda c\sqrt{c}}{3K_3}\sqrt{\frac{g-u}{\beta}}e^{-\lambda\sqrt{c}\sqrt{\frac{g-u}{\beta}}}$$

$$+\frac{5\lambda a^2c^2}{12K_3}\frac{g-u}{\beta}e^{-\lambda\sqrt{c}\sqrt{\frac{g-u}{\beta}}} + \frac{3\lambda a^3c^2\sqrt{c}}{20K_3}\sqrt{\frac{g-u}{\beta}}\frac{g-u}{\beta}e^{-\lambda\sqrt{c}\sqrt{\frac{g-u}{\beta}}}$$

$$+\frac{7\lambda a^4c^2}{720K_3}\left(\frac{g-u}{\beta}\right)^2 e^{-\lambda\sqrt{c}\sqrt{\frac{g-u}{\beta}}}+\frac{\lambda a^5c^3\sqrt{c}}{1800K_3}\sqrt{\frac{g-u}{\beta}}\left(\frac{g-u}{\beta}\right)^2 e^{-\lambda\sqrt{c}\sqrt{\frac{g-u}{\beta}}}$$

$$-\frac{\lambda bce^{-\lambda b}}{K_3}-\frac{\lambda^2b^2ce^{-\lambda b}}{2K_3}-\frac{\lambda^3b^3ce^{-\lambda b}}{6K_3}-\frac{7\lambda^4b^4ce^{-\lambda b}}{720K_3}-\frac{\lambda^5b^5ce^{-\lambda b}}{1800K_3}\Big\}I_{(g-\frac{\beta b^2}{c},g-\frac{\beta b^2}{d})}(u)$$

$$+\Big\{\frac{2\lambda c\sqrt{c}}{3K_3}\sqrt{\frac{g-u}{\beta}}e^{-\lambda\sqrt{c}\sqrt{\frac{g-u}{\beta}}}+\frac{5\lambda^2c^2}{12K_3}\frac{g-u}{\beta}e^{-\lambda\sqrt{c}\sqrt{\frac{g-u}{\beta}}}$$

$$+\frac{3\lambda^3c^2\sqrt{c}}{20K_3}\sqrt{\frac{g-u}{\beta}}\frac{g-u}{\beta}e^{-\lambda\sqrt{c}\sqrt{\frac{g-u}{\beta}}}+\frac{7\lambda^4c^3}{720K_3}\left(\frac{g-u}{\beta}\right)^2 e^{-\lambda\sqrt{c}\sqrt{\frac{g-u}{\beta}}}$$

$$+\frac{\lambda^5c^3\sqrt{c}}{1800K_3}\sqrt{\frac{g-u}{\beta}}\left(\frac{g-u}{\beta}\right)^2 e^{-\lambda\sqrt{c}\sqrt{\frac{g-u}{\beta}}}-\frac{2\lambda d\sqrt{d}}{3K_3}\sqrt{\frac{g-u}{\beta}}e^{-\lambda\sqrt{d}\sqrt{\frac{g-u}{\beta}}}$$

$$-\frac{5\lambda^2d^2}{12K_3}\frac{g-u}{\beta}e^{-\lambda\sqrt{d}\sqrt{\frac{g-u}{\beta}}}-\frac{3\lambda^3d^2\sqrt{d}}{20K_3}\sqrt{\frac{g-u}{\beta}}\frac{g-u}{\beta}e^{-\lambda\sqrt{d}\sqrt{\frac{g-u}{\beta}}}$$

$$-\frac{7\lambda^4d^3}{720K_3}\left(\frac{g-u}{\beta}\right)^2 e^{-\lambda\sqrt{d}\sqrt{\frac{g-u}{\beta}}}-\frac{\lambda^5d^3\sqrt{d}}{1800K_3}\sqrt{\frac{g-u}{\beta}}\left(\frac{g-u}{\beta}\right)^2 e^{-\lambda\sqrt{d}\sqrt{\frac{g-u}{\beta}}}$$

$$-\frac{\lambda bce^{-\lambda b}}{K_3}-\frac{\lambda^2b^2ce^{-\lambda b}}{2K_3}-\frac{\lambda^3b^3ce^{-\lambda b}}{6K_3}-\frac{7\lambda^4b^4ce^{-\lambda b}}{720K_3}-\frac{\lambda^5b^5ce^{-\lambda b}}{1800K_3}$$

$$+\frac{\lambda bde^{-\lambda b}}{K_3}+\frac{\lambda^2b^2de^{-\lambda b}}{2K_3}+\frac{\lambda^3b^3de^{-\lambda b}}{6K_3}+\frac{7\lambda^4b^4de^{-\lambda b}}{720K_3}+\frac{\lambda^5b^5de^{-\lambda b}}{1800K_3}\Big\}I_{(g-\frac{\beta b^2}{d},g-\frac{\beta a^2}{c})}(u)$$

$$+\Big\{-\frac{\lambda ae^{-\lambda a}(20a^2+5a^3\lambda+a^4\lambda^2)}{60K_3}\frac{\beta}{g-u}-\frac{2\lambda d\sqrt{d}}{3K_3}\sqrt{\frac{g-u}{\beta}}e^{-\lambda\sqrt{d}\sqrt{\frac{g-u}{\beta}}}$$

$$-\frac{5\lambda^2d^2}{12K_3}\frac{g-u}{\beta}e^{-\lambda\sqrt{d}\sqrt{\frac{g-u}{\beta}}}-\frac{3\lambda^3d^2\sqrt{d}}{20K_3}\sqrt{\frac{g-u}{\beta}}\frac{g-u}{\beta}e^{-\lambda\sqrt{d}\sqrt{\frac{g-u}{\beta}}}$$

$$-\frac{7\lambda^4d^3}{720K_3}\left(\frac{g-u}{\beta}\right)^2 e^{-\lambda\sqrt{d}\sqrt{\frac{g-u}{\beta}}}-\frac{\lambda^5d^3\sqrt{d}}{1800K_3}\sqrt{\frac{g-u}{\beta}}\left(\frac{g-u}{\beta}\right)^2 e^{-\lambda\sqrt{d}\sqrt{\frac{g-u}{\beta}}}$$

$$-\frac{\lambda bce^{-\lambda b}}{K_3}-\frac{\lambda^2b^2ce^{-\lambda b}}{2K_3}-\frac{\lambda^3b^3ce^{-\lambda b}}{6K_3}-\frac{7\lambda^4b^4ce^{-\lambda b}}{720K_3}-\frac{\lambda^5b^5ce^{-\lambda b}}{1800K_3}$$

$$+\frac{\lambda ace^{-\lambda a}}{K_3}+\frac{\lambda^2a^2ce^{-\lambda a}}{2K_3}+\frac{\lambda^3a^3ce^{-\lambda a}}{6K_3}+\frac{7\lambda^4a^4ce^{-\lambda a}}{720K_3}+\frac{\lambda^5a^5ce^{-\lambda a}}{1800K_3}$$

$$+\frac{\lambda bde^{-\lambda b}}{K_3}+\frac{\lambda^2b^2de^{-\lambda b}}{2K_3}+\frac{\lambda^3b^3de^{-\lambda b}}{6K_3}+\frac{7\lambda^4b^4de^{-\lambda b}}{720K_3}+\frac{\lambda^5b^5de^{-\lambda b}}{1800K_3}\Big\}I_{(g-\frac{\beta a^2}{c},g-\frac{\beta a^2}{d})}(u)$$

$$+\Big\{\frac{1}{(e^{-\lambda a}-e^{-\lambda b})(h-g)}\Big(\lambda be^{-\lambda b}-\lambda ae^{-\lambda a}+\frac{\lambda^2b^2e^{-\lambda b}}{2}-\frac{\lambda^2a^2e^{-\lambda a}}{2}+\frac{\lambda^3b^3e^{-\lambda b}}{6}-\frac{\lambda^3a^3e^{-\lambda a}}{6}$$

$$+\frac{\lambda^4b^4e^{-\lambda b}}{720}-\frac{\lambda^4a^4e^{-\lambda a}}{720}+\frac{\lambda^5b^5e^{-\lambda b}}{1800}-\frac{\lambda^5a^5e^{-\lambda a}}{1800}\Big)\Big\}I_{(g-\frac{\beta a^2}{d},h-\frac{\beta b^2}{c})}(u)$$

$$+\Big\{-\frac{\lambda be^{-\lambda b}(20b^2+5b^3\lambda+b^4\lambda^2)}{60K_3}\frac{\beta}{h-u}-\frac{2\lambda c\sqrt{c}}{3K_3}\sqrt{\frac{h-u}{\beta}}e^{-\lambda\sqrt{c}\sqrt{\frac{h-u}{\beta}}}$$

$$-\frac{5\lambda^2c^2}{12K_3}\frac{h-u}{\beta}e^{-\lambda\sqrt{c}\sqrt{\frac{h-u}{\beta}}}-\frac{3\lambda^3d^2\sqrt{c}}{20K_3}\sqrt{\frac{h-u}{\beta}}\frac{h-u}{\beta}e^{-\lambda\sqrt{c}\sqrt{\frac{h-u}{\beta}}}$$

$$-\frac{7\lambda^4c^3}{720K_3}\left(\frac{h-u}{\beta}\right)^2 e^{-\lambda\sqrt{c}\sqrt{\frac{h-u}{\beta}}}-\frac{\lambda^5c^3\sqrt{c}}{1800K_3}\sqrt{\frac{h-u}{\beta}}\left(\frac{h-u}{\beta}\right)^2 e^{-\lambda\sqrt{c}\sqrt{\frac{h-u}{\beta}}}$$

$$-\frac{\lambda ade^{-\lambda a}}{K_3}-\frac{\lambda^2a^2de^{-\lambda a}}{2K_3}-\frac{\lambda^3a^3de^{-\lambda a}}{6K_3}-\frac{7\lambda^4a^4de^{-\lambda a}}{720K_3}-\frac{\lambda^5a^5de^{-\lambda a}}{1800K_3}$$

$$+\frac{\lambda ace^{-\lambda a}}{K_3}+\frac{\lambda^2a^2ce^{-\lambda a}}{2K_3}+\frac{\lambda^3a^3ce^{-\lambda a}}{6K_3}+\frac{7\lambda^4a^4ce^{-\lambda a}}{720K_3}+\frac{\lambda^5a^5ce^{-\lambda a}}{1800K_3}$$

$$+\frac{\lambda bde^{-\lambda b}}{K_3}+\frac{\lambda^2b^2de^{-\lambda b}}{2K_3}+\frac{\lambda^3b^3de^{-\lambda b}}{6K_3}+\frac{7\lambda^4b^4de^{-\lambda b}}{720K_3}+\frac{\lambda^5b^5de^{-\lambda b}}{1800K_3}\}I_{(h-\frac{\beta b^2}{c},h-\frac{\beta b^2}{d})}(u)$$

$$+\{\frac{2\lambda d\sqrt{d}}{3K_3}\sqrt{\frac{h-u}{\beta}}e^{-\lambda\sqrt{d}\sqrt{\frac{h-u}{\beta}}}+\frac{5\lambda^2d^2}{12K_3}\frac{h-u}{\beta}e^{-\lambda\sqrt{d}\sqrt{\frac{h-u}{\beta}}}$$

$$+\frac{3\lambda^3d^2\sqrt{d}}{20K_3}\sqrt{\frac{h-u}{\beta}}\frac{h-u}{\beta}e^{-\lambda\sqrt{d}\sqrt{\frac{h-u}{\beta}}}+\frac{7\lambda^4d^3}{720K_3}(\frac{h-u}{\beta})^2e^{-\lambda\sqrt{d}\sqrt{\frac{h-u}{\beta}}}$$

$$+\frac{\lambda^5d^3\sqrt{d}}{1800K_3}\sqrt{\frac{h-u}{\beta}}(\frac{h-u}{\beta})^2e^{-\lambda\sqrt{d}\sqrt{\frac{h-u}{\beta}}}-\frac{2\sqrt{c}}{3K_3}\sqrt{\frac{h-u}{\beta}}e^{-\lambda\sqrt{c}\sqrt{\frac{h-u}{\beta}}}$$

$$-\frac{5\lambda^2c^2}{12K_3}\frac{h-u}{\beta}e^{-\lambda\sqrt{c}\sqrt{\frac{h-u}{\beta}}}-\frac{3\lambda^3d^2\sqrt{c}}{20K_3}\sqrt{\frac{h-u}{\beta}}\frac{h-u}{\beta}e^{-\lambda\sqrt{c}\sqrt{\frac{h-u}{\beta}}}$$

$$-\frac{7\lambda^4c^3}{720K_3}(\frac{h-u}{\beta})^2e^{-\lambda\sqrt{c}\sqrt{\frac{h-u}{\beta}}}-\frac{\lambda^5c^3\sqrt{c}}{1800K_3}\sqrt{\frac{h-u}{\beta}}(\frac{h-u}{\beta})^2e^{-\lambda\sqrt{c}\sqrt{\frac{h-u}{\beta}}}$$

$$-\frac{\lambda ade^{-\lambda a}}{K_3}-\frac{\lambda^2a^2de^{-\lambda a}}{2K_3}-\frac{\lambda^3a^3de^{-\lambda a}}{6K_3}-\frac{7\lambda^4a^4de^{-\lambda a}}{720K_3}-\frac{\lambda^5a^5de^{-\lambda a}}{1800K_3}$$

$$+\frac{\lambda ace^{-\lambda a}}{K_3}+\frac{\lambda^2a^2ce^{-\lambda a}}{2K_3}+\frac{\lambda^3a^3ce^{-\lambda a}}{6K_3}+\frac{7\lambda^4a^4ce^{-\lambda a}}{720K_3}+\frac{\lambda^5a^5ce^{-\lambda a}}{1800K_3}\}I_{(h-\frac{\beta b^2}{d},h-\frac{\beta a^2}{c})}(u)$$

$$+\{\frac{\lambda ace^{-\lambda a}(20a^2+5a^3\lambda+a^4\lambda^2)}{60K_3}\frac{\beta}{h-u}+\frac{2\lambda d\sqrt{d}}{3K_3}\sqrt{\frac{h-u}{\beta}}e^{-\lambda\sqrt{d}\sqrt{\frac{h-u}{\beta}}}$$

$$+\frac{5\lambda^2d^2}{12K_3}\frac{h-u}{\beta}e^{-\lambda\sqrt{d}\sqrt{\frac{h-u}{\beta}}}+\frac{3\lambda^3d^2\sqrt{d}}{20K_3}\sqrt{\frac{h-u}{\beta}}\frac{h-u}{\beta}e^{-\lambda\sqrt{d}\sqrt{\frac{h-u}{\beta}}}$$

$$+\frac{7\lambda^4d^3}{720K_3}(\frac{h-u}{\beta})^2e^{-\lambda\sqrt{d}\sqrt{\frac{h-u}{\beta}}}+\frac{\lambda^5d^3\sqrt{d}}{1800K_3}\sqrt{\frac{h-u}{\beta}}(\frac{h-u}{\beta})^2e^{-\lambda\sqrt{d}\sqrt{\frac{h-u}{\beta}}}$$

$$-\frac{\lambda ade^{-\lambda a}}{K_3}-\frac{\lambda^2a^2de^{-\lambda a}}{2K_3}-\frac{\lambda^3a^3de^{-\lambda a}}{6K_3}-\frac{7\lambda^4a^4de^{-\lambda a}}{720K_3}-\frac{\lambda^5a^5de^{-\lambda a}}{1800K_3}\}I_{(h-\frac{\beta a^2}{c},h-\frac{\beta a^2}{d})}(u)$$

All $f_U(u)$ derived so far have the following properties:

- $f_U(u) \geq 0$.
- Compute $\int_{-\infty}^{+\infty} f_U(u)du = 1$.
- $f_U(u)$ is piecewise continuous.
- For any interval (p,q) , $Pr(p \leq u \leq q) = \int_p^q f_U(u)du$.

## 3.3 Analysis of probability density functions in multi-pass cases

Each probability density function has a similar shape with others, but has a different slope. The probability of a surface roughness for the multi-pass cases is determined by the following procedures:

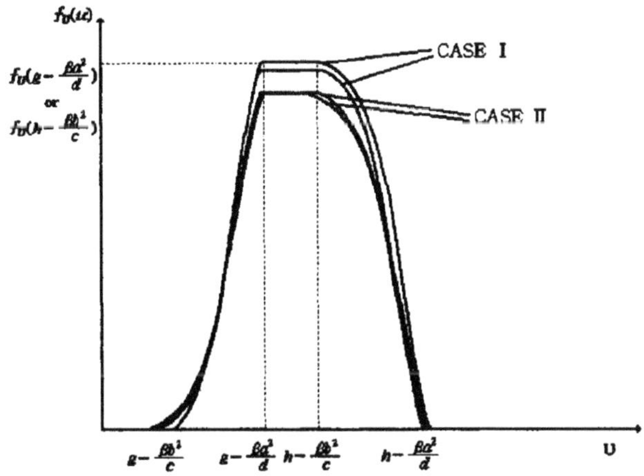


Figure 2: the shape of $f_U(u)$

- Define $V_w$ and $V_s$
- Define a, b, c, d, h, g, and $\lambda$
- Specify a surface roughness to be achieved: $p \leq u \leq q$
- Compute $\int_p^q f_U(u)du$

The detailed results can be summarized for multi-pass cases as follows:

1. If the distribution of $\{X|0 < a \leq x \leq b\}, \{Y|0 < c \leq y \leq d\}$, and $\{T|0 < g \leq t \leq h\}$is given, respectively, all the p.d.f $f_U(u)$ are similar shapes having a maximum probability value between $g - \frac{\beta a^2}{d}$ and $h - \frac{\beta b^2}{c}$ of U. Especially, the probability is constant in the middle stage of a curve when the roughness goes higher. This result can lead to set higher roughness values so that the grinding cost can be reduced.

2. As a reversed situation of 1., if $\Pr(p \leq u \leq q)$ is given, the corresponding surface roughness can be estimated in each case. Since the p.d.f $f_U(u)$ is a kind of parabolic curves, multiple roughness values are possible with an equal probability. The machining cost would be the most critical factor to select the appropriate surface roughness.

3. If a desired surface roughness along with the probability is given, some critical machining parameters such as $V_s$ and $V_w$ can be determined. Also, the

number of passes required to accomplish a given roughness can be derived as follows:

$$n < \frac{8 c g V_w^2}{b^2 V_w^2}$$

# 4 Measuring Distance and Wheel Radius

Both the distance between neighboring active grains and the wheel radius of a grinding wheel are the most critical characteristics used for estimating surface roughness in this study. The standard marking system[4] for abrasive wheels has either six or eight parameters dependent on wheel materials, for example, aluminum oxide and silicon carbide or diamond and CBN. Two parameters such as the abrasive grain size and concentration number(or structure) are directly related to this study. The grain size can be obtained by $d_g(mm) = 68M^{-1.4}$ where M is a value of the second parameter in the standard marking system. For the distance between adjacent active grains, the volumetric concentration of abrasive grain in the wheel can be determined first by $D_g(\%) = 2(32 - S)$ where S is a value of the fourth parameter(concentration number) in the marking system. Then, the distance between the active grains can be found by Equation (2).

$$\frac{\frac{\pi d_s}{\frac{\pi d_s D_g}{d_g}}} - d_g = \frac{d_g}{D_g} - d_g \qquad (2)$$

where $d_s$ is a wheel diameter.

# 5 Conclusion

The major focus of this study is the probabilistic estimation of surface roughness in the grinding operations when the characteristics of a grinding wheel are specified. The characteristics of the wheel are simplified to two factors: the distance between neighboring active grains and the wheel radius. Although the two characteristics are represented by statistical distributions, other important features of grinding such as vibration, thermal effect, friction, wheel dressing, etc. can be added to the current model for developing more realistic models. The authors have started working on this extension. Either mathematical or probabilistic representations is helpful to develop better grinding conditions, to forecast surface roughness, to minimize manufacturing cost and to be competitive in product quality.

# 6 Acknowledgement

The authors thanks to the Korea Science and Engineering Foundation for its financial support to this research. Research number is 961–1012–089–1

# 7 Biography

Hoo-Gon Choi is a professor in the Department of Industrial Engineering at Sung Kyun Kwan University in S. Korea. He received BS and MS degrees from Seoul National University, and MS and PhD degrees from Iowa State University. His research interests and publications are in CAPP and CIMS. He is a senior member of AIIE and SME.

Myung-Koo Yeo is a doctoral student in the Department of Industrial Engineering at Sung Kyun Kwan University in S. Korea. He received his BS and MS degrees from Sung Kyun Kwan University. His research interests are in Machining and CAPP.

Jae-Yoon Kim is a graduate student in the Department of Industrial Engineering at Sung Kyun Kwan University in S. Korea. He received his BS degree from Sung Kyun Kwan University. His research interests are in Machining and CAPP.

# References

[1] Boothroyd, G., (1975)*Fundamentals of Metal Machining and Machine Tools*, Scripta Book Company, Chap. 1, 5, 10.

[2] Kannappan, S., and Malkin, S., (1972) "Effects of Grain Size and Operating Parameters on the Mechanics of Grinding", *Journal of Engineering for Industry*, pp. 833–842.

[3] Law, S.S., Wu, S.M., and Joglekar, A.M., (1973) "On Building Models for the Grinding Process", *Journal of Engineering for Industry*, pp. 983–991.

[4] Malkin, S., (1989) *GRINDING TECHNOLOGY - Theory and Applications of Machining with Abrasives*. Ellis Horwood Ltd, Chap. 1, 2, 3, 4, 7.

[5] Peters, J., Inasaki, I., Paul, T., and Tonshoff, H.K., ( 1992 ) "Modeling and Simulation of Grinding Processes", *Annals of the CIRP*, VOL. 41, NO. 2, pp. 677–688.

[6] Xiao, G., Malkin, S., and Danai, K., ( 1992 ) "Intelligent Control of Cylindrical Plunge Grinding",*Proc. of 1992 American Control Conference*, pp. 391–398.

17

# SIMULATION STUDY OF THE PROCESS PARAMETERS OF A NEW PRECISION GRINDING METHOD

*Y. Wang, K. S. Moon and M. H. Miller*
*Department of Mechanical Engineering and Engineering Mechanics*
*Michigan Technological University*
*Houghton, MI 49931, U.S.A.*

**Abstract**

A new method for precision surface grinding which is termed "workpiece modulation" is studied in this paper. Simulations and experiments have shown that workpiece modulation improves ground surface quality. Simulations show that surface texture as quantified by 2D power spectrum for a single pass with modulation is similar to surface texture from a multiple pass grinding operation without modulation. The effect of process parameters of this new process is analyzed by factorially designed simulations. General rules for selecting grinding process parameters for this new method are given based on the simulation.

**Keywords**

Grinding, Simulation, Surface Texture.

## 1 INTRODUCTION

Grinding process is the common collective name for machining processes which utilize hard abrasive particles as the cutting medium. According to (Malkin, 1989), grinding is a major manufacturing process which accounts for about 20-25% of the total expenditures on machining operations in industrialized countries. The development of diamond and cubic boron nitride superabrasives, powerful machinery and machining technology has led to a considerably more efficient grinding process. Ground surface quality generally consists of two aspects: surface integrity and surface texture (Malkin, 1989). Surface integrity is associated with mechanical and metallurgical properties of the workpiece and is generally associated with the thermal damage caused by the excessive grinding temperature. Surface texture usually refers to the topography of machined surfaces. The fine-scale topography of ground surfaces shows overlapping cutting scratches in the direction of relative motion between the wheel and workpiece. There are also scallops in the workpiece feed direction which results from runout(Fig.1). Simulations and experiments have demonstrated that in surface grinding the roughness in the cross feed direction is larger than in the feed direction (Domala, 1995). Surface finish has an important role in the wear, lubricating and optical properties of products. Further improvement of the ground surface quality can be done by some non-conventional processes such as electro-polishing and finishing operations such as lapping and polishing; however, this usually involves high cost for the additional machinery and process.

Computer Applications in Production and Engineering. F. Plonka and G. Olling (Eds.)

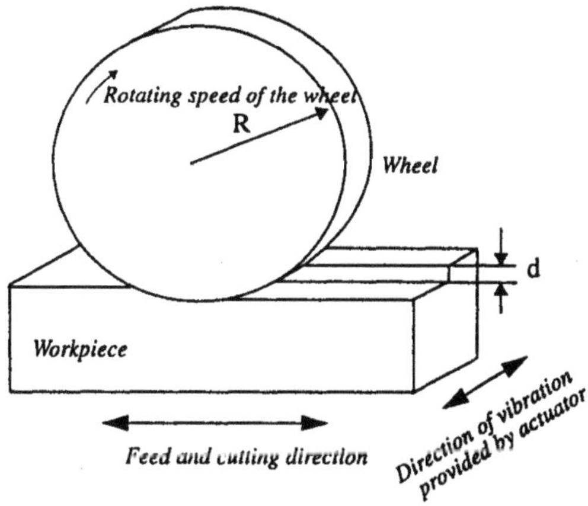


**Figure 1** Surface generation in a surface grinding process.

A new method (workpiece modulation) for improving the precision surface grinding quality was proposed recently (Wang, 1996). This method uses high-frequency vibratory movement of the workpiece in its cross feed direction can reduce the surface roughness in this direction and therefore the overall surface roughness. A micro-actuator based workpiece modulation system was implemented on a conventional surface grinding machine (Fig.2). Experimental results show that it offers an effective means of improving the quality of the ground surface texture.

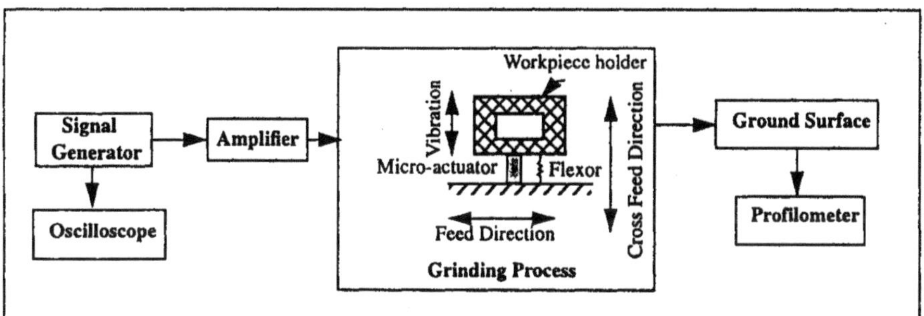


**Figure 2** System of workpiece modulation in precision grinding with workpiece actuator.

This paper studies the effect of workpiece modulation on the ground surface quality. The grinding process parameters which are workpiece feed, wheel speed, workpiece modulation frequency and workpiece modulation amplitude are studied by factorial designed experiments through a three dimensional simulation of the grinding process.

## 2. Simulation of the workpiece modulation in surface grinding process

The simulation method in this paper is illustrated in Figure 3. A three dimensional grinding simulation procedure was developed. The output simulation results are 3-D simulated ground surface data. During simulation, each grit on the wheel surface is checked for interference with the workpiece surface. If intereference occurs, the workpiece surface is modified accordingly and the chip thickness, cross sectional area and volume are recorded. At the end of the simulation, the parameters of the average chip geometry and its distribution can be obtained.

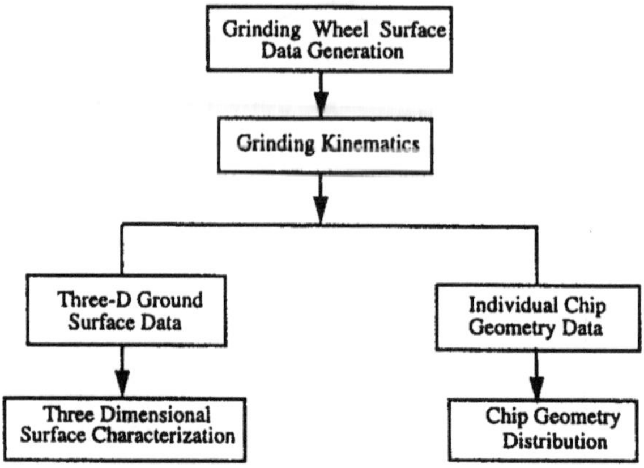


**Figure 3** Three dimensional simulation of grinding process

### 3. Simulated ground surface characterization

Simulations were conducted with and without workpiece modulation. The simulated ground surface data are analyzed by 2-D Fourier transformation. The simulated ground surface height data are denoted as $S(x,y)$, and the 2-D FFT can be done by:

$$F(\omega_p, \omega_q) = \frac{1}{MN} \sum_{y=1}^{N} \sum_{x=1}^{M} S(x, y) \cdot e^{-j2\pi\left(\frac{p}{M}x + \frac{q}{N}y\right)} \tag{1}$$

where: $p=0, 1,...M-1;\ q=0,1,...N-1;$ are the array coordinates of the surface heights. Correspondingly, $F(\omega_p, \omega_q)$ is a matrix of Fourier coefficients, $\omega_p$ and $\omega_q$ are the angular frequencies in the two orthogonal directions. The power spectrum density or the power associated with each frequency, $P(\omega_p, \omega_q)$ can be obtained by:

$$P(\omega_p, \omega_q) = F(\omega_p, \omega_q) \cdot F^*(\omega_p, \omega_q) \tag{2}$$

where $F^*$ is the complex conjugate of $F$. The magnitude of the power will determine the extent of significance of a certain frequency and hence can be used as a measure of relative importance. As reported by Domala et al (Domala, 1995), the spatial dynamics of the wheel and workpiece surfaces are related. Due to the kinematics of the straight surface grinding process (one-dimensional motion in the feed direction), the spectrum of the wheel surface is transformed into a distribution along a line perpendicular to the feed direction on the workpiece spectrum pattern. Further analysis indicates that additional grinding passes cause the power of the ground surfaces to decrease implying that the surface is getting smoother as would be expected.

Figures 4 and 5 show the power spectrum of simulated ground surfaces after a single pass without and with workpiece modulation in the cross direction. It can be seen clearly that introducing workpiece modulation lowers the power spectrum; therefore the ground surfaces are smoother with workpiece modulation than without. In other words, introducing workpiece modulation is similar in benefit as performing multiple-passes. Therefore, this new method has the potential to significantly improve the grinding efficiency.

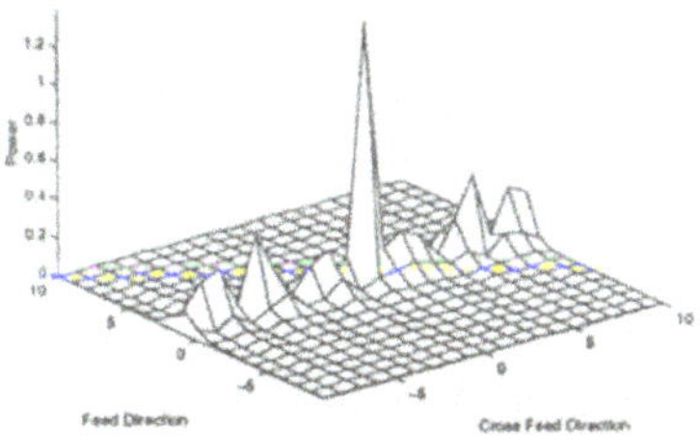


**Figure 4** Power spectrum of a ground surface in a single pass without actuation

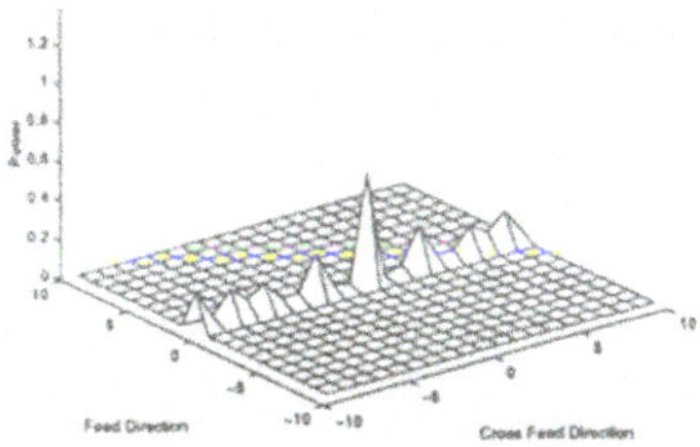


**Figure 5** Power spectrum of a ground surface in a single pass with actuation

Generally speaking, surfaces can be classified into homogeneous and inhomogeneous surfaces. The statistical properties of surface texture are invariant with respect to translation of area of examination for homogeneous surfaces. Homogeneous surfaces can be divided into deterministic and random surfaces. The texture of a deterministic surface has strong properties. Current surface evaluation practice is often based on the assumption that a surface in question is homogeneous and deterministic (Chao, 1995).

Based on an understanding of the intrinsic properties of surface topographic features and parameters, a primary three dimensional parameter set was proposed (Dong, 1994). Some of the parameters included in the primary parameter set are extended from their 2-D counterparts; others are specifically defined for characterizing 3-D surface topography. In this paper, we use the following three dimensional parameters similar to those introduced in (Chao, 1995 and Dong, 1994) to characterize the ground surfaces:

*Average Surface Height:*

$$S_a = \frac{1}{l_x l_y}\int_0^{l_x}\int_0^{l_y} (|S(x,y)|dxdy) = \frac{1}{MN}\sum_{j=1}^{N}\sum_{i=1}^{M}|S(x_i, y_j)| \tag{3}$$

where $l_x$ and $l_y$ are the side lengths of the sampling surface area of concern, $S(x_i,y_j)$ is the surface height data after substraction of the reference plane (usually a least square plane). This is a parameter similar to the 2-D arithmetic deviation parameter.

*Root Mean Square Deviation of Surface Topography:*

$$S_q = \sqrt{\frac{1}{l_x l_y}\int_0^{l_x}\int_0^{l_y} S^2(x,y)\,dxdy} = \sqrt{\frac{1}{MN}\sum_{j=1}^{N}\sum_{i=1}^{M} S^2(x_i, y_j)} \tag{4}$$

RMS deviation has a definite meaning in statistics, i.e. sample standard deviation, which can also be derived from the autocorrelation function.

*Skewness of Topography Height Distribution:*

$$S_{sk} = \frac{1}{S_q^3}\int_{-\infty}^{\infty}\int_{-\infty}^{\infty} S^3(x,y)\,p(\eta)\,dxdy \approx \frac{1}{MNS_q^3}\sum_{j=1}^{N}\sum_{i=1}^{M} S^3(x_i, y_j) \tag{5}$$

where $p(\eta)$ is the probability density function of the surface $S(x,y)$. Skewness can be used to describe certain aspects of the shape of a topographic height distribution. For a surface which has a symmetric distribution, the skewness is zero. For an asymmetric distribution of topography heights, the skewness is negative if the distribution has a longer tail at the lower side of the mean plane or positive if the distribution has a longer tail at the upper side of the plane.

*Kurtosis of Topography Height Distribution:*

$$S_{ku} = \frac{1}{S_q^4}\int_{-\infty}^{\infty}\int_{-\infty}^{\infty} S^4(x, y)\, p(\eta)\, dxdy = \frac{1}{MNS_q^4}\sum_{j=1}^{N}\sum_{i=1}^{M} S(x_i, y_j) \tag{6}$$

Kurtosis is always presented in conjunction with the skewness to describe the shape of the topography height distribution. It is a measure of the sharpness of the topography height distribution. A Gaussian surface has a kurtosis value of 3. A narrowly distributed topography height distribution has a kurtosis value larger than 3 whereas the kurtosis of a broad height distribution is smaller than 3.

The simulated ground surfaces with and without workpiece modulation are analyzed using the above four three dimensional surface characterization parameters. The results are documented in Table 1. It can be seen clearly that vibratory modulation reduces the three dimensional surface roughness both in terms of average surface height and RMS value. The skewness and kurtosis data indicate that the ground surfaces generated with modulation have some sharp peaks above the reference plane and this result needs to be investigated further.

| Grinding Method | $S_a$ | $S_q$ | $S_{sk}$ | $S_{ku}$ |
|---|---|---|---|---|
| Without Workpiece Modulation | 2.0 | 2.5 | 1.08 | 3.61 |
| With Workpiece Modulation | 1.1 | 1.4 | 1.34 | 4.26 |

**Table 1.** Ground surface characterization parameters (µm)

**4. Chip thickness distribution of the grinding process**

Almost all of the existing grinding chip thickness models are derived in an average sense. The random spacing and irregular shape of grinding grits makes an analytical derivation for chip thickness difficult. These models do not give a distribution of chip thickness and they cannot predict the effect of workpiece modulation on chip thickness; simulation was therefore used. The individual chip thickness is simply calculated by subtracts the current surface height from the previous one at the individual points where cutting happens.

Figures 6 and 7 show the chip size distribution with and without modulation. The distributions are similar although the number of the "small thickness" chips is slightly bigger for workpiece modulation than without. The effect of the process parameters on the average chip thickness will be discussed in the next section.

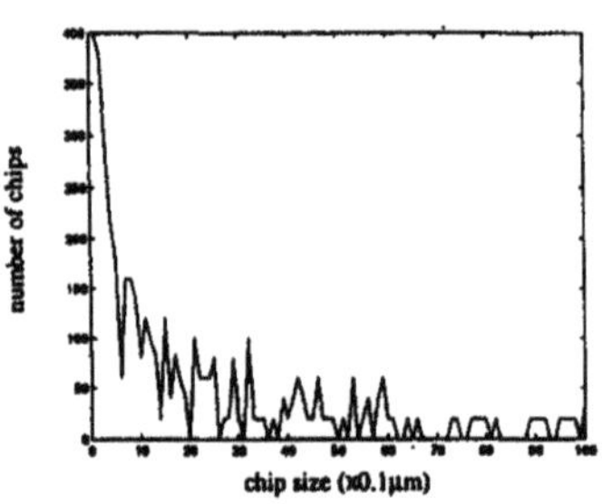


**Figure 6** Chip thickness distribution without workpiece actuation

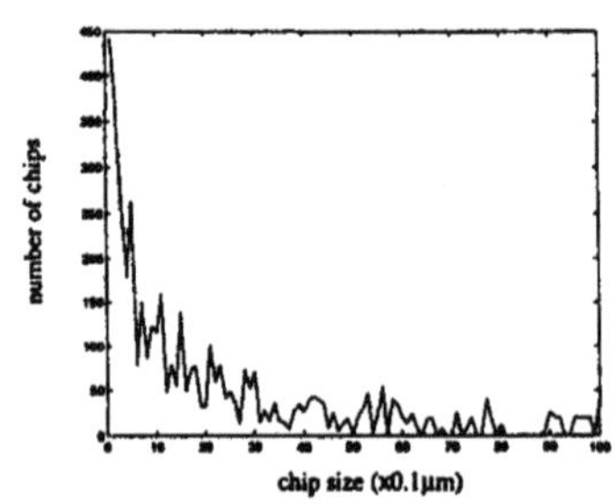


**Figure 7** Chip thickness distribution with workpiece actuation

**5. Study of the process parameters by factorially designed experiments**

The experimental design is focused on evaluating the influence of process parameters on surface roughness and chip size.

Four process parameters workpiece feed (factor *A*), wheel speed (factor *B*), workpiece modulation frequency (factor *C*) and workpiece modulation amplitude (factor *D*) were simulated in a $2^k$ factorial design experiment. Sixteen different combinations of the levels of the four process parameters are designed. With the help of normal probability plots, the significant effect of the parameters can be identified. The significant effect of the parameters can also be identified through the analysis of variance (ANOVA) by using Yates' algorithm (Montgometry, 1991).

*Surface Roughness:*

The normal probability plot of the residuals of the RMS values of the simulated ground surfaces for different combinations of the grinding parameters is plotted in figure 8. All of the effects that lie along the line are negligible, whereas the large effects are far from the line. The important effects that emerge from this analysis are the main effects *A, B, C* and the *AB* interaction. The ANOVA table of this analysis is shown in table 2. At the 0.05 level (which is the 95% confidence level), the *A, B, C* and *AB* have significant effect which agrees with the normal probability plot analysis. The surface roughness increases with an increase in workpiece feed or decrease in wheel speed. Therefore, a favorable approach to increasing production levels while maintaining the required surface finish would be to increase both the workpiece feed and the wheel speed. The frequency of the workpiece modulation frequency (factor *C*) has significant effect on the surface roughness. The surface roughness decreases with increasing modulation frequency as more grits have the opportunity to impact the same portion of the workpiece. Vibratory movement of the workpiece also has the effect of destroying the scratches generated in previous revolutions. The modulation amplitude is found to be insignificant to the surface roughness in this simulation. The *AB* interaction effect is plotted in figure 9. It means that at high wheel speeds the surface roughness is less sensitive to changes in feed rate.

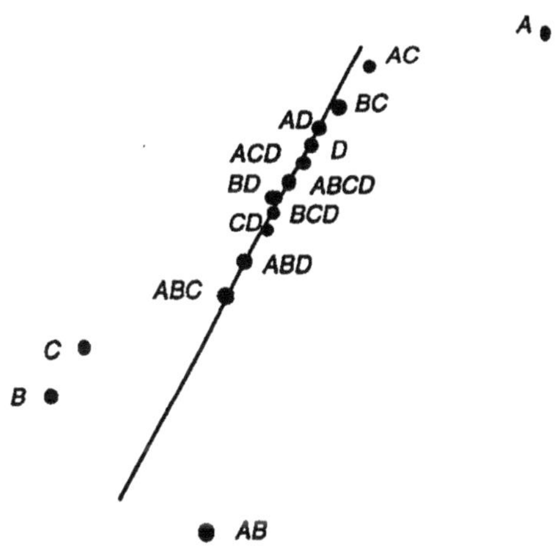


**Figure 8.** Normal probability plot of residuals for RMS surface roughness

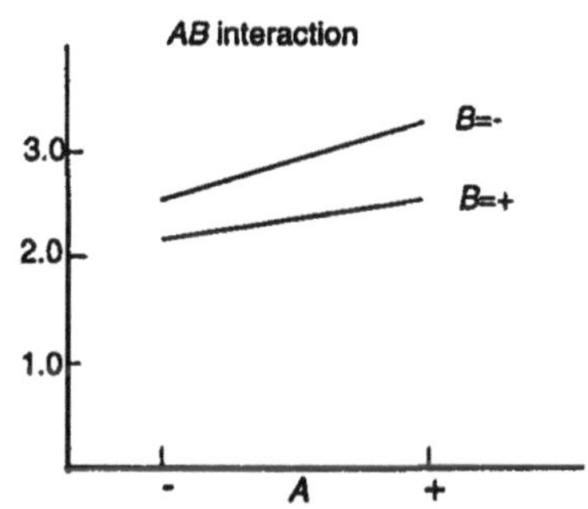


**Figure 9** Interaction effect of wheel speed and workpiece feed on surface roughness

| Source of Variation | Sum of Squares | Degrees of Freedom | Mean Square | $F_0$ |
|---|---|---|---|---|
| *A* | 2.4025 | 1 | 2.4025 | 40.72 (*) |
| *B* | 0.7225 | 1 | 0.7225 | 12.25 (*) |
| *C* | 0.6400 | 1 | 0.6400 | 10.84 (*) |
| *D* | 0.0025 | 1 | 0.0025 | 0.38 |
| *AB* | 1.4400 | 1 | 1.4400 | 24.40 (*) |
| *AC* | 0.2025 | 1 | 0.2025 | 3.43 |
| *AD* | 0.0400 | 1 | 0.0400 | 0.68 |
| *BC* | 0.0625 | 1 | 0.0625 | 1.06 |
| *BD* | 0.0100 | 1 | 0.0100 | 0.17 |
| *CD* | 0.0225 | 1 | 0.0225 | 0.38 |
| Error | 0.2950 | 5 | 0.0590 | |

**(*): Significant at 0.05 level.** $F_{0.05}(1, 5)=6.61$

**Table 2** ANOVA table for RMS surface roughness

| Source of Variation | Sum of Squares | Degrees of Freedom | Mean Square | $F_0$ |
|---|---|---|---|---|
| *A* | 0.4029 | 1 | 0.4029 | 149.22 (*) |
| *B* | 0.5948 | 1 | 0.5948 | 220.30 (*) |
| *C* | 0.0114 | 1 | 0.0114 | 4.22 |
| *D* | 0.0710 | 1 | 0.0710 | 26.30 (*) |
| *AB* | 0.0512 | 1 | 0.0512 | 18.96 (*) |
| *AC* | 0.0017 | 1 | 0.0017 | 0.63 |
| *AD* | 0.0086 | 1 | 0.0086 | 3.19 |
| *BC* | 0.0001 | 1 | 0.0001 | 0.04 |
| *BD* | 0.0223 | 1 | 0.0223 | 8.26 (*) |
| *CD* | 0.0015 | 1 | 0.0015 | 0.56 |
| Error | 0.0133 | 5 | 0.0027 | |

**(*): Significant at 0.05 level.** $F_{0.05}(1, 5)=6.61$

**Table 3** ANOVA table for the chip thickness

| Source of Variation | Sum of Squares | Degrees of Freedom | Mean Square | $F_0$ |
|---|---|---|---|---|
| *A* | 6.5850 | 1 | 6.5850 | 120.47 (*) |
| *B* | 8.1033 | 1 | 8.1033 | 142.51 (*) |
| *C* | 0.0888 | 1 | 0.0888 | 1.56 |
| *D* | 1.0784 | 1 | 1.0784 | 18.97 (*) |
| *AB* | 2.0675 | 1 | 2.0675 | 36.36 (*) |
| *AC* | 0.0319 | 1 | 0.0319 | 0.56 |
| *AD* | 0.3215 | 1 | 0.3215 | 5.65 |
| *BC* | 0.0074 | 1 | 0.0074 | 0.13 |
| *BD* | 0.6651 | 1 | 0.6651 | 11.7 (*) |
| *CD* | 0.0147 | 1 | 0.0147 | 0.26 |
| Error | 0.2843 | 5 | 0.0569 | |

(*): Significant at 0.05 level. $F_{0.05}(1, 5)$=6.61

**Table 4** ANOVA table for the chip area

| Source of Variation | Sum of Squares | Degrees of Freedom | Mean Square | $F_0$ |
|---|---|---|---|---|
| *A* | 1.9097 | 1 | 1.9097 | 289.35 (*) |
| *B* | 1.5029 | 1 | 1.5029 | 227.71 (*) |
| *C* | 0.0856 | 1 | 0.0856 | 12.97 (*) |
| *D* | 0.0376 | 1 | 0.0376 | 5.67 |
| *AB* | 0.2858 | 1 | 0.2858 | 43.30 (*) |
| *AC* | 0.0806 | 1 | 0.0806 | 12.21 (*) |
| *AD* | 0.0124 | 1 | 0.0124 | 1.88 |
| *BC* | 0.0114 | 1 | 0.0114 | 1.73 |
| *BD* | 0 | 1 | 0 | 0 |
| *CD* | 0.0041 | 1 | 0.0041 | 0.62 |
| Error | 0.0331 | 5 | 0.0067 | |

(*): Significant at 0.05 level. $F_{0.05}(1, 5)$=6.61

**Table 5** ANOVA table for the chip volume

*Chip Geometry*
In order to calculate the chip geometry in terms of chip thickness, chip area and chip volume, the grits of the wheel are assumed to be spherical and the procedure for calculating these parameters are given in (Miller, 1996). The ANOVA table for the chip geometry with the process parameters are shown in table 3 to table 5.

For the average chip thickness, the main factors that have significant effect are workpiece feed, wheel speed and modulation amplitude. The average chip thickness increases with increasing workpiece feed or decreasing wheel speed. The average chip thickness also increases with increasing modulation amplitude while the modulation frequency does not have a significant effect. The interaction between workpiece feed and wheel speed (*AB*) and between the wheel speed and modulation amplitude (*BD*) also have significant effect on chip thickness as shown in figure 10 and figure 11. The factors that affect the chip thickness have similar effect on the chip area, which can be seen from the ANOVA table 4.

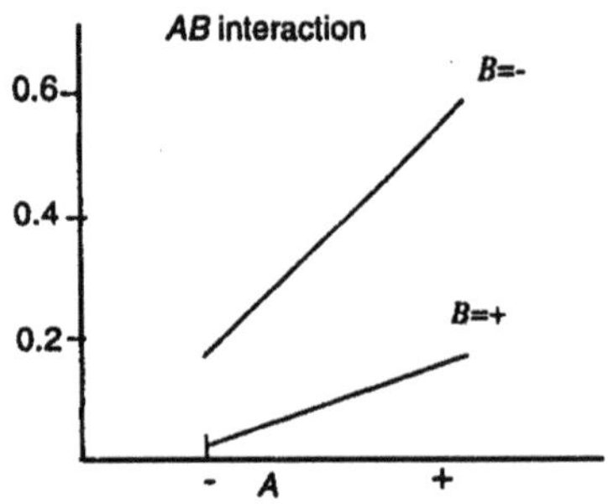


**Figure 10** Interaction effect of wheel speed and workpiece feed on chip thickness

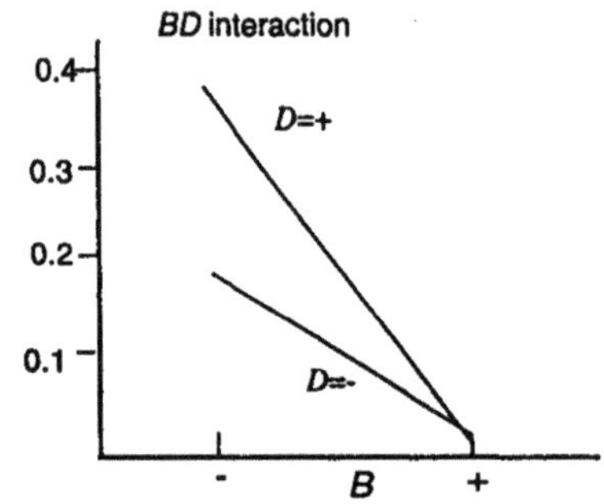


**Figure 11** Interaction effect of wheel speed and modulation amplitude on chip thickness

For the average chip volume, the main factors that have significant effect are workpiece feed, wheel speed and modulation frequency. The average chip volume increases with the increase of workpiece feed and decreases with the increase of wheel speed. An increase in modulation frequency generally decreases the average chip volume; however, there is a significant interaction effect between workpiece feed and modulation frequency (figure 12). The interaction between workpiece feed and wheel speed also has significant effect (figure 13).

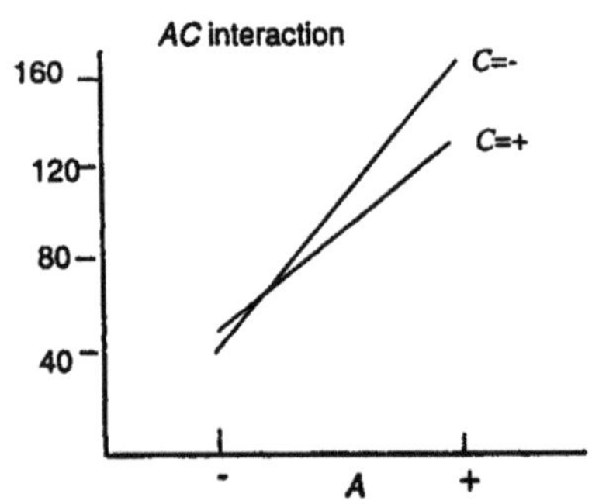


**Figure 12** Interaction effect of workpiece feed and modulation frequency on chip volume

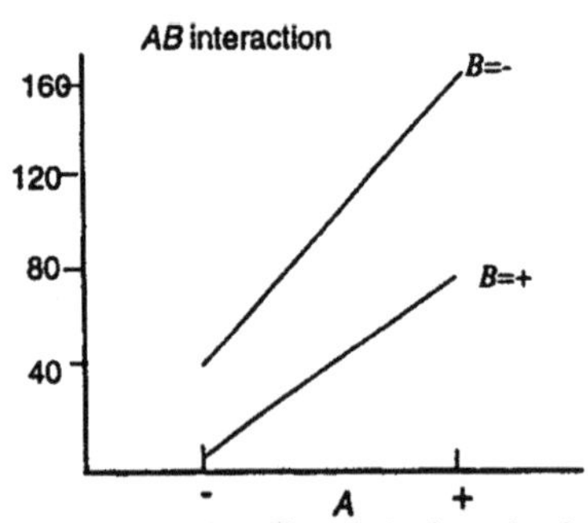


**Figure 13** Interaction effect of wheel speed and workpiece feed on chip volume

Based on the statistical analysis, we may conclude that a higher workpiece modulation frequency decreases surface roughness. Chip thickness and chip area do not change significantly with modulation frequency, but are impacted by a change of modulation amplitude. Therefore, for workpiece modulation in grinding, the favorable choice of the process parameters are: the wheel speed should be high, the workpiece feed should be slow, the modulation frequency should be high. The statistical analysis indicates that small vibration amplitude is favorable. However, a very small amplitude would be the same as grinding without modulation. Therefore, an optimum exists. Further analysis indicates that the optimum amplitude is approximately the grit radius (fig. 14).

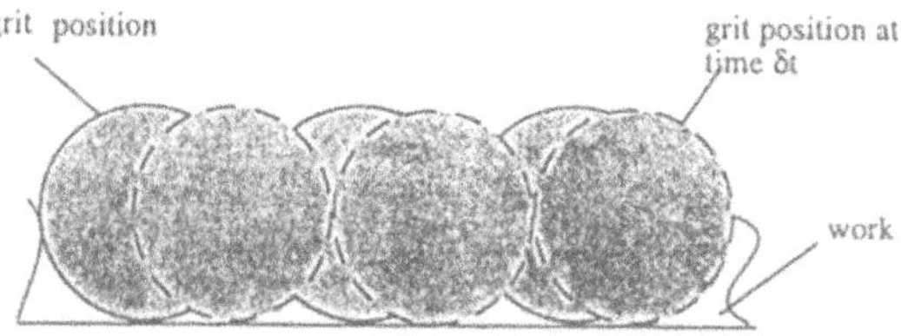


**Figure 14** Effect of modulation amplitude.

## 6. Conclusions

A new method for precision surface grinding which is termed "workpiece modulation" is analyzed in this paper. The grinding process is simulated in three dimensions.The simulated ground surface is analyzed using three-dimensional surface parameters. The results show that vibratory modulation in the workpiece cross feed direction can reduce the surface roughness. The grinding process parameters for this new method are analyzed by factorially designed simulations. The results show that for high quality surface grinding, a favorable way in choosing process parameters is: high wheel speed, low workpiece feed rate, high workpiece modulation frequency, the amplitude should be equal to the radius of the grit diameter of the wheel.

## 7. References

Chao, J., G. Zhou, M. C. Leu and E. Geskin. (1995). "*Characteristics of Abrasive Waterjet Generated Surfaces and Effects of Cutting Parameters and Structure Vibration.*" *Trans. of ASME, J. of Eng. for Ind.* Vol. 117. pp. 516-525.

Domala, K. V., K. S. Moon, E. J. Salisbury and J. W. Sutherland. (1995). "*A study of the Three-Dimensional Structure of a Ground Surface.*" *1st International Machining and Grinding Conference.* pp.847-863.

Dong, W. P., P. J. Sullivan and K. J. Stout. (1994). "*Comprehensive Study of Parameters for Characterizing three dimensional surface topography. III: Parameters for Characterizing Amplitude and Some Functional Properties.*" *Wear.* 178. pp. 29-43.

Hahn R. S. and R. P. Lindsay. (1969). "*The influence of Process Variables on Material Removal, Surface Finish and Vibration in Grinding.*" *Proc. of the 10th Int'l Mach. Tool Des. and Res. Conf.* pp. 677-681.

Malkin, S. (1989). *Grinding Technology: Theory and Application of Machining with Abrasives.* Ellis Horwood Limited.

Miller, M. H. and K. S. Moon (1996). "*The Effect of Workpiece Modulation on Grinding Kinematics.*" *Proceedings of the American Society for Precision Engineering,* Spring Topical Meeting.

Miller, M. H. (1994) *A Model for the Grinding of Brittle Materials.* Ph.D. Dissertation. North Carolina State University, Raleigh, NC.

Montgomery, D. C. (1991).*Design and Analysis of Experiments.* Third Edition. John Wiley & Sons, Inc.

Tonshoff, H. K., J. Peters, I. Inasaki and T. Paul. (1992). *Modelling and Simulation of Grinding Process.* Annals of the CIRP. Vol. 41/2. pp. 677-688.

Wang, Y. ,K. S. Moon and M. H. Miller. *(1996) Micro-actuation in Precision Grinding.* Proceeding of IMECE.

Yoshikawa, H. and T. Sata. (1968). *Simulated Grinding Process by Monte Carlo Method.* Annals of the CIRP. pp. 297-301.

Younis, M. A. and H. Alawi. (1984). *Probabilistic Analysis of the Surface Grinding Process.* Tans. of CSME. Vol. 8, No. 4, pp. 208-213.

# 18

# A computer model for tool management information system

*R. V. Narang*
*Manufacturing Technology, Indiana-Purdue University, Fort Wayne, USA*
*(219)481-6384,Fax:(219)481-5734*
*e-mail: narang@cvax.ipfw.indiana.edu*

**Abstract**

Tooling is an important and expensive part of any manufacturing enterprise. An application-based tool management system was developed for a machining company that had a total expenditure of over a million dollars per annum on tooling alone. The system was developed on a relational database system available on a PC network. All different types of tools, their cost, supplier location of the tooling, and other relevant information were built into the system for management to make the right decisions on tooling. The paper gives an overview of the tooling system and describes the individual modules and their interrelationships, including some of the important files. It also describes how the system helps the company controlling tool costs and inventory.

**Keywords**

Tooling management, automated manufacturing, data flow diagram, database, flexible manufacturing system, computer integrated manufacturing, management information system

## 1. INTRODUCTION

In a recent survey paper on tooling management, Gray *et al.* (1993) identified the lack of attention to tool management issues as the primary reason for the poor performance of

Computer Applications in Production and Engineering. F. Plonka and G. Olling (Eds.)

many manufacturing facilities. The management of the increased number of tool components and their application requirements has also hindered increases in productivity.

Implementation of an encompassing tool management system is one of the most essential aspects of an effective automated manufacturing system (AMS). As automated manufacturing systems, especially flexible manufacturing systems (FMS), have become more common, there is evidence that a lack of attention to structured tool management has resulted in an increase in machine downtime, leading to a decrease in productivity. Many companies today cannot achieve on-time delivery or operating efficiency, not because of the lack of materials, machines or labor, but because of not having the right tooling at the right time.

In addition to being an integral part of an automated manufacturing system, tool management also has direct cost implications. Industry data show that tooling could account for 25% to 30% of production costs in an automated manufacturing system (Chen *et al.*, 1993). Use of proper tool management methods in an AMS is thus critical in preventing losses due to operator error, overstocking and understocking of tooling, damaged tools, lost or misplaced tools, and poor quality parts. Indeed the growing recognition is that AMSs may operate with partial tool management, but the full potential of the new technology will not be realized without proper tool management.

The enthusiastic participation at the conferences on various issues of tool management demonstrates the pervasive interest among academia and practitioners. Because of the great interest directed toward tooling problems, papers addressing various issues of tool management have recently appeared in various journals including *International Journal of Production Research, International Journal of Flexible Manufacturing Systems, Journal of manufacturing Systems, and Journal of Operations Management (Chen et al.*, 1993). A computerized tool management system should be used by companies aspiring to ISO 9000, the Malcolm Baldridge Award or just cost cutting through better quality, organization and control. This paper describes a systematic way to design and develop a tool management relational model that can be adopted as a guide to develop tool management systems used in a computer integrated manufacturing (CIM) environment.

## 2. TOOL DATABASE

A tool database is the core of a tool management system in FMS. Tool management is not a single, simple activity, but it is composed of a complex and pervasive set of functions (Frechette, 1992). An important ingredient in management information systems is the database that represents the heart of the information system and provides a common data storage for consistency of application.

In particular a common database for all tools' data, which can be shared and retrieved by all work centers, will eliminate the redundancy and duplication of tool inventory, effort in tooling plans, and facilitate tool changeovers. For example, a production planner must know what tools can be used, how many useful tools exist and their whereabouts, otherwise a production plan cannot be scheduled properly. Production planning and process control systems must be updated or changed in real time, otherwise the operation of the system can be disrupted. Part programmers must know the actual sizes of the tools and their characteristics and behavior in different conditions, otherwise part programs cannot be generated properly, causing lower quality and productivity (Torvinen and Salminen, 1991).

A common database for all tooling and machining data provides the following advantages

First, it encourages tool standardization in the company, and this minimizes tool redundancy. Second, it can help to optimize tool selection. Third, it provides the user with a comprehensive pool of information with regard to cutting technology. It will aid in the selection of cutting tools, cutting fluid, speed, feed, depth of cut and tool change frequency for new operations. In addition, it improves tool inventory control and assists in rationalizing tool utilization. Furthermore, it increases the effectiveness of tool data monitoring and management systems. Finally, it provides valuable tool data for simulation studies (Elmaraghy, 1985). These benefits require a vast amount of analysis and system development work. Every piece of useful information must be identified so that the database can become the core of the tool management system in FMS.

Figure 1 illustrates the tool management system in a CIM environment. Note that from a tool management point of view, the links with the design and process planning must be emphasized. The links between tool management and other systems, such as accounting, purchases and inventory, are well known. In a complex CIM system, tooling information needs to be used at different times, for different purposes and by different users in a variety of subsystems, including production planning, process control, dynamic scheduling, part programming, tool preset and maintenance, assembly and stock control (Evershim, 1991).

Figure 1 Tool management system in CIM.

Figure 2 Modules in the tool management.

## 3. TOOL MANAGEMENT MODEL

The requirements of such a system were identified through integration of the collected information using tools such as IDEF0 functional analysis and data flow diagramming

(DFD) technique. This became the basis for the design of relations and the database, which was implemented using a based relational database management system.

The IDEF0 methodology is a top-down hierarchical method providing a technique for modeling a complex manufacturing system. It can help to identify the information needs of the manufacturing system. From the integration of information point of view, constructing an IDEF0 model of a manufacturing system is the first step to understanding, documentation and implementation of a manufacturing system (Goodwin, 1989). Revision of IDEF0 models is recommended before any further developments. Figure 2 shows the role of the different tool databases in the tool management function. The following is a brief description of the major elements of the system.

Tools are received and stored initially as components. The main components for assembling complete tools are tool-holders and tool Inserts. According to the tool setup specifications, tool components are assembled, preset and, in some case, measured for offsets. The offsets data are used by the machining centers to determine cutter compensation.

Groups of tools for specific operations are issued to the machine tool chain. Return of tools from machines can be due to wear-out, lack of immediate demand or lack of storage in the cell. Tools returning from the machines may be simply stored as assemblies, may be restored by regrinding or adjustment of inserts, or may be disassembled into components.

The geometric data of each tool-holder and tool insert are described by standard ISO codes (Shayan and Liu, 1995) which assist in designing an easy-to-use standardized database Figure 3 shows the parameters used to generate an ISO code for a turning tool-holder matching inserts for a CNC turning center.

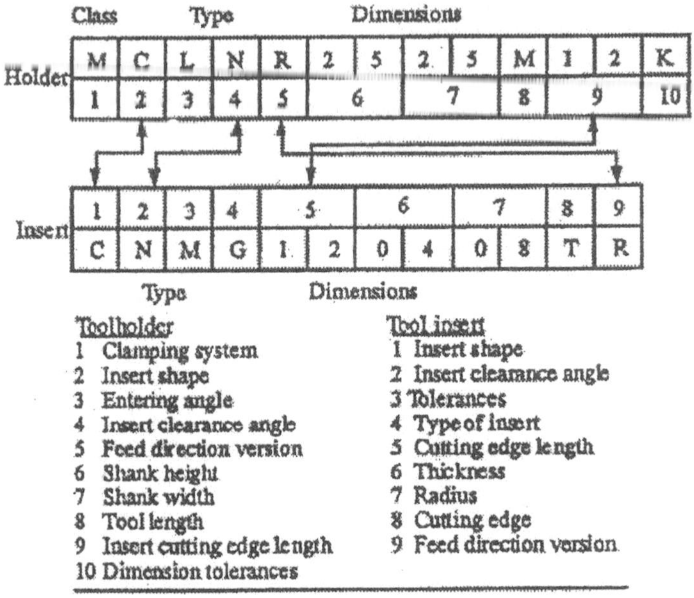


Figure 3 An ISO code for CNC turning center (Shayan and Liu, 1995).

A data flow diagram shows data moving about the system and being stored in data stores. DFDs yield a set, of data items of interest and their logical relationships. Figure 4 illustrates a data flow diagram for the tool receipts module. Every circle shows a process that may have a configuration of other activities.

The DFD diagramming technique is recognized as a good tool for logical database design by providing a natural and intuitive approach to model users' requirements, leading to system development. This forms the basis for further DFD analysis such as design of database files or tables and their fields. Some of the highlights of the tool management system are:

- Key fields in a table make that record unique in the entire table. For example, since serial number field is a key field in the Serial Tool table, different serial numbers will be required to be given to different tools.
- Stock category is the keyword by which a tool is classified such as, Hob, Drill, Insert, Shave Cutter, Blade, etc. The capital and small letters are critical for the system to identify the tools correctly. Table I shows some of tool category keywords.

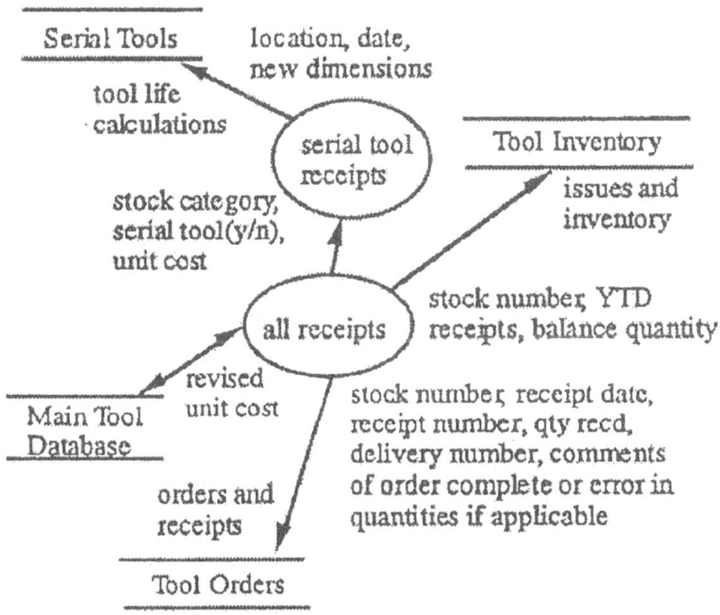


**Figure 4** A data flow diagram for tool receipts module.

- The Main Tool database consists of a tool's unique record in the table. Certain repetitive type of information is asked once when it is encountered for the first time. That is, stock category, stock description, serial tool (y/n), and vendor name are three specific items that are asked only once. Stock category, stock description, and serial tool are stored in Main Tool table. It also consists of important tool information, such as balance quantity, quantity on order, minimum quantity, system comments, total order costs, and total issue costs.

Table 1 Some examples of tool category

| TOOL CATEGORY |
|---|
| Angular Milling Cutters |
| Boring Bars |
| Convex Cutters |
| Corner Round Cutters |
| Countersink Cutters |
| Drills |

| |
|---|
| Endmills |
| Indexable Inserts |
| Milling Cutters |

- The "System Comments" in the Main Tool table are given automatically by the system. The two types of comments are: (a) "Order Now" when the system detects the sum of balance quantity and quantity on order to be less than or equal to the minimum quantity, and (b) "On Order" when the system detects that the quantity on order is greater than 0.

- Enter tool orders first and then their receipts. A purchase order may have multiple receipts. The system keeps track of the quantity received and closes the order automatically.

- If a particular information asked by the system is not available, the user can skip the question and can later update the table or form when the information becomes available.

- Tool issue summary by month is done in Tool Center table by the work center number and in Tool Category table by the tool category. Tool order summary by month is done in Tool Purchase table by the tool category. Year-to-date and the percentages are also calculated in these tables.

Tool management should provide information for decision making and problem resolution for:

- Manufacturing engineering: usage information will provide comparisons for new tool trials,
  check tool availability during fixture design, scrapped tool problem awareness.

- Industrial engineering: quickly locate tool numbers for process sheets, and utilize kits feature for process sheets.
- Accounting: tool expenditure accountability; inventory value.

- Purchasing: requisition review, vendor tracking, creation.

- Production Planning: check tooling availability for production schedule or "what if" forecasting.

- Product engineering: reference in-house tool standards during design.

- Production supervisors: eliminate time looking for tools, see problem areas by tool usage by work center.
- Tool-room: quick, easy tool ordering, no tool hunts, tool regrind or rework, know what work is in area by priority.

## 4. IMPLEMENTATION

Considering the properties of different database systems (network, hierarchical and relational) in terms of factors such as portability, ease of use, understanding and marketability, the choice was relational database (Elmasri, 1989). The choice of a PC-based database system was based on availability, size and reputation.

After the database was implemented, user interfaces to the database were developed. In order to design a user-friendly interface, development of forms-based applications for users to enter, query, update and print data is a desirable feature. Relational database management systems allow multiple views on the data. This property was exploited in generating different applications for a variety of potential users with the following requirements:

- Tool designers access the tool database to ensure that designs do not create new tool
- demands unnecessarily.
- Process planners access the database to ensure that only the available tools are specified
- for production
- Manufacturing engineering access the database to know where tools are used and monitor high volume users to ensure using the tools for the correct application and in an appropriate manner. They should be able to track the tool real-time data, such as remaining tool life and tool wear data from the tool database. They should also be able to qualify different grades for performance comparison, and costs can be more accurately assessed by
- product or work center.
- When tools are broken, the alternative tools should be identifiable in a very timely fashion.
- Part programmers access the database to find out the cutting parameters for specific tool inserts corresponding to specific work material.

The user selects the appropriate option from the top level menu to initialize the relevant module. The user can then query the database by the subsequent dialogue. It offers extensive tool life auditing capabilities based on tool wear. The major benefits are tracking of standard and serialized tooling through the regrind, and possibly, the inspection and coating areas, and
for certain types of serialized tools, recording and calculating usage, wear, and remaining production capacity.

Standard perishable tooling such as drills can be returned from the shop floor directly into regrind area. After the tools are reworked, they are transferred to tool-room stock. Reports show where tools are and what was reworked, how many, by which employees, and over what time period.

For serialized tooling such as hobs and punch sets, re-sharpening is the only way to regain use of the tool after it has been dulled. The regrinding process removes valuable cutting metal until repeated regrinds result in a scrapped tool. Knowing the current production capacity of a tool in parts before it needs regrinding helps in determining if more tools should be purchased without overbuying. Additionally, knowing the total production capacity in part quantity of all tools enables the production planner to schedule jobs. Information collected for serialized tooling is minimum, maximum, and current dimension, regrind date, parts produced, theoretical and actual grinds, in order to form a life history of each tool. On-screen and printed reports provide valuable data on:

- current condition and used/remaining capacity per tool;
- complete tool wear histories
- machine performance by part number and operation;
- overall production capacity per tool group.

## 5. CONCLUSION

The requirements of a tool management system were identified through integration of the collected information. The methodology used to develop the system was IDEF0 functional analysis technique and DFD diagramming. The system was developed and implemented according to the framework presented herein. By making such a tool database available in day-to-day operation, savings in tool costs have been considerable. It also provides ease of tool management in satisfying requests for tools required for production. The tool database is a real and essential ingredient in the integration for the AMS environment. The system developed provides a basis for further specific developments.

## 6. REFERENCES

Chen, I. J., Gupta, A. and Chung, C-H.(1993) Tool planning and control: A selected bibliography. *Production and Inventory Management Journal,* Third Quarter, 87-8.

Elmaraghy, H.A. (1985) Automated tools management in flexible manufacturing. Journal of *Manufacturing Systems,* 4, 1-13.

Elmasri, R. (1989) *Fundamentals of Database Systems.* Benjamin Cumminors, Redwood City,CA.

Evershim, W. (1991) Tool management: the present and the future. *Annals of the CIRP*, 40, 631-3 9.
Frechette, S. (1992) Open architecture for tool management. *Manufacturing International*, 319-34.
Goodwin, A.N., et al. (1989) An assessment of the IDEF notations as descriptive tools. *Information Systems*, **14**, 13-28.
Gray, A.E., Seldmann, A. and Stecke, K.E. (1993) A synthesis of decision models for tool management in automated manufacturing. *Management Science*, **39**, 549-67.
Shayan, E. and Liu, C-L. (1995) Tool management in flexible manufacturing systems. *Integrated Manufacturing Systems*, **6**, 26-3 5.
Torvinen, S.J. and Salminen, K. (1991) Integration of a CIM tool management system to an intelligent feature-based process planning system. *Computers in Industry*, 17, 207-16.

## 7. BIOGRAPHY

Prof. R. V. Narang is an associate professor at Indiana-Purdue University in the Manufacturing Technology department. He did his M.S. and Ph.D. in Industrial Engineering from the University of Iowa in 1975 and 1992 respectively. He has many years of industrial, teaching, and consulting experience. He is an ABET/TAC program evaluator for manufacturing engineering technology. He has presented a number of research papers in international conferences and published papers in reputed journals.

# A Comprehensive Modelling Methodology for the Development of Manufacturing Enterprise Systems

*Ang C. L.*
*Gintic Institute of Manufacturing Technology*
*Nanyang Technological University*
*71 Nanyang Drive*
*Singapore 638075*
*Tel: 65-799-4921*
*Fax: 65-791-6377*
*E-mail: clang@gintic.gov.sg*

**ABSTRACT**

To completely describe a manufacturing system, several models are usually created, each from a different viewpoint. Traditionally, these models are created independently using different methodologies and in different environments. This approach poses many problems, for example, time-consuming, inconsistency between models, difficulties in model maintenance, difficulties in ensuring a seamless transition in the system development life cycle, etc.. To overcome these problems, a comprehensive methodology termed IDEF* has been developed for the modelling of enterprise systems. The purpose of this paper is to introduce to the readers the features and concepts of the methodology.

**KEYWORDS**

Modeling methodology, manufacturing enterprise systems, CIMOSA, IDEF, IDEF*, IDEF0, IDEF1x, IDEF3, IDEF0-based IDEF2.

## 1. INTRODUCTION

Models are descriptions of systems. To completely describe a manufacturing enterprise, several models are usually created, each from a different viewpoint. According to CIMOSA reference architecture [AMICE 93], models from four complementary viewpoints are required: function, information, resource, and organisation. Traditionally, these models are built independently using different methodologies and in different environments. However, a methodology tailored to a particular viewpoint is incompatible with another. This traditional approach thus poses the following problems:

- The whole modelling process involves repeated capturing of the same information and is time-consuming.
- It is very difficult to identify the effect of any changes of one model on the others.
- Inconsistency between the different but interrelated models.
- Model maintenance is difficult.
- Seamless transition in the systems development life cycle is difficult.
- It is difficult for system users and system developers to communicate and work together.
- Similarly, it is difficult for several system developers who have different purposes and backgrounds, but who are working on the same system to communicate and work together.

Computer Applications in Production and Engineering. F. Plonka and G. Olling (Eds.)

To overcome these problems, a comprehensive modelling methodology termed IDEF* and an associated software tool are being developed in Gintic. The purpose of this paper is to explain to the readers the features and concepts of this methodology.

The methodology is termed IDEF* because it is basically an enhancement of the IDEF (ICAM DEFinition language) methodology, which was developed by the USAF ICAM programme in the 80's for CIM design and implementation. The IDEF methodology comprises IDEF0, IDEF1, IDEF2, and IDEF3 which are methodologies for functional, information, dynamic, and process modelling, respectively.

## 2. THE IDEF* METHODOLOGY

The main features of the IDEF* methodology are:

1) CIMOSA-compliant;
2) IDEF0-based; and
3) Integrated.

### 2.1 CIMOSA COMPLIANCE

The IDEF* methodology conforms to the CIMOSA modelling framework [AMICE 1993], which is a diagrammatic representation of three modelling views (Figure 1).

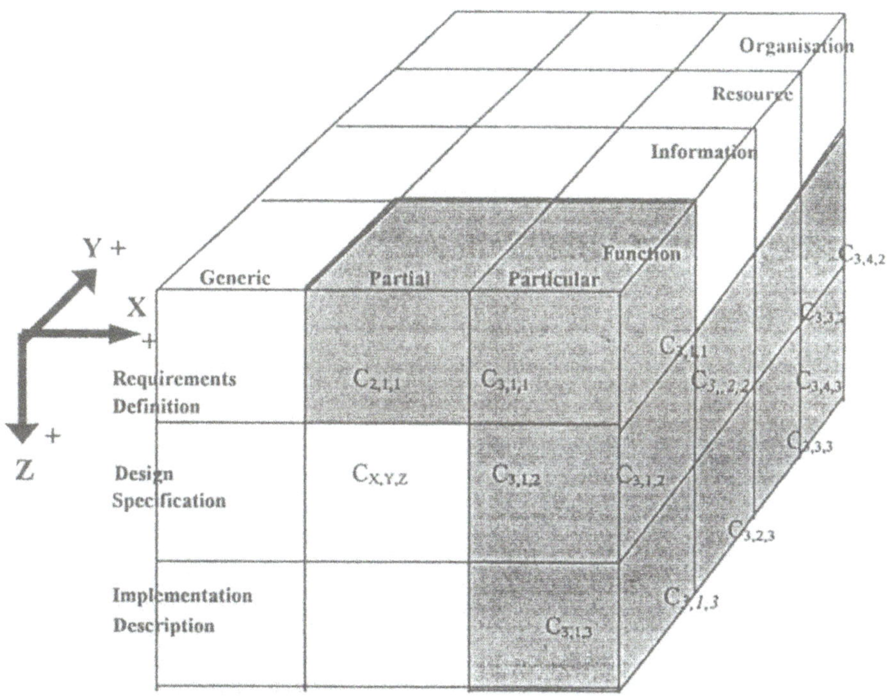


Figure 1: CIMOSA Modelling Framework

In one view, modelling is described as consisting of generic, partial, and particular requirements definition phases. In another view, modelling has function, information, resource, and organisation levels of analysis. Finally, in the third view, modelling is described as having requirements definition, design specification, and implementation description stages of development. The combination of each of these three views results in 36 different modelling domains or cubes $C_{x,y,z}$s, giving rise to many possible "routes" for enterprise system development. However, not all modelling domains are necessary. Some cubes are actually redundant. The IDEF* methodology supports the following route, which consists of four sections and is thought to be one of the "shortest" in terms of development effort.

*I.* $C_{2,1,1} \rightarrow C_{3,1,1} \rightarrow C_{3,1,2} \rightarrow C_{3,1,3}$
*II.* $C_{3,1,2} \rightarrow C_{3,2,2} \rightarrow C_{3,2,3}$
*III.* $C_{3,1,2} \rightarrow C_{3,3,2} \rightarrow C_{3,3,3}$
*IV.* $C_{3,1,2} \rightarrow C_{3,4,2} \rightarrow C_{3,4,3}$

In IDEF* methodology, section *I* of the development route involves: a) customising a partial function model into a particular function model at the requirement definition stage; b) extending the particular function model at the design specification stage to enable visual and computer workflow analysis; and c) further extending the particular function model at the implementation description stage to enable computer workflow execution. Section *II* involves the derivation of a particular information model from the particular function model at the design specification stage, and the development of relational databases at the implementation description stage. Sections *III* & *IV* involve extending the particular function model to include resource view and organisation view, respectively, at both the design specification stage and the implementation description stage.

## 2.2 IDEF0-BASED

IDEF0 is chosen as the basis of IDEF* methodology. In producing a complete system description model, an IDEF0 model is first built and other details are then added progressively onto the IDEF0 model so that:

- Functional description of the system can be achieved at any level of abstraction;
- Complete system description can be realised sequentially, and
- Models consistency can be maintained by using the same functions among the different models

Throughout the process, the IDEF0 model is used as a basis for the collection of relevant details. This helps to ensure that models resulting from the process will be compatible with the IDEF0 model, and that only function-related details are collected. This is in contrast with the traditional approach as mentioned in the §1. To meet these requirements of IDEF*, IDEF0 is extended syntactically and textually into IDEF0*.

## 2.3 INTEGRATION

It is integrated, meaning that it achieves four kinds of modelling integration simultaneously:

- Integration of five modelling processes: function, dynamics, information, resource, and organisation;
- Integration of three modelling stages: requirements definition, design specification, and implementation description;
- Integration of three modelling levels: generic, partial, and particular; and
- Integration of two modelling environments: computer-based enterprise engineering and enterprise operation.

The first two kinds of integration are achieved through an integrated modelling approach in which the different modelling processes share common information on business processes (see §.3, and §.4). The approach will help to reduce the time and effort needed to build the different models that are required for complete system description. It will also help to ensure consistency between these models, and will therefore allow system users and system developers to work together more easily than when using models that are built independently [Kim 1996].

The third kind of integration involves the use of a knowledge-based system to semi-automate the generation of IDEF0 models based on the concept of reference models (see §.5). The knowledge-based approach not only will greatly speed up the IDEF0 modelling process, but will also eliminate the problem of inconsistency that is associated with the traditional approach [Ang et al 1997; Luo 1997].

Finally, the last kind of integration involves extending the IDEF0 model, making it computer-processable not only for workflow analysis but also for workflow execution. This kind of integration enables real-time implementation of operational changes, hence providing a very flexible operation environment.

## 3. INTEGRATION OF MODELLING PROCESSES.

This is achieved through an integrated modelling approach in which IDEF0 is chosen as the basis of modelling. Thus an IDEF0 model is first built and other details are then added progressively so that a complete system description can be realised sequentially. To fulfill these requirements, IDEF0 is extended syntactically and textually into IDEF0* in order to accommodate process, dynamic, information, resource, and organisation modelling.

### 3.1 EXTENSION OF IDEF0 TO INCLUDE PROCESS FLOW MODELLING

To facilitate visual analysis of the IDEF0 models for BPR (business process re-engineering), IDEF0 is extended syntactically so that it can also be used to describe the temporal precedence relationships between the functional activities. In other words, IDEF0* not only can be used to describe what the processes do, but also how they work, i.e. the behaviour aspects.

In IDEF0*, precedence relationships between functional activities are modelled with precedence links (denoted by bold arrows), which connect functional activities by means of *AND* (&), *OR* (O), and ***Exclusive OR*** (XOR) junction boxes (see Table 1). Figure 2 shows an IDEF0 diagram and its corresponding IDEF0* diagram showing the precedence relationships.

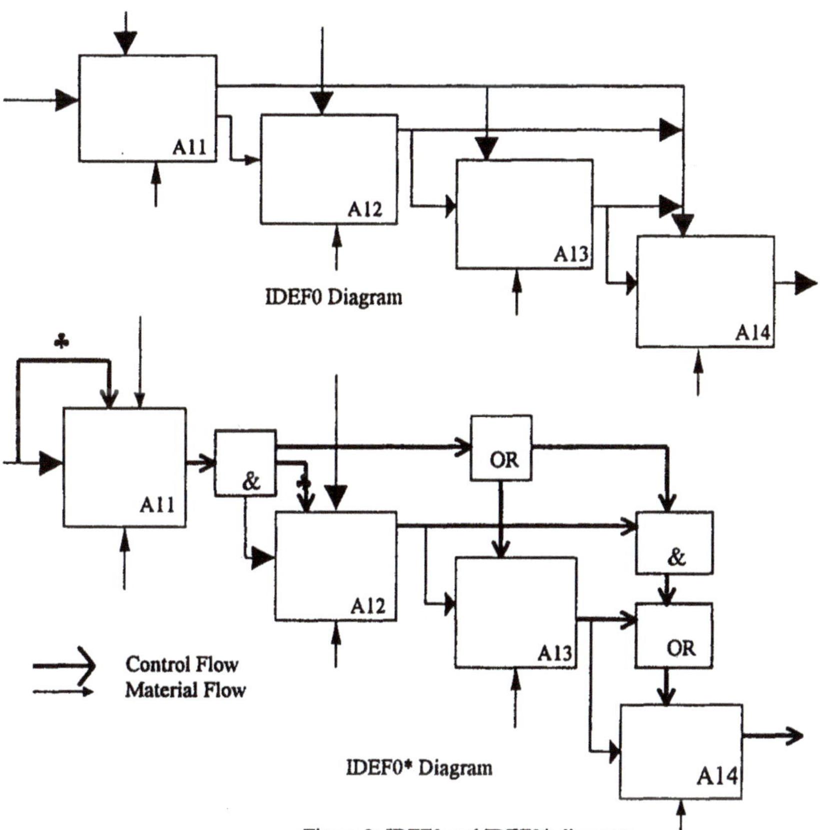


Figure 2: IDEF0 and IDEF0* diagrams.

As can be seen from Figure 2, the IDEF0* diagram is practically formed by superimposing the IDEF3 (PFD) diagram onto the IDEF0 diagram. In the IDEF0* diagram, additional precedence links (arrows marked ♣) are added to make explicit the fact that some material flows in the IDEF0 diagram are also control flows. This fact is implicit in the IDEF0 diagram.

## 3.2 EXTENSION OF IDEF0 TO INCLUDE DYNAMICS MODELLING

To facilitate performance analysis, dynamics parameters are incorporated into the IDEF0 model. They are incorporated as text files attached to the relevant functions or arrows of the IDEF0 model and contained within the Text or Glossary of the model. This has the advantages of not complicating the IDEF0 diagrams. Such performance-related parameters as arrival rate, quantity of each resource type, branching conditions or behaviour rules, etc. can be incorporated. The resulting IDEF0* model, which is basically an IDEF0-based IDEF2 model, can be simulated for workflow analysis [Shunk 1990, Popplewell et al 1994].

## 3.3 DERIVATION OF IDEF1x MODELS FROM IDEF0 MODELS

IDEF0 models describe the functions performed by business processes. A function transforms its inputs into outputs under the supervision of its controls by using its mechanisms. Although a function's inputs and outputs can be information or physical objects, they are represented only at the level of graphical labels and no actual information structures are attached to those labels. An IDEF1x model on the other hand graphically represents the information content and structure related to a business process or an enterprise. However, it is possible to derive an IDEF1x model from an appropriate IDEF0 model using the Glossary of the IDEF0 model as the entity pool for IDEF1x [Le Clair 1982, Smart et al 1996]. A procedure for the systematic derivation of IDEF1x models from IDEF0 models has been developed by the author [Ang 1997]. The procedure is adapted from the work of [Adam et al 1993].

## 3.4 EXTENSION OF IDEF0 TO INCLUDE RESOURCE MODELLING

The term resource is restricted to mechanisms in the sense of IDEF0, i.e. enterprise objects contributing to the realisation of the functionality of activities of business processes [Vernadat 1996]. In IDEF0*, description templates, which are subsets of those of the two CIMOSA resource modelling constructs: Capability Set and Resource [AMICE 1993], are used to deal with resource modelling (Figure 3). They are attached to the relevant mechanism arrows as text files and contained within the Glossary of the IDEF0 model. Again, they are input via pop-up boxes in the associated software tool being developed.

| | |
|---|---|
| <u>Capability Set</u> | |
| Design Authority: | [Name of person with authority to design/maintain this particular Capability Set]. |
| Capabilities | |
| Function Related: | [Capability elements] |
| Performance related: | [Capability elements] |
| Objective related: | [Capability elements] |
| <u>Resource</u> | |
| Design Authority: | [Name of person and department with authority to design/maintain this particular instance] |
| Capability Set: | [Name of Capability Set defining the provided capabilities of this Resource instance] |
| Class: | [Functional Entity or Resource Cell or Resource Set or Resource Component] |
| Operation Set: | [Functional operations valid for this Resource instance] |
| Object View: | [Name of Object View instance defining the characteristics (capacity, availability, location, etc.) of this Resource instance] |

Figure 3: Description templates for resource modeling.

## 3.5 EXTENSION OF IDEF0 TO INCLUDE ORGANISATION MODELLING

In IDEF*, IDEF0 is also extended both syntactically and textually to deal with organisation modelling. Thus an IDEF0* diagram may have, in addition to the *AND, OR, XOR* junction boxes as mentioned in

§3.1, eight basic elements (see Figure 4) which are defined as follows. Here distinction is made between line authority (control) and staff authority (authority), and between the person who owns the process and the person who executes the process [Born 1994]. The person who executes a process is a resource termed Functional Entity in CIMOSA [AMICE 1995].

- Process: A series of steps or actions which transform an object from an initial state (input) to a final state (output).
- Process owner The person or other agent responsible for the execution of a process.
- Organisation Cell (see below): The organisation cell to which the person is assigned.
- Staff authority (authority): The description, specification or justification of a process. It is shown entering the process box at the top right.
- Line authority (control): The conditions for activating process. It is shown entering the process box at the top left.
- Input: An object at the point of entry to a process.
- Output: An object at the point of exit from a process.
- Mechanisms: The resources used to execute the process.

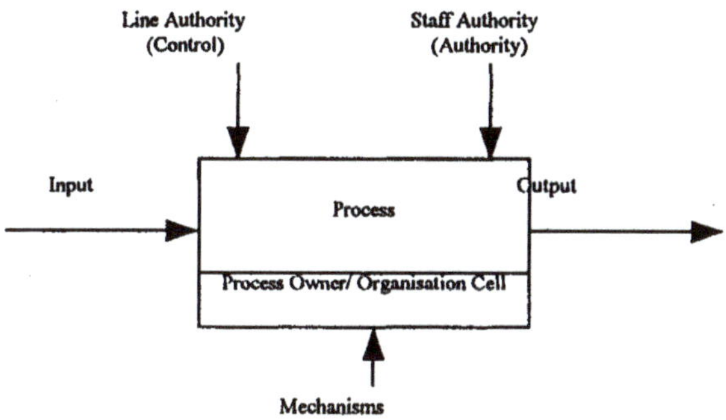


Figure 4: IDEF0* process notation

In addition, IDEF0* also uses two types of description templates for organisation modelling (Figure 5). They are attached to the relevant function boxes, again as text files, and contained within the Text of the IDEF0 model. These description templates are subsets of those of the two CIMOSA organisation modelling constructs, namely Organisation Unit and Organisation Cell [AMICE 1993].

| | |
|---|---|
| **Organization Unit** | |
| **Design Authority:** | [Name of person and department with authority to design/maintain this particular instance] |
| **Function Description** | |
| **Functional Entity:** | [Name of functional entity associated to this organization unit] |
| **Job Unit Description:** | [Textual description of the decision-making or problem solving job] |
| **Skill profile:** | [List of capabilities/skills which are needed to fulfill the job] |
| **Responsibilities:** | [List of responsibilities given to this organization unit] |
| **Authorities:** | [List of authorities necessary to fill the job] |
| **Structural Description** | |
| **Assigned to organization cell:** | [Name of organization cell to which the organization unit belongs] |
| **Organization Cell** | |
| **Design Authority:** | [Name of person and department with authority to design/maintain this particular instance] |
| **Function Description** | |
| **Cell Description:** | [Textual description of the purpose of the organization cell] |
| **Operational Authority/ Responsibility:** | [Organization unit responsible for the organization cell. Must be a person] |
| **Process Authorities/ Responsibilities:** | [List of function view constructs on which this organization cell has responsibility and authority] |
| **Information Authorities/** | |

| | |
|---|---|
| Responsibilities: | [List of information view constructs on which this organization cell has responsibility and authority] |
| Resource Authorities/ Responsibilities. | [List of resource view constructs on which this organization cell has responsibility and authority] |
| Organization Level: | [One of : "Enterprise", "Plant", "Shop", "Cell", "Workcenter", or "Equipment"] |

Figure 5: Description templates for organization modeling.

At this stage, the IDEF0* model contains sufficient information for the construction of an organisation chart (Figure 6).

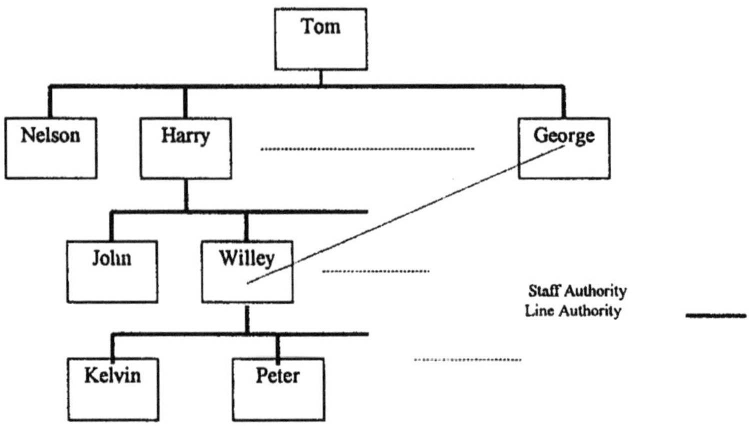


Figure 6: Organisation chart

## 4. INTEGRATION OF MODELLING STAGES

This section describes the integration of modelling stages of each of the four modelling processes.

### 4.1 FUNCTIONAL MODELLING

At the requirements definition stage, an IDEF0 model is first built. It is then extended into an IDEF0* model at the design specification stage to include details like time, resource, and behaviour of each enterprise activity and functional operation (resources in terms of functional entities providing the functional operations are also specified in the resource view using the description templates mentioned in §3.2). At the implementation description stage, the same IDEF0* model is used and enriched. In particular, ports for data communications are defined for each activity to indicate the exact entry points for receiving/sending linputs and outputs. Also, if messages are exchanged among activities, a communication channel and the format of messages must also be described. Finally, the IDEF0* model is supplemented by network diagrams and block diagrams to facilitate data communications system planning and facility layout planning, respectively.

### 4.2 INFORMATION MODELLING

Database design is more than just building entities and connecting them by relationships which only represent the static part of the information system. The dynamic part, i.e., the way data and information are going to be processed, must also be considered [Vernadat 1996]. In IDEF*, the static part is modelled by two constructs: Conceptual Schema and External Schema; while the dynamic part by another two constructs: Integrity Rule and Database Transaction. The modelling framework is compliant with the three-schema approach proposed by ANSI (American National Standards Institute) [ANSI 1976], which advocates for the use of a global conceptual schema implemented in terms of an internal schema and presented to the system users via external schema.

In IDEF* methodology, IDEF1x models are derived from IDEF0* models. At the design specification stage, an ERA-based global conceptual schema is first produced (see §3.3 and Figures 4c & 4d). From the conceptual schema, external schemata can then be derived. In addition, the integrity rules that constrain the possible values taken by attributes can also be specified. These rules are expressed in terms of natural language of expressions. They can be derived from the declarative rules of business processes or they can be specified by users as separate detailed information requirements.

Once the conceptual schema and its external schemata have been produced, data and database transactions, i.e. data processing functional operations or queries on data, can be specified using IDEF0*. Like the M* Process Description Model [Vernadat et al 1989], the IDEF0* model mentioned §3.2 is a formal model which can be used to specify data manipulation operations to be executed on data, either by application programs, or directly by users in the form of data transactions.

Implementation description involves both logical database design and physical database design. In logical database design, the conceptual schema is mapped onto a relational schema using the conversion rules developed by [Elmasri et al 1993](see §3.3). The relational schema is then implemented as an internal schema in physical database design using the Structured Query Language (SQL). Physical database design also involves coding the integrity rules, data and database transactions of applications programs, and on-line queries using SQL for data manipulation and query. SQL is both the data description language, and the data manipulation and query language for well-known relational database systems like Oracle, DB2, Ingres, and Informix.

## 4.3 RESOURCE MODELLING

For resource modelling, the same IDEF0* model as for functional modelling (see §3.1) is used and extended to include two types of description templates, namely Capability Set and Resource (see §3.4). At the requirements definition stage, only the Capability Set template is used to express resource requirements from the standpoint of enterprise activities (i.e. required capabilities). At the design specification stage and the implementation description stage, both the Capability Set and Resource templates are used and are respectively qualified as specified and implemented.

The Capability Set in CIMOSA is an essential construct for supporting the principle of process and resource decoupling (see §6). The principle is based on the fact that activities, and therefore processes, require capabilities for their execution while resources provide capabilities to execute functional operations of activities, if they are available and have the necessary capacity.

## 4.4 ORGANISATION MODELLING

For organisation modelling, the same IDEF0* model as for functional modelling (see § 3.1) is again used and extended. As described in §3.5, it is extended to include additional graphical notations, and two types of description templates:, namely Organisation Units and Organisation Cells. The additional graphical notations together with the description templates are supposed to apply at the design specification modelling stage and at the implementation description modelling stage. This is especially true for designing or restructuring an organisation. However, they can be used at the requirements definition stage in the case of the modelling of an existing system.

# 5. INTEGRATION OF MODELLING LEVELS

Integration of the generic, partial, and particular modelling levels is achieved by means of a knowledge-based system for the automated generation of IDEF0 models based on the concepts of reference models. Reference models represent structures and practices that are typical of a particular industry or a set of companies within that industry. They can be customised to partial models or company-specific models and hence can be shared and reused. It has been reported by Baines [1989], Weaver [1995], and Vernadat [1996] that the use of reference function models can facilitate and accelerate the functional modelling process.

An operational prototype of the knowledge-based system has been developed in Gintic [Ang et al 1997, Luo 1977]. The work involved: 1) the development of a structured methodology for the automated generation of IDEF0 models and its associated knowledge base; and 2) their implementation in computer software.

## 9. CONCLUSION

In this paper, a comprehensive modelling methodology IDEF* for manufacturing enterprise systems development has been proposed. The methodology, which is based on an integrated modelling approach, incorporates such robust modelling methodologies as IDEF0, IDEF3(PFD), and IDEF1x. It conforms to the CIMOSA modelling framework, and simultaneously achieves four kinds of integration, namely integration of modelling processes, integration of modelling stages, integration of modelling levels, and integration of modelling environments. When supported by appropriate software tools, it is expected to drastically reduce the time and effort of enterprise systems development.

## REFERENCES

Adam, N. R., and Ganopadhyay, A., Integrating Functional and Data Modeling in a Computer Integrated Manufacturing System, IEEE 9th International Conference on Data Engineering, 1993.

AMICE Consortium, CIMOSA Open Systems Architecture for CIM, Springer Verlag, Berlin 1993.

Ang, C.L., Luo M., and Gay Robert K.L., A Knowledge-Based Approach to the Generation of IDEF0 Models, International Journal of Production Research, Vol. 35, No 5, 1997.

Ang C.L., Derivation of IDEF1x Models from IDEF0 models, In-house Technical Report WP/RIC-U/SD/ST/ACL/97/03, Gintic Institute of Manufacturing Technology, 1977.

ANSI, ANSI/X3/SPARC, Study Group on Database Management Systems: Interim Report, 75-02-08, In: ACM SIGMOD Newsletter, FDT, Vol. 7, No. 2, 1975.

Baines, R.W., and Colquhourn, G. J., The Use of a Generic IDEF0 Model to Capture Process Planning Functional Information, Proceedings of the Sunderland Advanced Manufacturing Technology Conference, Sunderland, 1989.

Born, C., Process Management to Quality Improvement, Wiley, 1994.

FIPS PUBS, Integration Definition for Function Modeling (IDEF0), Federal Information Processing Standards Publication 183, National Institute of Standards and Technology, USA, 1993.

Kim J.I, Function, Information., Dynamics, and Organization Integrated Modeling Methodology for Enterprise Systems Integration, PhD Thesis, Arizona State University, 1996.

Luo, M., A Knowledge-Based Approach to the Automated Generation of IDEF0 Models, PhD Thesis, in advanced preparation, 1997.

Popplewell, K., et al, A Comprehensive Methodology for Factory Modeling, 1994.

Smart, A., Maull, R., Childe, S., Bennett, J., and Weaver, A., Guidelines for Linking Process and Information Models - IDEF0 to IDEF1x, Working Paper WP/GR/J95010-7, 1996.

Shunk, D.L., Creating an Integrated, Useful Systems Definition Technique, Optimization of Manufacturing Systems Design, Edited by Shunk, D. L., Elsevier Science Publishers B.V., 1993.

Vernadat, F., DiLeva, A., and Giolito, P., Organization and Information System Design of Manufacturing Environments: the New M* Approach, Journal of Computer-Integrated Manufacturing Systems, Vol. 2, No. 2, 1989.

Vernadat, F. B., Enterprise Modeling and Integration, Principles and Applications, Chapman & Hall. 1996.

Wang, W., Popplewell, K., and Bell, R., An Integrated Multi-View System Description Approach to Approximate Factory Modeling, International Journal of Computer Integrated Manufacturing, Vol. 6, No.2, 1993.

Weaver, A.M., Childe, S.J., Maul, R.S., and Smart, P.A., The Development and Application of a Generic "Order Fulfillment" Process Model, Proceedings of the Third International Conference on CIM, Singapore, July 1995.

# 20

# Using IDEF0 to develop Generic Business Process Models

*R. Maull, A Weaver, A Smart, S Childe,*
*School of Computing, University of Plymouth, Plymouth, UK*
*Telephone 01752 232545*
*Fax 01752 232540*
*E-Mail rmaull@plym.ac.uk*

**Abstract**

This paper has two main elements. Firstly, the research team based at the University of Plymouth have identified three 'sets' of processes: manage, operate and support and we have further sub-divided the operate processes into three: product development, order flow and after-sales service. Using a Soft Systems approach we have developed a root definition and a conceptual model for the order flow process. The paper will describe the conceptual model in detail, illustrated through the use of the IDEF0 modeling technique.

The second major element of the paper is an illustration of how we have used the process models in small companies. We will provide a case study with reflections on how the generic model may be applied to help small companies improve their business processes.

## 1. BACKGROUND TO THE RESEARCH

The basic idea of a hierarchy of processes is important when considering generic processes for an industry type and the core processes within a company. The hierarchy of processes provides the framework within which the analysis and redesign will take place.

In the majority of documented BPR methodologies, including those developed by Coopers & Lybrand (Johansson et al 1993), IBM (Kane 1986), British Telecom (Harvey 1994), Xerox and Lucas (Parnaby 1993), one of the initial activities is to identify the core business processes. In identifying the core processes the participants in the BPR project are defining boundaries within their organization using a process perspective. Examples of core process definition by companies can

Computer Applications in Production and Engineering. F. Plonka and G. Olling (Eds.)

be found in Davenport (1993) and the Business Intelligence report (Harvey 1994) on BPR and many case studies in journal articles (Shapiro et al 1992, Davenport and Short 1990). The number of core processes within a company is very much dependent on the level of abstraction at which the organization decides the core process definition will be meaningful.

## 2. BUSINESS PROCESSES

The Business Processes concept is closely linked with Enterprise Integration (EI). EI is associated with the development of reference architectures. Unfortunately, much of this reference architecture work is at the abstract level. They are very high level frameworks which enable users to take a complete enterprise wide perspective on the organization. Their great strength is that they develop activity (function), information and human/organizational views, all of which are capable of being integrated together. Their great weakness is that they are not equipped with models which users can quickly pick up and use. We would argue that what industry requires are tailorable models, building blocks on which they can quickly develop business process and integration models. It is these building block models that we have set out to develop. Real benefits are expected with the integration of examples such as ours within the all embracing reference architectures.

Given our interest in developing re-usable business process models and their subsequent integration within EI reference architectures, we set out to ensure some compatibility of our UK government sponsored research with the international developments in reference architectures.

This research project has used the CIM-OSA (AMICE ESPRIT, 1989) framework to identify three types of processes within an organization. CIM-OSA was used because it is the major European initiative in reference architectures. As Vernadat (1996) reports, has been developed from a number of European wide ESPRIT projects over the last ten years and has a wide range of academic and industrial project partners. In addition other Enterprise Integration architectures e.g. CEN ENV (1990) and ARIS (Scheer 1992) are based on CIM-OSA. Internationally, GERAM (Williams 1995) uses CIM-OSA as one of its core elements along with PERA (Williams 1994). CIM-OSA identifies three types of processes Operate processes that add value. Support processes that enable the value adding processes to function e.g. personnel and finance processes. Manage processes, which are the processes that develop a set of business objectives, a business strategy and manage the overall behavior of the organization.

We set out to identify a set of business process models for the operate processes.

## 2.1 The "Operate" processes

The "Operate" processes are those processes which directly produce value for customers, the core operational processes identified by Champy (1995) and Meyer (1993) for a business are "product development", "customer service" and "order fulfillment". The "product development" process transforms the actual or perceived requirements of a customer into a design that can be manufactured. The "customer service" process transforms knowledge of customer requirements and the market into customer orders. The "order fulfilment" process takes the order, manufactures and delivers the product to the customer.

The product development process adds value for the end customer by using knowledge to design a product to the customer's requirements. The customer service process adds value by translating customer requirements of a product into the value to be added by the other two operate processes. The order fulfillment process adds value by manufacturing and delivering a product to a customer.

The authors recognize that although the "operate" processes can be identified as individual processes it is the interaction of all three that results in the overall value added and hence the fulfillment of customer needs. However, it is not the purpose of this paper to describe these interactions. These are described more fully in a paper currently under preparation and available in draft form from the authors, see Smart et al (1997). This paper will focus on describing in detail one of the processes - the order fulfillment process. The generic model of the "order fulfillment" process has been developed using IDEF0 (CAM-I 1980).

## 2.2 The development and validation of the generic "order fulfillment" process model

Smart (1995 in a wide ranging survey of Process Analysis Tools identified three key issues that a process analysis method must support

1. The development of consensus regarding Weltanschauungs and objectives. Techniques must provide an easy to use/common language for communication and debate. The success of the technique depends upon the simplicity of the syntax and semantics employed by the technique. Consensus needs to be established regarding system boundary and purpose In addition, a coherent set of modeling rules are required to facilitate the modeling process itself:

2. The description of a process in terms of systems parameters. That is inputs, transformation, outputs, receivers and feedback.

3. The identification of a systems hierarchy. The idea of hierarchy is based on a systems concept in which systems are composed of sub-systems (and processes of sub-processes). Harrington (1992) has proposed a hierarchy of macroprocesses, sub-processes, activities and tasks each of which represents further hierarchical detailing of the process. Techniques must facilitate the identification of sub-processes, activities and tasks within the whole process. This is so that each element of the system is seen in its proper context. Abilities to represent hierarchical decomposition and ensure that the context for a part of a model under detailed analysis is always known is advantageous when using a generic model. A company can focus on a part of the generic model it is particularly interested in and develop a further levels of detail without losing an understanding of the whole process.

Given these requirements we concluded that IDEF0 was the most appropriate modeling method to support activity based business process analysis. We recognize that IDEF0 is unsuitable for both dynamic modeling and information modeling. However, for identifying and providing a basis for improving the activities in a business process model (i.e., the three requirements set out above) we contend that IDEF0 is the most suitable method. For a further discussion on this issue, see the PAT report.

Generic activities

The information used to develop the generic process model has been extracted and assimilated from a number of sources. The activities that are carried out within the "order fulfillment" process were adapted from a generic task model developed by Childe (1991). Childe's task model was based on the proposition that there are a key set of tasks or activities which are consistent throughout manufacturing companies (all manufacturing companies order materials, take orders from customers etc.).

Generic flows

The types of flows that are modeled in the generic process model can initially be divided into physical and information flows i.e. flows of physical materials which are transformed by value adding activities and information flows where the value is in the information and not the medium of transmission e.g. a paper proforma or an electronic signal. The information flows can be further divided into seven categories of information described by Jorysz and Vernadat (1990). These seven categories of information are

1) *Product information* describes what to produce e.g. Drawings, part lists
2) *Process Information* describes how the product should be produced e.g. process plans
3) *Production Information* describes the quantities to be produced and shop floor progress
4) *Planning Information* describes the schedules, inventories and plans
5) *Resource Information* describes the facilities that produce the products
6) *Administrative information* describes management information e.g. customer orders
7) *Organization information* describes responsibilities

The generic process model includes generic flows between activities representing the first six types of information. The seventh type of information about the organization and responsibilities is company specific. Although IDEF0 provides the facility to identify responsibilities by the addition of mechanism arrows on the bottom of activity boxes, the generic process model does not have any because of their company specific nature.

Generic flows were identified from IDEF0 models of manufacturing companies that had been produced by the authors in the course of their research work. Information was also distilled from other models produced in a number of different modeling techniques presented in literature.

## 2.3 The generic "order fulfillment" model

The generic "order fulfillment" model that has been developed currently includes over 110 activities integrated by the flows of physical and information entities. It is a model which has been validated with all industry types - although we recognize that the importance of certain activities in the model will differ depending on various organizational characteristics. A description and illustration of these characteristics is provided in Weaver (1995). The model below is a representation of the second highest level of abstraction of the "order fulfillment" process. The model extends to 5 lower levels of activities and flows. The complete model also includes a glossary of terms.

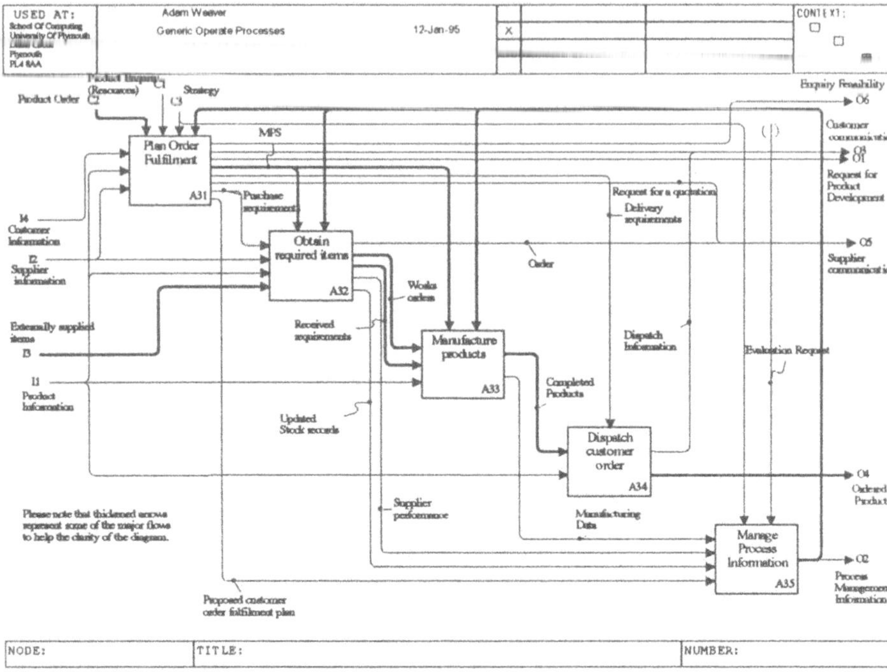


The event that triggers the commencement of activities within the order fulfillment process is arrival of an order for a product or an enquiry requesting feedback on the feasibility of fulfilling a possible order to a customer's requirements both events come from the "Get Order" process. The event that represents a full cycle of the process results in either an enquiry feasibility report sent to the "Get Order" process or an order delivered to a customer.

## 3. CASE STUDY

The objective of this phase of the validation approach was to find out if the model could be used by a company as a useful framework to help identify and understand their business processes. The idea of the model and its use as a framework was introduced to a local manufacturing company that was at the point of initiating a project to improve the management of what could be described as its order fulfillment process. The IT manager agreed to use the model as a starting point to develop a model of the company's existing order fulfillment process.

### Background of the company

The company manufactures printed circuit boards (PCBs) under contract for a variety of customers. The quantity and complexity of individual PCBs per order varies considerably. The company has expanded rapidly over the past 5 years and was seeking to improve the management of orders throughout the business.

Use of the model as a framework

The IT manager was the main point of contact within the company. He acted as facilitator to a team using the model. The model and its use as a framework were introduced to the IT manager during a single meeting that lasted approximately 2 hours. A set of guidelines for the use of the model was not available at that time so a brief outline of the context, viewpoint, structure of the model and proposed approach to its use was given verbally.

The model was used by the IT manager as a template. Key personnel were interviewed and during the interview the IT manager described the activities that the model represented and their context in the overall process. The IT manager focused on those activities which were similar in nature and content to those actual activities undertaken by the individual. This part of the interview could be described as a "walk through" of the process.

## 4. FEEDBACK ON THE USE OF THE MODEL IN THE COMPANY

Issues that were raised during the meetings while "walking through" the model and altering it to represent the existing "order fulfillment" process included:

Allocation of responsibility - When adding mechanisms to indicate who carried out activities, it was necessary to clarify who was responsible for doing them. This initiated discussions about who was and should be responsible for activities and supplying information.

'Taken for granted - "Walking through" the model, interviewees were provoked into thinking about some of the activities that they did but had never really considered properly before. For example, "Produce simulation for decision making" [A3132] was initially dismissed, however on reflection the interviewees realized that they did simulate "what if" scenarios although the activity was not formally documented. This realization provoked ideas on how some of the knowledge could be captured in the future.

Ideas for Improvements - Discussing the activities represented by the model resulted in the identification of activities that the company did not currently carry out but should be done. For example, no one in the company had the responsibility for performing the activity "confirm order to customer" under circumstances where there were no queries relating to order. The procedure for confirming to a customer that the company was accepting the customer's order was later reviewed.

## 5. DISCUSSION

As a result of this and other case studies applying the model the research team have identified a number of advantages of using a generic model.

1. It reduces the chance of the team reverting to a traditional functional view. As a result of the prevailing functional organizational mindset, process modeling teams can resort back to modeling departments e.g. Design or Manufacturing and to shy away from modeling the integrating elements. The scope of the model ensures that they focus on the whole process.
2. Reduces amount of modeling activity required. Process modeling can be a very time consuming task. Before we developed the generic model, the team have been involved in "fulfill order" process modeling, that has taken 12 - 18 man months of activity. Working from the generic model we estimate that this is reduced by 75%.
3. Provides greater momentum than starting from a "blank sheet of paper". Starting from scratch is a daunting experience. In some cases it has been a major task to move modeling teams from project management to process modeling. The advantage of the generic model is that teams begin with a model and only have to work onwards to modify activities and linkages.
4. The standard models are not influenced by any political issues in the company. Models that are developed "in-house" can be influenced by senior management, who either want to throw a complimentary perspective on their own activities or develop models that appear to point the blame at other departments. The generics are free from this bias.
5. Team should feel able to criticize the standard models. Modellers can quickly feel proprietorial about their models. They may resist all attempts to change them. The generics are used on the basis of "no pride of ownership" and company members are encouraged to criticize and modify the models.
6. The activity of comparison encourages communication and understanding through debate. By comparing what we do with the model, it encourages companies to think through why they carry out activities in that way. Often, in our experience, a discussion ensues which exposes many of the underlying reasons behind why processes work in specific ways. It can be that the reasons that caused a process to be changed have changed themselves and particular aspects of the process no longer need to be carried out in that way.

## 6. CONCLUSION

The objective of this paper was to describe the development of a framework that would help manufacturing organizations identify and understand their business processes.

A high level business process architecture has been developed from a study of various business process architectures defined by specific manufacturing organizations and general models suggested in the BPR literature. The high level business process architecture groups the business processes within an organization under three headings. A set of standard business processes has been identified and defined under the "Operate" heading.

To define the four processes in more detail a model of processes has been developed. The purpose of the model was to represent the activities and flows that when integrated form the four "Operate" processes in a typical manufacturing organization. The model is not meant to be prescriptive and is not intended to show how a business should operate.

The model has been validated by a number of practitioners. They found that it represented a view of standard "Operate" processes within a typical manufacturing company. It was then used in a manufacturing company as a framework to help the company identify and understand its business processes. A case study of the company and its findings from using the model has been provided. The framework proved useful to the company in developing a model of their existing order fulfillment process.

The framework consisting of the high level business process architecture and model are currently at a stage of completeness where they can be used within manufacturing organizations. They will benefit from further development to incorporate new information and views gained from subsequent applications.

## 7. ACKNOWLEDGEMENTS

The research described in this paper has been funded by the DIP directorate of the UK's Engineering and Physical Science Research Council.

## 8. REFERENCES

AMICE ESPRIT, 1989, CIM-OSA Reference Architecture CAM-I (1980), Architectecture Manual ICAM Definition Method "IDEF-0", Arlington, Texas

CEN (1990) ENV 40 003, Computer-Integrated manufacturing –Systems Architecture - Framework for Enterprise Modeling. CEN/CENELEC, Brussels.

Champy J (1995), Re-engineering Management, HarperBusiness, NY

Checkland P (1981), Systems thinking, systems practice, J Wiley & Sons

Childe S J (1991), The design and implementation of manufacturing infrastructure, PhD Thesis, Polytechnic South West, UK

Davenport T H and Short J E (1990), The new industrial engineering: information technology and Business Process Redesign, Sloan Management Review, Summer

Davenport H J (1993), Process Innovation, Harvard Business School Press
Hammer M. Re-engineering Work: Don't automate, Obliterate, Harvard Business Review, July-August, 1990
Harrington H J, (1992), Business Process Improvement, McGraw-Hill
Harvey D (1994), Re-engineering: The Critical Success Factors. , Business Intelligence
Johansson H J, McHugh P, Pendlebury A J, Wheeler W A (1993), Business Process Re-engineering- BreakPoint Strategies for market dominance, J Wiley & Sons
Jorysz H R, Vernadat F B (1990), CIM-OSA Part2: Information View, International Journal of Computer Integrated Manufacturing, vol. 3 No. 3
Kane E J (1986), IBM's Quality Focus on the Business Process, Quality Progress, April
Meyer C (1993), Fast Cycle Time, The Free Press, NY
Porter M E (1985), Competitive Advantage: Creating and Sustaining Superior Performance, The Free Press, NY
Parnaby J (1993), Business Process Systems Engineering, Lucas Industries plc, November
Scheer W A (1992) Architecture for Integrated Information Systems, Springer-Verlag, Berlin
Shapiro B P, Rangan V K, Sviokla J J (1992), Staple yourself to an order, Harvard Business Review, July-August
Smart PA, Maull R S, Childe S J, Bennett J, Weaver A M, (1995), Report on Process Analysis Tools, (Working Paper WP/GR/J/95010-3), EPSRC Grant No GR/J/95010, University of Plymouth, UK
Smart A Weaver A Maull R and Childe S (1997) A reference Model of Operate Processes for Process Based Change. Paper in preparation.
Weaver A M, (1995), A model based approach to the design and implementation of computer aided production management systems, PhD Thesis, University of Plymouth, UK
Vernadat F B, (1996) Enterprise Modeling and Integration. Chapman Hall
Williams T J (1994) The Purdue Enterprise Reference Architecture. Computers in Industry 24 (2-3).
Williams T J (1995) Development of GERAM, a Generic Enterprise Reference Architecture and enterprise Integration Methodology. In Integrated Manufacturing Systems Engineering, Chapman and Hall, London

# 21

# Process Assessment Method – an approach for business process development

*Terho Laakso*
*Helsinki University of Technology*
*TAI Research Center*
*PO BOX 9555, FIN-02015 Espoo*
*Tel: +358 9 451 2851 Fax: +358 9 451 3665*
*E-mail: terho.laakso@hut.fi*

**Abstract**

This paper introduces a method that facilitates the effective implementation of capable business processes. The capability of a business process is defined to be its ability to satisfy customers' expectations by using available resources as efficiently as possible and to be adaptive to changes in external and internal requirements. In the paper it is discussed "how companies could be helped to develop and implement capable business processes".

The proposed process assessment method combines hard system analysis techniques with participation of employees. It facilitates skills for productive communication, examines system structure, analyses system interrelationships and allows employees to participate in process redesign and implementation. The method has been developed during the EUREKA TIME GUIDE project (EU 11579). In Finland the project included eight pilot companies where the method has been tested.

**Keywords**

Business process assessment, Process modeling, Business process re-engineering, Organizational development

Computer Applications in Production and Engineering. F. Plonka and G. Olling (Eds.)

# 1 INTRODUCTION

Enterprises have become more and more aware of business processes. Business process performance is recognized to be the basis for the overall capability of the company. Clear evidence of this is the massive publicity business process re-engineering (BPR) has received in the 90's. The discussion about the BPR has been voluminous in journals and books (Davenport, 1995). One of the big issues in the BPR discussions has been how the company should develop its processes. There has been a distinction between incremental improvements advocated by the TQM school (Harrington 1991,Oakland 1993) and radical process redesigning advocated by BPR school (Hammer and Champy 1993, Davenport 1993). However, the reality is not so black and white as Stoddard and Jarvenpaa (1995) have proved in their case studies. They argue that both radical and incremental approaches are needed in different phases of business process development and process change management.

In this paper process development is seen as a system of nested development cycles. There is a cycle that continuously monitors how outputs of the processes fit the external requirements and adjust themselves to the changes, if they are able to. The main concern of this cycle is "do the processes deliver outputs that are needed at the market place at right time and the right price"? If not, processes should be redesigned, which typically involves heavy investments and high risks. The second cycle concerns "how efficiently resources are used in the process". The cycle is continuously seeking opportunities to improve process efficiency by eliminating non-value adding activities, implementing streamlined process structures, empowering employees and setting measures to monitor change. These activities have lower risks and do not require major investments. However, if the second cycle is well managed it could add up to considerable improvements, which could lead to a new competitive edge in the market place. The process assessment method introduced in this paper is developed to support nested process development cycles.

# 2 PROCESS CHANGE MANAGEMENT

According to Kettinger and Grover (1995) process change management is a strategy-driven organizational initiative to improve and redesign business processes to achieve competitive advantage in performance through changes in the relationships between management, information, technology, organizational structure and people.

A business process in this paper is defined to be: *"a structured, measured set of activities and flows that use necessary resources of the organization to provide specified output for a particular customer."*

## 2.1 Concept of process management

One of the main drivers for moving from a functional view to a team based process management is a necessity to bring planning and thinking back together with implementing and doing. To maximize the level of improvement in ownership for making things to happen, the thinking and doing are brought as close as possible to the customers and the people making, serving or supporting the organization's products and/or services (Turner, 1995). In addition, Rummler and Brache (1990) claim that the greatest opportunities for performance improvement often lie in the functional interfaces. These critical interfaces are visible only in the horizontal process view of an organization.

Harrington (1991) gives nine characteristics for a well defined and a well-managed process:

- it has someone who is held accountable for the process;
- the boundaries of the process are defined;
- its interfaces and responsibilities are clearly defined;
- it is documented;
- it has measurement and feedback controls;
- it has customer related measurements and targets;
- its cycle time is known;
- it has formalized change procedures;
- opportunities for improvements are continuously sought.

Following the list of Harrington (1991), seven contentions for process management are given:

1. There should be designated process owner who is responsible and accountable for managing and improving the process.
2. Team work is an important part of the process management and teams are the vehicles to bring together needed resources and skills.
3. The abstract concept of business process should be made tangible by using several modeling techniques. Models are used to visualize the structure and behavior of a business process.
4. Customer needs and requirements must be understood throughout the business process.
5. Performance measures, which are aligned with the process objectives, are important tools to drive process thinking and process improvement.
6. Process based organizations should commit themselves to continuous learning and capability development.
7. There must be harmony between vertical and horizontal dimensions of an organization and they must support each other.

## 2.2 Challenges in process change management

The shift from the functional to the process based organization is always a difficult task not only because it redistributes resources and power, but also because it brings into question employees' most basic assumptions about the nature of the organization.

Seven empirical studies (Bashein et al. 1994, Hall et al. 1994, Zairi and Sinclair 1995, Grover et al. 1995, Guimare and Bond 1996, Majchrzak and Wang 1996, Childe et al. 1996) have been analyzed by the author in order to identify the main challenges and problems faced during the shift from the functional to the process based organizations. The Burke-Litwin (Burke and Litwin, 1992) model has been used as a framework for the analysis. The model defines twelve variables that need to be considered in the change programs. See Figure 1.

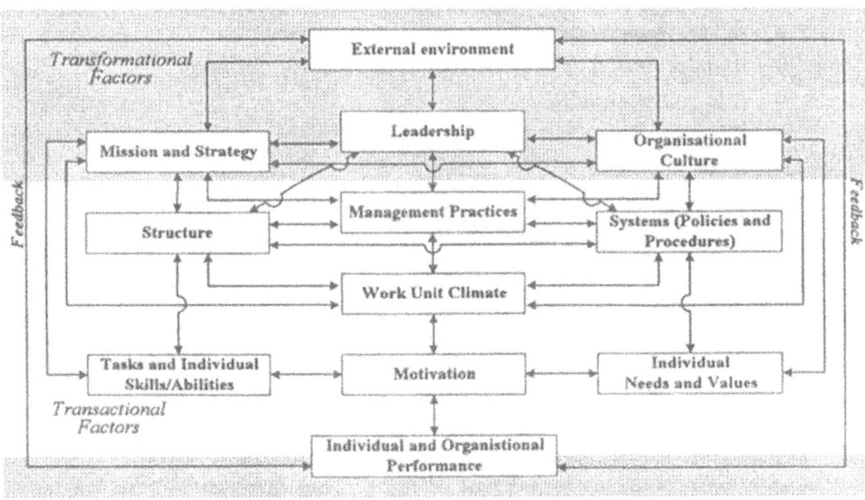


**Figure 1** Burke-Litwin model (Burke and Litwin, 1992)

According to the analysis three most difficult areas in process change management are related to:

1. *Structure* that is the arrangement of functions and people into specific areas and levels of responsibility, decision-making authority, communication, and relationship to assure effective implementation of the organizations mission and strategy. The issues related to this variable according to the studies were such as:
   - Project had a wrong sponsor;
   - The importance of communication was underestimated;
   - Re-engineering team was made-up narrowly;
   - Failure to anticipate and plan for the organizational resistance to change;
   - Jobs were not structured with overlapping responsibilities and rotation.

2. *Systems* that are standardized polices and mechanisms that are designed to facilitate work. They are typically embedded in an organization's reward system, management and information system, quality system and in such control systems as performance appraisal, goal and budget development and human resource allocation. The issues related to this variable according to the studies were such as:
   - Needed investments were hard to justify;
   - BPR was too disruptive to business operations;
   - Rewards were not based on the group performance;
   - Lack of tools and skills to promote collaboration horizontally and vertically;
   - Performance measures were not aligned according to the processes.
3. *Leadership* that is executive behavior providing overall direction and serving as role models for all employees about practices and values in the organization. It also encourages others to take needed action to accomplish the strategy. The issues related to this variable according to the studies were such as:
   - Failure to build support from line managers;
   - Project was run and done by an external "swat" team;
   - Lack of a strong director who was willing to make clear demands:
   - Senior executives were not fully committed for the BPR project;
   - BPR project was subjected to a stand-alone examination.

The review to the empirical studies denoted some requirements that should be taken account in the process assessment method development. Co-operation should be facilitated. Need for change should be understood among employees. The method should enhance reciprocal communication vertically and horizontally. In addition, the method should catalyze thinking on how the measurement system could be aligned according to the change objectives.

## 3 CAPABLE BUSINESS PROCESS DEVELOPMENT

A business process was previously defined to be "a structured, measured set of activities and flows that use necessary resources of the organization to provide specified output for a particular customer". Following this, business process capability is defined to be: *"the ability of a process to satisfy customers expectations by using resources as efficiently as possible. In addition, a capable process is adaptive to changes in external and internal requirements."*

In this paper the development of a capable business process relies on the taxonomy of systems thinking, organizational learning and proper interventions. This taxonomy is derived from the definition above and the ideas of Checkland (1981), Argyris (1992) and Garvin (1993).

A business process is a combination of technical and social systems with a multiplicity of objectives. In addition, it is in constant change. Checkland (1981) argues that systems thinking is an approach to study and understand such complex dynamic systems. Adaptation i.e. adjustment to environmental conditions needs constant reflection of environment and reflection of results of one's actions. This is a basic principle of the organizational learning loop of Argyris (1992). Garvin (1993) has stated that without the implementation of changes only the potential for improvement exists. To enter into an ongoing system in order to help it in change implementation or process adaptation some knowledge of interventions is needed.

*Understanding the business process as a dynamic system*

According to Senge et al. (1994) a new understanding of the process of change emerges not top-down or bottom-up, but participative at all levels - *aligned through common understanding of a system.* Senge (1990) adds that systems thinking aims at seeing interrelationships and continuums. It separates detail complexity from dynamic complexity. The detail complexity arises when there are many variables. The dynamic complexity arises when cause and effect are distant in time and space, and when the consequences of interventions over time are hidden and not obvious.

Systems thinking attempts to focus on areas of high leverage. Tackling a difficult problem is often a matter of seeing where the high leverage lies and where a change - with a minimum of effort - would lead to lasting and significant improvements (Senge, 1990).

Systems, hence business processes are dynamic when events occur that change their properties (Smith, 1982). Coyle (1977) argue that the dynamics of a system arise from three sources:

- Shocks imposed by the environment on the business process and/or on the markets i.e. customers and competitors;
- Operating polices within the business process;
- Policies and reactions within the markets.

According to Forrester (1975) three basic types of information are needed for studying dynamic systems: structure, delays in decisions and actions, and policies on managing material flows.

*Business process as a learning system*

In the absence of learning, processes simply repeat old practices. Change remains cosmetic, and improvements are either incidental or short-lived. Without implementation of changes in the ways of working only the potential for improvement exists (Garvin, 1993). Capable business processes require a commitment to learning.

According to Garvin (1993) organizational learning can usually be traced through the three overlapping stages. The first step is cognitive. Members of organization are discovering new ideas, expanding their knowledge and beginning to think differently. The second step is behavioral. Employees begin to internalize new insights and alter their behavior. The third step is performance improvement. Changes in behavior lead to measurable improvements in results: improved quality, shorter lead times or increased customer satisfaction, etc.

*Process interventions*

Different interventions have different dynamics. Interventions do different things because they are based on different causal mechanisms. Selection of an intervention type is dependent on the objectives and the target group of the intervention (French and Bell, 1995). However, the basic requirements and the primary tasks for any intervention activities regardless of the substantive issues involved are (Argyris, 1970):

- Generation of valid information that describes the factors and their interrelationships, that create problems for the client system (object of an intervention).
- To help the client system make free but informed and responsible choices. The client should remain responsible for their destiny and maintain their autonomy.
- To build client's internal commitment to the choices.

Intervention should help the client to create ownership and a feeling of responsibility about the selected choice and its implications. In addition, the client system should come to the point where it begins to change its behavior according to choice (Argyris, 1970).

## 4 A METHOD FOR BUSINESS PROCESS ASSESSMENT

The process assessment method (PAM) introduced in this paper combines qualitative and quantitative modeling methods. Qualitative models are graphical presentations of a business process. Quantitative models represent mathematical or logical relationships which are believed govern the behavior of the business process.

The objective of the PAM is to help companies to improve their understanding of business processes. One of the best ways to learn about organizational reality is to model current processes and through this examines an organization's operation and behavior patterns. An understanding of the company's current set of beliefs and values, and the unwritten but underlying business assumptions that are driving operations, is a prerequisite for the process development. Change is not possible without uncovering these assumptions (Laakso et al. 1996).

The process assessment method is a cyclical process and it is conducted by participative cross-functional and cross-hierarchical teams to ensure a broad knowledge sharing about the studied process. See Figure 2. The method consists of several individual interventions.

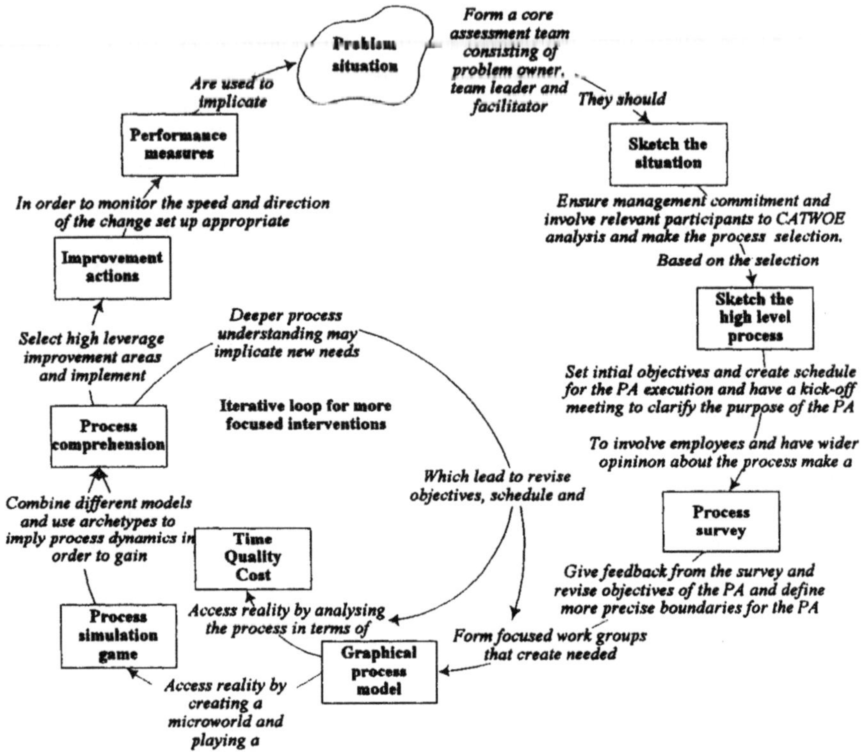


**Figure 2** The process assessment method (Laakso, 1997).

French and Bell (1995) have given six guidelines for managing multiple interventions. These guidelines are taken account in the development of PAM. They argue that several interventions should be managed in a way which:

1. *maximizes diagnostic data* by beginning with the intervention that provides data needed to make subsequent interventions;
2. *maximizes effectiveness* by sequencing the interventions so that early interventions enhance the effectiveness of subsequent interventions;
3. *maximizes efficiency* by sequencing the interventions to save resources such as time, people, material and money;
4. *maximizes speed* by sequencing the interventions in way that objectives of the project are attained in time;
5. *maximizes relevance* by beginning with intervention that tries to tackle the most immediate problem according to the management;
6. *minimizes psychological and organizational strain.*

As a result of the process assessment, a company should have a clear picture of what is happening in the business process. This consciousness is needed in process development where actions are taken and implemented based on the process understanding. Without implementation no changes will be realized. However, the aim of the PAM is to gain process understanding and to locate high leverage improvement areas that are needed in development of capable business processes. The scope of the PAM is not in the implementation phase. Yet, it provides useful tools for the implementation process.

## 5 CONCLUSIONS

The process assessment method is a tool for evaluating process structure and its performance, which is needed in process development and management. Clarification of a structure is achieved by creating qualitative process models that are graphical presentations of the process. Process performance and behavior are evaluated through qualitative process analysis.

The PAM offers an overall view of the business process - its flows (inputs and outputs), transformation, performance level, goals and the structure of an organization that performs the process. After the process assessment, the organization should have a clear picture what is happening in the business process. This consciousness is prerequisite for sensible process development and management. The actual process development work begins with the selection of the improvement areas that have the highest leverage. The PAM is a tool to identify these areas.

## 6 REFERENCES

Argyris, C. (1970) Intervention Theory and Method: A Behavioral Science View. Addison-Wesley, Publishing Company, Social Science and Administration Series, USA.

Bashein, B. and Markus, M. L. and Riley, P. (1994) Preconditions for BPR Success and How to Prevent Failures. *Information Systems Management*, Spring, pp. 98-110.

Burke, W. and Litwin (1992) A Casual Model of Organizational Performance and Change. *Journal of Management*, Vol. 18, No. 5, pp. 523-545.

Checkland, P. (1981) Systems Thinking, Systems Practice. John Wiley & Sons, UK.

Childe, S and Maull, R. and Mills, B. (1996) UK Experiences in Business Process Re-engineering; A Scoping study for the Innovative Manufacturing Initiative. Research Report for Grant No. GR/K67328, School of Computing, University of Plymouth.

Coyle, R. (1977) Management System Dynamics. John Wiley & Sons, UK.

Davenport, T. (1993) Process Innovation: Re-engineering Work trough Information Technology, Harvard Business School Press, Boston, Massachusetts.

Davenport, T. (1995) Business Process Re-engineering: Where It's Been, Where It's Going. In Grover, V and Kettinger, W. (eds.) *Business Process Change: Re-engineering Concepts, Methods and Technologies*. Harrisburg, PA: Idea Group Publishing.

Forrester, J. (1975) Collected Papers of Jay W. Forrester. Wright-Allen Press Inc., Massachusetts.

French, W. and Bell, C. (1995) Organization Development: Behavioral Science Interventions for Organization Improvement, Fifth Edition, Prentice-Hall Inc., USA.

Garvin, D. (1993) Building Learning Organization. *Harvard Business Review*, July-August, pp. 78-91.

Grover, V. and Jeong, S. and Kettinger, W. and Teng, J. (1995) The Implementation of Business Process Re-engineering. *Journal of Management Information Systems*, Vol. 12, No. 1, pp. 109-144.

Guimaraes, T. and Bond, W. (1996) Empirically Assessing the Impact of BPR on Manufacturing Firms, *International Journal of Operations & Production Management*, Vol. 16, No. 8, pp. 5-28.

Hall, E. and Rosenthal, J. and Wade, J. (1994) How to Make Re-engineering Really Work. *The McKinsey Quarterly*, No. 2, pp. 107-128.

Hammer, M. and Champy, J. (1993) Re-engineering the Corporation: A Manifesto for Business Revolution. Harper Collins Publisher Inc., USA.

Harrington, H J. (1991) Business Process Improvement. Quality Press, McGraw-Hill, Inc. New York.

Kettinger, W. and Grover, V. (1995) Toward a Theory of Business Process Change Management. *Journal of Management Information Systems*, Vol. 12, No. 1, pp. 9-30.

Laakso, T. (1997) Performance Evaluation and Process Interventions - A Method for Business Process Development. Acta Polytechnica Scandinavica, Mathematics and Computer Series, No. 86, The Finnish Academy of Technology, Espoo, Finland.

Laakso, T., Kleinhans, S., Smeds, R. and Doumeingts, G. (1996) Embedding the management of evolution into strategic learning. Ninth International Working Seminar on Production Economics, Innsbruck, Austria, February 19-23, 1996, 19 p.

Majchrzak, A. and Wang, Q. (1996) Breaking the Functional Mind-Set in Process Organizations. *Harvard Business Review*, September-October, pp. 93-99.

Oakland, J. (1993) Total Quality Management; The Route to Improving Performance. Second edition, Butterworth-Heinemann Ltd, Oxford, UK.

Rummler, G. and Brache, A. (1990) Improving Performance: How to Manage the White Space on the Organization Chart. Jossey-Bass, San Francisco.

Senge, P. (1990) The Leader's New Work: Building Learning Organizations. *Sloan Management Review*, Fall, pp. 7-23.

Senge, P. and Roberts, C. and Ross, R. and Smith, B. and Kleiner, A. (1994) The Fifth Discipline Fieldbook. Nicholas Brealey Publishing Ltd, London, UK.

Smith, A. (1982) Management Systems: Analyses and Applications. The Dryden Press, Japan,

Stoddard, D. and Jarvenpaa, S. (1995) Business Process Redesign: Tactics for Managing Radical Change. *Journal of Management Information Systems*, Vol. 12, No. 1, pp. 81-107.

Turner, R. (1995) Process Management: The Versatile Approach to Achieving Quality in Project Based Organizations. *Journal of General Management*, Vol. 21, No. 1, Autumn, pp. 47-61.

## 7 BIOGRAPHY

Terho Laakso received his Ph.D. from Helsinki University of Technology (HUT) in 1997. The subject of his thesis was in the area of business process development. After his M.Sc.(Eng.) graduation in 1989 he has worked as a system engineer and quality manager in Schneider Electric Oy for five years. Currently he is a senior researcher at HUT and undertaking research on business process development and change management.

# 22

# Information Transfers as a metric for Engineering processes

*M. P. Klapsis, V. Thomson*
*Department of Mechanical Engineering*
*McGill University*
*817 Sherbrooke Street West, Montreal, Canada, H3A 2K6*
*tel.: 1-514-398-2597, e-mail: thomson@mecheng.mcgill.ca*

**Abstract**

Engineering processes have been studied to understand better knowledge work processes, the scheduling of work, and the effects of certain engineering practices. In this study the concept of using information transfers as a measure of the performance of knowledge work processes was developed.

Most engineering projects are oriented towards producing deliverables. Work is organized by dividing projects into arbitrary work packages for assembly into some type of product. However, the focus on a small number of widely spaced deliverables makes it very difficult to measure project progress and work process performance due to the lack of suitable performance indicators.

The tracking of the transfer of information used to complete work provides an excellent measure of both project and process performance. Since engineering (knowledge work) is information intensive, the movement of information from one worker to another provides an excellent measure of task completion. An engineering design project was studied; the tracking of key information transfers showed project progress and provided insight into performance. The metric also aided analysis of resource loading and project timeliness. While only studied for engineering processes, information transfers should be a useful metric to track progress and to predict task completion in any information intensive process.

**Keywords**

Process management, metrics, engineering processes

## 1 INTRODUCTION

In order to maintain a competitive position in today's rapidly changing market environment, organizations are forced to deliver products and services in shorter and shorter time frames. This implies a greater emphasis on improving processes,

Computer Applications in Production and Engineering. F. Plonka and G. Olling (Eds.)

and therefore, better measurement of the processes involved. For manufacturing and engineering based companies, the focus for improvement is placed on engineering or knowledge work processes. For example, for new product introduction, engineered-to-order products and production planning, these knowledge intensive processes encompass most of the work involved and of the time to delivery. The processes need to be actively managed, which includes formalizing processes, scheduling activities, and defining metrics to improve knowledge worker productivity, and thus, overall process performance.

Measuring the performance of such processes is fundamental for controlling, and consequently, reducing the time-to-market, a crucial factor for a customer when an order is being considered. For large engineered-to-order projects, for example, a shorter delivery time becomes a competitive advantage and is often the key differentiating factor for securing a potential contract. Achieving the promised time-to-market is what gives the client confidence and satisfaction. There are several approaches currently used to ensure that the schedule developed to meet the desired delivery time is indeed met. These are predominantly project management methods which are focused on the control of resources.

In this paper a metrics approach is presented which allows the better management of knowledge work processes through the measurement of information transfers. This is a process management technique which provides an improved capability to control the use of time. This paper considers: first, the current practices used for managing the performance of an engineering project through deliverables and decision points; then, the concept of information transfers and the advantages that they provide in controlling completion time; and finally, a case study of General Electric Hydro which provides an example of the use of information transfers in a large, complex engineering project.

## 2 PHASE REVIEW AND STAGE-GATE PROCESSES

The phase review process was developed in the 1960's by the US military (Cooper, 1994). It is applicable to very large engineering projects, such as the procurement of military hardware and the construction of hydroelectric power dams. This approach provides the necessary means to a contractor to manage a project at all times. Projects get divided into phases according to work content. At the end of each phase there is a milestone, a very formal and usually lengthy review point, which is scheduled at the planning stage. Milestones lie far apart in time, and may be major, reflecting significant sections of work, or minor, set at intermediate points within a phase. They comprise a set of deliverables that contain or describe the work previously performed. These deliverables are carefully reviewed and approved in formal events, often by teams of cross-functional experts, only then, can work or funding resume.

A similar approach, the stage-gate process, was developed by industry later in the 1960's for new product development (Cooper, 1994). These engineering projects are characterized by a series of steps, starting from winning a bid through preparing product or service specifications and negotiating their approval with the customer, to the manufacture of the product or the handing over of the service. Like the phase review method, projects get divided into discrete stages, and a road-map for task completion is created from the beginning to the end of the project. Each stage is followed by a gate, which is a go/no-go type of decision point. Therefore, work at a later stage can proceed only if the work at all prerequisite ones has been approved at their respective gates. In case of non-approval, the project gets canceled.

Milestones permit an appropriate management of resources by controlling their use (cost). Timely completion of projects, while desirable, tends not to be the main purpose of project management by milestone. In practice, the use of milestone procedures often leads to poor performance through work discontinuity and significant time-to-market delay. Introducing stages and decision gates creates a rather linear, time consuming approach to managing a project. Indeed, each gate becomes a stopping point, where the next stage has to wait for the previous one to be completed and a subsequent decision taken in order to proceed. Furthermore, as teams rush to meet defined deadlines, serious resource fluctuations are observed, which can be attributed to poor forecasting of the work required or unanticipated changes. Also, during review periods resource demand drops to minimal levels, only to increase suddenly once more, when an approval is obtained. When deliverables do not get approved, the amount of rework increases dramatically, usually to comply with changing requirements. As resources get absorbed to resolve rework related issues, further progress is halted until all the work gets approved. The resulting delay is usually further compounded, since rework often occurs in multiple loops before a satisfactory solution is reached. Therefore, the use of milestones actually becomes a factor of disruption in a project or a process; these disruptions need to be minimized in order to ensure a stable resource utilization (Bhuiyan and Thomson, 1996). New process methods have been developed to overcome the shortcomings of phase review and stage-gate processes (Bhuiyan and Thomson, 1996; Cooper, 1994). This paper will not focus on these new methods, but on a new metric which will permit knowledge work processes to be measured better, and thus, allow the new process methods to succeed.

## 3 INFORMATION TRANSFERS

An information transfer is a hand-over of knowledge from one individual or group of individuals to another during a process or a project. This communication of information can be informal, over the phone or through electronic mail, as well as formal, when entire pieces of requisite work are transferred to allow the continuation of a process. The latter forms the basis for the use of information transfers, as the transfers tend to be more substantial and critical to the progress of a knowledge work process.

An information transfer indicates the completion of a piece of work. Furthermore, it shows the timeliness at any stage in the process, since the moment that a transfer is made can be compared to an original plan or schedule. It also denotes the instant when subsequent work dependent upon the information can commence. Hence, at an aggregate level, a group of information transfers measures the degree of completeness of an entire body of work. Therefore, a view of the requisite work completed at any point in the project is obtained, thus, demonstrating project progress and timeliness.

Knowledge intensive, engineering processes, such as new product introduction and engineered-to-order, are characterized by information intensive work, multiple activities and complex organizational structures. The driving force in these processes is the creation, movement and use of information. Hence, managing the flow of information becomes the key to timeliness. Information transfers highlight the path that information follows through a process, indicate subprocess dependencies, and allow the measurement of time-based activities. Consequently, the use of information transfers as a metric is a good process management tool, permitting process analysis beyond simple monitoring.

In general, engineering performance is defined by the degree of timeliness, process productivity and process predictability. For time critical knowledge work processes, there is a limited number of sources from which cycle time can be squeezed. These include reducing the span time and rework, as well as increasing the concurrency of activities. Better scheduling drives span time (project duration) closer to make time (temporal sum of all individual tasks). Better coordination and work discipline lead to reduced rework and more efficient resource utilization. More process concurrency reduces project duration. However, all these factors increase process complexity, and therefore, the difficulty of managing a project. Information transfers provide a mechanism to measure the effects of rework, span time and concurrency so that they can be controlled or used better.

As already mentioned, tracking information transfers is an excellent way to monitor task progress and to measure process characteristics such as rework. By capturing the amount of rework and the interconnection of activities, it is possible to use the metric of information transfers as a tool for predicting process or project duration. Indeed, the various subprocesses within a process are linked through information transfers, with the output of one activity becoming the input to a number of downstream ones. This coupling of activities can be captured in a step-by-step view of a process. However, tracking information transfers provides a mechanism to gauge the level of rework (recycling through additional process tasks) and the corresponding delay this causes to downstream activities. However, active management through measurement of information transfers provides a useful process management technique that greatly improves overall process coordination, which in turn increases process effectiveness. Furthermore, the application of this metric is flexible enough to permit measurement at the appropriate level of activity granularity to match the requirements of a particular process analysis.

The simple tracking of deliverables is neither a sufficient nor a satisfactory method for monitoring knowledge intensive, engineering processes. This is mainly due to the small number of entities that can be monitored, as well as the lack of a convenient mechanism to track the contribution of task completion to a specific deliverable, and the interdependencies among the completed deliverables. The organized tracking of information, visible to all participants, can enhance the traditional techniques used for the scheduling of large engineering projects, such as PERT and CPM (Malone and Crowston, 1994); information transfers do provide the means required. They are based on the flow of information in a process throughout time, rather than at widely separated discrete events, as in the case of deliverables. They allow the detailed measurement of a process, and thus, permit better management.

## 4 GE CASE STUDY

Studies were undertaken with General Electric Hydro (GE) to analyze their engineering specification approval (ESA) process. This process requires that, after a contract is won to design and build a hydroelectric turbine-generator system, GE must develop a complete set of engineering specifications for the system. This includes the creation of conceptual, layout and detailed designs, the approval of engineering specifications by the customer, and the hand-over of the requisite information to manufacturing for production, and to the site contractor for the installation of the integrated system. The main characteristics that define the ESA process are: high information content, high level of product complexity, low level of new technology development, large projects, and long time frames.

Throughout the ESA process a great deal of coordination is necessary among the various sections within GE, as well as between these sections and the customer, to ensure that engineering information is created and approved in a timely manner, as specified in the contractual agreement. The GE study investigated all the aspects of the ESA process and considered evidence from several projects, though it mainly focused on one large, international project, the ERTAN power dam project in Sichuan, China. A detailed stochastic model of the ESA process was developed using FirstSTEP™, a process modeling and simulation software tool from Interfacing Technologies Inc. (Montreal). The model encapsulated all the design and engineering activities associated with specifying all the components for a turbine-generator system for specification approval by the customer, and subsequent manufacture by GE. Actual activity data, such as work flow, effort, time, personnel involved, and communication patterns, were incorporated into the model. Many simulations were done to analyze the process.

A key element of the study was the investigation of the capability of information transfers to show task completion and to illustrate the effects of delays, rework and concurrent activities. The results from this work are presented below.

## 4.1 Results

One of the main subjects studied was rework. Multiple rework loops were simulated. These were due to either customer or GE engineer requested changes. Customer related rework caused more time delay than internal rework due to the lengthy and complicated approval procedures involved. Two scenarios were studied: first, a straightforward process with no rework; secondly, a triple rework

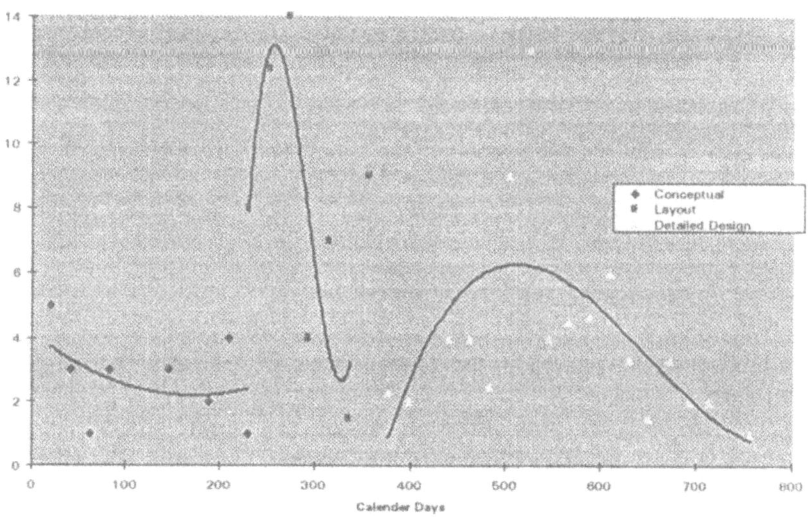


**Figure 1** Information transfers for the stages of the ESA process with no rework

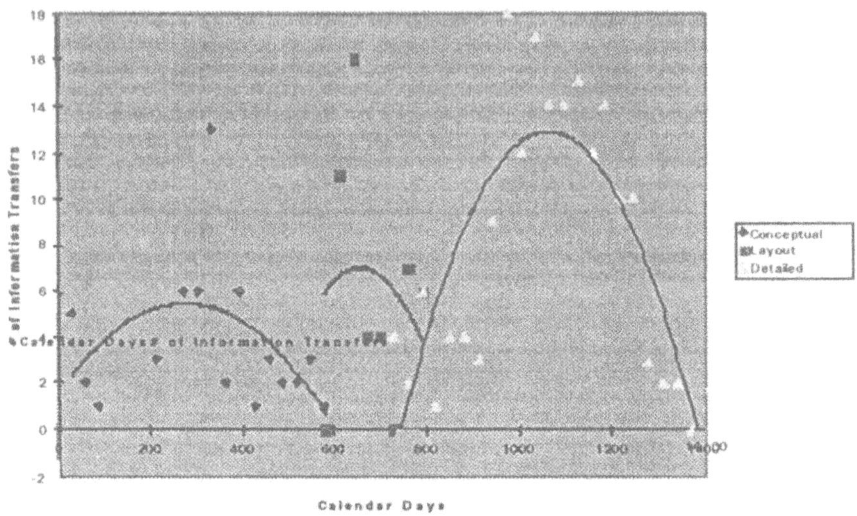


**Figure 2**Information transfers for the stages of the ESA process with multiple rework loops

loop pattern at every interface point with the customer. In reality, the latter was a modest assumption for rework since a greater number of rework loops were usually performed in most cases.

The occurrence of information transfers with respect to time for the no-rework and multiple rework scenarios is shown in Figures 1 and 2 respectively. The time axis is in calendar days; a week of forty working hours was used with holidays being neglected. The graphs in Figures 1 and 2 show the number of information transfers for the conceptual, layout and detailed design stages in the ESA process. Note that rework (Figure 2) approximately doubles the length of time of each design stage.

The general behavior of the information transfers with respect to time can be described by a second order, bell shaped curve. This conforms to the model developed by P.V. Norden (1964, 1970) which describes the level of design effort per unit time for a project; the model is effective when the design process is resource limited. Notice that the effort curve for conceptual design (Figure 1) is flat, which shows that the process is not resource limited.

Analysis was also done with weighted information transfers, i.e., each information transfer was multiplied by a factor which indicated the amount of effort

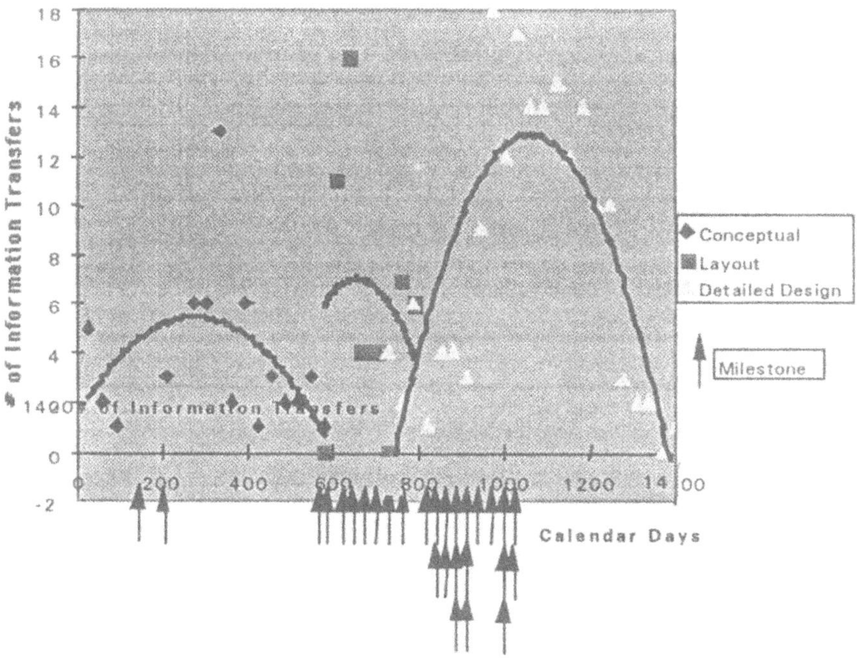


**Figure 3** Information transfers with major milestones indicated for the ESA process with multiple rework loops

needed to create a particular information transfer. With weighted information transfers, the difference in the curves for no-rework and rework was the extra effort caused by rework.

Major milestones are indicated in Figure 3 on the same plot of information transfers as given in Figure 2. Milestones at the end of the ESA process for the transfer of information to manufacturing are not shown. It is obvious that information transfers are a much better metric for monitoring the performance of the design process. They are more numerous and occur more uniformly throughout the process.

Information transfers which specifically contribute to a final deliverable for the design of two major components are shown in Figure 4. The transfers represent the data that has to be created and then delivered at each stage of the design process for the winding and rotor components of the generator.

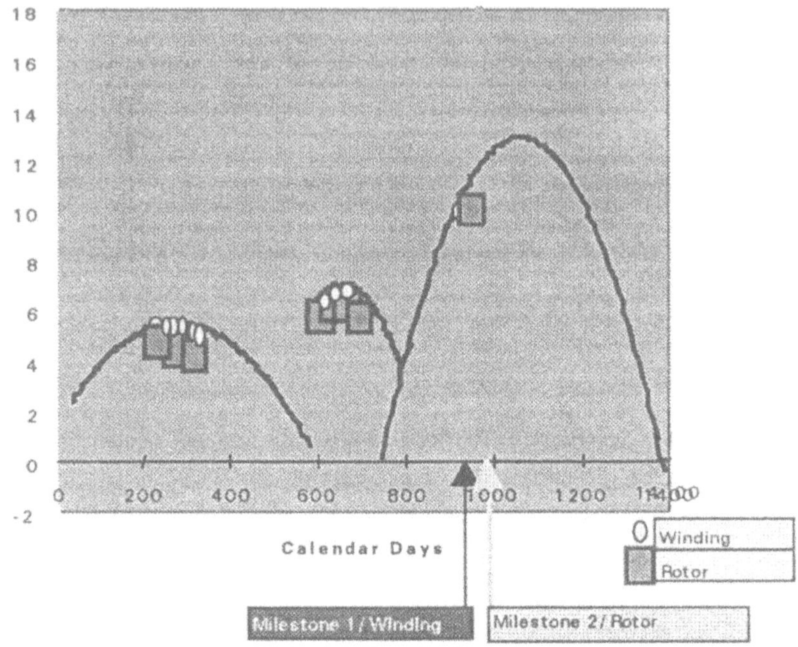


**Figure 4** Information transfers which relate to specific milestones are indicated at each design stage.

A complete set of information transfers is shown in Figure 5. The transfers start at the conceptual stage for the total design of a generator, followed by the separate information transfers during the layout stage for 5 major components. Some of the information transfers for the detailed design of the bracket are also shown. In addition, some of the dependencies between the information transfers are indicated. In this format, it is very apparent that information transfers can capture the flow of information, the interdependencies between different data streams, and how information contributes to deliverables.

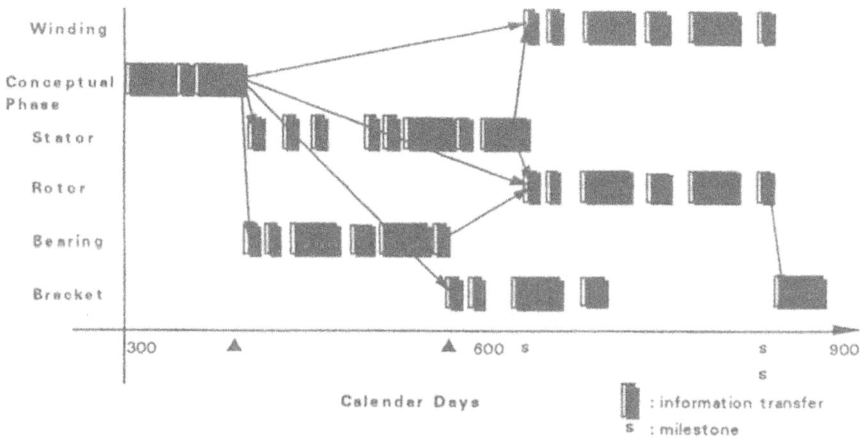


**Figure 5** A set of information transfers and milestones for the design of five generator components in the ESA process

## 5 CONCLUSIONS

Information transfers were found to be a very useful tool in the study of performance in engineering processes. They were able to show the timeliness of task completion and the dependency of downstream process steps to upstream information. As well, they measured the effects of other process characteristics, such as rework, span time, time delays and concurrency.

While Gantt charts can show some of the same things, they do so only with a view of how resources are used. This is usually not a measure of project timeliness, and certainly not, process performance. Information transfers are, however, a useful metric for indicating process timeliness, and thus, project timeliness. They are a direct measure of process performance.

Information transfers also highlight the path of information in a process showing the interrelationships and interdependencies of the process steps. This information path is the knowledge path through a process. Monitoring information transfers, then, tracks the essence of knowledge work processes, i.e., the creation, movement and use of information.

This metric should provide a direct technique to overcome some of the inadequacies in the emphasis on control of resources in phase review and stage-gate processes. With the greater emphasis on timely completion of projects, managers need new processes and new process measurement tools such as information transfers. While only studied for engineering processes, information transfers should be a useful metric for any information intensive process to monitor progress, predict task completion and measure performance.

## 6 REFERENCES

Bhuiyan, N., Thomson, V. (1996) Submitted to the *International Journal for Project Management.*

Cooper, RAG. 1994. Perspective: Third-Generation New Product Processes. *Journal of Production & Innovation Management* 11, 3-14

Klapsis, P.M., Thomson, V. (1996) The Engineering Specification Approval Process. *Proceedings of the Conference on Integration in Manufacturing* (IiM), Galway, Ireland

Malone, T.W., Crowston, K (1994) The Interdisciplinary Study of Coordination. *ACMComputing Surveys* 26, 1, 88-119

Norden, P.V. (1964) *Manpower Utilization Patterns in Research and Development Projects*, Ph.D. Dissertation, Columbia University

Norden, P.V. (1970) Useful tools for process management. *Management of Production* (Ed. M.K. Starr), Penguin Books, Baltimore, 71-101

## 7 BIOGRAPHY

Marios P. Klapsis is a Ph.D. student in Mechanical Engineering at McGill University studying process management in manufacturing and the coordination of knowledge work processes. He has a Master's degree in Mechanical Engineering (McGill). He has worked as a consultant for a number of projects with companies in Canada and Greece.

Vince Thomson is the Werner Graupe Professor for Manufacturing Automation in the Department of Mechanical Engineering at McGill University. He has been involved in manufacturing and information technology related research for 20 years at McGill and the National Research Council (Ottawa). His research has ranged from shop floor control and production scheduling to the present interest in process management in manufacturing.

# 23

# Consequences of current organizational concepts on Management Control and Design / Production Processes interactions

*O. Sénéchal, D. Raviart, C. Tahon*
*L.A.M.I.H., Université de Valenciennes*
*Le Mont Houy BP 311, 59304 VALENCIENNES, FRANCE*
*Tel : +33 3 27 14 13 54, Fax : +33 3 27 14 12 88*
*e-mail : senechal@univ-valenciennes.fr*

**Abstract**

In this paper, we first discuss the role of accounting, according to the current organizational concepts like Concurrent Engineering, Target Costing, and Value Analysis. In this context, we define the notions of measurement, estimation and evaluation, and situate them in the design / production process. Then we show the necessity of performance indicators between accountants, designers and producers and we deduce a set of conditions that a pertinent performance evaluation system has to fulfill. After a short description of the activity concept in Activity Based Costing (ABC) and Activity Based Management (ABM), we introduce a modeling methodology based on this concept, and we describe the associated Decision Support System (DSS). This proposal constitutes, in a concurrent engineering context, a support for communication about past, current and future performances of the design / production process. It is based on a double modeling of the firm for simulation, and on the exploitation of the results with a multi-criteria approach, allowing a multi-disciplinary team to participate to the design phase. This global approach has been implemented in an industrial site and we discuss first results.

**Keywords**

Costing, organization, integration, ABC, simulation.

Computer Applications in Production and Engineering. F. Plonka and G. Olling (Eds.)

# 1 INTRODUCTION

Nowadays, the evolution from a mass-economy to an economy of variety and reactivity forces the firms to be innovative while searching for control of costs, lead times, and quality in a continuous manner. As a result, design and production methods have to change, and some organizational concepts based on transformation and project management appears. This context implies to reconsidering cost structures, the role of costs in decision processes, and more globally, the vision of the control activity of the firm.

# 2 A POINT OF VIEW ON THE CONTROL OF THE ACTIVITY OF THE FIRM

Current constraints have direct consequences on organizational methods as much for production management (Just-in-Time, Cost Kaizen and Total Quality Control) as for development or design (Design to Cost, Value Analysis, and Design for Manufacturing...). These methods and concepts are characterized by a research of transformation, most common principles being decentralization, cooperation with suppliers, diagnostics, anticipation and distribution of responsibility.

This tendency induces us to reconsider the information system of the firm, and particularly the cost management system. Management control, as a specific function, results from the transfer of systems analysis coming from biology, and of cybernetics coming from electronics, towards social sciences, (Mévellec, 1991). Effectively, the firm can be considered as a global regulated system that has to satisfy objectives (order) generally dictated by the market (in terms of variety, cost, quality and lead times). For this, solutions must be proposed (or designed) with regard to these objectives and to the real performance of the firm (that must be previously measured). The proposed solutions must be compared after estimating the corresponding performances. When a decision is made (a set of solutions is chosen), a command is given to the manufacturing process that provides products or services satisfying the needs expressed by the market. Then the obtained performances must be measured to allow, on the one hand, to verify that estimates are confirmed (and to make corrective decisions, if necessary), and on the other hand, to provide information for the design of future products or services.

This very simplified vision of the firm, illustrated by Figure 1, points up what can appear as the main role of control managers in firms being their contribution to measurement, estimation and comparison of performances for making good decisions.

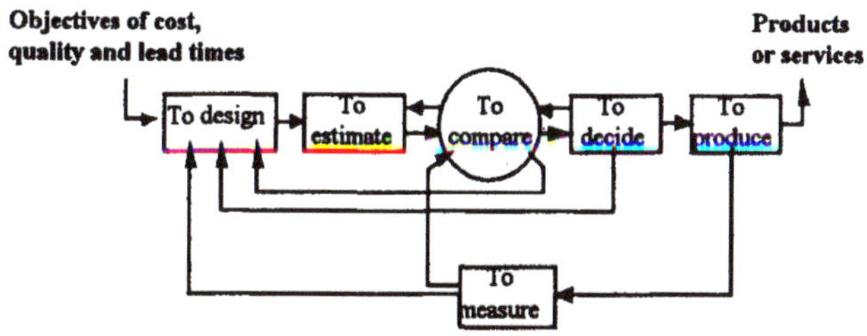


**Figure 1.** Cybernetic vision of control activity.

Some precautions must be taken about the implementation of the regulating notion. If the detection of unfavorable results must trigger corrective actions to achieve objectives, the detection of favorable results must not induce moderation on these efforts. On the contrary, the system must amplify the phenomena, to obtain continuous improvement of performances (Mévellec, 1991).

## 3 CONSEQUENCES ON THE PERFORMANCE INDICATION METHODS AND TOOLS

The previously introduced loop leads us to underline the consequences of growing cognitive and politic autonomy, that originates the transfer from a measurement problematic, to a diagnostic problematic, Lorino, 1996. Effectively, providing information on performance about given activities (in response to the question "how much?") is now useless without information on the reasons of these performances (response to the question "why?"). Where in the past, information had verification and repression finality; it must now be dedicated to the interpretation for action and apprenticeship. This reality induces that performance indication systems have to allow for cause-effect link comprehension.

Three consequences on the performance indication system can be found. First, it must be based on a model able to distinguish products (and their components), activities and resources. Each of these entities has effectively an impact on performances and can constitute the distinctive element of different tactical or operational choices. Second, indicators must be more economical and physical: the explanatory power of economical indicators is now recognized as not being sufficient to allow diagnostics, (Bescos and Mendoza, 1994), (Giard and Pellegrin, 1991), (Lorino, 1996). Finally, simulations must be performed due to the predictive significance given to the estimate notion.

In the first part of this paper, the role of the management controller in organizational structures that characterize current firms has been specified. These new decentralized organizations, where decision is distributed between several services and hierarchical levels, make even more pertinent the action of management controller, (Bescos and Mendoza, 1994). In a very global manner, the role of the management controller is to implement, in a concurrent approach; the regulating loop previously presented.

This objective can be defined in the following sub objectives:

- to ensure the communication between people having different skills (translating problematic) and/or coming within different hierarchical levels (deployment or aggregation problematic);
- to provide information allowing us to know the relevance, the efficiency, and the effectiveness of activities that are (or that will be) implemented in the firm;
- to make reliable estimations about future activities, and for this, to have a realistic image of the sub-systems of the firm (physical, information, decision, organization and economic system).

All these conditions must be fulfilled to guide good decisions, to generate continuous improvement of manufacturing processes ("Kaizen" approach) and of development/design processes ("concurrent engineering" or "design to cost" approach).

Since the last ten years, numerous reflections have been carried out about accounting models or methods allowing to join these objectives. It seems from these reflections that modeling of the activities, through methods like Activity Based Costing (ABC) and Activity Based Management (ABM) are emerging and constitute a potential response to the presented problematic.

## 4 ADVANTAGES OF ABC AND ABM

Activity Based Costing as a method appeared in the eighties owing to the works of Robin Cooper and Robert Kaplan, (Cooper and Kaplan, 1991), authors of the current mechanisms of the method, and owing to Michael Porter, inventor of the Value Chain, (Porter, 1986). The CAM-I introduced the theoretical approaches of Porter, Cooper and Kaplan in a practical and formalized methodology, in the Cost Management System (CMS) project, (Berliner and Brimson, 1986), (Troxel, 1986), (Lorino, 1991). Then the Activity Based Management (ABM) appeared, where the concept of activity is used for strategic control of the firm, and where a real management by activities is driven, with the implementation of a coordination logic, an organizational engineering logic, and of a set of dashboards, (Lebas, 1994).

Regarding the reliability of information, approaches like ABC and ABM avoid artificial allocations. The first advantage of ABC is that expenses of the firm are first assigned to a set of significant activities, using resource drivers. Resource drivers (for example, duration of an activity for assignation of wages) come from the information system of the firm (Computer Aided Manufacturing, internal invoicing, questioning...). Second, activity costs are assigned to cost objects (a cost object can be a product, or a component, a document, a service). This assignation is made with activity drivers, that are specific to each activity, and that allow quantifying the cost objects' consumption or demand for each activity.

In terms of relevance of information, ABC leads to a better understanding of the value creation and to a better cost mastering. The notion of activity favors a dynamic approach to decision making because it represents what the organization really does, (Bescos and Mendoza, 1994). To evaluate relevance and efficiency, what new management accounting has to do is: first to allow managers to know to what extend resources contribute to the value of the product, and second to allow each firm member to know what they can do to increase added value and to decrease cost. Activity Based Costing contributes to the vertical integration in providing operational performance indications, and in contributing to the identification of the key success factors of the company, and to strategic decision support.

A process is a set of activities linked by significant information or physical flows, and associated to provide a material or immaterial product. A process is so transversal in a functional, spatial and temporal point of view: it can need the participation of different skills in the firm (as for example, the process "improvement of quality"), use resources located everywhere in the firm (for example the process "to design and to implant information system") and be implemented in long term (as the process "to promote").

Following an approach based on the process analysis, each effort is made to optimize the global performance, (Lorino, 1996). Thus, if a process analysis is made in the previously quoted example, the first question will be "what are the costs and value added induced by the "data processing" process.

Concepts of activity and process seem to be theoretically relevant for a management controller to ensure his role of integration and decision support. Nevertheless, tools currently used to exploit these concepts are not quite adapted to the different data processing necessary for performance evaluation according to a tactical and operational point of view.

We propose so in the next part a methodology aiming to respond to these needs.

## 5 PROPOSAL OF A MODELLING METHODOLOGY

One of the basic principles of our modeling methodology is that an expense can only be determined when a given activity is performed by a given resource to obtain a given cost objective.

The second principle is that making decisions needs indication of performance on each of these categories. Designers need to know the production cost of a product with new features, which of these features influence costs, and to compare these costs to the corresponding added value for customers. Management has to know the profitability of resources, to make tactical decision on new investments, and operationals have to know the contribution of each of their activities to the global performance and, to feel implicated in the competition of the firm.

The main characteristic of our approach is the double modeling of the company, according to two further points of view, (Sénéchal, 1996): a top-down analysis of services and/or resources of the company, leaning on a representation of physical elements that implement these functions, and an analysis focused on the processes and not on their physical supports (resources). Successive refinements of the processes constituting "macro-activities" allow an analysis to be performed. The modeling of a firm according to this approach is shown in Figure 2

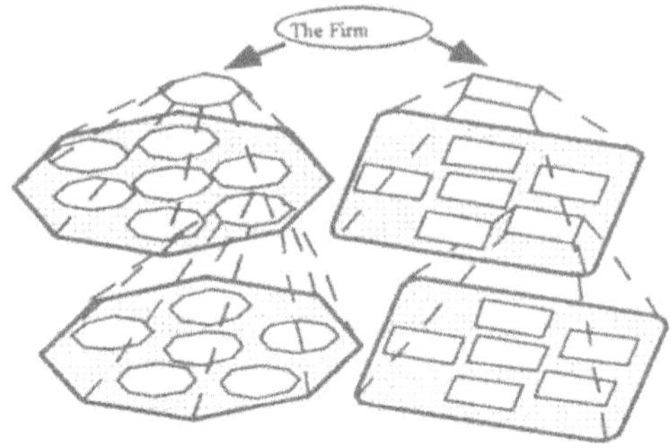


**Figure 2** A double modeling of the firm.

The influence of entities going through activities and resources is double: entities are consumed by activities, and their cost can be part of the cost of these activities (for example, the cost of oil for preventive maintenance activities); they also can influence the behavior of processes, according to their role in activities. For modeling these entities as a whole, we use the notion of *transformable entity,* and define the role of each *transformable entity* towards activities in using the modeling method Extended SADT (Feller 1989). This method was adapted to our economical analysis requirements. On Figure 3, we show the model of an activity "to make plan" and of a *transformable entity*, which constitute the interface with environment.

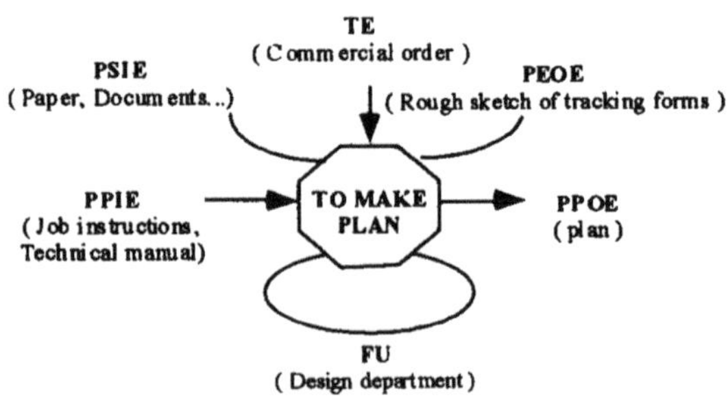


**Figure 3** Modelling of an activity and its interfaces.

The different interfaces between the activity and its environment are entities having specific roles and implementing some specific notions:

- The Processing Purpose Input Entity (PPIE): it is the principal input, its value is modified throughout the activity.
- The Processing Support Input Entities (PSIE): they represent the entities

necessary for the achievement of the activity, but they do not depend on the resource. These entities can be physical (e.g., some screws for an assembly activity) or informational (e.g., the assembly operation list).

- The Trigger Entities (TE): they correspond to the notion of trigger, they are entities necessary for the starting of the activity.
- The Processing Purpose Output Entity (PPOE): it is the main objective of the activity. It corresponds to the principal output, that is to say the entity whose value is modified. There is only one kind of PPEO for each activity, and it is common to each activity of the process.
- The Processing Effect Output Entities (PEOE): they represent the physical entities (waste, scraps...) and informational entities (resources release messages, trigger of other activities...) resulting from the performing of the activity. These entities are factors coming from the activity, and influencing activities of other processes.
- The resource notion is distinct from the input notion. It is a *functional unit*.

These models allow taking into account each element contributing to the costs and performances of the firm, as well as of their mutual interaction. Performances and costs are deduced from these simulations owing to notions stemming from automatic sciences.

## 6 INDUSTRIAL APPLICATION

The industrial site is a medium sized company (nearly 400 persons) producing ball and roller bearings, essentially from orders. Each product corresponds to a well identified customer, who waits for a precise technical and economic response to his needs. The principal added value is the technical know-how and the trade mastery. Production is made in little and middles series, products are various but with comparable technologies.
It is important to note that in the firm, the demand for concerning our project, came from the technical manager who expressed a need for tools, allowing designers to know the impact of their decisions on production costs, and more generally on performances. For the marketing manager, the need was about credibility and reliability of quotations. To make better products than competitors, he needed a means to distinguish products, and to identify for a given product its characteristics influencing the final production cost. For producers, the advantage was to be involved in the decision process of the firm, in giving some expectations on their future activities corresponding to the manufacturing of new product. The accounting manager saw in the project the opportunity to implement a performance evaluation system, allowing him to enrich his knowing of the operational processes of the firm. His interest was to be more implicated in the design and production processes, and to not "suffer" decisions in regarding costs of which he was not responsible.

The information for the members of the firm allowed presenting the objectives of the project, and the stakes of their participation. This task consisted in information and reflection meetings with the managers (technical, marketing, accounting...), and discussions with operational actors in their place of work, aiming to identify their activities and respective roles.

Grouping of activities in processes was made in analyzing flows existing in the firm (physical, information and decision flows). Models of processes have been validated by managers, and successive modifications obtained by consensus.

The different technical managers were quickly aware that this kind of cost approach might become a criterion for their decisions. The subjectivity part in decision making being reduced, the justification of choices with regard to the objectives of the firm were facilitated. For example, the choice was made for the investment in new equipment, for future products manufacturing, after consulting the information given by the estimation system (cost of set-up, of manufacturing, working factor.).

A dashboard composed of physical and/or economic performance indicators can be associated to each point of view, and adapted to users needs. The approach respects the cognitive autonomy of each in taking into account different points of view, and ensuring the evaluation coherence associated with a common model.

## 7 CONCLUSION

We have specified the principles that, according to us, must be applied to answer the current needs of engineers in term of performance evaluation. We made a proposal of performance estimation and evaluation approach, supported by a software environment. This approach does not assert to solve the problem on its own, but to contribute to some improvements. Its implementation being not totally completed, we can not give quantified and perpetuated results. Nevertheless, theoretical evaluation and partial practical results allow us to affirm its coherence with current industrial expectations, and to consider interesting perspectives.

## 8 REFERENCES

Berliner C., Brimson J. A. (1986) *Cost management for today's advanced manufacturing ; the CAM-I conceptual design.*, HBS Press, Boston.

Bescos P.L., Mendoza C. (1994) *Le management de la performance* Editions compatibles Malesherbes, Paris.

Cooper R., Kaplan R.S. (1991) *The Design of Cost Management Systems.* Robert KAPLAN Consulting Editor, Edition Prentice Hall.

Feller A. & Rucker R. (1989) Extending Structured Analysis Modelling with A.I.: An Application to MRPII Profiles and SFC Data Communications Requirements Specifications. *IFIPS Conference Paper*, November 1989.

Giard V., Pellegrin C. (1991) Fundaments de l'évaluation économique dans les modèles économiques de gestion, *3è congrès international de Génie Logiciel,*

Tours.

Lebas M. (1994) Du coût de revient au management par les activités. *Revue Française de Comptabilité*, 258, Juillet Août 1994.

Lorino P. (1991) *Le contrôle de gestion stratégique. La gestion par les activités.* Dunod, Paris.

Lorino P. (1996) Le pilotage de l'entreprise: de la mesure à l'interprétation, Cohérence, *Pertinence et Evaluation, ECOSIP,* Economica, Paris.

Mévellec P. (1991) *Outils de gestion. La pertinence retrouvée.* Editions Compatibles Malesherbes, Paris.

Porter M. (1986) *L'avantage concurrentiel.* inter Editions, Paris.

Sénéchal O. (1996) *Proposition d'une méthodologie pour l'aide à l'estimation des performances physico-économiques des systèmes de production dans une approche concourante.* Thèse de Doctorat, LAMIH - LGIL, Université de Valenciennes, 27 Février.

Troxel R. (1986) Performance Measurement, *Actes du colloque CAM-I: Cost Management System Project - Phase 1 Conceptual Design*, 8-9 Décembre Nice.

24

# Machining feature generation based on a facility model and manufacturing knowledge

*M. Matsuda*
*Department of Information and Computer Sciences*
*Faculty of Engineering, Kanagawa Institute of Technology*
*1030 Shimo-ogino, Atsugi-shi, Kanagawa 243-02, Japan*
*Telephone:81-462-41-1211, Fax:81-462-42-8490*
*E-mail:matsuda@ic.kanagawa-it.ac.jp*

*F. Kimura*
*Department of Precision Machinery Engineering*
*Graduate School of Engineering, The University of Tokyo*
*7-3-1 Hongo, Bunkyo-ku, Tokyo 113, Japan*
*Telephone:81-3-3812-2111, Fax:81-3-3812-8849*
*E-mail:kimura@cim.pe.u-tokyo.ac.jp*

**Abstract**

The derivation process of a product model for machining through the generation of machining features is discussed in this paper. Descriptions of the machining features are derived by applying machining constraints to the product model for design. Machining constraints consist of machine specifications, machine functions, and machining knowledge. Here the machine specification and functions are represented as a machine model, which is a type of facility model. The machine model is composed of a specification model and a process model. The specification model is the description of the static elements of the machine. The process model is the description of the actual operation by means of simulation. Manufacturing knowledge is used for listing candidates of machining methods, using tools, operation order, and machining conditions. A prototype system for milling feature generation using the milling machine model and machining knowledge is provided.

Computer Applications in Production and Engineering. F. Plonka and G. Olling (Eds.)

**Keywords**
Product modeling, machining feature description, machine model, virtual machining, machining preparation

# 1 INTRODUCTION

In a concurrent manufacturing system, a product model is used at various stages, such as product design and process/operation planning. However, the required product model differs depending on the stages. For example, a product model with machining feature description is required for the machining preparation or checking the process for machinability. This means that there is a product model for design, a product model for machining, a product model for assembly, and so on. In some cases, a product model for design is a product model with design feature descriptions, and a product model for machining is a product model with machining feature descriptions. In a concurrent manufacturing framework, all product models for XXX should be transformable between themselves, since all product models for XXX should be commonly usable as one product model at every manufacturing stage. Therefore, a framework for handling the product model is required, as pointed out in the literature. (Kimura, 1993) (Krause, 1993). This framework will provide flexible use and operation for product data, and as such, will provide one of the basic techniques for achieving concurrent manufacturing.

Usually, a product model is created at the design stage. At this stage, the product model is described using design features. When this product model with design features was automatically transformed to the product model with machining features, a total automatic machining system from product design to actual machining was realized (Matsuda, 1991). This transformation mechanism showed that descriptions of machining features were derived by applying machining constraints, such as usable machines and tools, to descriptions of design features (Matsuda, 1995) (Matsuda, 1996). A general methodology for handling the product model will be provided by expansion of this mechanism. This paper tries to provide the methodology which derives the product model for machining from the product model for design. Finally, this paper offers a proposal for the basic framework for handling the product model using manufacturing environment models.

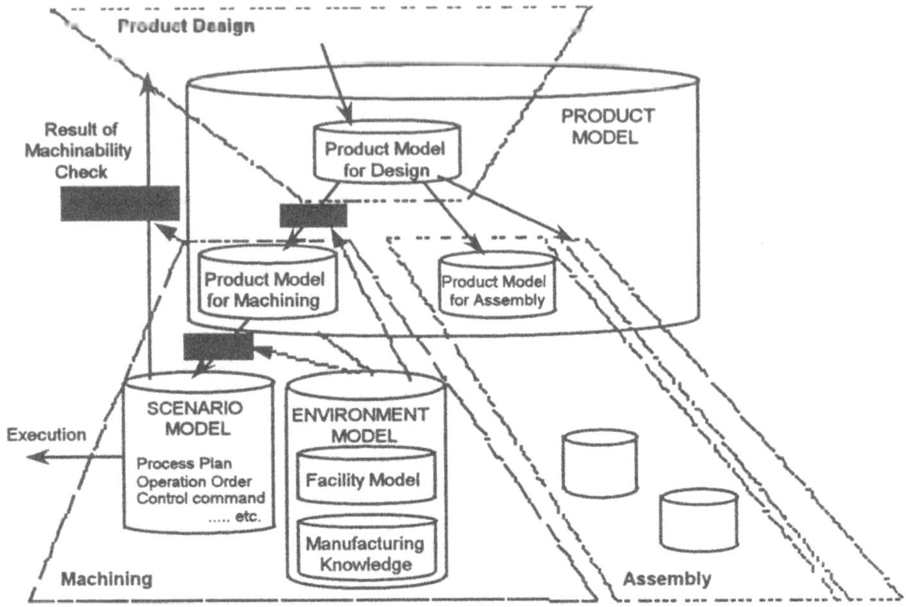


**Figure 1** Product model, scenario model and environment model.

## 2 INTEGRATION FRAMEWORK FOR PRODUCT, SCENARIO AND ENVIRONMENT MODELS

At the machining or assembly process/operation planning stage, it is required to focus on features which relate to operation units, such as a volume machined by a single tool or attaching faces at the assembly stage. The product model for machining or the product model for assembly is a product model which has explicit descriptions of adequate features. Similarly, there are product models for measuring, product models for quality control, and so on.

Usually, a computer system generates a machining or assembly process plan, the order of operation, operation condition and control commands are determined by using the above mentioned feature descriptions. These generated plans, operation sequences, conditions and commands are represented as scenario models. The scenario model is used not only for actual production but also for simulation or evaluation. In order to realize a concurrent manufacturing system, the first step is the generation of a product model with adequate feature descriptions based on the product model used at the product design stage, and then generate a scenario model based on a suitable product model.

Descriptions of adequate features, such as machining features or assembly features, are derived by consideration of the target facility, such as machines, tools, or robots used. Manufacturing knowledge is used when making decisions on selecting a target facility. In other words, the facility information and knowledge are used as manufacturing constraints for the derivation of feature descriptions.

Here, these manufacturing constraints are represented as an environment model. The environment model consists of facility models and manufacturing knowledge.

Figure 1 shows the relationship between the product model, the scenario model, and the environment model. If the designer wants to check for machinability or assemblability of the product, the following steps have to be executed. First, the system has to generate a product model with machining or assembly feature descriptions by using the environment model. Second, the system will have to generate a scenario model based on the product model while utilizing the environment model. Third, the system will have to simulate the scenario model and evaluate the result by again using the environment model. In order to achieve the actual production, the process which generates the scenario model via the product model including adequate feature descriptions will have to be executed. The environment model is required at every process stage.

## 3 ENVIRONMENT MODEL

### 3.1 Facility model

The facility model models the static and dynamic properties of equipment. As shown in Figure 2, a facility model has a hierarchical structure. At the highest level is the equipment model such as a machine model or a robot model. At the middle level are models of units, which are components of the equipment. A unit is one functional block such as a controller and mechanism in the machine, or an arm and hand in the robot. At the lowest level are the models of parts which compose a unit.

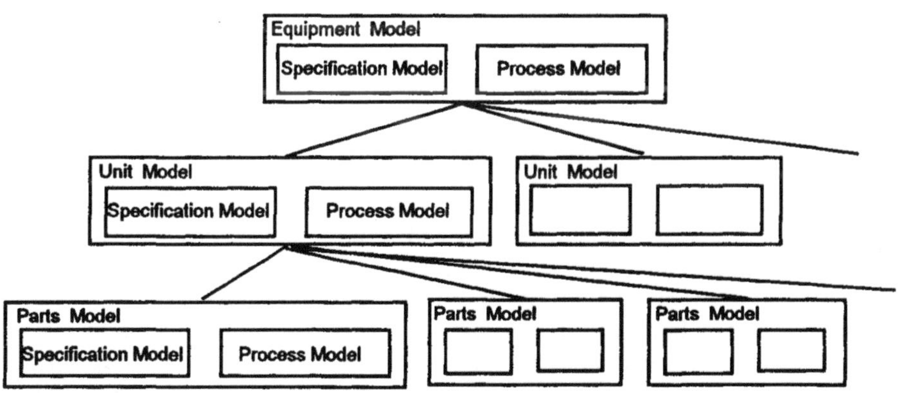


**Figure 2** Structure of facility model.

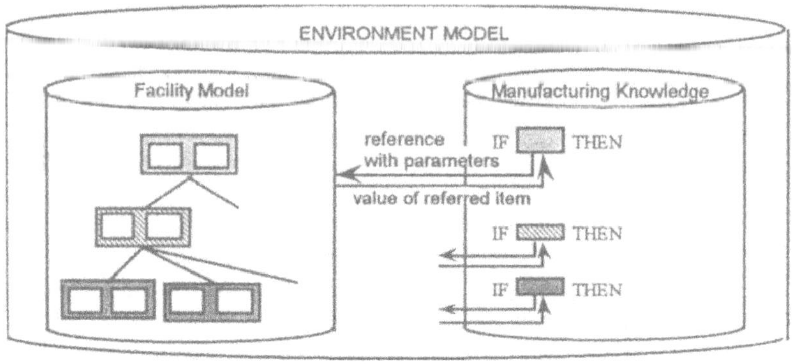


**Figure 3** Structure of environment model.

A part is one element of a unit such as a tool or a robot finger. In some cases, a facility model may have more or fewer levels in the hierarchy.

Each of the equipment, unit and part models are composed of a specification model and a process model. The specification model consists of a description of static data, such as name, type, size, speed, and weight. The process model consists of a description of dynamic data, such as the results of some operation or condition during an operation. The process model at the equipment level and unit level has itself a hierarchical structure, since the total behavior of the equipment is based on the combined behavior of the motion of its units, and similarly, the behavior of a unit is totally the result of the motion of its parts. In other words, the process model represents the function of the equipment, units and parts. The implementation of the process model includes a simulation process.

## 3.2 Manufacturing knowledge

Manufacturing knowledge is used for listing candidates for a manufacturing method using a machine and process/operation plan. Also manufacturing knowledge is used for decision making when selecting from the candidates and generating the actual operation order and control commands. Manufacturing knowledge consists of manufacturing know-how, decision rules, the basis for evaluation and so on. As shown in Figure 3, the manufacturing knowledge description has a hierarchical structure corresponding to the hierarchy of the facility model. Most manufacturing knowledge is described by IF-THEN rules. When applying a rule, the actual value for the condition of a part is provided by reference to the facility model at the corresponding level. For example, when selecting a device to be used, the equipment model is referred to, with parameters such as device identifier, product description, and reference item. The reference item indicates what kind of value is desired in this reference.

# 4 DERIVATION OF PRODUCT MODEL FOR MACHINING

In this paper, a product model for machining means a product model with machining feature descriptions. Similarly a machining feature means, for example, the volume which is machined by a single tool. Figure 4 shows the basic derivation process for the product model with machining features by using the machining environment model. All machines and tools in the factory are modeled as facility models in the machining environment model. Also, the machining knowledge is described in the machining environment model. The product description already exists as a product model for design. The derivation proceeds as follows:

1) Candidates of applicable machines are generated and listed. Under considerations of product shape, size, material, required finished accuracy, and so on, the system selects usable machines by referring to the machining environment model.
2) The machine for the actual production is selected, taking account of machining cost, schedule, and so on. While the decision process is taking place, the environment model, especially the process model and knowledge, are referenced.
3) Candidates of applicable tools are generated and listed, taking into consideration the product shape, product size, finished accuracy, cutting stage and so on. The system makes reference to tool models and related knowledge in the environment model.

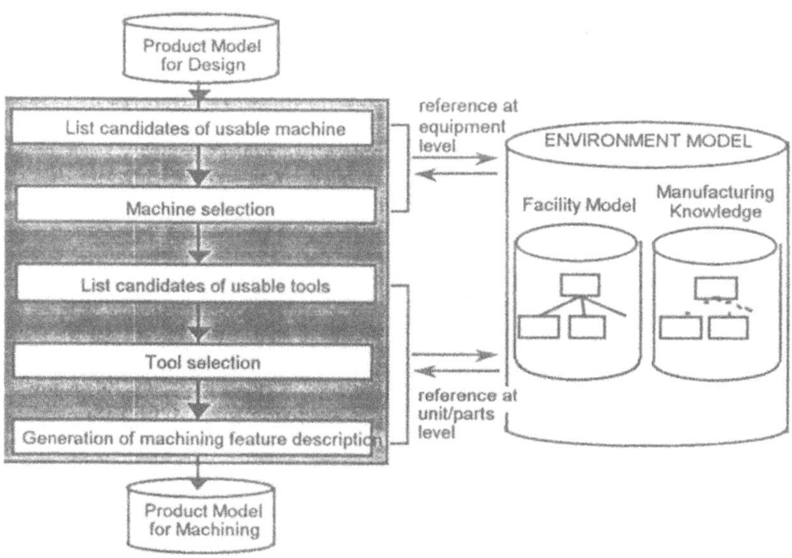


**Figure 4** Derivation process of machining feature.

4) The tools to be used are selected through rejection of candidate tools which have low cutting efficiency, such as a small machining area or long cutting time. During

the rejection process, process models for each tool model and knowledge are referenced.
5) Machining features are generated by means of calculations of machined volumes
corresponding to each of the selected tools.

# 5 MILLING DATA GENERATION SYSTEM

## 5.1 Structure of the system

The milling data generation system described is a prototype system under development by the authors. This system produces a process plan for cutting as well as NC data based on the derived milling features. A milling feature is one type of machining feature. This system considers milling of a cavity for a die or mold. A cavity is one kind of a pocket. This system treats only a pocket with a complicated 2 1/2 dimensional shape. A 2 1/2 dimensional shape means the combination of several volumes which are derived by sweeping a 2 dimensional figure. Usually, straight endmills are used for 2 1/2 dimensional shape cutting.

The structure of this system is shown in Figure 5. This system consists of two parts. One is the milling feature generator, and the other is the milling data generator. The product description which is obtained at the product design stage, provides inputs to the milling feature generator. In the milling feature generator, the milled cross section as milling area is determined based on the product shape. This is followed by the milling feature generation and tool selection, based on the milled cross section and making use of the milling environment model. Finally,

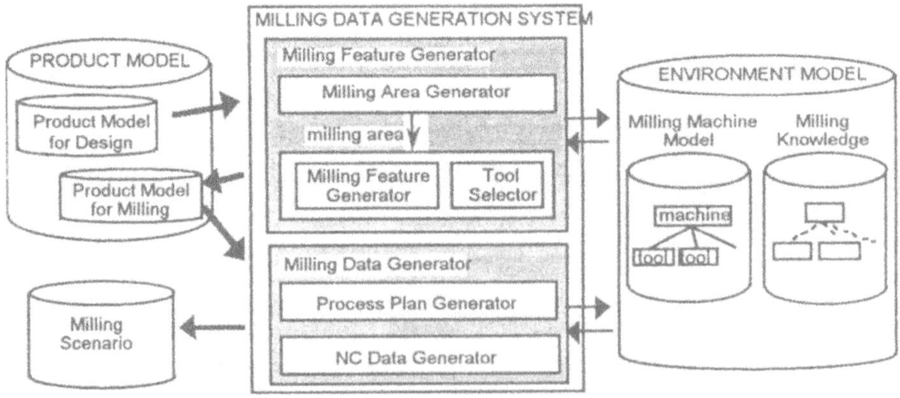


**Figure 5** Milling feature generation system.

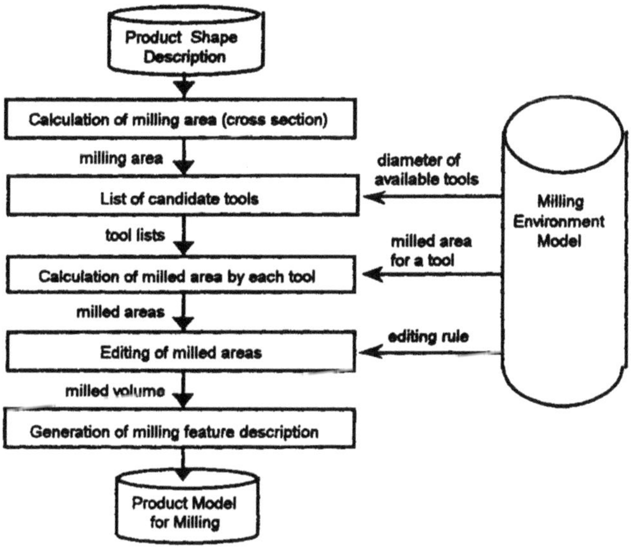


**Figure 6** Process of milling feature generation.

the milling feature description is provided. The milling environment model consists of the milling machine model and milling knowledge. The milling machine model has a two level hierarchy. The higher level is at the milling machine level, while the lower level is at the tool level which is a description of available tools. The milling data generator produces a cutting process plan and NC data as a milling scenario based on generated milling features by using the milling environment model.

## 5.2 Milling feature generation

The process flow for milling feature generation is shown in Figure 6. The generation process proceeds as follows:

1) The milled cross section at each bottom face depth is computed. Each milled cross section is considered independently as a milling area.
2) For one milling area, the candidate list of possible tools are selected in the form of tool diameters of a straight endmill. This selection process is based on the corner size, distance between island areas, and the diameter of the biggest available tool. List of available tools and selection rules are provided by the milling environment model. The final candidate list of applied tool diameters consists in an ordering of tools according to their diameters from largest to smallest, since the largest possible tool would provide optimum milling efficiency.
3) For each milling area, the list of milled areas are calculated by applying each tool on the corresponding candidate list. The milled area is the machinable 2

dimensional figure cut by the diameter of the candidate tool. The milled area is provided from the process model of the milling machine model with reference to the corresponding milling area and applied tool diameter. The result of this stage is a list of resulting milled areas, and a list of applied tools, ordered according to their diameters.

4) The milled areas are edited according to editing rules in order to obtain milled volumes. In each list of milled areas, the milled area for the bigger tool is subtracted from the milled area for the smaller tool. The result of the subtraction provides the actual milled area for the smaller tool, because actual cutting starts with the bigger tool. The result is registered as the correct milled area for the smaller tool on the list of milled areas. However, if the result of the subtraction is smaller than the threshold area, the milled area for smaller tool is eliminated from the list. The threshold value is decided based on the milling knowledge. Milled areas on all lists are divided into groups according to tool diameter. These groups of tools are ordered by size, largest to smallest. In one group, milled areas are ordered by depth, shallow to deep, and duplicated milled areas at each depth are eliminated. The volume cut by a single tool is obtained by sweeping the milled areas for one tool.
5) One milled volume corresponds to one milling feature. Milling feature descriptions are derived from the milled volumes.

## 6 CONCLUSIONS

A mechanism for deriving machining feature descriptions using a milling environment model was proposed, based on the concept that machining features are obtained by applying machining constraints to the product model for design, and that machining constraints are represented as an environment model. A prototype system developed showed the basic propriety and utility of the proposal.

Through using an environment model which is composed of facility models and manufacturing knowledge, the flexibility and expandability of the proposed system are increased. For example, when a new machine is added in a factory, only the addition of a new machine model and its related knowledge is required. Furthermore, it is possible to compare machinability by generating and simulating machining data for corresponding available machines, since the system has several facility models available at the same time. This means that the proposed system is one kind of a virtual manufacturing system.

## 7 REFERENCES


Kimura, F. (1993) Product and Process Modeling as a Kernel for Virtual Manufacturing Environment: Annals of CIRP, Vol.42, No.1, 147-150.

Krause, F.-L., Kimura, F., Kjellberg, T. and Lu, S.C.-Y. (1993) Product Modeling: Annals of CIRP, Vol.42, No.2, 695-706.

Matsuda, M. and Kimura, F. (1991) Extraction of machining feature for milling data generation: Proceeding of CAPE'91. IFIP TC5, North-Holland, 353-360.

Matsuda, M. and Kimura, F. (1995) Modeling of virtual manufacturing devices for machining data generation: Proceeding of CAPE'95.IFIP TC5, Chapman & Hall, 407-414.

Matsuda, M. and Kimura, F. (1997) Generation of milling data in a virtual manufacturing framework: The Design of Information Infrastructure Systems for Manufacturing, IFIP TC5, Chapman & Hall, in print.

## 8 BIOGRAPHY

*M.Matsuda* is an associate professor in the Department of Information and Computer Sciences of Kanagawa Institute of Technology. She received a Dr.Eng. degree in precision machinery engineering from the University of Tokyo in 1989. She was an associate professor in the Department of Computer Science of Sanno Institute of Management from 1991 to March 1997. She has been active in the field of CAD/CAM, process/operation planning, NC programming and numerical control. Her recent research interests include product modeling for manufacturing and virtual manufacturing. She is a member of Japan Society of Precision Engineering and Information Processing Society of Japan.

*F.Kimura* is a professor in the Department of Precision Machinery Engineering of the University of Tokyo. He received a Dr. Eng. Sci. degree in aeronautics from the University of Tokyo in 1974. He was a research associate at the Electroacoustics Laboratory of the Ministry of International Trade and Industry from 1974 to 1979. He then moved to the University of Tokyo, and was an associate professor from 1979 to 1987. He has been active in the field of solid modeling, free-form surface modeling and product modeling. His research interests now include the basic theory of CAD/CAM and CIM, concurrent engineering, engineering simulation, virtual manufacturing and life-cycle engineering. He is a member of IFIP WG5.2 and WG5.3, and a member of CIRP.

# 25

# Simulation of wires handling for the automation of industrial processes

*P. Denti, P. Dragoni, G. Frugoli, and C. Rizzi*
*KAEMaRT Group, Department of Industrial Engineering University of Parma,*
*Viale delle Scienze, 43100 Parma, Italy*
*Tel. +39 521 905701, Fax. +39 521 905705*
*E-mail: [denti, frugoli, rizzi]@ied.eng.unipr.it*

**Abstract**

This paper considers the automation of industrial processes; in particular we focus attention on those operations that require the manipulation of wires and cables, such as laying.

To this end, we used a software prototype, named *SoftWorld*, that provides a graphical environment to simulate the handling machinery integrated with the dynamic and static behavior of the material.

To fulfill our goal we proceeded in three steps: analysis of possible wire models, identification of possible approaches to simulate the handling process, and validation through experimental tests.

In order to cover most of the typical problems in wire simulation, different models have been considered to describe wires and simulate their behavior. The objective has been to investigate different approaches analyzing advantages and disadvantages with reference to the goal of the simulation.

In the same way, for the simulation of the handling process we considered different approaches that imply different computational costs and give different levels of accuracy.

Results obtained will be described as well as final considerations and future developments.

**Keywords**

Wire handling, nonrigid materials modeling and simulation, automation.

Computer Applications in Production and Engineering. F. Plonka and G. Olling (Eds.)

# 1 INTRODUCTION

Mainly in the automotive and aerospace sectors, wire and flexible tube laying design is getting more and more important. Several sensors and actuators are used even in low-cost vehicles both for safety and performance. Examples include diagnotic systems, ABSs, climate control systems, airbags, integrated hi-fi systems, and so on.

The automation of wire laying processes is usually considered as a 'geometrical' planning problem but, in general, this is not correct: several 'physical' parameters should be taken into account. Wires and flexible tubes in vehicles are exposed to damages due to high stress, high temperature, and vibration. Some of the damage causes could be eliminated during the design phase by taking into account the behavior of the vehicle under operating conditions. Tools for off-line analysis could be very effective in detecting design pitfalls.

In such a context, we developed a software prototype, named *SoftWorld*, that provides a graphical environment to simulate the handling machinery integrated with the dynamic and static behavior of the material. At first the system was experimented with considering typical operations in the clothing industry, e.g. pick and place of garment pieces or garment draping on digital mannequins (Cugini 1994, Denti 1996). Now we focus our attention on a different class of flexible objects, wires and cables, and on processes that require their manipulation, e.g., vehicle assembly or recycling.

Wire behavior simulation can be carried out at different levels of accuracy (and computational cost) depending on problem requirements. In the following, different approaches to model wires are shown with their advantages and disadvantages, in order to cover most of the typical problems in wire simulation.

Tests carried out to compare the potential of different wire models and approaches for process simulation will be described as well as final considerations on the results obtained.

# 2 NONRIGID MATERIALS REPRESENTATION

The approach adopted in *SoftWorld* (Denti, 1996) to model flexible materials is based on the known **particle-based** approach (Witkin, 1995, Volino, 1995, Eberhardt, 1996): with a particle-based representation, a deformable object is described as a set of mechanical elements (particles) and forces acting among them, representing the macro-behavior of the material (e.g., elasticity, plasticity). For example, a piece of fabric can be modeled as a grid of particles with a distribution of forces, like bending, stretching and repelling. Different materials are modeled using different:

- particle meshes;
- particle masses;
- sets of inter-particle forces.

In order to simulate a manufacturing process, it is not sufficient to model only the deformable objects but it is necessary to consider external forces that could be applied to the objects (e.g., the action of a gripper), constraints that must be respected (e.g., a predefined trajectory), and rigid obstacles (e.g., a worktable).

*SoftWorld* permits modeling not only different classes of flexible objects but also the physical environment surrounding them, in terms of external forces, constraints and rigid obstacles. Figure 1 portrays the high-level architecture of the prototype. Two main components can be identified: *SoftLand*, the modeling and simulation library, and *SoftInterface*, the graphical user interface.

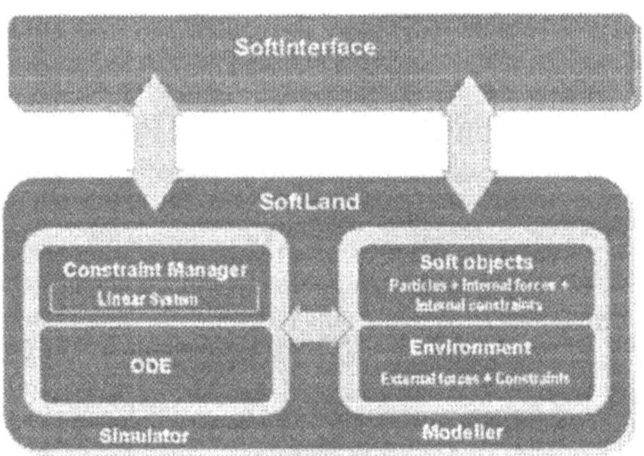


Figure 1 **High-level architecture of *SoftWorld***

SoftLand can be subdivided in two main modules: the **modeler** and the **simulator**. The modeler comprehends all the necessary functionalities for the definition of nonrigid objects and surrounding environment. As already stated, nonrigid objects are represented by a set of particles interconnected by internal forces and subjected to internal constraints, while the environment is a set of external forces and constraints. The simulator comprehends:

- an **ODE** (Ordinary Differential Equation) numerical solver;
- a **Constraint Manager**, whose aim is to manage constraints and obstacles during the simulation.

The system also provides the end-user with a graphical environment, SoftInterface, to model nonrigid materials and to simulate their behavior during handling processes. Through the user interface, the system allows a designer to:

- describe **nonrigid objects** together with their physical properties as a set of particles interconnected by internal forces (describing the physical behavior) and subjected to internal constraints;
- describe a **virtual physical environment** as a set of external forces (e.g., gravity), rigid obstacles, and constraints;
- simulate the **behavior of the objects** in the defined virtual physical environment, producing both numerical and graphical output;

- produce high-quality graphical outputs using different rendering techniques.

Up to now the prototype has been used:

- to model and simulate flexible industrial products, in this case wires;
- to simulate automated handling processes.

In the following, we illustrate different representations that can be adopted to model and simulate the behavior of wires during handling operations.

## 3 WIRES REPRESENTATION AND SIMULATION

To simulate wire handling two problems have to be considered:

- how to represent wires (in our case, how to do it using a particle-based model);
- how to describe the interaction with the environment in terms of external forces, constraints and obstacles.

The particle-based approach can be seen as a *macro-molecular* representation. The accuracy level needed for the simulation determines the particle mesh resolution of the model. Tending toward the exact molecular representation, both for particles and forces, we obtain simulation results that better approximate the real behavior. Of course, the exact molecular representation is too complicated to handle and, moreover, approximated solutions are in general good enough for common purposes; different levels of approximation are usually required for different problems.

Our objective has been to investigate different models for wire behavior simulation and find out which is the best suitable with reference to the goal of the simulation.

Different representations have been considered in order to describe wires and simulate their behavior:

- unidimensional;
- surface-like;
- solid-like.

Each model is characterized by a different level of realism and computational cost.

Even for the problem of the interactions with the environment, considerations can be done taking into account the level of realism required. Several parameters can be considered or ignored: in a simulation of a grasping operation we could take into account the roughness of the gripper fingers, the force exerted by the gripper (and therefore the deformation generated), and collisions with other parts of the robot arm.

Two approaches, corresponding to different problems, have been identified:

- imposing a trajectory constraint;
- considering the real gripper action.

In order to verify and evaluate the different models and simulation approaches, two tests have been carried out: simulation of automatic wire laying and simulation of wire deformation due to the action of a gripper.

In the following, wire models and simulation approaches will be described with reference to the tests considered.

The unidimensional model is the simplest representation of a wire or a cable, by which the object is represented as a string of particles, with stretching, repelling and bending forces that connect each particle to its previous and next neighbors. Due to the fact that only one of the three dimensions of the object is considered, this model is suitable for simulations in which computational speed is more important than realism of the object behavior or when the study of transversal deformations is not relevant. Therefore this model is not satisfactory enough for our tests.

## 4 SIMULATION OF AUTOMATIC WIRE LAYING

This test considers the simulation of wire laying operations: we suppose to grasp a wire and move it along a specified trajectory. Various obstacles represent the surrounding environment. Therefore, in this case the focus is on the behavior of the wire during the operation.

The **surface-like** model has been adopted to represent the wire. The object is modeled with a cylindrical surface: the process of discretization is carried out by positioning the particles on the intersection of the isoparametric curves of the surface (Figure 2). In this way, the model becomes a series of connected rings of particles distributed along the central axis of the object.

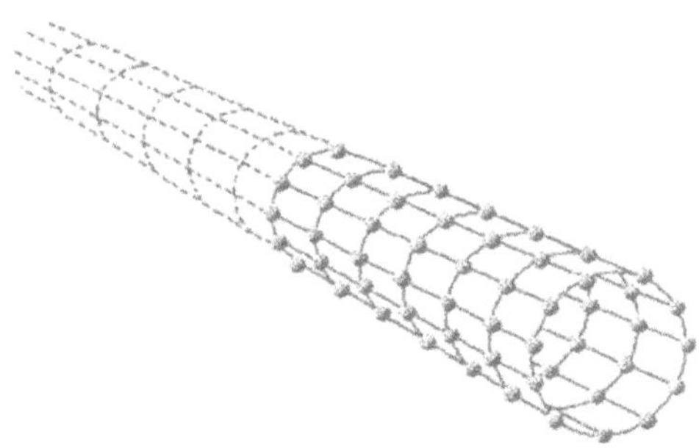

Figure 2 **Wire represented by a set of particles distributed on a cylindrical surface**

Between every pair of rings we set elastic forces simulating the resistance to pulling and compressive stress. Other forces are also set in order to simulate the bending resistance and the cross-section deformation tension.

This model offers a good level of realism and acceptable computational cost. With respect to the unidimensional model, it implies more complex collision detection due to a more complex geometry and a bigger set of parameters to be tuned in order to obtain the real behavior. However, this approach offers an average level of realism at an average computational cost and the possibility to take into account the torsional stress.

The simulation is carried out by imposing a trajectory constraint. This approach is based on the following assumptions:

- a grasped object, if the operation is correctly done, can be considered forming a single unit with the gripper;
- material deformations generated by the gripper action can be ignored.

The trajectory constraint has been considered in order to impose a particular motion law to some particles. In order to define the constraint, we first determine the area involved in the grasping operation and then the particles contained within this area are constrained to follow the gripper trajectory. In such a way, the grasping action is simulated imposing a predefined trajectory to the particles detected.

Main characteristics of this approach are:

- higher simulation speed, if compared with the other approach that will be described in the following;
- independence from the shape of the contact surface between object and gripper and from the friction coefficient;
- low level of realism, because the grasping action on the material is not simulated.

The layout used for the test is as follows (Figure 3):

- a wire laying on a table;
- a gripper that holds one end of the wire;
- obstacles represented by thin walls.

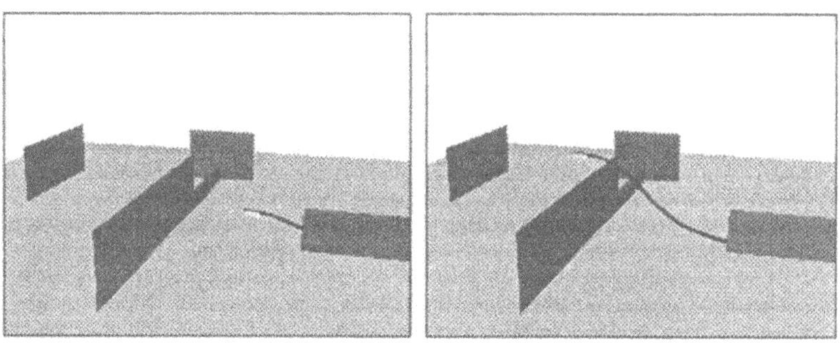

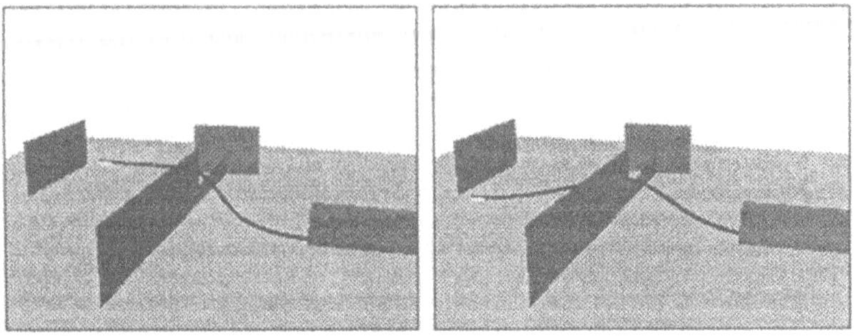

Figure 3 **Wire laying simulation**

The wire is grasped at one of its ends and moved along a predefined trajectory. The object is therefore constrained to follow the trajectory imposed by the gripper. Figure 3 shows some steps of the behavior of a wire when manipulated as described. In the sequence shown in Figure 3, it is possible to see the behavior of the wire when colliding with obstacles.

## 5 SIMULATION OF THE ACTION OF A GRIPPER

The second test considers the simulation of the action of a robot gripper. The most important aspect of this example is the deformation of the material due to the external forces applied.

A **three-dimensional** model of the wire is more suitable for this simulation since it offers a higher level of realism. A possible discretization can be the decomposition of the object into small cubes (in the same way as if we were using a *voxel* representation), which will be represented by particles (Figure 4a). Generality is the main characteristic of this type of discretization, in fact this model could be adopted for any shape, not only for cylinder-like objects.

However, we loose axial symmetry, and a purely homogeneous discretization may cause large irregularities of the object surface (especially when using a small number of particles).

A more suitable discretization for a cylindrical object such as a wire is to displace the particles radially within the cross-section as shown in Figure 4b: in this way the set of inter-particles forces is arranged in a symmetric way within the section.

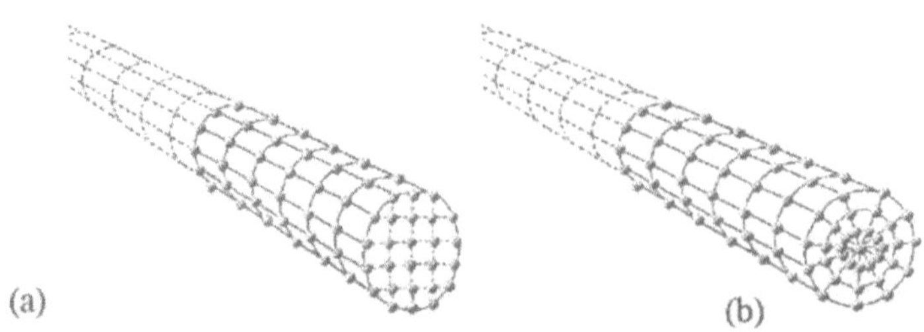


Figure 4 **3D representation of the wire: (a) cubic-based mesh, (b) radial-based mesh**

With respect to the previous model, this one implies:

- higher level of realism, because all the three dimensions of the object are considered;
- bigger number of particles and forces, that implies higher computational cost.

The gripper is represented as a set of rigid objects whose surfaces are characterized by a roughness value. The rigid objects defining the gripper must follow a given trajectory in the space and when they touch the wire, a mechanical action of compression and friction on the wire surface is accomplished.
With respect to the previous approach, we have:

- higher level of realism: in this case we take into account the friction between the wire and the rigid objects as well as the wire deformation;
- possibility to calculate the force and the medium/maximum momentum of the gripper during a time interval: this can be useful to properly quantify the mechanical characteristics of the gripper;
- generality: we can define a gripper or some other mobile rigid object that will interact with a generic nonrigid object in a proper way;
- higher computational cost: this approach implies complex collision detection between the gripper and the wire and the calculation of friction and compression;
- the simulation requires a model characterized by a high level of physical realism, otherwise the simulation can produce completely wrong results.

The end-effector of the gripper is modeled by two flat plates. The wire lays on a worktable and the gripper grasps and then translates it. The simulated action is simpler than the previous but the models of the objects present in the scene are more complex. Figure 5 shows the behavior of the wire when manipulated as described: the deformation due to the action of the gripper can be seen.

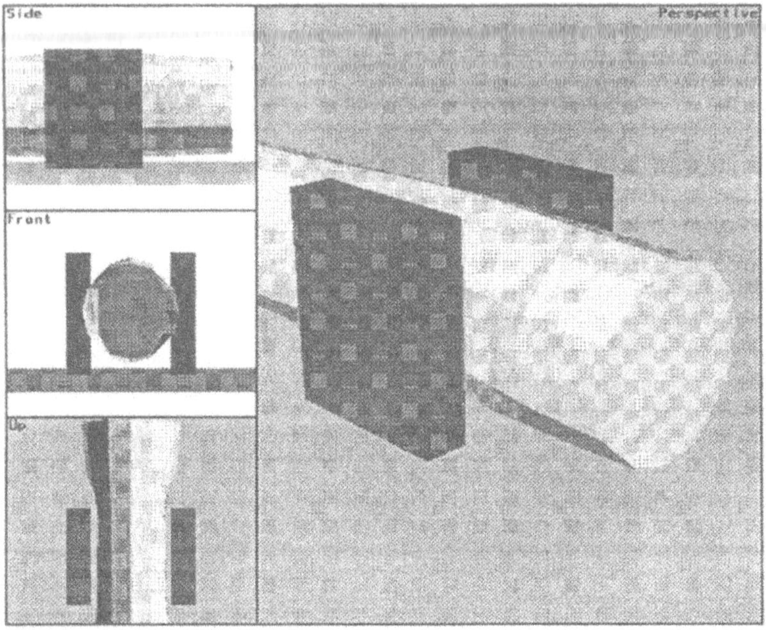


Figure 5 **Simulation of the action of the gripper**

## 6 CONSIDERATIONS

In some cases, it is convenient to adopt a combination of the described models. For example, in order to simulate a real electric cable, we can model the external shell as a cylindrical surface and use any of the other approaches to model the core. We can obtain different levels of realism and computational cost by using different combinations.

Even for the problem of the interaction it can be useful to adopt a mixed approach that is a combination of the two approaches described. It consists of two steps: at first we calculate the wire deformation, due to the gripper action, following the second approach; then, supposing the wire is fixed with respect to the gripper (that means it cannot slip away) and the deformation constant, we follow the first approach.

This technique is based on the following approximation: the pressure exerted by the gripper deforms the material only when it grasps it. Any further movement of the gripper does not change the effect of the finger pressure. This assumption is quite reasonable in several cases and it allows lowering significantly the computational cost of the second approach described.

Main characteristics are:

- possibility to take into account, even if partially, the wire deformation;
- average computational cost during the second phase of the simulation;
- more complex algorithm, because we must perform it in two different steps.

This mixed approach is currently under development.

## 7 CONCLUSIONS

We showed how wires and cables can be modeled and simulated using a particle-based approach. Analyzing the techniques studied, we can see that the particle-based representation exhibits a high level of generality and flexibility. The basic idea of discretizing the object into a set of particles does not limit very much the set of simulation techniques applicable. Several algorithms, very different among themselves, can be easily tested; even different levels of precision can be obtained using the same basic modeling idea. All the modeling and simulation approaches described here are based on the same software package (*SoftWorld*), but many other approaches to the wire manipulation problem can be tested.

## REFERENCES

Cugini, U. and Denti, P. and Ippolito, M. and Rizzi, C. (1994) Design and simulation of non-rigid materials handling systems, in *Proceedings of Euriscon 94*, **III**, 1424–1432, Malaga, Spain.

Denti, P. and Dragoni, P. and Frugoli, G. and Rizzi, C. (1996) SoftWorld: a system to simulate flexible products behaviour in industrial processes, in *Proceedings of ESS 1996*, **II**, 235–239, Genova, Italy.

Eberhardt, B., Weber, A., and Strasser, W. (1996) A fast, flexible, particle-system model for cloth draping, in *IEEE Computer Graphics and Applications*, **16**, **5**, 52–59.

Volino, P., Courchesne, M. and Magnenat Thalmann, N. (1995) Versatile and efficient techniques for simulating cloth and other deformable objects, in *Proceedings of SIGGRAPH 95*, Los Angeles, California, USA.

Witkin, A. et al. (1995) Physically based modeling, in *SIGGRAPH 95 Course Notes*, **34**, Los Angeles, California, USA.

## ACKNOWLEDGEMENTS

The authors would like to thank the EU Commission and all partners of SKILL-MART project for their invaluable support in this research.

## BIOGRAPHY

*Paolo Denti* is currently a post-doc fellow at the University of Parma, Department of Industrial Engineering. He received the Laurea Degree in Computer Science from University of Milan in 1991. His research interests include physically-based modeling and simulation, motion planning in robotics, computational geometry, and augmented reality.

*Paolo Dragoni* is currently a fellow at the University of Parma, Department of Industrial Engineering. He received the Laurea Degree in Electronic Engineering from Politecnico di Milano in 1995. Since 1995 he has been working in the field of modeling and simulation of nonrigid materials behavior for industrial applications. Current research interests include physically-based modeling and simulation, computational geometry, object-oriented programming.

*Giancarlo Frugoli* is currently a Ph.D. student at the University of Parma, Department of Industrial Engineering. He received the Laurea Degree in Electronic Engineering from Politecnico di Milano in 1996. Since 1995 he has been working in the field of modeling and simulation of nonrigid materials behavior for industrial applications. Current research interests include physically-based modeling and simulation, human-computer interaction, object-oriented programming.

*Caterina Rizzi* is currently Associate Professor of Computer Aided Design at the University of Parma, Faculty of Engineering. She received the Laurea Degree in Physics from University of Milan in 1985. She has been working in the area of CAD, CAM and CIM since 1985 with particular interest in the following topics: solid modeling, parametric surfaces, man-machine interaction in industrial applications, user interface development tools, nonrigid materials modeling and simulation, off-line programming.

26

# Integration of reverse engineering and rapid prototyping with data reduction

*Y. H. Chen, C. T. Ng, Y. Z. Wang*
*Dept. of Mechanical Engineering, The University of Hong Kong*
*Pokfulam Road, Hong Kong,*
*Tel: 852-28597910, Fax: 852-28585415,*
*E-mail: YHCHEN@hkucc.hku.hk*

**Abstract**

Reverse engineering is a methodology for constructing CAD models of physical parts by digitizing an existing part, creating a computer model and then using it to manufacture the component. When a digitized part is to be manufactured by means of rapid prototyping machines such as stereolithography apparatus (SLA) and selective laser sintering equipment (SLS), etc., it is not necessary to construct the CAD model of a digitized part. This will be described by the proposed novel method which can construct a STL file (the de facto file format for rapid prototyping machines) directly from digitized part data. Further more, the STL file can even be constructed in a way that significant data reduction can be achieved at the users' discretion.

**Keywords**

Reverse engineering, rapid prototyping, triangulation, STL

## 1 INTRODUCTION

Reverse engineering is an important process in the design and manufacturing context. This can be illustrated by two examples. First, a product that initially exists in a designer's medium such as clay and wood, must have its surfaces

Computer Applications in Production and Engineering. F. Plonka and G. Olling (Eds.)

digitized in order to convert the model to a computer-based representation(compatible with CAD/CAM systems). Secondly, if part drawings are not available in CAD form such as some proven old designs or antiques, CAD models of such parts can be constructed through reverse engineering techniques. Given a CAD model of a part, traditional methods such as CNC machining can be used to produce the parts. However, it is sometimes impossible for CNC machines to machine complicated surfaces both rapidly and cost-effectively. Over the past a few years, rapid prototyping machines have been widely used in industry. A variety of rapid prototyping technologies have emerged(Yan and Gu, 1989, Miller and Grote, 1995, Wallet et al., 1992). They include Stereolithography (SLA), Selective Laser Sintering (SLS), Fused Deposition Manufacturing (FDM), Laminated Object Manufacturing (LOM), Ballistic Particle Manufacturing (BPM), and Three Dimensional Printing (3D Printing). These technologies are capable of directly generating physical objects from a CAD model. They have an important common feature: physical parts are produced by adding materials layer by layer. This is opposite to traditional machining methods which make physical parts by removing material.

In rapid prototyping, STL file format has become the de facto standard(3D Systems, 1988). An STL file consists of a list of triangular facet data. Each facet is uniquely identified by a unit normal and three vertices. The normal and each vertex are specified by three coordinates each, so there is a total of 12 numbers stored for each facet. Apart from this, triangular facets in an STL file must also obey the following two rules.

*Facet orientation*

The facets define the surfaces of a 3-dimensional object. As such, each facet is part of the boundary between the interior and the exterior of the object. The orientation of the facet is specified redundantly in two ways which must be consistent. First, the direction of the normal is outward. Second, the vertices are listed in counter-clockwise order when looking at the object from the outside. This rule is illustrated in Figure 1.

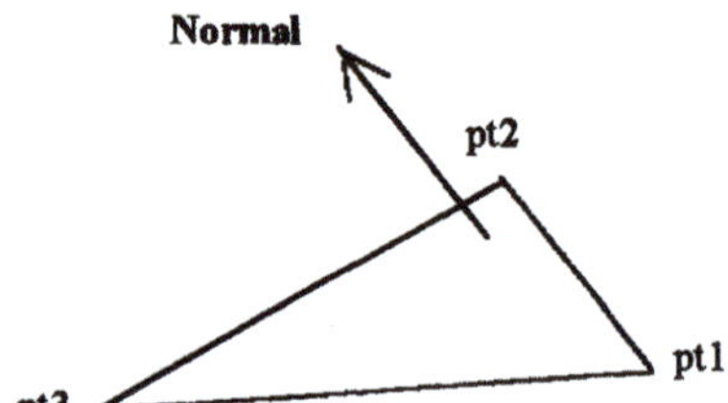


Figure 1 Orientation of a triangular facet.

*Vertex-to-vertex*

Each triangular facet must share two vertices with each of its adjacent triangles. In other words, a vertex of one triangle cannot lie on the side of another. This rule is illustrated in Figure 2.

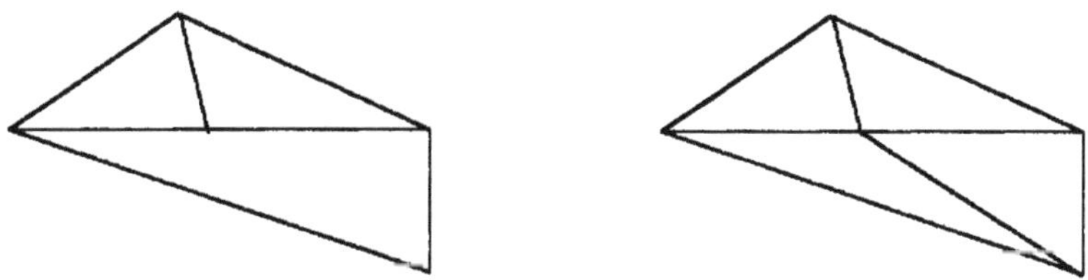

(a) Violation of vertex-to-vertex rule (b) Correct triangulation

Figure 2 The vertex-to-vertex rule.

Most recent commercial CAD/CAM software systems are capable of generating STL files directly from a surface model. The majority of triangulation methods are based on a known surface model(Schumaker, 1993, Sheng and Hirrch, 1992). Triangulation of scattered data in 3D space often has an objective of constructing smooth surfaces(Oxley, 1985, Park and Kim, 1995). Literature about optimized STL file generation from reverse engineering data cannot be found. The most relevant publication is found in Hamann paper(Humann, 1994). His proposal removes a triangle based on curvatures at the three vertices of a triangle. Again, his research has smooth surface fitting in mind. This paper describes a data reduction method for automatic STL file generation directly from reverse engineering data. The proposed method is based on surface normals of triangles that share a data point.

## 2 AUTOMATED STL FILE GENERATION

There are various methods for part digitization. The presented research utilizes a Mitutoyo BLN 122 coordinate measuring machine (CMM) to digitize a part. In order not to miss any detail of part geometry, a large number of measurement points are normally defined. If all points are used in STL file generation, the file can easily becomes huge that the whole rapid prototyping process will be slowed down significantly. In fact, keeping lots of data points in nearly planar regions is rather unsophisticated. Removal of data points in these regions would not affect the accuracy for rapid prototyping machines. A criterion based on normals of neighboring triangles has been defined as to which points can be removed in accordance with users' requirement.

Point data from CMM measurement is usually very regular and can be arranged in matrix form. If all measurement points are to be used for STL file construction, the problem becomes quite simple. In fact, the proposed method initially uses all points to form triangles in the following simple way:

```
Given a data point matrix M(i, j)
        where i = 1, ...m; j = 1, ...n
        For j = 1 to n
                for i = 1 to (m-1)
                        join M(i, j) to M(i+1, j);
        For j = 1 to (n - 1)
                for i = 1 to m
                        join M(i, j) to M(i, j+1);
                for i = 1 to (m-1)
                        join M(i, j) to M(i+1,j+1);
End.
```

With the above procedure, data points can be triangulated as shown in Figure 3. It can be seen that triangles formed in this ways conform to the STL file vertex-to-vertex rule.

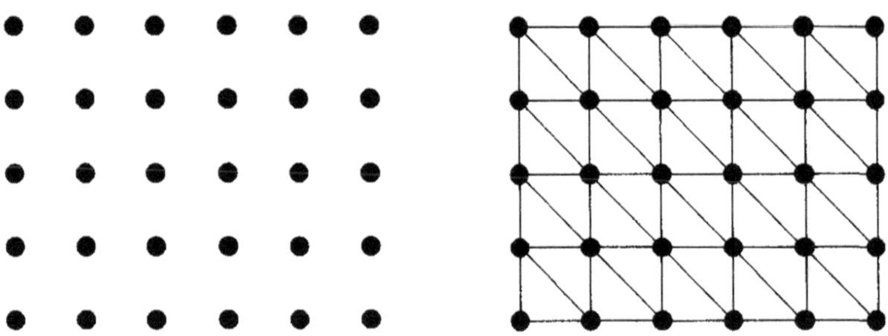

(a) Data points (b) Triangulation

Figure 3 Initial triangulation.

To generate a complete STL file, normalized surface normals of triangles must be specified. Given a triangle as shown in Figure 1 ($pt_1$, $pt_2$ and $pt_3$ must be arranged in counter-clockwise direction), normalized normals can be easily calculated from the following procedure.

(a) Form two vectors $\mathbf{V}_{31}$ and $\mathbf{V}_{32}$ by

$$\mathbf{V}_{31} = \mathbf{Pt}_1 - \mathbf{Pt}_3$$
$$\mathbf{V}_{32} = \mathbf{Pt}_2 - \mathbf{Pt}_3 \quad (1)$$

(b) Calculate surface normal from the cross product.

$$\mathbf{n} = \mathbf{V}_{31} \times \mathbf{V}_{32} \tag{2}$$

(c) Normalize **n** through the division.

$$\hat{\mathbf{n}} = \frac{\mathbf{n}}{|\mathbf{n}|} \tag{3}$$

With the above information, STL file can be readily generated.

# 3 DATA REDUCTION

## 3.1 Data reduction in percentage

If the digitized object has large planar or near planar regions, it is desirable to remove some of the points in these regions. In order to identify which points can be removed, a point weighting scheme based on a point surrounding triangles' normals is developed and described in the following:

(a) Search all triangles Δ that share the point in concern.
(b) Let one of the surface normal **U** in Δ be the reference vector, calculate subtractions of **U** with the rest of surface normals in Δ.

$$\begin{aligned}
\mathbf{UV}_1 &= \mathbf{V}_1 - \mathbf{U} \\
\mathbf{UV}_2 &= \mathbf{V}_2 - \mathbf{U} \\
&\bullet \\
&\bullet \\
&\bullet \\
\mathbf{UV}_n &= \mathbf{V}_n - \mathbf{U}
\end{aligned} \tag{4}$$

(c) Transform all resulting vectors to first quadrant by taking the absolute values of all vector components, e.g. $\mathbf{UV}_2 = a\mathbf{i} + b\mathbf{j} + c\mathbf{k}$ is transformed to $\mathbf{UV}_2 = |a|\mathbf{i} + |b|\mathbf{j} + |c|\mathbf{k}$.
(d) Sum up all the resulting vectors.

$$\mathbf{W} = \mathbf{UV}_1 + \mathbf{UV}_2 + \ldots + \mathbf{UV}_n \tag{5}$$

(e) Calculated the average quantity d by

$$d = \frac{|\mathbf{W}|}{n}\mathbf{V}_{\mathbf{n}} \tag{6}$$

If d is small for a given point, the point stands a higher chance of being removed. Which points are to be removed depends on users' specifications. If a user want 10% of the point data be removed, then points with the lowest 10% of d will be removed.

### 3.2 Data reduction by bounded error

In computer visualization, polygonal mesh, triangles in particular are usually used to approximate object surfaces. In the triangulation of an object surface, accuracy is often controlled by bounded error(Kalvin and Taylor, 1996). The bounded error concept is also adapted in this research to control errors resulting from data reduction of an STL file in rapid prototyping.

In data reduction, two strategies can be used. One is to remove the point one at a time. The other is to remove several points, or a patch at the same time. After consideration of error accumulation and computation efficiency, patch removal strategy is implemented in this research.

Suppose a patch has k triangles. The normals and areas of the k triangles are $\mathbf{n}_1$ to $\mathbf{n}_k$ and $S_1$ to $S_k$ respectively. Let

$$S = \sum_{i=1}^{k} S \tag{7}$$

The patch direction normal is calculated by:

$$\mathbf{n} = \sum_{i=1}^{k} \frac{S_i}{S}\mathbf{n}_i \tag{8}$$

$$\hat{\mathbf{n}} = \frac{\mathbf{n}}{|\mathbf{n}|} \tag{9}$$

The direction normal $\hat{\mathbf{n}}$ is an indication of the direction of maximum projection. Based on the patch direction normal, a minimum enclosing box of a patch can be calculated. For illustration purpose, Figure 4(a) shows a patch and its bounding box. After data reduction (Suppose the three points in the middle are removed), the new patch and its bounding box are shown in Figure 4(b). The bounded error $E_p$ is measured along the patch direction normal, that is

$$E_p = D_b - D_a \tag{10}$$

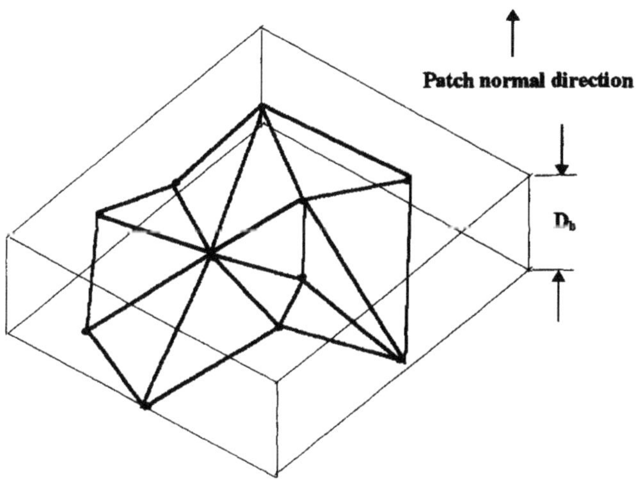


(A) Before removal

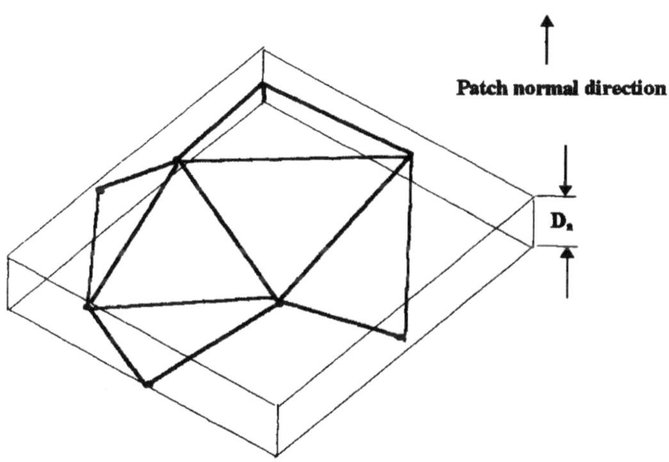


(B) After removal

Figure 4 Error definition.

This error can be specified by the user so that the accuracy after data reduction is still within control.

## 4 RE-TRIANGULATION

When a point is to be removed, triangles sharing this point must be removed too. This leaves a lank region’ which must be covered through re-triangulation. The implemented re-triangulation method is described in the following:

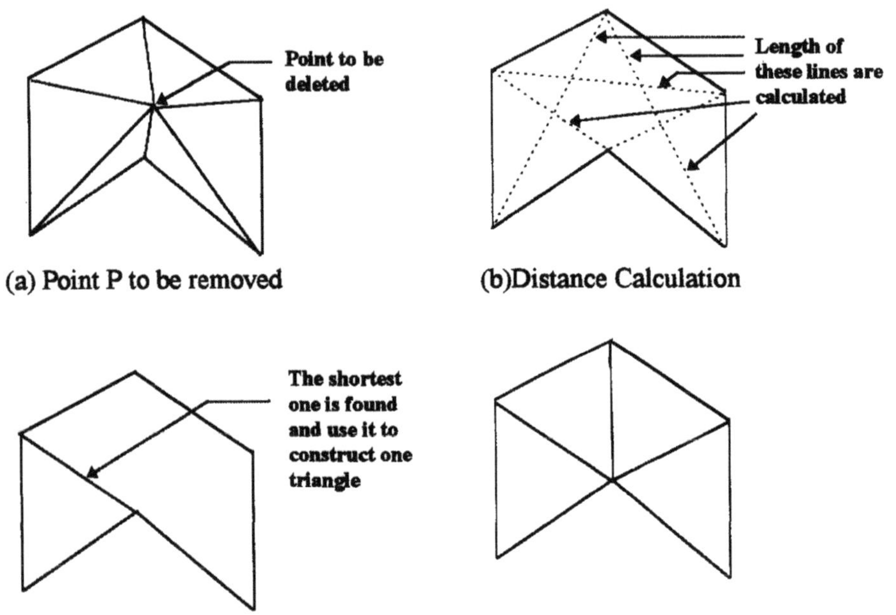


(a) Point P to be removed

(b)Distance Calculation

(c) Form a new triangle

(d) The rest of triangles are formed in the same way

Figure 5 Re-triangulation.

(1) Form a point list **L** that are affected by the removal of a point. In figure 5(a), if point P is to be removed, the affected point list will be **L** = {$P_1$, $P_2$, $P_3$, $P_4$, $P_5$, $P_6$}.
(2) Take three consecutive points from the point list **L** and check whether the triangle formed by the three points is inside or outside the region formed by **L**. If not, take another three consecutive points and check again.
(3) Calculate the length of the line formed by the first and the last point of the three points as shown in Figure 5(b) in dashed lines.
(4) Repeat (2) and (3) until all combinations of consecutive three points have been exhausted.
(5) Find the shortest length and use the corresponding three points to form a real triangle as shown in Figure 5(c). Calculate the normal of the newly formed triangle and delete the middle point of the three points from **L** have $\mathbf{L_1}$.
(6) Repeat from (2) with point list **L** until no more than four points left in $\mathbf{L_1}$.

Figure 5(d) shows a re-triangulated region after a point is removed. Point removal and re-triangulation will go on iteratively until certain criteria are met. Two criteria are given for users' specification. One is the percentage of points to be removed and the other is the bounded error caused by points removal.

## 5 EXPERIMENTAL RESULTS

With the implemented method, a number of examples have been tested. One of the example is a human face. It was digitized using a Mitutoyo BLN 122 coordinate measuring machine as shown in Figure 6. As some parts of the human face has very low curvature change, some data points can be removed. In the experiment, data reduction for 20%, 50% and 80% have been specified for

Figure 6 STL file without data reduction.

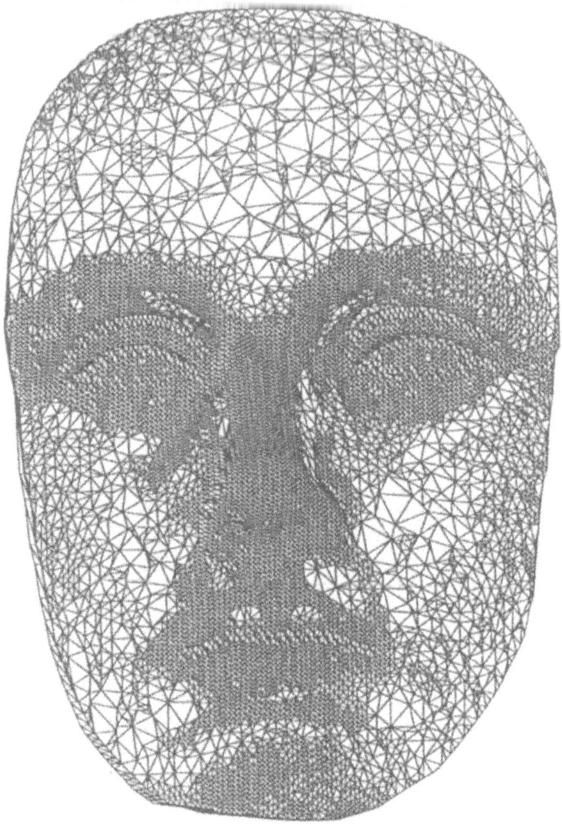

Figure 7 STL file after 50% data reduction.

prototype fabrication. Figure 7 shows the STL file after 50% of data reduction. It can be seen that regions with small curvature changes have large data reduction. This is exactly what is desired.

## 6 CONCLUSION

This paper has presented a novel method for STL file construction directly from CMM measurement data. When desired, the user can specify either the percentage of points to be removed or the bounded error caused by points removal in order to speed up computation and to reduce storage space. Several prototypes with different amounts of data reduction have been built using an SLS equipment which shows satisfactory results.

## 7 ACKNOWLEDGEMENT

This research is carried out with a CRCG grant (code:337/064/0023) from the University of Hong Kong.


## 8 REFERENCES


3D Systems (1988) Stereolithography interface specification. USA.

Hamann, B. (1994) A data reduction scheme for triangulated surfaces. *Computer Aided Geometric Design*, **11**, 197-214.

Kalvin, A.D. and Taylor, R.H. (1996) Superfaces: polygonal mesh simplification with bounded error. *IEEE Computer Graphics & Applications*, May, 64-77

Miller, J.L. and Grote, K.H. (1995) Solid freeform manufacturing technologies as an important step in the product development process. *Computers in Industry*, **28**, 11-16.

Oxley, A. (1985) Surface fitting by triangulation. *The Computer Journal*, **28**(3), 335-339.

Park, H. and Kim, K. (1995) An adaptive method for smooth surface approximation to scattered 3D points. *Computer-Aided Design*, **27**, 929-939.

Schumaker, L.L. (1993) Triangulations in CAGD. *IEEE Computer Graphics & Applications*, January, 47-52.

Sheng, X. and Hirrch, B.E. (1992) Triangulation of trimmed surfaces in parametric space. *Computer-Aided Design*, **24**(8), 437-444.

Wall, M.B., Ulrich, K.T. and Flowers, W.C. (1992) Evaluating prototyping technologies for product design. *Research in Engineering Design*, **3**, 163-177.

Yan, X. and Gu, P. (1996) A review of rapid prototyping technologies and systems. *Computer-Aided Design*, **28**(4), 307-318.


## 9 BIOGRAPH

Dr. Y.H. Chen is an assistant professor in The Department of Mechanical Engineering, The University of Hong Kong since 1993. Before joining The University of Hong Kong, Dr. Chen has worked in Motorola Electronics Pte, Ltd (Singapore), Asia Matshushita Electronics Pte, Led (Singapore), and Swire Technologies Pte, Ltd (Hong Kong) as senior automation engineer, senior research engineer and automation manager respectively. Dr. Chen research interest include CAD/CAM, reverse engineering and rapid prototyping.

Mr. C.T. Ng is an M.Phil research student under Dr. Chen.

Dr. Y.Z. Wang is currently a research associate working with Dr. Chen. He is a lecturer in The Department of Mechanical Engineering, Tianjin University, P.R. China.

# 27

# Performance Prediction of P/M Electrodes in EDM Using Artificial Neural Network

*P.K.Philip, Mathews P.Samuel, Thomas George,*
*G.Kuppuswamy*
*Department of Mechanical Engineering*
*Indian Institute of Technology, Madras 600 036, India*
*Tel: 2351365 Extn:3624, FAX: 91 44 2350509/2352545*
*E-Mail: philip@acer.iitm.ernet.in*

**Abstract**

Tool electrode is a vital factor in Electrical Discharge Machining (EDM). The non-availability of an ideal single tool material points to the Powder Metallurgy (P/M) process for combining the desirable properties of different tool materials. The properties of electrodes prepared by P/M route are determined by the powder characteristics as well as process variables. Due to the complex nature of electrical discharge machining, it is very difficult to determine the optimum conditions for improving machining performance. In this paper, a feed forward back-propagation neural network is used to correlate the process parameters with electrode performance. Experimental results have shown that the machining performance of EDM can be estimated and consequently improved upon by this method.

Keywords

EDM, P/M Electrodes, Performance indices ,Neural Network, Back Propagation, Machining estimation.

Computer Applications in Production and Engineering. F. Plonka and G. Olling (Eds.)

## 1. INTRODUCTION

The erosive effect of electrical discharges on metals has been known for a long time, but the first step to use it for machining was made by Lazarenko in 1946 (1). Now it is a well developed technique for the manufacture of dies and moulds. Due to the technological developments in the past few decades, Electrical Discharge Machining (EDM) can provide an effective solution for machining hard conductive materials and reproducing complex shapes. Sophisticated computer control with fully automated work handling systems have enhanced the capability of EDM process (2). Even in the midst of all these technical excellence, selection of various input parameters for obtaining higher performance is not yet fully solved (3,4).

Electrical discharge machining involves complicated phenomena such as spark initiation, dielectric breakdown, thermo-mechanical erosion of metal etc. (5). Due to the stochastic nature of EDM process, it is very difficult to map input factors to cutting performance using the conventional techniques. But neural networks are highly flexible modeling tools with an ability to learn the mapping between input and output variables (6-10). The advantage of neural network is utilised here to predict the machining performance of each electrode. A multi-layered, feed forward neural network with supervised learning has been used in the present work. The input-output data are normalised before the initiation of the neural network for better convergence and accuracy of the process. Since electrical discharge machining is basically a metal removal process, the amount of metal removed form the work piece in unit time and the electrode wear are the most important factors to be considered for evaluating the performance of a tool. For a comparative evaluation of such factors the conventional solid (forged) copper electrode is selected as a reference. Based on the performance of this conventional solid electrode. Powder Metallurgy (P/M) electrodes can be evaluated as described in the following pages.

## 2. POWDER METALLURGY ELECTRODES IN EDM

EDM is based on the controlled erosion of materials by elelctric sparks between tool and work piece submerged in a bath of dielectric medium. The EDM process as it is understood today, can be divided into three sub divisions.

1. Application of adequate electrical energy
2. Dielectric breakdown and spark phenomena
3. Expulsion (erosion) of materials.

Although this is a simple depiction of a complex process, it is sufficient to provide an overall perspective. Figure 1 shows the factors which affect the overall EDM performance. Among these factors, electrodes play a vital role in machining performance and accuracy (11,12).

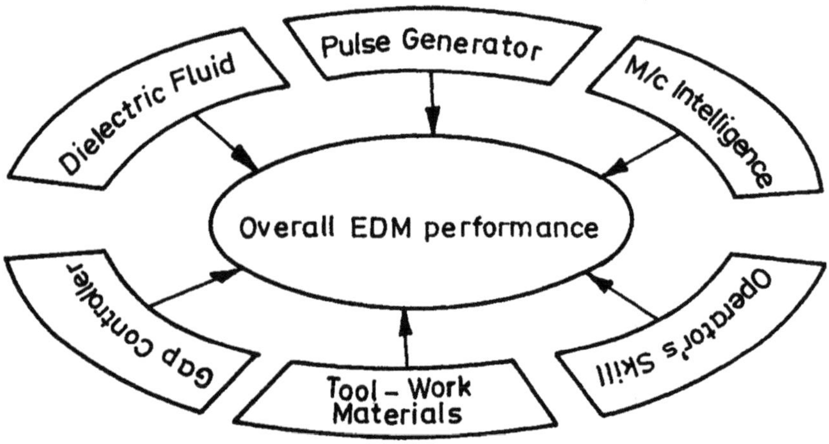


**Figure 1 EDM Performance as a function of different parameters**

The tool electrode material should not only be resistant to electric erosion, but also be capable of removing maximum material from the opposite electrode (work piece). Although an ideal single material with such a property does not exist, powder metallurgy (P/M) provides a means of combining desirable characteristics of different materials. In this process compacting and sintering conditions as well as powder characteristics are decisive factors. Judicious selection of operating variables results in optimum electrode performance.

The results of EDM with P/M electrodes do not match completely with the conventional. These electrodes produce varying responses depending on the powder metallurgy conditions employed in their manufacture. In short, powder metallurgy process variables control the electrode properties and thereby dictate the performance of P/M electrodes in EDM. In order to describe the performance behavior of P/M electrodes, following performance factors are defined in this paper.

1. Machining Index (MI): It is the ratio of metal removed by a P/M electrode to that of by the conventional solid copper electrode of same dimensions operating under similar conditions.

2. Electrode Performance Number (EPN). It is the ratio of the wear ratio of a P/M electrode to that of a conventional solid copper electrode of same dimensions operating under similar conditions.
3. Material Removal Rate (MRR): It is the amount of work material removed by the electrode per unit time.

MI and EPN of solid copper electrode is fixed as 100 and based on this reference P/M electrodes are graded. Negative value in any of these factors indicates metal deposition rather than metal removal.

## 3. EXPERIMENTAL DETAILS

Electrolytic copper (99.7% pure) powder was the starting material. A double cone blender was used for mixing the lubricant (1% zinc stearate by wt.) with the powder and the electrodes were prepared in a single acting press with die assembly. The electrodes prepared at different compacting pressures were sintered to different levels using a tubular furnace. The detailed specifications of compaction and sintering are given in table 1.

**Table 1 Specification of Compaction and Sintering**

COMPACTION

| | | |
|---|---|---|
| Press capacity | : | 20 Ton |
| Mode of compaction | : | Single action |
| Diameter of compact | : | 14 mm |
| Length of compact | : | 12 mm |
| Compaction range | : | 62 to 625 MPa |

SINTERING

| | | |
|---|---|---|
| Type of furnace | : | Tubular |
| Protective atmosphere | : | Argon gas |
| Heating Rate | : | 14° C/min. |
| Pre-sintering Temp. | : | 400°C |
| Max.Temperature | : | 950°C |
| Sintering time | : | 30 min. |

Performance evaluation of these P/M electrodes were carried out by Nassovia Krupp-31 discharge machine equipped with iso-frequent pulse generator. Kerosene was the dielectric medium and hardened steel (53 HRC) was used as work piece for all experiments. Experiments were conducted with different settings of Pulse current and pulse frequency. The voltage and current pulses were recorded simultaneously using a dual trace oscilloscope connected to a digital plotter. Metal erosion was determined by weighing the electrodes before and after the experiments.

## 4. NEURAL NETWORK MODELING

Neural networks are based on the working pattern of brain cells or neurons and represent models different from those related to physical symbol systems such as expert systems where artificial intelligence(AI) features refer to performance paradigm of human reasoning. Neural systems are associated with what is called brain paradigm of AI methods. Typically the network consists of nodes and arcs, each of the nodes or circles modeling a very simplified neuron and arcs treated as connections. The nodes compute by responding to its inputs and the weights on the concerned arcs by the weighted sum rule.

Neuron is basic to the operation of neural networks by serving as an information processing unit. Fig.2 illustrates the model of a typical neuron.

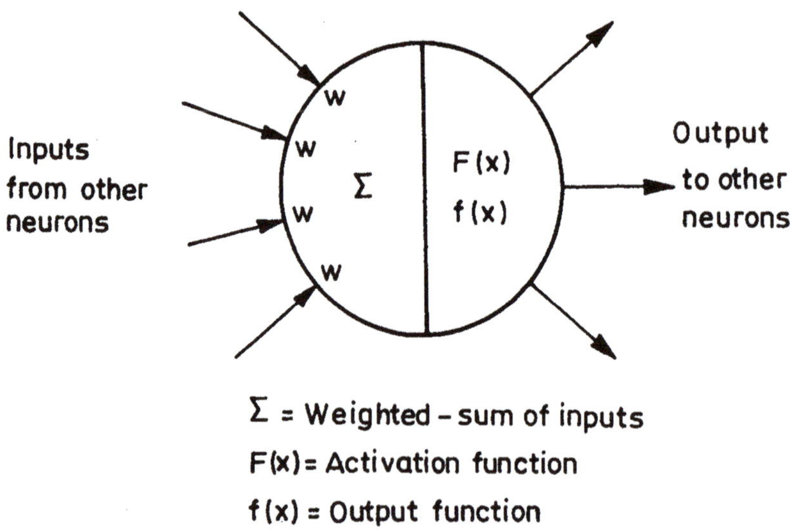


**Figure 2 Working of Neuron model**

The sum of weighted inputs from other neurons is processed based on specified threshold or activation and output functions to obtain the output to other neurons. The cells activation is determined by an activation function F(x) specifying how the input is combined with the current activation value in order to produce the new activation value, or activation level. The final output of the cell is on computation by another function, the output function f(x) on its activation level, typically by using a sigmoidal transfer function. This output value is further transmitted along the weighted outgoing connections as inputs to subsequent neurons.

Neural nets basically describe mathematical models of information processing and provide a method of representing relationships between input and output variables quite different from other computer methods with stored programs for functional models. The neural method had been chosen in the present study of performance of P/M electrodes in EDM since the problem is complex. The EDM output variables are not only dependent on pulse characteristics viz. frequency and current but also on electrode processing parameters, namely, powder size, compaction pressure and sintering temperature. The mathematical model formulation is thus difficult. Neural network model based on a typical sample data becomes a powerful simulation tool for further analysis regarding the influence of changes in parameters of the concerned variables on EDM performance indices, by providing reasonable output estimates.

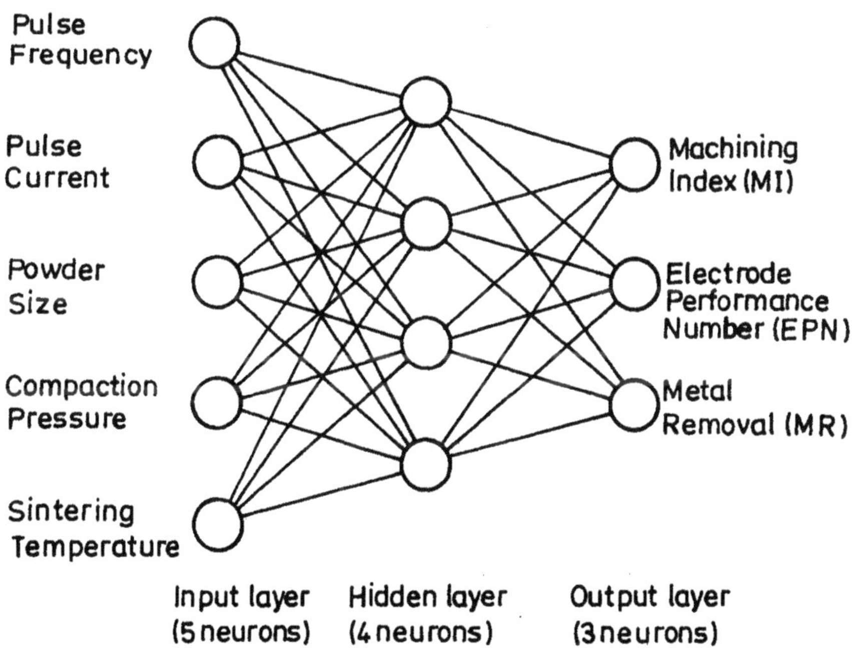


**Figure 3 A multi-layered (5-4-3) back propagation neural network model**

The feed-forward back propagation net is a popular architecture among different types of neural networks and finds applications in several areas in engineering.

Fig.3 represents a model having 5 neurons in the input layer, 4 neurons in the hidden layer and 3 neurons in the output layer. This network is used for analysis in the present study. Typically the network is trained for supervised learning with known input vector and output vector pairs to arrive at the arc weights for a prescribed error level, often requiring a large number of iterations or cycles of computation based on the back propagation algorithm. The backpropagation is a learning method that computes an error at each layer and propagates this error backward to determine appropriate improvements in weights.

For training the model, parameters for pulse frequency, pulse current, powder size, compaction pressure and sintering temperature have been used as inputs. Machining Index (MI) Electrode Performance Number (EPN) and Metal Removal (MR) are considered as outputs. A software written in C++ for the back propagation method (7) was run on a 486 PC/AT. Totally 15 K cycles of iterations were necessary to arrive at the cycle error of 7.78E-05. This session was carried out in four stages by modifying the learning rate, momentum and noise factors used in the algorithm. The first phase had been for 3.5 K iterations at a learning rate of 0.5, the second one for 1.5K iterations at a learning rate of 0.1 and the last two for 10 K iterations at a learning rate of 0.01. The error levels arrived at are 1.8E-04,1.28E-04,9.70E-05, and finally 7.78 E-05 after the respective phases.

Table 2 represents the data used for training the network, and the final output values obtained.

**Table 2 Data used for training and output results**

| Pulse Frequency kHz | Pulse Current Amp. | Powder Size µm | Compaction Pressure MPa | Sintering Temperature °C | MI Training Data | MI Output Result | EPN Training Data | EPN Output Result | MR mg Training Data | MR mg Output Result |
|---|---|---|---|---|---|---|---|---|---|---|
| 06 | 10 | 03 | 250 | 900 | 061 | 061 | 2.8 | 2.8 | 94.8 | 94.8 |
| 10 | 09 | 03 | 625 | 900 | 124 | 123.6 | 6.2 | 6.2 | 99.6 | 99.9 |
| 07 | 16 | 75 | 250 | 850 | 056 | 55.4 | 9.7 | 9.7 | 143 | 143.6 |
| 12 | 10 | 75 | 500 | 850 | 028 | 28.7 | 7.9 | 7.9 | 98.4 | 97.5 |

## 5. SIMULATION RESULTS

The neural network model developed is used as a simulation tool to evaluate the performance of P/M tool electrodes in EDM by estimating the MI, EPN and MR parameters. Table 3 shows the model output for a study on changes in powder size for a compaction pressure of 540 MPa, sintering temperature of 850°C at a pulse frequency of 8 KHz and pulse current of 10 A. The Table illustrates the use of the method to the manufacturing technologist. The model provides output estimates of the performance indices based on specified input parameters for further analysis. The model possesses potential for process monitoring, adaptive control as well as optimisation of electrode processing parameters. The results imply that the EDM performance is not only dependent on electrical pulse characateristics but also to a large extent on the electrode processing parameters. The model proves to be an appropriate tool for analysing the complex phenomena encountered in EDM involving a number of significant variables.

**Table 3 Model-estimates at different levels of powder size**

| Powder Size μm | MI | EPN | MR mg |
|---|---|---|---|
| 15 | 91.4 | 6.41 | 98.36 |
| 30 | 66.9 | 6.83 | 96.99 |
| 45 | 47.8 | 7.09 | 95.44 |
| 65 | 35.6 | 7.36 | 94.31 |

## 6. CONCLUSIONS

A multi-layered feed-forward back propagation neural network has been used to construct a model of Electrical Discharge Machining incorporating electrode manufacturing process parameters. The study illustrates that the network model can effectively map different process variables to machining performance of P/M electrodes in terms of machining index, electrode performance number and metal removal and be used as a simulation tool for further analysis and optimisation. The results endorse the application of P/M electrodes in EDM and the dependence of P/M processing variables on its performance.

# 7. REFERENCES

1. Lazarenko B.R.(1964) Electro spark machining of metals, Consultants Bureau, NY.

2. De Vries M.F, Duffie N.A, Kruth J, Dauw D.F, and Schumacher B (1990) Integration of EDM with CIM environment. *Annals of the CIRP*, Vol.39, pp 665-672

3. Bayramoglu M and Dufil A.W (1994) Systematic investigation on the use of cylindrical tools for the reduction of 3D complex shapes on CNC EDM machines. *Int.J.Mech.Tools Manuf.*Vol.34,No.3.pp 327-339.

4. Rajurkar K P.(1990) Technology and research in EDM and ECM. *ASME Fundamental Issue Mach*. Vol.453, pp 309-336.

5. Erden E.(1983) Effect of materials on the mechanism of EDM. *Trans of the ASME* Vol.105, pp 132-138.

6. Nayes, J.L.(1992) Artificial Intelligence with common lisp fundamentals of symbolic and numerric processing, D.C. Heath and Co., MA, USA.

7. Rao V and Rao H, (1994) C++ neural networks and fuzzy logic, *M&T Publishing Inc*. USA.

8. Lee B.Y, Tang Y.S.,Ma S.C.(1995) Modeling of the process damping force in chatter vibration, *Int.J.Mach Tools.Manufact.*Vol.35, No.7, pp 963-974.

9. Liao T.W. Chen L.J.(1994) A neural network approach for grinding process: Modeling and optimization, *Int.J Mach Tools Manufact.*Vol.34, No. 7, pp 919-937 .

10. Tang Y.S. Ma S.C.,Chung, I.K.(1995) Determination of optical cutting parameters in wire electrical discharge machining *Int. J.Mach.Tools Manufact.* Vol.46, No.12, pp 1693-1701.

11. Jeswani M.J. (1979) Dimensional analysis of tool wear in EDM, *Int.J. of Wear*, Vol.55, pp 153-161.

12. Meyrin S.A, Dauw D.F and Albert L (1992)About the evolution of wire tool performance in wire EDM, *Annals of the CIRP*, Vol.11/1, pp 221-225.

## 8. BIOGRAPHY

Prof.P.K.PHILIP is Professor of Manufacturing Engineering, Department of Mechanical Engineering, Indian Institute of Technology, Madras from 1984. He was a doctoral scholar under the German Academic Exchange Programme (1968-70) and a Post-doctoral Fellow of the Alexander von Humboldt Foundation, Bonn (1975-77) both at the University of Stuttgart, Germany. He has published a large number of papers in his field of interest, which is material removal processes. He is a life fellow of the Institution of Engineers, India and a senior member of the SME from 1988.

Mathews P.Samuel finished his M.S. research degree and is currently Scientist B at the Centre for Military Airworthiness and Certification, Bangalore 560 035.

Thomas George was M.Tech. student at IIT Madras and is at present Lecturer in Mechanical Engineering at M.A.College of Engineering, Kothamangalam, Kerala 686 666.

Dr.G.Kuppuswamy is Associate Professor in Manufacturing Engineering at IIT Madras.

# 28
# Rapid manufacturing of dinnerware

*R.K.L. Gay, C.K. Chua and W. Hoheisel*
*Gintic Institute of Manufacturing Technology*
*Nanyang Avenue, Singapore 639798*
*65-7995491(P), 65-7916377 (F), grobertgay@ntu.edu.sg*

**Abstract**

Computer usage in the ceramic dinnerware industry has largely been confined to word processing, spreadsheets, database, payroll, inventory and statistical process control. CAD/CAM or Computer Aided Design and Computer Aided Manufacturing is slowly gaining ground in this industry. The relatively high speed of generating physical designs from conceptualization using CAD/CAM and Rapid Prototyping has suggested their use for the decoration of ceramic dinnerware. A CAD/CAM system developed for the design and manufacture of patterns to be decorated on ceramic dinnerware is described in this paper.

An industrial case study featuring ceramic dinnerware prototypes is carried out and presented to illustrate the various advantages. These advantages include significant time and cost savings. It also avoids the heavy reliance on traditional practices, and the experience and skills of craftsmen. The major contribution of the research is an innovative approach from art to part or, from conceptualization to realization, for the decoration of ceramic dinnerware. The solution of 3 Dimensional decoration and application of rapid prototyping are also described.

**Keywords**

Ceramic dinner, rapid prototyping, rapid manufacturing, CAD/CAM, craftsmen

Computer Applications in Production and Engineering. F. Plonka and G. Olling (Eds.)

# 1 INTRODUCTION

There are presently several commercially-available software systems for product design for a particular range of industries which include ceramic tableware (Chua, et. al., 1993), glassware, bottle making, both plastic and glass, jewelry (Lee, et.al., 1992), packaging, food processing, for molded products and products produced from forming rolls, coins and badges, and embossing rollers. All of these industries share a common problem: most of their products have elements of complex engraving or low relief on them. Traditionally, such work is carried out by skilled engravers either in-house, or more often by a third-party sub-contractor, working from 2D artwork. This process is costly, open to unwanted misinterpretation of the design by the engraver and most importantly, lengthens the time of the design cycle.

The CAD/CAM revolution has boosted the production and the performance of many industries everywhere for the past 15 years. However, its applications in the above industries are still at their infancy stage. Prototyping is still very much a manual process, which relies largely on the skills of an experienced craftsman who uses handtools such as a small chisel to carve and shape the model out of a plaster block. Little attention has been focused on the use of quick and accurate rapid prototyping equipment for building prototypes in this industry.

The use of CAD/CAM and Rapid Prototyping (RP) technologies such as Stereolithography Apparatus (SLA) and Laminated Object Manufacturing (LOM) reduces the time required for design modifications and improvement of prototypes. The steps involved in the art to part process are described in the following sections.

# 2 SCANNING OF ARTWORK

The function of scanning software is to automatically or semi-automatically create a 2D image from 2D artwork. It would normally be applied in cases where it would be too complicated and time consuming to model the part from a drawing using existing CAD techniques.

The 2D artwork is first read into ArtCAM, the CAD/CAM system used for the project, using a Sharp JX A4 scanner. Figure 1 shows the 2D artwork of a floral design, which has been generated using the circular adaptation, routinely. This combination of hardware and software allows for the direct production of a standard image from the artwork, which can be read directly into ArtCAM. The 2D artwork in such instances represents the designs to be used on the face of tableware item such as a dinner plate.

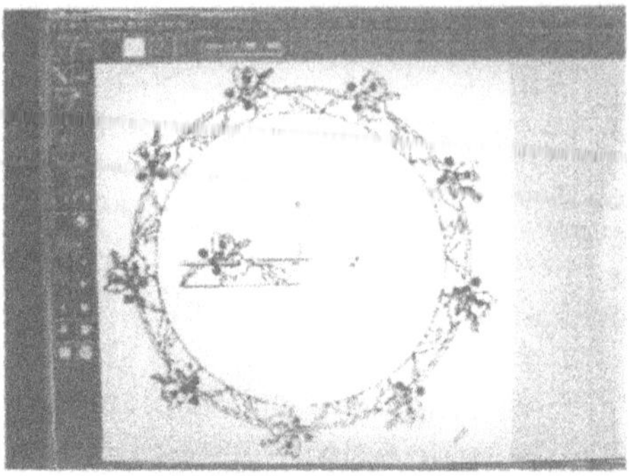

**Figure 1** 2D artwork.

In the ArtCAM environment, the scanned image is first reduced from a color image to a monochrome image with the fully automatic "Gary Scale" function. Alternatively, the number of colors in the image can be reduced using the "Reduce Color" function. A color palette is provided for color selection and the various areas of the images are colored either using different sizes/types of brushes or the automatic flood fills function.

## 3 GENERATION OF SURFACES

The shape of a dinnerware is modeled to the required dimensions in the CAD system for model building. A triangular mesh file is produced automatically from the 3D model. This is used as a base onto which the relief data is wrapped and later combined with the relief model to form the finished part.

## 4 GENERATION OF 3D DECORATION RELIEFS

The next stage in creating the 3D-decoration relief is to assign each color in the image a shape profile. There are various fields which control the shape profile of the selected colored region, namely, the overall general shape for the region, the curvatures of the profile (convex or concave), the maximum height, base height, angle and scale.

There are three possibilities for the overall general shape; a plane shape profile will appear completely flat, whereas a round shape profile will have a rounded cross section and lastly, the square shape profile will have straight angled sides. For each of these shapes, there is an option to define the profile as either convex or concave.

The square and round profiles can be given a maximum height. If the specified shape reaches this height, it will 'plateau' out at this height giving in effect a flat region with rounded or angled corners, depending on whether a round or square shape was selected for the overall profile respectively.

The overall profile height which covers the respective region can be controlled by specifying the required angle of the profile which represents the tangent angle of the curve at the edge of the region. An alternative to control the overall profile height is to use the 'scale' function to flatten out or elevate the height of the shape profile. The relief detail can be examined in a dynamic Graphic Window within the ArtCAM environment itself. Figure 2 illustrates the 3D-decoration relief of an artwork.

**Figure 2** 3D-decoration relieves of an artwork.

## 5 WRAPPING OF RELIEFS ON SURFACES

The 3D-decoration relief is next wrapped onto the triangular mesh file generated from the tableware plate surfaces using the command Wrap. This is a true surface wrap and not a simple projection. The wrapped relief is also converted into triangular mesh. The triangular mesh files can be used to produce 3D model suitable for color shading and machining. The two sets of triangular mesh files, of the relief and the coin shape, are automatically combined. The resultant model file can be color-shaded (see figure 3) and used by the SLA to build the prototype.

**Figure 3** Color-shaded resultant model file.

## 6 CONVERTING TRIANGULAR MESH FILES TO AN STL FILE

The STL format is originated by 3D System Inc. as the input format to the SLA, and has since been accepted as the *de facto* standard of input for Rapid Prototyping systems. Upon conversion to STL, the object's surfaces are triangulated, which means that the STL format essentially consists of a description of inter-joining triangles that enclose the object's volume. The triangular mesh files are also triangulated surfaces, however, of a slightly different format. Therefore, an interface program written in Turbo-C language is developed for the purpose of conversion. The converted triangular file adheres to the standard STL format. It has the capability of handling triangular files of huge memory size.

## 7 BUILDING OF MODEL BY RAPID PROTOTYPING METHODS

Many computer-aided manufacturing methods are available such as CNC machining and rapid prototyping (RP) methods. However, for complex 3D shapes, the CNC machining will be disadvantaged when compared to RP. Coupled with complex engineering relieves where a large amount of removal is required and yet the machining cutter diameter must be small to reach those small intricate relieves, rapid prototyping has a definite edge. Rapid prototyping, though, has the disadvantage of limited materials. If, however, given a restricted material type, the functions and applications - design, engineering and manufacturing (or tooling) - can still be carried out, then rapid prototyping would have proved its usefulness and relevance.

While many RP methods are available commercially (Chua, 1997), the world's top two selling RP machines are used in the study. They are the SLA (number 1) and LOM. The SLA has the advantages of being a pioneer and a proven technology with many excellent case studies available. It is also advantageous to use in tableware design as the material is translucent and thus, it allows designers to view the internal structure and details of tableware items like tea pot and gravy bowls. On the other hand, the use of LOM has also its own distinct advantages. Its material cost is much lower and because it does not need support in its process (unlike the SLA), it saves a lot of time in both pre-processing (deciding where and what supports to use) and postprocessing (removing the supports). The use of both systems allows the evaluation of both systems for ceramic tableware. The main criteria for evaluation are speed (time for pre-processing, building and postprocessing), accuracy and surface finish, and suitability for tooling applications.

## 7.1 Using the SLA

Californian company 3D System Inc., pioneered the RP technology when they released their commercial RP system in December 1988 - the SLA-250 model of their Stereolithography Apparatus (SLA). Stereolithography technology was first developed by Chuck Hall, 3D's founding president, in 1982. Stereolithography works by using a low-power Helium-Cadmium laser or an Argon laser to scan the surface of a vat of liquid photopolymer which solidifies when struck by a laser beam. The dinner plate design with its floral relieves is built using the SLA and the resin model is shown in figure 4.

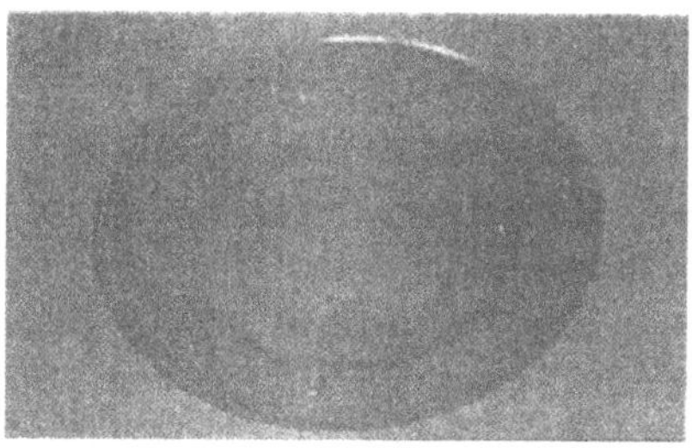

**Figure 4** Dinner plate design built using the SLA.

## 7.2 Using the LOM

Helisys, Inc. was founded in 1985 with a charter to provide state-of-the-art, three-dimensional modeling capability to a wide range of industrial applications. Early R&D activities were financed in large part by DARPA grants, resulting in the development of the Laminated Object Manufacturing (LOM) process. Helisys introduced the LOM machines in 1991. The dinner plate design with its floral reliefs are built using the LOM and the paper model is shown in figure 5.

**Figure 5** Dinner plate design built using the LOM.

# 8 EVALUATION OF THE SLA'S AND LOM'S MODELS AND PROCESSES

## 8.1 Technical evaluation

Technical evaluation is done through the execution of a benchmark test. The benchmark test piece, in this case the dinner plate, is analyzed through some tests including visual inspection and dimensional measurement. In general, two types of measurements can be taken namely, main (large) measurements and detailed (small) measurements.

The record of the measurement results is based on the deviations of the built part from the CAD model. These deviations of both the main and detailed measurements are tabulated for both the SLA and the LOM. The record of the time results is based on three components - data preparation, building time and postprocessing. The total time is based on the addition of the three components. A Table of all four times results can be tabulated for both the SLA and the LOM. The time component by itself gives one an idea of the length required for a task and directly affects the cost factor. Therefore, the time data can become useful for a full economic justification and cost analysis.

The measurements taken are linear dimensions - diameters, heights and thicknesses. Two parts of the test piece are considered for evaluation. The first part includes the plate's top and base surfaces. The second part is the delicate design of the floral patterns which includes the flowers, leaves and others. The results are sub-divided into main measurements (> 10 mm) and detailed measurements (<= 10 mm). For both the readings, the deviations from the actual reading are computed and tabulated. The deviations for both the measurements are compared.

## 8.2 Results of technical evaluation

From visual inspection, it is apparent that the floral patterns of the LOM part are more distinct and correctly formed than those of the SLA part. Even under close examination, the flowers, leaves and stems on the SLA model are indistinguishable. As the focus of the research is on the 3D decoration, this means that the LOM model meets the requirements whereas the SLA model does not. Tables 1 and 2 list the measurements taken and their deviations from the nominal values. The Cs (diameters) and Ts (thicknesses) are taken with a vernier caliper and the Hs (heights) a height gauge.

The reason for taking two values each of the diameter, for example, C1 and C2 is for the purpose of establishing the circularity of the plate. For the same reason, two values of the height H1 and H2 are taken as seen in Table 1. Similarly, in Table 2, several values of the plate thickness are taken off different parts of the plate. The results show that LOM displayed better accuracies or lower deviations as compared to the SLA for most of the main measurements and all of the detailed measurements. In particular, the T values for the LOM model are very consistent, unlike those of the SLA model.

**Table 1 Main** measurements (>10mm) of the 2 benchmark test pieces

| Main Measurements | | | | | | |
|---|---|---|---|---|---|---|
| Design Dimensions (mm) | | | Measurements (mm) | | Deviations (mm) | |
| | | | SLA | LOM | SLA | LOM |
| Top Surface of Dinner Plate | C1 | 186 | 187.00 | 185.62 | 1.00 | -0.38 |
| | C2 | 186 | 186.78 | 185.72 | 0.78 | 0.38 |
| | C3 | 130 | 129.65 | 129.28 | -0.35 | -0.72 |
| | C4 | 130 | 129.63 | 129.01 | -0.37 | -0.99 |
| | H1 | 27 | 27.58 | 27.05 | 0.58 | 0.05 |
| | H2 | 27 | 27.62 | 26.95 | 0.62 | -0.05 |
| Base Surface of Dinner Plate | C5 | 82 | 82.32 | 82.29 | 0.32 | 0.29 |
| | C6 | 82 | 82.56 | 82.31 | 0.56 | 0.31 |
| | H3 | 18 | 18.69 | 18.56 | 0.69 | 0.56 |
| | H4 | 18 | 19.06 | 18.71 | 1.06 | 0.71 |

**Table 2** Detailed measurements (<10mm) of the 2 benchmark test pieces

| Detailed Measurements | | | | | | |
|---|---|---|---|---|---|---|
| Design Dimensions (mm) | | | Measurements (mm) | | Deviations (mm) | |
| | | | SLA | LOM | SLA | LOM |
| Base Surface of Dinner Plate | T1 | 4.00 | 4.87 | 4.51 | 0.87 | 0.51 |
| | T2 | 4.00 | 4.85 | 4.48 | 0.85 | 0.48 |
| | T3 | 4.00 | 3.29 | 3.99 | -0.71 | -0.01 |
| | T4 | 4.00 | 3.19 | 3.95 | -0.81 | -0.05 |
| | H5 | 3.50 | 3.21 | 3.58 | -0.29 | 0.08 |
| | H6 | 3.50 | 3.28 | 3.59 | -0.22 | 0.09 |
| Floral Patterns on Plate | Flowers | | Not distin-guish-able | Dis-tinctly repro-duced | NA | |
| | Leaves | | | | | |
| | Stems | | | | | |
| | Others | | | | | |

## 8.3 Economical evaluation and other considerations

Besides technical evaluation, economical evaluation is also important. The cost of a machine or a part made by the machine is an important factor. Compared to SLA, the LOM is a much cheaper machine, at about US$100,000 cheaper. In addition, the material cost of paper used by the LOM is cheaper than the photosensitive polymer used by SLA. In fact, amongst all commercial rapid prototyping systems, the LOM has probably the lowest material cost.

In terms of the speed of processing and building a part, it is typical to categorize into: Pre-processing, Building and Postprocessing times. Pre-processing time is the time taken to prepare, verify and correct the data file (usually an STL file), as well as the time taken to specify slicing and building parameters and setup the machine for building. Building time is strictly the time taken for the machine to build the part from beginning to end. Finally, postprocessing is taken to include all activities after building. For example, activities such as removal of excess resin, cleaning using solvent, removal of supports, posturing, etc., are required for the SLA model. For the LOM process, it means removing all the excess wood/paper which can be fairly tedious because care is needed not to damage the part.

Table 3 shows the results obtained from the building of the dinner plate model. In all categories, the LOM takes longer than the SLA. However, the difference is not very significant. Thus, though in terms of the labor cost, the SLA will cost less, the higher cost of the SLA and its photosensitive resin make it more economical to use the LOM. This is also confirmed by service bureau sources in Singapore and Germany, where the typical charge for a SLA model is 1½ - 2 times more costly than a LOM model for the same part.

**Table 3** Results of processing times for the SLA and LOM models

| Times | SLA | LOM |
|---|---|---|
| Pre-processing | 0.5 hours | 5 minutes |
| Building | 15.5 hours | 18 hours |
| Postprocessing | 2 hours | 4 hours |
| Total | 18 hours | 22 hours and 5 minutes |

Other advantages associated with the LOM process includes the fact that it is clean and can operate in an office environment. Material used such as paper need not be shielded from sunlight and does not have an objection smell. Finally, supports are not required in the process, making it less constrained in the decision process of orientating a part for building.

## 9 CONCLUSION

The research and development work carried out indicates that a tableware designer can use CADCAM for the decoration of tableware items by molded or incised decoration. Patterns are 3-dimensional (3D) and lie on the surface of a 3D-tableware item. Using commercial relief creation software, the 3D patterns are generated and mapped onto an already modeled tableware item such as dinner plate. Experiments using rapid prototyping (RP) technology have proven to be successful. Amongst the many RP methods, the SLA and LOM were used for the trials. From the results and based on technical and economical evaluation, the LOM was chosen for its better performance and affordability.

## 10 REFERENCES

Chua, C.K., Hoheisel, W., Keller, G., and Werling, E. (1993) Adapting decorative patterns for ceramic tableware. *Computing and Control Engineering Journal* 4(5): 209-217.

Lee H.B., Ko, M.S.H., Gay, R.K.L., Leong K.F. and Chua C.K. (1992) Using computer-based tools and technology to improve jewelry design and manufacturing. *International Journal of Computer Applications in Technology* 5(1): 72-80.

Lee, Han Boon. (1993) Computer-aided and manufacturing for the jewelry industry. M.Eng. diss., Nanyang Technological University, Singapore.

Chua, C.K. and Leong K.F. (1997) Rapid prototyping: Principles and applications in manufacturing *John Wiley*.

## 11 BIOGRAPHY

Dr Robert Gay is the Director of Postgraduate Studies at the Gintic Institute of Manufacturing Technology, Singapore. Dr Chua Chee Kai is a senior lecturer with the School of Mechanical and Production Engineering in Nanyang Technological University, Singapore. Prof Wolfgang Hoheisel is the Director of the Steinbeis Centre of Computer Integrated Manufacturing at Karlsruhe, Germany.

# 29

# Design issues of an integrated software workbench supporting the manufacturing systems design process

*M. Garetti*[†], *A. Bartolotta*[†], *E. Corradi*[†], *M. Rabe*[‡] *and A. Raimondo*[§]

[†]*Politecnico di Milano*
*piazza Leonardo Da Vinci 32, I-20133 Milano, Italy*

[‡]*IPK Fraunhofer Gesellschaft*
*Pascalstraße 8-9, D-80636 Berlin, Germany*

[§]*Candy Elettrodomestici,*
*via privata E. Fumagalli, I-20047 Brugherio (MI), Italy*

**Abstract**

This paper describes an ongoing research project, funded by the EC, Esprit program, aiming at developing a "workbench" for the computer-aided design of manufacturing systems. The system provides an user-friendly and powerful environment in which tools supporting the conception, design and evaluation of manufacturing systems will be integrated in a common framework. The workbench has its foundation on a descriptive method of the domain of manufacturing systems (based on the object-oriented methodology), enabling the description of all the aspects of a generic manufacturing system. The paper gives a general overview on the project: after a short introduction on the drawbacks of the current IT tools supporting the manufacturing system engineering process, the logical architecture of the software workbench is presented; then the expected benefits arising from the employment of the system are underlined.

**Keywords**

Manufacturing system engineering, object-oriented modeling

Computer Applications in Production and Engineering. F. Plonka and G. Olling (Eds.)

# 1 INTRODUCTION

Manufacturing systems engineering (MSE) is a recently recognized multidisciplinary engineering function covering all traditional forms of engineering concerned with production: it ranges from design of manufacturing systems, to logistics design, to flow control philosophy selection, to production organization. Recently the need for frequent restructuring of manufacturing systems and for faster new product-to-market cycles is calling for MSE process optimization. Really today the manufacturing system engineering process is still poorly formalized and requires relevant effort and time for the production engineer to deal with, while speed, accuracy, co-ordination and integration of this activity with other business processes could have dramatic impact on overall company performances. An interesting survey, conducted in the UK (Devereux *et al.*, 1994) over a sample of 50 organizations, discovered that only about half of the sample actually uses a formal, structured method when restructuring their operations, mainly a method developed in-house, then concluding that there is no existing single widespread design method currently in common use.
The survey also revealed that there is a widespread usage of some tools and techniques in the design process. Due to the multidisciplinary nature of MSE, available tools come from different disciplines: i.e. from manufacturing technology (such as group technology and production flow analysis), from operations research (such as queue theory or scheduling algorithms), from system theory (such as Petri nets and control theory) and from computer science (ranging from simulation software, to concurrent programming techniques, to simple tools such as spreadsheets).
So while in the product design area CAD/CAM/CAE technologies provide powerful and comprehensive support to the design process, and in the production management area a lot of IT tools are supporting the production planning process, a lack does exist in the MSE area where it is not available a single approach yet, offering a complete framework (a "platform") to handle the brain intensive work of design for a modern manufacturing system. At a large extent, the MSE process continues to be left to the intuitive judgment of the production managers' mind. In the meantime, production decentralization and internationalization of enterprises, involving remote plants and distributed engineering offices, all stress the importance of a standardized and integrated approach to the MSE process. Last but not least, the absence of a MSE platform means the lack of a method to store in a suitable manner data on manufacturing systems architecture, entailing a missing link between product design and production management processes (while these processes structurally share a great amount of data with the MSE process).
In this context, an integrated system enabling the management of all relevant information and knowledge associated with the manufacturing system design is needed.

## 1.1 Related work

Ongoing projects, strictly related to this research subject are briefly outlined herewith.
In the USA, at the National Institute of Standards and Technology (NIST), work on 'Computer-Aided Manufacturing System Engineering' is underway since 1992. The NIST project is aimed "at advancing the development of software environments and tools for the design and engineering of manufacturing systems"; such an environment "will improve the productivity of manufacturing/industrial engineers", who would use it "to design and implement future manufacturing systems and subsystems" (Mc Lean, 1993).
At the Oklahoma State University an underway project, funded by National Science Foundation, involves the conceptualization and development of an integrated, object-oriented modeling and analysis environment for aiding manufacturing engineers in the detailed design and rapid configuration of discrete part manufacturing systems. The environment should provide the integration of a variety of appropriate analysis and optimization tools which lye in different domains (Mize *et al.*, 1992).
At the Ohio University, a research team has designed a virtual environment for manufacturing systems design, integrating the many existing manufacturing systems design tools; the suggested architecture for the Integrated Manufacturing Systems Design (IMDE) co-ordinates the design and modeling on familiar design tools, thanks to a unified meta-model (UDMM), containing the entities and relationships commonly shared among the tools included within the environment (Koonce *et al.*, 1996).
Although the basic principle addressed by these projects, i.e. to provide some kind of support to the designer of manufacturing system, is basically the same, the projects present different focuses: the IMDE project focuses on communication mechanisms among the different manufacturing systems design tools, able to facilitate the sharing and exchange of information between them and ensure the consistency and coherence among the different data models; the project, developed at the Oklahoma State University, focuses on the kernel of the system, an object-oriented modeling environment that emphasizes model reusability; the NIST project addresses ambitiously a more global environment, that includes tools not strictly related to the manufacturing system design, like hazardous analysis, budget planning, benchmarking tools and so on, focusing on the technical issues and incompatibilities which hinder the interaction between commercial software packages.

# 2 SYSTEM ISSUES

## 2.1 Modeling and re-engineering of the MSE process

The objective to enhance production engineer's work productivity can be achieved by re-engineering the manufacturing systems engineering process, through the use of a suitable computer-aided software workbench. Therefore the manufacturing systems engineering process has to be examined, according to a model-based approach: sub-processes must be identified and each sub-process has to be modeled in terms of input-output specifications (Spur *et al.*, 1996). This kind of analysis leads to the identification of main process weaknesses and to the proposal of a re-engineered MSE process when supported by a computer-aided workbench: these requirements lead to the definition of tools and models necessary to support the designer in the MSE process.

## 2.2 Formal representation of manufacturing systems

As widely described in the following sections, in order to effectively support the designer in the manufacturing systems engineering process, many tools and models were identified. In fact, during the design process several models are developed; all these models are abstractions (with different objectives and at different levels of detail) of the same reality: the manufacturing system under design. The idea is that, through an analysis of the manufacturing systems domain, it is possible to identify the building blocks of a generic system, which can be used to build these models. From this consideration, the need to develop a descriptive method of the domain of manufacturing systems, which enables the definition of a structure of objects (building blocks) describing a generic manufacturing system, becomes evident. So a formal method to describe all relevant aspects of a generic manufacturing system is necessary. This descriptive method can also provide the semantic unification necessary for the sharing of information among the different tools/models that have to be integrated.

*The concept of 'manufacturing entity structure'*

The descriptive method we propose allows to define a structured representation of the domain of manufacturing systems (that we call *manufacturing entity structure,* MES), i.e. an unifying abstraction enabling the management of all relevant information and knowledge associated with the process of manufacturing systems design. In other words it can be considered as a *metamodel* of the manufacturing systems domain: it contains not only the type of entities, i.e. the building blocks of the models, but also the relationships among the entities; it specifies the format for the entities, the attributes and the relations it contains, defining a standardized data format for manufacturing systems description.

The descriptive method defines three different aspects of a manufacturing system:

1. the *structural aspect*: it contains the structural (static) definition of the system including workers, production facilities (including tools, jigs and fixtures), material handling equipment and other supplementary devices;
2. the *technological aspect*: it defines the transformational (functional) view of the system, considering the conversion process of the factors of production;
3. the *management aspect* defines the operating procedures of production, constituting the so-called management cycle, i.e. planning, implementation and control.

Each aspect only captures some features of the manufacturing system reality, whereas the whole system is exhaustively described by putting the three aspects together. The *manufacturing entity structure* contains the building blocks for the modeling of all the three aspects above explained.

As regards the implementation of the descriptive method, the object-oriented approach presents characteristics that make it particularly suitable to meet the requirements of the manufacturing entity structure, as already discussed in detail previously (Bartolotta and Garetti, 1996). In fact, the object-oriented paradigm provides an excellent approach to manage and express complex systems: the concepts of encapsulation and inheritance provide the object-oriented approach with characteristics of flexibility, realistic view, extensibility and reusability, all characteristics necessary for the descriptive method of the manufacturing systems.

## 3 THE SYSTEM LOGICAL ARCHITECTURE

In figure 1, the software architecture of a workbench implementing the descriptive method is reported. It is mainly a logical architecture: apart from the interfaces to external system (in particular CAD and simulation), the kernel of the system, named CAMSE (*Computer-Aided Manufacturing Systems Engineering*), accessed through the user interface, contains a series of logical modules corresponding to the functionalities provided by the system. Accordingly the system logical architecture should be seen as a set of tools the designer will freely use in his activity. Let's illustrate this picture considering the involved data structures first and the logical modules performing the various functions afterwards.

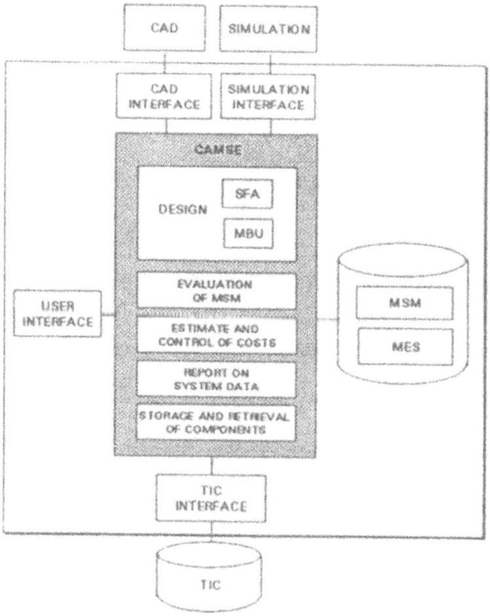


**Figure 1** The system logical architecture

## 3.1 Data structures

Two different data structures have been depicted in the logical architecture: the *system database*, internal to the architecture, and the *technical information catalogue*, external to the system.

*System database*

The persistent part of the database stores the *manufacturing entity structure* (MES), i.e. all the building blocks, to build the different models of any manufacturing system, while the temporary part of the database contains the models, called *manufacturing system models* (MSM), built during the design process instancing the classes contained in the MES.

In spite of this distinction between temporary and permanent part within the system database, the designer has the possibility to enrich the object structure of the database, during the operative use of the system, both with basic objects, called *components*, not included in the MES, and with composite objects, called *subsystems*, which are aggregates of basic objects particularly frequent within a specific industry.

*Technical Information Catalogue*

An archive of information on manufacturing systems, subsystems and components stored in different formats, as an electronic format, or as a pointer to traditional archives (folders, floppy disks, etc.) is provided as a consulting support for the plant engineer.

## 3.2 Logical modules

The following is the list of main modules obtained identifying the needs of MSE.

*A. Design*

Within the design module, the following modules are established:

- a *system flow analysis* (SFA) module, that, starting from data on products to be manufactured in the production system (production mix, bills of material and process plans), will allow the generation of the model of the production flow within the manufacturing system, that we will call *system flow model*;
- a *model building and updating* (MBU) module supporting the designer in the construction of the manufacturing system models by properly selecting objects from the MES and setting their links.

*B. Storage and retrieval of Components*

This module is necessary to store and retrieve information about manufacturing systems, subsystems, components. This module must provide the designer with the possibility to customize for a specific industry the content of the databases, foreseeing the possibility to add new classes (both components and subsystems) at the MES or new links to documents.

*C. Evaluation of Manufacturing systems Models.*

This module must allow the interfacing to external systems, like queue theory or simulation tools, able to evaluate the performances of the *manufacturing system models.*

*D. Estimate and control of plant costs*

Such a module must allow to estimate the costs of the designed production system.

*E. Report on System Data.*

This module is necessary to make information available as input data external systems (procurement, detailed design, etc.).

# 4 THE REVISED MSE PROCESS

Before describing how the design process can be performed through the use of the proposed workbench, it should be cleared that it doesn't mean to provide the designer with a rigid methodology for manufacturing system design, due to the consideration that the methodologies followed in each company can be very different and proprietary, but the workbench must offer a framework supporting the design activity, i.e. a logical route the designer can follow during the design activity.

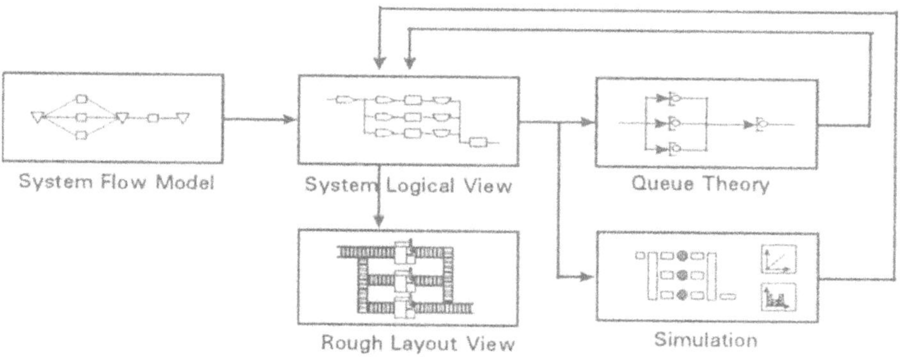


**Figure 2** General description of the MSE process supported by the proposed software workbench

Within the workbench environment, the manufacturing systems design process is seen as carried out in some steps, in which several models, more and more detailed, of the manufacturing system are generated and evaluated and a satisfying solution is identified through an iterative process (see fig. 2).
In particular two different type of models are foreseen:

- *system flow model* (SFM): it will model the production flows, generated on the basis of data on production mix, bills of material and process plans of products to manufacture/assemble, giving information about the required production capacity for each kind of required resource and on the quantity of material flow linking production resources;
- *manufacturing system model* (MSM): it is the object model of the manufacturing system, of which two different views are foreseen: i) the *system logical view* (SLV), representing the logical view of the manufacturing system model in terms of logical objects and relationships among them (described by choosing symbolic icons representing specific machines, handling systems and other plant elements from the "catalogue" of objects corresponding to different plant components, technological and management methods); ii) the *rough layout view* (RLV) representing the physical view of the manufacturing system, obtained through the embedding to the logical view of further data for layout drawing.

Once the *manufacturing system model* is defined, its performances shall be evaluated through the link to external computer tools, like queue theory and simulation. On the basis of the results coming from their evaluation, the models will be modified and refined, until a satisfying solution is obtained.

## 5 EXPECTED BENEFITS

After having outlined the architecture and the functionalities of the proposed approach, that we are suggesting for the design of manufacturing systems, let's describe the expected benefits:

- *reduction of the effort of creating and evaluating the model of a manufacturing system*: a large library of reusable components and subsystems could be created for configuring plant models at different levels of detail for specific purposes, then plant configuration could be developed by properly selecting previously stored objects from library;
- *enforcement of standardization in manufacturing system design*: the knowledge-base of the software workbench could be used for urging the designer to choose standard components during the project development;
- *enhancement of coherence and co-ordination among different engineering teams*, whether they are dislocated in different geographical sites (multi-site design), or they are working, in a design site, on modules of the same manufacturing system: in fact, referring to a common database, every design team could be easily acquainted with the ongoing projects developed by other teams;
- *minimization of the retro-fitting and fine tuning associated with implementation of a manufacturing system*: the possibility of carrying out a fast computer-aided analysis and evaluation of a designer idea could entail presumably a better-quality solution; it's then foreseeable that failures occurring during the phase of start-up/runtime of a manufacturing system (up to 100 times more expensive to correct once a system is installed) could be significantly reduced;
- *reduction of the time spent in re-design and reconfiguration of manufacturing systems*: once made the one-time strain of creating the initial base model of a manufacturing system, the incremental effort to make a change in the current plant, such as the introduction of a new machine, could be slight, thank to the possibility to utilize and update the model previously stored;
- *reduction of inconsistency and redundancy of manufacturing system data*: during the development of the manufacturing system engineering process, the same common base representation could be employed by different modeling tools;
- *encouragement of production engineers in the direct use of modeling/analysis tools*: the software workbench could provide the access to model utilization by designers, who typically aren't modeling specialists, but have a very good knowledge of the manufacturing system to be analyzed;
- *enhancement of integration between product design and production management tools*: information on product details and routing could stem directly from CAD/CAM/CAPP packages; while plant data, such as machine type, machine throughput, buffer dimensions, could be automatically forwarded into production planning packages (i.e. master production schedule, material requirements planning, short term scheduling).

## 6 REFERENCES

Bartolotta, A. and Garetti, M. (1996) Object-oriented representation of manufacturing systems: trends and perspectives. *Proceedings of the Advances in Production Management Systems conference*, IFIP, Kyoto

Devereux S., Smith P., and Wood D.(1994) A survey of the use of design methodologies for implemented change in manufacturing companies in the United Kingdom. *International Journal of Manufacturing System Design*, 1(1), 51-58

Koonce, D. A., Judd, R. P. and Parks, C. M., (1996) Manufacturing systems engineering and design: an intelligent, multi-model, integration architecture. *International Journal of Computer Integrated Manufacturing*, 9(6), 443-453

McLean, C.R. (1993) Computer-Aided Manufacturing System Engineering, in *Advances in Production Management Systems* (eds. I.A. Pappas and I.P. Tatsiopoulos), Netherlands: Elsevier Science.

Mize, J. H., Bhuskute, H. C., Pratt, D. B. and Kamath M. (1992). Modeling of integrated manufacturing systems using an object-oriented approach. *IIE Transactions*, 24(3), 14-26.

Spur, G., Mertins K. and Jochem R. (1996) *Integrated Enterprise Modeling*, DIN, Germany.

---

The authors fully agree on the contents of the paper. However, M. Rabe wrote the section 2.1, A. Raimondo wrote the section 4, while the rest of the paper is due to the joint work of the other authors.

*This work has been supported by the EC project "Plantfaber: An integrated software workbench as a tool for the re-engineering of the Manufacturing System Engineering Process", co-sponsored by the European Commission, IV Framework Program - DG III- ESPRIT program. The partners of the project are two industrial users (Candy Elettrodomestici (I) and Convey Satafim (E)), two research institutes (MIP of Politecnico di Milano (I) and IPK Fraunhofer Institute of Berlin (D)) and two software developers (LIPRO from Berlin (D) and Spaziosystem (I). The Plantfaber project started in May 1996 and is due for October 1998.*

30

# World Wide Simulation Environment (WISE)

## Web-based simulation using three dimensional models for manufacturing and material handling

*Kazuo Morita, Koji Kawashima, Junya Saito, Yoshinori Naruko*
*Mitsui Engineering & Shipbuilding Co., LTD.*
*Makuhari Techno Garden 1-3-D7, Nakase, Mihama-ku,*
*Chiba-City, Chiba 261, Japan*
*Phone +81-43-274-0321, Fax +81-43-274-0324*
*e-mail: kmorita@mes.co.jp, kkawshi@mes.co.jp*

*Masahiro Okamoto*
*Toyada Machine Works, LTD.*

*Hiromasa Suzuki*
*Department of Precision Machinery Engineering*
*The University of Tokyo*

**Abstract**

This paper describes a Web-based simulation using three-dimensional models for manufacturing and material handling. The goal of this study is to construct a simulation environment that builds a virtual machine representing real equipment and a virtual factory collecting the virtual machine through a global communication network and executes them. This simulation environment is called World Wide Simulation Environment(WISE). The simulation environment is built with a new object-oriented language and architecture.

In this paper, arguments about simulation in manufacturing are clarified in order to identify requirements for next-generation manufacturing simulation systems. Then, models that meet the requirements of this concept are reviewed and, where suitable,

Computer Applications in Production and Engineering. F. Plonka and G. Olling (Eds.)

are proposed for WISE. Furthermore, a system for demonstrating a Web-based virtual manufacturing simulator system is described in order to verify the operability of the system.

**Keywords**
WWW(World Wide Web), simulation, object oriented technology, product model, INTERNET

# 1 INTRODUCTION

Under increasingly competitive conditions in manufacturing sector, process engineering requires drastic improvements in all process. Simulation-based design is a new approach which, at the design stage, aims at developing a new environment for design, creation and operation of virtual and real products and process, focused on increasing real product value and reducing life cycle cost.

The main object of such a manufacturing simulation is a virtual environment which can provide support, information and control during all parts of the production cycle. Furthermore, this environment has to support internationalization and decentralization of the design and production activities, and simulation technology is very effective tool for this purpose. On the other hand, the tool is not good enough to support all parts of all production process. Therefore, to construct the next generation manufacturing system, a virtual environment is required that will support the life cycle of product, ranging from the planning to production, maintenance and reuse.

The goal of this study is to construct an environment that simulates a virtual manufacturing through a global communication network. This simulation environment is called the World Wide Simulation Environment(WISE), and it is built with a new object-oriented language and architecture called Umbel.[1)]

In this project, physically meáningful models or product models with behavior, are built in a distributed environment and distributed throughout a network. The models are made to represent the function, behavior, and performance of real parts and manufacturing equipment ( such as robots, NC machines, AGVs, AS/RS, controllers, sensors) and human beings, by giving behaviors to three dimensional CAD models which represent real parts and equipment and correspond to the "behavioral product catalogs" of real equipment.

Users can thereby collect such pieces of equipment through a wide-area network and construct a manufacturing system. Since the physical model through the communication networks is simulated as a virtual machine representing a real equipment, so that a virtual plant built on such a network represents a real manufacturing plant and can be utilized to control an actual factory. The virtual factory can communicate through a network and support collaborative engineering among the enterprises and facilities distributed worldwide. So, We call this environment as WISE.

## 2 WISE MODEL AND FUNDAMENTAL STUCTURE

### 2.1 WISE ARCHITECTURE.

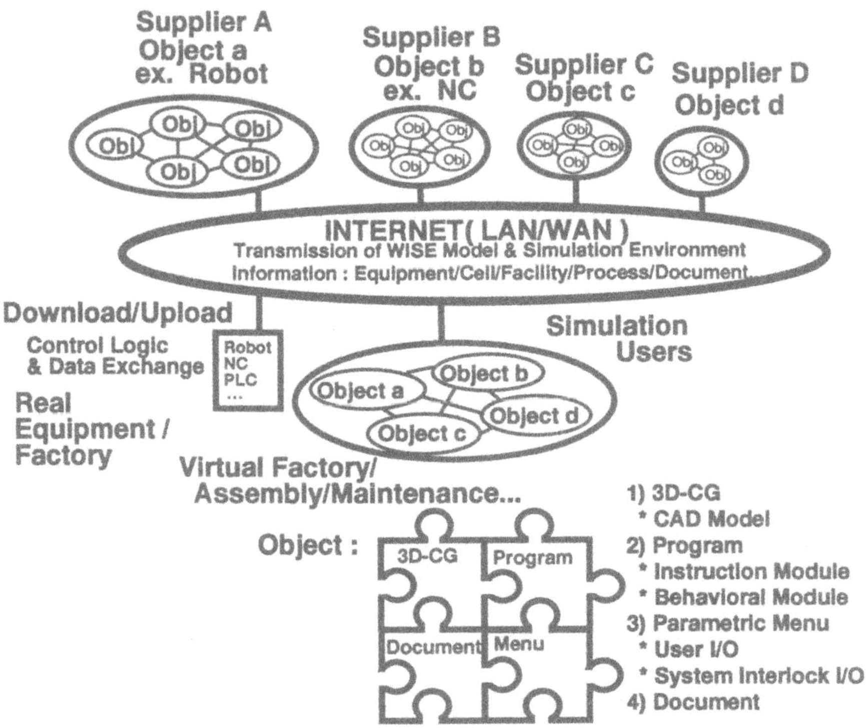


Figure1 World Wide Simulation Environment(WISE) Architecture

The WISE networking based simulation architecture is shown in Figure 1. The system has to distribute electronic catalogs to the client side where factory product engineer can construct a virtual factory in client-sever environment via INTERNET. The communication environment can transfer the WISE model by designating the URL address in the WWW browser based on the HTTP protocol. The WISE model is constructed as an integrated file which is taken in by designating the URL address and constructed by a three-dimensional model, the objects oriented program showing it's behavior and HTML multi-documents for GUI. In such a virtual factory

construction environment, a factory engineer can execute the simulation by communicating via HTML multi-documents after acquiring the electric catalog through the INTERNET.
This simulation environment is investigated from the language to application level using Inflorescence, Inc.'s Umbel.

## 2.2 STANDARD MODEL OF WISE

The Basic requirements necessary for WISE model are defined below

.

### (1) Configuration of simulation model

### a) Basic WISE model requirements

Software language environment requires:

- The creation of a three dimensional model in order to represent the product model of each machine.
- Hierarchical programming, which is handled as a unit, and creating a new program combining the existing program, and the object oriented language which can create a reusable object encapsulating data and function.
- A concurrent environment with a scheduler function, for control the autonomous behavior of each machine object, and the ability to define and communicate by signal to control behavior.
- Interpreter and compiler language for creating the program flexibly and quickly.
- Transmission of the electronic catalog via the INTERNET by designating the URL address, accessing to the programs on the Web which implement the programs in HTML function and execute the simulation using these programs.
- An animation function that operates while simulation is running to enable the products engineer to easily understand the behavior of the virtual machine and activity of the virtual factory.

### b) WISE model and its basic configuration

On the basis of these requirements, a simulation model is proposed that can support a plant life cycle from conceptualization to operation. The proposed model is a physical model that considers equipment and operations in a real plant from the software engineering viewpoint. The proposed model is not abstract mathematical model like a stochastic queuing network model in which entities representing products flow in a network between nodes which correspond to equipment.

An example of a detailed robot object for a WISE model consisting of links and each servo motor for the links is shown in Figure 2. This equipment class represents the physical model of the equipment. For example, if a servo motor is attached to a link, the motor rotates with the link. This robot class consists of the inverse kinematics and the synchronized function which represents real behavior. The relationship between objects are shown in Figure 3 [2)] and represent dependency between equipment, along with standard job( behavior) and parts. First, equipment is conceived as an abstracted model which performs processing with the lapse of time. Then, a physical model based on the abstract model is derived. This physical model is a three-dimensional model with actual behavior and is branched into robot model and so on. In this way, a simulation environment is constructed that is consisted through all stage from conceptual design to a detail design reflecting actual operational behavior. One of jobs shows the relationship between current jobs and next jobs.

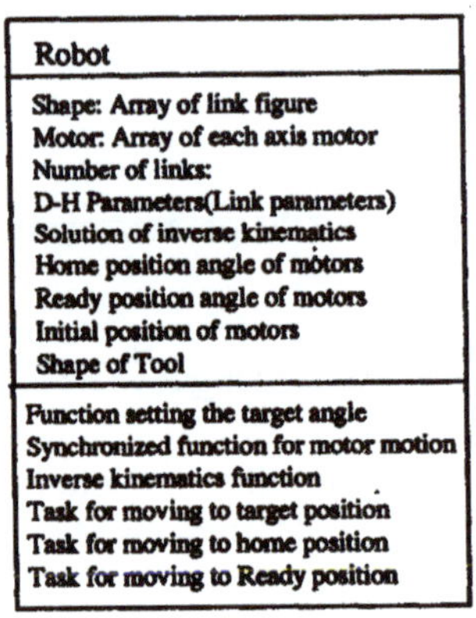


Figure2 Robot class

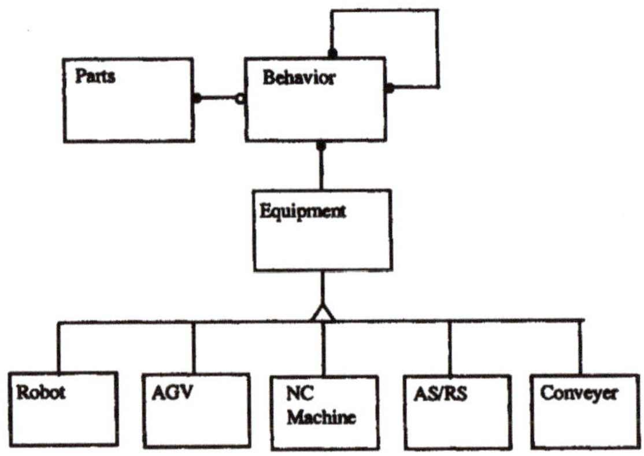


Figure3 Relationships between objects

Each individual object is a primitive object within the whole system. Therefore, behaviors can be defined as combinations of the methods of these primitive objects. In other words, all behavior is expressed by primitive methods in the same manner as real equipment is composed of individual components. This is the reverse to of complicated behavior being divided into simple behaviors and then further into primitive behaviors. In each behavior, signals are embedded in such a way that a behavior can cause other behaviors in a chain. A control object can perform centralized or parallel control. Consequently:

- Product model and Sequential behaviors can be defined as 1:n.
- Individual behavior can be combined arbitrarily sequences by signals.
- Each process is started up by signal to drive any objects.

  Here, a process is an aggregate of behavior sequences and shows collaborative behavior. As a result, the user can have an environment that allows selection of arbitrary behaviors and processes against defined figures, and along with immediate execute.

## 3 WWW BROWSER-BASED DEMONSTRATION SYSTEM

First, Robots, NC machines and AGV are constructed as each electronic catalog to simulate a factory. Next, a factory cell is constructed in local site after loading each electronic catalog, and the behavior of the machine is taught by the product engineer, and the simulation of cell is executed.

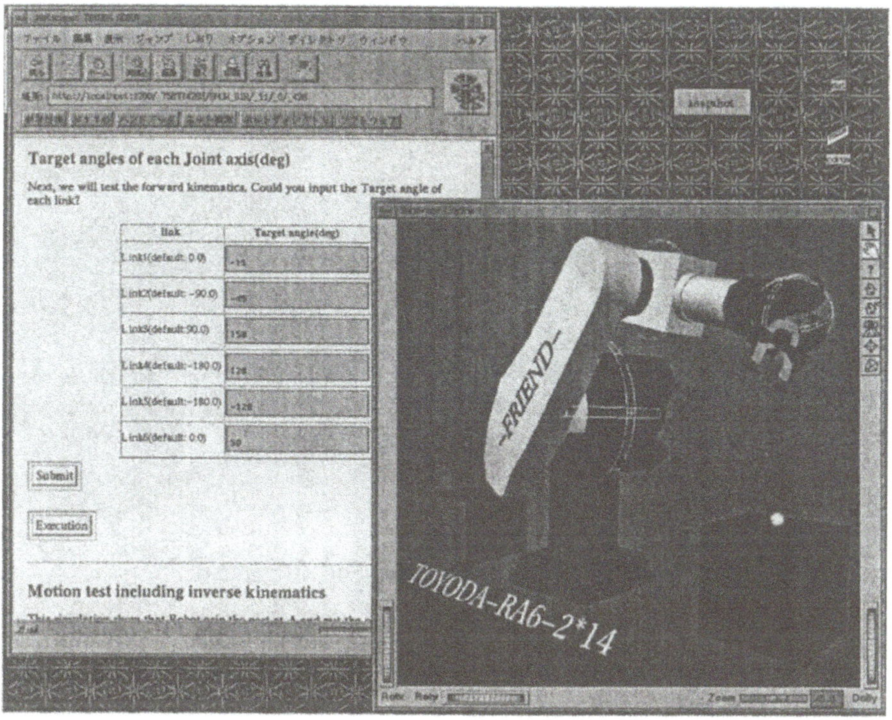


Figure 4 The electronic catalog of robot

The electronic catalog consists of equipment class, behavior programs, three dimensional models by Open Inventor, and an input panel for teaching and executing behaviors by HTML. It can communicate through INTERNET.

(1) Robot

An electronic catalog of the robot with six joints is shown in Figure 4. The input panel divides into three areas.

(a) Definition of acceleration, velocity and deceleration of each servo motor.
(b) Execution of forward kinematics by setting the target angle.
(c) Execution of a behavior series solving the inverse kinematics for the target position and gripping the target part.

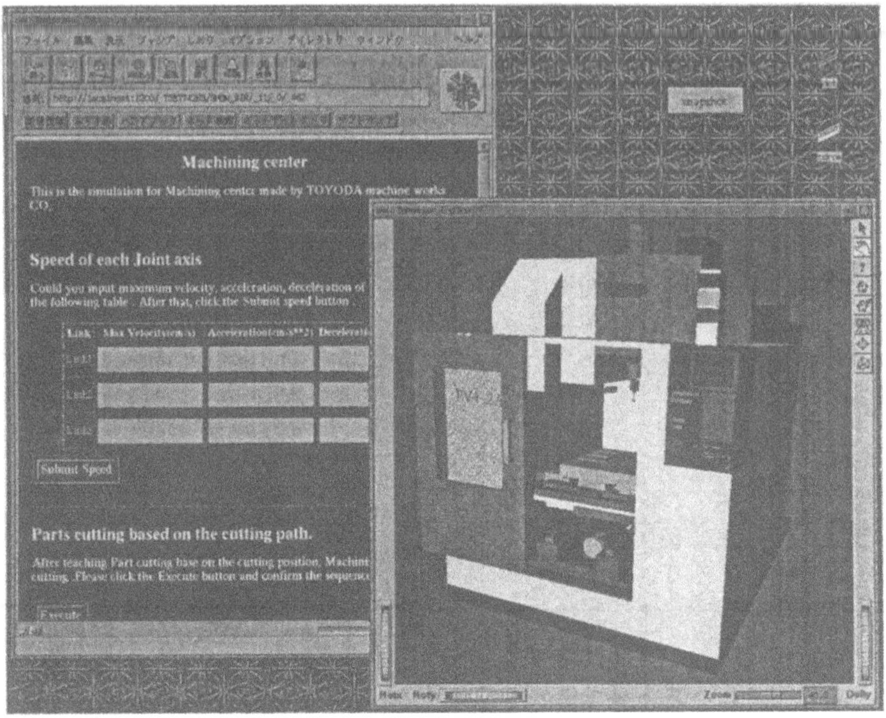


Figure 5 The electronic catalog of NC machine

(2) NC machine

The electronic catalog of a three axis NC machine is shown in Figure 5. The input panel divides into two parts.

(a) Definition of acceleration, velocity, and deceleration of each axis.

(b) Execution of a behavior series required for cutting a part based on inverse kinematics for cutting position on the part.

(3) AGV

The input panel is divides into two areas.

(a) Definition of translation acceleration, velocity, and velocity on the curved rail.

(b) Execution of behavior moving on guided path.

(4) FA cell simulation

The FA cell is constructed by robot, NC machine and AGV electronic catalogs. In this process a product engineer constructs an FA cell after evaluating the performance of each machine using the electronic catalog for each piece of equipment. First, the product engineer loads the file integrating the machine model and behavior program of each machine, then teaches the behavior using an HTML menu and executes the simulation concurrently. By these process, the virtual simulation shown in Figure 6 can execute while taking the real performance of each machine and activity of the factory into consideration.

The simulation sequence shown in Figure 7 represent relationships among dynamic behaviors in an expansion of IDEF3[3]. The part flow is shown by a doted line, and the control signal flow is shown by a solid line. This is representative job flows expressed by a chain of behaviors. Such behavior divided into primitive behavior elements ( motion). The junction in IDEF3 can be also executed. Each behavior represents the autonomous behavior which is encapsulated object with input and output control ports. The connection between the input and output ports defines the simulation sequence. All behavior and related signal shows in Figure 8.

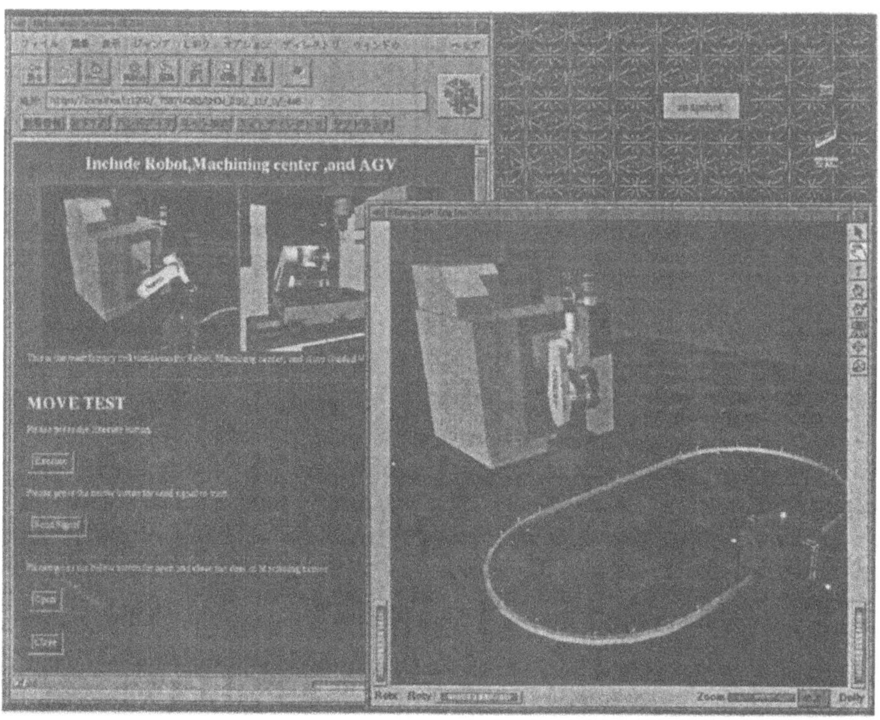


Figure 6 Executing simulation of FA cell

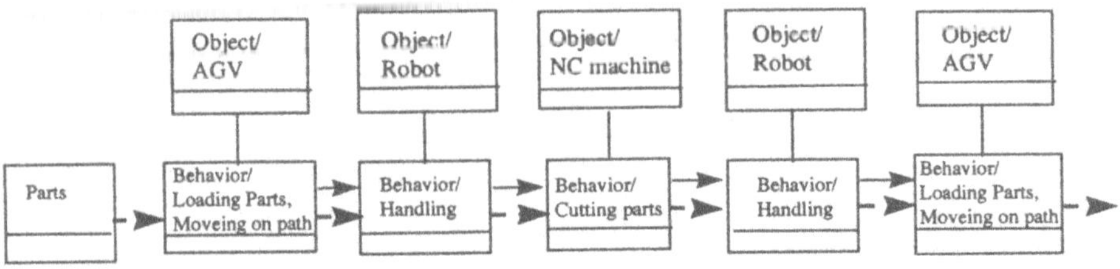


Figure 7 Simulation sequence by IDEF3

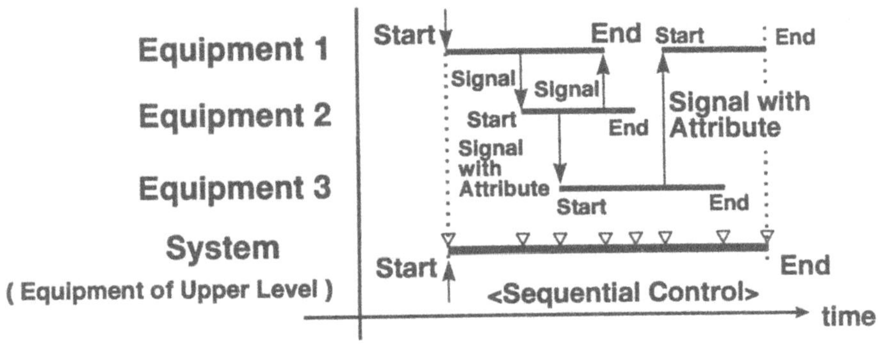


Figure 8 Signal interaction among behaviors

Definition of manufacturing Scenario/Process

Concurrent process Control using Message among Objects

(Autonomous Sequential and Central Control )

## 4 CONCLUSION

A networking based simulation architecture and its configuration for a communication model (WISE model ) that can exactly represent real equipment in the software is presented. A WWW browser-based FA simulation demonstration system is then developed and the workability of the principle demonstrated and validated.

The purpose of the study is to create such an environment that can execute a virtual plant simulation in accordance with a scenario through INTERNET. The simulation follows a procedure in which the parts or equipment manufacturer provides its own WISE model as a "product catalog" that behaves autonomously, and the user collects catalogs and assembles them together to construct an actual plant by using interlock signal. Furthermore, the virtual plant itself provides, through communication, wide-area collaborative engineering support environment in order to support the virtual enterprise.

At Mitsui Engineering & Shipbuilding Co., Ltd., this concept will be used as the next step for the virtual operation training and remote maintenance etc. through INTERNET in order to achieve the virtual enterprise.

Finally, this research and development is being implemented as a part of Globman21 project under the umbrella of International IMS program.

## 6 REFERENCES

1) Chris Goad, "A Language-Level Attack on Compositional Simulation" http://www.inflor.com/compsim.html
2) James Rumbaugh, et al.(1991) "Object-Oriented modeling and Design", Prentice-Hall International, Inc.
3) Richard J. Mayer, et al. (1992) "Information Integration For Concurrent Engineering(IICE) IDEF3 Process Description Capture Method Report", Knowledge Based System, Inc.

## 7 BIOGRAPHY

Kazuo Morita is an Assistant Manager for Advanced Machine & System Div. of Mitsui Engineering & Shipbuilding Co., Ltd. He received a Bachelor's degree in Mechanical Engineering and a Master of Engineering from Nihon University. He is developing a new object oriented simulator for manufacturing and material handling.

# 31

# A Scenario Simulation Methodology for Re-engineering Potential Assessment

*J-M Lehtonen, K. Marttila*
*Helsinki University of Technology, TAI Research Centre*
*Po. Box 9555, 02015 Espoo, Finland*
*Tel: + 358 9 451 1, fax: + 358 9 451 3665*
*email: jmlehto@tuta.hut.fi, kmartti@tuta.hut.fi*

**Abstract**

The research objective of this paper is to experiment the applicability of scenario simulation methodology in a paper industry distribution problem. The methodology proved to be able to assess the re-engineering potential by producing quantifiable results for the performance measures. The methodology itself does not provide optimal re-engineering actions. Its function is to assess the improvement potential of re-engineering actions derived elsewhere.

**Keywords**

Simulation, modeling, logistics

## 1 SIMULATION AS A RESEARCH METHOD IN LOGISTICS

Today, the use of discrete event simulation as a research method is commonplace in logistics research. In fact, the importance of simulation can be described by the viewpoint that there are three pillars in scientific and technology research; analytic methods, experimental methods and numerical simulation (Strandhagen, 1994).

According to Bowersox (1986), the main advantage of discrete event simulation in logistics is that it incorporates the impact of time into performance evaluation. Hoover and Perry (1989) view simulation as a powerful problem solving method. According to Mott and Tumay (1992), simulation is a thorough and economic way

Computer Applications in Production and Engineering. F. Plonka and G. Olling (Eds.)

to express and evaluate ideas and alternatives before implementation. Simulation, however, will provide merely the best answer of the solutions tried and thus it is limited in its ability find the "best" answer (Menzer, 1989).

The popularity of simulation can partly be explained also by the following advantages of simulation in logistics research:

- In comparison to analytical models, it is flexible. You can include details, which are impossible with analytical models (Hoover and Perry, 1989). Even in simple systems analytical modelling of queuing disciplines and priority rules is extremely difficult (Johnsson, 1992)
- In comparison to the real system, the researcher has control over the other variables (Johnsson, 1992). In fact, simulation could be viewed as a test laboratory of logistics research.
- Non-existent systems can also be studied (Hoover and Perry, 1989).

## 2 SIMULATION PROJECT MODELS

A few authors have attempted to give guidelines for carrying out a simulation modeling project. Strandhagen (1994) has a summary of the simulation project models and he concludes that for many purposes it is convenient to distinguish only three major tasks:

- feeding information into a system
- running the model
- extracting information from the system

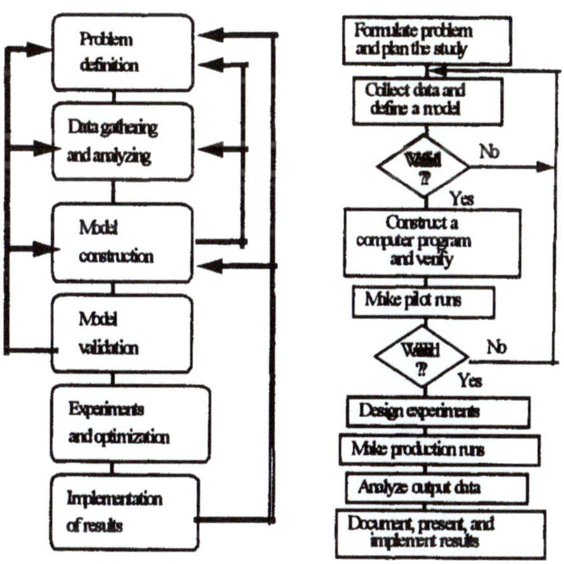


**Figure 1** Simulation project models, left:Hoover and Perry, right: Law and Kelton.

Figure 1 shows two simulation project models by Hoover and Perry (1989) and Law and Kelton (1991). Both project models are almost in perfect agreement on how to perform simulation study, although Hoover and Perry view the project even more iteratively than Law and Kelton. Also Law and Kelton add finer detail in some of the phases than Hoover and Perry. Also Banks & Carlson (1984) give similar project guidelines. In the following, the major stages in simulation project models are discussed.

*Problem definition*

The problem definition is very important and as Hoover and Perry (1989) put it, one is not likely to find good solutions to ill-defined problems. Simulation textbooks and literature that cover simulation project, however, give only very vague guidelines concerning problem definition. For example, according to Law and Kelton (1991) a model should contain only **enough** detail to capture the **essence** of the system and Mitrani's (1982) advises it is necessary to abstract from the real system **all** those components that are considered **important** enough for inclusion in the model.

*Model definition and data gathering and analyzing*

According to Hoover and Perry (1989), an important part of model definition is to define system inputs, that can either be decision variables or given variables and outputs. Hoover and Perry (1989) advise to first make a conceptual model by either drawing a flowchart or by using a state change approach before implementing it. Defining the model is almost as vaguely covered as problem definition. According to Robinson (1994) there is a tendency to want to model everything without stopping to consider exactly what is **necessary**. He advises to include the minimum amount of detail to achieve the project's objectives. Law and Kelton (1991) advise that one should not have more detail in a model than is necessary to address the issues of interest.

*Validation*

A valid model corresponds to the real system. As Strandhagen (1994) points out, no model is ever completely valid corresponding perfectly to the real system. One approach, that is shown in Figure 2, to validating a simulation model is to see whether the simulation model can produce similar results as the real system has produced (Hoover and Perry, 1989). Law and Kelton (1991) call this the correlated inspection approach.

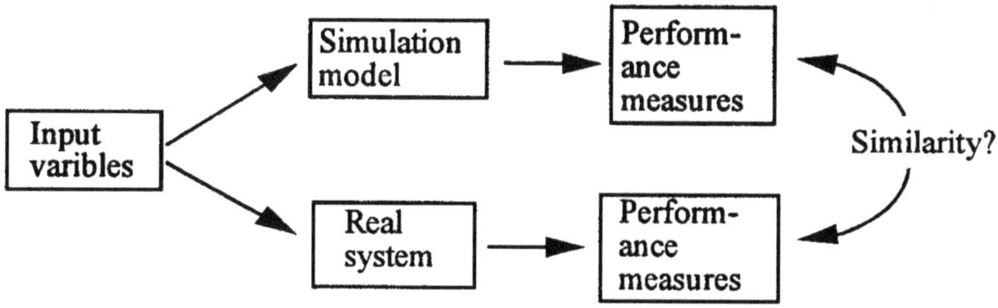


**Figure 2** Correlated inspection approach to simulation model validation (Hoover and Perry, 1989)

According to Naylor et al. (1966) the ultimate test of a simulation model is the degree of accuracy with which it predicts the behavior of the actual system in the future.

*Result analysis and experiments*

A Simulation model as such does not give any indication of the possible changes in order to improve desired logistics system performance measures. There are a number of techniques for finding improved or optimized values for the decision variables that are based on probability and statistics theory.

The outcome of a particular stochastic simulation is a random variable. However, the usual independence of errors assumption of standard statistical methods is normally not met in a simulation study (Hoover and Perry, 1989). Both serial correlation of errors and heteroscedasticity can be present (Hoover and Perry, 1989). It can be proved (Pindyck and Rubinfeld, 1991) that the expected values still remain the same but confidence intervals are affected. Another problem is when input data is taken from the real figures the data itself is random variable and does not represent a true value in the statistical formula meaning (Vaughan, 1996). This means that the confidence interval of a performance measure represents the confidence interval inside that model and not the modeled system.

In a "what-if" experimental setting we need to decide between different scenarios and also estimate their difference. This can be achieved by establishing the confidence interval of the performance measure in question. The situation becomes much more complicated if the research objective is to find out how, given a set of decision variables, the performance measures could be improved or optimized. One possibility to deal with multiple input variables is to apply the statistical design of experiments approach. Other possibilities in analyzing the model include optimization methods (response surface methodology) and gradient method (Law and Kelton, 1991). Goldberg (1989) even suggests genetic algorithms for search of a local optimum. However, all these methods are ill developed in a non-independent errors environment (Hoover and Perry, 1989). The situation can be further complicated when there are more than one performance measure that cannot be combined into a single measure.

*Implementation*

Both Hoover and Perry (1989) and Law and Kelton (1991) ambitiously include implementation in their simulation project models. Unfortunately, the researcher in logistics has no control over the real system and cannot implement any changes. Gaining knowledge of systems functioning is less challenging than implementation, but still a good enough reason for building the simulation model.

## 3 THE SCENARIO SIMULATION METHODOLOGY

The research objective was to experiment with the applicability of scenario the simulation methodology in a paper industry distribution problem. The immediate objective was to evaluate the re-engineering potential. For this purpose, the scenario simulation methodology was applied. The steps of scenario simulation methodology are defined:

1) Analyze the existing system. If not possible, use interviews and documents.
2) Arrive at the improvement actions to test. System analysis, existing logistics theory and experience will help.
3) Define model scope and create conceptual model.
4) Create computer simulation model of the present system, called base case model.
5) Compare the results to the existing system.
6) Implement the changes to the present model to make it the scenario model.
7) Assess the improvement potential by comparing the present and scenario model results

The applicability of the scenario simulation methodolgy is experimented in a case in the following chapter. At the same time, the steps of the methodology are demonstrated during the case.

## 4 SIMULATION MODELING CASE

### 4.1 The existing system

The case included three Nordic paper mills that manufactured printing and writing papers and newsprint that were delivered in reels cut to customer specific widths at the mills. The main markets for all the mills were in Western Europe although mill 1 had large overseas sales. The mills share a common shipping arrangement to Western Europe that is shown in figure 3. The case mills have a customer dedicated call-off stock at the port terminal from which deliveries can be made by customer call-off. This is shown with (B) in figure 3. This port terminal stock is replenished from the paper machines. Mills 1 and 3 manufactured standard grades and had no notable production cycle. Mill 2, however, had a three-week-production cycle. The production cycle in the mill 2 was not included in the simulation models.

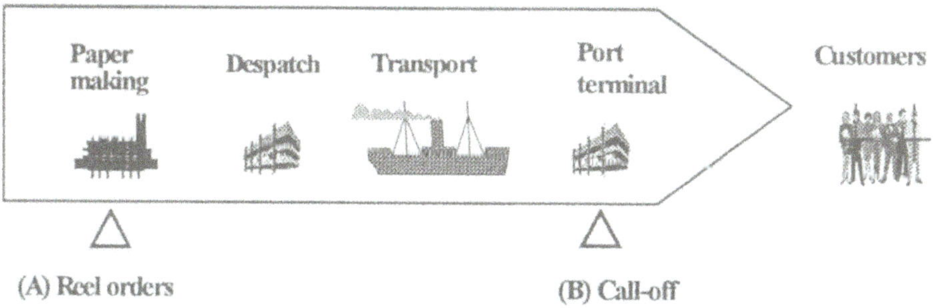


**Figure 3** The logistical chain of the case.

### 4.2 The improvement actions to test

The problem statement for the simulation study was formulated

1) to find out the inventory savings achievable by an alternative transport arrangement.
2) to study the feasibility of make-to-order deliveries instead of having customer dedicated call-off stock at the port terminals.

### 4.3 Model scope

The simulation study was carried out by making five independent one-year simulations with both the present model and scenario transport model arrangement. The comparisons between the models were made at equal availability levels.
Customer demand was modeled by 60 customers. Each of the customers had an expected demand of 24 tons per day. Twelve customers have a highly variable demand, 24 customers have medium demand variance and 24 customers have low demand variance. The foreign port terminal call-off inventory replenishment logic was reorder point control. Production control logic at each mill was FIFO. The mill was shut down when the order book was empty and reopened after there were enough orders for a few days' production. Reorder points and replenishment quantities for the call-off inventories were set so that a 95% availability level was achieved.

### 4.4 Simulation model of the present system

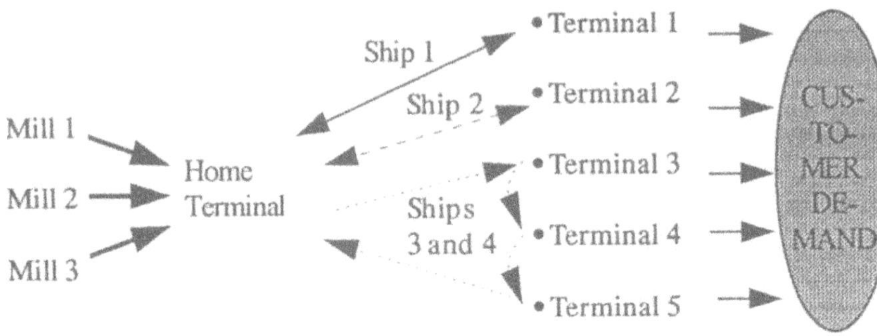


**Figure 4** Base case logistical system.

Figure 4 shows the base case transportation system. Ship 1 serves terminal 1 and takes only paper form mill 1. Ship 1 can make a back and forth trip in five days. Ships 2 serves terminal 2 and makes a back and forth trip in five days. Ship 3 makes a seven-day round trip serving terminals 3-5. While the capacity of ship 3 is not enough to handle all the volume to terminals 3-5, ship 4 helps by making four additional round trips a year. This arrangement is also close to the present operating practice.

**Table 1** Base case simulation results

| | Inventory (tn) | | | | | Lead time (days) | |
|---|---|---|---|---|---|---|---|
| | Home terminal | In-transit | Foreign Terminal | Availability | Order book (tn) | 1 and 2 | Others |
| Average | 4741 | 4042 | 24 624 | 94.5% | 3590 | 8.8 | 11.4 |
| 2.5% | 4375 | 3749 | 24 202 | 94.0% | 3357 | 8.8 | 11.2 |
| 97.5% | 5106 | 4334 | 25 046 | 95.1% | 3824 | 8.9 | 11.7 |

The base case simulation results are shown in Table 1. The average-row gives the average of the five runs. Rows marked 2.5 % and 97.5 % give the 95 % confidence interval on the average under the assumption that the average is normally distributed.

Availability in the base case was a little under the target level of 95 %, but the target level was inside the 95 % confidence interval. Average lead time in the base case is 11.4 days to terminals 3-5 and 8.8 days to terminals 1 and 2.

The base case inventory in the first simulation run during its last half is shown in Figure 5. The total inventory in the base case model was 33 400 tn.

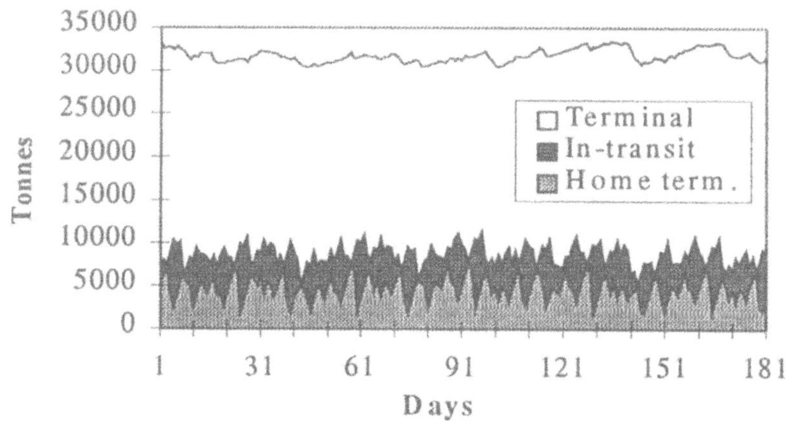


**Figure 5** Base case inventory in the last half of one of the simulation runs.

### 4.5 Scenario model

The alternative transport arrangement used in the scenario model is shown in figure 6. The number of foreign port terminals is consolidated to three. All the remaining terminals are served three times a week. Each of the three ships visits all the terminals during each trip. A round trip takes seven days.

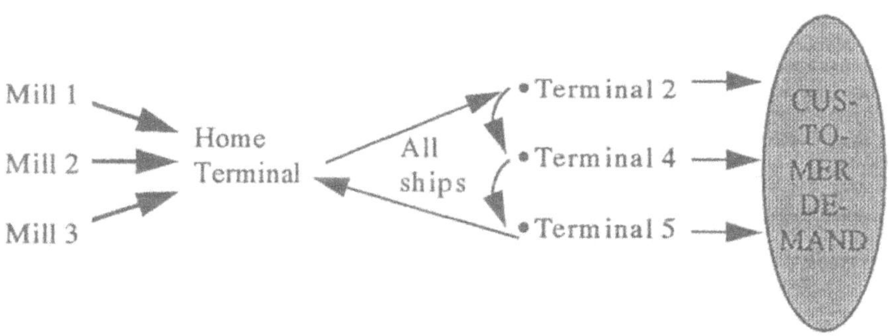


**Figure 6** Scenario logistical system.

The existing ships do not have enough capacity because some capacity is lost due to longer travel time in new systems vs. short terminal 2 trips. This was noticed during the first trial of simulating the scenario model. The home terminal inventory increased wildly. When the results were studied further, it was found out that the ship utilization was 99.9 %. The transport capacity formed a bottleneck in the logistical chain.
Based on the results of the first simulation, the transport capacity needs were recalculated. To handle the production capacity of the mills, the smaller ship 1 is replaced by a new ship with 1400 tons more capacity. The total shipping capacity

then exceeds the total production capacity. The scenario simulation results are shown in Table 2.

**Table 2** Scenario simulation results

| | Inventory (tn) | | | | | Lead time (days) |
|---|---|---|---|---|---|---|
| | Home terminal | In-transit | Foreign Terminal | Avail-ability | Order book (tn) | All terminals |
| Average | 1569 | 4864 | 17 245 | 95.4% | 3430 | 7.8 |
| 2.5% | 1058 | 3659 | 16 707 | 95.0% | 3220 | 7.7 |
| 97.5% | 2080 | 6069 | 17 783 | 95.7% | 3640 | 7.9 |

## 4.6 Assessment of the improvement potential

Average lead time for the scenario model was 7.8 days. The scenario model average lead time reduction to base case terminals 3-5 is 3.6 days or 32 %. A large part of the difference is due to the increased shipping frequency from once a week to three times a week. For terminal 2 the lead time reduction is less, down only one day from 8.8 days or 10 %. The shipping time to terminal 2 remains the same because it is the first terminal to be visited during the round trip. The lead time is affected also by a little larger base case order book, due to larger replenishment quantities which have a small effect on the average lead time.

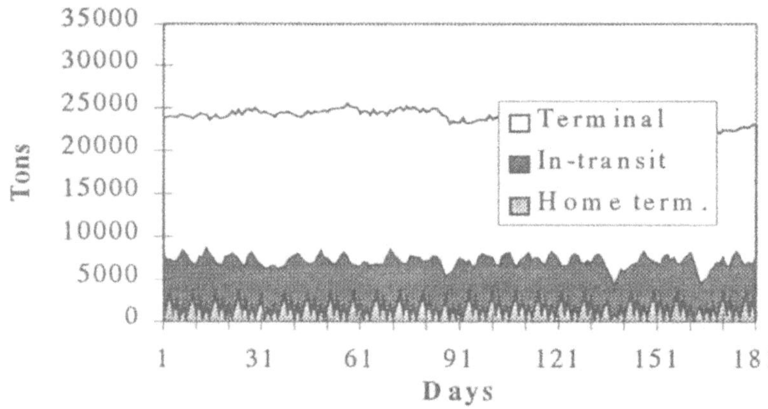


**Figure 7** Scenario inventory in the last half of one of the simulation runs.

The scenario inventory in the first simulation run during its last half is shown in figure 7. The alternative transport arrangement achieves a reduction of 9700 tn or almost 30 % reduction in the total inventory when compared to the base case.
The foreign port terminal inventory reduction in the scenario model is 7400 tn or 30 % as compared to the base case. Because the lead time is shorter, the

replenishment uncertainty and therefore safety stock needed is less. The cycle inventory is also decreased because the increased transport frequency in the scenario model allowed decreasing the replenishment quantity.
In the scenario model the home terminal inventory is greatly reduced as compared to the base case. A reduction of 3100 tons or 67 % was achieved. As can be seen from figures 5 and 7, the base case home terminal inventory is all the time larger than in the scenario model and has more cyclic variation. This is due to two reasons. First, the cycle inventory for all destinations is longer because ships leave less frequently to all destinations in the base case. Secondly, it sometimes happens that mills produce orders assigned to the same ship thus exceeding the capacity of the ship during a short period and forming a home terminal inventory. In the scenario model only a small cycle inventory accumulates between the three weekly sailings because all the ships visit all the terminals.
In-transit inventory is slightly increased in the scenario. The transit time to terminal 4 in the scenario model is about one day longer than in terminals 1 and 2. The increase in the in-transit inventory is 800 tons or 20 %.

## 5 CONCLUSIONS

The scenario simulation methodology was able to assess the improvement potential. It produced quantifiable results for the chosen performance measures. It also warned of possible problems like the inadequate shipping capacity.
Scenario simulation methodology calls for few models only: the base case model and the scenarios. The benefit of the scenario simulation technique compared to other results analysis techniques like the design of experiments or steepest ascent is that it reduces the time-consuming sets of simulation runs and elaborate results analysis. This is in line with the view that simulation is an economic way to evaluate alternatives before implementation (Mott and Tumay, 1992), although perhaps not as thorough as they claim. In their extensive article on production scheduling approaches, Rodammer and White (1988) reach the conclusion that once a problem has been defined and suitable candidates generated, the performance of candidate schedules could be verified using simulation models. This is the same approach used in the scenario simulation methodology.
One drawback of simulation is that model optimum is not found (Mentzer, 1989). This applies to the scenario simulation methodology also. However, not all re-engineering actions are found by optimizing present system parameters. The alternative shipping arrangement was not a part of the original, base case simulation model and cannot therefore be found by optimizing the base case model decision variables like reorder point and replenishment quantity. Simulation as such did not prove to be a powerful problem solving method, as Hoover and Perry (1989) believe. Instead, the improvement actions were discovered from the researcher's previous experience or from existing logistics theory.
The correlated inspection approach to validate the simulation models as suggested by Kelton and Law (1991) or Hoover and Perry (1989) to validate the base case models was not properly carried out. The exact replenishment policies and demand

structures were not known for a stock, so the actual system inventory level data was used to fine-tune replenishment policies. After this fine-tuning is done, comparing the model inventory level to the actual system inventory level is no longer a test of validity.

Another consideration is that the role of simulation modeling can be a decision support tool. The improvement actions are decided elsewhere. Then the function of the model is to assess the improvement potential of the suggested improvement actions. For this purpose, scenario simulation methodology is suitable.

## REFERENCES

Banks J. and Carson J (1984) *Discrete-event System Simulation*, Prentice-Hall, New Jersey.

Bowersox, Donald J., Closs, David J., and Helferich, Omar K. (1986) *Logistical Management - A Systems Integration of Physical Distribution, Manufacturing Support and Materials Procurement*, 3rd edition, MacMillian Publishing, U.S.A.

Goldberg, D. (1989) *Genetic Algorithms in Search, Optimization, and Machine Learning*, Addison-Wesley, Massachusetts.

Hoover S. and Perry R. (1989) *Simulation - A problem-solving approach*, Addison-Wesley, USA.

Johnsson M. (1992) *Discrete Event Simulation, An Evaluation Tool for Logistic Systems*, Lund Institute of Technology, Lund, Sweden.

Law, A and Kelton, W. (1991) *Simulation Modeling & Analysis*, McGraw-Hill, U.S.A.

Menzer, J. (1989) Symposium Feature: Approaches to Logistics Modeling, *Journal of Business Logistics*, vol. 10, no 1.

Mott J. and Tumay K. (1992) Developing A Strategy For Justifying Simulation, *Industrial Engineering*, July 1992.

Naylor, T., Balintfy, J., Burdick, D. and Kong, C. (1966) *Computer Simulation Techniques*, John Wiley, U.S.A.

Pindyck R. and Rubinfeld D. (1991) *Econometric Models & Economic Forecasts*, McGraw-Hill, Singapore.

Rodammer, F. and White, P. (1988) A recent survey on production scheduling, *IEEE transactions on systems, man and cybernetics*, Vol. 18, no.6.

Strandhagen, J. (1994) *Operative simulation in production management*, Doctoral thesis, NTH Trondheim, Norway.

Vaughan, T. (1995) The effect of sampling variability on statistical order point computation, *Production and inventory management journal*, 3rd quarter.

## 7 BIOGRAPHY

PhD Juha-Matti Lehtonen is currently working as a senior researcher in TAI Research Centre at Helsinki University of Technology. Currently he is responsible for modeling food industry production facilities in a national food industry logistics research project. He was project leader in a Finnish paper industry distributon research project that ended in 1995.

M.Sc. and M.Ph. Kari Marttila has been working as a senior researcher researcher in TAI Research Centre at Helsinki University of Technology since 1996. Previously he has been working in industry, developing production control software for paper industry applications.

# 32

# Group Technology: Generation and Selection of the Best Multi-Criteria Alternative

*Behnam B. Malakooti, Ziyong Yang, Evan C. Tandler, and Jumah Al-Alwani*

*Systems, Control and Industrial Engineering Department*
*Center for Automation and Intelligent Systems Research*
*Case Western Reserve University*
*Cleveland, Ohio 44106*

**Abstract**

Group technology is a modern manufacturing approach which has been widely used in many industries. This paper addresses the machine-part cell formation problem while several criteria are considered for the evaluation of alternatives. The criteria include the number of work stations or cells, the cost of set-up and operation of different designs, and the volume of inter-flow traffic. Methods are presented for generation of efficient alternatives, evaluation of alternatives, and selection of the best alternative. This paper develops an approach to determine the machine-part cells and to choose the part processing plans minimizing the inter-cell part flow. The proposed approach solves the problem iteratively until a set of plans and the machine-part cells are obtained with minimal inter-cell part flow.

## 1. INTRODUCTION

Many US firms are utilizing the cellular manufacturing technology to increase their productivity and quicken their responses to market change. The design of a cellular manufacturing system consists of three major stages: 1) economical and technical feasibility study; 2) design of manufacturing systems; and 3) systems implementation (Wemmerlov and Hyer 1987). A cellular manufacturing system (CMS) can be designed by applying group technology and just-in-time concepts. One of the first problems to be solved in the system design stage is the machine-part cell formation. According to similarities in design features or processing requirements, the parts are grouped into families, and machines into cells. Families of parts can then be completely processed in their corresponding machine cells. The design procedures based on design features of parts require a classification and coding system that is time-consuming and demands additional expertise

Computer Applications in Production and Engineering. F. Plonka and G. Olling (Eds.)

to develop. Most design methods use the processing requirements of parts to form machine-part cells (King and Nakornchai 1982; Kusiak 1987; Srinivasan and Narendran 1991).

The processing requirements of parts on machines can be represented in the form of a matrix $\{a_{ij}\}$ which is called the machine-part incidence matrix. The incidence matrix has m rows representing the machines and n columns representing the parts. An element $a_{ij}$ in the incidence matrix is 1 if part j requires an operation to be performed on machine i; otherwise $a_{ij}$ is zero. The grouping of parts into families and machines into cells results in row and column exchanges of the incidence matrix. The expected solution is a block-diagonal matrix. But in most cases, the final grouped cells are not mutually exclusive. A few entries outside the diagonal blocks represent operations to be performed outside the assigned machine cells. These elements are called exceptional elements. The corresponding machine is called a bottleneck machine, and the corresponding part is called an exceptional part.

During the past two decades, numerous research papers have been published for cell formation. These methods are based on the following approaches:

1) Coding and classification (Bedworth et al. 1991, Xu and Wang 1989); 2) Machine-part group analysis (Burbidge 1971, King 1980, Chan and Milner 1982, Chandrasekaran and Rajagopalan 1986); 3) Similarity coefficients (Seifoddini and Wolfe 1986, Askin et al. 1991); 4) Knowledge-based (ElMaraghy and Gu 1988, Singh and Qi 1991); 5) Mathematical programming (Choobineh 1988, Rajamani et al. 1992, Logendran 1990); 6) Fuzzy clustering (Li et al. 1988, Xu and Wang 1989).

Most of these methods concentrate on forming the machine-part cells. If there exist exceptional elements in the final cell structure, these methods suggest duplicating all bottleneck machines or to subcontracting exceptional parts. They do not provide systematic means to handle the cell structure with exceptional elements.

In this paper, we propose a multiple criteria decision making (MCDM) framework for generating alternative cell structures and selecting the best one. The approach includes three levels. First, the seed alternative is formed by using our ANN-based clustering method (Malakooti and Yang 1995). Next, a heuristic procedure is proposed to generate alternatives from the seed alternative. This approach can generate alternatives for any feasible number of cells. Finally, the best machine-cell structure is found with considerations of maximizing the machine utilization rate, minimizing the number of duplicated machines, and minimizing the number of exceptional elements. We investigate relationships among several criteria and report experimental results.

The rest of the paper is organized as follows. In section 2, we give the multiple criteria approach for the machine-part cell formation problem. In section 3, an example is solved and the relationship among several criteria is also investigated. Section 4 is the conclusions.

## 2. MULTIPLE CRITERIA DECISION MAKING DESIGN APPROACH FOR MACHINE-PART CELL FORMATION IN CELLULAR MANUFACTURING

From our experiments and other researchers' experiments, we note that the final cell structures for most practical problems include some exceptional elements. These exceptional parts need to be moved among different machine cells. To decrease this kind of intercell part flow, the corresponding bottleneck machines could be duplicated, but this could result in increased capital cost and decreased machine utilization rate. Thus, there is a trade-off among intercell part flow and the number of duplicated machines, as well as other criteria such as machine utilization, cell utilization, machine loading, etc. We propose a multiple criteria decision making approach to design the machine-part cells to minimize the exceptional elements, to minimize the number of duplicated machines (capital cost), to maximize the machine utilization rate, and to find the best number of machine-part cells.

Most methods require the number of cells, K, as a known parameter. But in the practical design, the optimal number of cells is unknown and needs to be determined. Clearly, to put all machines and parts into one single cell, or to put only one machine into each cell does not make any sense. We assume that the minimum number of machine-part cells $R_{min}$ is two.

## 2.1. Model Formulation

2.1.1. Definitions

1) An alternative $a_i$ is a machine-part cell structure which can be represented as $\{(m_{ir}, p_{ir}), r = 1, 2, ..., R\}$, where $m_{ir}$ is the index set of machines in cell r, $p_{ir}$ is the index set of parts in cell r, and R is the number of cells.

2) $R_{min}$ is the minimum possible number of cells and $R_{max}$ the maximum possible number of cells.

3) Machine Utilization (MU)

MU can be computed as (Chandrasekharan and Rajagopalan 1986):

$$MU = N1/( \sum_{r=1}^{R} m_r n_r )$$

where N1 is the total number of 1's within the groups, R is the number of groups, $m_r$ is the number of machines in the *rth* group, and $n_r$ is the number of components in the *rth* group. Generally speaking, the higher the MU, the better the machines are being utilized, and the better the machine-part cell structure.

2.1.2. Model

1) P1 (multiple criteria problem):

From the set of q alternatives (machine-part cell structures) $A = \{a_i, i = 1, 2, ... , q\}$, find the alternative with the best number of cells which optimizes the following objectives:

min $f_1(a_i)$ = number of duplicated machines

min $f_2(a_i)$ = number of exceptional elements

max $f_3(a_i)$ = machine utilization rate

$$a_i \in A$$

The problem formulated above is a discrete multiple criteria decision making one. There are two kinds of approaches to solving discrete MCDM problems (Malakooti 1988): a) One assumes that there exists a utility function for a given Decision Maker (DM) that can predict his/her behavior and interest; b) One makes no assumptions regarding the existence of a utility function, but provides the DM with a set of simple but effective tools and lets him/her, by trial and error, and if-then type of statements, obtain the best alternative.

Under the assumption of an additive utility function:

$$U(a_i) = U(f_1^*(a_i), f_2^*(a_i), f_3^*(a_i)) = w_1 f_1^*(a_i) + w_2 f_2^*(a_i) + w_3 f_3^*(a_i)$$

where $w_1$, $w_2$, and $w3$ are weights representing the importance of each criterion to the DM; and $f_1^*(a_i)$, $f_2^*(a_i)$, and $f_3^*(a_i)$ are normalized values of $f_1(a_i)$, $f_2(a_i)$, and $f_3(a_i)$. P1 can be transformed into the following single objective problem P2. Under the above formulation, an alternative $a_i \in A$ is quasi-nondominated if and only if another alternative $a_{i'} \in A$ such that $f_1^*(a_{i'}) > f_1^*(a_i)$, $f_2^*(a_{i'}) > f_2^*(a_i)$ does not exist.

2) P2 (additive utility problem):

From the set of alternatives $A = \{a_i, i = 1, 2, ..., q\}$ find the alternative with the best number of cells which maximizes the utility function:

$$\text{Maximize } U(a_i) = w_1 f_1^*(a_i) + w_2 f_2^*(a_i) + w_3 f_3^*(a_i)$$

$$a_i \in A,$$

where $w_1 + w_2 + w_3 = 1$ and $w_1, w_2, w_3 \geq 0$;

$$f_1^*(a_i) = (f_{1max}(a_i) - f_1(a_i)) / (f_{1max}(a_i) - f_{1min}(a_i)) \quad (2\text{-}1)$$

and $f_2^*(a_i) = (f_{2max}(a_i) - f_2(a_i)) / (f_{2max}(a_i) - f_{2min}(a_i))$. (2-2)

$f_3^*(a_i) = f_3(a_i)$ (2-3)

Our purpose in solving this problem is to find an alternative $a_i \in A$ such that $U(a_i) \geq U(a_{i'})$ for any $a_{i'} \in A$.

### 2.2. A Three-Level Approach to Find the Best Alternative

Level 1: An artificial neural network (ANN) approach for Family Formation of Group Technology (Malakooti and Yang 1995) can be used to solve P2 to generate a seed alternative $a_0$ for each given number of cells, R. We start cell number at R = 2 and increase the cell number by one for each iteration until the cell structure has a cell containing only one machine or one part.

Clearly, $a_0$ is a quasi-nondominated alternative because $f_1^*(a_0) = 1$ is the maximum value of $f_1^*$ (Steuer 1986).

Level 2: Generate a set of local nondominated alternatives from the seed alternative $a_0$.

The heuristic procedure to generate alternatives from the seed alternative is as follows:

1) Check if there exist exceptional elements in thr seed alternative $a_0$. If there are none, stop.

2) Find the bottleneck machine j* associated with the most exceptional elements.

3) Find the corresponding machine-part cell $C_r^*$ in which the highest number of parts need to be processed on bottleneck machine j*.

4) Duplicate machine j*, and put it in cell $C_r^*$ to generate an alternative. Go to step 1).

From this heuristic procedure, we know that each new alternative is generated by duplicating one bottleneck machine to decrease the number of exceptional elements. Although $f_1^*$ of a new alternative decreases, the corresponding $f_2^*$ increases. We conclude that the generated alternatives are always local nondominated (or global quasi-nondominated). The best alternative is one of those quasi-nondominated alternatives.

Level 3: Evaluate the alternatives based on P2 to find the best alternative (the one having the highest utility value).

In order to evaluate all alternatives, we need to assess the importance weights $w_1$, $w_2$, and $w_3$ that the DM attaches to the criteria. There are a number of methods available, such as directly rating or ranking the criteria, or using indifference tradeoffs. In this paper, we assume that $w_1$, $w_2$, and $w_3$ are known, so the set of alternatives can be evaluated by their utility values. An alternative $a_i \in A$ is the best one when $U(a_i) \geq U(a_{i'})$ for any $a_{i'} \in A$.

## 3. AN EXAMPLE TO EXPLAIN THE THREE-LEVEL MCDM APPROACH

Problem 3 in this section is solved by our approach. We generate alternatives for each seed alternative and represent them using three objective values (number of duplicated machines $f_1$, number of exceptional elements $f_2$, machine utilization rate $f_3$, and their corresponding normalized values $f_1^*$, $f_2^*$, $f_3^*$). We also calculate utility values for each alternative using two sets of preference values: 1) $w_1 = w_2 = w_3 = 1/3$; 2) $w_1 = 0.2$, $w_2 = 0.4$, and $w_3 = 0.4$. The purpose of using two sets of preference values is to show that the best machine-part cell structure is chosen based on the Decision Maker's preference to each objective. The best machine-part cell structure corresponding to each set of preference values is also given.

Problem 3 (5x7) (Waghodekar and Sahu 1984)

The initial incidence matrix:

| | 1 | 2 | 3 | 4 | 5 | 6 | 7 |
|---|---|---|---|---|---|---|---|
| 01 | | 1 | | 1 | | | 1 |
| 02 | | | 1 | | 1 | | |
| 03 | 1 | 1 | | 1 | | | 1 |
| 04 | 1 | | 1 | | | 1 | |
| 05 | | | 1 | 1 | 1 | 1 | |

The seed alternative $a_0$ for R = 2:

| | 1 | 2 | 4 | 7 | 3 | 5 | 6 |
|---|---|---|---|---|---|---|---|
| 01 | | 1 | 1 | 1 | | | |
| 03 | 1 | 1 | 1 | 1 | | | |
| 02 | | | | | 1 | 1 | |
| 04 | 1 | | | | 1 | | 1 |
| 05 | | | 1 | | 1 | 1 | 1 |

The seed alternative $a_0$ for R = 3:

| | 1 | 2 | 4 | 7 | 3 | 5 | 6 |
|---|---|---|---|---|---|---|---|
| 01 | | 1 | 1 | 1 | | | |
| 03 | 1 | 1 | 1 | 1 | | | |
| 02 | | | | | 1 | 1 | |
| 05 | 1 | | | | 1 | 1 | 1 |
| 04 | | | 1 | | 1 | | 1 |

The 8 alternatives are:

| | R=2 | | | R=3 | | | | |
|---|---|---|---|---|---|---|---|---|
| | $a_0$ | $a_1$ | $a_2$ | $a_0$ | $a_1$ | $a_2$ | $a_3$ | $a_4$ |
| $f_1$ | 0 | 1 | 2 | 0 | 1 | 2 | 3 | 4 |
| $f_2$ | 2 | 1 | 0 | 4 | 3 | 2 | 1 | 0 |
| $f_3$ | 0.82 | 0.71 | 0.64 | 0.92 | 0.92 | 0.88 | 0.75 | 0.67 |
| $f_1^*$ | 1.00 | 0.91 | 0.82 | 0.73 | 0.64 | 0.55 | 0.45 | 0.36 |
| $f_2^*$ | 0.25 | 0.40 | 0.50 | 0.60 | 0.70 | 0.80 | 0.85 | 0.90 |
| $f_3^*$ | 0.93 | 0.93 | 0.93 | 0.90 | 0.88 | 0.83 | 0.79 | 0.78 |
| $U_1$ | 0.77 | 0.74 | 0.71 | 0.64 | 0.64 | 0.63 | 0.58 | 0.56 |
| $U_2$ | 0.73 | 0.73 | 0.76 | 0.57 | 0.62 | 0.64 | 0.65 | 0.67 |

Note

R: Number of cells

$f_1$: Number of duplicated machines

$f_2$: Number of exceptional elements

$f_3$: Machine utilization rate

$f_1^*$: Normalized value of $f_1$ using (2-1)

$f_2^*$: Normalized value of $f_2$ using (2-2)

$f_3^*$: Normalized value of $f_3$ using (2-3)

$U_1 = 1/3(f_1^*) + 1/3(f_2^*) + 1/3(f_3^*)$

$U_2 = 0.2(f_1^*) + 0.4(f_2^*) + 0.4(f_3^*)$

The best cell structure is $a_0$ with R=2 when $w_1 = w_2 = w_3 = 1/3$:

| | 1 | 2 | 4 | 7 | 3 | 5 | 6 |
|---|---|---|---|---|---|---|---|
| 01 | | 1 | 1 | 1 | | | |
| 03 | 1 | 1 | 1 | 1 | | | |
| 02 | | | | | 1 | 1 | |
| 04 | 1 | | | | 1 | | 1 |
| 05 | | | 1 | | 1 | 1 | 1 |

The best cell structure is $a_2$ with R=2 (machines 02 and 05 are duplicated) when $w_1 = 0.2$, $w_2 = 0.4$, and $w_3 = 0.4$:

| | 1 | 2 | 4 | 7 | 3 | 5 | 6 |
|---|---|---|---|---|---|---|---|
| 01 | | 1 | 1 | 1 | | | |
| 03 | 1 | 1 | 1 | 1 | | | |
| 02' | 1 | | | | | | |
| 05' | | | 1 | | | | |
| 02 | | | | | 1 | 1 | |
| 04 | | | | | 1 | | 1 |
| 05 | | | | | 1 | 1 | 1 |

We observe the following:

1) Regardless of the weights $w_1$, $w_2$, $w_3$, the machine utilization rate, $f_3$, for the best cell structure is higher when R=3 than it is when R=2. Thus, as the number of cells decreases, the machine utilization rate decreases.

2) $f_3$, - machine utilization rate, always decreases as f1, number of duplicated machines, increases.

3) $f_2$, the number of exceptional elements, is higher when R=3.

## 4. CONCLUSIONS

In this paper, we proposed a multiple criteria decision making approach to solve machine-part cell formation problems, especially those problems with exceptional elements. This three-level method generates a seed machine-part cell structure, and alternative structures from the seed, for every feasible number of cells. These alternative machine-part cell structures were evaluated by several criteria: the number of duplicated machines, the number of exceptional elements, and the machine utilization rate. An example was solved to show that the proposed approach can successfully solve the problems. We investigated the relationship among these criteria. We have the following observations from our experiment: 1) Machine utilization rate will decrease when the number of cells decreases; 2) Machine utilization rate will decrease when the number of duplicated machines increases; 3) Number of exceptional elements will increase when the number of cells increases. We gave experimental results on several problems from the literature.

## REFERENCES


Askin, R. G. et al., "A Hamiltonian path approach to recording the part-machine matrix for cellular manufacturing", *International Journal of Production Research*, **29**, 1081-1100, 1991.

Bedworth, D. D. et al., *Computer Integrated Design and Manufacturing*, McGraw-Hill, New York, 1991.

Burbidge, J. L., "Production flow analysis", *Production Engineer*, **50**, 139-152, 1971.

Chan, H. M. and Milner, D. A., "Direct Clustering Algorithm for Group Formation in Cellular Manufacture," *Journal of Manufacturing Systems*, 65-75, 1982.

Chandrsekharam, M. P. and Rajagopalan, R. "MODROC: An Extension of Rank Order Clustering for Group Technology," *International Journal of Production Research*, **24**, 1221-1233, 1986.

Choobineh, F., "A framework for the design of cellular manufacturing systems", *International Journal. of Production Research*, **26**, 1161-1172, 1988.

ElMaraghy, H. A. et al., "Knowledge-based system for assignment of parts to machines", *International Journal of Advanced Manufacturing Technology*, **3**, 1988.

King, J. R., "Machine-component Group Formation in Group Technology," *OMEGA*, **8**, 193-199, 1980.

King, J. R., "Machine-component Grouping in Production Flow Analysis: An Approach using a Rank Order Clustering Algorithm," *International Journal of Production Research.*, **18**, 213-232, 1980.

King, J. R. and Nakornchai, V., "Machine-component Group Formation in Group Technology: Review and Extension," *International Journal of Production Research*, **20**, 117-133, 1982.

Kusiak, A., "The Generalized Group Technology Concepts," *International Journal of Production Research*, **25**, 561-569, 1987.

Kusiak, A. and Heragu, S., "Group Technology," *Computer in Industry*, **9**, 83-91, 1987.

Kusiak, A. et al., "Similarity coefficient algorithms for solving the group technology problem", *International Journal of Production Research*, **30**, 2633-2646, 1992.

Li, J. et al., "Fuzzy cluster analysis and fuzzy pattern recognition method for formation of part families", *Proceeding of 16th North American Manufacturing Research Conference*, 558-563, 1988.

Logendran, R., "A workload based model for minimizing total intercell and intracell moves in cellular manufacturing", *International Journal of Production Research*, **28**, 913-925, 1990.

Malakooti, B. "Screening and Ranking Alternatives with Partial Information on Additive Multi-Attribute Utility Function for Discrete Sets and Multiple Objective Linear Programming Problems," *IEEE Transactions on Systems. Man. and Cybernetics*, **19**, 95-107, 1989.

Malakooti, B. and Yang, Z., "A Variable-Parameter Unsupervised Learning Neural Network Clustering Systems for Machine-Part Group Formation", *International Journal of Production Research*, **33**, 2395-2413, 1995.

Rajamani, D. et al., "A model for cell formation in manufacturing systems with sequence dependence", *International Journal of Production Research*, **30**, 1227-1235, 1992.

Seifoddini, H., "Duplication process in machine cells formation in group technology", *IIE Transactions*, **21**, 382-388, 1989.

Shafer, S. and Rogers, D., "Similarity and Distance Measures for Cellular Manufacturing. Part I. A Survey," *International Journal of Production Research*, **31**, 1133-1142, 1993.

Singh, N. et al., "Fuzzy multi-objective routing problem with application to process planning in manufacturing systems", *International Journal of Production Research*, **29**, 1161-1170, 1991.

Srinivasan, G. et al., "An assignment model for the part families problem in group technology", *International Journal of Production Research*, **28**, 145-152, 1990.

Waghodekar, P. H. and Sahu, S., "Machine-component Cell Formation in Group Technology: MACE," *International Journal of Production Research*, **22**, 937-948, 1984.

Wemmerlov, U. and Hyer, N., "Cellular Manufacturing in the US Industry: A Survey of Users," *International Journal of Production Research*, **27**, 1511-1530, 1989.

Xu, H. and Wang, H. P., "Part family formation for GT application based on fuzzy mathematics", *International Journal of Production Research*, **27**, 1637-1651, 1989.

# 33
# Reduction of cycle time in manufacturing using simulation

*A.W. Chan*
*Integrated Manufacturing Technologies Institute*
*National Research Council of Canada*
*Montreal Road M50, Ottawa, Canada, K1A 0R6*
*tel: 1-613-993-9437, fax: 1-613-941-1571*
*e-mail: albert.chan@nrc.ca*

*A. Satir*
*Department of Decision Sciences and MIS*
*Concordia University*
*Montreal, Canada, H3G 1M8*
*tel: 1-514-848-2974, fax: 1-514-848-2824*
*e-mail: ats@vax2.concordia.ca*

*V. J. Thomson*
*Department of Mechanical Engineering*
*McGill University*
*817 Sherbrooke Street West, Montreal, Canada, H3A 2K6*
*tel: 1-514-398-2597, fax: 1-514-398-7365*
*e-mail: thomson@mecheng.mcgill.ca*

**Abstract**

A shop floor model of a large electronics manufacturer was developed to study the reduction of manufacturing cycle time. The model followed the manufacture of electronic systems from printed circuit board preparation, through board assembly and test, to final system assembly and system testing.

Simulation allowed the evaluation of four different tactics for manufacturing cycle time reduction. These were: the effect of setup, breakdown and lot size on printed circuit board (PCB) assembly; the implementation of a total pull tactic on a

Computer Applications in Production and Engineering. F. Plonka and G. Olling (Eds.)

production line; the comparison of improved quality in manufacture and rework; and the effect of balancing personnel across shifts.

The study used actual production data. Conclusions about the study and the effectiveness of alternative tactics are presented.

**Keywords**
Shop floor simulation, manufacturing cycle time, electronics manufacturing

## 1 INTRODUCTION

The spectrum of manufacturing operations can be classified from make-to-stock (MTS), where all products are standardized, at one extreme, to engineer-to-order (ETO), where the customer specifies the purpose of the product, at the other. In between these extremes in the manufacturing spectrum are assemble to-order (ATO) and make-to-order (MTO) type operations. ATO involves an environment where major components and subassemblies are held in stock awaiting customer orders and can be treated either as a unique environment by itself or the first step from an MTS to an MTO environment. In an MTO environment, products are made to customer requests, usually involving a large engineering component.

The manufacturing technologies (such as FMS, robotics, CIM) and management based approaches (such as supply chain management, JIT, BPR) that have been implemented over the last two decades enable enterprises to compete on time-based performance, especially in ETO, ATO and MTO environments. Time reduction at all phases and levels of manufacturing from order processing to shipment is emerging as a pivotal issue in this respect.

Modeling and analytical aspects of cycle time reduction are studied in Karmarkar (1987), Kingsman et al (1989), Hill and Khosla (1992), Lockamy III (1993) as well as Miltenburg and Sparling (1996) among others. Frameworks for analyzing lead time related issues are developed in Kingsman et al (1989) incorporating a hierarchy of lead times that add up to total delivery lead time. Certain input/output control procedures are proposed. A cost/benefit analysis based framework for lead time reduction is argued in Hill and Khosla (1992). Lockamy III's framework, on the other hand, is based on a study of six large manufacturing organizations. Performance measures by various functions are proposed for lead time management. Mathematical models are developed to study cycle time in Karmarkar (1987) and Miltenburg and Sparling (1996). In the former study, the impact of lot sizing and work-in-process stocks on lead time is studied. In the latter article, three models in the form of a stochastic, Markov chain and a queuing model are developed to study cycle time management in MTO, ATO and MTS environments.

Approaches and techniques for lead time reduction are discussed in Hopp et al (1990). The overall conclusion is that the most effective factors in lead time reduction are the decrease in mean flow time and flow time variance. A study by Handfield and Pannesi (1995) focuses on how firms can achieve a time-based advantage in MTO manufacturing environments through: i) cross functional design participation, ii) just-in-time purchasing, iii) improved supplier delivery and quality performance, and iv) lot size reduction. A structural model and relevant measures were developed. The model was tested using interview data with managers in forty plants from nine industries. Findings suggest the significance of factors (ii) and (iii) on lead time based competitiveness.

Rather than focusing on a limited number of factors as in many of the articles reviewed, this study covers a wider range of operational factors and analyzes their impact on lead time. The production line studied in this article operates in a hybrid environment of MTS and MTO. The study objectives, factors studied and their impact on cycle time are discussed in the following sections.

## 2 STUDY OBJECTIVE

The authors in collaboration with a large manufacturer of electronics equipment developed a computer model/simulation of the supplier's manufacturing operations in order to assess the potential benefits of applying simulation technologies to the study of its manufacturing and business operations, as well as to understand how overall manufacturing cycle time can be shortened. The project examined the drivers and the effects of reducing manufacturing cycle time, where manufacturing cycle time was defined as the time from work orders arriving on the shop floor to the point when fabricated items are deemed to be finished goods. The study had two major objectives: a) to determine how to achieve a reduced manufacturing cycle time, and b) to investigate the effects that reduced time would have on other functions in the enterprise, e.g., order fulfillment, production planning, etc.

A Manufacturing Enterprise Model was developed, comprising three submodels: an Order Fulfillment Submodel, an Inventory Submodel, and a Shop Floor Submodel. The Order Fulfillment Submodel was composed of those business processes from receiving a customer order to invoicing of the customer including order entry, custom product configuration, material planning, production scheduling, and distribution. The Shop Floor Submodel was composed of those processes from reception of work orders to placing finished goods into inventory. A separate Inventory Submodel was created to track ordered components, work-in-process (WIP), and finished goods. The points of communication between the submodels are the work orders which come from the central planning function, the components which are controlled and purchased by the planning and purchasing functions, and which are drawn upon by the shop floor, and finished goods which are placed in inventory by the shop floor, and then, delivered to the customer by distribution as part of the order fulfillment function. More detail about this integrated modeling approach is in Chan and Thomson (1997).

The present paper deals with the study of tactics which allow the reduction of manufacturing cycle time and discusses the Shop Floor Submodel only.

## 3 SHOP FLOOR STUDIES

The Shop Floor Submodel was developed using ProModel, a Windows based tool for simulating and analyzing discrete part manufacturing systems. The model was based on the production facility of the participating electronics manufacturer. A typical line starts with board preparation and screen printing (application of solder). A number of automated steps for component placement, including surface mount, automatic insertion, mold seal, and connector assembly is performed. These are, then, followed by a before-wave, wave (soldering) and after-wave assembly sequence. In-circuit testing is performed next, followed by mechanical assembly into system units. The system units are, then, passed through a series of testing stages, including functional test, post-functional test and environmental test, where they have to be tested in conjunction with other system units. Having passed all the foregoing tests, a system may still undergo system test and customer requested field acceptance testing. The model terminates at finished goods inventory. A schematic of this process is shown in Figure 1.

The specific studies for manufacturing cycle time reduction were based on data supplied by the electronics manufacturer for several days of production. Four different tactics to reduce cycle time were investigated:

1. variation of setup, breakdowns, and lot size parameters
2. use of a complete 'pull' tactic across the assembly and test sections
3. improvement of quality, and
4. changes in the distribution of personnel employed across shifts.

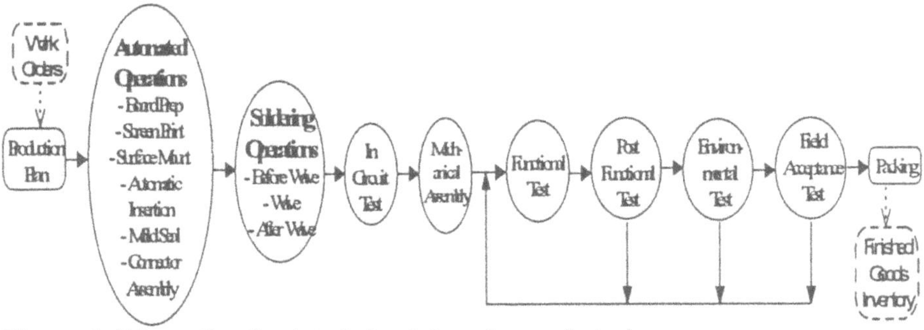

Figure 1 Schematic of printed circuit board manufacturing processes

### 4.1 Impact of lot size, setup times and downtimes

The Shop Floor Submodel was used to study the impact of lot size, setup time, breakdown frequencies and repair times on the assembly time for the assembly section of the PCB production line as described above. Products assembled on the line were grouped into six families. Data for setup, processing and repair times and breakdown frequencies were gathered for each station/product combination from company files and through stopwatch studies in certain cases. All parameters of the model were assumed to be deterministic, with the exception of breakdown occurrences, which were assumed to follow a Poisson distribution. The model was validated to assess the degree to which it corresponded to the real system being simulated. The comparison between the model's findings in term of the distribution of various times and the company's actual data for the validation period was quite favorable, as illustrated in Table 1. The comparison was for one machine which was typical of other machines in the line. Since the line was balanced, the idle time was completely due to the effects of setup and downtime from other machines, i.e., machines were either blocked or starved for work. Downtime was the sum of intervention time to failed stations and repair time.

**Table 1** Distribution of operating times for a typical workstation

| | Setup (%) | Processing (%) | Idle (%) | Downtime (%) |
|---|---|---|---|---|
| Model | 14.5 | 19.5 | 50.0 | 16.0 |
| Actual | 14.0 | 20.0 | 48.0 | 18. 0 |

Two separate days of operations were simulated on the line. Each 24 hour day is denoted by sample 1 and sample 2. The input data used to simulate these two days was deemed to be appropriate since the data cover most of the product types made by the manufacturer. Also, the total number of boards processed in both days was quite large. The performance measures used to evaluate the impact of a given factor were: i) throughput time, i.e., the number of hours required to process 275 and 295 PCBs, in sample 1 and 2, respectively, and ii) throughput rate per day, i.e., the number of PCBs assembled per 24 hours. When the former measure was of concern, a terminating type simulation was run, where the simulation starts and ends at a defined state/time. In such a case, the behavior of the system over this particular period of time is of interest, rather than its steady state behavior.

While all other parameters were at base levels and breakdowns were disabled, simulations with lot sizes of 14, 10, 7, 5, 3 over a 24 hour period provided the throughput rates in terms of PCBs assembled given in Table 2. A lot size of 7 was used in other scenarios since it was the actual lot size used by the manufacturer.

**Table 2** Variation in output with change in lot size

| Lot size | Sample 1 (Number of PCBs) | Sample 2 (Number of PCBs) |
|---|---|---|
| 14 | 378 | 392 |
| 10 | 355 | 351 |
| 7 | 327 | 345 |
| 5 | 280 | 285 |
| 3 | 226 | 235 |

The impact of varying setup time was tested at three levels, while breakdowns were disabled: base (current) level (1), half of base level (0.5), and zero setup time

(0). The total throughput time for assembling 275 and 295 PCBs in sample 1 and 2 for each setup time is given in Table 3.

**Table 3** Reduction in production time with a reduction in setup

| Setup time | Sample 1 (Hours) | Sample 2 (Hours) |
|---|---|---|
| Base (1) | 17.63 | 19.27 |
| Half (0.5) | 16.81 | 16.61. |
| Zero (0) | 13.91 | 14.56 |

Another set of experiments was carried out by varying the degree of downtime due to breakdowns at three levels: base (current) level (1), half of base level (0.5) and zero downtime (0). The throughput time required to assemble the 275 and 295 PCBs in sample 1 and 2, respectively, is given in Table 4.

**Table 4** Reduction in production time with a reduction in downtime

| Downtime | Sample 1 (Hours) | Sample 2 (Hours) |
|---|---|---|
| Base (1) | 30.17 | 29.30 |
| Half (0.5) | 22.73 | 23.20 |
| Zero (0) | 17.63 | 19.27 |

Table 5 shows the relative increase in production for setup time and downtime reductions using a lot size of 7.

**Table 5** Proportion of production increase with reductions in setup and downtime

| | Sample 1 | Sample 2 | Average |
|---|---|---|---|
| Half setup time | 1.05 | 1.16 | 1.11 |
| Zero setup time | 1.27 | 1.32 | 1.30 |
| Half downtime | 1.33 | 1.26 | 1.30 |
| Zero downtime | 1.71 | 1.52 | 1.62 |

It is evident that increases in production are higher when downtime is reduced compared to similar, proportional decreases in setup time. This indicates that quicker intervention to breakdowns and reduced repair times would have a larger impact in reducing the assembly time. This finding has implications for the company in terms of its preventive maintenance and repair practices.

## 4.2 Total pull tactic

The Shop Floor Submodel was used to study the effects of using a complete 'pull' tactic from finished goods to the start of the board assembly section. The actual production line being studied operated by pulling orders from finished goods to the start of the testing section and by 'pushing' lots of circuit boards through the assembly section. There was a small buffer between the board assembly and testing sections which acted as a 'regulator' between the processing of lots of boards and the assembly and test of systems.

The following assumptions were incorporated into the model:

a) a pull of 1 was defined as the boards required to build a complete system,
b) like boards were processed as one lot, i.e., while one system of boards was pulled each time, there were multiples of certain boards.

The original system had a lot size of 7 boards which was used during the assembly section of the line and into the in-circuit test station. In the simulations for a pull system, scenarios with lot sizes of 1, 4 and 7 boards were performed. The results for lot sizes of 1 and 4 are compared to those of a lot size of 7 in Table 6.

**Table 6** The effect of a pull tactic for different lot sizes

| Tactic | Reduction in cycle time | Reduction in throughput |
|---|---|---|
| Pull with lot size 1 | 45% | 35% |
| Pull with lot size 4 | 15% | 5% |

As can be seen from Table 6, manufacturing cycle time can be reduced by 45% through the use of a total pull tactic. This was due to two main factors: first, the elimination in some cases or a reduction in the use of buffers in others along the production line, and secondly, a reduction in delay times for the various groups of boards where they waited for testing facilities, i.e., essentially, waiting times in queues which operated on a first-in-first-out basis. There were no substantial reduction in actual workstation processing times.

Nevertheless, three drawbacks were noted. First, adopting a complete pull system meant that the effective lot size was reduced; this increased the amount of setup time, thereby, reducing assembly line utilization and throughput. This had a large effect. Secondly, the reduction in the use of buffers in the testing area did reduce cycle time, but it also decreased testing facility utilization and throughput; this had a small effect. Overall, throughput was reduced due to these two factors as indicated in the above results. A third factor was the increased exposure to downtime due to possible component shortages. This was not simulated in the scenarios, but is an obvious consequence of reduced buffer size. This could be overcome by having an appropriate ordered component stocking policy.

While studying the different lot sizes, especially the lot size of 1, different operating rules for the testing facilities were tried in order to overcome some of the observed shortcomings and to determine optimum procedures. These different operating rules had minimum effect (less than 5%) on the cycle time or throughput.

## 4.3 Quality

Due to product variety and complexity many errors occur during the assembly of circuit boards. This is the state-of-the-art in the circuit board manufacture and will probably remain so since the desire for more variety and complexity is always pushing the capabilities of assembly lines.

In the production line studied, there were four test areas: in-circuit test, functional test, post-functional test and environmental test. The first pass yield rate of the complete testing section was about 40%, i.e., 40% of the boards tested successfully passed the tests at all four test areas the first time. The yield was this low due to the high component density and requirement for high precision placement. The effects of two different tactics that address quality were studied: first, an improved assembly quality or better first pass yield rate; second, different repair tactics leaving the first pass yield rate alone.

For the first tactic, the first pass yield rate was individually improved at each of the four different test areas. This had very little effect on reducing the overall cycle time. It was also noted in the simulations that any improvement in any single workstation, assembly or test, had very little effect on decreasing cycle time due to the highly balanced nature of the line. First pass yield rates were improved at all test areas uniformly by 10%; this gave a first pass yield rate in the testing section of the production line of about 58%. This improved overall yield rate resulted in a reduced total cycle time of about 6.5%.

When PCBs fail tests at the testing areas, they are sent to repair stations for rework. Repair operations are such that boards being repaired can take a number of repair cycles for them to pass successfully through the testing section. Simulations were done assuming that the number of repair cycles at each test center was reduced by one repair cycle. This reduced total manufacturing cycle time by 6%.

Due to some simplifying assumptions in the original models, the magnitude of the reduction in cycle time for simulations of quality improvement is underestimated. However, the interesting conclusion from the study is not so much the magnitude of cycle time reduction, but that improved repair tactics can have the same effect as significantly improving the first pass yield rate. Significantly improving rates is very difficult, if not impossible, due to the determination of precise causes for failures and the cost or inviolability of better equipment, but it is most often feasible to improve repair processes so that total rework is lowered.

## 4.4 Balancing personnel across shifts

One of the important considerations for operating the production lines is the allocation of workers to the various stages of the assembly and testing processes. While the utilization of human resources on the automated portion of the production line is fairly routine, the assignment of operators to the manual portion of the production line, particularly to the various assembly and test stations, could have a significant impact on productivity. As well, the balancing of the number of workers for the different shifts in a day (or week) could have a dramatic effect on the formation of bottlenecks, and thus, WIP and throughput. Yet any changes to current practices must be justified to the work force. The Shop Floor Submodel helped to address this important issue.

The Shop Floor Submodel was applied to study the impact of various resource allocation strategies on overall manufacturing cycle time. One of the studies involved the balancing of workers across the different shifts in a working day. The assembly operations on a printed circuit board production line include before-wave and after-wave, which are labor intensive operations, and a large number of manual workstations are involved. As well, the functional testing operation is a key step in the testing sequence for any printed circuit board. Not only is this a labor intensive operation, but the testing equipment deployed is highly dependent on the type of circuit board being tested. Again, a large number of manual workstations with technicians of various skill levels have to be utilized. The Shop Floor Submodel was designed so that the number of workstations (thus, workers) deployed on any shift during the day/week for these locations can be varied easily via a spreadsheet, thereby, facilitating the experimentation of different worker assignment strategies.

In order to focus the study on the effects of shift balancing, a series of experiments was conducted to identify the needed levels of resources that are commensurate with given input volumes. The number of workstations at various locations along the production line was successively reduced until the utilization rate was reasonable (75 to 100%), and not an excessive amount of slack was experienced for a given quantity of blank circuit boards being pushed from the beginning of the production line. Once this level was identified, it was used as a reference level for shift balancing experiments. Suppose this level was found to be 15 workstations per day for the Functional Testing operation for a certain type of circuit board. In this case, the fully balanced scenario would call for a deployment of 5 workstations for each of the 3 shifts in a day. One unbalanced scenario could involve using 7, 5 and 3 workstations respectively for the 3 shifts in a day. Assuming there were actually 7 workstations available for this type of Functional Testing on the shop floor, then a highly unbalanced scenario could be 7, 7 and 1 workstations respectively for the 3 shifts.

An appropriate level of resource allocation was first identified separately for each of the operations on the production line where shift balancing strategies were being considered. Where different workstations or test sets were involved for different board types, this level was identified for each of those board types as well. With these levels serving as reference points, personnel balancing strategies for each group of workstations were tried individually as well as aggregately. In each case, the effect on overall production cycle time was compared. Multiple replications were run to even out the effects of random fluctuations in processing times and probabilistic failure rates.

The results of shift balancing experiments showed that if strategies to balance the deployment of workers over the 3 shifts of a day were applied to individual groups of workstations, such as before-wave, or after-wave, or functional testing, the impact on cycle time was not significant. However, if the same strategies were applied to multiple groups of workstations, i.e., on a larger scale, then, the difference in cycle time could be significant. Specifically, if a shift balancing strategy was applied across the board to all applicable workstations on the production line, there was a reduction in overall cycle time for the fully balanced scenario over the highly unbalanced scenario of between 15 to 20%. This result is both intuitive and conforms to theoretical analysis. In other words, it is reasonable to expect that the overall cycle time on the production line to be shorter when the 3 shifts are fully balanced when compared to a highly unbalanced scenario. The 15 to 20% reduction is lower than the theoretical difference because the shift balancing strategy is applicable only to some of the workstations on the line.

## 5 SUMMARY

Simulation was an excellent method for evaluating different tactics for the reduction of manufacturing cycle time. The favorable comparison of validated models to actual production results gave a high degree of confidence to the findings.

*Lot size, setup and downtime*
Lot size showed no optimum value; lower values gave lower cycle times, but reduced throughput also occurred. The ability to reduce manufacturing cycle time by decreasing downtime showed much greater potential than reducing setup time.

*A total pull tactic*
A total pull tactic greatly reduced manufacturing cycle time; however, there was a significant, simultaneous reduction in throughput. More studies are being undertaken to determine if this can be overcome.

*Quality*
The interesting conclusion that improved repair procedures can have as large an effect as an improved first pass yield rate for reducing cycle time was obtained. This is being investigated by the company and further research is ongoing in order to better predict the magnitude of the reduction.

*Shift balance*
Balancing personnel and equipment utilization across shifts reduced manufacturing cycle time compared to unbalanced operations. Only a 15 to 20% reduction was observed since balance/imbalance was only applicable to a few workstations.

## REFERENCES

Chan, A.W. and Thomson, V. (1997) Simulating a Manufacturing Enterprise Using Integrated Process Models, *Proceedings of IFAC Workshop on Manufacturing Systems: Modeling, Management and Control*, (MIM '97) Vienna, Austria, 3-5 February 1997, 397-402.

Handfield, R.B. and Pannesi, R.T. (1995) Antecedents of Leadtime Competitiveness in Make-to-Order Manufacturing Firms, *International Journal of Production Research*, **33**, No. 2, 511–37.

Hill, A.V. and Khosla, I.S. (1992) Models for Optimal Lead Time Reduction, *Production and Operations Management*, **1**, No. 2, 185–97.

Hopp, W.J., Spearman, M.L. and Woodruff, D.L. (1990) Practical Strategies for Lead Time Reduction, *Manufacturing Review*, **3**, No. 2, 78–84.

Karmarkar, U.S. (1987) Lot Sizes, Lead Times and In-Process Inventories, *Management Science*, **33**, No. 3, 409–18.

Kingsman, B.G., Tatsiopoulos, I.P. and Hendry, L.C. (1989) A Structural Methodology for Managing Manufacturing Lead Times in Make-to-Order Companies, *European Journal of Operational Research*, **40**, No. 2, 196–209.

Lockamy III, A. (1993) A Conceptual Framework for Value-Delivery System Lead Time Management, *International Journal of Production Research*, **31**, No. 1, 223–33.

Miltenburg, J. and Sparling, D. (December 1996) Managing and Reducing Total Cycle Time: Models and Analysis, *International Journal of Production Economics*, **46**, 89–108.

## BIOGRAPHY

Albert W. Chan is a Senior Research Officer in the Integrated Manufacturing Technologies Institute at the National Research Council of Canada. He received a B.Sc. in Mathematics from the University of Minnesota, and a M.Sc. and Ph.D. in Industrial Engineering from the University of Florida. His research interests include simulation and computer modeling, decision support systems, and process modeling and re-engineering of business and industrial systems.

Ahmet Satir is a professor of production/operations management at Concordia University. His current research interests focus on supply chain management and just-in-time manufacturing systems.

Vince Thomson is the Werner Graupe Professor for Manufacturing Automation in the Department of Mechanical Engineering at McGill University. He has been involved in manufacturing and information technology related research for 20 years at McGill and the National Research Council (Ottawa). His research has ranged from shop floor control and production scheduling to the present interest in process management in manufacturing.

# 34

# Experiments with a knowledge-based simulator and scheduler system

*G. L. Kovács*
*Computer and Automation Research Institute, Hungarian Academy of Sciences*
*H-1111 Budapest, Kende u. 13-17., Hungary,*
*Fax: 36-1-1667-503; E-mail: h673kov@ella.hu*

**Abstract**
Computer aided simulation can assist in Flexible Manufacturing Systems' (FMS) design (planning), scheduling and operation as well. The knowledge for planning and controlling of FMS can be built into knowledge based (KB) systems. KB, intelligent control of FMS can be done by using the results of scheduling (production planning based on process plans). Intelligent control and supervision of a system can be solved by real-time, intelligent environments. In this paper two KB simulation-scheduler systems will be discussed. In the first one the simulation system is implemented in SIMAN/Cinema, while in the second one in G2. The simulation is connected to preparation, evaluation and scheduling advisory systems implemented in G2 in both systems. The paper gives details on scheduling results using both systems with the same two test cases.

**Keywords**
Simulation, scheduling, knowledge-based system, flexible manufacturing

## 1 INTRODUCTION

The production process in a manufacturing system is based on the manufacturing schedule which is created from a process plan. A process plan consists of the operation order, the identifiers of the machines, tools, etc. and the time period of each operation on the given manufacturing equipment. The manufacturing schedule contains the previous information plus the start and end times of all the

Computer Applications in Production and Engineering. F. Plonka and G. Olling (Eds.)

operations. A good scheduler can take into account the transportation and set-up times as well. A scheduler also has to consider the due dates (or due times). There are different solutions to obtain appropriate production schedules. Some of them are in the following categories: mathematical programming, multi-criterion decision making, heuristic approach, graph-theoretical approach, application of simulation, application of AI tools.

Our approach is a combination of the last two methods, when a simulation system will be connected to a KB scheduler.

## 2 APPLICATION OF KB SIMULATION FOR SCHEDULING

Scheduling with simulation is usually fast and reliable. During the simulated manufacturing process the starting and finishing time of each operation can be recorded, and later on a schedule can be built up based on these information.

If we create a manufacturing schedule with simulation, there are several decision points - even if only simple algorithms are used - in the process of the simulation. For example:

- if there are more than one workpieces in a parallel buffer (temporary storage), the question is which workpiece can leave the buffer first, or
- more than one machine tools are suitable for a certain operation, which machine to choose,
- more than one workpieces are waiting for the same resource, which will be served first, - etc.

In traditional languages and in most of the simulation languages these kind of decisions can be made by using the if-then-else structure only. It is rather difficult to write decision rules if we have a large number of conditions to be satisfied at the same time. Using the traditional languages even not too complicated scheduling rules as LIFO or FIFO are hard to manage. Combining simulation and knowledge based (KB) systems will result in the so called knowledge based simulation to solve the problem of decision making during simulation. In such a combination the scheduling power will be defined by the KB.

## 3 KB PROTOTYPE FMS SIMULATION-SCHEDULER SYSTEMS

Our first KB FMS Simulation system was written in CS-PROLOG (Communicating Sequential Prolog) [1]. The next version was based on the traditional SIMAN/Cinema simulation-animation [2] package connected with advisory systems implemented in the ALL-EX [3] expert system shell. Then ALL-EX was substituted by the G2, real-time, object oriented expert system environment [4] (Hybrid System). Finally the simulation was implemented in G2 as well, this way the same object definitions and some part of the knowledge could be used for all subsystems and there were no communication problems between the simulation and the KB (KB System). [5] gives a detailed description of system development and implementation problems including some comparisons of the above KB simulation-scheduler systems.

## 3.1 Simulation and advisory systems in the same G2 environment

The natural advantage of the system where the simulation and the interconnected expert systems (preparation, evaluation and scheduler) are implemented in the same G2 environment is that neither interfacing nor co-operation problems appeared as in the previous prototypes, where G2 had to cooperate with SIMAN/Cinema. The biggest difference was caused by the G2's object-oriented view. All elements of the simulated system are now represented by G2 objects with a hierarchy between them to make attribute inheritance possible.

# 4 EXPERIMENTS USING THE G2 ENVIRONMENT

[6] gives a good summary of scheduling (and dispatching or priority) rules which are often applied in experimental systems. There is a distinction between dispatching (or priority) and scheduling rules, which is the following according to a simplified definition: Dispatching rules assign scalar values to all waiting jobs, while scheduling rules select the job to be scheduled next in preference to the other waiting jobs. However in most practical implementations priority rules are used for both purposes. In the following we shall use only the scheduling rules for both terms, and we do not distinguish between pre-release decisions, part-release decisions and part-routing decisions which are the essence of dispatching.

Some of the possible scheduling priorities and rules associated to them are the following:

- Processing time (shortest/longest next operation, shortest/longest remaining time, etc.)
- Due date (earliest, earliest operation, etc.)
- Number of operations (fewest/most remaining, etc.)
- Random arrival time (FIFO, LIFO, random, earliest available, etc.)
- Cost rules (minimum tardiness, etc.)
- Setup time rules (highest/lowest setup time, etc.)
- Slack rules (least amount of slack, least static slack, etc.)
- Machine (shortest processing time, shortest queue behind, etc.)
- Tool (least number of tool movement, etc.)

These priorities and the rules belonging to them freely can be combined in the hope of getting better results. The "better result" means better according to some given goal functions or expectations. Such expectations can be the shortest total production time, cheapest production, uniform load of resources, maximal (or minimal) load of the most expensive/cheapest machine, etc. These can be simple or combined, and they may be contradictory is some cases. And - naturally - they are represented by the applied scheduling algorithm (rules).

Application of expert systems allows to use contradictory rules simultaneously, and probabilities and uncertainties can be applied, too. This way the power of the system can be increased and programming is easier. For our experiments we applied simple rules of different priorities with a goal function of having the shortest throughput time (total production time). The results are evaluated based on total throughput times. Scheduling was divided into two consecutive steps. We separately tried to optimize the sequence, as raw parts arrive into the input buffers of the FMS (pre-schedule), and then optimization is done when the parts are moving in the FMS (schedule).

## 4.1 Optimizing the input sequence of raw parts arriving into the FMS

In this phase a preliminary sequence of the raw parts is determined how to arrive into the input storage of the FMS to see the effects of these sequences to the final schedule.

The following rules/priorities were used:

- MQ, type of maximum quantity first (always that part type has the highest priority from which the biggest number is required, the basis of comparison is the number of required parts minus number of parts under /plus after/) processing of the given types)
- MC, multicolor input (all types of parts should be in the input storage as long as possible)
- UD, uniform distribution input (the distribution of different parts in the input storage corresponds to the distribution of quantities of different part types to be produced)

## 4.2 Application of different scheduling algorithms

As it was mentioned, earlier only the well-known Round Robin strategy was built into the SIMAN simulation system itself and a LIFO and a FIFO algorithms were implemented in the Scheduling Advisor first. Later on we changed these algorithms, and for the experiments the following ones were implemented:

- SP, job (part) with shortest process plan first
- LP, job (part) with longest process plan first
- SI, job (part) with the shortest next operation time first
- LI, job (part) with longest next operation time first
- ED, job (part) with the earliest due date first
- SR, job with the shortest remaining processing time first
- LR, job with the longest remaining processing time first

(Jobs are always associated to parts.)

The time-spans of individual process-plans are measured by generating individual schedules for each part as they were the only single parts in the system.

### 4.3 Tests with the GoldStar FMS, application of the hybrid system

The goal of the experiments was twofold: to test the hybrid simulation-scheduler and to make test runs with a real industrial example. The FMS works in the workshop of the GoldStar Heavy Industries Cable factory near Seoul. There are 8 CNC machining centers with palette exchanger and tool magazine in the system. The machine tools are situated in one long line, there are seven buffers for temporary palette storage, with 6 slots each. One transport carriage is moving on rails, with a speed of 60 m/min if loaded and with 80 m/min if empty and its accuracy is 0.2 mm. The palette size is 1mx1m, the maximum weight of the workpiece is 3000 kg (3 tons), there is room only for one palette in the carriage. There is a load/unload station with four slots where parts are fixed on the palettes, and where they are unfixed to leave the system. Fixing/defixing is done manually.

To demonstrate the size of the workshop we give the distances of the machine tools from the load/unload station, as machine identifier (distance in meters):

1(12), 2(27), 3(26), 4(33), 5(40), 6(47), 7(54), 8(61)

The production task in a shift (one week) are given in Table 1.

Table 1. Production tasks of the GoldStar system

| color | batch size | package size | due date | setup time | operation times (min) | | |
|---|---|---|---|---|---|---|---|
| | | | (day) | (min) | op1 | op2 | sum |
| red | 100 | 6 | 6 | 5 | 105 | 77 | 182 |
| yellow | 100 | 5 | 6 | 5 | 65 | 50 | 115 |
| blue | 90 | 10 | 6 | 5 | 30 | 225 | 255 |
| brown | 30 | 3 | 6 | 5 | 60 | 120 | 180 |
| green | 10 | 2 | 3 | 5 | 70 | 65 | 135 |
| white | 10 | 2 | 3 | 5 | 80 | 65 | 145 |
| Total | 340 | | | | | | |

We use the Cinema animation colors instead of the names of the parts to identify them. There are two operations to be done on every part. An operation is defined as all CNC programs on one machine tool with one palette position. The two operations can be done at any machine tools, and there is a need of a new fixing of the part between them.

If we calculate the total amount of time which is theoretically necessary for the production we have:

100x182+100x115+90x255+30x180+10x135+10x145= 60850

If we add two setup times to each workpiece we get:

TSUM=60850+340x10= 64250 min

TSUM in days is 64250/60/24= 44.6 days if we suppose 1 machine tool only, but as we have 8 similar purpose machine tools

TSUM8= 44.6/8= 5.57 days

We can say that to produce all parts in a shift 5.57 days were necessary if every machine tool worked full load all the time, i.e. theoretically the production could be done in a working week with 6 days to work with 24 hours work a day. The high amount (42) of buffer places makes such a vision realistic. As the speed of the AGV is high enough to say that the time periods which the palettes spend on the AGV are one-two order smaller than the machining times, transportation times are neglected or we can say that they are included into the setup times.

## 4.4 Tests on the CIM plant of the TUB, application of the KB program

For these experiments the pure G2 program was used with the goal of checking as many test runs as possible with a complicated, 4-cell FMS, with simple, but realistic production tasks, to find out the differences between the possible combinations of pre-scheduling and scheduling rules. Several different batch sizes of all parts were checked with several scheduling algorithms available (in the Scheduling Advisor system). We made test runs with a real production task where 4 different parts should be produced and checked on the CIM pilot plant of the Technical University of Budapest (TUB). This flexible manufacturing system consists of 4 different cells (manufacturing, storage and AGV, measurement and assembly). The manufacturing cell contains a CNC lathe and a CNC machining center served by two different robots. There is an AGV moving on given traces to carry one palette with one workpiece at a time. All parts have different process plans (Table 2.). The meaning of the abbreviations are the following: fix-fixing, turn-turning, mill-milling, asm-assembly, meas-measurement, dfix-defixing.

Table 2. Process-plans of the four parts of the TUB system

| part | operations time (min) | timespan (min) |
|---|---|---|
| red | fix(15)-turn(25)-mill(30)-dfix(5) | 75 |
| yellow | fix(15)-mill(18)-asm(30)-dfix(5) | 68 |
| blue | fix(15)-meas(25)-asm(30)-dfix(5) | 75 |
| green | fix(30)-turn(20)-meas(10)-mill(20)-meas(10)-mill(20)-asm(30)-dfix(5) | 145 |

We use the different colors to identify the different parts as it was implemented in the animation of the process. The respective due-date priorities of the part type were given instead of real due dates and they order was the same in all experiments: yellow-green-blue-red. The yellow parts are the most important, the red ones are the least important, if due dates are concerned.

The batch sizes varied from 0 to 30 during the experiments. As the Input Storage of the system has 10 slots the experiments would have been meaningless if the sum of the four batch sizes had not been bigger than 10. We made runs with several combinations of the priorities (3 x 4= 12 runs for each production task.

All the three input sequence algorithms and the following scheduling algorithms were used: LP, SI, LI, ED) with the following 8 sets of batch sizes:

| | | | | | | | | |
|---|---|---|---|---|---|---|---|---|
| yellow | 3 | 4 | 5 | 6 | 7 | 8 | 9 | 10 |
| green | 3 | 4 | 5 | 6 | 7 | 8 | 9 | 10 |
| blue | 3 | 4 | 5 | 6 | 7 | 8 | 9 | 10 |
| red | 3 | 4 | 5 | 6 | 7 | 8 | 9 | 10 |

and then with the same numbers, but one part was always missing. As example we give the table without yellow parts.

| | | | | | | | | |
|---|---|---|---|---|---|---|---|---|
| yellow | 0 | 0 | 0 | 0 | 0 | 0 | 0 | 0 |
| green | 3 | 4 | 5 | 6 | 7 | 8 | 9 | 10 |
| blue | 3 | 4 | 5 | 6 | 7 | 8 | 9 | 10 |
| red | 3 | 4 | 5 | 6 | 7 | 8 | 9 | 10 |

We had one group of experiments with all part types, one with yellow missing, one with green missing, etc. This way we had 8 times 12=96 runs for each group, i. e. altogether we made 5 times 96 = 480 experimental runs, which took several hours. Comparisons are made only within the same groups, i. e. if the final evaluation will be done we expect results for five distinct types of production, what is naturally far from an exhaustive examination. The results are rather interesting, the statistical evaluation will take some more time, as no direct relationships could yet be determined.

Similar results were gotten with the application of the hybrid system on the same FMS (TUB).

## 4.5 Some basic features of the test problems

There are some basic differences between the two problems we made experiments with:

- The layout of the TUB system is really two-dimensional, with complicated trace for the AGV to follow.
- The layout of the GoldStar system is one-dimensional, the machine tools are in one row, and there is a parallel row for the buffers, while the AGV moves on rails between the two parallel rows to easily serve both of them.
- The task of the TUB system is more complicated as not only machining, but measurement and assembly functions are done, too, and the system is cell-based.
- The GoldStar system does only machining with equivalent machine-tools
- There is no substitution possibility for any of the resources in the TUB system, thus there cannot be alternative routings for the workpieces.
- There is an almost infinite substitution possibility in the GoldStar system as all machine tools (and all buffers) are of the same type, thus alternative routings can be essential.
- The TUB system has a 10 slot I/O buffer and each resource has a 2 slot buffer for palette exchange.

- The GoldStar system has a 4 slot I/O buffer and each machine tool has a 1 slot buffer, and the system has 42 further buffer storage places for temporary storage of palettes.

Based on the above differences it is clear that we had completely different goals with the two sets of experiments:

- We had the goal of trying to approach to the theoretical value of 5.57 days, which is a lower limit to the given production task in the GoldStar system.
- The goal of the several test-runs on the TUB system was to figure out whether there are relationships between the different production tasks and different pre-scheduling and scheduling algorithms on a given FMS.

## 4.6 Evaluation of the test-run results

<u>4.6.1 The GoldStar system</u>. For this example we did not deal with the sequence of filling up the 4 slot I/O buffer, but a fixed sequence was used for all test-runs. This was the following: 2xWhite, 2xGreen, 6xBrown, 18xBlue, 20xYellow and 20xRed. This set of 68 workpieces was repeated 5 times. We made runs where the following algorithms (priority rules) were checked: the original embedded scheduling algorithm of SIMAN, and SI, LI, SR, LR, and LP. It is interesting, that the SI and SR rules gave exactly the same results, as well as the application of the LI and LR rules. It was surprising that all runs gave results within the range of 5.6 to 6.1 days, i. e. all were very closed to the theoretical minimum, to the 5.57 days. The differences are so small that no reason to specially evaluate them. But, as we know that the FMS was designed to optimally produce the given parts in the given amounts we can tell that the results are not really surprising. There are two main factors that influence these results: the high speed, and neglected times of the AGV and the high amount (42) of temporary buffers. This way the full load of all machine tools can be reached for all time except of starting and finishing the shift. Similar results were gotten with the application of the KB system on the same FMS (GoldStar).

Now we are in the process of checking whether that FMS is really flexible or not, and we try to make test runs with different production tasks of the same magnitude, as the real one is. The evaluation of the results will take a longer time.

<u>4.6.2 The TUB system.</u> In spite of the very high amount of test-runs we still do not have enough results to have any kind of final conclusions concerning the FMS and the given production tasks on it. Just to give an idea on the measured time values some results were the following (see Table 3.) :

Table 3. Some scheduling results of the TUB system

| Scheduling rules | workpieces: 5,5,5,5 <u>input sequence</u> | workpieces: 10,10,10,10 <u>input sequence</u> |
|---|---|---|

| | MQ | UD | MC | MQ | UD | MC |
|---|---|---|---|---|---|---|
| ED | 624 | 638 | 587 | 1119 | 1158 | 1142 |
| SI | 591 | 653 | 605 | 1143 | 1159 | 1175 |
| LI | 625 | 622 | 604 | 1162 | 1183 | 1207 |
| LP | 619 | 625 | 617 | 1170 | 1191 | 1194 |

Based on the above and several similar tables we can get only rather general conclusions on the given FMS: generally the ED algorithms are better than the LI ones, there are no significant differences between MQ, UD and MC, etc.

## 5 SOME REMARKS ON THE APPLICATION OF SIMAN

Since SIMAN is a language developed directly for FMS simulation it has some very pleasant properties which are missing from G2. For instance, in SIMAN it is very convenient to define a transport-device to follow a zigzag route - it is only necessary to define the route in the animation module. Then the transport-device can follow the route only by telling it the start and final station. On the contrary, in G2 a route following algorithm had to be implemented and it did not reach the quality of the SIMAN animation (Cinema), of course it was not our goal, either. Another feature that would be of great use in G2, too, were the presence of predefined statistics and distribution functions. Statistics functions are used in numerical evaluation of the simulation results and distribution functions are required when we wish to randomly generate numbers with a given distribution.

On the other hand program development and model building are definitively easier in G2 than in SIMAN - even for simulation. The object oriented feature of G2 is one of its great advantages.

## 6 CONCLUSIONS

The implementation of our programs in SIMAN and G2 was fast enough, G2 was excellent to make the different experimental program runs. Data preparation is - however - a tedious and time-consuming activity.

There is a basic problem to be solved: if G2 and SIMAN are used together most data of the production plant, products and of the production have to be duplicated to be there in both systems. This should be avoided by using some kind of automatic data conversion between the object oriented G2 and the traditional SIMAN. This is one of the interesting challenges for our future research and development - if we decide to keep SIMAN/Cinema for simulation and animation. Even if an object-oriented simulation package (e.g. ARENA, the recent version of SIMAN) is used, the problem is not solved automatically.

Based on the test-runs we have to admit that experiments should be designed more carefully, and then more characteristic results can be obtained. In the recent set of tests we tested our programs, and we can conclude that they can be used for checking different possible production schedules of given FMS. On the other hand the test results are strongly FMS and production task related, so we could not yet find general ideas to suggest for scheduling new tasks. Further experiments should be done on different FMS with different production tasks to be able to define quality differences between the scheduling and dispatching algorithms (rules) discussed in this paper. On the other hand, differences between the pure G2 and the hybrid programs should be further analyzed.

## 7 ACKNOWLEDGMENTS

This work was partially supported by the Hungarian OTKA (National Scientific Fund) fund, contract No. T014549.

## 8 REFERENCES

[1] I. Futó: "AI and Simulation on PROLOG Basis", Proc. of the Int. Symp. on AI, Expert Systems and Languages in Modeling and Simulation, Barcelona, Spain, June 2-4., 1987., pp. 117-124.

[2] C.D. Pegden, R.E. Shannon, R.P. Sadowski: "Introduction to Simulation Using SIMAN", McGraw-Hill Inc., New York, 1990.

[3] "ALL-EX Reference Guide", Multilogic Computing Ltd, 1991.

[4] "G2 Reference Manual", G2 Version 2.0, Gensym Corporation, Cambridge, MA, USA, 1990.

[5] Kovács, G., Mezgár, I., Nacsa, J., Kopácsi, S., Gavalcová: "A Knowledge Based and a Hybrid Simulation - Scheduling System", Proceedings of the 1994 Japan - USA Symposium on Flexible Automation, Kobe, Japan, July 11-18, 1994, Vol. 2. pp. 783-790.

[6] Gupta, Y. P. et al: "A Review of Scheduling Rules in Flexible Manufacturing Systems", Int. J. Computer Integrated Manufacturing, 1989, Vol., 2. No. 6, pp. 356-377.

KEYNOTE PAPER

# Inverse Manufacturing: from products to services

# 35

# Inverse Manufacturing: from products to services

*Fumihiko Kimura*
*Department of Precision Machinery Engineering*
*The University of Tokyo*
*Hongo 7-3-1, Bunkyo-ku, Tokyo 113, Japan*
*Tel. +81-3-3812-2111 ext. 6455 Fax +81-3-3812-8849*

Keywords: Inverse manufacturing, life-cycle engineering, maintenance engineering, service engineering, re-use engineering

Manufacturing is an activity for enriching the quality of human life by supplying various kinds of artifacts which provide us with more services than nature. However, with the increase of human activity, as a by-product of manufacturing, our natural environment is being degraded or polluted. These phenomena come mainly from too much consumption of energy and natural resources, and the disposal of waste. The probable effect of manufacturing activity today may be too much for the natural preserving capacity of the earth to absorb. If we can reduce the volume of industrial production, the problem may be solved. But, it is fundamentally difficult to reduce our industrial activity in spite of the natural human desire to attain a high quality of life. Therefore, the feasible solution should seek to keep the quality and volume of industrial activity while reducing the environmental burden of manufacturing. Towards this aim, we propose a concept of inverse manufacturing, where physical substances are re-used as much as possible, while the services or functions of products are maintained appropriately.

To cope with the above issue, it is effective not only to consider the product design and manufacturing preparation concurrently, but also to design the total product life cycle as a whole from product planning, and through product design and manufacturing, to product usage, maintenance and re-use/recycling/disposal. A comprehensive strategy for product maintenance and improvement during product usage should be established, and all life cycle processes should be controlled. With such an approach, re-use/cycling activities can be rationalized. The whole product life cycle can be made visible and controllable. We call this approach Inverse

Computer Applications in Production and Engineering. F. Plonka and G. Olling (Eds.)

Manufacturing by stressing the controllability of re-use/recycling processes, where close cycles of manufacturing activity are preplanned and controlled. Inverse manufacturing is practically implemented today in maintenance-centered products such as aircrafts or heavy industrial machinery. This concept can be extended into commodity products, such as household appliances or personal computers, etc.

Inverse manufacturing can be the basis not only for the change of product life cycle into a closed cycle, but also for an innovative paradigm shift of industrial structure. Traditionally, manufacturing companies supply physical products to fulfil customer's demands. Once physical products are in customer's hands, they are used, and finally they are disposed. But, the real demands of customers are not to possess physical products, but to receive appropriate services from products. In this sense, the new role of the manufacturing industry can be defined as a supplying industry, where manufacturing companies maintain the total product operating environment, and customers only buy services in such an environment. This type of service environment is common in some industry areas, for example, in telephone and communication. Copy machines are another example. People rarely buy copy machines, but they just lease machines and pay for services. However, due to several technical, social, economical and political reasons, this new style of manufacturing is not totally popular for automobiles or electronic appliances. If this style is accepted by society, the environmental issues concerning manufacturing will be greatly reduced, because the environmental burden can be controlled explicitly and independently with the services for customers. Thus we re-define the manufacturing industry as a service industry.

It is now almost obvious that the service industry concept based on inverse manufacturing will be a definite solution for our environmental problems caused by manufacturing. In addition to social, economical and political problems, there are many technical problems, such as, product life cycle modeling and management, deterioration modeling, re-use/recycling processes, monitoring of operations etc. Further research is desired for such problems.

# 36
# Advances in Measurement systems integration

*J. Lenner.*
*Rockwell Automation*
*1 Allen-Bradley Drive*
*Mayfield Heights, Ohio 44124*
*Ph. 216-646-5114, Fax. 216-646-5116*
*Email:Joseph.Lenner@ab.com*

*F.E. Plonka, Ph.D.*
*Wayne State University*
*Dept. of Industrial & Manufacturing Engineering*
*4815 Fourth Street*
*Detroit, MI 48202*
*Ph. 313-577-4846*
*Fax. 313-577-8833*
*Email:fplonka@mie.eng.wayne.edu*

*D. Carnahan, P.E.*
*Rockwell Automation*
*1 Allen-Bradley Drive*
*Mayfield Heights, Ohio 44124*
*Ph. 216-646-5106, Fax. 216-646-5116*
*Email: Dan.Carnahan@ab.com*

*R. Jaikumar, CMfgT.*
*Wayne State University*
*Dept. of Industrial & Manufacturing Engineering*
*4815 Fourth Street*
*Detroit, MI 48202*
*Ph. 313-577-3821*
*Fax. 313-577-8833*
*Email: rkj1@roogna.eng.wayne.edu*

**Abstract**

Two major goals of the Auto Body Consortium(ABC) are to increase precision of automobile bodies and improve the agility of automotive manufacturing plants. To address the agility issues, ABC has targeted specific processes in automotive manufacturing to facilitate the information integration and exchange among manufacturing entities. These processes, in conjunction with new technology, provide overall quality improvement in the automotive assembly, while reducing the amount of time to develop a new product.

The purpose of this paper is to outline processes for improvement in agility using emerging methods and standards. This paper will focus on the identification of critical parameters and the communication of these parameters throughout the design and manufacturing processes. Key standards will be identified for use and extension.

**Keywords**

Information Integration, Agile Manufacturing, Auto Body Consortium, Computer Aided Design, Measurement Systems, Standard for the Exchange of Product Model Data (STEP).

Computer Applications in Production and Engineering. F. Plonka and G. Olling (Eds.)

## 1. INTRODUCTION

As companies are adopting strategies to reduce cycle time with leaner organizations, collaborative projects and information integration are frequently mentioned as methods for improving manufacturing productivity and agility. However, many times the communications among organizational functions are impeded by a lack of common tools and methodologies used to identify and communicate the important product features. This leads to a lack of understanding of the items and features that are critical to the overall manufacturing process.
One of the major goals of the Auto Body Consortium (ABC)[1] is to increase the precision of automobile bodies and improve the agility of automotive manufacturing plants. To address these issues, the ABC has targeted specific processes in automotive manufacturing to facilitate information integration exchange among manufacturing entities. These processes, in conjunction with new technology, provide overall quality improvement in automobile body assembly, while reducing the amount of time to develop a new product.
The Standard for the Exchange of Product Model Data (STEP), ISO 10303[2], was developed to enable effective data exchange between commercial and proprietary product and process design systems. To achieve this communication the standard permits the definition of data models, creation of a database and linkages to programming languages. This paper proposes to use this capability to integrate design and measurement systems. The opportunity exists to enhance communication between individuals performing product design, process design and verification activities. A further opportunity exists to permit intelligent communication between application languages and programmable devices. By extending STEP in this direction, people to people communications among all levels of the industry and the capture of knowledge will be enhanced.

## 2. MEASUREMENT SYSTEMS ACTIVITY MODEL

The overall process for transfer of component design information to the downstream processes for designing and constructing dies, assembly fixtures, part handling equipment, measurement fixtures and measurement procedures requires many different information models. For instance, the sub-assembly instructions for joining of components parts and the "checking" or measurement instructions for critical dimensions in the sub-assemblies, involves the transfer of design information among many different types of design and manufacturing systems. To set the context of the information needs for the various systems, an "activity model", shown in figure 1, is used to describe the design, manufacturing and measurement operations that are required in each functional area.

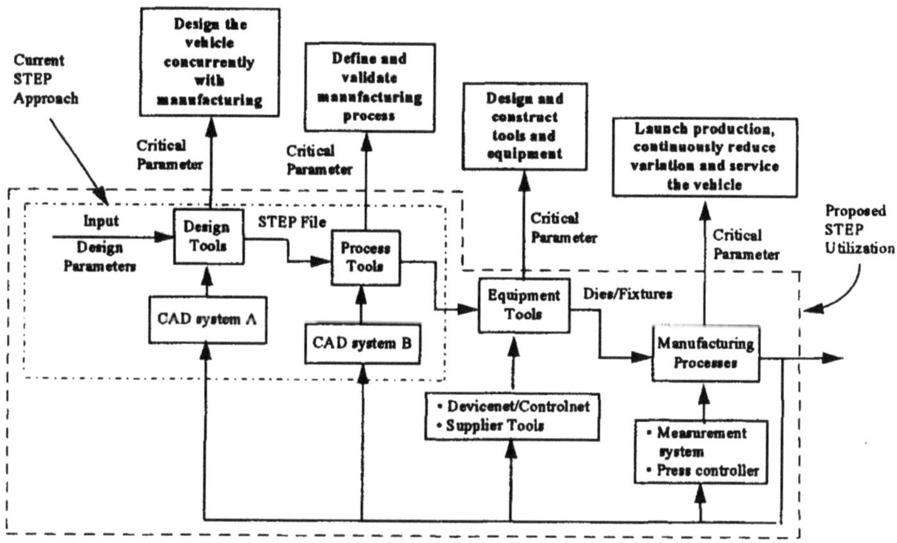


**Figure 1** Activity Model

At each stage, the designers will need to identify critical parameters for fabrication and verification. These may be end customer features, assembly features or individual part tooling features. The use of labels in addition to Geometric Dimensioning and Tolerancing (GD & T) for each critical feature will permit all of the disciplines involved in the processes to effectively interact by supporting a continuity of understanding. These "feature labels" are used to identify critical parameters both for the upstream and the downstream systems and they enable both on-line and off-line measurements to be integrated and communicated to all parties.

In the example shown in Figure 2, a sheet metal assembly is made by joining two sheet metal stamping parts. The product designer has identified the overall width as one of the critical dimensions for assembly to be made from two pieces. The assembly tooling engineers have specified holes and slots to accommodate pins for joining in subsequent assembly operations. The same holes are used to locate the assembly for measurement purposes and identify the relationships between the form and the holes as critical. The die engineers create the form in the first die operation and locate features such as flanges and holes relative to the form.

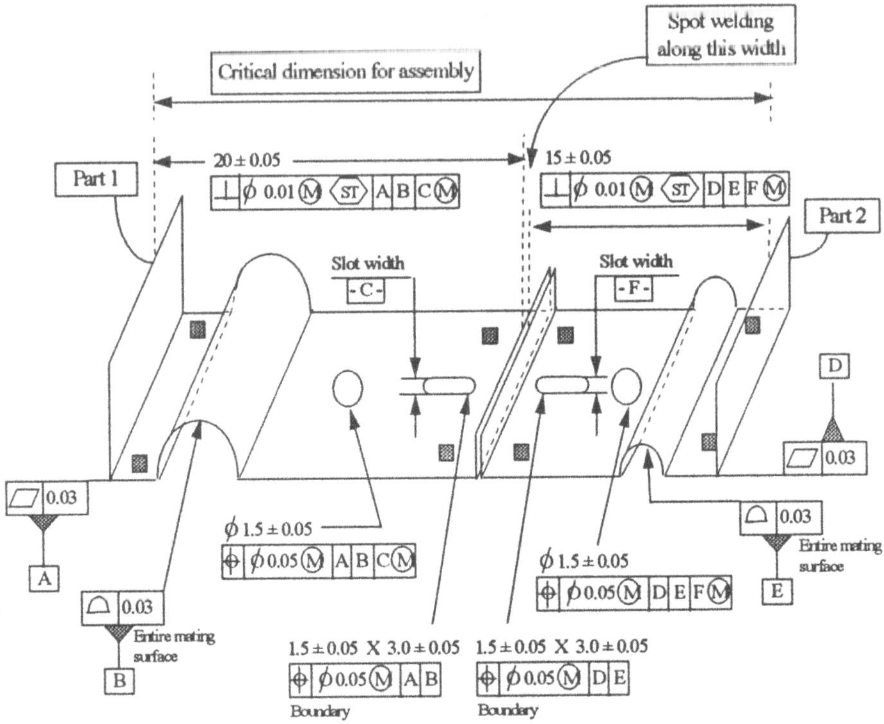


**Figure 2** Example of sheet metal stamping and joining operation

The measurement systems that the quality groups will use for the verification at the different process steps must have knowledge of these critical dimensions and their relationships throughout the various process stages. If there is an easily identifiable label associated with each critical feature contained in the drawing, the measurement system will be simplified, minimize unnecessary measurements and contribute to producing quality parts.

The identification of the critical features will also allow the different disciplines to consider the impact that their designs will have on the product. As the product moves through production the consistent identification will enhance the ability of the process engineers to communicate problems, and improvement suggestions effectively to the upstream design personal.

In today's systems there is a gap in our ability to identify and transfer this data to different systems. There are standards which aid in the transfer of the configuration and graphical information, but these standards will need to be enhanced to transfer the identification of critical features.

# 3. CURRENT SYSTEM FOR MEASUREMENTS SYSTEM INFORMATION INTEGRATION

Many tools for product design today provide the capability to model parts in a 3-D rendering which enables enhanced capabilities for integration of the "component parts" into the total assembly. As these component parts are integrated into a sub-assembly, the product designer can add additional detail to the parts to specify critical dimensions that must be met in the sub-assembly. These critical dimensions can be utilized to develop a "dimensional measurement" strategy to be used by the downstream measurement systems.

These systems are highly dependent upon manual generation of "paper-based" documentation to define the critical measurements to be made on parts and sub-assemblies. The documentation is of the form of instructions and sequences of steps to perform the measurements. If new or different measurements are required, "new" instructions need to be developed and communicated.

As the first pilot components and assemblies are built, certain manufacturing considerations may impact the component and assembly design. The ability to relate those manufacturing considerations back to the component or sub-assembly model require annotated changes to be included in the elemental design of the part.

## 3.1 Impediments to information integration

Improving the agility of a manufacturing organization many times requires significant changes in the process as well as the tools used in the process. Technology has enabled many improvements in the tools used in the manufacturing processes. Technology has also enabled more information about local processes to be gathered, stored, and retrieved. However, if this information cannot be clearly shared across functional areas, then only local improvements can be made.

Many of the "information sharing" problems have been addressed by "concurrent" engineering tools[ii]. This has enabled some of the problems associated with the "waterfall" model of product development to be solved. However, many of these tools simply "import" information from an "upstream" tool into a unique proprietary environment. This requires as many information "import" formats as there are tools. Conversely, the tool typically exports information in only one format unique to that tool environment. Additional problems that may be encountered are:

- **Data transformation issues** - When measurement systems are used, differences in data formats require a specific re-formatting process. System accuracy issues may impact the translation process.
- **Measurement systems integration** - Measurement systems are primarily used for local process improvements. When measurement systems are used to feed information concerning the manufacturing process to upstream design functions, the information is not resilient;

that is, changes in measurement steps and the number of measurements require setting up new procedures.

- **Communication of measurement system information** - Because of the need to support a distributed and changing supplier base, the communication of new measurement system requirements requires a configuration system to make it available to the "downstream" user measurement systems.

## 4. EMERGING SYSTEMS IN INFORMATION SHARING AMONG CAD VENDORS

Currently in the CAD tool environment, the above problems has been addressed for multiple users of CAD tools, shown in figure 3, in different design environments such as mechanical, electrical, electronic, etc. by developing standards which enable the "sharing" of information in a common way. An emerging standard, STEP provides a methodology for describing common aspects of a product, which are specific to a particular design discipline[iii].
STEP is an international standard for the computer-interpretable representation and exchange of product information. The objective of this International Standard is to provide a mechanism that is capable of describing product data throughout the life of a product, independent of any particular computer system.

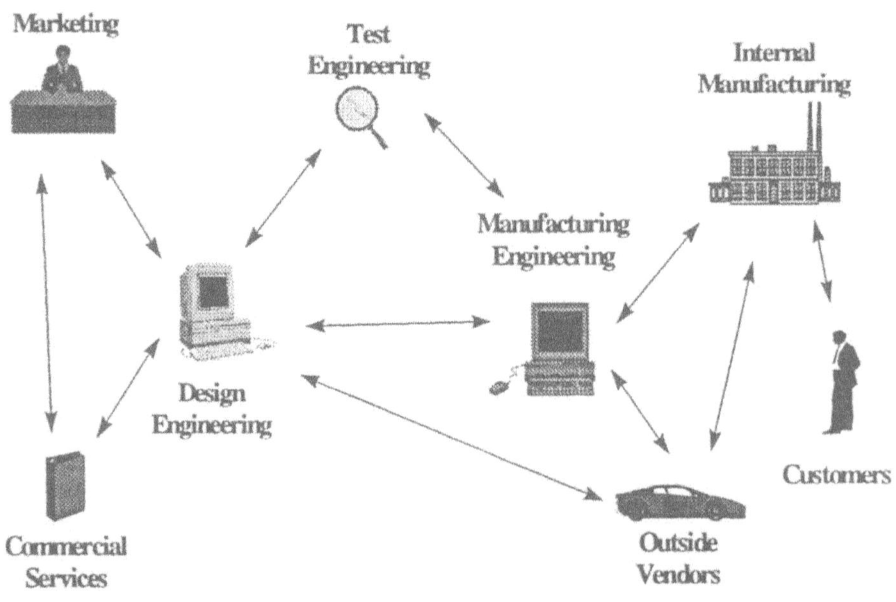


**Figure 3** Information sharing among CAD users

STEP is composed of many parts as shown in figure 4. At the core of the standard are the Integrated Resources (parts 40-199, ISO 10303-40 through 199). The

Integrated Resources define the elements that would be common in many places such as shapes, product structure and geometric dimensioning and tolerancing.
The common language used in all parts of the standard is EXPRESS (part 11). The EXPRESS language specifies data representations in both graphical and textual forms. EXPRESS is a data definition language and as such is not directly executable, but parsers and bindings are available for several of the most commonly used application languages.
The Application Protocols (parts 200-1999) are the parts of the standard that put the basics in the context of the working engineer. The Applications Protocol contains several parts, Scope, Application Resource Model(ARM), Application Integrated Model(AIM), Conformance and Validation, and User Documentation. The scope defines the field of application and bounds the problem. The ARM defines the information requirements in terms an engineer in the specific field would understand. The AIM translates the ARM into EXPRESS for application software developers. The Conformance and Validation sections specify test suites and conformance classes that will be used to compare different applications and implementations by the prospective end users.

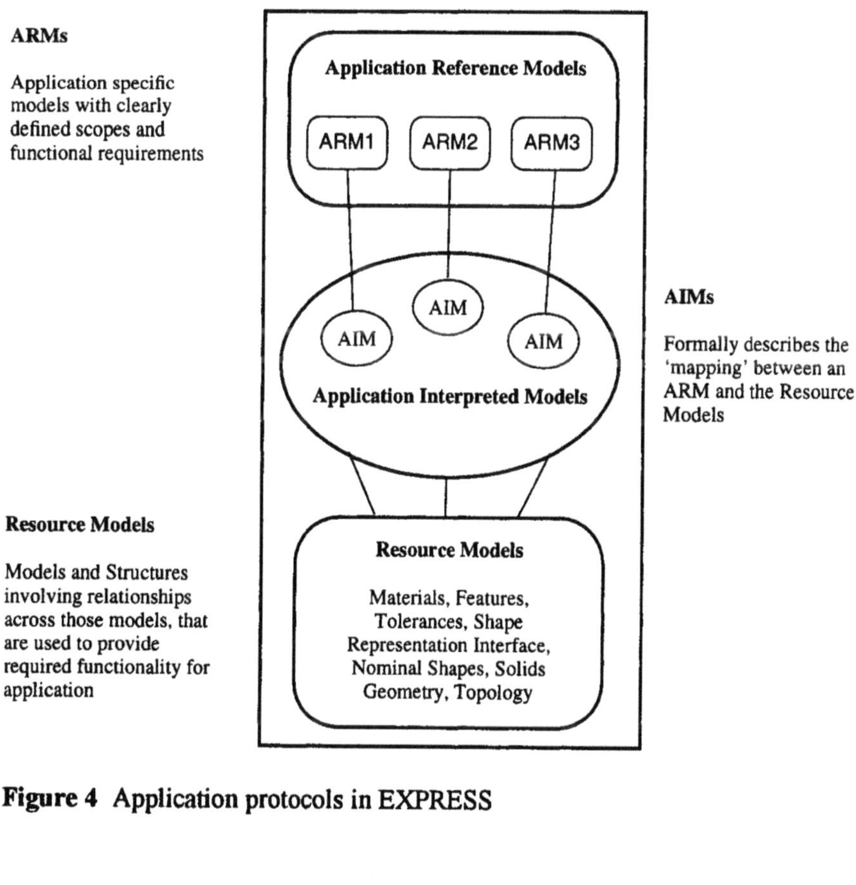


**Figure 4** Application protocols in EXPRESS

The actual exchange mechanisms that are in place at this time are for a flat physical file (ISO 10303 part 21) and an Application Programming Interface (API) to databases. The STEP Data Access Interface (SDAI) (SDAI-Part 22) also includes bindings for programming languages such as C, C++ and Common Object Request Broker Architecture (CORBA) interface description languages (idl's).

While the first versions or implementation of the standard were primarily designed to accommodate exchanges between different CAD vendors of the same discipline(such as mechanical), the methodology also provides the mechanism to define information exchange to different disciplines (such as electrical, electronic, pneumatic, etc.).

## 5. CURRENT EMERGING SYSTEMS FOR MEASUREMENTS SYSTEM INFORMATION INTEGRATION

New systems are emerging to couple the measurement system information to provide access to the design systems. The accuracy information is maintained by keeping the information in a common software environment, as shown in figure 5, or "homogeneous-monolithic" system, or a "math-based" model of the information. Issues with data translation and transformation are minimized because, the "syntax" (the format) and the "semantics" (the meaning) of information are based upon the only one "user interface" in the system.

This common view of the process information enables the upstream/ downstream flow of information to be handled quite efficiently. However, as new tool and/or features are added to the system, the "homogeneous" system must define all of the information that is necessary to describe the product. This creates a tremendous burden for the developers of the "monolithic system" user interface tool environment, because the "user interface" for the design tools need to continually adapt as new requirements are identified.

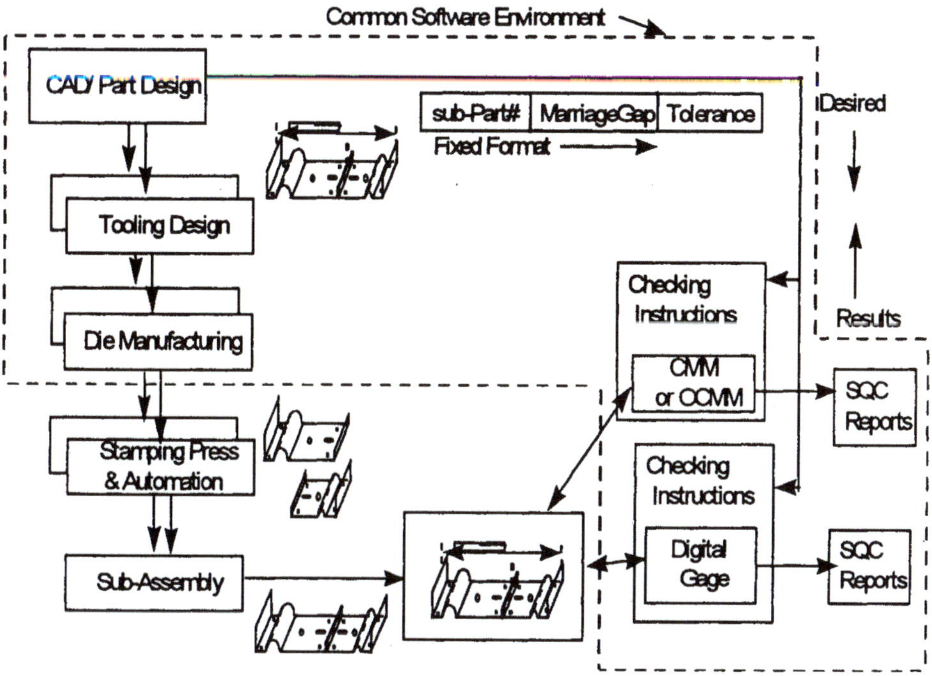


**Figure 5** Current emerging systems

## 6. PROPOSED SYSTEM FOR MEASUREMENTS SYSTEM INFORMATION INTEGRATION

This proposal builds upon this concept by first describing standard conventions and guidelines to be used from a particular discipline (such as mechanical design), to the measurement system environment. Inclusion of the information to describe a particular "critical" dimension on a part enables the "downstream" process to "read" the desired information for measurement (see Figure 6 ).

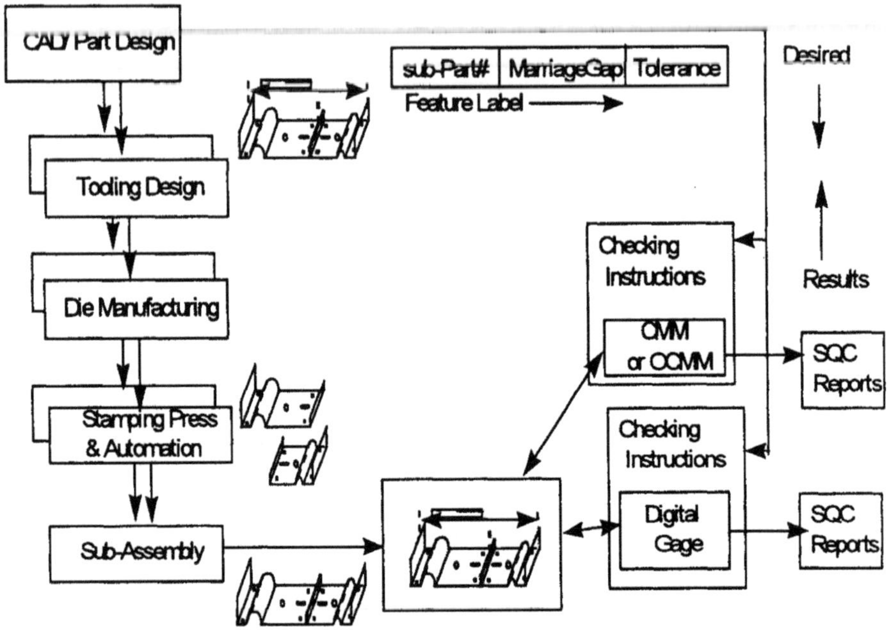


**Figure 6** Proposed systems

The proposed system builds upon much of the work completed in the standards and methodologies for the exchange of product information, STEP. This proposal suggest methods for development of guidelines and conventions for the use of those standards to enable the downstream activities to "capture" information from the "upstream" design processes, and to add value to this information by validation of "real measurement" information.

One way that critical features could be identified using STEP is by adding the appropriate identifiers to the entities identifying shape and relationship. Figure 7[iv], shows one possible way of doing this. The identifiers for "aspect_criticality" and "aspect_relationship_criticality" could be added to the STEP AP-203 Data model as shown. This will allow features and spatial relationships to be identified as critical.

```
ENTITY shape_aspect
	name : label;
	description : text;
	of_shape : product_definition_shape;
	product_definitional : LOGICAL;
	aspect_criticality : LOGICAL;
END_ENTITY

ENTITY shape_aspect_relationship
	name : label;
	description : text;
	aspect_relationship_criticality : LOGICAL;
	related_shape_aspect	: shape_aspect;
	relating_shape_aspect	: shape_aspect;
END_ENTITY
```

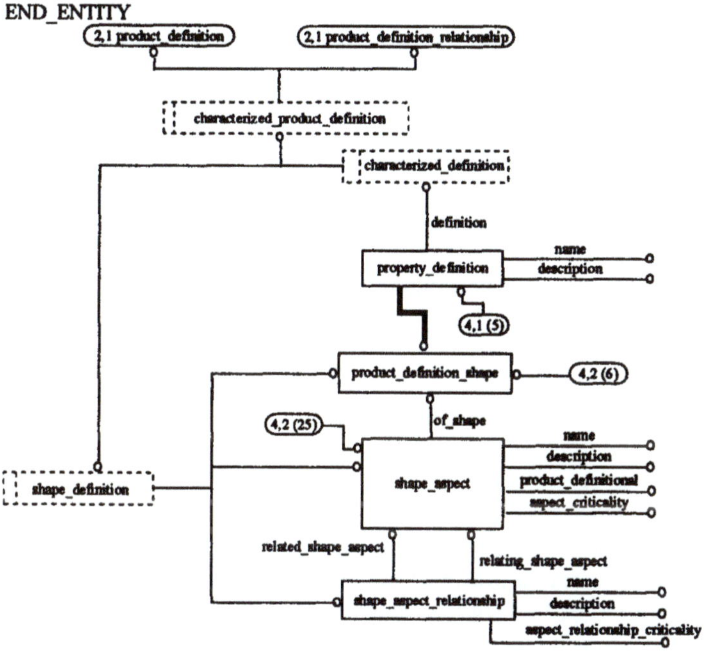


**Figure 7** Fragment of AP-203 Data Model

The ideal place for the identification of critical features to occur is in the Integrated Resources. The inclusion of this identification in the integrated Resources would allow for the propagation of the identification mechanism throughout the appropriate Application Protocols (AP). This inclusion would also facilitate interpretation of differing Mechanical AP's, such as Associative Drafting, 3-D Configuration Controlled Design and a possible future AP for measurement systems.

The development of the 'measurement process" or "instructions" are then developed independently of the "design process." Changes to the design can then be "earmarked" for the measurement system (to denote needed changes to the instructions). While the sequence of instructions for measurement of the part are not important to the designer, the resultant information may provide information to the manufacturing process engineer in terms of process capability, and information to the Statistical Quality Control (SQC) tools.

## 7. SUMMARY

Information Integration from both upstream/ downstream design and manufacturing activities will become more complex as the capabilities of the tools at each stage of the process improve. The key to controlling and enhancing this process is the utilization of information standards. The clear definitions of the data in the STEP standards will allow information to be shared and clearly understood by both upstream and downstream systems. The sharing and integration of this data eliminates redundant entry of data, speeds the process, increase capability and increases quality.

The use of standard methodologies enables technology improvements to occur at each stage of the design and manufacturing process without requiring all improvements to take place at once. As each process tool improves, the process improvements can be made incrementally. New design and analysis functions can be added without disruption to the manufacturing process provided that the tool supports the appropriate interfaces.

Much as the GD & T standards have enhanced the ability of the designers to communicate the design information clearly and easily, information standards will continue to facilitate the communications.

The continued enhancement and use of these standards in design and manufacturing tools will offer manufacturers several advantages.

- Common identification of critical features will minimize tooling and measurement errors and expedite the problem solving process when production problems occur.
- Manufacturers will be able to draw from a wider supplier base due to increased information transmission capabilities.
- Manufacturers will be able to choose the best tool at the time, not the best tool that can accept the existing format.

By first adding the ability to identify the critical relationships in the STEP data model the ground work is being laid for the future development of a STEP Application Protocol (AP) for Measurement Systems. The development of a Measurement Systems AP will allow the seamless information integration with of the manufacturing systems, quality systems, product design systems and tooling systems. This level of integration will allow manufactures to realize significant performance and quality improvements while maintaining or decreasing overall costs.

## 8. REFERENCES

[i] NIST/ATP Near Zero Stamping, 7-95

[ii] Manufacturing System, July 1996

[iii] PDES Presentation, 1993

[4] ISO 10303-203, Configuration Controlled 3-D Designs of Mechanical Parts and Assemblies

BIOGRAPHY

Francis E. Plonka

Frank is a professor in the department of Industrial and Manufacturing Engineering at Wayne State University in Detroit, MI. He presently teaches courses in Operations Management, Manufacturing Information Systems and Senior Design Projects. His research interests include the application of computer methods to designing processes, constructing tooling and running manufacturing operations.

Prior to joining the faculty in September 1991, he was Manager, Technical Systems Development on the Advanced Manufacturing Operations Staff of the Chrysler Corporation. In this capacity he was responsible for integrating computers for design, machining, process planning, simulation and factory monitoring into manufacturing operations and training associates in their use.

Raja Jaikumar

Raja is a graduate research assistant in the department of Industrial and Manufacturing Engineering at Wayne State University in Detroit, MI. He is pursuing his Master of Science degree in Manufacturing Engineering with a specialization in Metal Forming and Stamping process engineering. He has worked in the Near Zero Stamping Project of the Auto Body Consortium, Inc., undertaking research projects involving on-line and off-line measurement strategies.

# 37

# Sensor-Fusion methodology for reducing product quality variation

*J. Mou*
*Department of I&MSE*
*Arizona State University*
*Tempe, AZ 85287*

*S. D. Jones*
*R. J. Furness*
*Manufacturing Systems Department*
*Ford Scientific Research Laboratory*
*Dearborn, MI 48121*

**Abstract**

As competitive pressures demand higher levels of productivity and product quality, the accuracy and reliability of products remains important but becomes increasingly more difficult to achieve. The dimensional inaccuracy of any manufactured part is a combined effect of several degradation factors including process related errors, machine related errors, fixturing related errors, material property variation, and dimensional variation of the incoming parts or raw material. The inspection processes have become an integral part of the manufacturing processes and form the metrology anchor to determine the quality of manufactured products and to certify the performance of manufacturing processes. However, there still remains a lack of a comprehensive methodology, to identify and assess the contribution of those factors that cause variation in product quality, based solely on inspection data.

The objective of this study is to advance the technology, precision, and functionality of machining centers by developing a sensor-fusion methodology that integrates pre-process, on-machine, and post-process measurement and analysis technology to cost-effectively enhance the accuracy and precision of both manufacturing and inspection processes. The primary effort is directed at the development of a sensor fusion methodology that captures the part error signature. Non-traditional sensory data analysis algorithms will also be developed to identify

Computer Applications in Production and Engineering. F. Plonka and G. Olling (Eds.)

the contribution of each degradation factor, based solely on the error signature. Finally, an adaptive machining process control algorithms will be derived to reduce product quality variation.

**Keywords**
Sensor-fusion, Error modeling, Error correction, Product variation reduction.

# 1 INTRODUCTION

A significant portion of the cost in small batch manufacturing results from verifying workpiece form, finish, and dimensions, and then scrapping or reworking rejected parts. Historically, inspection data was used to determine whether or not a manufactured part met specifications. If it did not, it was reworked or rejected. Recently, significant progress has been made in determining the quality of manufacturing products and certifying the performance of manufacturing process (ANSI, 1985, 1990, 1992, 1994). Inspection procedures are commonly used to identify the resultant variation in product quality. Now inspection devices like coordinate measuring machines (CMMs) can provide data about how far a part is in or out of tolerance. This data is now being used to make manual adjustments to machining offsets and process parameters.

Ideally, the same inspection data should also be used for controlling and reducing the process variation. In reality, it is a very difficult task due to the lack of methodology that leads to the determination of the actual contribution of each degradation factor in affecting the product quality variation. In anticipation of the future of manufacturing technology, when machine tools are equipped with open-architecture controls and advanced sensing technology, the information from these sensors must be processed and used to make adjustments at the machine level. Therefore, there is a critical need to develop such methodology to identify the contribution of each degradation factor by innovatively interpreting the inspection results. In order for this vision to be realized, it is necessary to develop analytical models between dimensional measurement sensor data and the factors that result in increased process variations. These models do not yet exist, but can be developed from in-depth analysis encompassing advances in machine tool metrology, dimensional metrology, and process control.

To achieve this goal, sensor-fusion technology and non-traditional inspection analysis techniques are needed to identify the signature and contribution of various factors that cause variation of product quality in dimension [Swyt, 1992], form (Menq, et. al., 1990), surface finish (Shin, et. al., 1995), and sub-surface material properties (Nguyen, et. al., 1995). Meanwhile, part features produced by different machines with specific manufacturing processes will have different signatures. Therefore, there is a need to develop algorithms to assist the process of selecting the proper sensors, sampling procedures, and the sampling size for each feature (Woo & Liang, 1993; Lee & Mou, 1996). To ensure the quality and reliability of inspection process, measurement uncertainty and error needs to be addressed for all data acquisition activities (Hocken, 1995).

The efforts of this study are to develop a sensor-fusion methodology that integrates the aforementioned technologies to capture the signature of part quality variation. Innovative sensory data analysis algorithms also need to be developed to identify the contribution of each degradation factor, solely based on its individual error signature. Further, adaptive machining process control algorithms need to be derived to reduce product quality variation. The result could significantly advance the accuracy and functionality of automated machinery. This study is trying to provide a means for integrating more sensing and analyzing capabilities at the machine level, and to generate methods for deriving information describing machine, process, and fixturing related errors from various sensor-fusion techniques. From gauging the part where it is machined, to post-process fixture gauging that can be tied into on-machine gauging to audit the machine, the methodology developed under this study could reduce cost and dramatically improve manufacturing performance.

A major goal is to make high quality parts with the least amount of scrap. Other objectives of this project are to integrate data acquisition and evaluation functions with machining functions, provide on-line quality analysis and feedback, and develop methods of using sensor data to perform real-time adaptive sensor feedback process controls to reduce overall product variations. Since more accurate and on-time product monitoring and control will be achieved, the methodology will improve part-to-part repeatability, increase flexibility, reduce cycle time, and increase the accuracy of the machined features. The resulting technology advancement and implementation will benefit industry in reducing production costs and increasing competitiveness.

Given that the research is successfully executed, the cause and effect relationship of product and process variation resulting from machine related errors, process related errors, and fixturing related errors can be identified and then minimized. Meanwhile, the results of developing non-traditional measurement procedures and sampling strategies will advance the technology in extracting information that truly represents the actual dimensions and the form of measured features. Therefore, the accuracy and reliability of both manufacturing and inspection processes can be improved dramatically. The developed methodology that integrates sensor-fusion technologies could significantly facilitate the implementation of the error modeling and correction techniques in performance monitoring and tracking for manufacturing processes. The developed algorithms can then be implemented on a PC-based open-architecture controller (Wright, et. al., 1996) to receive information from various sensors, assess the status of the process, determine the proper action, and deliver the command to actuators for task execution. This will enhance a CNC machine's capability to produce workpieces within the imposed dimension tolerances.

This project has proceeded in several dimensions in parallel. In the following sections, only selected major elements are discussed in detail.

## 2 METHODOLOGY

Multi-axis machines are typically composed of a sequence of elements or links connected by joints, providing either rotational or translational motion. By means of a kinematic analysis, each link and joint can be modeled as a link transformation matrix and a joint constraint matrix, respectively. There are two types of kinematic relationship between two adjacent components: stationary transformation and motion transformation. Machine errors result from both imperfect stationary configuration and imperfect motion of those components. The spatial displacement error of the cutting tool or end effector is affected by the translational and rotational errors in each individual axis.

A kinematics-based analytical model is derived to describe the degradation effect of machine error (i.e., spindle growth, linear displacement error, straightness error, etc.) on a part's dimensional and form accuracy. A generic model generator has been developed to enable analysts to systematically formulate an appropriate error model that establishes the relationship between the component errors and the observed volumetric errors for various machine configurations. An explicit, parametrically represented generic function describing the machine error is therefore obtained. For error compensation, the corrective matrix and modified input command is also derived using this generic function. The generic model generator is based upon the concepts of functional variation, rigid body kinematics, and homogeneous transformation.

To include the physical imperfections of a multi-axis machine, the link transformation matrix, $L_i$, is used to describe the relative position of two coordinate systems on an inaccurate link (Mou & Liu, 1992). The joint constraint matrix, $J_i$, is used to describe the relative motion of two coordinate systems along an imperfect prismatic or revolute joint. A homogeneous transformation matrix, $A_i$, for an inaccurate positioning element is then expressed as $A_i = L_i * J_i$. Given any multi-axis machine with an arbitrary combination of prismatic and revolute joints, this homogeneous transformation matrix is used to build a mathematical model describing the resultant positioning errors as follows:

$$[\bar{e}_w] = [T - I][\bar{r}_{ideal}] = \left[\left[\prod_{i=1}^{n}[A_i]\right] - [I]\right][\bar{r}_{ideal}] \quad (1)$$

The input to the error model includes the nominal tool positions, temperature profile of the machine structure, and machine configuration constants. The output of the error model is the predicted machine tool error within the designated workspace.

The major advantage of this modeling approach is that a kinematics based model provides a systematic way to model, estimate, and compensate for the positioning error of a multi-axis machine. By using the inverse kinematics technique, the contribution of each error component in each axis can be systematically determined. The information is subsequently used to calculate the error compensation signal for each axis to correct machine error. For machine error correction, the relationship between the error compensation signal and the corrected position vector of the tool tip is expressed as

$$[\bar{r}_{compensated}] = [T][\bar{r}_{tool} + \bar{e}_c] \tag{2}$$

Rearranging the matrices, the error compensation signal is then obtained as

$$[\bar{e}_c] = [T^{-1} - I][\bar{r}_{tool}] \tag{3}$$

Commercially available software (for example, MAPLE or MATHEMATICA) with symbolic manipulation functions are used in developing the proposed generic model generator. Boolean algebra are used to eliminate the cross over terms in stepwise fashion and, thus, to reduce the complexity involved in the derivation of the model. A window based graphical interface is currently been developed to help the analysts graphically formulate the manipulating sequence of transformation matrices for various machine configurations. Once the sequence for matrix manipulation is determined, the developed generic function can then automatically generate the corresponding resultant transformation matrices for both machine error modeling and compensation.

To fully utilize the derived generic model for machining system performance assessment, the appropriate sensors and sampling techniques for capturing the signature of various degradation factors need to be determined. In this project, touch-trigger probes are used in on-machine gauging and post-process inspection to determine the dimensional accuracy of manufactured parts. Analog scanning probes are used in on-machine gauging and post-process inspection to determine the form accuracy of manufactured parts. In a second phase of this project, a video probe will be used to inspect surface texture, burr formation, chip breaking, and tool wear. The inspection data collected from different sensors not only provide information on part quality variation but also on machine performance variation. For example, by comparing the data obtained from on-machine measurement and post-process inspection, the variation in machine accuracy at various thermal states can also be captured. The degradation effect of process related errors (i.e., tool deflection, tool wear, cutting force related workpiece deformation, chatter, etc.) on a part's dimensional accuracy, form accuracy, surface texture, and surface finishing can also be characterized.

For any monitoring or inspection activity, sampling methods used in data collection will affect the precision of the measurement results. Because the analysis model and algorithms consider only those data points that are sampled, any valuable information represented by the unsampled points will be overlooked. Therefore, sampling strategies should be carefully considered during the data collection. From a statistical viewpoint, sampling methods and their designs are the keys to permit valid inferences about any inspection result. Each set of measured data contains a certain amount of information about the inspected object. The quantity of information obtained in the sample depends on the number of data points sampled and on the amount of variation in the data.

Since different features produced by a particular type of machine or machining process will have different signatures, algorithms need to be developed to assist the process of selecting the proper sampling strategy and the sampling size for various features. A feature-based sampling strategy (Lee & Mou, 1996), based on the Hammersley sequence (Woo & Liang, 1993) and the stratified sampling method, is implemented to locate sampling points on different geometric features. The design of the sampling strategies and the sample size determine the quantity of information in the sample pertinent to a population parameter, provided that accurate measurements are obtained on each sampled element. Usually, the best design for a given problem is the one that provides the necessary precision in terms of a bound on the error of estimation for a minimum cost. Statistical methods are used to determine the proper sampling rate. Meanwhile, the number of specified measuring points and its relation to time, cost, and accuracy is currently been investigated.

For all data collection activities, measurement uncertainty needs to be understood and minimized. Since various sensors will be used in this sensor-fusion based projects, the measurement uncertainty assessment becomes more complex especially when machine errors are present. Case studies are conducted to investigate the effect of both individual and confounded measurement uncertainties resulting from sensors and measurement procedures. For example, in most inspection operations using a CMM, the data acquisition process is conducted while controlling each axis either individually or simultaneously. Nevertheless, for all operation modes, the errors in each axis will affect the measurement accuracy. The degradation effect will vary as a function of the characteristics of the machine error and the geometric feature of the measured artifact. As shown in Figure 1, when a designated nominal point $N = (x_N, y_N)$ on the workpiece is measured, the measuring process can be divided into two stages. In the first stage, the probe is quickly moved to a temporary point $N_I = (x_{NI}, y_{NI})$ which is a nominal point relative to $N$. Usually, for every measuring machine, the distance between $N$ and $N_I$ is the default or user selected approach distance $d$. From point $N_I$, the probe is then moved slowly toward the designated measurement point $N$ in the second stage to assure an accurate measurement.

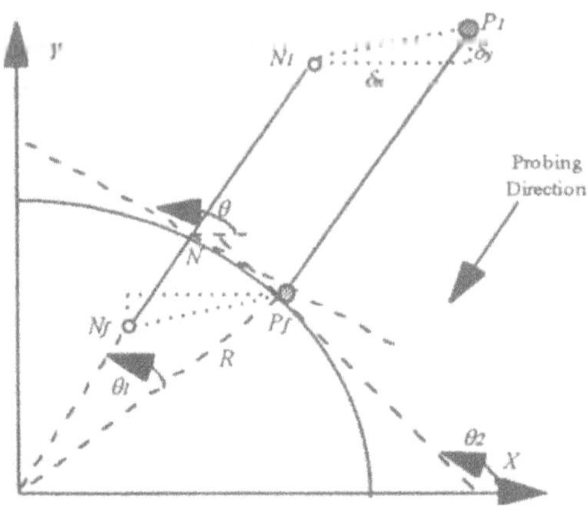


**Figure 1** Potential error in measuring a circular feature along the normal direction.

If there are machine errors ($\delta_x$ and $\delta_y$) in both x-axis and y-axis, the probe may not be exactly located at the point $N_1$, but will be located at $P_1$ instead. Then, the probe will be moved along the designated approach direction that is usually parallel to x-axis, y-axis, or normal to the feature surface until a contact occurs. However, due to machine related error, the machine controller cannot detect the error and may command the probe to move along a path slightly different from the designated path. The offset of the new path is a function of machine errors. Depending on the relative measurement direction and geometric characteristics of the measured feature, the inspection data will be contaminated by different types of confounded uncertainties. For example, when the probe finally contacts the measured feature at point $P_f$, the machine controller may interpret the point $P_f$ as point $N_f$ based on the distance the probe traveled. Therefore, the uncertainties result from the machine errors and the geometry characteristics of the measured feature, as well as the dimensional imperfection of the measured feature.

Generic analytical models and computational algorithms are derived to assess the confounded effect of various types of uncertainties occurring in common measurement procedures. To improve the effectiveness of machine performance calibration and on-machine inspection process, analytical methods are derived to assess the confounded effect of machine errors, geometric characteristics of measured features, and dimensional imperfection of measured features. The development of the analytical models and computational algorithms is carried out in several sequential steps. In the first step, the uncertainty effect of an imperfect measuring device is considered while assuming the measured features have perfect dimensions and forms. Therefore, the confound effect is a joint product of the equipment imperfection and geometric characteristics of the measured features. In the second step, the uncertainty effect of an imperfect measuring device, the geometric characteristics, and dimensional imperfection of the measured features are considered.

After analytical models are derived for various uncertainty effects, new measurement methods and algorithms for uncertainty decoupling and reduction need to be developed. The effectiveness and the limitation of the derived uncertainty models, the uncertainty decoupling and reduction algorithms need to be investigated. Simulation and experimental analysis are then conducted to validate the effectiveness of the derived method (Lee, et. al., 1997a, b).

Since the dimensions and the form of each manufactured feature always differ from the nominal dimensions and the perfect form, most existing fitting algorithms cannot provide the information needed for part error signature characterization. For part error signature characterization, we need to know the actual dimensions and the geometric form of the manufactured feature instead of the substitute features of perfect geometric forms. Therefore, an alternative way of sampling and analyzing data is needed to extract feature parameters that truly represent the actual dimensions and the form of measured features.

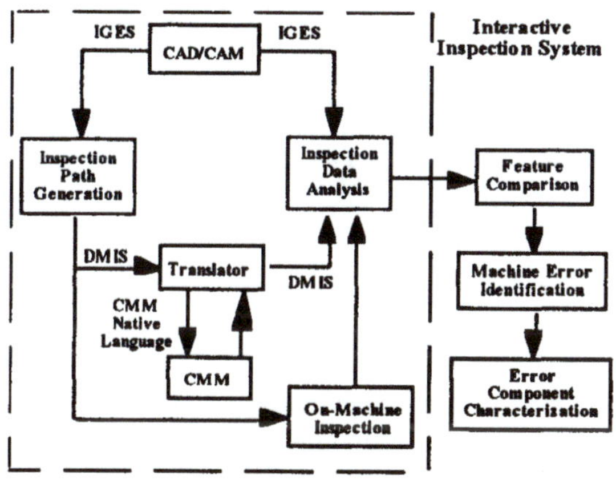


**Figure 2** Interactive inspection system and part error characterization.

An interactive inspection algorithm, as shown in Figure 2 (Mou, et. al., 1995), is developed to compare the inspection data obtained from both on-machine sensing and post-process inspection to identify systematic dimensional and form errors. The results of the proposed interactive inspection algorithm will be used to i) compare the data obtained from on-machine and post-process inspections, ii) decouple the machine related error and process related error, and iii) identify the contribution of each error component.

To characterize the machine related error, the geometric inaccuracy must be related to the error components that compose the volumetric machine error. A feature-based analysis method is developed to decompose the geometry of any part into a collection of basic geometric features (such as cylinders, cones, circles, hemispheres, planes, etc.) as defined in Dimension Measurement Interface Standard (DMIS, 1990). A feature-based comparison method is also developed to identify and then decouple the effect of machine related and process related errors.

The same inspection information is used to verify the effectiveness of the on-machine inspection and machine error characterization.

After the degradation effect of machine error and process error are identified and decoupled, the inspection analysis results can then be used to extract information regarding error resulted from tool wear, tool deflection, chatter, and fixture/workpiece deformation. The dimensional inaccuracies of different features can be used to extract information regarding the systematic machine error and process error. For a particular type of machining process, the potential error sources for each feature can be categorized and used to derive a set of diagnostic equations to identify the individual degradation factor. As the contribution of each degradation factor to part quality is determined, the results can be used by the adaptive error correction system to iteratively improve the machine performance.

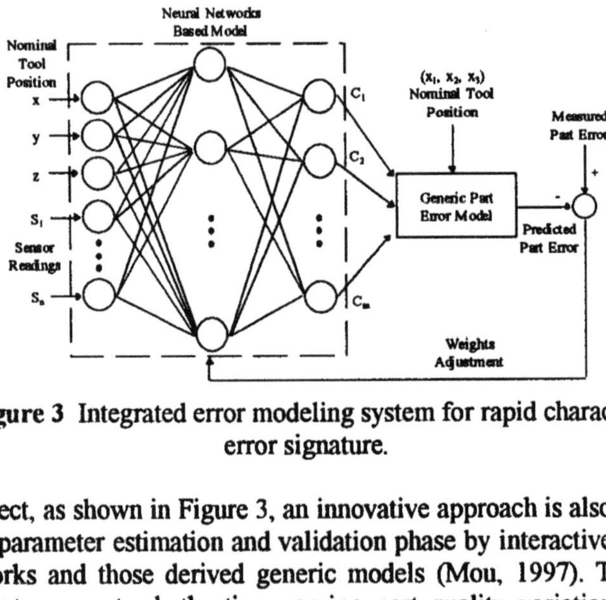


**Figure 3** Integrated error modeling system for rapid characterization of error signature.

In this project, as shown in Figure 3, an innovative approach is also developed to simplify the parameter estimation and validation phase by interactively integrating neural networks and those derived generic models (Mou, 1997). The developed integrated system can track the time-varying part quality variation by adapting current inspection results obtained from various sensors. The goal is to develop a fast characterization process to build a model for characterizing the variation of the production process by adopting a sensor-fusion approach.

In deriving the coefficients of the proposed integrated system, there is no measured data available for direct comparison with the neural network output. Instead, the difference between the predicted value from generic models and the measured value is used to train the neural network. Therefore, a new training algorithm is developed for this integrated error modeling system. For data-adaptive updating purposes, the gradient-descent direction method is adopted in deriving the training algorithm. Issues related to convergence rate, stability, training rate, and number of hidden nodes are also investigated.

A methodology is currently being developed for using on-machine inspection techniques to identify the fixturing related error in terms of offset in part datum coordinates and the deformation of the workpiece and fixturing components due to the clamping forces and clamping sequence. The goal is to develop a method for shop floor personnel to conduct a quick checking, after clamping forces are applied, on the deformation of critical machining surfaces.

An adaptive algorithm is currently being derived for iteratively identifying the contribution of each degradation factor. The output of the adaptive algorithm will be merged with the cutting force prediction model, next generation inspection system (Jones, et. al., 1996), and the plug-and-play software development environment of Figure 4 (Furness, et.al., 1996) that is currently under development by Ford's research engineers to determine the proper setting of NC tool path, tooling, fixturing, and machining parameters to minimize the variation in part quality and production cost.

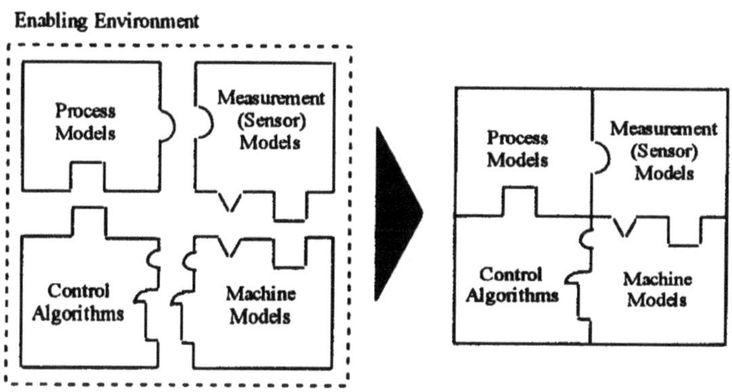


**Figure 4** Plug-and-play software development environment.

A recursive fine-tuning algorithm, as shown in Figure 5 (Mou, et. al., 1995a, b), is also being derived to iteratively refine the model. The objective is to investigate a concept for developing an adaptive error correction system that integrates the methods and algorithms proposed in previous sections to facilitate the following procedures: (1) identification of the systematic degradation factors, (2) development of the multi-variable model for part error estimation and compensation, (3) detection of the residual systematic errors that are not considered by the model using information obtained from both on-machine sensing and post-process inspection processes, (4) identification and characterization of the contribution of each residual systematic degradation factor, and (5) fine-tuning the model parameter for more accurate part error estimation and compensation.

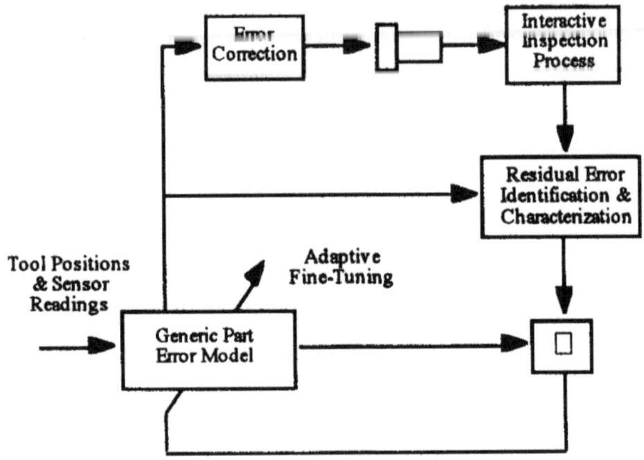


**Figure 5** Recursively fine-tuning the model for part error estimation and compensation.

By using the feature-based analysis method discussed in the previous section, the contribution of the degradation factor can be iteratively monitored and determined. As the manufacturing process proceeds, this process is iteratively executed as more information regarding the part error signature becomes available. Therefore, the inference space of the proposed integrated part error modeling system is continuously updated.

## 3 CONCLUSION

This research is motivated by the need to develop innovative and cost-effective methods to advance the machine technology for precision and agile manufacturing applications. The impacts of the research can be summarized as follows.

The results of the research will significantly advance the accuracy and functionality of manufacturing and measuring equipment. This research effort is devoted to the improvement of the precision of machining centers through advances in dimensional measurement and analysis techniques. This research provides methods for integrating more sensing and analysis capabilities at the machine level. The developed sensor-fusion methodology provides the mechanism for determining the degradation effect of machine error, process error, and fixturing error on part quality variation. The derivation of uncertainty models for sensor setting and measuring processes will significantly contribute to the development of novel techniques for data sampling and analysis, and thus will have a significant impact on precision manufacturing.

The results of advancing the on-machine and post-process sensing and analysis techniques will have significant impact on research into precision and agile engineering applications. The research results can be used to identify, decouple, and then minimize confounded measurement uncertainties. The results of developing innovative measurement procedures and sampling strategies will advance the technology in extracting information that truly represents the actual dimensions and the form of measured features. Therefore, the quality and reliability of the inspection data can be improved dramatically and a more accurate and meaningful conclusion can be drawn.

The development of an adaptive error modeling system with sensor-fusion technologies will significantly facilitate the implementation of the error modeling and correction techniques for various manufacturing equipment. The adaptive error modeling system can be easily implemented on a PC based open-architecture controller to receive information from various sensors, assess the status of the process, determine the proper action, and deliver the command to actuators for task execution. This will enhance machine capabilities to produce workpieces within the imposed dimension tolerances.

## 4 REFERENCES

ANSI/ASME PTC 19.1-1985, 1985, Measuring Uncertainty, ASME, New York.

ANSI/ASME B89.1.12M-1990, 1990, Methods for Performance Evaluation of Coordinate Measuring Machines, ASME, New York.

ANSI/ASME B5.54-1992, 1992, Methods for Performance Evaluation of Computer Numerically Controlled Machining Centers, ASME, New York.

ANSI/ASME Y14.5M-1994, 1994, Dimensional and Tolerancing, ASME, New York.

DMIS, 1990, "DMIS 2.1," Specification CAM-I Standard 101, CAM-I, Inc., Arlington, TX.

Furness, R.J., Jones, S.D., Rankin, J.S., Muth, M.J., Wei, K.C., and Copper, J.C., 1996, "Control System Requirements to Support Intelligent Sensor-Based Manufacturing," *Proceedings of the 1996 IPC Conference and Exposition*, pp.55-62.

Hocken, R.J., 1995, "Measurement Integration," in Coordinate Measuring Machines and Systems, edited by Bosch, J.A., Marcel Dekker, Inc., New York.

Jones, S.D., Furness, R.J., Muth, M.J., and Rankin, J.S., 1996, "Agile Metrology: The Next Generation of Measuring Machines," *Proceedings of the 1996 IPC Conference and Exposition*, pp.97-102.

Lee, G. and J. Mou, 1996, "Design the Sampling Strategy for Dimensional Measurement of Geometric Features using Coordinate Measuring Machine," *Proceedings of Japan-U.S.A. Symposium on Flexible Automation*, pp.1193-1200.

Lee, G., J. Mou, and Y. Shen, 1997a, "An Analytical Assessment of Measurement Uncertainty in Precision Inspection and Machine Calibration," *International Journal of Machine Tool and Manufacture*, Vol. 37, No. 3, pp. 263-276.

Lee, G., J. Mou, and Y. Shen, 1997b, "Decoupling the Confounded Effect of Machine Error and Geometric Characteristics of Artifacts in Precision Measurement and Machine Calibration," submitted to *ASME Transactions on Journal of Manufacturing Science and Engineering*.

Menq, C.-H., Yau, H.-T., Lai, G.-Y., and Miller R.A., 1990, "Statistical Evaluation of Form Tolerances Using Discrete Measurement Data," *Proceedings of ASME Winter Annual Meeting*, pp.135-149.

Mou, J, and Liu, C.R., 1992, "A Method for Enhancing the Accuracy of CNC Machine Tools for On-Machine Inspection," *Journal of Manufacturing Systems*, Vol.11, No.4, pp.229-237.

Mou, J., Donmez, M.A., and Cetinkunt, S., 1995a, "An Adaptive Methodology Using Features-Based Analysis Techniques for Machine Performance Improvement: Part I - Theory Derivation," *ASME Transactions on Journal of Engineering for Industry*, Vol.117, No.4, pp.584-590.

Mou, J., Donmez, M.A., and Cetinkunt, S., 1995b, "An Adaptive Methodology Using Features-Based Analysis Techniques for Machine Performance Improvement: Part II - Experimental Verification," *ASME Transactions on Journal of Engineering for Industry*, Vol.117, No.4, pp.591-600.

Mou, J., 1997, "A Method of Using Neural Network and Inverse Kinematics for Machine Tool Error Estimation and Correction," *ASME Transactions on Journal of Manufacturing Science and Engineering*, Vol.119, No.2, pp.247-254.

Nguyen, T.L., Furgason, E.S., and Shin, Y.C., 1995, "Feasibility Assessment of Residual Stress Measurement by an Ultrasonic Technique," *Transactions of the North American Manufacturing Research Institution of SME*, pp.287-292.

Shin, Y.C., Oh, S.J., and Coker, S.A., 1995, " Surface Roughness Measurement by Ultrasonic Sensing for In-Process Monitoring," *ASME Transactions on Journal of Engineering for Industry*, Vol.117, No.3, pp.439-447.

Swyt, D.A., 1992, Challenges to NIST in Dimensional Metrology: The Impact of Tightening Tolerances in the U.S. Discrete-Part Manufacturing Industry, *NISTIR 4757*, National Institute of Standards and Technology, MD.

Woo, T.C., and Liang, R., 1993, "Dimensional Measurement of Surfaces and Their Sampling," *Computer-Aided Design*, Vol.25, No.4, pp.233-239.

Wright, P., Schofield, S., and Wang F.-C., "Open Architecture Control For Machine Tools," *Proceedings of 13th Symposium on Engineering Applications of Mechanics: Manufacturing Science and Engineering of 1996 CSME Forum*, pp.1-17.

38

# Evaluation of roughness of machined surfaces using vision system by phase shifting method

*M.B.Kiran B.Ramamoorthy V.Radhakrishnan*
Department of Mechanical Engineering
Indian Institute of Technology
Madras- 600 036, India.
**Tel : 044-2351365 Ex: 3632 ; Fax : 91 44 2350509 / 2352545**
**E-mail : ramu@acer.iitm.ernet.in**

**Abstract**

Evaluation of surface roughness has assumed considerable significance due to the better understanding of its role on the performance of the components. To overcome some of the drawbacks of the stylus method, optical methods were developed, which include using principle of interferometry. In this work an attempt is made to evaluate the surface roughness of machined surfaces by phase shifting method.

**Key words**

Vision inspection, Roughness evaluation, Phase shifting method.

## 1. INTRODUCTION

Surface roughness evaluation has assumed considerable significance due to better understanding of its role on the performance of the component. The most popular method of surface roughness evaluation is by stylus method. The stylus method is

Computer Applications in Production and Engineering. F. Plonka and G. Olling (Eds.)

contact in nature which has a limitation in measuring speed. In order to overcome some of the drawbacks of the stylus method, other methods were developed and most of them are optical. The electro- optical methods though fast do not provide enough information for the full characterisation of the surface.

One of the methods employed widely for the surface roughness assessment is by using the principle of interference of light. Interferometry produces interference fringe pattern when two or more light waves combine in phase after travelling different path lenghts. interact with each other. Traditionally, interferometry has been used to determine surface roughness (Bruning, *et al.*,1974; Bennett, 1976; Cheng and Wyant, 1985; Ai and Wyant, 1987;Larkin and Oreb, 1992) and construct the topography of the surface. The reconstruction of the surface topography from fringe patterns has been accomplished by several different methods. Perry *et al.* (1983) created the topographic map of the surface using the undulations of the fringe centre lines. Bruning *et al.* (1974) introduced the phase shift interferometry which uses surface reconstruction method. The phase shift of each point on the fringe is calculated and converted into height thus creating the topographic map of the surface.

Many phase shifting algorithms that perform well with sinusoidal or near sinusoidal periodic wave fronts have been developed (Gierloff,1987). In this work an attempt is made to evaluate the surface roughness by phase shifting method. A vision system is used to grab and analyse the fringe patterns. It is different from the previous methods in that the method does not use complex optical set-ups. Moreover the conventional interferometric measurements are restricted to highly reflecting surfaces.

## 2. PRINCIPLE

The interference concept is based on the superposition property of the coherent light waves. For example, if two waves of initial amplitudes 'a' and 'b' with the same wavelength 'λ' leave a source and travel by different paths and then arrive at the same point in space, where superposition occurs, the complex amplitudes of the resultant waves is given by the sum of the complex amplitudes of the initial waves. Consider two wave trains '$E_1$' and '$E_2$' that are given by

$$E_1(x,y) = ae^{2ikl} \tag{1}$$

$$E_2(x,y) = be^{2ikw(x,y)} \tag{2}$$

where a and b is denote the wavefront amplitudes and

$$k = \frac{2\pi}{\lambda} \tag{3}$$

where, 'k' is the wave number and 'λ' is the wave length of light.

'l' is the mean path length from the reference surface and the 'w(x,y)' is the mean path length of the test surface. These two waves join together and produces the resultant wave '$E_p$'. which is given as

$$E_p(x, y) = E_1(x, y) + E_2(x, y) \quad (4)$$

The energy flux or intensity of a wave is proportional to the square of the amplitude of the wave field or $E_p * E_p^*$, $E_p^*$ is the complex conjugate of $E_p$. From this the intensity distribution in the interference pattern is given as

$$I(x, y) = A + B\cos(\phi(x, y) + \alpha) \quad (5)$$

where, 'A' is an unknown constant due to background intensity, 'B' is an unknown constant due to fringe contrast, '$\phi$' is the required phase difference and '$\alpha$' is the added phase difference.

The intensity distribution, I, can be used to reconstruct the surface topography of the specimen. For each position (x,y) in the interference pattern, the phase or the wavefront that corresponds to the surface height w(x,y) can be found within some multiple of $2\pi$.

$$\phi(x,y) = \arctan\left[\frac{I_4(x,y) - I_2(x,y)}{I_1(x,y) - I_3(x,y)}\right] \quad (6)$$

Since the phase $\phi$ (x,y) is determined by using an arctangent function, it is restricted between $-\pi$ and $\pi$. Hence a consistency may arise in determining the fringe order. This constitutes the unwrapping phase problem, which is important in digital fringe analysis (Bone, 1991; Asundi and Chan, 1994). The one dimensional phase unwrapping problem is simpler. These algorithms have been extended to two dimensions (Macy, 1983). They are based on addition or subtraction of $2\pi$ when the phase difference between the two adjacent points is greater than $\pi$. First, each row is scanned and then the process is repeated into each column and depth of surface points is calculated using the following equation.

$$Depth = \frac{p}{2\pi}\left[\frac{\phi_{obj} - \phi_{ref}}{\tan\theta}\right] \quad (7)$$

Where 'p' is the pitch and '$\theta$' is the angle of projection.

## 3. EXPERIMENTAL PROCEDURE

In this method a micro computer based vision system is used for image acquisition and analysis. In the measurement process, a projector is used to project a computer generated grating pattern onto the surface to be inspected. The pitch and the type of the intensity distribution can be varied using a software. Specimens are made to varied roughness by different manufacturing processes, which include shaping, milling, EDM, casting and sandblasting. The specimens are made to different roughness by using different machining parameters ( speed, feed and depth of cut). Figure 1 shows the images of the different specimens used in the experiment.

Figure 2 shows the experimental set-up. The specimen to be inspected is kept in position and is illuminated using grating projector at 45 degrees. The projected pattern will be deformed in accordance with the surface irregularities. The deformed grating pattern is captured using a CCD camera. Figure 3 shows the projected grating patterns on sand blasted surfaces as seen through the CCD camera.

The digitised image is stored in one of the four frame buffers. The specimen to be inspected is then moved by distances equal to p/4, p/8 and p/16. where 'p' is the pitch of the grating. Thus in all four images are grabbed. The specimen is then replaced with the reference surface and the above procedure is repeated. Thus, in all, eight images are grabbed. The algorithm will then compute the phase values at each pixel within a window of 32x32 pixels.

## 4. PHASE UNWRAPPING PROCEDURE

Since the phase is determined using an arctangent function it is restricted between $-\pi$ and $\pi$. Hence, a consistency is maintained in determining the fringe order. This constitutes the unwrapping phase problem, which is of interest in digital fringe analysis.

A serious problem confronting all the phase shifting techniques is the phase unwrapping after arctangent calculations. If each phase point is unwrapped along some fixed direction, it always propagates errors from bad quality points to good quality points. The method of phase unwrapping is known as ordered phase unwrapping procedure. For such processing it needs quality factor in determining the quality point (Q). Quality factor is defined as

$$Q_i = \sum_{m=1}^{4} \left| P_m - P_i \right| \tag{8}$$

where '$Q_i$' is the quality factor of phase point '$P_i$' and '$P_m$' is the one of four adjacent points around '$P_i$'. While getting the absolute phase differences, the

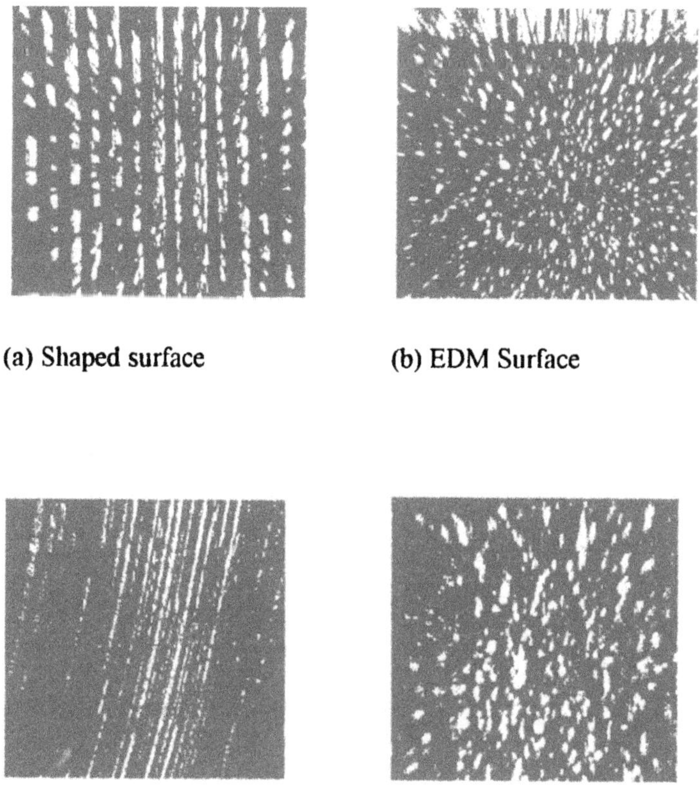

(a) Shaped surface (b) EDM Surface

(c) Milled surface (d) Sand blasted Surface

**Figure 1** Different texture images.

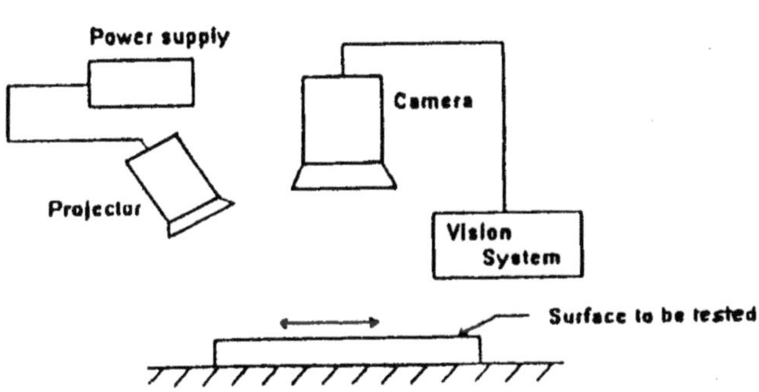


**Figure 2** Experimental set-up.

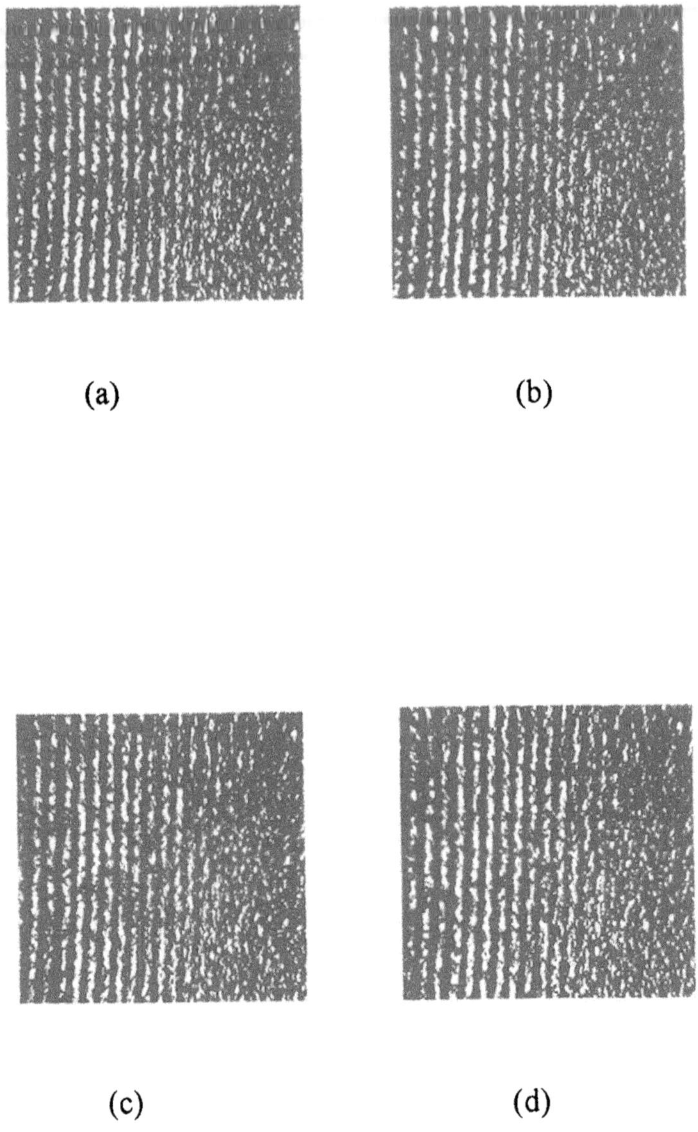

**Figure 3** Projected grating pattern on a typical sandblasted surface.

$2\pi$ jumps should be excluded, if they exist. With the quality factor, an optimal order for unwrapping all the phase points can be determined automatically and the propagation of the errors can be kept as low as possible. In order to get results, representing the good phase points, bad region recognition can be performed on the $-\pi$ and $\pi$ wrapped phase map. It is because, no fringe areas and the poor quality fringe areas are most obvious during processing. The main feature in the wrapped phase maps is the phase values jumping randomly in high spatial frequency. So a rectangular region around an inspected phase point is selected and the surrounding points whose phase differences to the inspecting point satisfying the following conditions are encountered. The condition is given as

$$\delta p < |P - P_0| < 2\pi - \delta p \qquad (9)$$

Where 'P' is the phase point in the surrounding area, '$P_0$' is the inspected phase point and $\delta_p$ is the allowance of legal amplitude of phase variations. If the number counted is greater than the given threshold, the inspected point will be marked as a bad point and will not be processed during phase unwrapping.

## 5. RESULTS AND DISCUSSIONS

The software computes the depth of the surface points using the equation (7) and plots it as a 3D plot. Figure 4 shows the 3D plots of machined surfaces.

1. Specimens are made to different roughness by different manufacturing processes. They are made of shaping, milling, EDM and sandblasting processes. It was found that there was a good correlation between the average roughness and those computed from vision methods. Figure 5 shows the correlation between the vision roughness and the average roughness obtained from the stylus instrument.
2. The method is fast in computing surface roughness parameter and is applicable for on-line inspection of surface roughness. The method can be used to evaluate the surface roughness of rough surfaces. These include surfaces made of milling, shaping, EDM, sand blasting, and casting processes.
3. The accuracy of the proposed method depends on the pitch of the grating used. The smaller the pitch the better will be the accuracy. The equation for computing the phase values is derived with the assumption of the sinusoidal intensity distribution. In reality, the actual profile is not truly sinusoidal. The effect of the non sinusoidal intensity distribution on the computed values will be minimised by using the grating of smaller pitch.

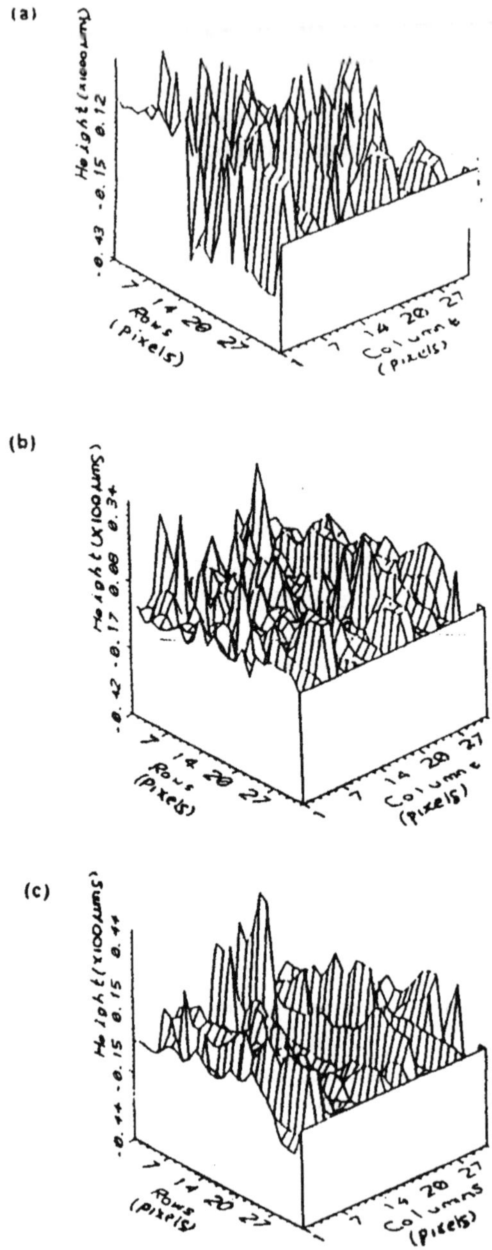


**Figure 4** 3D plots of typical (a) cast (b) EDM and (c) sandblasted surface.

4. Coefficient of variation increases with decreasing roughness, suggesting that the method is not applicable for smooth surfaces. Accuracy of measurement can be improved by using the Liquid Crystal Display (L.C.D) Projector.

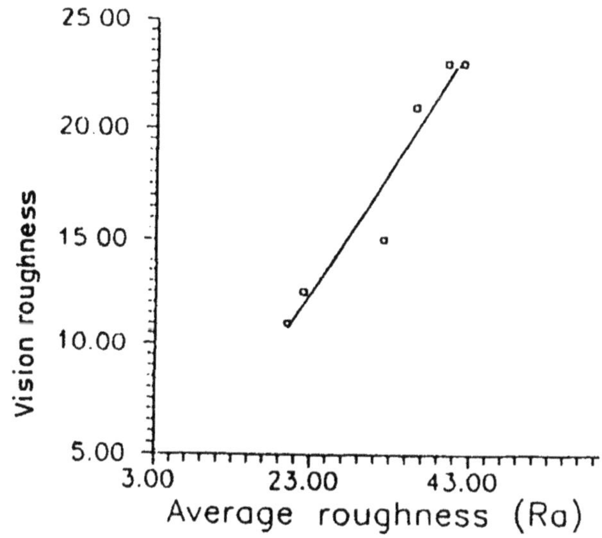


**Figure 5** Correlation curve of shaped surfaces.

## 6. CONCLUSIONS

In this work an attempt is made to evaluate the surface roughness of machined surfaces by phase shifting method. A micro computer based vision system is used for surface image acquisition and analysis. Phase values are computed using the bucket equation. The unwrapped phase values are then used to compute the depth of the surface points. It was found that there was a good correlation between the average roughness and the vision roughness computed from the vision method. The method is quick, reliable and finds application in high speed and automated inspection of machined surfaces.

## 7. ACKNOWLEDGEMENT

Work reported in this paper forms a part of a project on Application of Vision System for Surface and Dimensional Inspection, sponsored by the CSIR, Government of India.

## 8. REFERENCES

1. **Ai, C. and Wyant, J.C.** (1987) Effect of piezo electric transducer non-linearity on phase shift interferometry, *Applied Optics*, **26**, 1112- 1116.
2. **Asundi, A and Chan, C.S.** ( 1994) Phase shifted projection grid - effect of pitch and profile, *Optics and Lasers in Engineering*, **21**, 31-47.

3. **Bennett, J.M.** (1976) Measurement of rms roughness, autocovariance function and other optical properties of surfaces using FECO scanning interferometer, *Applied Optics*,**15**, No.11, 2705-2721.
4. **Bone, D.J** ( 1991) Fourier fringe analysis : the two dimensional phase unwrapping problem, *Applied optics*, **30**, 3627-3632.
5. **Bruning, J.H., Herriott, D.R., Gallagher, J.E., Rosenfeld, D.P., White, A.D. and Brangaccio** (1974) Digital wavefront measuring interferometer for testing optical surfaces and lenses, *Applied Optics*, **13**, 2693-2703.
6. **Cheng, Y.Y and Wyant, J.C.** (1985) Phase shifter calibration in phase shifting interferometry, *Applied Optics*, **24**, 3049-3052.
7. **Gierloff, J.J** ( 1987) Phase unwrapping by regions, Current developments in Optical Engineering II , *Proceedings of SPIE*, **818**, 2-9.
8. **Larin, K.G and Oreb, B.F.** ( 1992) Design and assessment of symmetrical phase shifting Algorithms, *Journal of Optical Society of America*, **9**, No.10, 1740-1748.
9. **Macy, W.W** (1983) Two dimensional fringe pattern Analysis, *Applied Optics*, **22**, 3898- 3901.
10. **Perry, D.M., Peterson, R.W. and Robinson,G.M.** ( 1983) Measurement of surface topography of magnetic recording materials through computer analysed microscopic interferometry, *IEEE Transactions on Magnetics*, **19**, No.5,1656- 1700.

## 9. BIOGRAPHY

Dr.V.Radhakrishnan, Professor at the Manufacturing Engineering section, Department of Mechanical Engineering , Indian Institute of Technology, Madras, India. He has to his credit over 200 research papers in international journals and conferences, national journals and conferences. He is working in the area of Metrology, Grinding and CIM.

Dr.B.Ramamoorthy Associate professor and presently the head of the Manufacturing Engineering section, Department of Mechanical Engineering, Indian Institute of Technology, Madras, India. He has to his credit over 40 research papers in international journals and conferences, national journals and conferences. He is working in the area of Metrology and Machine vision.

M.B.Kiran is presently working as Senior research fellow in the CSIR project, Mechanical Engineering Department at Indian Institute of Technology, Madras, India. He is currently working towards Ph.D. He is working in the area of surface roughness evaluation using machine vision.

# 39
# A novel method to create intelligent sensors with learning capabilities to improve modern production systems

*A. Mahajan*
*Associate Professor*
*School of engineering and Mathematics*
*Lake Superior State University, Sault Ste. Marie, Aff 49 783, USA*
*Tel: 906-635-2598*
*Fax: 906-635-6663*
*Email: amahajan@lakers.Issu.edu*

**Abstract**

A formal theory for the development of a generic model of an autonomous sensor is proposed and implemented. An autonomous sensor is defined as an intelligent sensor that has machine learning capabilities. It not only interprets the acquired data in accordance with an embedded expert system knowledge base, but is also capable of using this data to modify and enhance this knowledge base. Hence, the system is capable of learning and thereby improving its performance over time. The main objective of the model is to combine the capabilities of the physical sensor and an expert operator monitoring the sensor in real-time. The system has been successfully tested using various simulated data sets as well as a real thermistor that has been developed as an autonomous sensor. This work has significant impact on modem production systems since sensors form an integral part of all closed loop control systems, and modem manufacturing processes rely heavily on sensor based control systems. The long range aim of this work is to develop highly autonomous production systems that have self diagnostic, maintenance, self correction, and learning capabilities embedded at the local and global levels. This work builds upon work on a formalized theory for autonomous

Computer Applications in Production and Engineering. F. Plonka and G. Olling (Eds.)

sensing called Dynamic Across Time Autonomous Sensing, Interpretation, Model learning and Maintenance Theory (DATA-SEIALAMT) that has been supported by the NSF and the SME Education Foundation.

**Keywords**
Intelligent sensors, learning, autonomous, modem production systems

# 1. INTRODUCTION

Sensing has become increasingly important in the control of complex and sophisticated systems of today's technology. There is an increased interest in developing a general theory to treat intelligent sensor systems [1,2,3]. Parallel work has been done in industry where sensors have been developed with built in expert systems and look-up tables [4,5]. These sensors, called *smart sensors, are* described as simple sensing devices with built-in intelligence. This intelligence includes decision making capabilities, data processing, conflict resolution, communications, or distribution of information. Again, there is no generic model, and the sensors and their built-in-intelligence usually very specific towards their field of application.

*The autonomous sensor* is defined as a sensor that has an expert system with extensive qualitative tools that allow it to evolve with time into a better and more efficient system [6]. It differs from the above mentioned models by having a dynamic knowledge base as well as embedded qualitative and analytical functions that give it a higher degree of operational independence, self-sufficiency and robustness. The underlying philosophy behind the autonomous sensor is probably closest to Henderson's [7,8] *logical* sensor models that also endeavor to give more problem solving capabilities to the sensor.

Multisensor integration and fusion has always been an attractive method to reduce the ambiguity in the sensed data, and considerable work has been done in this area [9,10,11,12]. The autonomous sensor model can reduce the need for redundant sensors, and give more accurate information for integration and fusion purposes. Recent work in qualitative reasoning regarding physical systems has been published in a special volume of Artificial Intelligence [13]. This volume focuses on the development and use of qualitative reasoning methods to cope with fundamental engineering tasks. A link has been forged between qualitative reasoning and the traditional numeric and analytic methods.

DeCoste [14] describes a system, called DATMI, that dynamically maintains a concise representation of the space of local and global interpretations across time that are consistent with the observations. Each of the observations is obtained from a sensor, and therefore the number of observations is equal to the number of sensors in the control system. The truth of the observations and the validity of the sensors is obtained by cross-referencing with possible and impossible states of the system (envisionments). DATMI is designed for a complete control system comprising of multiple sensors and actuators, and is the inspiration for the formalized theory developed by the authors [15]. This theory is called DATA-SE\4LAMT *(Dynamic Across Time Autonomous Sensing, Interpretation, Model Learning and Maintenance Theory)* and is designed for and is applicable to each sensor in the control system.

Brooks [16,17] states that a truly intelligent system would perform its own abstraction of the problem and then solve it. He has also presented the subsumption architecture and used it successfully on various mobile robots developed at the MIT Laboratory of Artificial Intelligence. The central theme is that there is no central representation or an overall intelligent controller. This entire philosophy of perception and reaction without a specific intelligent controller is also in keeping with the philosophy underlying the autonomous sensor that allows more decision making and problem solving at the sensor level rather than at the controller level in a robotic, or other control system.

The autonomous sensor model is really a combination of a sensor and an operator monitoring it in real time. The operator has a basic understanding of the sensor and the measurand (entity being measured), and as time passes he learns more about the sensor and measurand behaviors and uses his knowledge to keep running the sensor in as perfect a condition as possible. It is the operator's part that has to be embedded in existing sensors to make them autonomous.

The autonomous sensor finds applications in any physical system that uses sensors since the sensors themselves become more robust and reliable. It is particularly suited for applications where the installed sensors can not be accessed for long periods of time, e.g. nuclear power plants, space structures, etc. In such applications the autonomous sensor could function for long periods of time fairly well without going through hard calibrations at short intervals of time. It would also be able to better handle itself in adverse conditions. Autonomous sensors are also useful in situations where the system has a large number of sensors, since installation, calibration and monitoring done by the sensor itself can greatly decrease the complexity of the system's operation. Examples are automated systems in industry, ships, airplanes, shuttles, etc.

## 2. DATA-SIMLAMT (Formalized Theory)

DATA-SAMT is a philosophy that has been inspired by the need for autonomous sensors, and these in turn were inspired by the need for autonomous systems. DATA-SEQLAMT, as presented in this paper, is a formalized theory to create autonomous agents, and the autonomous sensor is an application of this theory.

## 2.1 The Different Types of Databases

DATA-SIMLAMT defines two types of databases for the autonomous sensor. These databases keep a running history of the sensed value in the quantitative and qualitative domain.

a) Quantitative Database: This consists of a history of the actual numerical values sensed by the sensing element, and some pertinent statistical parameters and their numerical values, e.g. mean, std. dev., etc.

b) Qualitative Database: This database consists of qualitative symbols that represent some situation of a relevant aspect of the system at that particular instant. These symbols are defined based on limiting quantitative parameters. These relevant aspects are called properties, and the symbolic representations are called state values.

Some of the terms that will be used in this paper are defined as follows:
<u>Property</u> - is a parameter, e.g. amplitude check.
<u>Concept</u> - is a set of same properties, e.g. amplitude is high for a duration of time.
Behavior - is a set of concepts, e.g. a normal operation followed by a very high amplitude may be a spike.
<u>Envisionment</u> - is a known, hence pre-defined, concept or behavior similar to a known *pattern in the pattern recognition* problem.

## 2.2 Windowing

DATA-SIMLAMT uses three types of windows to determine the number of samples that must be used to define the properties, concepts and behaviors. These windows operate on the various databases described in the previous sections. Windowing is an important feature of DATASIMLAMT, and provides observation histories of appropriate length to identify the different

behaviors in the sensor and measurand domain. These are dynamic windows, i.e., they can change size under various circumstances.

**Measurand Identification Window:** This window is used to obtain the instantaneous model of the behavior of the measurand. This is essential for the sensor to identify problems in its own operation. DATA-SE\4LAMT attempts to give the sensor with various analytical modeling and tracking routines so that it can use the one that best captures the instantaneous behavior of the measurand.

**Quantitative Database Window:** The main function of this window is to capture transitions. This window operates on the raw data as is sensed by the physical sensing device, and carries out pre-defined statistical and identification functions so as to supply enough information for the creation of the qualitative database. This window sets the number of points to be used in functions such as standard deviations, moving averages, etc.

**Qualitative Database Window (QLW):** This window acts upon the qualitative data base which has been created based upon the properties and their state values. This is the most important window as it matches the real-time qualitative data to the envisionments in the knowledge bases to come up with interpretations and identify sensor and measurand behaviors. Essentially, each behavior has a window which is dictated by the combination and sequence of its associated concepts.

## 2.3 DATA-SIMLAMT knowledge bases

DATA-SFMLAMT has two types of knowledge bases that are described below.

**Internal knowledge base:** This consists of the basic knowledge that is required to distinguish between the normal behavior of the sensor and any other behavior that differs from the pre-defined normal behavior. This knowledge base also has knowledge such as the time response of the sensor, the time required for a change in the measurand, appropriate methodologies for changing the size of the windows, analytical tools such as statistical routines, fast fourier transform routines, curve fitting routines, least-mean-square adaptive algorithm, etc. The internal knowledge base is a generic part of the model that can only be changed at the software level, i.e., it requires some programming effort on the source code.

**External knowledge base:** This knowledge base is the key feature of DATA-SIMLAMT, and hence, of the autonomous sensor. This knowledge base resides in external data files that may be created by the operator, and includes the specification sheet of the sensor and files containing the concepts and behaviors. These may be modified and updated by the operator as new behaviors are discovered, or the process may be automated, i.e., the knowledge base may be updated by the sensor as it discovers new behaviors that do not match the normal behavior of the sensor. The sensor memorizes new behaviors, identifies appropriate countermeasures for them, and categorizes them such that it may use them the next time they appear. This constitutes the learning mechanism of DATA-SIMLAMT, and will be discussed in a later section.

## 2.4 The Generic Model for an Autonomous sensor

This section gives the operational model of an autonomous sensor. The model has sensing, interpretation, truth maintenance and model learning capabilities embedded in it as can be seen in Figure 1. Data travels from the physical sensing element to the interpretation module, and then the maintenance and learning modules. These modules obtain knowledge to act upon the sensor data from the various knowledge bases in the sensor as well as the measurand domains.

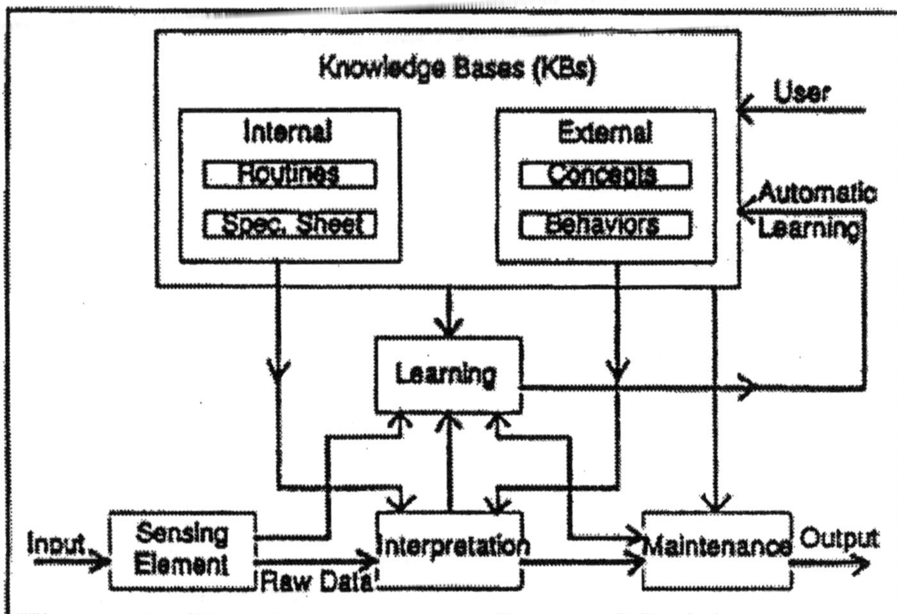


**Figure 1 The Autonomous Sensor Model**

## 3. ENVISIONINIENTS (or Patterns)

The envisionments are the most important feature of DATA-SIMLAMT, and were introduced before as part of the external knowledge base. These envisionments describe measurand behaviors such as step changes, etc., and abnormal sensor problems such as spikes, disturbances, dead sensors, etc. The sensor must distinguish between the behaviors that encompass the two different domains (measurand and sensor), since the sensor needs to take appropriate countermeasures if there is a sensor problem, but simply follow faithfully a valid change in the measurand behavior. These envisionments reside in external ASCII data files and can be created by the operator or by the sensor itself with the help of specialized machine learning algorithms. The sensor can use these precompiled envisionments, or it can start with a blank external knowledge base and create the very same envisionments during its operation when the learning mechanism is switched on.

Let us investigate a sudden jump in the signal from a normal value to a very high value. When there is a sudden jump in the signal it could have been caused by one of the following three occurrences:

a) It could be caused due to a problem in the internal circuitry of the sensor due to a surge of current, or a short circuit. It must be noted here that there are sometimes two distinct circuits, one associated with the sensor, and the other associated with the data-acquisition system. For simplicity, the effect of both will be grouped together under sensor behaviors.

b) It could be a start of a valid step change in the measurand.

c) It could be due to an external disturbance.

How does one quantify the term *sudden?* The sensor and the measurand time constants should always be checked against the actual time taken for the measurand to change from one value to another. A step change is the "most sudden" possible change in the measurand behavior. Hence, the following four possibilities can arise out of the comparison of the actual time (AT) with sensor time constant (STC) and the measurand time constant (MTC). Remember, the sensor time constant is always less than the measurand time constant (STC < MTC).

i) If the actual time elapsed during a change in the sensed signal is faster than the sensor time constant (AT < STC), then it has definitely been caused by a problem in the internal circuitry of the sensor due to a problem such as a surge of current, or a short circuit. This behavior can confidently be interpreted as a **Spike.** If this continues for more than one or two samples then the behavior is an internal disturbance due to a sensor problem, and will be denoted by the following behavior and state value - **Disturbance(Sensor).**

ii) If the time elapsed during a change in the sensed signal is greater than the sensor time constant but less than the measurand time constant (STC < AT < MTC), then it is definitely an external disturbance due to foreign body. This is because the sensor is responding to a valid change in a measurand behavior and hence does not violate the sensor time constant condition, but does violate the measurand time constant condition. This will be denoted by the following behavior and state value - **Disturbance(Measurand).**

iii) If the time elapsed during a change in the sensed signal is equal to the measurand time constant (AT = MTC), then it can be presumed that the measurand has gone through a valid **Step Change,** and the sensor is operating normally.

iv) If the time elapsed during a change in the sensed signal is greater than the measurand time constant (AT > MTC), then it can be assumed that the sensor is operating normally and is following the measurand behavior. It could also be disturbance from a foreign body whose time constant is greater than the measurand, but there is little one can do in this case except follow the change.

## 4, DATA-SIMLAMT AT WORK

There are some basic assumptions that must be made for the smooth and valid operation of the autonomous sensor, and these are:

a) The measurand behavior must be continuous in time, and if not, should be modeled as such. A thermistor measuring the room temperature continuously for some control system can easily be instantiated as an autonomous sensor. But, if this thermistor is used to measure the temperature for intermittent periods of time then the time intervals when the thermistor is not being used should be treated as zero-time gaps.

b) Since the measurand is itself usually a controlled variable it has its own response time to a step change. The sensor time constant, defined as the time for it to change 63.2 percent of the total difference between its initial and final value when subjected to a step change, should be less than the measurand time constant.

c) The sampling time of the data acquisition system should be less than the sensor time constant.
This is essential in capturing transitions in the measurand behavior, and is a necessary design criterion.

d) The sensor should have some idea about the frequency content of a harmonic signal. This is essential to extract and identify the principle frequencies of the signal and to be able to isolate it from a possible high frequency noise in the signal. In a non-harmonic signal this is not necessary, since the high frequency components can be assumed to be the noise contents.

DATA-SIMLAMT has four main tasks associated with it, these being sensing, interpretation, maintenance and learning (Figure 1 shows the different modules as well as the flow of information). The autonomous sensor model will be demonstrated using a specific sensor, i.e., a thermistor. This thermistor may be part of a control system that needs to know the room temperature for control purposes, and is using the thermistor to measure it.

**Sensing** includes two stages based on the traditional model of a sensor that consists of a physical sensing device that senses the measurand in some manner, and an analytical model that converts the sensed quantity into a digital value representative of the measurand.

**Interpretation** is the process which includes the creation of the quantitative database, then the qualitative database, and then the final matching of the real-time qualitative database with the envisionments to come up with the final interpreted behaviors in the sensor and measurand domain. This is similar to the pattern recognition problem as mentioned earlier. The matching is done by incrementing a *Matching Function* (MF) every time a property and its state value is matched. A perfect match means that MF=100%. A behavior can only be interpreted if the associated W has a value of 100. This process can also be termed as the diagnostic component of DATA-SE\4LAMT. This is the process very similar to a typical pattern recognition process.

**Maintenance** is the process of correcting the sensed value in some manner if a sensor problem has been interpreted, filling gaps in the quantitative database, and resolving conflicts by consulting possible and impossible states of the system and the recent history of the sensor and measurand behavior. The main hindrance to the autonomous sensor is that it does not have a model of the measurand behavior so it infers a reliable instantaneous model of the measurand behavior at all times, and only then can it identify its own problems as they occur. This instantaneous model is obtained by using various modeling tools available to the autonomous sensor, and is done within the Measurand Identification Window. The various analytical tools available to the autonomous sensor are FFT analysis routines, FIR filter design routines, curve fitting routines, LMS adaptive predicting routines, etc. The maintenance process uses knowledge from the, envisionments and the specification sheet that includes the quantitative parameters, tables for drift, and other data.

**Machine learning** is an important capability for any autonomous system, but one needs to know what constitutes learning before one can call it learning. The following definition of learning is proposed by the authors:

***Learning,*** as applied to physical systems, may be defined as a process in which the system *modifies its existing model (the structure itse6C or simply the parameters of the existing structure) based on the information extracted from the input data according to pre-defined guidelines or principles (performance measure/critic), memorizes the change, and has the ability to use this acquired knowledge in the future. 7he system should be able to adapt in some manner while it is operating even when there is no human involved in the closed loop system.*

The autonomous sensor has two levels of learning. The first is the learning of quantitative parameters, and the second is the learning of qualitative behaviors that comprise the external knowledge base.

**Learning of Quantitative parameters:** This is a lower level of learning in which the sensor parameters are fine tuned against an assumed measurand behavior. This is similar to system identification, except that the sensor does not have an exact model of the input, but has an assumed instantaneous model of the measurand behavior. Usually, the analytical model of the sensor should only be changed during a hard calibration done against known input signals. However, there are cases where some of the sensor constants can be changed with a fair degree of confidence. For example, whenever the sensor is certain that a step change has occurred, then the currently recorded measurand response time can be used in the future rather than the initially recorded one.

**Learning of Qualitative behaviors:** This is a higher level of learning in which the sensor can recognize new behaviors that differ from the normal behavior, classify them according to predefined principles and guidelines, memorize them, and use this acquired knowledge in the future. The aim, of course, is that the sensor continuously improves with time. This is manifested in a reduced amount of time spent on interpreting previously learned behaviors, and in an improved performance in countering problems.

The autonomous sensor model is based on the philosophy of making the sensor self-sufficient One can make the sensor self-sufficient by defining a perfect model for it under all circumstances, incorporating all the possible problems that it could encounter in its operation, and all the possible measurand models that it could encounter. But, this assumes the fact that the knowledge about sensor and the measurand is absolutely complete and can be coded in without mistakes and missing pieces. If for any reason this assumption does not hold, then one has to assume that the sensor is not self-sufficient, and needs expert human support.

The envisionment of the normal behavior of the sensor is used as a critic, called the *Normal Behavior Segment.* All real-time segments in the qualitative data base are compared to this envisionment, and if the *matching function* (MF) has a value of 100%, then the segment is said to have passed the *Normal Behavior Interpretation Test.* This algorithm to distinguish between a valid change in the measurand behavior and an abnormal sensor behavior is based on the assumption that if there is a sensor problem then there has to be a recovery some time in the future.

Formalizing a methodology to distinguish between a sensor problem caused due to the internal circuitry and one caused due to the actual physical sensing element is a difficult task. DATASIMLAMT provides an initial attempt to do so by watching trends in the quantitative corrected raw data base to capture a possible problem in the physical sensing device. This problem occurs over a long period of time and usually manifests itself as a drift in the sensed values. It is usually compounded by high temperature violations and repeated harmonic cycles. If pre-compiled tables for drift are not available then the sensor can, under certain circumstances, compile its own tables.

Since drift is compounded by harmonic cycles, DATA-SEMLAMT keeps track of the harmonic cycles and an average value obtained by recording successive local maximas and minimas, and then finding a correlation between them. This high level approach is only valid for a periodic signal. The advantage of this algorithm is that the signal need not be a perfect sinusoid, but can be any periodic signal with various frequencies and noise components.

## 5. SIMULATIONS AND EXPERIMENTS

This section presents the performance results of the autonomous sensor implementation. The following three figures show the raw data (dotted lines) and the corrected data (solid lines).

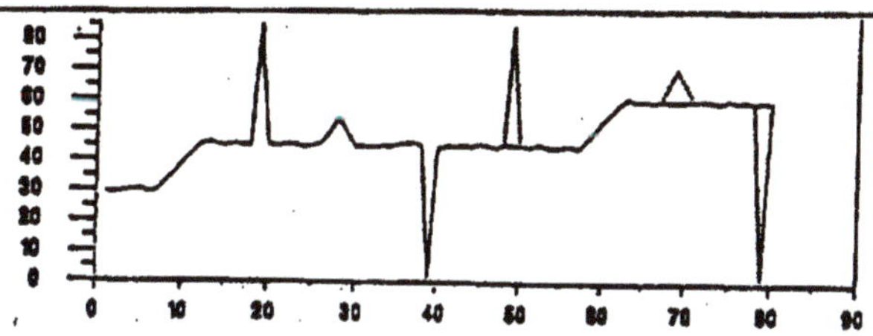


**Figure 2 Simulation of a Non-Harmonic Signal**

Figure 2 shows the raw signal with numerous faulty data points due to problems such as spikes, etc. Notice, the sensor is able to follow a step change, and learns about spikes and dead sensors the first time, and uses the knowledge later on to correct the original data.

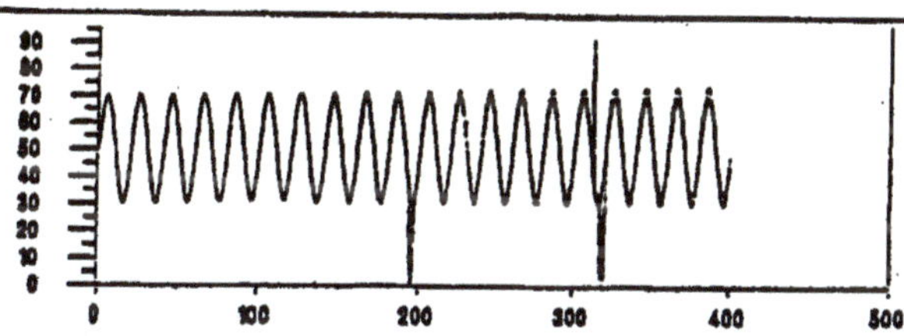


**Figure 3 Simulation of a harmonic signal with drift**

Figure 3 shows a harmonic signal that has drifted with time, and has spikes. The sensor recognizes the spikes and the drift, and compensates for the faulty raw data.

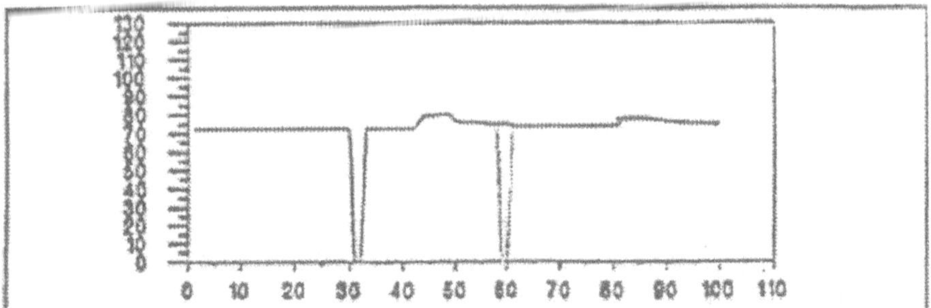


Figure 4 An Actual Experiment with a Thermistor

Figure 4 shows the results of an experiment in which the autonomous sensor model was used in conjunction with an actual thermistor measuring room temperature. The sensor was deliberately switched off twice and the temperature changed. Notice, the sensor follows the first problem, but then learns about it and compensates for the problem the second time around. It also recognizes the changes in the room temperature, and follows them faithfully.

## 6. CONCLUSIONS AND RECOMMENDATIONS

A formal theory for the development of a generic model for an autonomous sensor has been proposed and implemented. This theory, called *DA TA-SIMLAMT,* attempts to formalize knowledge that had formerly remained in the domain of the human operator. The autonomous sensor model is an advanced version of the existing smart or expert sensors that only include an embedded expert system. The improvement is in the form of learning capabilities that allow the model to evolve with time for improved performance. Future work entails increasing the number of analytical tools 'lable to the sensor in modeling the measurand behavior as well as using optimization techniques for the interpretation process. The autonomous sensor model will be used to improve the accuracy of an ultrasonic 3D position sensing system being currently developed at LSSU.

## 7. ACKNOWLEDGMENTS

The authors wish to thank the National Science Foundation (Grant #HU-9119178) and the Society of Manufacturing Engineers Education Foundation (SME 596-233 1) for supporting this work.

## 8. REFERENCES

1. Ghani, N., "Sensor integration in ESPRIT," *IFAC Proceedings,* Karlsruhe, FDR 1988, pp. 323-328.
2. Pinkava, J., "Towards a theory of sensory robotics," *Robotica,* Vol. 8, 1989, pp. 245-256.
3. Lozano-Perez, T., Mason, M. T., and Taylor, R., "Automatic synthesis of fine motion strategies for robots," *Int. J ofrobotics Research,* Vol. 3, No. 1, 1984, pp. 2-24.
4. AbdelRahman, M. and Smith M. L., "The Impact of AI On Sensing Technology," *SENSORS,* September 199 1, pp. 16-22.
5. Studt, T., "Smart Sensors Widen Views on Measuring Data," *R&D Magazine,* March 1994, pp. 18-20.
6. Figueroa, F. and Mahajan, A., "Generic Model of an Autonomous Sensor," *Mechatronics, Vol.* 4, No. 3, pp. 295-315, 1994.
7. Henderson, T and Shilcrat, E., "Logical Sensor Systems," *Journal of Robotic Systems, 1(2),* 1984, pp. 169-193.
8. Henderson, T., Hansen, C. and Bhanu, B., "The Specification of Distributed Sensing and Control," *Journal ofrobotic Systems,* 2(4),1985, pp. 387-396.
9. Dur-rant-Whyte, H. F., "Sensor Models and Multisensor Integration," *International Journal of Robotics Research,* Vol. 7, No. 6, 1988, pp. 97-113.
10. Luo, R. C. and Kay, M. G., "Multisensor integration and Fusion in Intelligent Sytems," *IEEE Transactions on Systems, Man, and Cybernetics,* Vol. 19, No. 5, September, 1989, pp. 901-93 1.
11. Kuc, R. and Siegel, M. W., "Physically Based Simulation Model for Acoustic Sensor Robot Navigation," *IEEE Transactions on Pattern Analysis and Machine Intelligence,* Vol. PAMI-9, No. 6, November 1987, pp. 766-778.
12. Elfes, E., "Sonar-Based Real-World Mapping and Navigation," *IEEE Journal of Robotics and Automation,* Vol. RA-3, No. 3, June 1987, pp. 249-265.
13. Guest Editors: de Kleer, J. and Williams, B. C., "Qualitative Reasoning about Physical Systems," *Artificial Intelligence, Vol.* 5 1, No. 1-3, October 199 1.
14. DeCoste, D., "Dynamic Across-Time Measurement and Interpretation," *Artificial Intelligence,* Vol. 51, 1991, pp. 273-341.

15. Mahajan, A. and Figueroa, F., "Dynamic Across Time Autonomous - Sensing, Interpretation, Model learning and Maintenance theory (DATA-SIMLAMT)," *Mechatronies, Vol.* 5, No. 6, 1995, pp. 665-693.
16. Brooks, R. A., "Intelligence without representation," *Artificial Intelligence,* Vol. 47, 199 1, pp. 139-159.
17. Brooks, R. A., "Robot Insect - Attila," *Popular Science,* March 199 1, pp.52-55, 86.

40

# Model and simulation based flexible production management system

*Prof. Dr.-Ing. W. Maßberg*
*Michael Bäcker*
*Harald Schallner*
*Ingo Thiem*
*Lehrstuhl für Produktionssysteme und Prozeßleitttechnik*
*Universitätsstraße 150*
*Gebäude IB 2/28*
*D-44780 Bochum*
*Telephone: 0234/700-6310*
*Telefax: 0234/7094-157*
*E-Mail: massberg@lps.ruhr-uni-bochum.de*

**Abstract**

The objective of the project MOBILEIT-S is to develop a model based toolbox that offers the possibility of designing and configuring integrated manufacturing control systems with simulation kernel. The basis of this production management system is a metamodel that provides the structural framework for general reference models of the manufacturing order processing for different organizations such as single item or serial productions. The metamodel of the manufacturing control is derived from the general organizational 'Viable System Model' and describes the minimum requirements of an information system from the perspective of information, communication and control. It is a cybernetic model that is based on the ideas of Second Order Cybernetics which makes it possible to design the necessary communication and control structures for an organization from a sociotechnical perspective.

Computer Applications in Production and Engineering. F. Plonka and G. Olling (Eds.)

**Keywords**

Model, Second Order Cybernetics, manufacturing control, Viable System Model, simulation

# 1 INTRODUCTION

In order to compete successfully in the global market companies have to control all factors such as costs innovation, quality and time. For this reason tasks in companies are being allocated in a new way and increasingly solved by team work. Many companies have started with extensive reorganization processes. In this context, decentralization is an important objective of the organizational design. The reorganization process is characterized by the following principles (*Figure 1*) (Hiersch, 1996):

**Employee orientation:**
Since the phase of Taylorism, the focus of attention has shifted to the individual with his intelligence, creativity and talent to improvise has moved again in the center of interest. The entrepreneurial goal is to use these capabilities to open new potentials of rationalization. The capabilities of the employee can best be developed and used in the scope of decentralized organizational structures.

**The ability to co-operate with internal and external partners:**
The success of the company depends not only on their products and services but increasingly on the processes used to produce them. Therefore, the focus has to be on the optimization of entrepreneurial business processes with respect to the satisfaction of internal and external customers (Grabowski, 1995). The objective is to increase customer satisfaction. Thus, the processes in a company have to be oriented towards the customer and continuously adjusted to his demands.

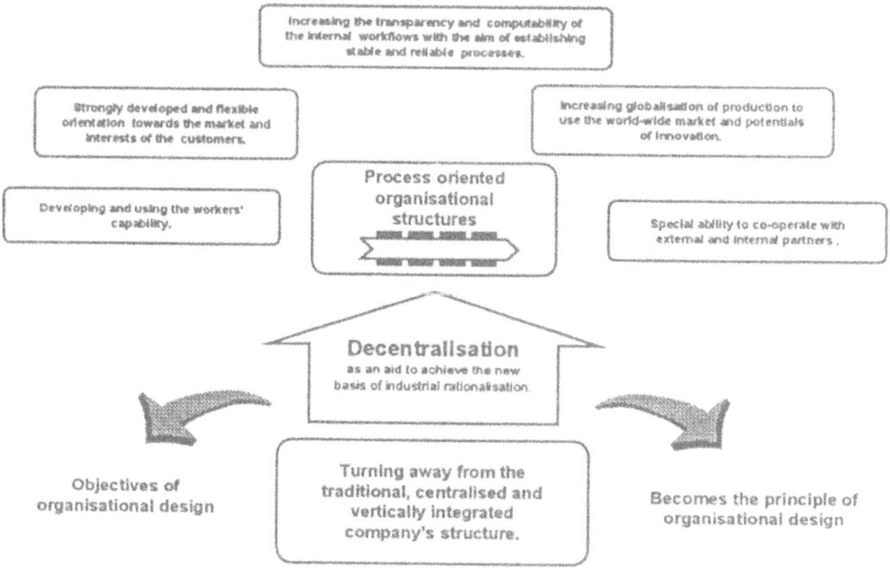


Figure 1 **Principles of organizational rationalization**

**Strongly developed and flexible orientation towards the market:**
The ability to co-operate is inseparably connected with the orientation toward the market. For this reason it is necessary to reorganize in a process-oriented way the operational sequences in a company according to the requests and demands of the customer (Wiegershaus, 1996). The organizational design must optimize the activities of a process. This process orientation is the prerequisite for a customer orientation. Moreover, this approach can lead to a considerable improvement of the processes (Eversheim, 1995). An orientation of the entrepreneurial activities towards the value-creating process provides greater transparency of the internal operational sequences.

In manufacturing, such a process-oriented organization is realized by hybrid manufacturing structures. In these structures partly autonomous, decentralized-scheduled manufacturing units work together with centralized-scheduled units within internal customer-supplier-relations in the manufacturing order processing. This future-oriented factory structure is based on the principle of modularity, the building of network structures as well as the implementation of team- and group-work (Wildemann, 1996).

## 2 SITUATION OF MANUFACTURING CONTROL SYSTEMS

Appropriate aids are required to support the employees in their new work environment and in the realization of their new additional responsibilities. Control and information systems are therefore needed, that are oriented towards the total process and adjusted to continuously changing operational sequences (Poensgen, 1994). PPC and manufacturing control systems that are currently available do not keep up with the flexibility of business processes. Current PPC- and manufacturing control systems do not have appropriate structures and operational sequences that fulfill the requirements of the new forms of organizations (*Table 1*).

The causes for the critics are, on the one hand, the inflexible and old soft- and hardware structures (DLR, 94) and on the other hand, the out-dated models of manufacturing control which are only of limited use but upon which the present systems are based (Linsen, 1995) (Herrmann, 1995). Often they are too inflexible and cannot be adapted to the current requirements of new organizational structures because they are oriented by old organizational models (Linsen, 1995). The functional technical design of the PPC- and manufacturing control systems corresponds to the organizational structures that are based on the division of labor and the division orientation (Poensgen, 1995). For the user the often oversized systems have a confusing offer of functions (VDW, 1995) (Herrmann, 1995). Often the weak points of a functional enterprise are reflected in particular by the software used (Poensgen, 1995).

Table 1 **Future oriented change in manufacturing control**

| *Weak points of classic control systems* | *Characteristics of advanced systems* |
|---|---|
| are oriented by old organizational models. | are decentralized. |
| are not adjustable to new requirements. | are process oriented. |
| support only isolated activities and not connected processes. | follow customer-supplier-principle. |
| handle complexity with the aid of an EDP-system. | provide continuous improvement process. |
| integrate new functions to face continuously increasing complexity. | are partially autonomous. |
| work functionally oriented. | are customer oriented. |
| are inaccurate because planning results are soon out of date. | have fast and networked control loops. |
| | manage complexity. |
| | are object oriented. |

In conclusion, it can be said that the available PPC- as well the manufacturing control systems do not meet the requirements of decentralized organizational structures. However, control and planing tools should decisively support decentralization (VDW, 1995). Information systems have to fit into the chosen organizational structures and processes without changing the general conditions. It is not the operational sequence in manufacturing that should be adjusted to the information system but the other way round. For this reason there is need for IT-systems for the manufacturing control that correspond to decentralize manufacturing structures.

IT-systems for manufacturing control no longer need to be designed from a purely technical perspective. Similar to the design of working systems it is required that the design of information systems has to be oriented to the needs of the individual. The role of the manufacturing control systems has changed. It should not make decisions for the employee but support him at his work. In this context the employee has an important position as the final decision-maker. So far the shop floor control has been perceived as a technical system in general. The role of the employee and the resulting consequences for the design of the manufacturing control and the supporting information systems have been neglected. The essential objective of previous approaches for shop floor control was to describe the complex processes using mathematical models which should lead to a more exact planning. By the developing of these planning methods far away from the shop floor (Herrmann, 1995) the sociotechnical approach was mainly ignored.

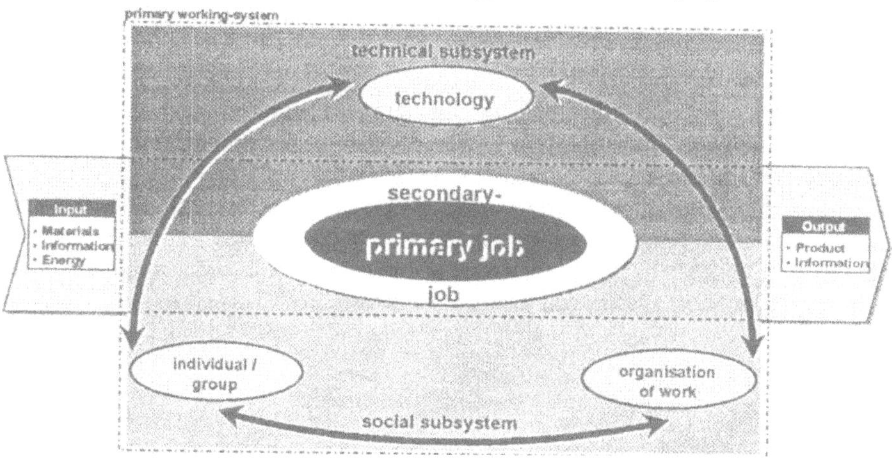


Figure 2 **The social technical system**

Therefore new information systems should be designed which consider the triangle relationship that is used in the sociotechnical system design (*Figure 2*): individual, technology and organization.

The concept of the sociotechnical system approach proceeds on the assumption that a working system consists of a technical and social subsystem. The technical subsystem comprises the technological and spatial conditions of the working system (Ulrich, 1994). The social subsystem consists of the organizational members with their individual and group related needs.

A working system is build to fulfill a primary job which transforms material, information and energy to a product or information of value. The secondary job of a working system is to maintain itself and to control the primary job.

The sociotechnical system approach forms an essential theoretical basis of the modern psychology of labor. According to it primary working systems are considered as goal oriented, open and dynamic systems that are in contact with their environment by the exchange of in- and outputs.

The sociotechnical concept demands an holistic approach to the solution of a problem. It accepts the complexity resulting from the interaction of human being and technique (Sydow, 1985).

An information system for the manufacturing control has to consider the needs of the group members, the organizational restrictions as well as the effect of technical systems. Likewise, it has to enable the complexity of an organization, resulting from the different factors of influence, to operate.

Bearing in mind these designing fields and the criticisms mentioned the following aspects have to be considered when previously designing information systems (*Figure 3*):

**Organization as a design aspect for a control system**

The organization of a system means its planned design. It represents a basis for the connections and interactions between the workers, the used technique and the information that is necessary to process the task. For this purpose the organization states rules that determine these relationships (Probst, 1993). The objective of such an organized working system is to fulfill the purpose of the system.

Consequently, the manufacturing organization represents the basis of the relationship between the employees that participate in the manufacturing process, the machines and the necessary information. Organization and technology have to be co-ordinated according to the overall purpose of the system. They have to provide a common basis for self-organization, self-control and autonomy. Only in this way is it possible to use the potential of the employee in order to continuously optimize the working system and to reach set targets.

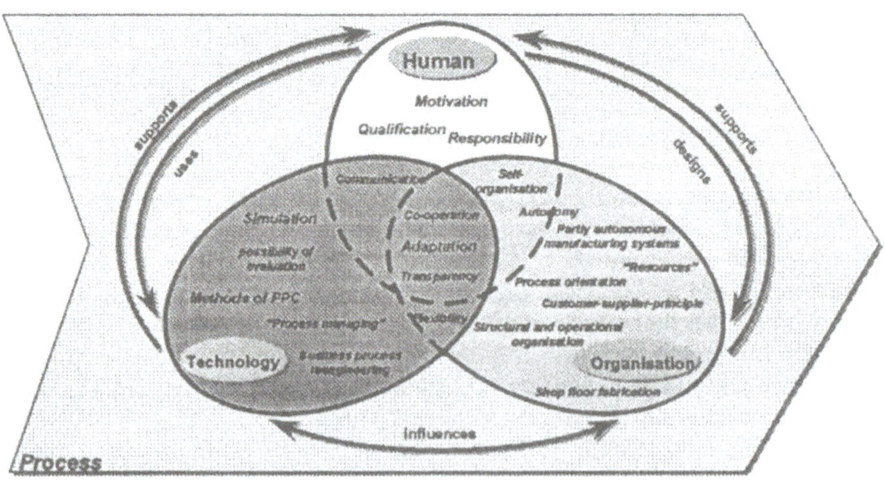


**Figure 3** Interaction between human, technology and organizational factors

For this reason the information, planning and control functions must be by and large shifted into the individual working area (Schwaninger, 1994). The information systems for the support of decentralized manufacturing structures have to be adapted to the organizational structures. Consequently, demands on the design of the manufacturing control must be analyzed with respect to autonomy and self-organization. In this way, the information processes can be closely approximated to the real processes.

**The individual as designing aspect for control systems**

The individual is the focus of labor oriented designing concepts. In order to use his potential for the optimization of the working system it is necessary to design systems and their tasks according to work and human oriented characteristics. The working task is the core of the sociotechnical view. It is the intersection between organization and individual (Volpert, 1987). The task has to meet different requirements to induce motivation which leads to the optimal realization of the task. The worker has to posses the skills needed for the working processes and the necessary aids. (Ulrich, 1994). The structural features of any task must be designed in a way to activate the worker to either continue or to finish their work In other words they should motivate the acting person to fulfill his task.

The following characteristics of a task design produce motivation: holistic work, variety of demands, possibilities of social interaction, autonomy, as well as possibilities for learning and development.

When designing a manufacturing system which fulfills the requirements of a human oriented design, it is therefore necessary to check which influences these characteristics have on the design of the manufacturing control and which consequences this again has on the design of an information system. In particular, information flows must be checked and communication structures have to be designed to support the self-organization and co-operation with other manufacturing sections.

**Technology as design aspect for a control system**

Here, technology is considered as an aid for the purpose 'manufacturing control'. For the realization of his task the employee needs informational technical aids which provide him with the necessary information and supporting functions for the planning and control of his task.

The design of shop floor information systems should be widely decentralized in order to increase the self-controlling ability of the decentralized manufacturing sections as well as to promote the interest of the employees in their work, their competence and their motivation.(Schwaninger, 1990).

This corresponds to the demand for the design of holistic tasks which include goal finding, planning and control functions. It follows that information systems have to offer these functions to make an integrated task design possible. In this context it is also necessary to clarify the type of information, communication and control structures used. For this reason the demands on the tools for manufacturing control systems from the perspective of the individuals and the decentralized organization must be examined.

## 3 SOLUTION APPROACH

Usually production management systems are based on implicit or explicit models that depict the characteristics of the controlled manufacturing system. A model is always a simplified copy of reality. Models for scheduling and control are open or closed control loops. Nowadays, EDP-systems for production planning and control as well as manufacturing control systems are based on these principles. For many new research projects the feedback control loop is still the basic concept. In order to describe the different scheduling levels of production planning and control as well as of manufacturing control, multistage feedback control loop systems have been developed.

This feedback control loop is also the basic principle of cybernetics. Cybernetics is the science of communication and control processes in living beings and machines. Its methods make it possible to look at structures in a wide sense and to depict different kind of systems from the perspective of their control structure (Probs., 1985).

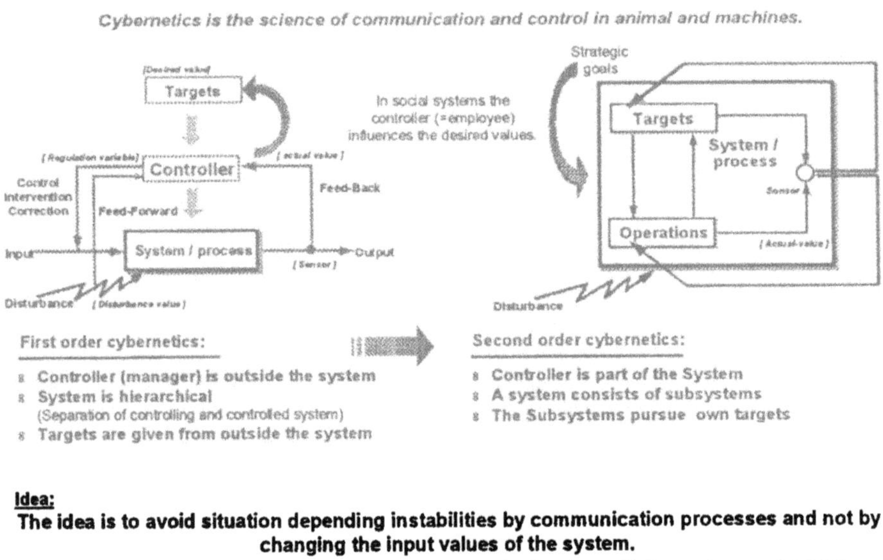


**Figure 4** First and Second Order Cybernetics [following (Schwaninger, 1994)]

*Figure 4* shows the control of a process from the cybernetics perspective. Current output values of the process are fed back to the controller. The controller carries out a comparison between current and desired values. Based on this difference the controller generates correcting input data which are transmitted into the process. By the principle of feedforward it is possible to consider the effect of future disturbances on the process and to use this information for control decisions (Schwaninger, 1994).

This concept presented here is called 'First order cybernetics' (=cybernetics of mechanical systems).

**Definition of First Order cybernetics:**
*'The cybernetics of systems that are observed from the outside as opposed to the cybernetics of systems involving their observers. First order cybernetics is concerned with circular causal processes, e.g. control, negative feedback, computing, adaption.'* (Kippendorff, 1997)

The decisive interest in developing this approach was only of a technical nature (Espejo, 1993). Characteristic of the First Order Cybernetics is that the controller (e.g. the manufacturing controller) stands outside the controlled system and the targets are given from outside the system (Schwaninger, 1994). The application of cybernetic models on social systems demands a special view because first order cybernetics is not appropriate to meet the characteristics of individuals constituting an organization. In hierarchical social systems the controller actively influences the desired values of the system from outside. This is represented by the curved arrow in the left hand side of figure 4. The outside controller is responsible to reach the given targets.

In contrast to technical systems in social systems similar to autonomous biological systems the principle of self-control gains in importance over the one of external control. Advanced manufacturing should be designed similar to such biological systems of high autonomy.

One example for an autonomous biological system is the balancing of the body temperature: Independent from outside disturbances - e.g. environmental temperature - the body temperatures are kept stable. In the same way manufacturing cells or islands should be able to keep their goals independently from external disturbances. Principles like autonomy, self-control, self-organization and self-reference acquire decisive organizational importance (Schwaninger, 1994). Hence, First and Second Order Cybernetics must be differentiated.

**Definition of Second Order Cybernetics:**
*'The cybernetics of systems involving their observers as opposed to the cybernetics of systems that are observed from the outside. Second-order cybernetics is a more recent development, which involves the observer as a constitutive part of a circular organization and is concerned with Self-reference, Epistemology, Autonomy, Self-Government, Autopoiesis.'* (Kippendorff, 1997)

In First Order Cybernetics the controller itself (i.e. the employee) is part of the system. The system is working goal oriented and consists of subsystems that pursue their own goals. The difference between the two points of views could be characterized as follows:

**First Order Cybernetics ('The cybernetics of observed systems')**

- The controller (manager) is outside the system.
- The system is purpose orientated, i.e. the goals are given from outside into the system.

**Second Order Cybernetics ('The Cybernetics of observing systems')**

- The controller (manager) himself is part of the system.
- The system is goal oriented and it consists of subsystems, that pursue their own goals.

By the introduction of Second Order Cybernetics the concept of the feedback control loop is not replaced, but instead completed and acquires partly new meanings (Schwaninger, 1994).

The cybernetics of mechanical systems is based on the assumption of a clearly defined 'Black-Box' that can be used to handle the goals as well as the control and communication mechanism of the system.

The planning and control of a conventionally organized manufacture is based on a similar assumption. It was assumed that detailed planning targets of the controller or the PPC-System could be used to control the manufacturing process. It has transpired that rules for centralized detailed planning are not appropriate for the planning and control of modern decentralized manufacturing. Only unsatisfactory results could be obtained.

This conclusion corresponds to the knowledge we have of cybernetics. Scientific publications in the field of Second Order Cybernetics have demonstrated that the assumption of a clearly defined 'Black-Box' is not justified in the context of human activities and actions (Espejo, 1993).

From the perspective of the Second Order Cybernetics the handling that is to say, the management of situations is not primarily the result of decisions that are based on abstract models of the situation, but on communication processes that make a common interaction of all involved persons in the process possible.

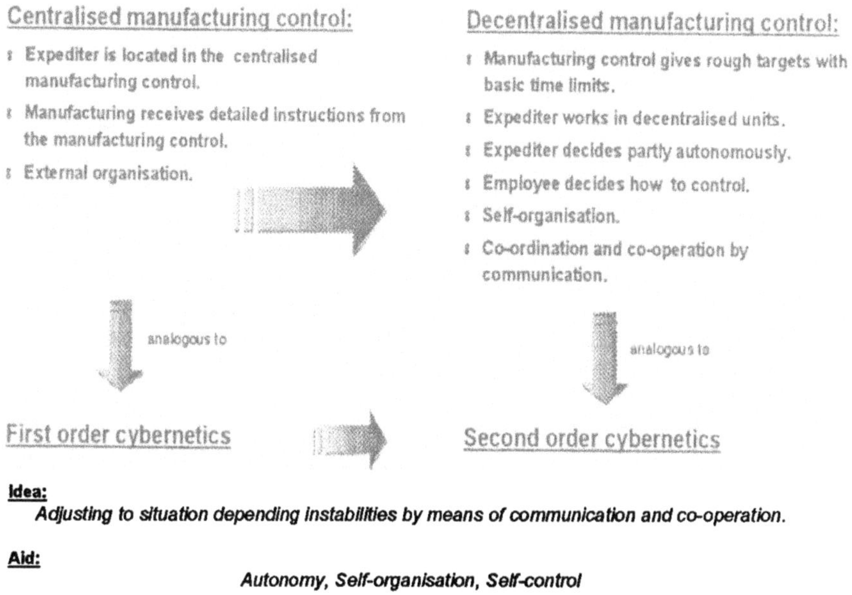


Figure 5 **Manufacturing control and Cybernetics**

The principle idea is to avoid having situation depending instabilities by means of communication processes and not by changing the input values of the 'Black-Box'. To co-operate as a community and to solve problems the knowledge of the persons that are involved in the process has to be included in the communication processes.

The distributed manufacturing control is based on this principle. The control does not happen by a detailed plan which is centrally scheduled but by manufacturing order pools with basic time limits which constitute targets for the decentralized organizational units. The realization of work is planned and controlled by the workers themselves in the decentralized units. As a result, experience and knowledge of the employee and the informal processes in the working system bear an important influence on the design and management of the control system. Therefore, it is necessary to consider the communication mechanism in these structures as well as the experience and knowledge of the workers. These forms of organizations work according to the principle of autonomy, self-organization and self-control. For this purpose the Second Order Cybernetics tries to offer appropriate mechanisms. A comparison of the characteristics of centralized and decentralized manufacturing control shows parallels between the situation of the manufacturing control in distributed organizational units and the characteristics of Second Order Cybernetics.

The importance of cybernetics for the design of problem solving and of decision making activities in sociotechnical systems has long since been recognized. Cybernetics makes it possible to model sociotechnical systems from the perspective of communication and control by analyzing and systematically designing communication processes and information flows. Therefore, cybernetics constitutes an ideal instrument for interdisciplinary co-operation (Gomez, 1981).

Consequently, it is possible to consider the different designing aspects of manufacturing control and to develop an integrated approach in order to design the control tasks in a manufacturing system using an appropriate cybernetic method.

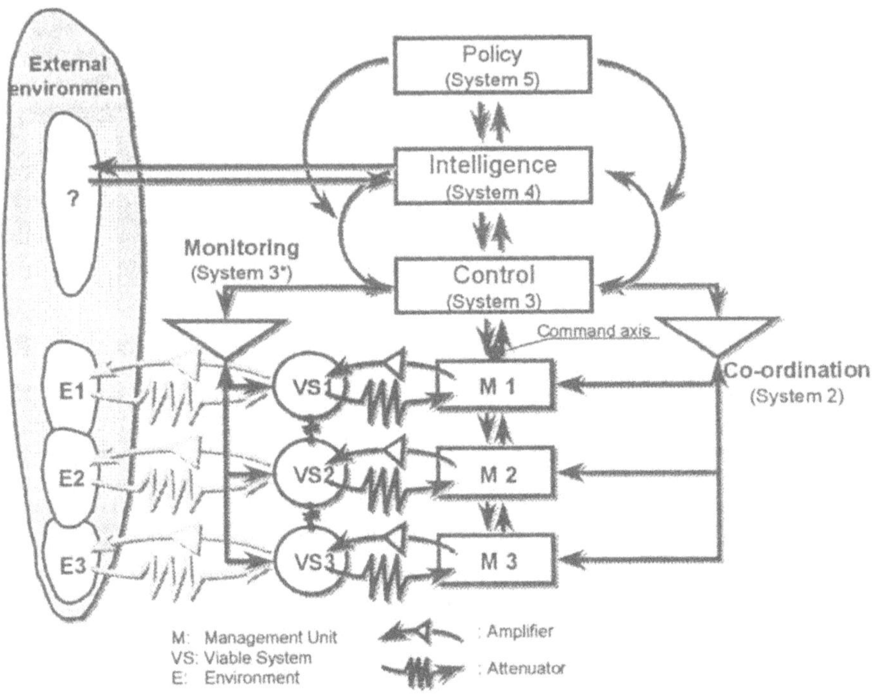


**Figure 6 The structure of the Viable System Model [according to (Espejo, 1993)]**

The 'Viable System Model (VSM)' is such a method (*Figure 6*). It was developed by the economist Stafford Beer to model and analyze sociotechnical systems and in particular, to model the control mechanism of such systems. The starting point was the question: Which communication structures and control mechanisms are necessary for an organization so that it may adapt to changing conditions as well as make use of experiences - i.e. to learn, to keep its identity and to develop - in other words to be viable (Malik, 1996).

To formalize the structural minimum requirements Beer used the human nerve system as an analogy. Based on the human nerve system he developed a structurally similar (homomorphist) model, which views at sociotechnical systems from the perspective of control. From Beer's point of view every viable system like the human nerve system is characterized by five subsystems of control, which express the necessary and minimal conditions to survive.(Probst, 1985). The model is based on the principles of viability, recursion and autonomy. *Table 2* describes the control mechanisms that are included in the model.

**Table 2 Systems and their functions**

| *System* | *Function* |
|---|---|
| One | (partly) autonomous organizational units are controlled within their environment. Every system One has to be a viable unit. It means that by the principle of recursion each system One again consists of five subsystems (system One to Five). |
| Two | Co-ordination to achieve a higher goal using a network of communication connections between the individual control mechanisms of the partly autonomous units. |
| Three | A "higher" control mechanism serves the co-ordination and optimization of any current activity in the system as a whole. This control mechanism is responsible for the internal balance. |
| Four | A control mechanism that integrates the information from the system's environment with the aim of establishing an external balance. |
| Five | A superposed control mechanism co-ordinates the control activities for the internal stabilization of the whole system (System Three) plus the control activities which achieve a balance with the system's environment depending on the targets and the purpose of the whole system. |

The Viable System Model provides a means of analyzing distributed organizations. It is a method to depict communication mechanisms that make the co-operation of the workers in a system possible. The model can be used for the design of 'viable' organizational structures (Espejo, 1993). The specific stress on the information connections between the systems and the recursion levels make the model an organization-theoretical basis for the architecture of information systems (Schuhmann, 1991).

Manufacturing control is done by certain activities of the workers (*Figure 7*). On the level of the machine operator a control activity is for example to sort the manufacturing orders according to certain targets. On the level of the expediter a control activity is for example the allocation of manufacturing orders to the different manufacturing areas. These activities are supported by certain (supporting) functions of the manufacturing control.

The necessary information and communication structures as well as supporting functions which realize these activities are structured by the Viable System Model. The result is a metamodel of the manufacturing control that fulfills the minimum requirement of an information system from the perspective of information, communication and control.

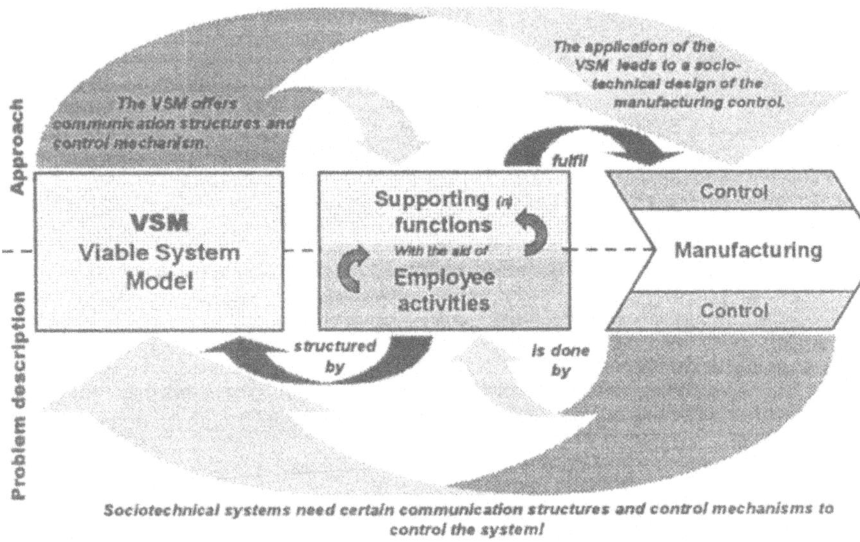


**Figure 7 Solution approach with the VSM**

The structure of the model makes it possible to model the manufacturing control from a sociotechnical perspective and to design the secondary task "manufacturing control" for the worker from a perspective of an integrated task design. That means that every worker should contribute to the target finding, planning, and control process. To support the worker by means of an information system from the perspective of cybernetics it is necessary that the target finding, planning and control processes correspond with the organizational structure (Schwaninger, 1994). The minimal organizational structure necessary for the manufacturing control which is required for that purpose is shown in *Figure8.*

To guarantee a wide autonomy the '**Decentralized Scheduling Mechanism**' receives a stock of orders with basic time limits over the command axis. Inside the '**Decentralized Scheduling Mechanism**' the detailed planning for the order processing in the decentralized manufacturing unit is carried out. By means of a calculated distribution of the stock of orders to the individual partly autonomous units the cohesion of these units in the sense of a given target is striven for. This vertical co-ordination function is the task of the control mechanism '**Control**'.

The function of the co-ordination mechanism '**Order Co-ordination**' is to avoid and regulate disturbances between the individual decentralized units. This mechanism pursues the goal of achieving synergy effects which are striven for by the plan of the mechanism '**Control**'. So the control demands on the system '**Control**' are reduced. The more powerful the horizontal co-ordination function is, the more autonomy can be guaranteed for the distributed manufacturing units.

In order to realize its co-ordination function the '**Order Co-ordination**' receives information about the stock of orders of the individually scheduled decentralized units from the system '**Control**'. The '**Decentralized Scheduling Mechanisms**' inform the '**Order Co-ordination**' about their current status of the detailed planning, their current progress of orders as well as about possible derivations from time targets and eventually resulting new order sequences.

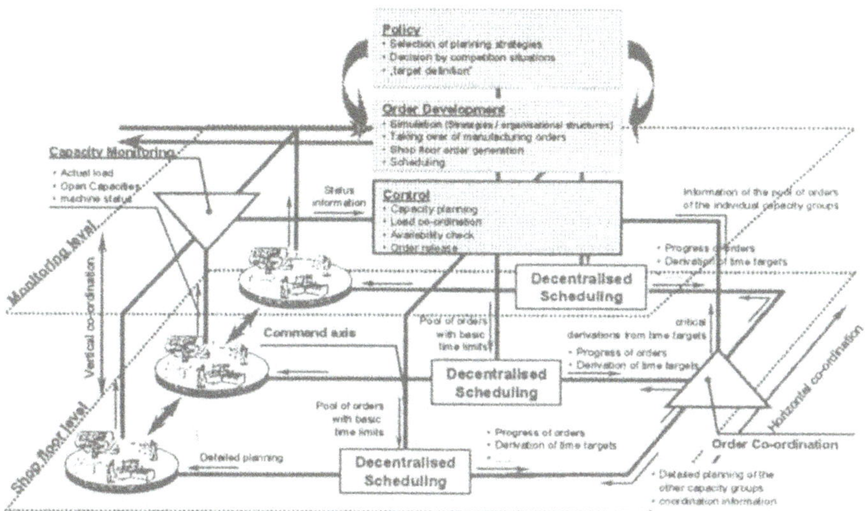


Figure 8 **Organizational structure of the shop-floor management**

The '**Order Co-ordination**' informs every '**Decentralized Scheduling Mechanism**' about the current detailed planning situation of the other units. It also derives co-ordination information to regulate possible disturbances, as a result of the comparison between the targets of the '**Control**' and the current progress of orders that is to say derivations from time targets of the decentralized units.

The '**Order Co-ordination**' only passes information about derivations from time targets that will lead to inadjustable disturbances to the '**Control**'. However, to fulfill the control function it is necessary for the system '**Control**' to obtain unfiltered information of the real status of the decentralized units (Espejo, 1989). For this to happen, a monitoring function is necessary. In the model this monitoring-mechanism is represented by the '**Capacity Monitoring**'. It belongs to the system '**Control**'.

The '**Capacity Monitoring**' delivers information to the '**Control**' about the real status of the decentralized manufacturing units, global targets such as capacity utilization or a certain throughput time. For this reason it monitors the current loading with manufacturing orders, possible open capacities as well as possible disturbances of machines or workers and passes is information to the system '**Control**'. With this information it is possible for the '**Control**' to cross-check the information of the '**Order Co-ordination**' and the direct information of the '**Decentralized Scheduling Mechanism**'. The described communication channels of the control mechanism '**Control**' (including '**Capacity Monitoring**'), the '**Decentralized Scheduling Mechanism**' and '**Order Co-ordination**' set up the monitoring and control mechanism of the manufacturing control and correspond to the systems 'Three', 'Two' and 'One' of the Viable System Model.

To adapt the manufacturing and the control mechanism to new situations, which result from, changed market conditions, it is necessary to provide appropriate mechanisms for the shop floor management in the organization structure. This is the task of the meta system that consists of the control mechanisms '**Control**', '**Order Development**' and '**Policy**'. These mechanisms correspond to the systems 'Three', 'Four' and 'Five' of the Viable System Model.

The task of the control mechanism '**Policy**' is to determine the basic goals and strategic rules for the whole job shop management. It derives the basic behavior of the job shop management from targets of system five of the higher recursion level and from the information of the external (=market) respectively internal (=manufacturing) environment. In the sense of the manufacturing control this could be for example planning strategies or setting of long-term targets for capacity balancing. In the long term the establishment of specific forms of manufacturing organizations are feasible as a target of the control mechanism '**Policy**'. Another task of system Five is the co-ordination of the internal environment and the external environment. This is necessary to remain viable in the future and to be able to compete with new market conditions.

The control mechanism '**Order Development**' has the function to process the orders and to develop possibilities to push the manufacturing orders through the production on time. That includes the optimization of planning strategies and the manufacturing organization itself. In the short term different order sequences can be simulated to evaluate the different effects on the manufacturing process.

Supporting functions from the perspective of the manufacturing control are for example. the time scheduling as well the taking over or splitting of manufacturing orders. In the medium-term the suitability of different planning methods can be examined. In the long-term the task is to optimize the manufacturing organization for instance by simulating of different organizational structures and orders of operations.

The solution proposals developed by the '**Order Development**' are transmitted to the operative '**Control**' that examines the proposals from the perspective of the internal situation in the manufacturing area. In the same way the '**Order Development**' examines proposals of the '**Control**' from its perspective. It is a continuous co-ordination process between these two systems.

From the perspective of the manufacturing control the capacity planning, the load co-ordination, the availability check as well as the order release are all functions that support the task of the system '**Control**'. In general the co-ordination process takes place in the short and medium term. The co-ordination of these two control mechanisms is monitored by the control mechanism '**Policy**' according to global company targets. If there is a conflict this mechanism is the highest authority.

The previous description demonstrates the transfer of the control mechanism of the manufacturing control to the Viable System Model of Stafford Beer. In the following chapter the realization of an information system that is based on this approach is presented.

## 4 MOBILEIT-S

The model based toolbox for integrated manufacturing control systems with simulation kernel is a concept for an information system that offers the possibility to configure system functions by designing a factory model.

For this reason the organizational structure of the job shop management that was mentioned with the VSM in the previous chapter, is described in form of general structures in a metamodel. This model offers the structural framework for general reference models of the manufacturing order processing for different manufacturing organizations like single item and serial production.

The model elements that are described in the reference model correspond to the ones in reality. In this way a machine in the model correspond to a machine in reality and the depicted control processes correspond to the ones that are necessary to control the shop floor. The elements are oriented to existing notations of a companies hierarchy, operation resources, manufacturing aids, order structures and working-papers.

From the perspective of the manufacturing control the behavior of the real manufacturing elements is reproduced by the methods and attributes of each corresponding model object. Factory objects with the same or similar structure and behavior are objects of the same class.

The building of a specific factory model is done by deriving the model elements from the reference model. The object-oriented concept offers a way to refine the model step by step by specifying the necessary changes in each case.

Since it is easy to alter the factory model and the included control processes during the run-time it is possible to adjust the model according to changing demands.

Various control strategies and factory behavior are implemented by the use of event-driven simulation and interaction of the factory objects. Therefore, it is possible to analyze planned manufacturing structures new control strategies and different order sequences for the job shop scheduling. In the same way it is possible to identify dependencies and conformities to laws of the processes and to use the results for planning and control in the meaning of continuous optimization.

The prototype of the system represents an integrated solution that offers functions of current monitoring system as well as certain functions of factory planning systems.

By combining a generally used factory model with a powerful model based simulation as well as with the application of an object-oriented software architecture a flexible information system is formed that allows the user a continuous adaptation to changing production conditions. As a result a continuous improvement process is provided. The use of simulation offers an aid that supports the preparation and evaluation of decisions in the manufacturing area. This ranges from the short-term manufacturing control to long-term investment decisions.

The development of this system is sponsored by the development-program 'Production 2000 - Strategies for the production in the 21. Century'. It is promoted by the German federal ministry of education, science, research and technology (BMBF). Four companies, two software houses and two departments of different universities are involved in this project.

## 5 REFERENCES


DLR/Projektträgerschaft: Arbeit und Technik, Leitstände für die Werkstatt.; Bremerhaven: Wirtschaftsverlag, 1994.

Espejo, R.: The VSM revisited. In: The Viable System Model - Interpretations and Applications of Stafford Beer's VSM.Espejo, R.; Harden, R. (Hrsg.).Chichester, New York: John Wiley & Sons Ltd., 1989.

Espejo, R.; Schwaninger, M.: Organizational fitness: corporate effectiveness through management cybernetics. Frankfurt a.M.; New York: Campus Verlag 1993.

Gomez, P.: Modelle und Methoden des systemorientierten Management. Bern; Stuttgart: Verlag Paul Haupt, 1981.

Grabowski, H.; Grein, G.; Milde, P.; Weber, U.: Unternehmensmodelle zur Konzeption von Informationssystemen. ZWF 90 (1995) 7-8, S. 354 – 356.

Herrmann,W.; Hug, B.: Werkstattnahes Produktionsmanagement und PPS. CIM-Management 11 (1995) 3, S. 47 – 51.

Hirsch-Kreinsen, H.: Restrukturierung von Unternehmen – Ziele, Formen und Probleme dezentraler Organisation in: Produzieren im 21. Jahrhundert – Herausforderungen für die deutsche Industrie. Lutz, B.; Hartmann, M.; Hirsch-Kreinsen, H. (Hrsg.), Campus-Verlag, Frankfurt am Main, New-York 1996.

Kippendorff, K.: Klaus Krippendorff's Dictionary of Cybernetics. Principa Cybernetica Web: URL:http://pespmc1.vub.ac.be/ASC/First-_cyber.html; Email: fkk@asc.upenn.edu; [Online: June 1997]

Linsen, M.: Fit für die Zukunft – Wohin geht der Trend bei PPS? AV 32 (1995) 2, S. 112 – 114.

Malik, F.: Strategie des Managements komplexer Systeme – Ein Beitrag zur Management-Kybernetik evolutionärer Systeme. Paul Haupt Verlag, Bern, Stuttgart, Wien; 1996.

Maßberg, W.; Thiem, I.: Objektorientiertes Referenzmodell der Auftragsbearbeitung. ZWF 92 (1997) 1-2, S. 38 – 41.

Poensgen, W.: Vom Taylorismus zum Prozeßmanagement – Individuelles Gestalten von Organisationen, Prozessen, Funktionen und Daten. AV 31 (1994) 6, S. 372 – 373.

Poensgen, W.: Informationstechnik für das Re-Engineering. ZWF 90 (1995) 3, S. 98 – 99.

Probst, G. J. B.: Die Entwicklung zu modernen systemorientierten Organisationsmodellen; in: Unternehmensorganisation - Entwicklungen in Theorie und Praxis. Ulrich, H.; Probst, G. (Hrsg.). Bern; Stuttgart: Verlag Paul Haupt, 1985.

Rohloff, M.: Produktionsmanagement in modularen Organisationsstrukturen: Reorganisation der Produktion und objektorientierte Informationssysteme für verteilte Planungsinstrumente. München, Wien: Oldenbourg, 1995.

Schumann, W.: Informationsmanagement - Unternehmensführung und Informationssysteme aus systemtheoretischer Sicht. Frankfurt a. M.: Campus Verlag, 1991.

Schwaninger, M.: Managementsysteme. Frankfurt a. M.: Campus Verlag, 1994.

Ulich, E.:Arbeitspsychologie.3., überarbeitete und erweiterte Auflage. Stuttgart: Schäffer Poeschel, 1994.

Verein Deutscher Werkzeugmaschinenfabriken: Autonome, Kooperative Produktionssysteme. Frankfurt 1995.

Wiegershaus, U.; Hagen, A.; Lackner, U.: Marktführerschaft durch kundenorientierte Servicestrukturen. VDI-Z 138 (1996), Nr. 6 – June, S. 94 – 97.

Wildemann, H.: Netzwerkstrukturen als neue Form der Unternehmensorganisation. ZWF 91 (1996) 1-2, S.12-16.

## 7 BIOGRAPHY

Prof. Dr.-Ing. Maßberg:
Born 11. May 1932 at Karlsruhe, Germany. Electrical Engineering studies at the University RWTH Aachen; 1965 Doctor of Mechanical Engineering by Prof. Dr.-Ing. H. Opitz at the RWTH Aachen; From 1965 to 1975 leading positions in several companies; Since 1976 holder of the chair 'Production Systems' and member of the Board of Automation Research Institute Ruhr-University Bochum. From 1990 till 1993 Rector of the Ruhr-University Bochum; From 1993 till 1997 Chairman of the German Academic Society for Production Engineering (WGP).

Michael Bäcker:
Born 21. July 1970 at Siegen, Germany. Mechanical Engineering studies at the Ruhr-University Bochum; Since April 1997 research assistant at the Automation Research Institute (Ruhr-University Bochum).

Harald Schallner:
Born 22. September 1969 at Münster, Germany. Computer Science studies at the University Paderborn; Since October 1996 research assistant at the Automation Research Institute (Ruhr-University Bochum).

Ingo Thiem:
Born 4. December 1964 at Wattenscheid, Germany. Study of Mechanical Engineering at the Ruhr-University Bochum and University Dortmund; From 1990 till 1993 engineer for logistics at FLACHGLAS AG; Since 1993 research assistant at the Automation Research Institute (Ruhr-University Bochum).

# 41
# Integration of process planning and production management

*G. Halevi* , H.J.J. Kals***
** Technician -- Israel Institute of Technology, Dobnov St. 20a Tel-Aviv 64369 ISRAEL, Tel/Fax. + 972 3 696 2833*
*E-mail merhlev@techunix.technion.ac.il*
***Director of the Center for Integrated Manufacturing & development, CIPV*
*University of Twente WB. Z.208 P.O. Box 217 7500 AE Enschede Tel. + 31 53 489 2534 Fax. + 31 53 489 3631*
*E-mail h.j.j.kals@utwpue.wb.utwente.nl*

**Abstract**

New markets' demand objectives call for the integration of process planning in production management, which means that the process plan must be regarded as a variable, to be generated within seconds and with no human intervention. The matrix method, aims at introducing flexibility by integrating process planning and production management. The routing is presented by an Operation-Resources Matrix, which represents many possible routing, However, the selection of the routing is deferred to the moment of need. The method does a Material Requirements Planning (finite capacity) and Capacity Planning in one run, keeping the product network (Bill of Material) at all times. In this paper the concept of the matrix method is described.

**Keywords**

Process planning, MRP, MRPII, Production Planning, Capacity Planning, Scheduling.

## 1. INTRODUCTION

The Production Management (PM) task is to plan and produce the products according to management orders and policy. The major objectives of the task are:

- Meeting the delivery dates
- Keeping the capital, tied down in production, to a minimum
- Minimizing the manufacturing lead time

Computer Applications in Production and Engineering. F. Plonka and G. Olling (Eds.)

- Minimizing the idle times of the resources

The traditional method to perform this task is divided into several stages (Hal, 1980). The orders are initially converted to required manufacturing activities, which defines what should be produced at the shop, and what should be purchased or outsourced. This stage is called MRP - Material Requirement Planning/Material Resource Planning. The material and the items that are made outside the company are taking care of by purchasing. The items that are produced in shop are handled in the next step: CP - Capacity Planning. In this step a long-range plan is made, planning the capacity required at each work center and helping to allocate the machines and manpower required to meet the goals of PM. The immediate short periods are scheduled in order to determine what jobs should be dispatched to the shop floor for execution in a certain time period. The Job Release (dispatch) step is the link between planning and execution. It initiates the production activities by the issue of orders to the shop floor, according to a short-term schedule taken from the capacity plan.

The main inputs to the PM are:

- The orders and tasks, including quantity and the delivery date
- The bill of materials for each product
- The routing for each component
- Inventory and resources

The planning and execution, in the traditional method, as described above, regards the routing as static and unalterable. Thus, the planning is simple, but it robs the shop from production flexibility and efficiency. [Seo and Egbelu 1996], [Hal, 1980]

Today's competitive market imposes new demands and objectives on the manufacturing process. Example of these demands is: delivery speed to market; product diversity and options; competitive product quality; customer satisfaction; and naturally, a competitive price. Since the traditional control methods do not supply solutions to these new demands, new methods and solutions are proposed. The main trend is to integrate technology with Production Management. Current Production Management often runs into problems such as: not meeting due dates, finite-capacity planning, overload, under-utilization and bottlenecks. Such problems occur mainly due to the fact that the routing (process plan) is regarded as unalterable. Anyone who has actually managed a production facility knows that this is not really the case. If the process routing is viewed as a variable, then many of the above problems can be solved by elimination. For example: An overload situation occurs in the Capacity Planning System. Traditional methods attempt to resolve this situation by transferring jobs to under-utilized periods or deferring operations to a later period. The result is increased Work In Process (WIP) and not meeting the due dates. By the dynamic routing method, this situation can often be solved by using a different routing that takes advantage of the under-utilized machines. Traditionally, internal due dates are set by the MRP system. They are not accurate as MRP considers infinite capacity. This causes unrealistic due dates, that in turn creates unrealistic capacity plans and schedules.

With a dynamic system that can generate process plans within seconds without human intervention, there is no need to run the MRP system with infinite capacity. By employing a dynamic CAPP system the MRP system can be run considering finite capacity. These are only a few examples of how the use of a dynamic CAPP system may revolutionize production management procedures.

The manufacturing process is a dynamic one as resources change, machines fail, tools break, employees are unavailable, orders change, parts are rejected and reworked, power failures occur, etc. This dynamic nature calls for dynamic planning and flexibility of operation. Flexibility calls for immediate adaptation of process plans to the availability of resources. Furthermore, there are many optimization criteria for production planning and process planning. Each criterion calls for modification of the process plan. Thus a process plan should be dynamically adjusted to meet the criteria of the situation at hand.

This paper presents a dynamic system that integrates process planning with production management. The system integrates all stages, i.e. MRP, CP and SFC(shop flow control) with one dynamic logistics program. The dynamic and flexible behavior is obtained by employing the matrix method in process planning. The philosophy of this method is that a process planner is neither an economist nor a production planner. Therefore he should not make decisions, that is beyond his field of expertise. His task should be to prepare a matrix, covering all feasible routings, and subsequently let the expert in production planning decide which route to use, considering order size, plant load and shop floor state at the moment of decision making. The product tree (network) is being kept throughout all the planning steps.

## 2 THE MATRIX PROCESS PLANNING CONCEPT

The proposed CAPP system is composed of three stages: technology, transformation, and decision (mathematics). The technology stage generates Theoretical Processes (TP). The transformation stage constructs a matrix. The decision (mathematics) stage solves the matrix and generates a dynamic process plan according to the immediate requirements of the production facility.

The matrix represents an almost infinite number of possible routings. The decision of which routing to use is deferred to the time of execution. The routing decision making has been transformed from a technological into a mathematics decision. The decision-maker does not need to posses any technical knowledge, he has just to understand the capabilities of the matrix. The matrix solution time is less then a second.

The construction of the matrix has been discussed in several papers and a book (Hal 1995). In this paper, only the usage of the matrix is described.

The concept is based on the Operation - Machine matrix, where the entries are $T_{i,j}$ or $C_{i,j}$, depending on the requested criteria of optimization. $T_{i,j}$ represents the time to perform operation i on machine j, and $C_{i,j}$ means the cost of performing operation i on machine j. The matrix is shown in Table 1. The sequence of entering operations into the matrix can be casual. The priority row indicates the constraints on the actual sequence of machining operations on a path. The number in this row indicates which operation must precede the considered operation. It does not have to follow this operation immediately. Priority number 0 means that this operation may be the first machining operation or be performed anywhere. For example, the priority of operation 010 is 000; the priority of operation 020 is 010; the priority of operation 030 is 020; the priority of operation 040 is also 010. This means that the sequence of operations may be: 010; 020; 030; 040 or 020; 030; 010; 040, or 020; 010, 040; 030.

Due to tolerance demands, some operations must be performed on the same machine or with the same fixture. These requirements are indicated in the row marked as relation.

Process planning is a technological decision-making process. By using the matrix method process planning is transformed from a technological into a mathematical process. The definition of the mathematical problem is as follows: Given a list of operations to be performed and a list of available facilities, a decision is required as to which machine (or machines) to use, which operation(s) to perform on each machine, what their sequence should be, and what cutting conditions to employ. The optimization criterion is either maximum production, or minimum cost. A penalty is added for extra time or expense, whenever a change in machine or set-up takes place. This penalty should cover the extra cost of: set-up, transfer of parts between machines, additional complications in capacity planning, job recording and inspection, etc. Note that the "penalty" is for a batch and thus is a function of the quantity to be produced. The larger the batch, the lower the penalty, and thus the higher the probability of selecting the best machine for each specific operation. The sequence (priority) and the relationship (relation) between operations must be maintained. That means that the sequence of operations may be altered, if by doing so the number of machine changes is reduced. However, the priority indicated in the matrix should be obeyed. This effect can be appreciated by reviewing Table 1.

**Table 1: The matrix format**

| | **Oper# 010** | **Oper# 020** | **Oper #030** | **Oper #040** | **Oper #050** | **Oper #060** | **Total** |
|---|---|---|---|---|---|---|---|
| Priority | 00 | 010 | 020 | 030 | 020 | 050 | **Cost Time** |
| Relation | 0 | 0 | 0 | 0 | 2 | 0 | |
| TP | 2.02 | 0.05 | 0.39 | 0.20 | 0.18 | 0.41 | |
| | C | O | S | T | $ | | |
| Mach #1 | 12.48 | 4.60 | 5.96 | 5.20 | 5.12 | 6.04 | 39.40 9.85 |
| Mach#2 | 9.51 | 3.60 | 4.59 | 4.05 | 3.99 | 4.68 | 30.42 10.14 |
| Mach#3 | 5.15 | 2.39 | 2.87 | 2.60 | 2.58 | 2.90 | 18.49 13.21 |
| Mach#4 | 999 | 999 | 999 | 1.86 | 999 | 999 | 999 |
| Mach#5 | 4.02 | 2.05 | 999 | 2.20 | 2.18 | 999 | 999 |
| Mach#6 | 6.54 | 2.00 | 3.28 | 2.90 | 2.86 | 3.32 | 21.50 10.75 |

Machine #5 ; 4.02 + 2.05 + 2.18 = $8.25 = 8.25 Min
Machine #3 ; 2.87 + 2.90 = $5.77 = 4.12 Min

| | | | |
|---|---|---|---|
| Machine #4 ; 1.86 | = $1.86 | = 1.86 Min | |
| Sub total | $15.88 | | 14.23 Min |
| Total * | | $17.08 | 15.43 Min |

* Three penalties of $0.4 each

By using an unaltered process and the best machine for each operation, as indicated by the shaded numbers, five penalties have to be added to the cost of the process. (Machine # 5 - 6 - 3 - 4 - 5 - 3). However, the sequence of operation might be changed to the one shown by the arrows. (The penalty to use machine #6 is greater than the machining cost difference between machine #5 & 6). In this case only two penalties have to be added to the cost of the process.

The solution for the maximum production ( minimum time ) criterion (the upper matrix) results in only one machine (machine #1) to perform all operations. The optimum process is a compromise between all the expenses and the individual operation cost. For solving this matrix problem, a special technique has been devised. The matrix solution is done within seconds.

Table 1 shows two optimum processes. The maximum production optimum will take 9.85 minutes and a cost of $39.4. The minimum cost optimum will take 15.43 minutes and a cost of $17.08. The difference between the two processes is, that for maximum production machine #1 is selected, which is a powerful modern machining center that can perform all the operations in one chucking, while the minimum cost process uses rough, old, inaccurate machines for roughing operations and an accurate and stable machine for the finishing operations. Which process to select, depends on the shop floor load. For rush orders, the shortest production process is best, while in a slack situation the minimum cost alternative is the best. One can make such a decision only at the production management stage, and not at the process planning stage.

Currently the information transferred to production management contains usually the final decisions. For example : Use machine #5 for 8.25 min. (performing operations No. 010; 020; & 050). Next, use Machine #3 for 4.12 min. (performing operations No. 030; & 050). Finally, use machine #4 for 1.86 min. (performing operation No. 040). Production management has to work with this information and subsequently will get into a lot of planning problems.

With the use of the matrix method, the process planner's task is to be a data provider and not a decision-maker. He only constructs the matrix. There is no optimum process that fulfills both the time and the cost optimum. One has to determine which one to use. Naturally, it is not a decision for the process planner to make.

The flexibility provided by the use of the matrix method, allows us to regard routing as a variable and not as a fixed one. Therefore, an improved production management method can be constructed. Such a method is proposed in the next section.

## 3 THE MATRIX METHOD - GENERAL ARCHITECTURE

The matrix method is based upon the following concepts:

- Each decision is made by a qualified expert
- Each decision is based on real facts and not on assumptions
- Each decision is made at the time of execution, independent of the other decisions
- Each decision may be changed when circumstances change
- Keep the system simple

## 3.1 Factory completed dates planning

Traditional practice is that Production Management activities start with customer orders as input. Order delivery date is part of the order information. Delivery date plays a major role in PM stages. The MRP uses it for determining due dates for purchased and in house production orders. CP uses MRP due dates for in house machine loading. The complete date is one of the determining factors in establishing the quality of the shop performance. However, no one questions how the delivery date was determined. In many cases, sales promise non-realistic delivery dates, but PM regards them as a constraint.

In the proposed set up, the matrix system may be used by Sales and/or Management to establish realistic delivery dates. The matrix may be used as part of a larger control architecture as shown in Figure 1. The algorithm is as follows: the last machine capacity plan will be referred to as "load profile" (see Figure 7). The load profile is a result of a finite capacity machine loading process. The loading method will be described in section 3.3. The load profile shows the existing jobs planned on all the available resources. In any plan there might be some resource idle time. When a new order arrives, the matrix generates the best routing for the order. Considering the available inventory and the bill of materials, the system attempts to load the new order by using the idle spaces. This loading will be based on the minimum cost criterion (if the routing was generated for minimum cost optimization criteria). However as the order is loaded only at idle time or at the end of the loading period, the complete date might be far ahead. The matrix method may generate alternative processes, by using different machines. As an alternate process cannot be as efficient as the best process, the cost of producing the order will increase. But on the other hand, the idle time of the alternate machines might become shorter and the due date may become nearer. The matrix method has two features that might be handy in this case. One is the "Machine blocking option", were the scheduler is asked to ignore certain machines. The other is "Forced process planning option" were the machines to use are dictated externally. These features are used to generate alternatives. A list of alternative due dates and cost will be generated by the matrix method, as shown in Figure 2. Negotiation with the customer may be used to establish realistic delivery dates.

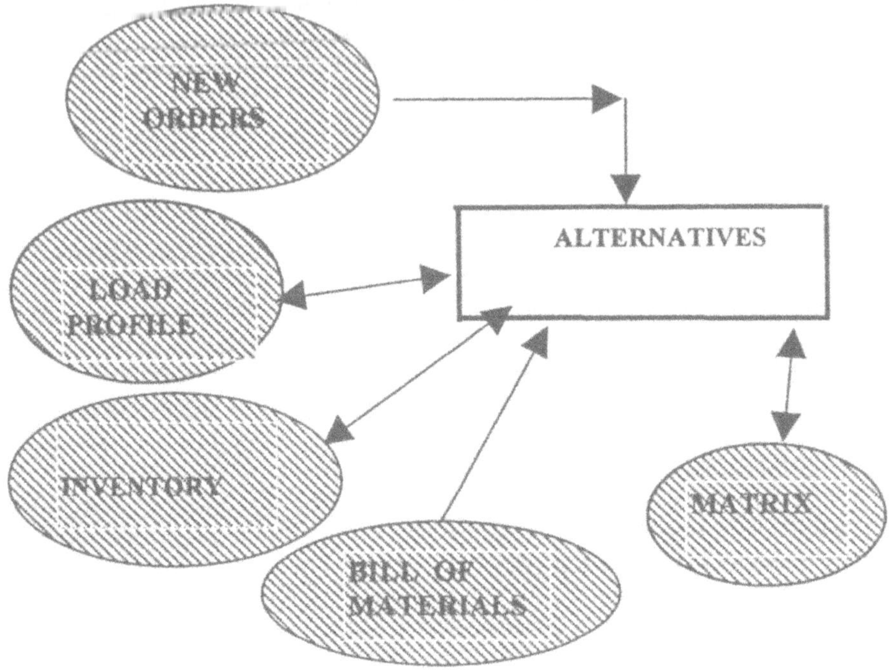


**Figure 1** Control architecture using the matrix method

| ALTERN | COST | DUE DATE | NOTES |
|---|---|---|---|
| 1 | 30 | 120 | New order super imposed on load profile with minimum cost optimization |
| 2 | 35 | 100 | New order super imposed on load profile with maximum production optimization |
| 3 | 40 | 70 | With dynamic process plan |
| 4 - n | 46 | 68 | Several dynamic alternatives |
| n - J | 50 | 50 | Combinations of delaying existing orders |

**Figure 2** Alternative Due Date Planning

## 3.2 Production Planning - Job Release

The objective of this stage is to plan the activities on the shop floor, in order to meet delivery dates. The outcome of this planning is the order release to the shop floor for execution. In the matrix method, the order release must be practical. The planning is with finite capacity and with the use of the product tree. The detailed capacity plan has to be transformed into a real schedule.
The planning steps and method are as follows:

a. Determination of priorities
   For each order build a time-element tree, using data from the product structure. The tree is constructed from the order due-date backwards. Starting with the order, call the matrix indicating the item and the required quantity and retrieve the execution time. Transfer the total time to the time scale (in, let say, days) and subtract the time from the delivery date of the order. This yields the starting time for the job. Next, retrieve the following sub-assembly or component from the bill of materials and compute its required quantity. Call the matrix indicating the item name and the required quantity and follow the same procedure as above, calculate the starting time of that job. Continue the same procedure for all the items of the order and for all orders in the logbook.
b. Stock allocation.
   The objective of this step is to allocate the available items in inventory to the available orders and adjust the early starting dates accordingly. It is done by scanning all the orders and finding the critical item i.e. the item where the starting day is the nearest one. Run over the tree of this item to find the product and the order. Search inventory and see if such product is available in stock. If available, allocate it to this order. Reduce the quantity of the order by the available quantity and rebuild the product tree with new quantities per item and new starting dates. In this case the starting time of the lowest level item will be changed and another order might become the critical one. Repeat the procedure of scanning all the orders to find the "new" critical item. In the case that there is no stock of the product, examine the stock availability for the next item using the same procedure.
c. Adjust quantities by economic considerations
   Compute the EOQ - the Economic Order Quantity, either by the matrix method or by any other method or by external constraints. Split or compose orders if required, and recompile the product time base tree.
d. Capacity planning - machine loading
   Machine loading is forward planning. The availability in time of each resource is symbolized by a row, were each slot in the row represents a planning period. The current date periods are shorter - say one hour- than the more distant periods, which each may cover two hours or more. The first ones, covering together a period of a few hours or a few days, depending on the kind of jobs and the average job time, serve as a scheduling period. The more distant slots, which together may take from a few hours up to weeks or months serve as a capacity planning period. When a job is allocated to the resource, the appropriate position(s) in the row hold(s) the order and the item code. Empty positions indicate idle resources. A critical planning path is defined as the path starting at the lowest independent item in the product structure with the earliest starting date, through its sub-assemblies up to the product. The critical path will have priority in machine loading. However, all the items for the sub-assembly have to be available before the assembly can start, i.e. all independent items that go into the critical sub-assembly will

have a priority greater than the sub-assembly. The priority of such items is related to their starting date.

In the case of items for which the starting date falls in the past or which have a slack of 10% or more, the maximum production criteria is used for solving the matrix. (mind that the initial starting dates were established with the use of the cost criterion, which results in a longer processing time). For all others items, the minimum cost optimization criteria is used.

The loading procedure is as follows:

Scan all the orders and find the item with the nearest starting day. Run over the time-tree to find the product and the order. This order has the priority in machine loading. The loading is done from the lowest level item, from its last machining operation and forward. Subsequently, the matrix with the item name and quantity can retrieve a process. The retrieved process indicates the number of resources, the name of each resource and the time for the operation (including set-up and penalties). Start with the last operation, multiply its time by the quantity and divide by the period scale of the row. Determine how many periods are needed for this operation. Run over the row of the appropriate resource and search for an idle period. The search starts at the operation early start period (depends on the previous operations and the product tree). When the idle time is found, the name of the item is inserted in the row. In the case that the early available idle period is too far ahead of the early start period, the matrix will be called to generate an alternate process. The alternative process will attempt to reduce the waiting time by employing a different resource, which is idle at the required periods, and that it is economical to change. The initial proposed process is based on the minimum value of the matrix solution. However, in many cases the difference between the minimum value and the next higher value is negligible. Blocking the occupied resource (using the "machine blocking" feature) and resolving the matrix, will generate the next alternate routing. If a known machine is idle, the "forced process plan" feature will be used and the economics of using that process plan are examined. This process may be continued until the available space is found. Carrying out the planning actions as described above, results in a capacity plan, which includes a resource-utilization-optimized schedule for the short-term periods.

e. Job release.

The capacity planning is a very important planning task, bridging the gap between long and short term planning. To carry out the production plan, jobs have to be released to the shop floor for execution. Different companies may have a different strategy regarding the length of the period for which the jobs are released to the shop floor. A long period might result in exceeding the delivery dates, while a short period might cause idle time at shop floor level. The auxiliary job dispatching strategy influences significantly the required length of the period. A period of 1-6 days is commonly used.

Before job execution can start, some auxiliary jobs have to be performed. Some of the auxiliary jobs might take a long period of time. One can distinguish two main strategies in dispatching auxiliary jobs. The first one, which is to be preferred when the execution of these jobs is relatively long when compared to the main jobs, deals with an early release during capacity planning. In this case, the main job is dispatched only after the auxiliary job has been reported ready. When the auxiliary job times are relatively short, one can dispatch these jobs at the beginning of the scheduling period.

## 3.3 Execution

The execution is divided into two stages:

1. Execution - auxiliary jobs
2. Execution - shop floor control

### 3.3.1 Execution - auxiliary jobs

The auxiliary jobs are: fixture design and construction, tool preparation, NC-program generation, material preparation (inventory management and control), material handling (transport), quality control ( inspection), set-up instructions and set-up itself.

When jobs are assigned to or arrive at the medium range periods in the row, the auxiliary jobs attached to them are released. These jobs are given a due date situated before the scheduling or dispatching time of the main job. At this stage, the routing of the main jobs is known. However, the operators on the shop floor are allowed to alter the process when necessary to overcome disruptions. This means that the execution of the auxiliary jobs has to be flexible as well; otherwise the flexibility in routing cannot be realized. The matrix method can significantly contribute to the required auxiliary job flexibility.

The matrix contains all the required information about the process and its parameters. This information can be used to prepare an NC-program (G-functions). The TP in the matrix holds all the operation specifications. The resource-file contains the machine specifications, including the controller data. Constructing the matrix when the TP is known takes a few seconds. Therefore, with the matrix method no information is stored, it is created whenever needed. The same applies for the NC-program preparation from CL-Data. Such as NC-program can be generated at the instance of job allocation just before starting production. Nowadays, the possibilities to generate complete new NC-programs instantly are rapidly increasing.

Tools are assembled and preset in the tool room. Each tool is a accompanied by a certificate stating its dimensions. This information is used to offset the machine controller.

Set-up and job instructions are the result of the process selection made with the assistance of the matrix. Hence the matrix method can generate this data dynamically. Quality control is usually independent of the selected process. The same applies for material preparation. The TP process plan indicates alternative datum surfaces. These datum surfaces are used to design the fixture. At the release stage, the datum surfaces, the tool access constraints and the candidate machines are known. This information is transferred to the fixture design office. The information is considered during fixture design. The design might be based on the pallet concept, the modular concept or the Group Technology concept, in order to allow for the flexibility to transfer jobs from one machine to another.

### 3.3.2 Execution - shop floor control

Conditions on the shop floor are dynamic and occur when a machine fails, a tool breaks, employees are missing, orders change, parts are rejected and reworked, power failures take place, etc. So, a practical execution of the jobs, it must be allowed to deviate from the planned schedule. Therefore, the decision to release a job must take into account the immediate shop floor situation.

Figure 3 represents a schematic presentation of shop floor planning and control. The control architecture is based on the shop floor control architecture as presented by [Tiemersma,1990].

The *Scheduling* function covers a short time slot of the capacity plan. The introduction of the scheduling module between capacity planning and dispatching enables the release of partial production orders. The production suborders can be merged or split before capacity planning on the cell level. The scheduling function extracts the required auxiliary jobs from the technical information, and checks their availability. Free operations are defined as the operations that are ready for immediate execution. The free operations list is transferred to dispatching for execution.

The *Dispatching* function is responsible for the release of jobs to the workstations. The dispatching concept includes, that whenever a resource is free, it searches for a job to be performed. If it is economical, a priority is given to the next operation of the same item. If not, the system scans the matrices of all parts in this particular machine column, and lists all free operations that the specific machine can do best. If the list is empty, a “look ahead” feature is used to determine when such an operation will become "free". The system will search for a free operation that the free machine can perform less efficiently, but economically. One method to compute the economics of using an “inefficient” operation, is to compute the difference in time between the “best” and the alternative operation time and comparing it to the time that the free machine will otherwise be idle. If such a free operation is found, it is allocated to the free machine. For more information see [Tiemersma, 1992] and [Hal, 1993].

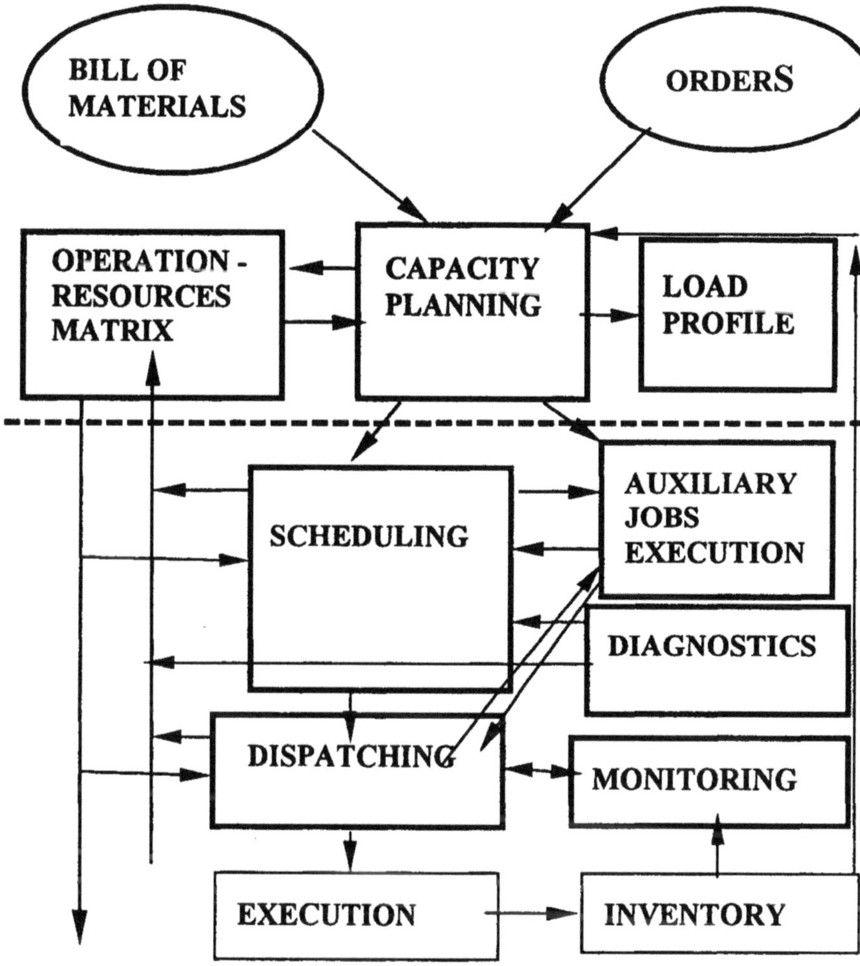


**Figure 3** System architecture for Shop Floor Planning and Control

The *Monitoring* function is to collect the status of either a job, an operation or a workstation. For auxiliary jobs, the "released" phase is followed by the "completed" phase, to indicate that the related main job may be started. When a job is dispatched to a workstation, its status changes from "not released" to "released" and the first operation becomes a "free operation". When an operation is finished, the next operation becomes a "free operation". If the operation was the last operation on a job, the part is transferred to inventory and the job status is set to "complete". The status of the workstation normally changes between "idle" and "busy". The monitoring function informs the dispatching function of unexpected changes in status and of disruptions.

The *Diagnostic* function has to determine, in the case of disruptions, the consequences for the work plan. A delay of a job can have a snowball effect. In such a case of local disruption, the scheduling function will possibly have to generate an alternative work plan. In the case of a permanent disruption (due to improper routing), a permanent correction will be done on the matrix, in order to improve future work plans.

## 4. THE MATRIX APPROACH - EXAMPLE

To validate the feasibility of the proposed system and to check the execution time, a computer program has been prepared The program may handle several orders and parts. However, for simplicity and clarification of demonstration, two orders, 12 parts and 15 machines are considered in the example.

The assumed company makes two kind of cylinders: spring-return and double acting. Figure 4 shows the product.

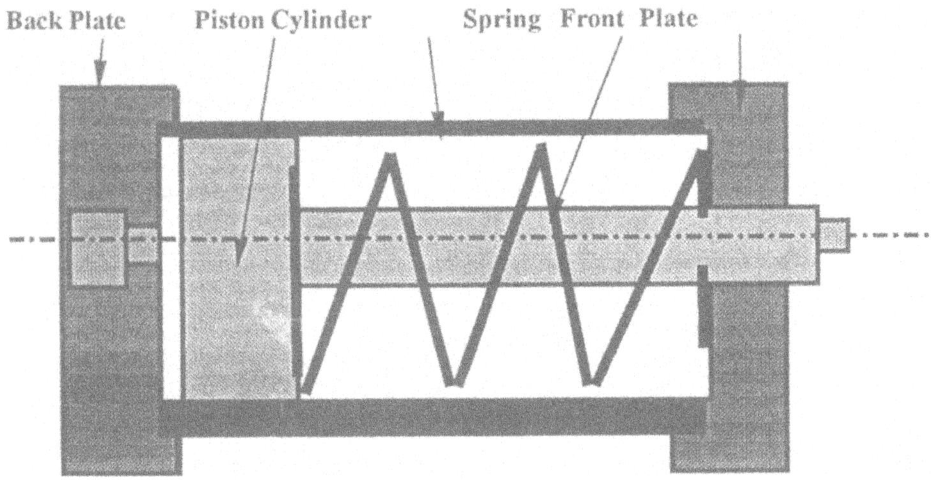


**Figure 4** Pneumatic Cylinder Spring Return

The main menu of the computer program is used to choose: Order updating, Bill of material updating and Running mode. In the sample test two orders are introduced. They are: 80 spring return cylinders for delivery on day 40; and 40 double acting cylinder to be delivered on day 35.

An TP process was made for each one of the cylinder items. An example of the TP for the front plate is shown in Table 2. The available 15 resources are detailed in Table 3. The TP process plan has been transformed into a matrix as shown in Table 4. The method used was detailed in section #3.

**Table 2: TP Process for the Front Plate of the Spring Return Cylinder**

| No. | Operation | Pr | Tool | L | a | Feed | V | kW | T min |
|---|---|---|---|---|---|---|---|---|---|
| 1 | Sawing | 00 | B | | | | | | 2.8 |
| | | | | | | | | | |
| 2 | Side milling | 10 | 50 | 113x2 | 2.5 | 304 | 88 | 1.0 | 2.02 |
| 3 | Face milling - R | 10 | 80 | 76 | 1.59 | 1428 | 118 | 6.63 | 0.05 |
| 4 | Face milling - F | 30 | 80 | 143 | 0.41 | 900 | 147 | 1.34 | 0.16 |
| 5 | Assembly Holes | 20 | 10 | 20 x4 | | 0.2 | 25 | 0.6 | 0.96 |
| | | | | | | | | | |
| 6 | Side milling | 10 | 50 | 113x2 | 2.5 | 304 | 88 | 1.0 | 2.02 |
| 7 | Face milling - R | 10 | 80 | 76 | 1.79 | 1401 | 116 | 7.34 | 0.05 |
| 8 | Face milling - F | 70 | 80 | 143 | 0.21 | 370 | 164 | 0.37 | 0.39 |
| 9 | Drill U 46∅ | 10 | 44 | 4 | | 0.27 | 114 | 10.3 | 0.2 |
| 10 | Boring 46∅ - Mr | 90 | 40 | 4 | | 804 | 93 | 0.22 | 0.18 |
| 11 | Boring 46∅ - Mf | 10 | 40 | 4 | | 359 | 106 | .07 | 0.41 |
| 12 | piston hole | 11 | 16 | 16 | | | | 2.0 | 0.34 |
| | | | | | | | | | |

The steps of the module are as follows:

a. Product Bill-of-Material Explosion - Quantity and Time.

The objective of this step is to set priorities for stock allocation. It works from the delivery date of each order backward. It starts with the assembly of order number one, i.e. item #1. The matrix is called to generate a process with minimum cost criteria, for the assembly of 80 items of product #1. The output of the matrix module gives the total time, and the detailed operations, including the time on each individual machine. The total time is multiplied by the quantity, and translated into days. The duration in days of the assembly product #1 is subtracted from the delivery date. The result is the starting date of the assembly (day 39.10). The next item on the Bill-of-Materials (see Figure 5) is the Back Plate item #2. The quantity per unit assembly is 1. Therefore the quantity of item #2 is 80. The matrix is called to generate a process with minimum cost criteria, for processing 80 pieces of item #2. The output of the matrix module gives the total time and the detailed operations, including the time on each individual machine. The detailed operation data are used to generate a report on the load of each machine, indicating starting and ending days of each item on each machine and the total load on each machine. This report is for general use only. The total time is multiplied by the quantity, and translated into days. The duration in days required to produce item #2 is subtracted from the starting date of the assembly, item #1, and sets the starting day for item #2 (day 36.43). This process continues till the last item of the second order has been dealt with. (in total 20 retrievals from the matrices, which took 3 seconds on a 33 MHz computer). A summary report is given in Figure 5. The bold numbers indicate the starting date of each item. The number in brackets indicates the quantity of each item whose number is given as (#).

**Table 3: The Available Machines**

| Mac No. | Machine description | Power kW | Speed RPM | Handle time | Relat cost |
|---|---|---|---|---|---|
| 1 | Milling Machining center | 35 | 1500 | 0.10 | 4 |
| 2 | Large CNC Milling | 35 | 1200 | 0.15 | 3 |
| 3 | Manual milling machine | 15 | 1500 | 0.66 | 1.4 |
| 4 | Small drill press | 1 | 1200 | 0.66 | 1 |
| 5 | Old milling machine | 15 | 2400 | 1.0 | 1 |
| 6 | Small CNC milling | 10 | 3000 | 0.25 | 2 |
| 7 | CNC Lathe | 25 | 3000 | 0.15 | 3 |
| 8 | Manual Lathe new | 15 | 3000 | 0.42 | 2 |
| 9 | Manual Lathe old | 10 | 2400 | 0.66 | 1 |
| 10 | Circular Saw | | | | 1 |
| 11 | Band Saw | | | | 1 |
| 12 | Hack Saw | | | | 1 |
| 13 | Manual assembly | | | | 1 |
| 14 | Machine assembly | | | | 1.5 |
| 15 | Robotics assembly | | | | 3 |

b. Stock allocation.

The objective of this step is to allocate available stock and to adjust the quantities of each item on the ordered products. The allocation is carried out with the product tree and gives priority to the critical path. The program scans all paths of the Bill-of-Material trees in a search for a low-level item of which the starting day is the nearest one. In this example, as indicated in Figure 5, item #7 of order 2 has a starting date of 31.18, which is the nearest one.

**Table 4 : The Time Matrix Content**

| Op. | Pri. | M# 1 | M# 2 | M# 3 | M# 4 | M# 5 | M# 6 | M# 7 | M# 8 | M# 9 | M# 10 | M# 11 | M# 12 | M# 13 | M# 14 | M# 15 |
|---|---|---|---|---|---|---|---|---|---|---|---|---|---|---|---|---|
| B A C K P L A T E #4 | | | | | | | | | | | | | | | | |
| 10 | 60 | 99 | 99 | 99 | 99 | 99 | 99 | 99 | 99 | 99 | 7.8 | 6.6 | 12.2 | 99 | 99 | 99 |
| B A C K P L A T E #3 | | | | | | | | | | | | | | | | |
| 10 | 00 | 3.12 | 3.17 | 3.68 | 99 | 4.02 | 3.27 | 99 | 99 | 99 | 99 | 99 | 99 | 99 | 99 | 99 |
| 20 | 10 | 1.15 | 1.2 | 1.71 | 99 | 2.05 | 1.3 | 99 | 99 | 99 | 99 | 99 | 99 | 99 | 99 | 99 |
| 30 | 20 | 1.26 | 1.31 | 1.82 | 99 | 99 | 1.41 | 99 | 99 | 99 | 99 | 99 | 99 | 99 | 99 | 99 |
| 40 | 10 | 1.37 | 1.62 | 2.13 | 2.53 | 2.47 | 1.72 | 99 | 99 | 99 | 99 | 99 | 99 | 99 | 99 | 99 |
| 50 | 10 | 2.06 | 2.11 | 2.62 | 2.62 | 2.96 | 2.21 | 99 | 99 | 99 | 99 | 99 | 99 | 99 | 99 | 99 |
| B A C K P L A T E #2 | | | | | | | | | | | | | | | | |
| 10 | 00 | 3.12 | 3.17 | 3.68 | 99 | 4.02 | 3.27 | 99 | 99 | 99 | 99 | 99 | 99 | 99 | 99 | 99 |
| 20 | 00 | 1.15 | 1.2 | 1.71 | 99 | 2.05 | 1.3 | 99 | 99 | 99 | 99 | 99 | 99 | 99 | 99 | 99 |
| 30 | 20 | 1.49 | 1.53 | 2.05 | 99 | 99 | 1.64 | 99 | 99 | 99 | 99 | 99 | 99 | 99 | 99 | 99 |
| 40 | 10 | 1.30 | 1.35 | 1.86 | 1.86 | 2.2 | 1.45 | 99 | 99 | 99 | 99 | 99 | 99 | 99 | 99 | 99 |
| 50 | 40 | 1.28 | 1.33 | 1.84 | 99 | 2.18 | 1.43 | 99 | 99 | 99 | 99 | 99 | 99 | 99 | 99 | 99 |
| 60 | 50 | 1.51 | 1.56 | 2.07 | 99 | 99 | 1.66 | 99 | 99 | 99 | 99 | 99 | 99 | 99 | 99 | 99 |
| F R O N T P L A T E #7 | | | | | | | | | | | | | | | | |
| 10 | 0 | 99 | 99 | 99 | 99 | 99 | 99 | 99 | 99 | 99 | 7.8 | 6.6 | 12.2 | 99 | 99 | 99 |
| F R O N T P L A T E #6 | | | | | | | | | | | | | | | | |
| 10 | 0 | 3.12 | 3.17 | 3.68 | 99 | 4.02 | 3.27 | 99 | 99 | 99 | 99 | 99 | 99 | 99 | 99 | 99 |
| 20 | 10 | 1.15 | 1.2 | 1.71 | 99 | 2.05 | 1.3 | 99 | 99 | 99 | 99 | 99 | 99 | 99 | 99 | 99 |
| 30 | 20 | 1.26 | 1.31 | 1.82 | 99 | 99 | 1.41 | 99 | 99 | 99 | 99 | 99 | 99 | 99 | 99 | 99 |
| 40 | 10 | 2.06 | 2.11 | 2.62 | 2.62 | 2.96 | 2.21 | 99 | 99 | 99 | 99 | 99 | 99 | 99 | 99 | 99 |
| F R O N T P L A T E #5 | | | | | | | | | | | | | | | | |
| 10 | 0 | 3.12 | 3.17 | 3.68 | 99 | 4.02 | 3.27 | 99 | 99 | 99 | 99 | 99 | 99 | 99 | 99 | 99 |
| 20 | 0 | 1.15 | 1.2 | 1.71 | 99 | 2.05 | 1.3 | 99 | 99 | 99 | 99 | 99 | 99 | 99 | 99 | 99 |
| 30 | 20 | 1.49 | 1.53 | 2.05 | 99 | 99 | 1.64 | 99 | 99 | 99 | 99 | 99 | 99 | 99 | 99 | 99 |
| 40 | 10 | 1.30 | 1.35 | 1.86 | 1.86 | 2.2 | 1.45 | 99 | 99 | 99 | 99 | 99 | 99 | 99 | 99 | 99 |
| 50 | 50 | 1.28 | 1.33 | 1.84 | 99 | 2.18 | 1.43 | 99 | 99 | 99 | 99 | 99 | 99 | 99 | 99 | 99 |
| 60 | 60 | 1.51 | 1.56 | 2.07 | 99 | 99 | 1.66 | 99 | 99 | 99 | 99 | 99 | 99 | 99 | 99 | 99 |
| 70 | 40 | 1.44 | 1.49 | 1.0 | 99 | 99 | 1.59 | 99 | 99 | 99 | 99 | 99 | 99 | 99 | 99 | 99 |
| P I S T O N #9 | | | | | | | | | | | | | | | | |
| 10 | 0 | 99 | 99 | 99 | 99 | 99 | 99 | 2.03 | 2.33 | 2.57 | 99 | 99 | 99 | 99 | 99 | 99 |
| 20 | 10 | 99 | 99 | 99 | 99 | 99 | 99 | 1.91 | 1.85 | 99 | | | | | | |
| P I S T O N #8 | | | | | | | | | | | | | | | | |
| 10 | 0 | 99 | 99 | 99 | 99 | 99 | 99 | 1.45 | 1.72 | [illegible] | 99 | 99 | 99 | 99 | 99 | 99 |
| 20 | 10 | 99 | 99 | 99 | 99 | 99 | 99 | 1.45 | 1.72 | 99 | 99 | 99 | 99 | 99 | 99 | 99 |
| C Y L I N D E R #1 0 | | | | | | | | | | | | | | | | |
| 10 | 0 | 99 | 99 | 99 | 99 | 99 | 99 | 2.86 | 3.12 | 99 | 99 | 99 | 99 | 99 | 99 | 99 |
| A S S E M B L Y #1 & #11 | | | | | | | | | | | | | | | | |
| 10 | 0 | 99 | 99 | 99 | 99 | 99 | 99 | 99 | 99 | 99 | 99 | 99 | 99 | 3.0 | 4.0 | 3.0 |

Following the Bill-of-Material tree, from this item onwards, indicates that this item is part of product #11, order number 2. Therefore, order #2 is the critical one and stock allocation will start with this order. It starts with the high level items and proceeds towards the low-level items. Hence, initially product #11 will search for available stock. In this example the available stock shows:

| Item | 1 | 2 | 3 | 5 | 8 | 10 | 11 |
|---|---|---|---|---|---|---|---|
| Quantity | 3 | 3 | 13 | 14 | 10 | 3 | 20 |

Therefore, the quantity for item #11 will be reduced to 20 pieces. and the quantities of all items in the product tree will be adjusted accordingly. The matrix will be called to generate a process plan for the new quantity, in the same manner as before. The adjusted starting date of item #7 is now 33.19, which is shown in Figure 6. Figure 6 shows an intermittent stage of the stock allocation module. The critical path is now item #4 (32.90) of product #1 in order #1. Subsequently, product #1 will search for available stock. There are 3 products of item #1. Its quantity, and the quantity of all the items on the product tree will be adjusted. Next, the starting date will be recomputed. After the adjustment, the new lowest starting day is on item #4 of product #1 (33.15) and is on the critical path (33.15 is compared to 33.19 of item #7 of product #11). Following the product tree, brings us to item #2 of product #1 to become the critical one. The procedure continues till stock has been allocated to all items. This step took 5 seconds on a 33 MHz personal computer.

c. Capacity Planning - Machine loading

An array mac(15,400) was defined. The number '15' represents the resources as detailed in Table 3. The number '400' represents the periods. For this demonstration only 23 periods are used. The machine loading is forward planning. When a job is allocated to the resource, the appropriate positions in the row hold the order and item code. In this example the two digits are used: The first indicates the item number (as defined in Figure 5) and the second digit represents the order number. The critical path has priority in machine loading. To determine the critical order, the program scans all paths of the Bill-of-Material tree in a search for the minimum value. In this example, item #4 of product #1, order #1 is the critical one. The matrix is called to generate a process for 74 units of item #4 ( see Figure 7). As seen from Table 4, the process calls for 6.6 minutes on machine #11. This time is multiplied by the quantity and divided by the period scale. As it is the first item to be loaded, it starts at period #1. Figure 7 shows that machine #11 are loaded at periods 1 & 2 with 41. ( item #4 of order #1). Next, the matrix is called to generate a process for 74 units of item #3. The retrieved process calls for: machine #5 for 6.07 min., then for machine #3 for 1.82 min, ending with machine #4 with 5.15 min. (In consulting the reasoning of the generated process, remember that Table 4 gives the time, while the process is regarded for minimum cost).

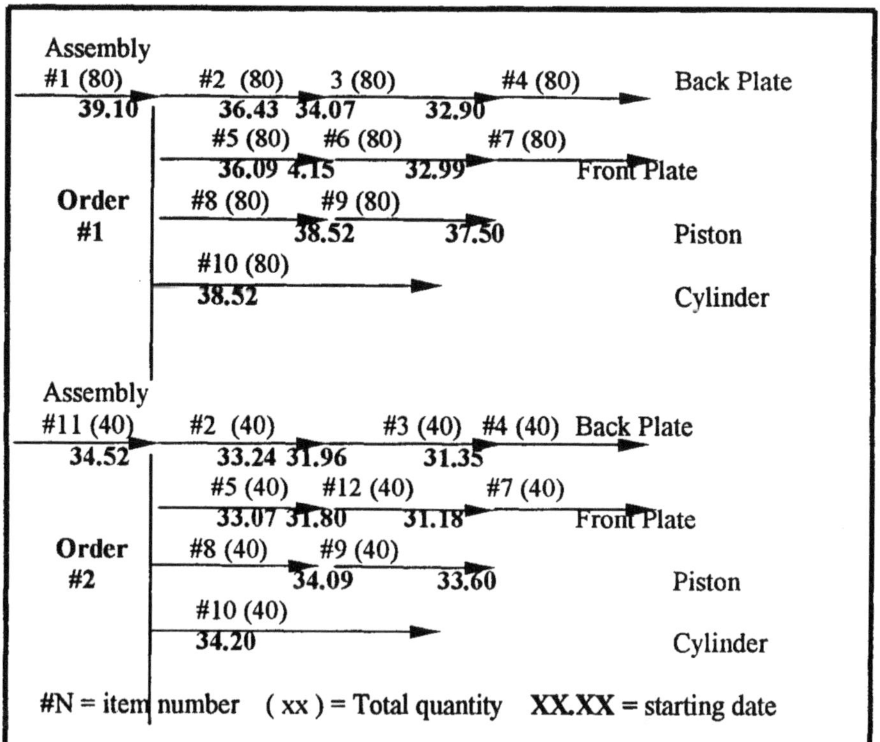


**Figure 5: Order Product Tree with Basic Quantity Per item and Starting Date**

Machine loading starts with the last operation, in this case with machine #4 for 2 periods. It may start only after item #4 is finished, i.e. at period #3. The array shows this through the symbol of "31" in the periods 3 & 4 on machine #4. The next operation calls for 1 period on machine #3 and then for 2 periods on machine #5. This process continues for item #2. As item #1 is an assembly, it will start only after all the components are available. Therefore, machine loading will proceed to item #7. Item #7 can be assigned to period #1, as it is an independent item. The matrix recommends a process of 6.6 minutes (2 periods) on machine #11. However, the machine is occupied till period #3; therefore it is loaded at periods #4 & #5. Next, item #6 is treated.

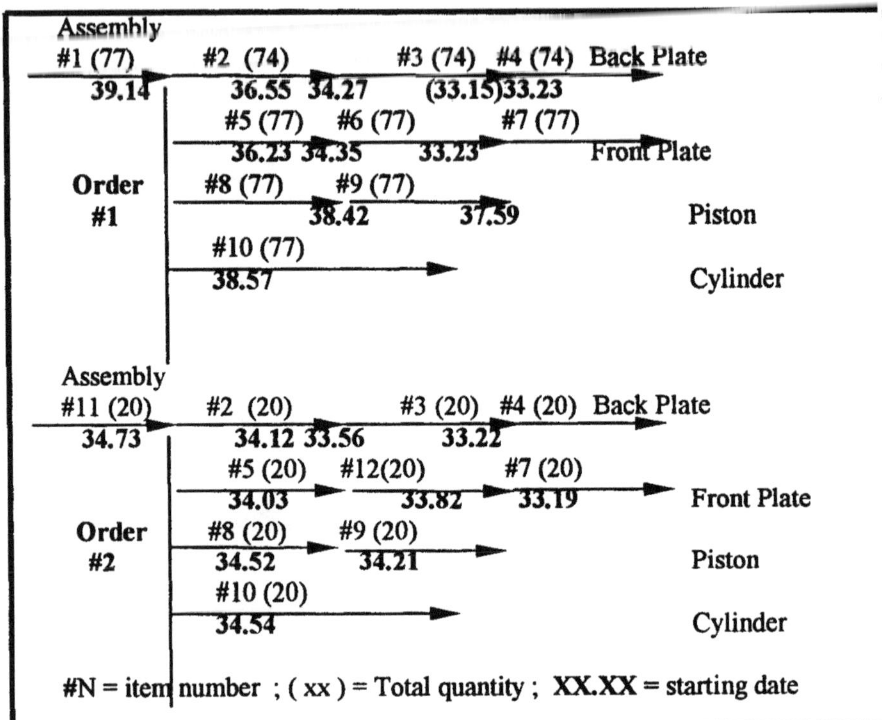


**Figure 6. Product Tree with Quantity and Starting Date after 3 Cycles**

Its last operation is on machine #4 for one period; it is loaded on period #5. Then Machine #3 for one period, and is loaded in period #6. Next operation calls for machine #5 for two periods. The available space is on period #14. The loading process continues going through all the items and orders. The resulting loading scheme is shown in Figure 7a, which deals with the unaltered routing. It takes 23 periods to fill up the 2 orders. The matrix method is a dynamic system, and the routing is regarded as a variable. When the required machine is not idle at the desired period, the matrix will look for an alternative. In the case of item #7, the work can be done by machine #10, which is idle. For item #6 the matrix system will look for an alternative process. The proposed machine is machine #6.

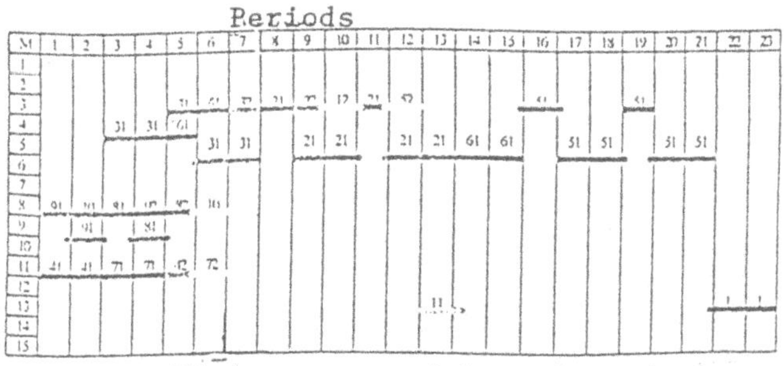


a. Minimum cost with unaltered process

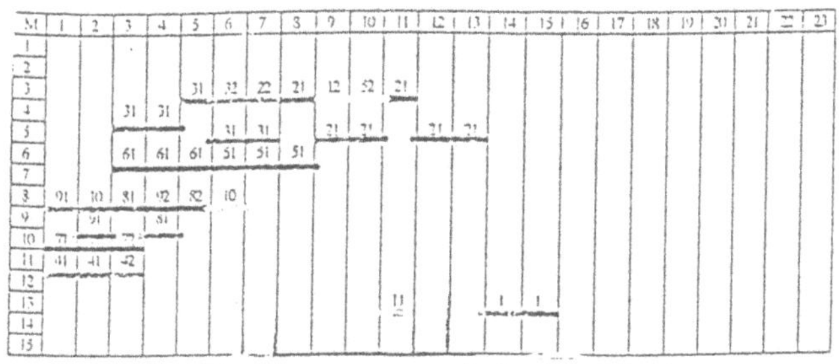

b. Minimum cost with local improvement

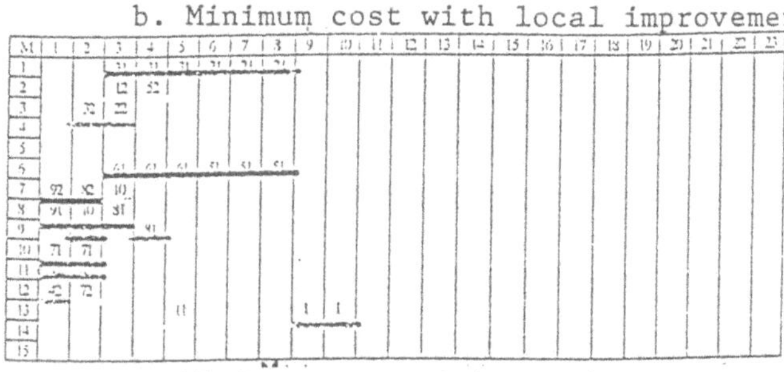

c. Minimum cost with total improvement

**Figure 7 : Load Profile of Machine Loading**

Machine #6 is idle. By choosing this alternative, the cost of machining the part will increase from 12.01 to 16.38. It was decided that this increase in cost is acceptable. Similar logic and procedures are applied to all other items. By introducing the concept of dynamic routing, the two orders can be finished after 15 periods, instead of 23 periods as shown in Figure 7b. The load profile in Figure 7b uses the first alternative. If an additional reduction of the delivery date is required, other alternatives can be employed, like the ones shown in Figure 7c. In this case, the two orders can be finished within 10 periods. The machine loading cycle of those two orders takes 4 seconds on a 33 MHz PC computer.

Using the maximum production optimization criteria instead of the minimum cost optimization criteria, as the retrieved process plan, does not make much difference. It is clear that for each part, the best machine has been selected, i.e. machine #1. As a result of this, a long queue of work piles up at machine #1.

## 5. CONCLUSIONS

The manufacturing process is flexible by nature. However, the manufacturing practice developed over the years, characterized by separated departments and manual planning and management methods, has led to complicated and rigid procedures. Especially in small batch manufacturing, present practice is still merely based on traditional planning and management methods. As an example, capacity plans of a finite number of resources as a procedure preceding scheduling, is hardly applied in industry. However, in the era of the computers and global competition in terms of cost and time to market, the manufacturing methods must be adapted to the new tools and demands. The matrix method presents the basis for an overall planning method, covering the needs of company management strategic planning, factory planning, operations management planning and production. Planning on all these levels can be based on the same basic principle, the matrix. The manufacturing process is composed of many disciplines, were each calling for a particular expertise. The basic concept of the matrix method is that decisions should be made only by the various experts in their own field and at the moment of execution. No one should make decisions that are out of his field of expertise and that may effect other disciplines and disturb the course of the logic decision making. This may seem contradictory with the present trend of integration of manufacturing processes, but it is not. The first step in any true integration process must always be the entanglement of (non-transparent) relations and separation of concerns in order to be able to design transparent processes.

Process planning is not an execution task. Process planners should only prepare data for the production planners. The process planner is an expert in technology, but not an economist, neither business administrator nor a production manager. However, process-planning decisions effect the level of competitiveness of the company. Communication and information transfer between disciplines should merely be of the nature of basic information, alternatives, etc., facilitating the separation of decisions and making subsequent decision making possible without negatively effecting the overall performance (which creates true flexibility). In this context, the matrix method provides an effective tool. It presents many possible process plans without making a decision. Each discipline may use the matrix in the manner it suits best. Company management may use the matrix for resource planning or for rating the company's level of competitiveness. The factory management may use the matrix for negotiation with customers regarding cost and delivery dates. The production management may use the matrix for stock allocation and capacity planning. The shop floor management can use the matrix for scheduling and job release. All the disciplines can work with the same information.

The solution of the matrix is done in seconds on a PC. Therefore, there is no need to store decisions. Decisions can be reproduced much faster by the matrix method then by storage and retrieval systems. The administration becomes simpler and more efficient as the amount of document storage is reduced. The problem of keeping track of versions, and releases is eliminated. Furthermore, decisions may be adapted to the dynamic situation of the business. The flexibility and dynamics introduced by the matrix method improves significantly production management. It has been shown that delivery dates may be shortened drastically using the matrix method. The matrix method works with the b method all the time. This feature permits the modification of the production plan for a whole product instead of for an individual item. When disruptions occur in one item, the system adjusts the working plan for all items on the product tree. The results of the experimental prototype of the computer program, written in Q-basic, proves that the matrix method is a realistic one. Running two orders with 10 parts each and in an assumed plant with 15 machines, it takes about 20 seconds to perform stock allocation and capacity planning on a 33 MHz PC.

The additional degree of freedom introduced by the matrix method, raises many operational options. In this work, certain decisions were made before hand, such as, using the minimum cost criteria as the initial working process plan. The reason is that it leaves spare time for rush orders, or in the case of disruptions, moving to maximum production optimization criteria. The critical path was defined by the path in the product tree for which the starting date is the lowest one. However, many other options are possible normally:

- the product that uses a bottleneck machine,
- the product with the minimum quantity required,
- the product for which the penalty for not meeting the delivery date is the greatest,
- the part with the maximum number of operations,
- the product with the least slack,
- the product that does not have an alternate process.

The work so far, proved that the objectives around the matrix method are feasible. Future plans are, to carry the research further, considering more options and coming up with rules, that can be embedded in the program.

## 6. REFERENCES AND BIBLIOGRAPHY:

Cho, H., Derebail, A., Hale, T., Wysk, R.A. (1994) A formal approach to integrating CAPP and SFC, Transactions of the ASME, Department of Industrial Engineering, Texas A&M University, Texas, USA, 1994, vol. 116, p.108-116.

Detand, J., (1993), A CAPP system generating Non-Linear Process Plans, Ph.D. Thesis, KU Leuven, October (ISBN 90-73802-23-7)

Halevi G., (1980). *The Role of Computers in Manufacturing Processes,* John-Wiley &Sons, NY

Halevi, G. (1993). The magic matrix as a smart scheduler, Computer in Industry 21, 1993, 245-253

Halevi G., (1995). *Principles of process planning - A logistic approach*. Chapman & Hall, London
Halevi, G. (1997). The magic matrix as a smart machine evaluator, International Journal of Production Planning & Control, Vol. 8, No. 4
Halevi, G. (1997). The magic matrix as a smart resource planner. International Journal of Reduction Engineering and Computers , Vol.1 , No. 1, PP- 21-28
Halevi, G. (1996). Computerized benchmarking as a deduction of practical industrial project, Modeling techniques, Business Process Re-Engineering(BPR) and Benchmarking, Ed. Guy Doumeingts & J. Browne, Chapman & Hall 1997 , pp. 359-374

Huang, S.H., Zhang, H.C., Smith, M.L. (1995). A progressive approach for the integration of Process Planning and Scheduling, IIE Transactions, Department of Industrial Engineering, Texas Tech. University, Lubbock, Texas, USA, vol. 27, p. 456-464.
Kempenaers, J., Pinte, J., Detand, J., Kruth, J.-P., (1996). A collaborative process planning and scheduling system, Advances in Engineering Software, Vol. 25 , p. 3-8.
Laliberty, T.J., et al..(1996), A blackboard architecture for integrated process planning/production scheduling, Proceedings of ASME Design for Manufacturing, August
Larsen, N.E., Clausen, J., (1992). Applied methods for integration of process planning and production control, Manufacturing International, pp.349-364.
Nasr, N., Elsayed, E.A.,(1990) Job shop scheduling with alternative machines, Int. J. Prod. Res., Vol. 28, No. 9, p. 1595-1609
Seo ,Y., Egbelu, P.J., (1996), Process plan selection based on product mix and production volume, Int. J. PROD. RES , Vol. 34, No. 9 2639-2655
Tiemersma, J.J., Kals, H.J.J..(1990). A real-time monitoring and control system for small batch part manufacturing. Proc. of the ASME Manufacturing-International '90 conference. Atlanta USA, March 1990, pp. 41-48.
Tiemersma, J.J.,(1992). Shop Floor Control in small Batch Part Manufacturing, Ph.D. Thesis, University of Twente, Enschede, The Netherlands, 1992
Tonshoff, H.K., Beckendorff, U., Andres, N., (1989) FLEXPLAN: A Concept for Intelligent Process Planning and Scheduling, The CIRP International Workshop, Hannover, Germany, September 1989.

## 7. BIOGRAPHY

**Gideon Halevi** received his M.Sc in Mechanical Engineering from the University of Pennsylvania (1959) and his Doctor of Science in Technology from the Technion (1973). He is as adjunct professor at the Technion (1981), teaching mostly at the graduate school on CAD/CAM and Robotics. For more than 30 years he has been active in industry in production development, Combine Technical

Operations, heading the corporate computing center and as manager and director of the CAD/CAM Research and Development Center. He has developed the All Embracing Technology, which was published in his book "The Role of Computers in Manufacturing Processes ( Wiley 1980). He developed the process planning matrix system, which was published in his book "Principles of Process Planning - A logical approach" Chapman & Hall. 1994 . He is an active member of the CIRP, Israeli representative to IFIP TC5, a member of IFIP WG5.3 and WG5.7, past chairman of SME chapter 319 and past chairman of IPICS.

**H.J.J. Kals**

Prof.Dr.ir. H.J.J.Kals is the Director of the Center of Integrated Manufacturing & development, CIPV. He is also the Head of the Laboratory of Production and Design Engineering at the University of Twente, Netherlands.
He is the president of the CIRP - International Institution of Production Engineering Research.

# 42

# An approach for the evaluation of an integrated process and production planning and control system

*P.F. Cunha [1] and R.M. Mesquita [2]*

*[1] Escola Superior de Tecnologia*
*Rua Vale de Chaves, Estefanilha, 2910 Setúbal; Portugal;*
*Email: pcunha@bocage.ips.pt*

*[2] Instituto Nacional de Engenharia e Tecnologia Industrial*
*Estrada do Paço do Lumiar; 1699 Lisboa; Portugal;*
*Email: ruy.mesquita@imp.ineti.pt*

**Abstract**

This paper presents a research project under development, aiming to integrate Production Planning and Control functions and Process Planning functions with the support of a Discrete Event Simulation tool. This integrated system will be targeted to typical metalworking companies, manufacturing small to medium sized batches. Planning and control of large production systems involves the resolution of very difficult problems, normally demanding a high degree of human intervention. Through this approach we aim to improve the effectiveness of each planning function and also to simplify the decision-making tasks when dealing with unexpected events at shop floor level.

**Keywords**

Process Planning, Production Planning and Control and Discrete Event Simulation.

Computer Applications in Production and Engineering. F. Plonka and G. Olling (Eds.)

# 1 INTRODUCTION

New challenges are forcing companies to improve manufacturing system performance in order to maintain their competitiveness. A more demanding requirement for new and more complex products has been forcing the companies to concentrate in reducing, both, the design and manufacturing cycle time. Customer satisfaction is a key objective. Consequently, flexibility, quality, cost and on-time delivery are the main requirements in the design and management of the overall manufacturing system. According to the type of manufacturing process (from mass to job-shop production) the use of Advanced Manufacturing Technology offers new chances in the level of integration and in new approaches for the implemented operational strategies. With the development and the spread of the CIM concept, the need for the integration of an increasing number of functions was established. Many specialized methods and procedures were developed, enabling each individual system to work more effectively with data generated from the different functions.

Manufacturing planning decisions are made on different phases of the product and process development cycle, such as process planning, master production scheduling, capacity planning and production order scheduling. In fact, the integration of planning functions has been referred to as a key issue in state-of-art manufacturing systems. Particularly, Process and Production Planning, which are two multi-task activities of particular importance in the batch manufacturing environment, are the candidates for the integration effort. In this type of production system the number and the variety of products to be manufactured will have influence in the chosen technology together with the management approaches used. Process and Production Planning integration will result in shorter lead-times, more efficient manufacturing systems and a high competitive advantage (ElSayed, 1996).

# 2 REASONS FOR THE INTEGRATION OF PROCESS AND PRODUCTION PLANNING

Integration of Process and Production Planning is an approach that enables each system to function more effectively, especially in organizations where production-to-order is dominant or an increasing number of different parts, to be manufactured in lower lot sizes, is required. Any production system is characterized by a set of technologies and organization structures which is determined by the diversity of products that they are able to manufacture and the expected demand. Additional strategic decisions should be done setting the manufacturing facilities (e.g., equipment and layout) and the operational strategies, such as lot sizes and workflow, to couple the customer orders.

The rapidly changing situations that happen in real manufacturing environments, involving some aspects like materials availability, order due dates/lot sizes, route sheets, lead times and manufacturing resources, result in difficulties in carrying out the daily plan. The competitiveness of each manufacturing system will be dependent on the capability to manage the dynamic changes that will occur during a normal run. As an example, many causes can be identified which influence the delivery time. The Cause-and-Effect diagram as shown in Figure 1 provides a structured view of the disturbing influences on on-time deliveries, guiding manufacturing managers on the definition of strategies for continuous improvements.

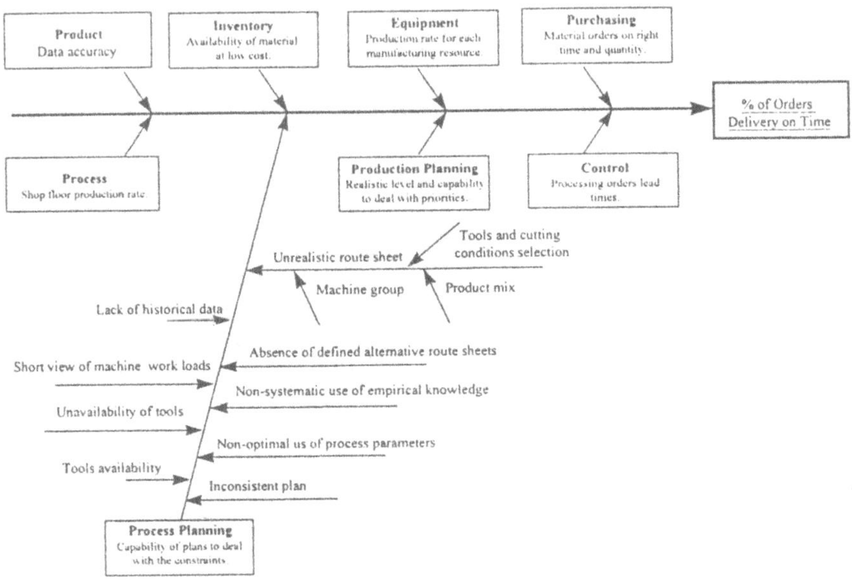


**Figure 1** Example of using Cause-and-Effect diagram for the analysis of the process planning task

Process planning as a stand-alone function does not consider the *available* resources at the shop floor. An event in the shop floor, such as bottlenecks, unavailability of tools and equipment breakdown, influences the execution of the manufacturing orders. In this case available pre-developed process plans are no longer adequate. The common procedure is to change the process plan at the shop floor, which can result in an inefficient (non-optimal) plan or the need for the utilization of alternative sequences of operations and resources. So, the process plan or route sheet, as a static and linear sequence of operations, does not cope with the shop-floor dynamic behavior. Process planning must be carried out considering the specific machine and tooling capacities, determined by the parts to be manufactured, on an underlying dynamic shop-floor scenario. The real scenario in manufacturing environments includes simultaneous in progress work, sharing finite resources, scheduled works and unexpected events that affect the production capacity. Process planning systems must interact, in this context, with shop floor scheduling and monitoring systems, recognizing the actual conditions and modifying the production plan, using alternative and "optimal" process plans. These difficulties are amplified by the lack of ability that the manufacturing planning and control systems have to operate with the process plan. The ability to communicate effectively between each system allow to create process plans dedicated to problematic situations (Cunha, 1996).

Considering the above mentioned events, the absence of materials or any changes in orders or route sheets, requires that some changes have to be proposed by shop-floor managers or schedulers, in most of the cases based in their empirical knowledge of the manufacturing system. This traditional approach requires that very skilled managers have to be involved in this level of decision. The influence of such decisions sometimes can be seen in an increasing level of entropy due to the resources that are shared and the clear competition between each order in reach of their operational objectives.

From our own experience, other topics can be presented, showing some weakness in the traditional approach to deal with Process and Production Planning tasks to run the manufacturing process. These can be summarized in the following:

a. Most of manufacturing planning and control systems do not include facilities to allow an efficient visibility of existing problems, as a support for an optimization of manufacturing resources;

b. Operational managers in general don't have enough data to deal with the increasing complexity of decisions required to manage the manufacturing process;

c. It is usual to observe a lack of data aggregation, processing and understanding at shop-floor level;

d. It is common the low level of quality, accuracy and effectiveness of feed-back data from shop-floor;

e. There are no guarantees for an uniform use of resources, meeting the due dates and working at minimum cost;

f. Limited capacity to answer to "what...if...?" questions, specially of a fuzzy pattern;

g. Most of the decisions in managing the manufacturing process are based on an empirical knowledge of the system;

h. The way that the lead times are defined does not guarantee validity and introduce difficulties to meet the due dates;

i. The traditional approach does not allow a dynamic scheduling of events, which should be done according to the real manufacturing environment;

j. Changes in due dates in an open order, involve a sequence of procedures within the company where it is difficult to find out which actions should be taken, specifying clearly when and how each operational staff should act.

## 3 INTEGRATION OF PROCESS AND PRODUCTION PLANNING

State-of-art computer aided Process Planning (CAPP) systems support the main functionalities that are required for the work planning in the production process. The capabilities include the creation of process plans, the design of raw materials, the selection of operation sequences, machine-tools, cutting tools, fixtures and machining parameters as well as the determination of manufacturing times. All technically feasible manufacturing routings and the necessary manufacturing resources are described and can be made available. CAPP systems for generating process plans operate based on data that are related to the customer order, manufacturing and technical know-how and an appropriate planning logic. Some systems retrieve existing process plans assigned to particular part families and allow the revision of these existing plans to develop new ones (variant process planning). In other systems, a new process plan is generated for every part, based on the description of part geometry and other part characteristics, through the application of a particular manufacturing logic coded into a suitable computer program. According to Kuhnle (1994) most of the available systems on the market are technologically oriented, rule-, or knowledge-based systems. They operate semi-automatically based on data that is related to the customer orders, manufacturing and technical know-how and an appropriate planning logic.

Production Planning and Control (PPC) systems are responsible for planning the utilization of production resources (e.g., machines capacities, labor, production quantities), which are required to satisfy some performance criteria, over some planning horizon, within some demand pattern. PPC systems are based on a description of the product, a description of the necessary operations, required production resources and dynamic information (e.g. varying with time) with regard to demand and the availability of resources. The complete scheduling and controlling of the production process are performed within the PPC system allowing a vertical integration of some planning tasks (e.g. from upper levels of decision to operational level). From master scheduling to material and capacity planning, order quantities and timing for placing orders are determined. At different time scales, schedules are produced with the aim to co-ordinate the necessary resources to fulfill production orders. Figure 2 shows the time scales and different planning time-horizons identified in Process and Production Planning and Control systems.

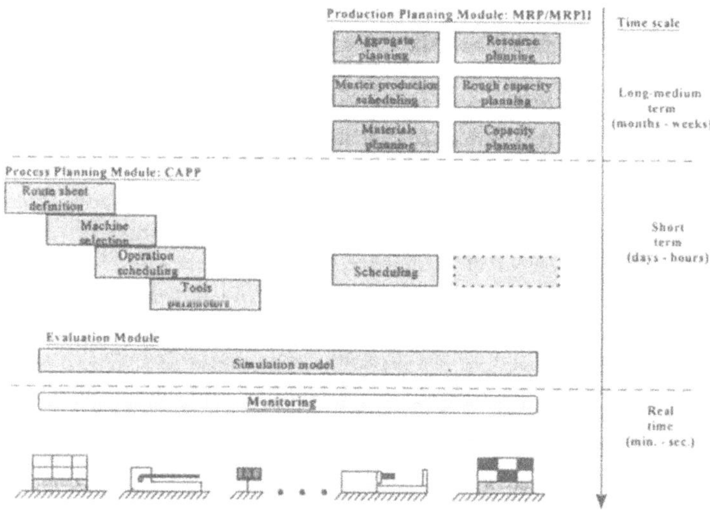


**Figure 2** Time scale associated with different functions with the PPP-Integrated Approach.

Planning objectives, manufacturing resources and performance measures or decision variables should be shared between the Process and Production planning tasks. Such an assumption yields a good foundation for integrating those tasks in a single multi-objective planning system (Elwany, 1996). Synergies can be generated from changing the traditional and non-integrated use of those systems into collaborative tasks, where advantages are obtained from the functions performed by each system together with the shared use of information.

The integration or collaboration of process planning and production planning, through the scheduling function, has been the focus of some work in recent years. The objective to implement dynamic Process Planning systems, has been presented through the developments of links between a CAPP system and Production Planning (scheduling), where three basic research approaches are being followed: non-linear process planning, closed loop process planning and distributed process planning (Wiendahl 1995, Leung, 1996).

CAPP and PPC systems are both modeling a part of the manufacturing process. From this manufacturing model, planning of production flow and employment of resources is required in order to assess manufacturing system performance. Process planning systems still rely on a *static* understanding of the plant. They are process dependent but time invariant functions. On the other hand, Production Planning and Control systems are both, process and time oriented and they lead to the use a *dynamic* view of the production process. The common element between both components is represented today by the process plan, which can be made available to the PPC system from the CAPP system by means of a data interface (Kuhnle, 1994).

As it has been pointed out, in the integration of CAPP with scheduling, some of the key aspects in this link are the choice of an optimal route, the determination of cycle and set-up times and the dependency of process planning on the loading conditions. However, the existence of a set of random events that occur in the real manufacturing environment, doesn't allow getting optimal solutions but searching for better alternatives. Discrete Events Simulation (DES) system by itself has an important role in dealing with stochastic systems allowing the representation of that randomness. Also, through the simulation, a set of equipment, labor and other facilities can be built into a model. This kind of system can easily allow the evaluation of produced schedules closer to a real scenario. Different process plans can be tested trying to reduce the effect of shop floor unexpected occurrences. Simulation can also provide managers with both qualitative and quantitative data on the effects of real-time constraints on the manufacturing system performance for decision making. Its facilities can minimize the lack of confidence in the expected results when a specific strategy is implemented, which has been a restriction for an effective management system. Through DES, a model of the manufacturing process can be developed and analyzed, generating data for decision making. Figure 3 illustrates the concept for CAPP/PPC/DES functional link.

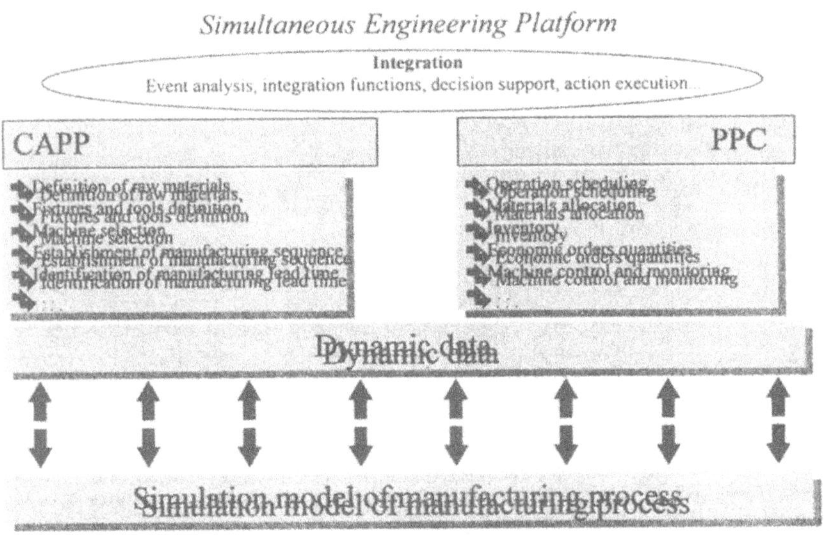


**Figure 3** Functional use of PPC, CAPP and DES techniques.

In the proposed architecture, commercial software packages are being used. A variant CAPP system, an MRP/MRPII system and a graphical simulation tool were selected. Our main purpose, in this selection, was to use the software applications that were compatible with the tools and methodologies used by Portuguese batch manufacturing companies. These applications are the core of each module identified in our proposed architecture (Figure 4).

As an interface approach a production relational database (RDB) platform will be used to link the different applications. In the RDB exist different folders with product and process-oriented data as well as the time and event-dependent data collected from shop-floor behavior. A shop-floor control system (SFC) can implement the required monitoring functions allowing the gathering of on-time and accurate data to be used in the evaluation of manufacturing system performance, as well as in the re-scheduling function. This database will be used to share data between each system and function. The RDB will allow the production scheduler to produce new alternative plans taking into account the status of the shop floor. In this integrated environment it is possible to develop and maintain effective schedules of manufacturing orders.

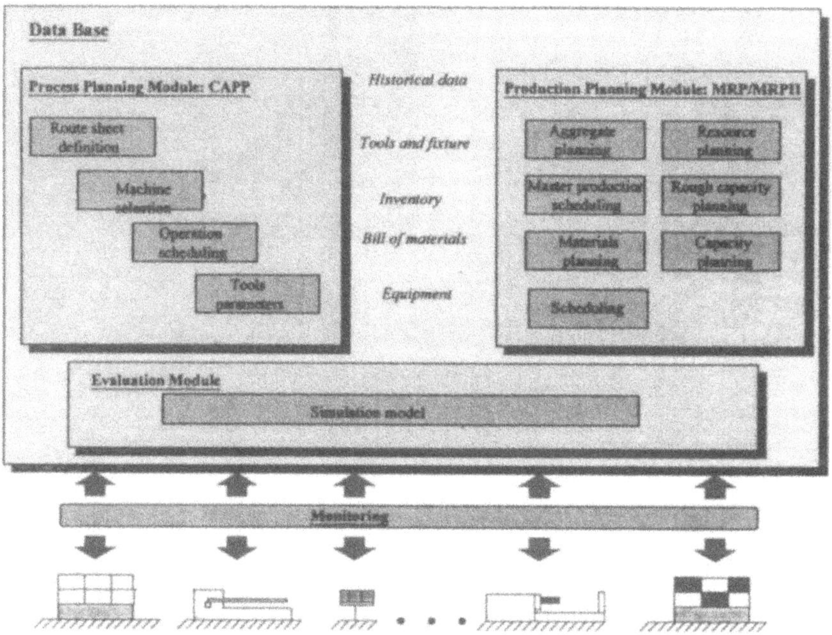


**Figure 4** Functional architecture for an integrated Process and Production Planning and Control system.

The functional architecture presented permits potential links to be established between each function. It includes not only the Process Planning - Production Planning link, but also the Process Planning - Capacity Planning and Process Planning - Shop Floor Control integration.

Figure 5, presents some of the commercial tools that are being used in our integrated approach. At this stage of development, work has been done on the integration of a CAPP system (MetCAPP/1 from IAMS) with the simulation system WITNESS (AT&T – ISTEL). For a given set of parts to be processed in our manufacturing system, a model is defined in the simulation system. The CAPP system generates the sequence of operations to be carried out at each workstation (in the future the alternative process plans will be generated also by the CAPP system). The integrated system approach allows that every new set of route plans, cycle and set-up times, when required, will be delivered to the simulation system. At this moment the alternative route sheets are defined in the simulation model but it should be transferred for the planning task.

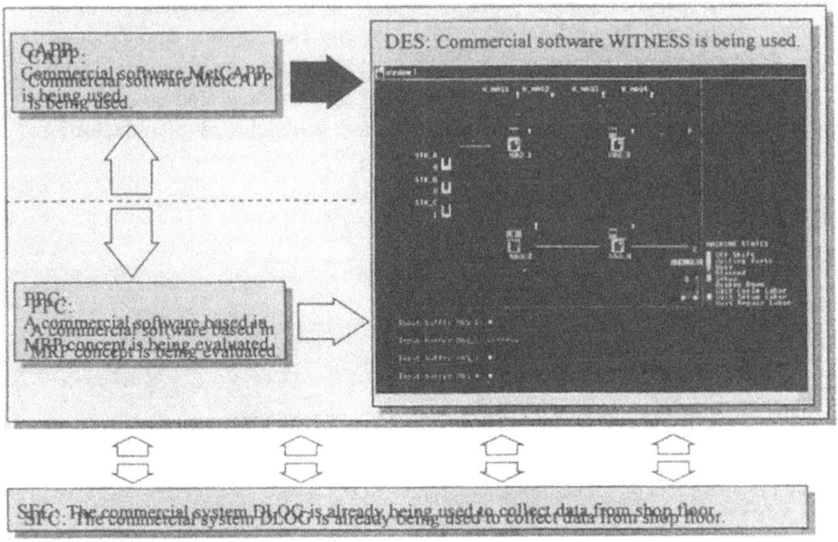


**Figure 5** Experimental use of integrated Process and Production Planning functions

In our approach, we focused our integration effort in short-term to real-time scales, e.g. the operational level. Here the monitoring requires the existence of a Shop Floor Control (SFC) system for an effective data collection. The feedback of data to the integrated Process and Production Planning and Control system should be based on measures (e.g. variables) which allow the scheduler or any other user to evaluate the performance of the manufacturing system. The performance measures also allow communicating up to each level of the integrated system on the manufacturing system behavior. The CAPP, PPC/SFC and DES systems are the backbone that integrates vertically up and down the company organization chart and horizontally across functions. At each level of decision making, the evaluation of different strategic and/or operational objectives is required. Consequently, several specifically designed performance measures are required for evaluation and for guiding the management of the manufacturing process.

## 3 DEVELOPMENT OF THE EVALUATION MODULE

The evaluation module has core relevance in the presented architecture. Having access to the collected data from the shop-floor we plan that this module will evaluate the operational performance of shop floor and test the effectiveness and reliability of process and production planning, whenever they are used to run the manufacturing process. The evaluation module should be flexible enough to assess the capability of each individual function or the overall system in dealing with unexpected events. In Figure 6 it is possible to observe some of the facilities planned for the evaluation module.

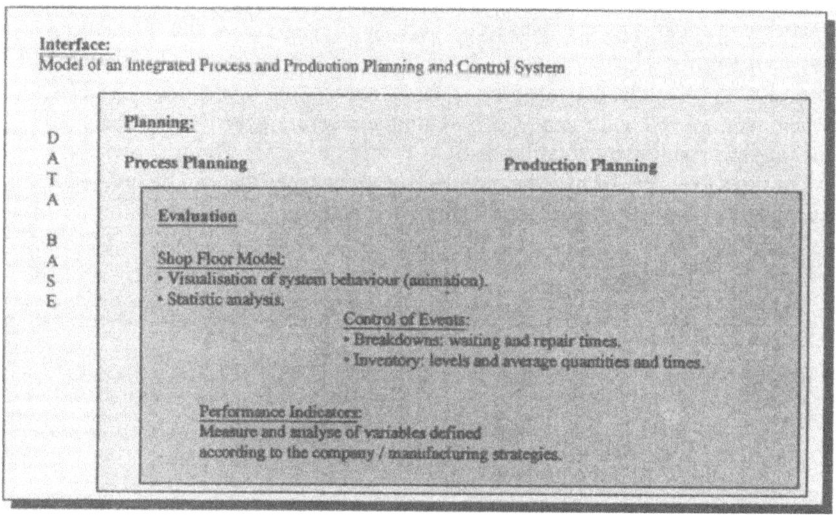


**Figure 6** Evaluation module in an integrated Process and Production Planning and Control system environment.

The use of Discrete Event Simulation in the evaluation module as well as statistical analysis tools is supported by the understanding that the efficient management of the manufacturing system requires system performance prediction rather than system failure or malfunction assessment after the occurrence of problems. The effective use of simulation requires that a validated model of the manufacturing process be built. Its animation capabilities will help to observe and understand the results of each simulation run. Also the model can always be updated with data that is being collected from the shop floor, allowing a better confidence on the results of the simulation. For an effective data processing and statistical analysis, in the implementation of the evaluation module, an effective link with the shop floor control system will be required. This system should allow observing in real time the value of some shop floor events. Those events can determine a set of performance measures to be used in the evaluation of the manufacturing system behavior.

Performance measures are interrelated throughout the organization. They should be implemented in order to articulate company strategies and monitoring the business results. The linkage between the established strategy and of required performance measures becomes very important as performance measures are pushed down the organization (Grady, 1991). Operational and tactical decision making without regard to strategy can be very costly and can result in a non-competitive position. In spite of already existing methodologies for defining performance measures we believe that its consistency with strategies are not achieved easily (e.g. they need to be linked to ensure they support and do not inhibit strategy implementation). Also single measures comparisons are dangerous because they overlook the interactions between specific objectives at different levels of the organization. In such a complex system, characterized by a large number of interacting variables, which are related with many different manufacturing activities, decision-making can result in the establishment of conflicting goals. Figure 7 presents a set of objectives, performance measures and event types that can be defined at each level of the hierarchical organization of a company.

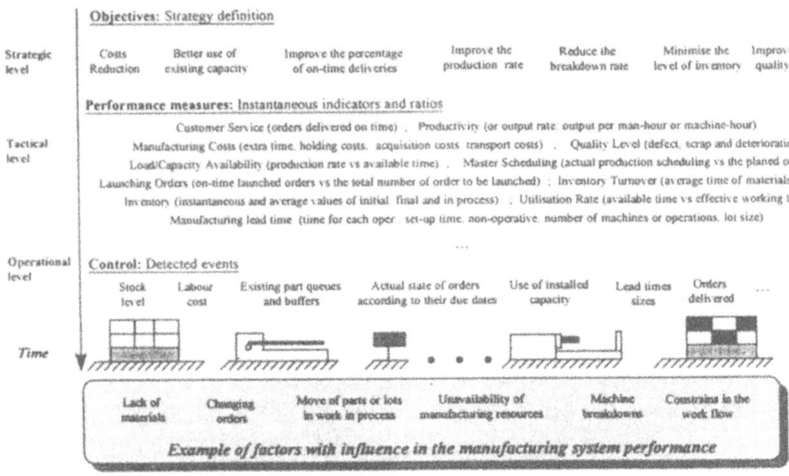


**Figure 7** Levels of decision making within a manufacturing environment.

When we consider the difficulties presented above, we propose a new approach to define the performance measures, in order to avoid loosing the information that exists in each performance measure. This approach is still under development requiring further validation.

The following study has the objective to test the possibility of reducing the amount of data for decision making, without losing relevant information about the manufacturing process. This data reduction is based on a set of new variables that are defined from the initial set of manufacturing variables. The technique used is know as Principal Components Technique and is considered to be a part of Multivariate Statistics.

The study was applied on a simulation model of a typical batch manufacturing company, for which we defined the following variables:

- TEMP.EXEC - Time required to manufacture the total demand of parts;
- OUTPUT - Number of parts manufactured without defects;
- AVWIP - Average number of parts in process;
- AVTIME_A, AVTIME_B, AVTIME_C - Average time the part **A**, **B** and **C** spent in process;
- P_MBUSY, P_MSETUP - Percentage of time the machines were occupied and in set-up;
- P_MBLOCK, P_MREPAIR - Percentage of time the machines were blocked and in repair;
- P_DEFEITOS - Percentage of part defects;
- OCUP.M.O. - Labor utilization rate.

Using the simulation system, the company model was built with the following characteristics:

- *Machines* - A set of 4 machines (resources), each with an input buffer of limited capacity, was considered. The operations executed for each part type in each machine, has a specific cycle time and set-up time. The resources are subjected to failures, which are characterized by the mean time between failures (MTBF) and the mean time to repair (MTTR).

- *Parts* - A set of 3 types of parts was assumed to be possible to manufacture with the existing facilities. For the completion of each part a given number and a pre-determined sequence of operations are required. For each part, a percentage of defects was defined at the end of the process as well as when each failure occurs. Every part type has a demand value, however we assumed that in each simulation run a total demand of 300 units exists.

- *Labors* - A set of 4 human resources required for the machines set-up and operation was defined. The allocation of each human resource to the machines was changed influencing the times for those operations.

Due to the necessity to have a sample of significant size we planned 100 experiments (e.g. simulation runs). In each experiment, we change the initial condition of the model, such as the part mix, the launch sequence, the cycle and set-up times and labor allocation, machine failure and part defect rates. Table 1 presents the results obtained from the simulation run.

**Table 1** Part of data matrix

| n | temp.exe | output | avwip | avtime_a | avtime_b | avtime_c | p_mbusy | p_defeit | ocup.m.o |
|---|---|---|---|---|---|---|---|---|---|
| 1 | 1471,7 | 288 | 151,9 | 745 | 0 | 0 | 73 | 4 | 75 |
| 2 | 1337,8 | 235 | 149 | 664,3 | 0 | 0 | 73,3 | 21,7 | 76,5 |
| 3 | 1123 | 183 | 148,1 | 554,5 | 0 | 0 | 76,7 | 39 | 79,1 |
| 4 | 1036,4 | 137 | 151,3 | 522,6 | 0 | 0 | 74,9 | 54,3 | 79,3 |
| 5 | 900,93 | 102 | 150,39 | 451,65 | 0 | 0 | 78 | 66 | 79,4 |
| 6 | 1478,4 | 293 | 150,1 | 0 | 739,5 | 0 | 43,4 | 2,3 | 44,5 |
| 7 | 1370,5 | 262 | 152,9 | 0 | 698,7 | 0 | 44,9 | 12,7 | 46,6 |
| 8 | 1253 | 232 | 151,8 | 0 | 634 | 0 | 47,3 | 22,7 | 48,2 |
| 9 | 1212,3 | 204 | 151,8 | 0 | 613,4 | 0 | 47 | 32 | 49,3 |
| 10 | 1156,7 | 179 | 153,7 | 0 | 592,8 | 0 | 47,2 | 40,3 | 49,2 |
| ... | ... | ... | ... | ... | ... | ... | ... | ... | ... |

n - Experiment number.

With the data matrix obtained from the simulation (Table 1) the Principal Components technique was used to reduce the dimensionality of data. Using this technique a new data matrix was obtained (Table 2) with the contribution of the initial variables for the principal components. Each principal component (*comp.i*) corresponds to a new variable. Based on the theory of Principal Component technique more than 80% of the information is in the first four principal components. Consequently we have reduced the number of variables to be dealt with.

**Table 2** Contribution of variables for the principal components.

| | Comp.1 | Comp.2 | Comp.3 | Comp.4 | Comp.5 | Comp.6 |
|---|---|---|---|---|---|---|
| AVTIME_A | 0,38887 | 0,83217 | 0,05313 | 0,21388 | 0,2054 | 0,04897 |
| AVTIME_B | 0,1064 | 0,09589 | 0,08182 | -0,05257 | 0,02328 | 0,27666 |
| AVTIME_C | 0,42941 | 0,5892 | 0,04627 | 0,06729 | 0,19344 | 0,02789 |
| AVWIP | -0,11326 | 0,89371 | 0,0571 | 0,20611 | 0,14323 | 0,1664 |
| OCUP.M.O | -0,05517 | 0,25755 | -0,04437 | 0,94372 | 0,17384 | -0,06087 |
| OUTPUT | -0,30915 | -0,51575 | 0,71503 | -0,04588 | -0,22383 | -0,06024 |
| P_DEFEIT | -0,21602 | -0,22828 | -0,93926 | 0,0212 | -0,02179 | -0,06313 |
| P_MBLOCK | 0,09262 | 0,13039 | 0,02993 | -0,05673 | -0,03391 | 0,94476 |
| P_MBUSY | -0,8896 | -0,13883 | 0,09015 | 0,26088 | -0,25022 | -0,05759 |
| P_MSETUP | 0,80032 | 0,42493 | 0,07227 | 0,30547 | -0,07135 | 0,04532 |
| P_REPAIR | 0,27192 | 0,25663 | -0,06938 | 0,19678 | 0,89852 | -0,04143 |
| TEMP.EXE | 0,95403 | -0,05647 | 0,13209 | -0,0206 | 0,17886 | 0,06631 |
| | **Comp.7** | **Comp.8** | **Comp.9** | **Comp.10** | **Comp.11** | **Comp.12** |
| AVTIME_A | 0,04121 | -0,03659 | 0,2407 | -0,02965 | 0,03348 | 0,01174 |
| AVTIME_B | 0,94465 | 0,02379 | -0,00129 | 0,00198 | 0,00143 | -0,00148 |
| AVTIME_C | 0,05572 | 0,6483 | -0,00685 | 0,00779 | -0,00885 | -0,00165 |
| AVWIP | 0,13159 | 0,21045 | -0,17342 | 0,03914 | -0,03163 | -0,01729 |
| OCUP.M.O | -0,05693 | 0,02885 | 0,00348 | 0,00605 | -0,00174 | 0,00157 |
| OUTPUT | 0,06576 | -0,09118 | 0,04116 | -0,01337 | 0,23822 | 0,00838 |
| P_DEFEIT | -0,06347 | -0,05826 | 0,01317 | -0,00735 | 0,08032 | -0,00061 |
| P_MBLOCK | 0,27637 | 0,01371 | -0,0012 | 0,00154 | -0,00342 | -0,00039 |
| P_MBUSY | -0,12351 | -0,10313 | 0,06008 | 0,0006 | 0,03946 | 0,12717 |
| P_MSETUP | 0,05055 | 0,10947 | -0,03622 | 0,23923 | -0,01278 | -0,00173 |
| P_REPAIR | 0,02473 | 0,08301 | 0,00463 | -0,00495 | -0,00801 | -0,00048 |
| TEMP.EXE | 0,0302 | 0,04987 | 0,08992 | -0,10622 | 0,01046 | 0,0975 |

Our understanding of the meaning of these four new variables is presented in table 3. In this Table, only the initial variables with a larger contribution for the new ones are presented.

**Table 3** Summary of results based on the Principal Components technique.

| Principal Components | Initial Variables | New Meaning |
|---|---|---|
| Comp.1 | TEMP.EXE, P_MBUSY and P_MSETUP | Process effectiveness |
| Comp.2 | AVWIP, AVTIME_A and AVTIME_C | Material flow constraint |
| Comp.3 | P_DEFEITOS and OUTPUT | Amount produced |
| Comp.4 | OCUP.M.O. | Labor utilization |

These new variables contain all the relevant information about the behaviour of the manufacturing system and should be considered as the decision-making variables.

Further steps have to be carried out for the validation of the use of the Principal Components Technique as well as for the establishment of a set of criteria for comparing performance measures.

## 4. CONCLUSIONS

The architecture of an integrated Process Planning, Production Planning and Control system was presented. The integrated system makes use of several manufacturing functions enabling the conditions to effectively manage the whole manufacturing system. Minimizing the manufacturing costs, reducing the lead times and improving system flexibility were the targeted objectives.

The approach that was implemented aimed at avoiding rushing orders and the guesswork usually required when the pre-defined route sheets and production plans are to be changed due to unexpected events. The use of DES linked to the Process and Production Planning system allowed the generation of several manufacturing scenarios closely related with the actual shop-floor behavior, since the appropriate linkage with a control system was established. The possibility to know in advance the performance of the system through the use of the results of the simulation run, allowed the analysis of several manufacturing alternatives (e.g. new production schedules), before the proposed changes are implemented.

Simulation tools showed to be very efficient as a data generator, supporting the development of other statistical analyses. The use of new variables as a performance measure was briefly presented. The approach that uses the Principal Components technique needs to be further validated.

## 5 REFERENCES

Cunha, P. F. and Mesquita, R.M.; "The Role of Discrete Event Simulation in the Improvement of Manufacturing Systems Performance", in "Balanced Automation Systems II - Implementation challenges for anthropocentric manufacturing", pp. 137-145, Ed. L. M. Camarinha-Matos e H. Afsarmanesh, Chapman & Hall, 1996.

ElSayed, A.E.; Elwany, M.H.; PPP: A Hybrid System for Integrating Process and Production Planning in Batch Part Manufacturing; Journal of Materials Processing Technology; 61;pp.113-119 (1996)

Grady M.W.; "Performance Measurement. Implementing Strategy"; Management Accounting; June 1991; pp. 49-53

Kuhnle, H.; Braun, H.J. and Buhring, J.; Integration of CAPP and PPC - Interfusion Manufacturing Management; Integrated Manufacturing Systems; Vol.5; nº2; pp.21-27 (1994)

Leung, H.C.; "Annotated Bibliography on Computer-Aided Process Planning"; Int. Journal of Advanced Manufacturing Technology; 12; pp.309-329 (1996)

Wiendahl H., Schmidt B.; A System Solution to Integrated Process Planning and Workshop Scheduling using Manufacturing Alternatives, in Production Engineering, Vol.II/2 (1995).

## 6 BIOGRAPHY

**M.Sc. Pedro Filipe do Carmo Cunha**

received his Master degree in Computer Aided Engineering from Staffordshire University in U.K in 1993. Current work is on his Ph.D. at Instituto Superior Técnico (IST-Higher Technical Institute), with the topic in Integration of Production and Process Planning.

**Professor, Ph.D. Ruy Manuel Dias Mesquita**

received his Ph.D. in Mechanical Engineering at the Technical University of Lisbon in 1988. He is an associate professor in Mechanical Technology at IST since 1991. His research activity has been developed in the area of Production Engineering. At present, he is the director of the Institute of Materials and Production Technologies at INETI-National Institute of Engineering and Industrial Technology.

# Implementation of executive information systems around traditional manufacturing control system packages

*J. Fisher and A K Kochhar*
*Department of Mechanical Engineering*
*UMIST*
*Manchester M60 1QD, United Kingdom.*
*Tel: +44 (0) 161 200 3801 Fax: +44 (0) 161 200 8721*
*Email:* mcjmscc@umist.ac.uk

*M. Reilley*
*Manufacturing Products and Services Limited*
*The Coach House*
*Drighlington, West Yorkshire BD11 LN*
*United Kingdom.*
*Tel: +44 (0) 113 285 3385 Fax: +44 (0) 113 285 2636*
*Email: miker@maps.co.uk*

**Abstract**

In common with most traditional data processing systems, a vast majority of manufacturing control systems' packages simply process and store large amounts of manufacturing data. This data can hold significant strategic value for an organization if it can be transformed into meaningful information.

This paper describes the main features of a prototype executive information system, based on the application of On-Line Analytical Processing techniques for extracting strategic performance data, suitable for making executive decisions, from standard manufacturing control system databases. The results of critical evaluation by users are described.

**Keywords**

Manufacturing control systems, Performance measurement, Executive information systems, On-line analytical processing.

Computer Applications in Production and Engineering. F. Plonka and G. Olling (Eds.)

## 1. INTRODUCTION

Within manufacturing organizations, often one of the largest and most important sources of information is the manufacturing planning and control (MPC) system. MPC systems are concerned with the planning and control of the manufacturing process, and an effective MPC system can provide substantial strategic advantage for a company in its markets (Vollman 1992). Although activities within manufacturing planning and control can be undertaken manually, the complexity of modern day systems demands the use of computers to manage them effectively. Such systems are, by their very nature, both consumers and creators of detailed operational data. They are vital for the daily running of organizations but are not appropriate for establishing the overall picture, making comparisons and deciding on change (Kelly 1996).

In efforts to provide solutions to the maze of information held within organizations, information regarded to be of strategic importance to decision making has been presented to executives by means of computerized executive information systems (EIS). These systems, originally aimed solely at executives, provide highly summarized information in a graphical and/or textual format. Such systems have achieved various levels of success (Taylor 1994, Nord 1995) at addressing the needs of executives, but have been fairly inflexible in being able to manipulate data for more detailed analysis.

## 2. ON-LINE ANALYTICAL PROCESSING

OLAP (On-Line Analytical Processing) is a new name for a set of proven concepts. The concept that most distinguishes OLAP from many other decision support categories is that of multidimensionality. Instead of the information being arranged in a set of flat tables or spreadsheets, multidimensional models present data in terms of the actual business dimensions of an organization. This is the type of analysis required by both managers and executives, so as to assess the variables which effect the performance of their organizations. OLAP is now becoming the technique used for data access and manipulation within EIS (Messina 1995, Ferguson 1996).

As the OLAP approach is amenable to providing a flexible, top down, view of an organization, it is postulated that it would be appropriate to apply OLAP to provide information relating to functions carried within manufacturing planning and control systems. By presenting a set of performance measures which are of strategic benefit to an organization, managers should be able to make more informed and timely decisions thus providing strategic advantage for their organizations. This paper describes a prototype Executive Information System, interfaced to an existing MRPII system, to obtain a variety of information in a very flexible manner.

## 3. SYSTEM INVESTIGATION AND DEVELOPMENT

The prototype executive information system has been developed within a research group consisting of an academic institution, two software houses and a manufacturing company, to assess the potential of the approach. It is based around a traditional MRPII framework. Within this framework, the prototype was developed around the key areas of inventory control and purchasing. A survey was conducted within the manufacturing company. This was designed to determine typical performance measures which were used to judge the performance of the company and the resulting actions taken, and assess the usefulness of an EIS and the types of analysis and features which would be of benefit.

The findings of the surveys are summarized below:

- Few measures used to assess the performance of the company related to operational activities. Instead they concentrated on broad financial issues and did little to help identify sources of problems. Measures used to assess performance provided a fixed picture and did not stimulate action
- Large numbers of reports were generated and filed with no specific aim in mind
- EIS would provide a useful means of only retaining data useful for specific purposes
- Drilling down through various layers of information would provide the greatest benefit in identifying problems and opportunities.

Perhaps the most important conclusion from the survey was:
"A manageable set of performance measures is required which will be of practical use in establishing the route causes of problems and which provide a true representation of an organization. The measures should be represented in an easy to understand format in a timely manner".

### *Executive Information System Development*

The development of the EIS essentially involved a two stage process. Firstly, an initial set of performance measures was developed which aimed to illustrate the activities of the areas under investigation. From this initial set of measures, attention was then focused on how they could be represented using multidimensional analysis, employing on-line analytical processing (OLAP).

### *Development of Performance Measures*

The initial set of performance measures for inventory control is shown in Table 1.

| **Measure** | **Objective** |
|---|---|
| Service Level | Measures parts that are available in the stores when required |
| Parts availability | Measures the level of availability of parts |
| Customer dissatisfaction | Measures the number of customers suffering from unavailability of parts in a given period |
| Inventory accuracy | Measures the accuracy of stock records |
| Sequencing of parts issue | Measure how well stock issuing procedures are followed |
| Shelf life control | Measures how much stock is wasted due to expiry of shelf life |
| Time a part is in stock | Determines slow moving or obsolete stock |
| Increase in inventory levels as a proportion of rate of increase of sales | Measures contribution of increased level of inventory to sales |
| Average value of inventory | Measures the value of inventory held |
| Inventory turnovers | Measures the frequency with which inventory is turned over |
| Frequency of stockouts | Measures how often parts are unavailable in inventory and thus cause disruptions to production |

**Table 1.** List of Performance Measures for Inventory Control

### *Model Design*

For the system to be considered as a beneficial and effective tool, the following functional requirements were specified:

1. Managers and executives should be able to rapidly access information relating to pre-defined performance measures, as well as perform ad-hoc enquiries from information available within the MPC system. This information should be presented in a variety of formats.
2. The system should provide relevant information which can be used to aid in making more informed decisions.
3. The system should be reasonably simple and straightforward to use.

4. Simple navigation through different business dimensions should be provided to enhance the ease of use.
5. Highlighting of exceptional information should be available to draw the attention of the user to important issues.

*Conceptual Design*

The system is modular in design (Figure 1), so that individual components can be modified without affecting others, and to facilitate future development. Individual elements of the system are now discussed.

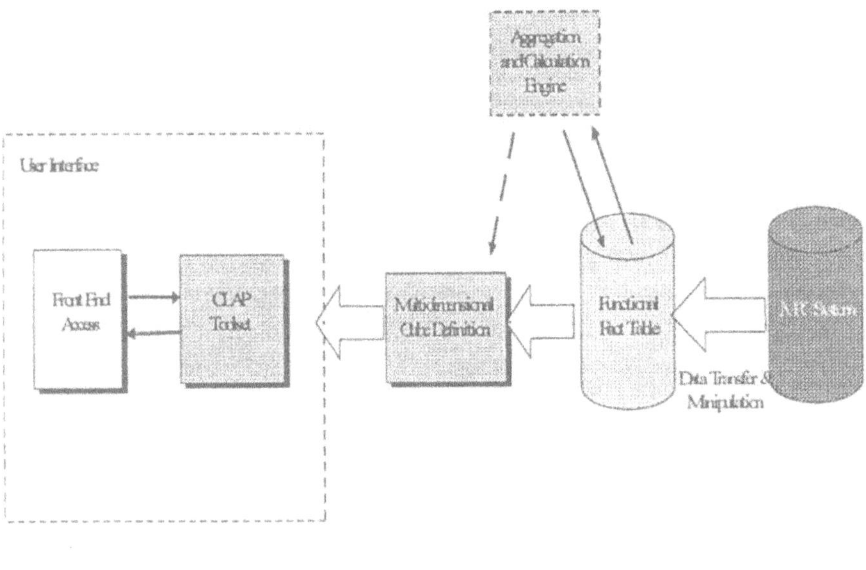


**Figure 1.** Representation of System Architecture

*MPC System*

The MPC system is the operational system from which manufacturing data is extracted. It consists of a number of different relational tables containing transactional information. In this form the data provides little value for decision making. The data required by the EIS, typically resides in a number of different tables within the MPC system. It is therefore necessary to create links between these tables so that the appropriate data may be extracted. The data held within the MPC system may also require a certain amount of manipulation before it can be extracted.

*Functional Fact Table*

Although the system uses the same data as the MPC system, it does not use the same image of it. Data is extracted from the operational system, manipulated as required and stored in tables relating to the specific function module. These tables, called functional fact tables, are used by the analysis tools as their source of information.

*Aggregation and Calculation Engine*

The aggregation and calculation engine (ACE) is used to populate the fact tables with pre-aggregated data for hierarchical dimensions and pre-calculated data for equations. ACE allows for the aggregation of the complete data set, or if required, a subset of the original.

*Multidimensional Cube Definition*

The multidimensional cube definition involves the creation of a definition 'layer' of the existing functional fact tables. The layer is in essence a mapping process whereby fields are identified within the fact tables and are mapped onto master tables. Each master table is equivalent to a dimension within the cube definition.

*OLAP Toolset*

The OLAP toolset is the main element of the system with which the end-user comes into contact. Users are able to view multiple charts and reports, rotate dimensions, drill up or down, rank information, highlight variances, change presentation formats and define new calculations.

*Front-End Access*

The front-end access provides a simple method to access the OLAP toolset through a Windows environment. Access is obtained by clicking on an icon.

*Example*

The application of the system is perhaps best illustrated by means of an example. One of the multidimensional 'cubes' relates to inventory movement around the system. Within the cube definition process, a graphical entity relationship diagram (ERD) is used to illustrate the relationship between dimension tables and central fact table. The multidimensional model provides a representation of all the relationships between different dimensions and portrays the types of analysis available. Figure 2 shows the entity relationship diagram for the inventory movements cube which is used for the analysis of raw materials and components control. The dimension tables contain information which describes the transaction data held in the fact table, or transaction file. As each cube has only one fact table, the cube definition can be said to have a 'one-to-one' relationship with the fact table.

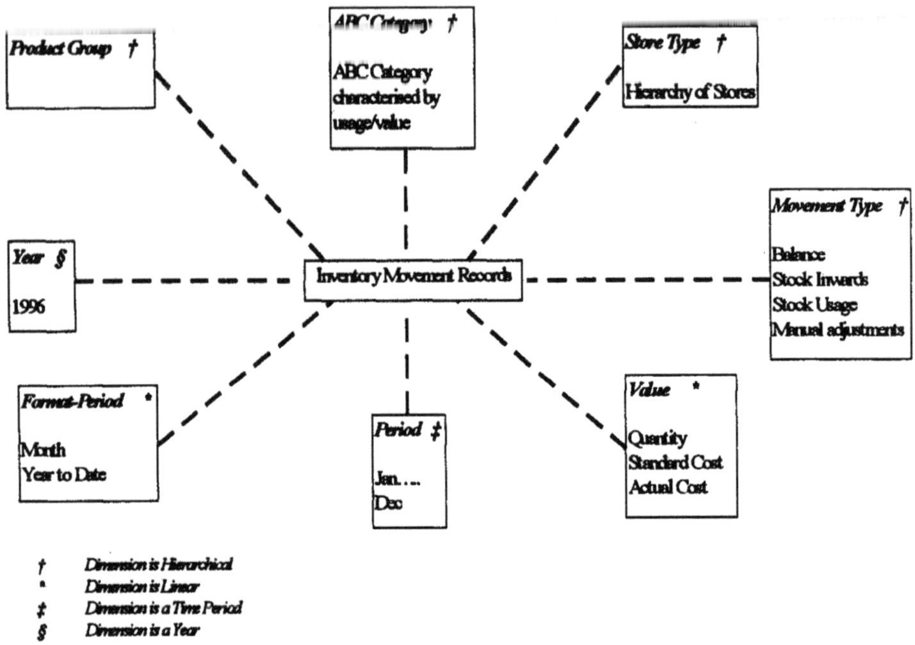


**Figure 2.** Entity Relationship Diagram for Inventory Movements Cube

The objective of the cube is to provide analysis relating to the dynamic inventory movements by utilizing data held within stock movement records. Analysis can be conducted for any combination of the dimensions shown in figure 2.

There are essentially two types of dimension, either 'list' or 'hierarchical.' List type dimensions are a simple list and are straight forward. However hierarchical dimensions contain a parent/child structure where data for parent items is aggregated across several child items. When specifying hierarchical dimensions, it is necessary to define the parent item of each child. For example, figure 3 illustrates the hierarchy for a dimension containing stock movement types, as taken from the *inventory movements cube.*

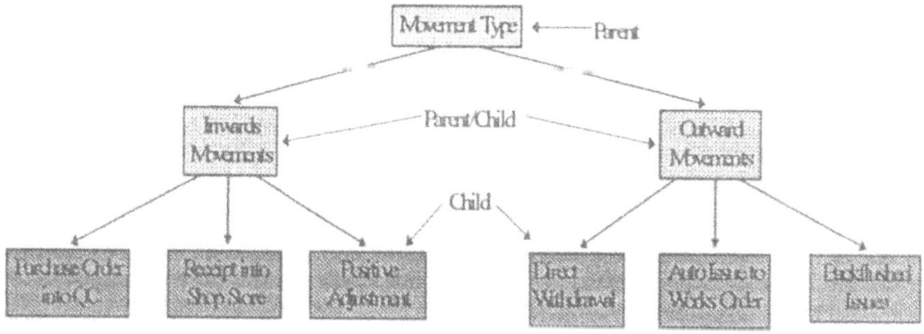


**Figure 3.** Example of a hierarchical dimension containing details of movement types.

*System Implementation*

The whole system has been implemented in a Windows environment and presents information in a highly visual and easily understandable environment. The system has an open architecture in that it can access information from any standard relational database. On-line analytical processing (OLAP is used to analyze the data so as to present meaningful information to users.

## 4. SYSTEM ASSESSMENT

The assessment of the system was carried out by means of a multi-part questionnaire, and feedback was obtained from a number of potential users. The results of the assessment are summarized below:

- It is possible to view manufacturing data in a way which has previously been unavailable from MPC systems.
- Companies are being run by fewer people who require information on the performance of their companies in a format which allows different perspectives of it to be analyzed.
- The EIS system developed represents the activities which occur within the areas under investigation effectively, and provides relevant and useful information which can be used to highlight problems and aid in decision making.
- The level of detail of the information is sufficient for general analysis, but more detailed information is required to identify individual problems.
- The facilities of drill down and exception reporting were considered to be of most benefit to people when analyzing data.

## 5. CONCLUSIONS

OLAP is very much user driven. It is not of great benefit if what is required is a rigid set of reports which present a fixed set of performance measures. The strength of this approach lies within the ability to view data from a number of different perspectives and thus navigate through different data slices. From the models developed during this research, a number of conclusions can be drawn with respect to the suitability of presenting performance measurement information using OLAP:

- OLAP provides an effective way of presenting manufacturing data, in a simple, intuitive form, and provides powerful manipulation and analysis of such data.
- Not all types of performance measures are conducive to multidimensional analysis. As the range of dimensions restricts the scope of the analysis, it is necessary to assess the benefits which would be attained from representing information multidimensionally , and the costs required to create the cubes.
- Cubes should be developed to incorporate those measures which are of greatest importance to a company.
- As the number of unrelated dimension items increases, sparsity within the models increases exponentially.
- The manufacturing data itself must be accurate and used in the way it is intended, for the system to be useful.

## 6. REFERENCES

Kelly, S. [1996] *Data Warehousing: The Route to Mass Customization.* John Wiley & Sons.

Ferguson, N. [1996] The Data Warehousing Boom, *Conspectus*, February, 2-5.

Messina, F. M.; Singh, S. [1995] Executive Information Systems: Not just for Executives Anymore!, *Management Accounting*, July, 60-63.

Nord, J. N.; Nord, G. D. [1995] Why managers use executive support systems, *Industrial Management and Data Systems*, **95** *No. 9*, 24-28.

Taylor, D. [1994] EIS is Dead, Long Live EIS, Technology, *Management Today*, May, 89.

Vollman T. E.; Berry W. L.; Whybark D. C. [1992] *Manufacturing Planning and Control Systems.* Irwin.

## 7. BIOGRAPHY

Jim Fisher holds a Bachelor's Degree in Mechanical Engineering from the University of Nottingham, and a Master's Degree in Advanced Manufacturing Technology and Systems Management from UMIST. He is currently a Manufacturing Engineering at Rover Group Limited.

Ashok Kochhar is the Lucas Professor of Manufacturing Systems Engineering, and Head of the Manufacturing Division at the University of Manchester Institute of Science and Technology (UMIST). His main research interests are in the areas of Competitive Manufacturing, Manufacturing Control Systems, Performance Measurement and Benchmarking.

Mike Reilly is the Principal Manufacturing Consultant at Manufacturing Products and Services (MAPS) who are one of the UK's leading developers and providers of Manufacturing Control Systems.

44

# An Architecture for aggregating real and virtual models in manufacturing systems

*ASAMORI Motoo, KAMIO Youichi*
*Toyo Engineering Corporation*
*8-1, Akanehama 2-chome, Narashino-shi, Chiba 275, Japan*
*asamori@is.toyo-eng.co.jp*

*MORI Kenichiro, YOSHIKAWA Norio, HOTTA Tadaaki*
*OMRON Corporation*
*2-5-48, Tadao, Machida-shi, Tokyo 194, Japan*
*Kenichiro_Mori@omron.co.jp*

*KIMURA Toshiaki, GOTO Hiroyuki*
*Technical Research Institute, Japan Society for the Promotion of Machine Industry*
*1-1-12, Hachiman-cho, Higashikurume-shi, Tokyo 203, Japan*
*kimura@tri.jspmi.or.jp*

*FUKUDA Yoshiro*
*Hosei University*
*3-7-2 Kagino-cho, Koganei-shi, Tokyo 184, Japan*
*fukuda@is.hosei.ac.jp*

**Abstract**

A manufacturing system needs to adapt or renew itself rapidly in order to produce better and cheaper products that customers require. In this paper a new architecture is proposed that features "renewal" within the life cycle of production

Computer Applications in Production and Engineering. F. Plonka and G. Olling (Eds.)

system. In order to support renewal effectively the architecture includes not only the feed-forward structure of plan, design, construction, operation, and maintenance, but also feedback information about know-how and experiences of field operations. The architecture assumes a virtual enterprise environment which accounts for and unifies both design and manufacturing even though they typically operate remotely. The architecture supports gathering and categorizing multimedia data such as signals from equipment, trouble information, quality management information, operators' know-how, etc. A demonstration, based on actual field-gathered multimedia data and its associated renewal activities, will verify the feasibility of the renewal-centered architecture. The demonstration will use object-oriented models and simulators.

**Keywords**
Renewal, Virtual Manufacturing, Real Model, Virtual Model, KAIZEN Activity

## 1 INTRODUCTION

The environment surrounding the manufacturing industries is changing substantially. These changes include structural changes in supply and demand, development and applications of new technology, and various new measures for environmental conservation. Under these changes, the life of manufacturing systems tends to become relatively longer compared with that of product. As the industries policy for manufacturing system changes from scrap and build to improvement, renewal activity in production life cycle is recognized more important than ever.

Although facility life cycle and virtual manufacturing system are studied, the industries are not sufficiently equipped with tools, evaluation methodology and technology that should systematically support all phases from planning, designing, construction, operation, maintenance to disposal of manufacturing devices. As production activities of enterprises become more international, it is often observed that a manufacturing system is operated remotely from the designing department. In such a case, remote operation and virtual enterprise are studied to ensure smooth information exchange between departments and to modify or change the system efficiently and at a low cost in accordance with changes in manufacturing environment. Advances in information technology proceed rapidly, and new tools and technology are introduced in market to apply to every phase of the life cycle of manufacturing system.

In view of these trends, a new platform was proposed which aggregates real and virtual models without the consciousness of geographical distance, and can compose, operate and evaluate a manufacturing system of shop floor level in design, operation, maintenance, and improvement phases. Through experimental evaluation, we verified that the platform is feasible and can efficiently realize the improvement of productivity of manufacturing systems. On the basis of this result, a new reference architecture focused on renewal activity of manufacturing system is proposed, which consists of a function model and an implementation model. Modeling discussed in this paper is limited to manufacturing systems which include devices, operators, materials, and information processed in the shop floor level.

In this paper, Chapter 2 defines renewal activity which we focus on. Chapter 3 describes the definition of real and virtual models, and the need for aggregation of them. Chapter 4 introduces the requirements for renewal activity, and Chapter 5 proposes a new reference architecture of renewal activity.

This study has been made as "the Globeman 21 project", a part of IMS International R&D Project.

## 2 KAIZEN ACTIVITY AND RENEWAL ACTIVITY

Nowadays the product life is shorter than ever. The production system adopts or renews itself in accordance with the change of product. Some of module units, which compose manufacturing equipment, are replaced frequently. It is important to keep the same or better performance by continuously monitoring and maintaining the facilities in normal condition in the operation phase as defined in the design phase even though the system configuration of the manufacturing facilities is changed. In many Japanese companies, the manufacturing system is kept well through continuous KAIZEN activity. KAIZEN activity is based on the local shop floor level, and has been carried out in a small group of several operators and maintenance persons. Therefore, KAIZEN activity can not always be applied to the global manufacturing environment, because it is not fully supported by the information system technology.

This research is intended to realize the environment which supports KAIZEN activity using up-to-date information technology. It is supposed that the model of manufacturing system is built in the design phase and that the information of it is kept in the electronic data. The operating information is monitored from the running manufacturing facilities. If any difference between the model information and the monitored data is observed, the monitored data is transferred to the model. Through the simulation carried out using the monitored data, the cause of the difference is investigated and counter measure is considered and decided for implementation. The manufacturing system is re-configured to cope with the situation (major change). This activity is carried out in the environment which has already been proposed in our R&D activity. In case there is no need of re-configuration, another solution is taken so that some parameters are changed to meet the situation (minor change). These activities are called " RENEWAL " as shown in figure 1.

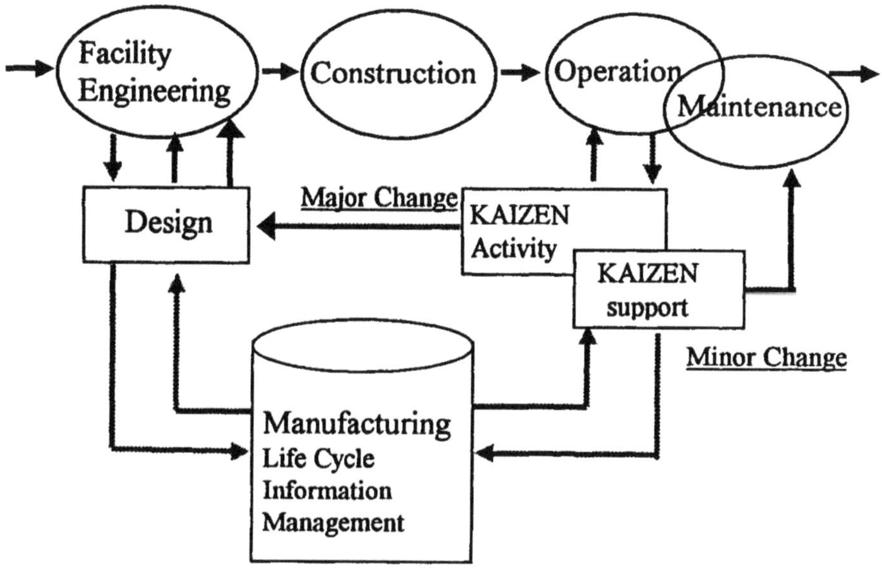


**Figure 1** Life Cycle of Manufacturing System and Renewals.

## 3 AGGREGATION OF REAL AND VIRTUAL MODELS

An actually existing manufacturing system is composed of devices, control information, management information, material flow, and transaction processes among them. Design, implementation and operation of a manufacturing system are very complicated because all the elements above are handled together, and therefore problems are difficult to identify if they occur. In order to identify a problem, a specific viewpoint must be established, and the model is built from that point which is selected from many viewpoints such as productivity of manufacturing system, operability of devices, quality of products, etc. relating to the problem.

A model represents the behavior of manufacturing system on several types of simulators or in other information processing world. It is called a virtual model. The virtual model in design phase is made, tested and evaluated from a critical point of view in manufacturing system. Many case studies are carried out using the model until the model is fixed to meet the requirements. A virtual model expresses the ideal states and their transition of manufacturing facilities under given conditions in the virtual world.

The virtual model of a manufacturing system has been built and used as a part of designing tools, and it is considered sufficient only in the workflow from designing, implementation to operation of manufacturing system. But taking account of renewal activity, the model needs to represent an existing manufacturing system in the real world. It is called a real model which is made up of the monitored and measured data of running devices from the viewpoint of specific information. The behavior of a manufacturing system in the real world can be described using the real data.

The virtual model is made and used mainly in design phase, while the real model is in operation phase. In renewal activity, a new environment is required where the real and virtual models are aggregated as mentioned in Chapter 2 "Kaizen Activity and Renewal Activity." The manufacturing system is evaluated more efficiently and effectively.

## 4 REQUIREMENTS FOR RENEWAL ACTIVITY

A manufacturing system consists of various devices which have their own information items and structures. Information of a device is independently defined and is not compatible with that of others, and it is difficult to exchange information among devices. To realize information exchange, an interface program is needed, which is not general but particular. Therefore a template is needed which shows the generic meaning of information independent of the structure dedicated to the device. There is too much information to be treated in a lump, and it is difficult to find out the necessary information. To simplify the problem, the template should be individually built in the specific point of view, however it should be furnished with common information items and structure.

The information of these models tends to be exchanged at different places in global manufacturing environment rather than in the same factory. The communication function is required in global manufacturing environment independent of the spatial distance.

Renewal activity is intended to be the same activity as Japanese KAIZEN activity. So the reference model deals with not only on-off signal information of the manufacturing devices but also human oriented information such as audio and visual signals treated by operators and maintenance persons. In addition to the character and numerical data processed on the computer, multimedia information such as picture, image, voice, animation, etc. is required to be treated in integrated and inter-related forms for the purpose of renewal activity.

# 5 REFERENCE ARCHITECTURE

The importance of aggregating the real and virtual models in renewal activity is described in Chapter 3 " Aggregation of Real Model and Virtual Model" in this paper. In order to realize that, two new reference architectures are proposed, one for building models and the other for implementing models.

## 5.1 Reference architecture for building models

The necessity of template in building models is described in Chapter 4 "Requirements for Renewal Activity" in this paper. A new reference architecture is shown in Figure 2 as a conceptual platform for building models of a manufacturing system.

The template is necessary for smooth exchange of information not only between real models in manufacturing system but also between real and virtual models. The template is an interface model of information exchange. It is not a functional model, but includes a functional aspect. The template is created from various points of views, such as productivity, manageability, operability, maintainability, quality assurance and so on, in manufacturing system. It describes briefly the meanings of information in order not to depend on the information items and its structure dedicated to manufacturing devices. It is common to all communication interfaces of real and virtual models, and is provided as a library based on object-oriented methodology. The instance of real and virtual models is created using this class library from the specific point of view.

## 5.2 Reference architecture for implementing models

The other reference architecture is proposed as shown in Figure 3 as a conceptual platform for implementation of manufacturing system.

This architecture consists of the following four layers:

Layer 1 : Common Platform – Represents communication network of data exchanges.

Layer 2 : Object Models - Represents information models of real and virtual manufacturing systems with communication interfaces through which data is transferred to the communication network, including multimedia database.

Layer 3 : Tools - Represents manufacturing equipment and devices including its controller such as NC and robot, data gathering devices like POP (point of production), and simulation tools for design engineering.

Layer 4 : Users - Represents designer, operator and manager who use the information of manufacturing system.

This architecture provides solutions for the requirements mentioned in Chapter 4 "Requirements for Renewal Activity."

The information exchange between the instances of real and virtual is carried out through Layer 1 (Common Platform). The communication in remote manufacturing environment is realized through Layer 1 and Layer 2 (Object Models). Communication network is realized based on information technology of Internet and LAN (Local Area Network) in the factory, etc., and interfaces are built using common off-the-shelf tools such as JAVA, C++, and so on. This is an infrastructure for data exchange between engineering department and manufacturing one. It removes the restrictions of time and space, and leads to promotion of smooth business activities in the global manufacturing environment.

There are many useful data in the real manufacturing system, and operators have knowledge and know-how about it. Such information leads to needs and seeds for renewal activity of manufacturing system. But it is buried in the files of field operation reports or in the head of operator. Two steps are needed for the utilization of information in the field, one is to get information, and the other is to store it and retrieve necessary pieces. The former is realized in layer 3 (Tools), where multimedia devices, e.g. video camera and voice recorder, are used for gathering information from operators in the real manufacturing field. The latter belongs to database in layer 2. Database archives raw data as they were. In renewal activity field data are analyzed from various points of view, and they leads to creation of new idea for improving the manufacturing system.

Object model is built using the template, and has an interface structure common for communication with other object models. In renewal activity, there are two cases of aggregation of real and virtual models. One is that real model is treated in the same manner as the virtual model in the virtual world. The other is that virtual data is replaced or incorporated with real data in the virtual model. These aggregations are realized in layers 2 & 3 of the virtual world.

Tools stand for data gathering and displaying devices through which an operator monitors the status of manufacturing facilities and inputs control/management information in real world. They express simulator and calculation software in virtual world. This layer includes multimedia equipment and graphical user interface for supporting virtual reality.

Users mean operators and field managers in the factory, and engineers and designers in product and process engineering. They have knowledge and know-how, and they decide what and how to perform renewal activity.

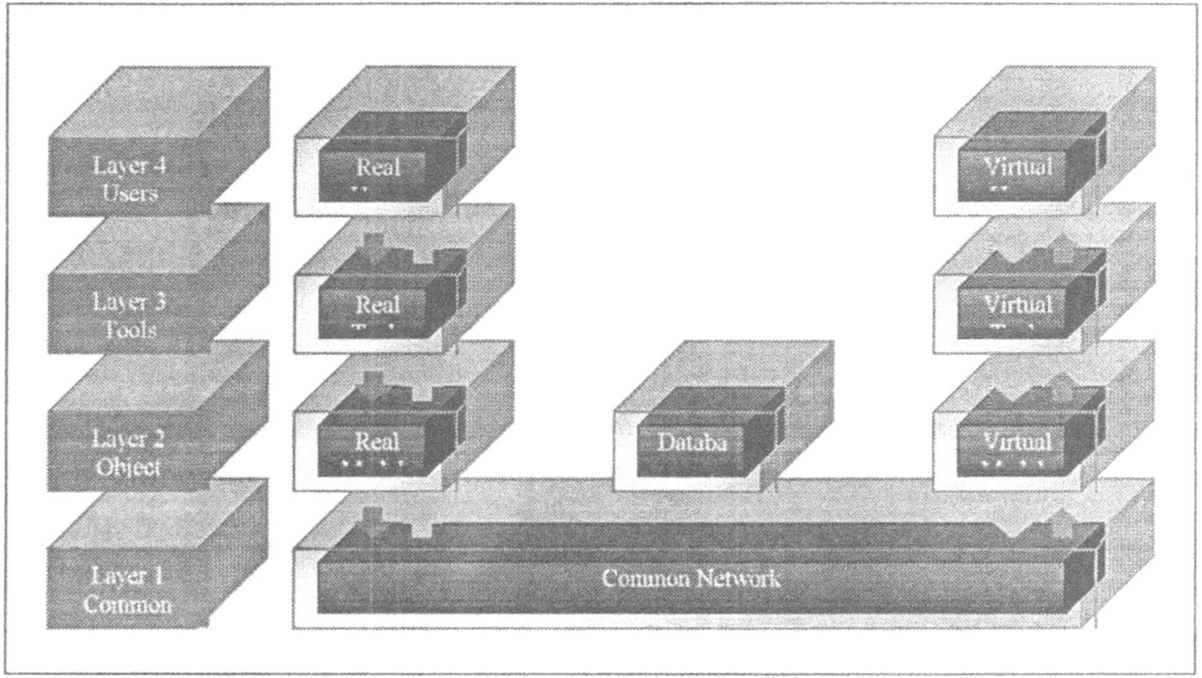


**Figure 2** Reference Architecture

## 6 CONCLUDING REMARKS

Two new reference architectures are proposed in focus on renewal activity in the life cycle of manufacturing system. A demonstration system is prepared for validation of the reference architectures. A sample manufacturing system is selected as a candidate for demonstration, and information of its features and specifications are gathered from designing section and operation field in the factory.

We are now under designing, and in near future we will build a demonstration system and will report the result.

## REFERENCES


Iwata, K. et al. (1995). Proceedings of EI '95, pp.154-167.

Onosato, M. and Iwata, K. (1993). Annals of the CIRP Vol.42, No1, pp.475-478, CIRP

Mitsuishi, M. et al. (1995). Proceedings of IROS' 95, pp.13-20, IEEE

NIIIP. (1995). NIIIP cycle0, Revision 6, The National Industrial Information Infrastructure Protocols Consortium.

IMS Promotion Center (1996). Enterprise Integration for Global Manufacturing Towards 21st Century

Mori, K. et al. (1996). Proceedings of APMS'96, pp.309-314, IFIP (http://ims.toyo-eng.co.jp/pub/gm21pub/PUBLICATION/apms/apms.htm)

# 45

# Concurrent Engineering Applications in Mexico: two case studies

*A. Molina, E. Gomez, D. Guerra*
*Centro de Sistemas Integrados de Manufactura,*
*ITESM, Campus Monterrey, CP 64849,*
*Monterrey, N.L. Mexico*
*fax: +52 (8) 358-1209, e-mail:*
*armolina@campus.mty.itesm.mx*

**Abstract**

The result of a study in the area of Concurrent Engineering in Mexican Companies is presented in this paper. This study identified the following major issues: the need to train/educate engineers in CE and to support design process automation, the lack of standardized product definitions and design for manufacture rules, and the necessity to introduce social-technical design concepts and cooperative design methods. From the 12 companies analyzed, two were selected to reengineer their design process in order to improve their product development processes. The process and information collected was used to develop two Computer Aided Engineering Systems to support Concurrent Engineering: Concurrent Design System for Automotive Part Dies and Integrated Development Environment of Glass Products.

**Keywords**

Concurrent Engineering, Assessment Tool, Process Models, Information Models, CAE System

## 1 INTRODUCTION

Mexico is playing a leading role in the Latin American manufacturing industry. The NAFTA agreement has forced Mexican companies, especially Automotive Parts Manufacturers, to implement new philosophies in order to become more competitive. The major approaches being used are: Concurrent Engineering/Simultaneous Engineering and Agile Manufacturing.

In order to support Mexican Manufacturing Companies, ITESM (Instituto Tecnológico y de Estudios Superiores de Monterrey), the largest private university

Computer Applications in Production and Engineering. F. Plonka and G. Olling (Eds.)

system in Latin America, created the CSIM (Centro de Sistemas Integrados de Manufactura) with the mission to train engineers with specialized knowledge in new manufacturing paradigms, methodologies and computer tools, and to develop and transfer new technologies to Mexican Industry. A new multidisciplinary research team has been created within CSIM named GI-INCIVI (acronym in Spanish for Life Cycle Engineering Research Group). The objective of the group is to explore the following areas with a unique integrated approach in Life Cycle Research (Molina, 1996):

1. Enterprise Life Cycle which comprises the strategic management process, enterprise engineering/integration process and enterprise lifetime process.
2. Product Life Cycle that involves the product development process from its conception to its disposal.
3. Technology Life Cycle related to the technology management process to identify technologies at different stage of evolution (emerging, pacing, key and basis) to be used to support the previous life cycle processes.

This paper presents the results achieved so far at CSIM by GI-INCIVI in the area of Product Life Cycle research.

## 2 PRODUCT LIFE CYCLE RESEARCH

The projects related to Product Life Cycle were targeted to introduce and implement the concept of Concurrent Engineering in Mexican Companies. The following projects have been developed:

1. Assessment Tool for Concurrent Engineering: An assessment tool was modified and applied to 12 Mexican companies in order to identify areas of opportunity to introduce Concurrent Engineering concepts, methodologies and tools (Gomez and Molina, 1996).

2. Methodology for Re-engineering the Design Process: based on the results of our study in Mexican companies the need to create a methodology to re-engineer the design process was identified. The aim of the methodology is to formalize and integrate the design process in order to standardize and improve the development of products within manufacturing companies (Gomez 1996, Guerra 1996). The methodology integrates the concepts of core processes, core competencies, strategic and technology planning in order to define the necessary learning and technical capabilities to support product development processes (Hamel and Prahalad 1990). This methodology is being extended to tackle the Enterprise Life Cycle process as well (Bernus and Nemes, 1994).

3. Development of Computer Aided Engineering Systems for Concurrent Engineering: once the methodology was developed and applied to two companies, prototype CAE Systems to support Concurrent Engineering were created to automate the design process using an object oriented language called AML (Adaptive Modeling Language) by applying the concept of data driven applications (Molina et al., 1995). Data driven applications use two information models to support decision making in product development. These models are: Product and Manufacturing Model. The Product Model represents all the information required of a product through its life cycle. The information concerning the manufacturing capability and capacity of a firm's facility is captured in the Manufacturing Model. The use of these two models allows the designer to have readily access to all the information required to achieve concurrent design of products supported by design for X applications (Molina and Chemaly, 1996).

Two case studies has been completed in two companies. In the next sections detailed descriptions of the results achieved so far are presented.

## 3 ASSESSMENT TOOL FOR CONCURRENT ENGINEERING

The first phase in our research project was targeted to identify the areas of opportunity in Mexican Companies and how companies' product development environments are set. The Concurrent Engineering (CE) Assessment Tool created by Carter and Baker (1992) was selected to support our work in studying 12 Mexican companies. No specific criterion was chosen to select the companies for the study. The companies selected were: engineering companies for capital goods (2), glass manufacturers (2), automotive part's manufacturer (6), and house ware manufacturers (2).

The CE Assessment Tool allows the user to have an idea of what kinds of changes are necessary in a company to create a concurrent engineering environment. The CE Assessment Tools has four elements (Figure 1):

1. A questionnaire to assess the company's current product development environment
2. A Matrix to determine the CE methods the company needs in order to develop a give product successfully
3. A Dimension Map to determine where a company is and where it should be
4. A Priority Map to define the priorities to transform the current product development environment into a CE environment

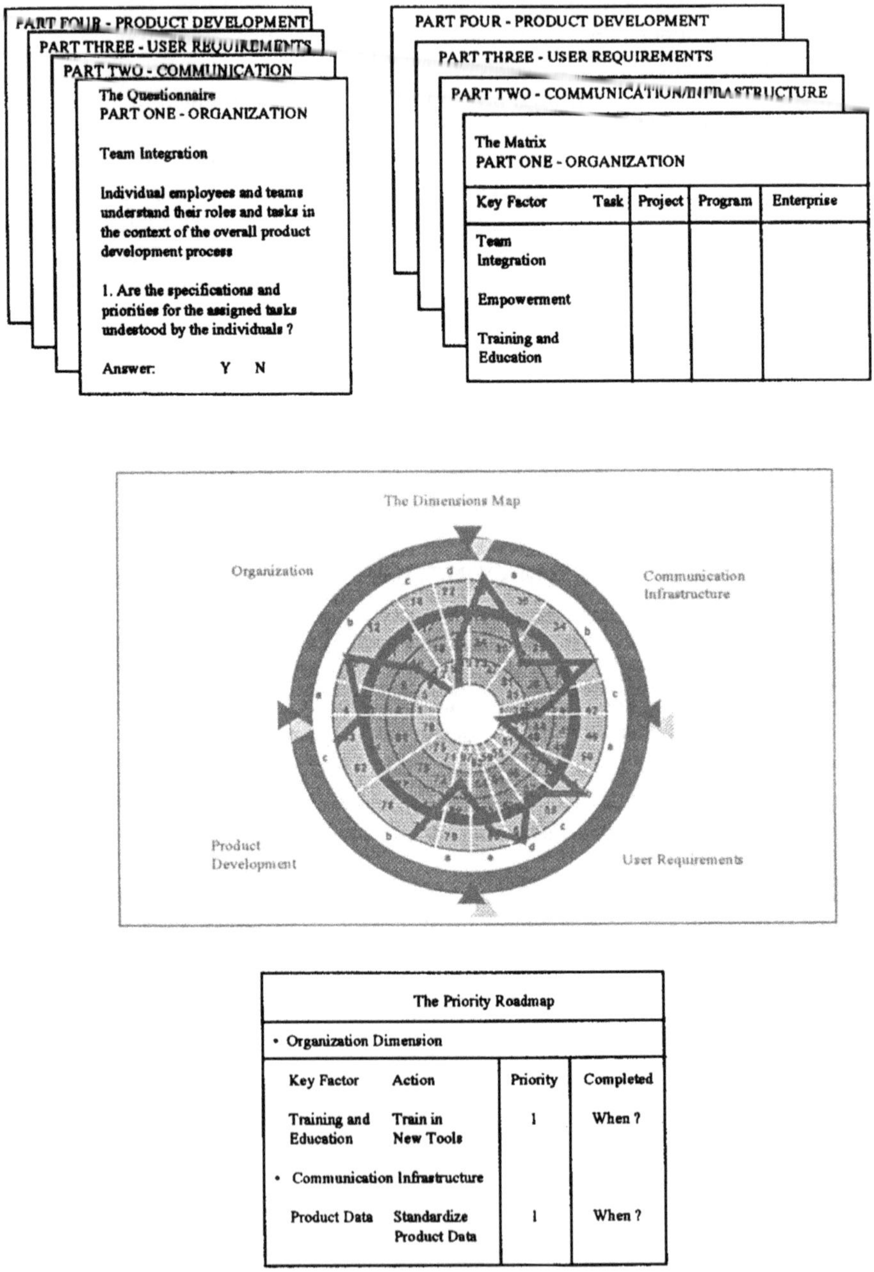


**Figure 1** Concurrent Engineering Assessment Tool (Carter and Baker 1992).

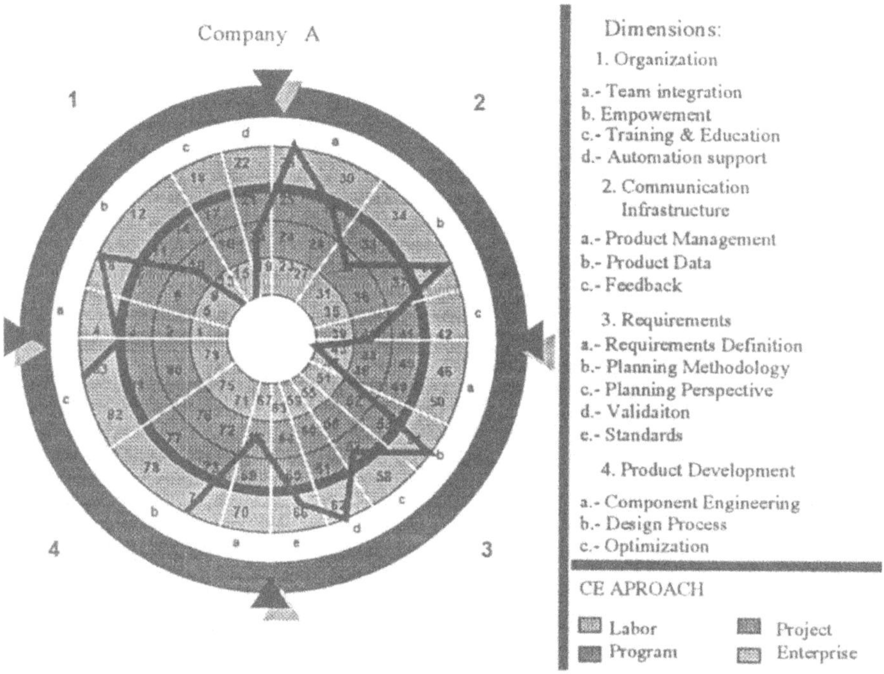


**Figure 2** Concurrent Engineering Assessment of Company A

The dimensions of change are related to the organization, communication infrastructure, user requirements and product development. These changes can be made at different levels of teamwork: task, project, program and enterprise. Details of the methodology can be found in Carter and Baker (1992).

For each individual company an assessment was carried out (Figure 2). Key factors defined by the companies for the implementation of CE environments were tabulated. The following major issues were identified: the need to train/educate engineers and to support the automation of the design process, the lack of standardized product definitions and design for manufacture rules, and the necessity to introduce social-technical design concepts and cooperative design methods (Table 1).

## 4 METHODOLOGY FOR RE-ENGINEERING THE DESIGN PROCESS

A methodology has been developed in order to support companies in the introduction of Concurrent Engineering, especially to tackle the following issues:

**Table 1** Areas of Opportunity identified by Mexican Companies

| Key Factors Identified by Companies | Number of Companies |
|---|---|
| Training and Education | 9 |
| Automation Support | 9 |
| Product Data | 9 |
| Standards | 8 |
| Component Engineering | 8 |
| Design Process | 8 |
| Empowerment | 7 |
| Product Management | 6 |
| Planning Methodology | 6 |
| Requirements Definition | 6 |
| Feedback Protocol | 6 |
| Optimization Policy | 6 |
| Team Integration | 4 |
| Validation of Requirements | 4 |
| Planning Perspective | 1 |

The necessity to introduce social-technical design concepts and cooperative design methods, and the need to train/educate engineers. This methodology has the following phases:

1. Diagnosis of Company's Product Value Chain (Suppliers-Products-Clients): evaluation of the characteristics of products being delivery to the client and being acquired from suppliers (material and components).
2. Analysis of Product Development Process Measures: definition and measure of key variables to evaluate the performance of the product development process, for example: product development lead time, extent of co-engineering, number of people in product development, etc.
3. Identification of Product Development Core Processes: detail description of processes within product development that are key to the success of product designs, for example: product research, product engineering and design, co-engineering, etc. These processes are modeled using IDEF0 (ICAM, 1980).
4. Identification of Product Design Core Competencies: definition, evaluation and allocation of technological capabilities of humans and technical resources necessary to achieve Concurrent Engineering. The concept of core competencies from Prahalad and Hamel (1990) is used to establish the criteria for their identification, acquisition, building and deployment.
5. Strategic Planning of Technology: definition of the situation "as-is" and situation "to-be" in the product development process, and establishment of the

transition plans to achieve Concurrent Engineering. The strategic planning methodology is based on the Purdue Reference Architecture (Williams, 1993).
6. Implementation of Technology Integration Plans to achieve Concurrent Engineering.

The above methodology has been applied to two of the companies that participated in the assessment study: Automotive Parts Die Design Company and Glass Manufacturing Company.

## 5 COMPUTER AIDED ENGINEERING SYSTEMS FOR CONCURRENT ENGINEERING

Prototype systems, for two company's re-engineered product development process, are being developed to explore how to overcome the lack of standardized product definitions and design for manufacture rules, and to support the automation of the design process. The following tasks are involved in these projects:

1. Modeling the Product Development Process using IDEF0 (ICAM, 1980).
2. Definition/Documentation of Product and Manufacturing Models using EXPRESS (ISO CD 10303 - 11)
3. Implementation of Product and Manufacturing Models using the object oriented environment for Knowledge Based Engineering AML - Adaptive Modeling Language (Molina and Chemaly, 1996).
4. Automation of the design process by implementing Design for Manufacture applications using AML

The idea behind this methodology is based on the fact that Concurrent Engineering can be effectively supported by computer technologies (e.g. CAE systems) if reliable and high quality data is provided to the engineers at all the stages of the product development. The methodologies to develop Product and Manufacturing Models can be found in Molina and Chemaly (1996). The work related to the implementation of the prototype systems for the two companies is at different stages of development. The following subsections describe the results achieved so far.

### 5.1 Concurrent Die Design for Automotive Parts

The objective of this project is to automate the design of dies for internal and external automotive parts. The analysis, standardization and documentation of the design process have been completed and the construction of the Product Model is being implemented in AML. Important comments on this case study are:

- There was a need to redefine the design process and create new structures for the design teams and incorporate product management techniques.
- The information required to develop the dies was not structured causing a lot of errors in the communication of product data between the designer, technical

sketcher and process designer. Therefore checklists were introduced to control the exchange of drawings and technical data.

- The Product Model being constructed incorporates the following technical data: die features, die components, and manufacturing technology data.
- An integrated system is being developed based on AML to allow the automated generation of die' drawings, NC code and manufacturing process data.

## 5.2 Integrated Environment for Glass Products

The prototype is complete for a family of water glass products. The system is able to design lemonade glasses and verifies the manufacturability of the product being designed. It can also produce the process plan for their production in order to estimate production time and sales cost. Finally, the system can automatically generate the drawing for tooling for the Machine Drive Press glass process. Figure 3 shows different aspects of the prototype system. Some key technical aspects in the development of this prototype were:

- Knowledge elicitation is the hardest work in the development of automated systems. Experts are always busy and are reluctant to share their knowledge.
- The core knowledge of the glass design is in the tool system, therefore the Product Model has to be built around this knowledge.
- Not all the DFM rules can be captured, but the benefit of building such a system is that new rules can easily be incorporated or old rules updated.

# 6 CONCLUSIONS

Global competition has forced Mexican Industry to look for new concepts in order to become competitive and being able to survive. In this paper first attempts to support Mexican companies in this survival endeavor have been presented. GI-INCIVI of CSIM-ITESM has defined a three phase research project in order to introduce Concurrent Engineering (CE) in Mexican Companies. The results of the first phase are the identification of key factors for a successful introduction of CE. This study allowed GI-INCIVI to define a methodology to help companies to implement CE by introducing new social-technical design concepts and cooperative design methods. It also helped in the identification of major topics for the development of CE training programs for company's engineers. Finally, prototype systems were developed to have standardized product definitions, improve the level of automation and apply proven design for manufacture rules in the design process. Two case study has been briefly described: Automotive Part Die Design and Design of Glasses for Machine Drive Press process.

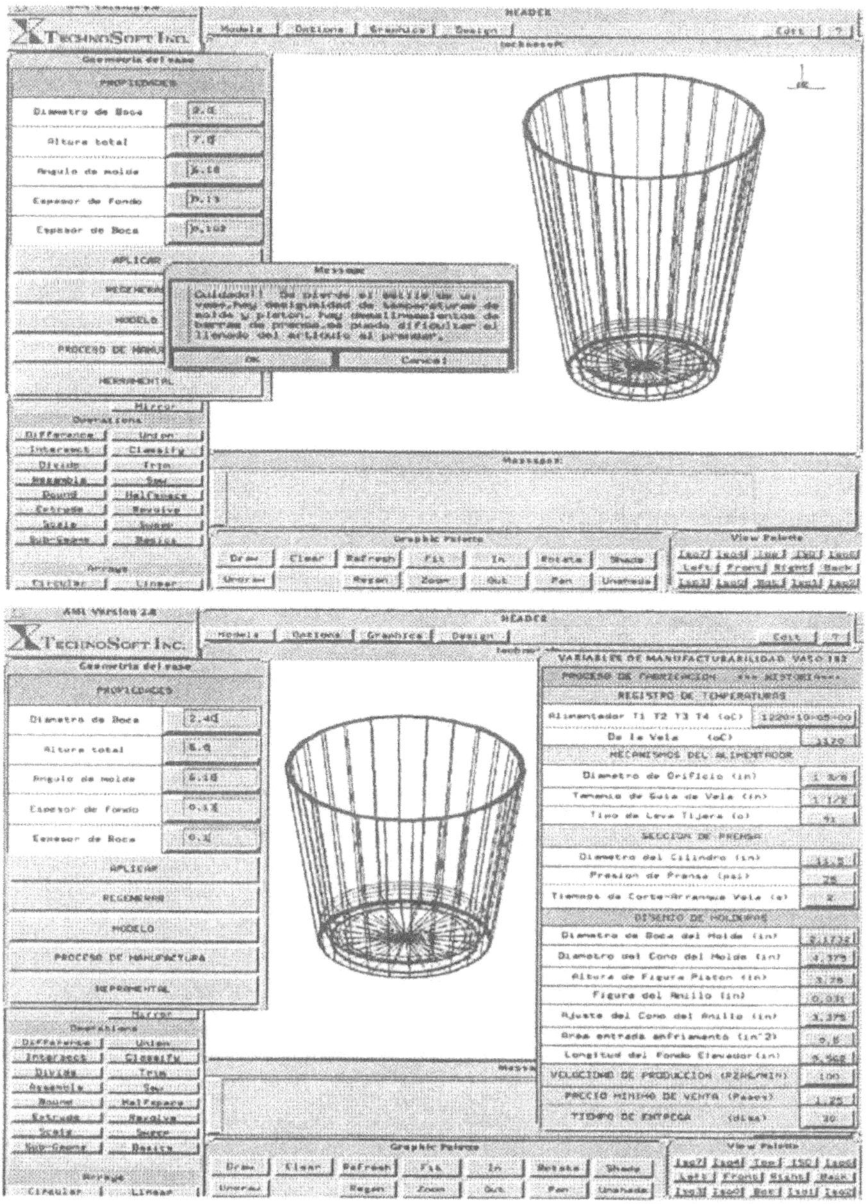

**Figure 3** Prototype System of the Integrated Development Environment of Glass Products: a) DFM applications to advise designer in defining manufacturable glass dimensions b) Automatic generation of production plans to advise on production variables, production time and sales cost.

## 7 ACKNOWLEDGEMENTS

The authors want to acknowledge the following members of the GI-INCIVI who helped to developed the prototype systems: Luis Alberto Rodriguez, Juan de Dios Rodriguez, Jose Luis Acosta, Julio Jaime Scheib and Mario de Diego.

## 8 REFERENCES

Bernus, P. and Nemes, L. (1994) A Framework to Define a Generic Enterprise Reference Architecture and Methodology. *Draft proposal, IFAC/IFIP Task Force on Architectures for Enterprise Integration*, Eight Workshop Meeting, Vienna, Austria, June 11-12.

Carter D. and Baker B. (1992) *Concurrent Engineering: The product Development Environment for the 1990s.* Addison-Wesley Publishing. USA.

Gomez E., and Molina A. (1996) Concurrent Engineering in Mexican Companies, *Revista Transferencia*, Año 9, Número 35, Julio de 1996, pp. 23-25, in Spanish.

Gomez E. (1996) Methodology for the Creation of Product Models, *Master Thesis*, Manufacturing Engineering, December 1996, ITESM., in Spanish.

Guerra D. (1996) Methodology for the elicitation and representation of Design for Manufacturing Rules in a Family of Machine Drive Press Glasses and it's Impact in the Development of New Product, *Master Thesis*, Manufacturing Engineering, December 1996, ITESM., in Spanish.

ICAM (1980) Architects' *Manual ICAM Definition Method* (IDEF0), DR-80-ATPCol.

ISO CD 10303 - 11, *Industrial automation systems and integration - Product data representation and exchange - Part 11: Description methods: The EXPRESS language reference manual.*

Molina, A. et al. (1995) A Review of Computer Aided Simultaneous Engineering Systems, *Research in Engineering Design*, 7:38-63.

Molina A., and Chemaly A. (1996) Information Models to Support Computer Aided Simultaneous Engineering, *Proceedings of the TMCE'96 Conference*, Budapest, Hungary, June 29-31, pp. 231-42.

Molina A. (1996) Report on Enterprise Integration Research at CSIM-ITESM, Presented at the *14th Workshop Meeting of the Task Force on Architectures for Enterprise Integration*, San Francisco California, July 2, 1996.

Prahalad C.K. and Hamel G. (1990) Harvard Business Review, May-June, pp. 79-91.

Williams, T.J. et al. (1993) Architectures for Integrating Manufacturing Activities and Enterprises, in H. Yoshikawa and J. Goossenaerts (eds.), Information Infrastructure Systems for Manufacturing, *Proceedings, JSPE/IFIP TC5/WG5.3 Workshop on the Design of Information Infrastructure Systems for Manufacturing*, DIISM'93, Tokyo, 8-10 November, 1993, North-Holland, pp. 3-16.

# 9 BIOGRAPHY

Dr. Arturo Molina is an Associate Professor in the Integrated Manufacturing System Center at Monterrey Institute of Technology (ITESM), Campus Monterrey, Mexico. He received his M.Sc. degree in Computer Science from ITESM, Campus Monterrey in December 1990, his University Doctor degree in Mechanical Engineering at the Technical University of Budapest in November 1992, and Phd in Manufacturing Engineering from Loughborough University of Technology in 1995 His current research interests include information systems support for concurrent engineering, information modeling, enterprise modeling and integration.

Enrique Gomez is associate consultant of A.T.Kearney. He received his M. Sc. degree in Manufacturing Engineering from ITESM Campus Monterrey in December 1997 and B. Sc in Industrial Engineering at ITSON, Sonora, Mexico.

David Guerra is an employee of VITROCRISA SA de CV, company from the VITRO Group in Monterrey, Mexico. He is working in the product development group of the Technology Department. He received his M.Sc. in Manufacturing Engineering in December 1996 and M.Sc. in Mechanical Engineering in May 1992 from ITESM Campus Monterrey.

46

# Parallel MRP system

*T.Tsukishima, M.Sato, M.Takata, H.Matoba*
*Production Information System Department*
*Production Engineering Research Laboratory,*
*Hitachi, Ltd.*
*292 Yoshida-cho, Totsuka-ku, Yokohama-shi 244 Japan*
*TEL : 81-45-860-1651, FAX : 81-45-860-1621*
*E-mail : tsuki@perl.hitachi.co.jp*

**Abstract**

Within an environment of rapid demand fluctuations, production planning changes are frequent and reductions in the plan proposal/revision cycle are sought. Also, an enlarged production planning scale is urgently sought to deal with integrated management of multiple, globally spread production points. To handle these demands, rapid processing of large scale data has become a major theme of Material Requirements Planning (MRP). In this paper a Parallel MRP System, using a loosely connected parallel computer, is described. A newly developed parallel algorithm, data transfer method and load balancing method are used and the system can reduce the 10 hours or more required by a conventional main frame computer for MRP calculations, on the 120,000 item level, to within 9 minutes using a structure with 6 WS servers. The processing speed of the 6 machine structure is 5.98 times the speed of 1 machine and the capabilities increase in a linear fashion. In this way simulated applications are possible for MRP in the workstation integrated management of multiple factories.

**Keywords**

Production Planning, MRP, Parallel Processing

## 1 INTRODUCTION

Within an environment of rapid demand fluctuations, production planning changes caused by design changes, part shortages and other problems are frequent

Computer Applications in Production and Engineering. F. Plonka and G. Olling (Eds.)

and reductions in the plan proposal/revision cycle are sought. Also, an enlarged production planning scale is urgently sought to deal with the integrated management of multiple, globally spread production points and other changes. To handle these demands, rapid processing of large scale data has become a major theme of Material Requirements Planning (MRP).

In relation to this, the research detailed here has carried out the development of a Parallel MRP System which allows the rapid processing of large-scale data, based on the premise of using a parallel processing computer.

## 2 TARGETS FOR INCREASING MRP PROCESSING SPEED

The targets for increasing MRP processing speed are given in Figure 1. The horizontal axis is processing time and the vertical axis is number of items, which gives an idea of the scale of the MRP, with the MRP processing speed being indicated by the line in the figure. Traditionally an MRP on the scale of 100,000 items would require at least ten hours on a mainframe, and be carried out once a week. With this being carried out several times a day, if an attempt was made to carry out the integrated management of multiple factories then more than 100 times the processing speed would be required. This research has set a goal of a speed increase with a wide range from 10- to over 100-times the traditional speed, by increasing the number of processing units of a parallel computer.

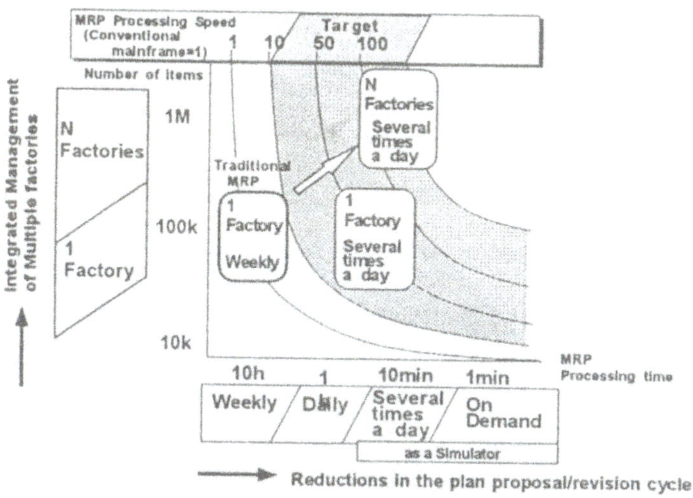


**Figure 1** Targets for increasing MRP processing speed.

## 3 BASIC STRUCTURE AND TECHNICAL PROBLEMS

In MRP, in order to repeat the calculation of the requirements for all items that make up the product, dividing the items that must be calculated amongst the processing units and carrying out the processing in parallel is the basic idea behind this system. The basic structure of this system is given in Figure 2. The hardware consists of multiple Work Stations (WS) connected to a high-speed network. From here on work stations connected to a network will be referred to as Processing Elements (PE). This system has for each PE one MRP calculation process that calculates the require amount of items, and overall a single control process which controls the entire progress. In order to increase the processing speed, the necessary data is moved to the MRP calculation processes internal memory before the calculation commences, and reside there.

The technical problems are the three points listed below. Details will be explained in the following sections.

(1) High-speed data access,

(2) Load balance, and

(3) Parallel algorithm.

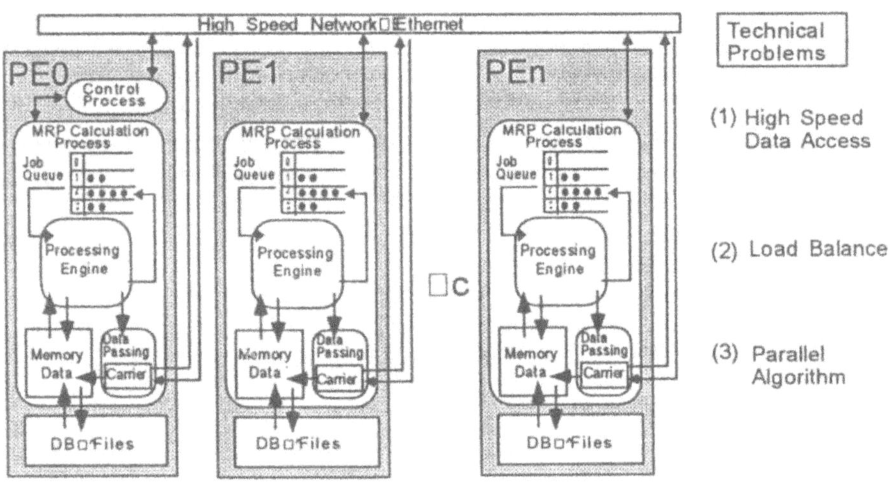


**Figure 2** The Basic structure and technical problems.

## 4 HIGH-SPEED DATA ACCESS

A loosely connected parallel computer has been selected this time. The data is spread amongst the PEs and stored in their memories. Generally, with a loosely connected computer the data transfer between PEs is more than ten times greater in comparison to accesses confined to within a PE and it becomes an overhead for parallel processing. In this system, a reduction in the overhead that accompanies the parallelization has been achieved by transferring the requirements data for multiple items as a group, as shown in Figure 3. It will be referred to as the Requirements Carrier. The effectiveness of this buffering transferal is detailed along with the evaluation of the load balance method in the next section.

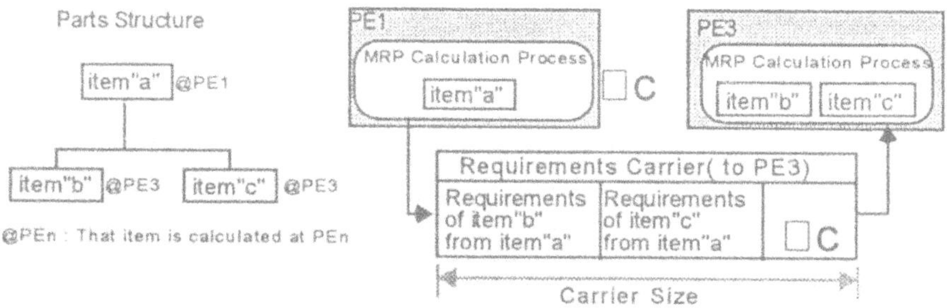


**Figure 3** Data Transfer by the Requirements Carrier.

# 5 LOAD BALANCE

## 5.1 Load balance method

In order to increase the effectiveness of parallel processing it is necessary to make the amount of processing of each PE uniform. Basically with MRP, the number of items to be calculated is made uniform, but in developing this system the following two points were taken into consideration.

(i) When parent items and child items are allotted to different PE, a transfer of requirements data occurs. It is possible that if not only the number of items are unified for each PE here, but also parent/child items are allotted to the same PE wherever possible, then there will be a decrease in the overhead from data transfers between PE.

(ii) In the course of the actual process there will be items that do not require to be calculated because of an inventory allocation and so on. Because of this, there is the possibility that even if each item is allocated uniformly beforehand the load balance will be lost and there will be a decrease in processing speed.

Next, detailed explanations of the two load balance methods developed by this system will be given.

*Parent/child based method*

The parent/child based method is a load balance method developed in order to investigate the possibility (i) given above. This method processes parent and child in the same PE wherever possible, as well as making the number of items uniform between PE, and is a static load balance method which decides beforehand which PE should process each item, before execution of the MRP.

*Dynamic load balance method*

This is a load balance method developed to solve the problem (ii ) given above. With a loosely connected parallel computer, dynamic load balance methods of the type which centrally manage the jobs in one PE result in a large overhead from data transmission. In relation to this, this system uses a method of leveling the load by moving items during the processing that have been assigned beforehand by static load balance. An outline of this function is shown in Fig. 4.

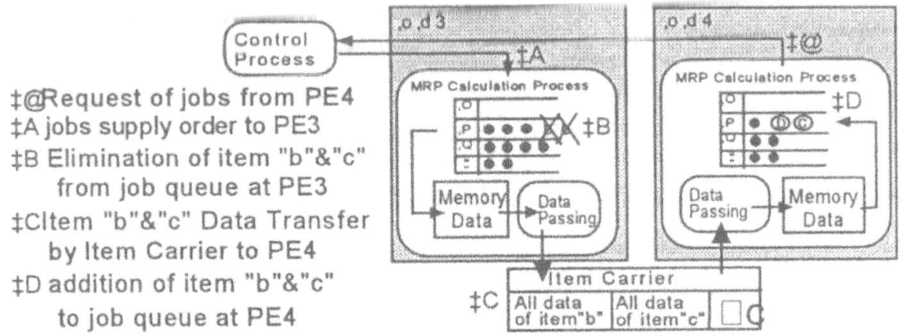


**Figure 4** Dynamic load balance method.

## 5.2 Evaluation of methods

*Parent/child based method*

An evaluation will be given of the reduction in MRP calculation time by assigning parent/child items to the same PE. This result comes from the ability to reduce the amount of data transferred. As the transmission overhead per item here varies depending upon the number of items loaded on the Requirements Carrier shown in Figure 2, this result is affected by the carrier size.

The simple balance method here does not take into account parent/child relationships and is a method that only makes the number of items uniform.

The results of the experiments in Table 1 are shown in Figure 5(a). For a carrier size of 10 the difference between both is only a few percent. Because a greater reduction in the inter-PE data transmission overhead was achieved than originally predicted, the difference between them was reduced. Taking into consideration the processing time of the load balance program itself, the simple load balance method which only makes the number of items uniform is of sufficient use.

*Dynamic load balance*

Under the conditions in Table 1, this method's performance was evaluated, with the load balanced unevenly so that for each level the assigned units of a specific PE was three times that of the others (Figure 5(b)). As will be explained later, with the hierarical parallel method, where the processing of each PE is done level-by-level at the same time, performance does degrade when there is a lack of uniformity in the load between levels. However, by adding the dynamic load balance function performance can be maintained of upto 90% of that at the time when the load is balanced uniformly.

Table 1 Experimental Condition

| *Hardware* | *MPS* | *Parts Num.* | *Parts Structure* | *Inventory Data* |
|---|---|---|---|---|
| WS(131 MIPS) x 6 | 2000 | 120,000 | 12 levels | Nothing |

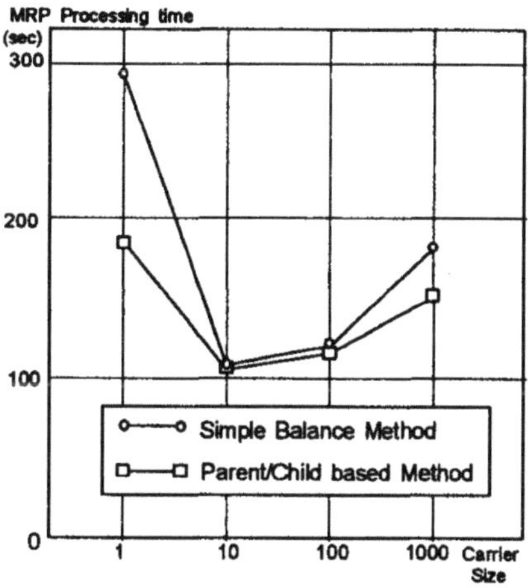


(a) Carrier size and processing time

**Figure 5** Performance of load balance method.

# 6 PARALLEL ALGORITHM

## 6.1 Two methods of Parallel Algorithm

In MRP there exists a restriction on the order of calculations such that the calculation for an item must be commenced after the calculation of requirements for that item's parent has been completed. In a parallel algorithm a synchronous mechanism is provided which fulfills the above restriction on the order of calculations. Furthermore there is a need to reduce two overheads mentioned below which is results from the parallelization.

(a) Processing time required by the synchronous mechanism itself

(b) The waiting time that occurs in the synchronization

In this system two methods have been developed for the parallel algorithm, the "hierarchical parallel method" and the "part parallel method", and their comparative evaluation was carried out. The details of these two methods are given below:

*Hierarchical parallel method*

The hierarchical parallel method simply applies the level-by-level calculation order, which uses the low level code of conventional non-parallel processing, as it is to the parallel algorithm. An outline of the process is shown in Figure 6. The calculation procedure repeats the calculation of items synchronizing them at each level.

Do until the final level
‡@When level n is finished, report and suspend. (a MRP Calculation Process)
‡A When all finish level n, order to resume. (Control Process)
‡B start level (n+1). (a MRP Calculation Process).

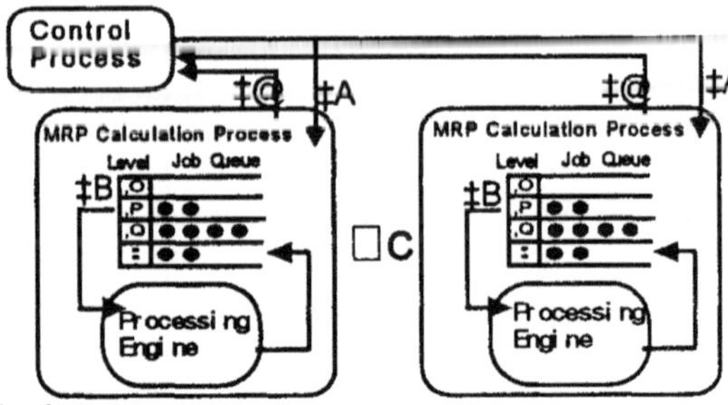


**Figure 6** Hierarchical parallel method

*Part parallel method*

The part parallel method is a new method which differs from the level-by-level calculation order which uses conventional low level code. An outline of the process is shown in Figure 7.

By controlling the progress of the calculation at the item level in this way, items that can be calculated are regularly stored in the job queue, reducing the chance of synchronization waits occurring. Also, this method does not use any low level code. Because of this, while conventionally when there was some design change several hours were required to process updates to the low level code, now there is no need to carry out this processing. In other words, there is a smooth integration of design and manufacture.

Do until all items are finished
‡@Write the child items' requirements data directly or via the network.
‡ACheck whether all parent items have written to each child item when writing.
‡BIf so,add the child item in the job queue at the PE.

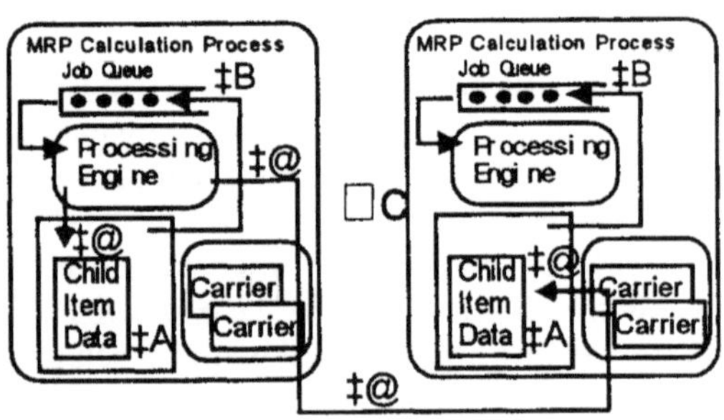


**Figure 7** Part parallel method

## 6.2 Evaluation of the parallel algorithm method

A comparative evaluation of the hierarchical parallel method and part parallel method was carried out from the following viewpoint:

(1) Synchronization mechanism

The amount of calculation for each MRP calculation unit was made uniform for each level in advance. Table 1 shows the experiment conditions, and Figure 8(a) shows the experiment results.

The performance of the part parallel method was equal to or greater than the hierarchical parallel method. From this, it can be seen that although the part parallel method's synchronization mechanism is complex, the processing time when the program is actually installed is the same as that of the hierarchical parallel method.

(2) Synchronization wait

The performance, under the conditions in Table 1, when the load is balanced so that for each level the number of items assigned to a particular PE is three times that of others is shown in Figure 8(b).

The part parallel method reduced the synchronization wait to the same level as the hierarchical parallel method using dynamic load balancing. Even if the amount of calculation for each PE is not uniform at each part level, if the load is balanced so that the total amount of calculation is uniform, as with these experiments, the part parallel method is thought to be superior from the simplicity of its mechanism.

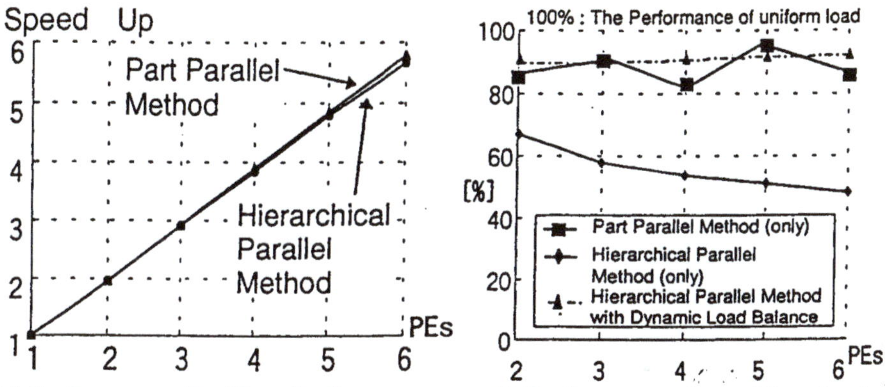


(a) Performance of uniform load at each level (Totally uniform)

(b) Performance of ununiform load at each level (Totally uniform)

**Figure 8** Evaluation of parallel algorithm

## 7 OVERALL PERFORMANCE EVALUATION

Based on the evaluation of each process method in the previous sections, an evaluation of the parallel MRP system's overall performance was carried out. The experiment conditions are shown in Table 1. The following was gained from the experiment results.

1) As shown in Figure 9, the system reduced the 10 hours or more required by a conventional main frame computer for MRP calculations, on the 120,000 item level, to within 9 minutes (67 times the processing speed including DB access) using a structure with 6 WS servers.

2) As shown in Figure 8(a) and 9, the processing speed of the 6 machine structure is 5.98 times the speed of 1 machine and the capabilities increase in a linear fashion. Also, a highly efficient parallelization of 95% or more was achieved for a wide variety of Bill of Materials (BOM) forms such as shown in Table 2.

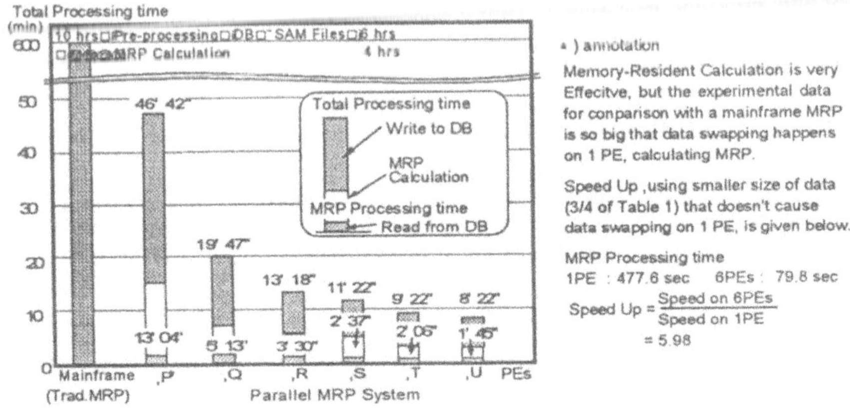


**Figure 9** Performance of parallel MRP system

Table 2 Parallel efficiency (6PE against 2PE) with a wide variety of BOM form

| *BOM Form* | *Rough Sketch* | *Parts Num.* | *Speed Up(6PE/2PE) (Ideal = 3)* | *Efficiency (SpeedUp/Ideal)* |
|---|---|---|---|---|
| |  | | | |
| | | | | |
| | | | | |
| | | | | |

## 8 CONCLUSION

A parallel MRP system has been developed for the high-speed processing of large-scale data. This system can reduce the 10 hours or more required for conventional MRP calculations, on the 120,000 item level, to within 9 minutes using a structure with 6 WS servers. Also, the capabilities increase in a linear fashion.

## REFERENCES

D.N.P.Murthy, L.Ma (1991) MRP with Uncertainty: A Review and Some Extensions. *International Journal of Production Economics*, **25** pp.51-64

D.Turbide (1995) MRP II. *IIE SOLUTION* **July** pp.28-31

W.Chamberlain, G.Thomas (1995) The Future of MRP II. *IIE SOLUTION* **July** pp.32-39

N.Carriero, D.Gelernter (1990) How to write Parallel Programs. The M.I.T. Press, Boston

## BIOGRAPHIES

**Takahiro Tsukishima** was born in 1965. He received a B.S. degree in 1988 and a M.S. degree in 1990 in Precision Engineering from Tokyo University. He is a researcher at the Production Research Engineering Laboratory, Hitachi, Ltd. His present interests include supply chain management and parallel processing. He is a member of JSPE and JIMA.

**Masahiro Sato** was born in 1969. He graduated from Hitachi Keihin College of Technology in 1994. He is a researcher at the Production Research Engineering Laboratory, Hitachi, Ltd. His present interests include supply chain management and parallel processing. He is a member of JIMA.

**Masahito Takata** was born in 1966. He graduated from Hitachi Keihin College of Technology in 1988. He is a researcher at the Production Research Engineering Laboratory, Hitachi, Ltd. His present interests include supply chain management and network computing.

**Hideaki Matoba** was born in 1954. He received a B.S. degree in 1977 and a M.S. degree in 1979 in Mechanical Engineering from Kobe University. He is a senior researcher at the Production Research Engineering Laboratory, Hitachi, Ltd. His present interests include supply chain management and agent systems. He is a member of JSME and JIMA.

# 47

# The practical limits for J.I.T.

*Prof. Dr. Javier Borda Elejabarrieta*
*C.E.O. of Datalde Sisteplant, S.A., Professor of Production and Engineering. Management Deusto University, Member of I.F.I.P. WG 5.7.*
*Parque Tecnológico Edificio 105 48170 ZAMUDIO Spain*
*Phone: (34) 4 452 06 11 Fax. (34) 4 452 12 66*
*E-mail: datalde@redestb.es*

**Abstract**

Zero Inventories (Z.I.) or near zero inventories, are we doing the right thing? Some years ago going along with inventory reduction beyond the more or less apparent economic optimal level has been justified in terms of getting the synergistic effects of flexibility, productivity and quality, and we all have seen the very famous diagram representing a company as a ship crashing into reefs when low tide (low inventories) comes.

That is really true, and till a certain limit, clear savings in expenses are obtained from this policy simply doing things right with no significative investment. Therefore, you normally are forced to reduce lead-times, with synergistics effects.

This is a path to be walked at a fastpace, at what point do we stop ? The paper establishes the practical limits for inventory reduction using the concept of the "economic transfer lot" that is affected, among other factors, by the practical economic level of the "minimum production lot", that is calculated in terms of the "manufacturing system decision triangle"

**Keywords**

J.I.T, Z.I., Manufacturing Strategy

Computer Applications in Production and Engineering. F. Plonka and G. Olling (Eds.)

# 1. INTRODUCTION

Car component makers are particularly forced to make continuous improvements in lead-times and costs reduction. Figure 1 represents a very attractive interaction in which cleverly focused lead-time reduction leads to dramatically reduced costs simultaneously improving quality and service. But is this an absolute linear non-ending model, suggesting Z.I. (Zero Inventories) as the panacea for best manufacturing practices. The answer is no. The multiplying links of the figure works out only from an initial manufacturing system given situation to another in which the maximum limit achievable manufacturing flexibility is a function of the involved machines technology.

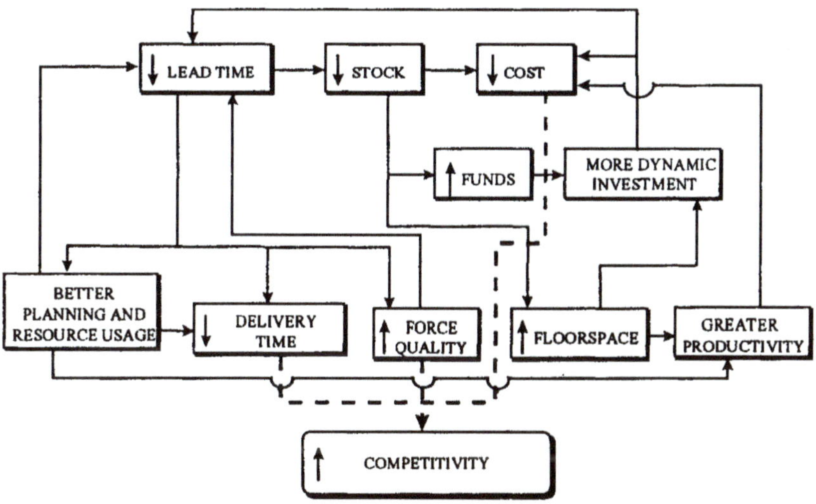


FIG. 1: LEAD TIME, ITS REDUCTION AND COMPETIVITY IMPROVEMENT
Note the "multiplying" characteristics of the links.

Going onreducing set-up times beyond this point is just a waste of precious time and money. Therefore, the minimum level of inventory you can have depends only on the Technology Strategy you are practicing. The confusion stands because the problem in real life is identification of the inventory sources. Taking that into account if you reduce the level of the inventory related to a lot-sizing practice of (roughly ½ EOQ), and you compare the figure with plant obtained samples, the surprise is that theoretical inventory is only one third (or less) than the sampled. Where is the difference? Very easy; on things that must be dramatically eradicated; machine breakdowns, inadequate and suppressive CPK's, scrap and rework, under controlled process adjustments of setting up with loss of expensive material, or inadequate or very slow operating planning and scheduling systems. Z.I. that must be pursued most is the inventory you have because all these things more or less randomly occur. This is the limit of linear behaviour of the model showed in Figure 1, and what we call P.Z.I. (practical zero inventories).

Proper identification and removal of these scraps requires the previous setting of logistics model and a coupled technology strategy for the involved machines and plant physical systems.

## 2. THE LOGISTIC MODEL AND THE MANUFACTURING DECISION TRIANGLE

Supposed defined if you are an assemble to order (ATO), manufacturing to order (MTO) or a manufacturing to stock (MTS), the identification of main and auxiliary lines is the key o issue. The Figure 2 represents the layout of lines.

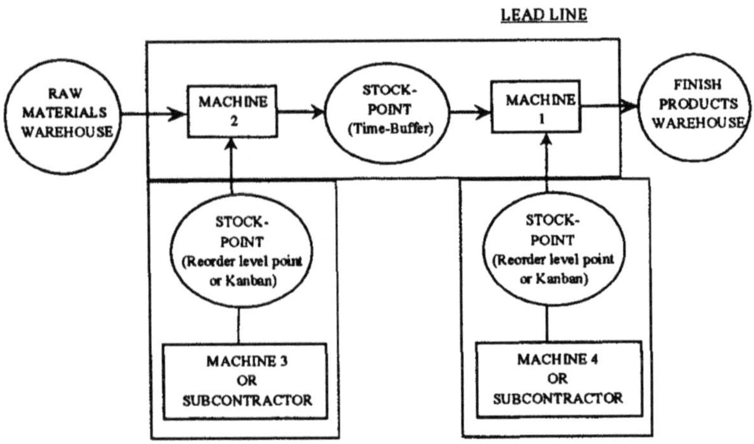


FIG. 2. LEAD AND AUXILIARY LINES. A SIMPLE MODEL

The main line is synchronized, as a time buffered inventory, contains the most value added product parts and process technology, and sets the manufacturing lead-times. The main lines contains the reserve capacity for differentiation of product inventory, quality, flexibility and service, and cost reduction for the future. The auxiliary lines (machines or subcontractors) are decoupled systems likely producing any of the rest of the areas represented in Figure 3, and performing JIT or reorder-level-point operating practices.

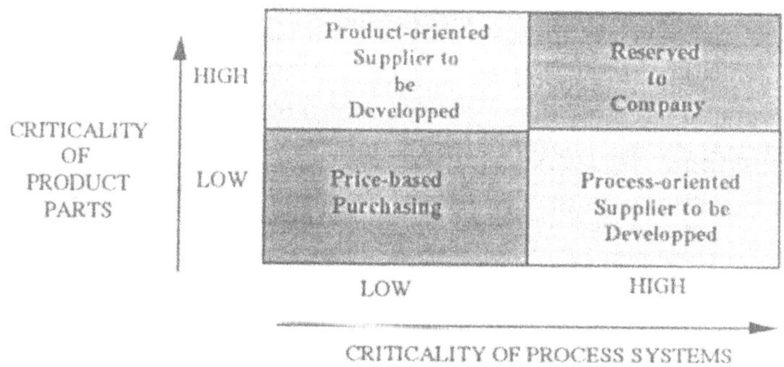


FIG. 3. THE ADDED-VALUE MATRIX

Main lines are the places to perform PZI, and doing this hierarchically through the logistic model is extremely useful, given that it channels product and process innovation and more intensive continuous improvement management efforts.
Which is the most convenient practical lot-size in the main-line? If you can manufacture as small as you rationally can move, you get the following:

- If the customer is fixed orders window is small (and in fact is decreasing continuously), there is a clear trend to order what is reasonable to move and deliver in manufacturing lots equal the main line remains syncronized along process stages.
- Operative integration of production and material handling personnel with decreasing labour costs through polivalence and self-balancing.
- Extremely simple and straight planning, scheduling and control systems, complemented by easy work in progress visual traceability.
- Everything in the plant must be moving (with exception of safety time-buffer-stock) and assigned to a customer order.
- Safety time-buffer stock size, convenience and lead-time added is clearly and continuously visually identified so decisions about definitive or occasional removal of safety are very easy to take.
- With the exception of some given scheduling conveniences (grouping for savings in set-up times), customer orders priorities or changes have reduced productivity.

So, it is clear that in the main line manufacturing technology must be coupled with the idea of doing manufacturing lot size equal to transfer lot size. The level of the transfer lot-size is selected with the criteria of minimizing handling costs, and depends on the product morphology, distances, and transport device design (selected for minimum handling costs).

With these conditions, we have to select the manufacturing technology for the main line. Minimum theoretical set-up times have to be reasonable for producing transfer lot sizes, and are calculated reversing the well known "Wilson" or "Coverage" formula (Coverage analysis is more appropriated for a family of products produced in expensive main lines). With deduced convenient set-up times, maximum admitted direct and labour costs, and product life cycle, we move to the Figure 4; the machine decision triangle.

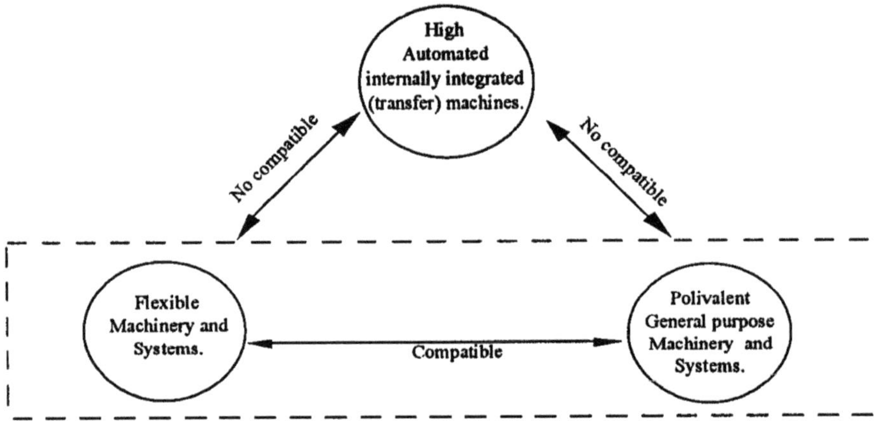


FIG. 4. MANUFACTURING SYSTEM DECISION TRIANGLE

Looking at the figure, and if needed flexibility is given by the transfer-lot, what we have to do is move as much as possible to automation but keeping the ability for rapidity in changeovers. This contradictory trade-off can be alter in own favour with good integrated product and process engineering practices. The Table 1 represents how to decide on the different alternatives, and Figure 5 situates them on an interline flow-chart.

# TABLE 1

[illegible]

**HOW TO BALANCE THE "MACHINE TRIANGLE" OR THE "DECISION'S CUBE" IN PRACTICE (for the key-machines of the lead syncronized line)**

F = Flexibility    H = Human
P = Polivalence    C = Economic comparison
I = Investment

| | (6) Cell including general purpose | | (7) Manipulate orientated cell including general purpose | | (8) Diminish set up oriented cell including general purpose machines | | (9) Set up oriented cell including general purpose machines | |
|---|---|---|---|---|---|---|---|---|
| | Value | Technical Comments | Value | Technical Comments | Value | Technical Comments | Value | Technical Comments |
| (F) • Set-up time | | | | | | | | |
| • Material cost in set up times | | | | | | | | |
| • Optimum manufacturing batches | | | | | | | | |
| • Set-ups/year | | | | | | | | |
| • Transfer batch | | | | | | | | |
| • Theoretical lead-times: Tp+tu.L | | | | | | | | |
| • Lead-time or terms (adjusted with (6)) | | | | | | | | |
| • Stocks's level (1) | | | | | | | | |
| • Set-up total cost (mat+MO) | | | | | | | | |
| (AI) • Typical optimum frequent limit (Tf) | | | | | | | | |
| • Material scrap/hour | | | | | | | | |
| • Variable operation cost/hour (without amortization) | | | | | | | | |
| • Variable maintenance cost and stocks/hour | | | | | | | | |
| • MOD cost/hour (4) | | | | | | | | |
| • MOI cost of supporting/hour | | | | | | | | |
| • MTBF | | | | | | | | |
| • MTTR | | | | | | | | |
| • Aviability % $\frac{MTBF}{MTBF+MTTR}$ (6) | | | | | | | | |
| • Operation total cost/hour | | | | | | | | |
| • Number of hours/year | | | | | | | | |
| (P) • Target process cycle life without changes | | | | | | | | |
| • (2) Investment in process in periods 1, 2, 3, 4 (Until target) | | | | | | | | |
| (H) • Differential cost/hour (4) | | | | | | | | |
| • Training cost (5) | | | | | | | | |
| • Improvement capacity (A,M,B). | | | | | | | | |
| • Investments according to current situation | | | | | | | | |
| (I) • Net investment (3)-(1) ≠ (2) + (5) | | | | | | | | |
| (C) • Comparison of alternatives: VAN/TIR in marginal target of costs | | | | | | | | |

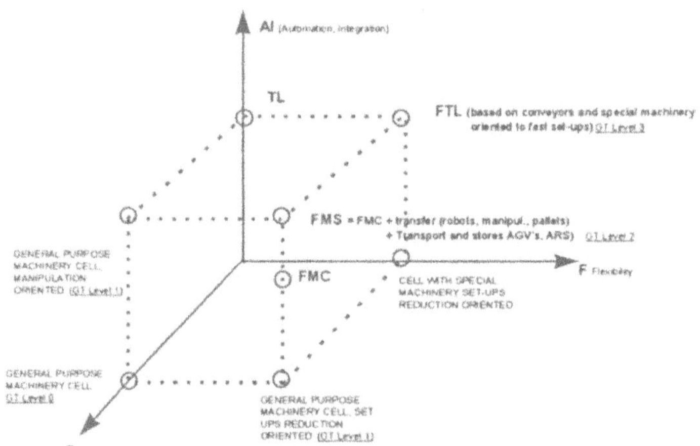


FIG. 5. THE DECISION CUBE

TL = transfer-line
FTL = flexible transfer - line
FMS = flexible manufacturing system
FMC = flexible manufacturing cell

## 3. DEDUCTION OF PZI AND RELATED M.I.S (management information system)

The size of PZI can be calculated in a roughly way (formula-based) or by simulation of optimal sequences in scheduling systems software that has the input of the MPS (master-plan) for the main-line (FIG. 6). The difference is that in the first, products are independently pipe-lined along the main line, and that with simulation grouping and changeover savings-and then some finish product inventory excess-arises. Depending on real cases, both are valid tactics, and their results are the ideal limits for plant management performance indicators.
The formula for deducting PZI for one part in terms of time is:

$$\underset{\text{(time)}}{PZI} = \underset{\text{(process stages)}}{\Sigma} \text{(Set up time+Transfer lot*Production-time+Transport-time+Minimum Safety lead-time)}$$

$$\underset{\text{(money)}}{PZI} = \underset{\text{(time)}}{PZI} * \frac{\text{unit cost * Annual Demand (units)}}{365}$$

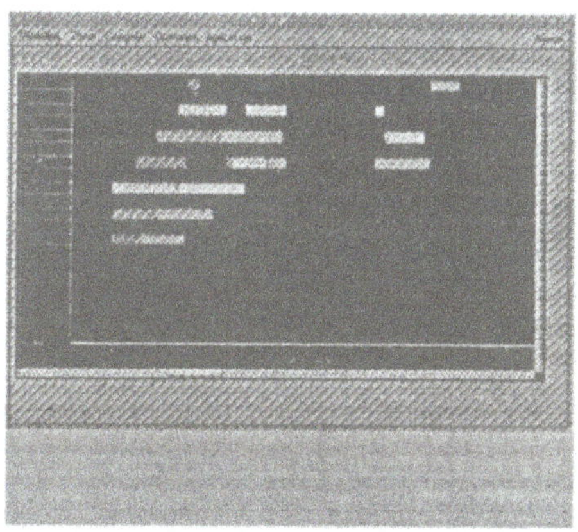

FIG. 6. GANTT CHART OF AN SCHEDULING SYSTEM SOFTWARE

Finally, a convenient M.I.S. for managing ZPI could be as follows:

- ● PZI excess (see FIG. 7) =
- +● Time EDI - Time dispatching.
- +●Time breakdowns and shortages - Time scheduled for buffering.
- +● Time scrap+rework - Time scheduled for buffering.
- +● Non-identified .

This non-identified piece of excess must also be continuously traced for deducting not so obvious problems.

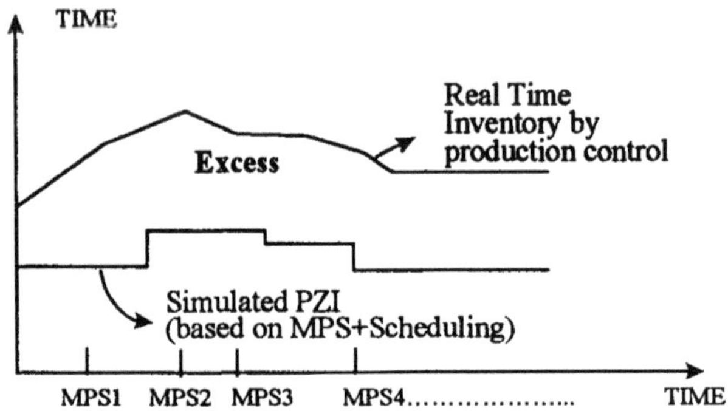


FIG. 7: INVENTORY EXCESS FROM PZI

## 4. CONCLUSIONS

The paper concludes saying that Z.I. is not, general speaking, a consistent strategy, but very interesting approach is arised if you fight Z.I. only for these all elements that are not part of the manufacturing system decision triangle strategy, and that push to you to have, sometimes, much more inventory than optimized correspondent set-up times EOQ would.

## 5. BIOGRAPHY

Prof. Dr. Javier Borda Elejabarrieta has been working as plant Engineer and Production Manager staff for 7 years, and from 1984 he is the managing director and C.E.O. of DATALDE, S.A., a spanish 35 people industrial engineering company, sited in the Basque Country. He read in 1989 the Doctoral Mechanical Engineering dissertation on "CIM for plastic injection workshops". He is also Professor of Production and Engineering Management in the University of Deusto, Bilbao, and the author of several international papers and a book titled: "Advanced Maintenance Techniques" (1990). He has become recently an IFIP WG 5.7 member.

## 6. REFERENCES


- (1987) (Dow Jones Irwin). "Zero Inventories", pp. 450 HALL .
- (1993) (R.E. Dauch) “Passion for Manufacturing” SME.
- (1988) (Th. J. Drozda) “Flexible Manufacturing Systems” SME.
- (1996) (Borda J.) "MRP-3 Concurrent integration of planning and scheduling in OKP". IFIP International Congress Kyoto-Japan.

- (1997) (Borda J.) "How to do in high competitive surpresive markets"- MATADOR CONGRESS- UMIST
- (1997) (Borda J.) "An extended coverage analysis for lot sizing group technology cells production environment"- ITAMS'91 CHINA (ELSEVIER)

# 48

# Network middleware for enterprise enhanced operation

*W. Loeve, M.E.S. Vogels, H. van der Ven, E.H. Baalbergen*
*National Aerospace Laboratory (NLR), The Netherlands*
*Anthony Fokkerweg 2, 1059 CM Amsterdam, NL*
*tel. 31 (0)20 5113421, fax 31 (0)20 5113210,*

**Abstract**

Enterprises are confronted with the challenge to lower cost of R&D and product engineering. More efficient transfer of know-how from R&D to engineering and between (generations of) engineers facilitates facing the challenge. Enterprise know-how has to be conserved in enterprises in the form of software such as for simulation, electronic documents and data. IT can enhance enterprise operation by giving engineers that work in or for the enterprise, easy access to the enterprise know-how. This requires a combination of distributed and centralized computing, a suitable network strategy and IT tools for management, control and use of the conserved enterprise know-how. In the paper the middleware SPINE for UNIX networks is described by which the network presents itself to the engineers as one single virtual computer. In the paper the considerations and the technical principles are illustrated by examples from two applications: a national virtual centre for Computational Fluid Dynamics for engineering and an IT framework for distributed multi-discipline design, analysis and optimisation of industry products. An estimation is given of the effort to be spent to realize and maintain such virtual single computers for a cooperating group.

**Keywords**

Enterprise network, middleware, IT, enterprise automation, engineering.

**List of abbreviations**

| | |
|---|---|
| AQAP | NATO Quality Assurance Requirements for Design/Development and Production |
| CFD | Computational Fluid Dynamics |
| DOC | Direct Operating Cost |
| ESTEC | European Space Research and Technology Centre |
| HFS | Nation Wide Virtual Centre for Flow Simulation in The Netherlands |
| HPCN | High Performance Computing and Networking |

Computer Applications in Production and Engineering. F. Plonka and G. Olling (Eds.)

| | |
|---|---|
| IBM SP2 | American Parallel Scalar Computer with Distributed Memory |
| ISNaS | Computer Based Working Environment for CFD |
| ismo | Computer Based Cooperative Working Environment for MDO |
| ISO | International Organization for Standardization |
| IT | Information Technology |
| MDO | Multi-disciplinary Design, Analysis and Optimization of Aerospace Vehicles, Project |
| MFLOP/s | Mega Floating Point Operations per second |
| NEC SX-4 | Japanese Parallel Vector Computer with Shared Memory |
| NICE | Project aiming at a Nation Wide Virtual Centre for CFD in The Netherlands |
| NLR | National Aerospace Laboratory in The Netherlands |
| PSUE | Parallel Simulation User Environment, Software Utility |
| R&D | Research and Development |
| SPINE | Software Utility for Presenting a Computer Network as one Single Virtual Computer to Users |
| sx4dev | A Collection of Tools for Development of Software for the SX-4 |
| TCP/IP | Computer Communication Standard |
| TNO-TPD | Technical Physical Institute in The Netherlands |
| UNIX | Computer Operating System, Trademark |

## 1 INTRODUCTION

Enterprises are confronted with the challenge to lower cost of product engineering. In this context engineering staff is minimized. Increasing the efficiency of enterprises by minimizing staff requires increased attention for management and control of engineering know-how. In view of this engineering know-how has to be conserved in enterprises in the form of software such as for simulation, electronic documents and data on electronic carriers. For engineering know-how in these forms it is possible to make use of Information Technology (IT) for management, development control, access and application.

R&D has to lead to production of products that are appreciated better by customers, that can be delivered at lower cost and for which engineering and production is possible in shorter time. For R&D results to become useful for an industrial enterprise, R&D results have to become enterprise know-how. This means that R&D results have to be transferred from R&D organisations to industrial enterprises as ready to use software, documents and data.

Enhancing enterprise operations in engineering is possible by enhancing accessibility and applicability of enterprise know-how. Minimizing staff to lower enterprise cost nowadays very often means that engineers are only hired to perform specific jobs. This means that it is required to enhance accessibility and applicability of enterprise know-how for engineering with partly temporary staff members. Using IT makes it possible to transfer more efficiently know-how between (generations of) engineers at various geographical locations.

It is a task of the enterprise itself to control the use of IT for enhancing operations. As a consequence IT is at least a required core competence of the enterprise. In chapter 2 a UNIX network and network middleware is described by which enterprise enhanced operation is possible. In chapter 3 and chapter 4 the use of the network and the middleware is illustrated to generate IT based working environments for application of computational fluid mechanics and for application of a combination of computational fluid mechanics and computational solid mechanics respectively. Chapter 5 contains information concerning effort to be spent by any participating company for establishing the working environment and for maintaining it.

# 2 A UNIX NETWORK FOR OPTIMAL ENGINEERING SUPPORT

## 2.1 Computer network required for engineering

When we look at the most powerful compute servers installed in the world (Dongarra, 1996) we see, at the top of the list, massively parallel computers with many scalar processors and distributed memory and vector computers with several processors and shared memory. The vector computers are easier to use than the distributed memory computers, especially with computational mechanics software that is frequently used in engineering (Vogels 1995).

The most advanced industrially applicable computational fluid mechanics (CFD) software for aerodynamic analysis in aircraft engineering at the moment is based on the Reynolds-Averaged Navier-Stokes equations (Rubbert, 1994). One not too detailed computation for a full aircraft configuration requires about 5 hours in case of a sustained computer performance of about 500MFLOP/s. One of the interesting applications of these computations for the near future is support of aerodynamic optimization (Borland, 1994). Optimization requires more computer performance than analysis, because for optimization for instance about 40 times solution of the flow equations in combination with an optimization algorithm is required. With a NEC SX-4/16 (a vector computer with 16 processors and shared memory) it is possible to realize for CFD a computational performance on 14 processors of 8,500MFLOP/s (Ven van der, 1997). With knowledge of only a few techniques on vectorization and coarse grained parallelization, this is realized with relatively little effort (only DO-loop parallelization). One aerodynamic optimization of 40 analysis runs then takes about 10 hours. Based on this reasoning NLR decided to procure a NEC SX-4/16 for R&D and for support of engineering in The Netherlands (Loeve 1996, Hameetman 1997).

The process of engineering an aircraft is characterised by a large number of activities executed by engineers from various disciplines mostly located at different geographical locations. The engineers use a variety of simulation software tools. Engineers need workstations for graphical interaction with their tools. Sharing of know-how between specialists has to be safeguarded which means that information servers and intranet servers are required in addition to compute servers and workstations. The network has to give access, for all involved persons and groups, to the computers as well as the software, data and electronic documents that are stored on the computers. Computers, workstations and information servers such as data management servers with tape robots have UNIX operating systems. Complexity of the computer networks and of the collections of software systems used in engineering processes both increase continuously in industry.

## 2.2 The need to present the network to engineers as a unity

Many problems occur in practice when engineers try to use a network:

- Remote access to computers is difficult to organize.
- Programs lack uniformity in user interface and data interface. Incidental use is practically impossible because of time required to familiarize.
- Problems with programs on different computers can be:
  - finding out on which computer a specific program may run,
  - remote login and remote execution, facing the user with aspects such as authentication and accounting,
  - operation of different operating systems or variants of the "same" operating system cause incompatible utilities,
  - exchange of files between computers,
  - incompatible data formats due to different byte ordering and representation of real numbers in different computers.
- Users have to organize, manage, and find a way through more on-line information than that is accessible on a single computer.

Removal of the technical and organizational shortcomings mentioned above will enhance the enterprise operation for simulation in engineering. Information about know-how (data, documents and software) shall be made available on-line. Information shall be managed and controlled in such a way that reconstruction of old information is possible and information can be exchanged between specialists in the same way as if they all make use of one computer. Accessibility and applicability of the software has to be such that the user does not have to be skilled in areas such as, computer programming, computer operating systems and computer network tools. Finally the user has to be assisted in organizing, re-using and integrating a continuously growing amount of software, data and supporting help information.

Only by making high performance computing a natural part of desktop workstation applications, the use of high performance computing in engineering will spread according to the need for competitive enterprise operation.

## 2.3 Network middleware for enterprise enhanced operation

Since computers were introduced at NLR in the late fifties this institute has applied a centralized IT approach. The main reasons were economy of scale and the need to be able to procure the computing power that is required for the most demanding applications (Loeve 1976). In addition productizing of software developed by NLR for CFD in industry is performed by IT professionals. In this development much attention was paid always to quality management. This resulted in an ISO 9001 and AQAP-110 certificate for development of simulation software. It also resulted in development of architecture and construction principles for development of CFD software according to industry needs (Vogels 1997).

Finally, quality management resulted in the development of a software utility called SPINE that supports the construction of general as well as application-oriented working environments (Baalbergen 1994). A SPINE-based working environment gives access to local and remote computing resources and information in a network. The network presents itself with SPINE as one single computer (a "metacomputer") to its users. In addition to hiding the networking details, SPINE provides mechanisms for easy customization of the metacomputer (to the needs of a particular user, group of users, or application area), for easy operation of the metacomputer by the user, and for management and control of information. SPINE is being further productized jointly by NEC and NLR. Currently, SPINE is based on, and targeted towards UNIX computer networks, in which the individual computers run vendor-supplied UNIX and standard TCP/IP-based networking software and tools.

The working environments constructed using SPINE are highly portable and easy to customize. Moreover, the working environments are open and extendible, in that any UNIX and TCP/IP based computing system can easily be integrated, and that existing software and other forms of electronically available information can easily be integrated. To support the operational use of a working environment, SPINE comprises technical solutions for the key elements of a metacomputer: an easy-to-use desk top, facilities for the management of information, and middleware.

The desk top provides the user of a working environment with a graphical integrated user shell. The shell provides a uniform and consistent view with respect to presentation and manipulation of data files, documents, and source code, and with respect to execution of tools. The data management and processing operations are available in terms of point-and-click and drag-and-drop operations on windows and icons. The shell provides control over multiple windows in combination with multi-tasking. This makes it possible to have several tools running simultaneously. The shell also provides the user with contextual on-line help, both on the operational aspects of the working environment as well as on the applications.

In addition to the Windows look-and-feel of SPINE, the shell supports data-oriented, tool-oriented, as well as work-flow driven modes of working. The work-flow capability of the shell supports work-flow management, in which data and tools can be configured in a network that supports, or even may enforce, certain scenarios or activities. Work flows are considered to resemble an engineer's way of working, and to provide an intuitive means of specifying jobs and controlling the execution of the jobs. Work-flow management also enables transparent and automated information management, e.g., to enforce synchronization and reconstruction of activities and results.

SPINE supports the Computer Supported Cooperative Working aspects of information management by providing tools for managing storage, access to, and modifications of data, documents, software and any information related to this, and for the exchange of information among users. The task of SPINE's middleware is to manage the available resources in order to accomplish the single computer look-and-feel, and to exploit the potentials of the underlying computer network. The middleware also takes care of the application of data conversions required to deal with hardware and data-format heterogeneity.

SPINE, by being based on standard UNIX and TCP/IP software, has proved to be applicable for realization of environments that span both local-area and wide-area networks. For example, the NICE environment (see chapter 3) spans the local area networks of the NICE partners, but also gives access from remote workstations to NLR's SX-4 vector computer and CFD software as well as the compute power and software in other partners in the NICE project, over the Internet. In this way, a Netherlands-wide CFD working environment has been realized.

At the moment, several systems exist that support realization of, mostly only part of the aspects of, metacomputing. For example, the Parallel Simulation User Environment (PSUE), aims to provide a software platform that can be customized for particular simulations. However, PSUE provides a particular desk-top model, which leaves hardly any freedom with respect to customization, and which enforces a tool-oriented mode of working, whereas the SPINE desk-top model supports data-oriented, tool-oriented, as well as work-flow driven modes. Another example is SiFrame, an open working environment that aims at supporting design-process management in a multi-user environment. SiFrame, however, concentrates mainly on the work-flow driven way of system interaction.

Most developments in metacomputing are primarily driven by research in computer science, which has resulted in a gap between scientifically well-founded metacomputing solutions and industrial needs. This gap often leads to products that do not meet the demands from engineers. SPINE, although including results of scientific research, has its roots in a practical engineering environment, viz. ISNaS (Section 3.1) at NLR, has proved to be the solution that meets the demands in modern engineering. Examples of SPINE applications are given in the next chapters.

# 3 THE USE OF THE UNIX NETWORK AND MIDDLEWARE FOR COMPUTATIONAL FLUID MECHANICS

## 3.1 CFD working environment in one organisation

Since the earliest developments of SPINE it has been applied to ISNaS, a working environment for flow simulations (Vogels 1989). At first, the working environment was aimed to support the use of flow simulation packages across the NLR network that connects the two NLR establishments. The distance between the establishments is 100 km. The network consists of workstations and terminals that give access to mainframes acting as compute-, intranet-, internet- and data management servers. The centralized automation policy at NLR made it economically possible also to integrate a supercomputer in the network since 1987. Because of its success, more functionality was and is added continuously to the network and to the network middleware of SPINE.

ISNaS now supports both use and development of simulation software. The use of the simulation software is supported by integrating the entire pipeline of simulation analysis: geometry modellers, grid generators, flow solvers, and postprocessors. File transfer and remote logins are hidden from the user. Exchange of different file formats between the various tools is made transparent to the user using the SPINE facility for implicit file conversion. Exchange of documents and data is made possible through easy-interface databases. Feedback to the developers of both the working environment and the simulation software is made easy by the use of electronic forms.

The development of simulation software is supported by providing via SPINE a software version management tool, and a toolpack sx4dev which integrates several development tools on the NEC SX-4 (more about the toolpack in Section 3.2). A framework for the creation of a regression test suite is available within the working environments. For support of development control, electronic forms are used to manage error reports.

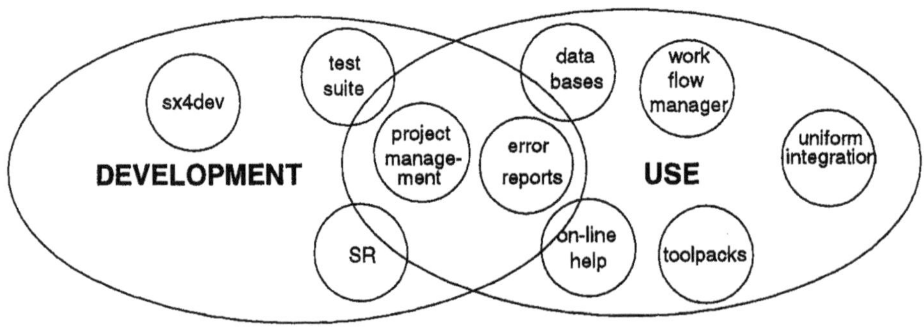


**Figure 1** Building blocks for both use and development of engineering software.

For both users and developers project management systems can be set up. Such a project management system consists of an electronic project archive, a search engine on this archive, a drag-and-drop mechanism to submit documents to the archive, and a database for electronic forms. We will see an example of such a project management system in Section 3.2.

The building blocks of the working environment supporting both use and development of CFD software are shown schematically in Figure 1. As is clear from the figure development and use interact and overlap.
The development of a working environment is dominated by two principles:
- an integrated tool has added value to the user,
- the working environment shall adapt to the user and not vice versa.

This also implies that integrated tools do not stand alone in the working environment: they are surrounded by tools that either supply input or use the output of the specific tool. This integration of tools greatly facilitates their use.

The success of the present working environment is probably best exemplified by the following. A CFD trainee was asked to perform an analysis of air heater flow. The trainee had a thorough knowledge of flow physics, and numerical mathematics. But he was less familiar with supercomputers, networks, UNIX and postprocessing. Using the working environment he was able to perform and analyze a specific flow configuration within one week. The analysis consisted of the entire pipeline from preprocessing up to visualization.

## 3.2 National CFD working environment

To enhance the use of HPCN techniques the Dutch government partly finances the project NICE, Netherlands Initiative for CFD in Engineering. NICE aims to promote the use of CFD methods, developed at universities and large technological institutes, to industry and small and medium enterprises. On the one hand, new (parallel) algorithms are developed motivated by the needs and wishes from the industry, on the other hand, these algorithms are used to analyze flow problems from the same industry. Development and use are combined in a single initiative.

In order to facilitate the use of remote resources NICE develops a nationwide virtual centre for flow simulation HFS based on SPINE. HFS consists of two parts: a common part to all NICE partners, and a part specifically tuned to the needs and wishes of a NICE partner. The network on which HFS operates consists of the local network of the partner and the NEC SX-4 at NLR. HFS is a specialized 'ISNaS' at each partner, extended with a common set of tools for both project management and development on and use of the NEC SX-4.

Management of the project NICE is facilitated through HFS. A project management system is part of the common tools in HFS. The system consists of an electronic project archive, electronic error reports, and search engines to search both the project archive and the error report database. The project archive has a technical report repository. Development on and use of the NEC SX-4 is supported by the toolpack sx4dev that integrates tools for compiling, executing, analysing and debugging source. Automatic makefile generation allows for manipulation of the source code. Options of the tools are based on the experience of experts in supercomputing. Using this tool the computational kernel of a flow solver of TNO-TPD was compiled, executed and analyzed within a quarter of an hour. Before that, TNO-TPD had never worked on an NEC supercomputer.

By supporting both development and use of CFD software HFS is suited for a wide range of customers. From novice users inexperienced with CFD, through experienced users with a need of more powerful resources, up to developers of new algorithms and software.

An example of a customer needing more powerful resources is ESTEC. For a time-accurate simulation using a multi grid, multi block structured solver they required more memory than their IBM SP2 could supply. Moreover, throughput times became prohibitive. Even though the code was originally written for scalar machines, a porting effort of roughly three manweeks increased the megaflop rate from 80 MFLOP/s on the IBM SP2 to 500 MFLOP/s on the NEC SX-4.

# 4 THE USE OF THE UNIX NETWORK AND MIDDLEWARE FOR MULTI-DISCIPLINE ANALYSIS AND OPTIMIZATION

## 4.1 Problem analysis

To effectively resolve cross-discipline trade-offs both to improve aircraft performance and reduce development timescales and costs, concurrent engineering principles are under investigation for the preliminary design stage.

In Europe, the MDO Consortium [1] is addressing integration of design and analysis tools creating a Multi-Disciplinary Optimisation (MDO) capability (MDO Consortium,1996). The purpose is to develop and demonstrate the viability of MDO and validate this for simplified but realistic aircraft preliminary design tasks concerning the design of a large civil aircraft where a non-trivial interaction is expected between the mono-disciplines of aerodynamics and structures. NLR, one of the Consortium members, carries out the work in a multi-disciplinary team with specialists from aerodynamics, flight mechanics, structures, and information technology.

---

[1] The MDO project (Multi-Disciplinary Design, Analysis and Optimization of Aerospace Vehicles) is a collaboration between British Aerospace, Aerospatiale, DASA, Dassault, SAAB, CASA, Alenia, Aermacchi, HAI, NLR, DERA, ONERA, and the Universities of Delft and Cranfield. The project is managed by the British Aerospace and is funded by the CEC under the BRITE-EURAM initiative (Project Ref: BE95-2056).

In the MDO problem, different aircraft designs are compared by comparing the Direct Operating Cost (DOC) for the aircraft design. For the problem at hand, the DOC is simplified in a model containing drag and total weight. The problem of DOC evaluation for an aircraft design can be solved in more than one process, each leading to a different approximation of the DOC. Therefore a DOC value for an aircraft design can only be interpreted in the context of the process in which it was achieved.

## *Process model*

The process is modelled in so-called $N^2$ diagrams where the *(N)* contributing disciplines form the diagonal of an $N*N$ matrix, the off-diagonal entries show the dependencies between the disciplines. An above-diagonal entry denotes a feedforward coupling, a below-diagonal entry denotes a feed backward coupling.

The top-level $N_2$ diagram for the NLR process for the early problem is given in figure 2. The figure shows the involvement of the disciplines. On lower levels, similar $N_2$ diagrams show the detailed processes. The level of detail of the $N^2$ diagrams is dictated by its usefulness for the MDO-process and usually stops at the level of a mono-discipline.

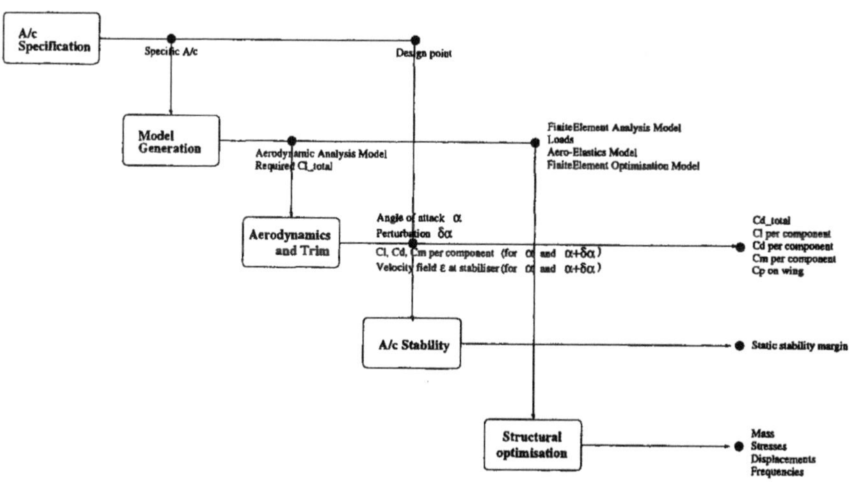


**Figure 2** Multi-discipline analysis process

## *Changes in the mono-discipline software for the multidiscipline context*

On the MDO level, it is assumed that all disciplines have their own (mono-disciplinary) application software. The application software runs on the NLR heterogeneous UNIX network, involving e.g. SGI work stations, CD4810 scalar compute server, and the NEC SX-4 parallel vector machine. Data, documents and software are stored via a data management server on a tape robot. Most software is home-brew, implemented in Fortran and C. The software frequently changes to satisfy additional requirements.

Three types of changes are required for the mono-discipline software to function in the multi-discipline context. First, the mono-discipline software has to accommodate for the communication with the other disciplines, on the level of detail and in the terminology specified in the $N^2$ diagrams. Whenever possible, this accommodation consists of interface programs which translate between the MDO-parameters/results and the mono-discipline's parameters/results.

In this way, the mono-discipline application software can remain unchanged, and can be used for solving mono- and multi-discipline problems.

Second, whereas in mono-disciplinary work it may be acceptable that the work halts when a specialist is unavailable, in multi-disciplinary work carried out in a team, it is not acceptable. The work may be taken over by a colleague less familiar with the MDO problem, or by a multi-discipline team member of a different discipline. A prerequisite for enabling someone else to perform the absent specialist's work, is accessibility to the mono-discipline software. This is organised in the MDO environment "ismo" (Section 4.2).

And, finally, again because of the team character of the multi-disciplinary work, it is required that the application software, used for the MDO work, is identified and reproducible.

## 4.2 Set-up of MDO environment

One of the purposes of the MDO environment is, as explained above to provide access to all mono- and multi-discipline application software of the MDO team. This includes the shielding of the computer network, and providing the virtual computer feel. For this purpose, the mono- and multi-discipline application software is integrated into an MDO environment based on SPINE.

Application software which is unchanged by the multi-discipline context, and which is already under version management, is considered to be identified and reproducible. Newly developed application software (such as the interface programs with the MDO-level), and changes in existing application software are version managed in the MDO environment.

The challenge for information technology is not only to capture the process as in $N^2$ diagrams, but also to supply an MDO environment which supports the work according to the MDO process view of the disciplines involved. The application software in the MDO environment is structured (in levels and groups) according to the $N^2$ diagrams. In this way, the MDO environment reflects the MDO team's view on the MDO process. In Figure 3, the highest level of MDO programs is given, showing the elements (in alphabetical order): 1 ac-performance; 2 ac-specification; 3 ac-stability; 4 aerodynamics-and-trim; 5 model-generation; 6 multi-inspection; 7 structural-optimisation.

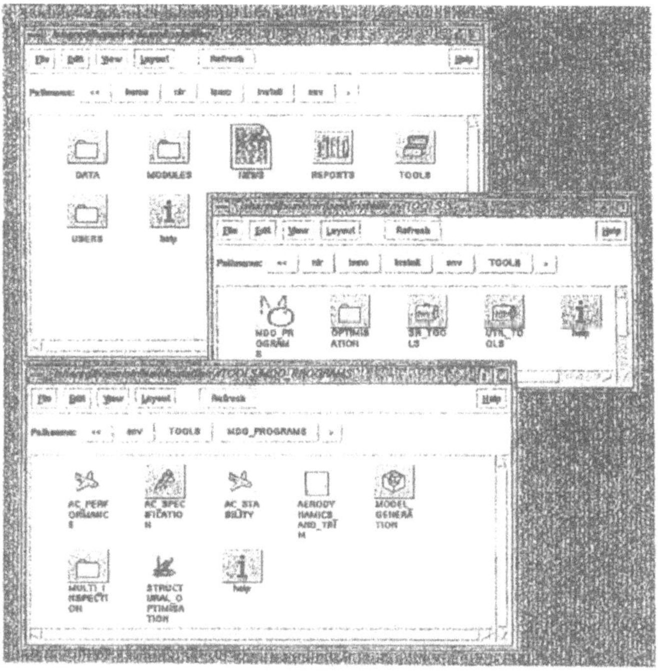

**Figure 3** Screen-dump of"ismo" showing the top-level of MDO programs.

The diagonal elements in the MDO process (Figure 2) correspond to the "ismo" elements 2, 5, 4, 3, 7 respectively. The "ismo" elements 1 and 6 are additional compared to the diagonal elements in the MDO process; they are included in the environment "ismo" because:

- "ac-performance" has been identified as a contributing discipline, but has been left empty for the problem at hand,
- "multi-inspection" is a passive process, not producing any information to the DOC formula.

## 5 EFFORT TO EFFECTUATE AN IT SUPPORTED COOPERATIVE WORKING ENVIRONMENT

The common working environments for cooperating groups of engineers as described above are based on the principle that members of a cooperating group are willing and able to share information that is made available by members of the group via procurement or development. This concerns information in the form of software, data or document. Sharing information means that development control of information is applied by each originator. This concerns such aspects as version control as well as planning of activities and communication about planning issues. Also standards for the structure of information that support access of information, and maintenance procedures have been agreed upon by the group and are being applied. The information has been described preferably in such a way that the descriptions can be provided as help information for non-regular users or even be provided in the form of tools that facilitate or support execution of the procedures. Rules have been developed with regard to authority to modify, release, consult and apply information. Control mechanisms for access to the computers have been implemented to support application of the rules.

The effort to be spent to realize that specialists are willing to cooperate, to share information and to make this also possible strongly depends on the degree of application of process and product control in the concerning enterprise(s). It may require a costly change of mentality such as when for instance process and product control according to the ISO 9000 industry standard has to be introduced in an individualistic R&D environment. One of the reasons to spend the effort in such cases may be the need of transformation of the situation with operation mainly based on input financing to the situation with operation mainly based on output financing in a competitive environment. The effort may take several calendar years and may cost several manyears even for a department with less than 20 people. Realization of an IT supported cooperative working environment requires that all concerning individuals have a desktop computer that is connected to a common network. This may require an additional effort for enterprises with many isolated desktop computers.

Installation of the SPINE software and a working environment containing a small number of tools takes only one day effort by experts. Maintenance and extension of functionality of the working environment take roughly four manweeks a year, and depend on the number of users and the number of tools. These figures are based on several years' experience at NLR and at organisations that NLR cooperates with on the basis of SPINE working environments. For new working environment managers a day's course introduces them to the concepts and structures of SPINE. In our experience UNIX experts quickly grasp the potential of SPINE. SPINE is currently extended with functionality for support of working environment modifications. This will significantly reduce the effort required for maintenance and modification. It appears that using a SPINE based working environment even for a limited number of activities in an enterprise may facilitate further introduction of product and process control according to the ISO 9001 standard in the enterprise.

## 6 CONCLUDING REMARKS

Hiring engineering staff when needed requires that enterprise know-how is conserved in software for simulation, electronic documents and data.

For engineering in industry it is essential that cooperating engineers can use the computer network of the enterprise as the central nerve system for exchanging, accessing and using enterprise know-how.

Network middleware such as in SPINE can be used to realize that for cooperating engineers a complicated (national) high performance computer network can be accessed and used as one single virtual computer.

## 7 REFERENCES

Baalbergen, E.H. and Loeve, W. (1994) SPINE: software platform for computer supported cooperative work in heterogeneous computer and software environments, NLR TP 94359, National Aerospace Laboratory Amsterdam.

Borland, C.J., Benton, J.R., Frank, P.D., Kao, T.J., Mastro, R.A. and Barthelemy, J.F.M. (1994) Multidisciplinary design optimization of a Commercial Aircraft Wing - An Exploratory Study. 5th Symposium on Multidisciplinary Analysis and Optimization, Panama City Beach, Sept. 7-9, 1994. AIAA-94-4305-CP, pp 505-519.

Dongarra, J.J., Meuer, H.W. and Strohmaier, E (1996) TOP500 Supercomputer Sites November 1996; retrievable from internet by anonymous ftp to www.netlib.org/benchmark/top500.ps.

Hameetman, G.J., Loeve, W., Poppinga, G., Potma, K. (1997) Early bench mark results on the NEC SX-4 supercomputer; in *Parallel Computational Fluid Dynamics (Algorithms and results using advanced computers)* (ed P. Schiano et al), Elsevier ISBN 0 444 82327 1.

Loeve, W. (1976) A hierarchical network linking two research laboratories; Computer Networks 1 North-Holland Publishing Company.

Loeve, W. (1996) From parallel CFD to a tool for computer aided engineering; in *Parallel Computational Fluid Dynamics* (ed A. Ecer et al) Elsevier ISBN 0 444 82322 0.

MDO Consortium (1996), http://www.telecall.co.uk/~srcbae/mdo.

Rubbert, P.E. (1994) CFD and the Changing World of Airplane Design; AIAA Wright Brothers Lecture, Anaheim California; September 18-23.

Ven, van der H. and Vegt van der J.J.W. (1997) Experience with advanced CFD algorithms on NEC SX-4; in *VECPAR '96 selected papers from the 2nd International Meeting on Vector and Parallel Processing (Systems and Applications)* (ed Laginha M. Palma et al), Lecture Notes in Computer Science 1215, Springer 1997.

Vogels, M.E.S. and Loeve, W. (1989) Development of ISNaS: An Information System for Flow Simulation in Design, in *Computer Applications in Production and Engineering* (ed F. Kimural) North-Holland ISBN 0 444 88089 5.

Vogels, M.E.S., Ven van der H., Hameetman, G.J. (1995) The need for super computers in aerospace research and industry, in *Proceedings HPCN Europe 1995 Milano*.

Vogels, M.E.S. (1997) Architecture and construction principles for computational fluid dynamics software for engineering in industry; Thesis, ISBN 90-9010295-7; M.E.S Vogels, National Aerospace Laboratory Amsterdam.

### *BIOGRAPHY*

W. Loeve's university degree is in aeronautical engineering. He is head of NLRs IT Division, IT consultant and responsible for quality management in the development by NLR of aerospace information systems for customers.

Dr M.E.S. Vogels's PhD thesis concerns architecture and construction principles of CFD software for engineering in industry. She is IT consultant and projectleader at NLR, responsible for the development of the IT framework in the MDO project.
Dr H. van der Ven's PhD thesis concerns harmonic analysis on Lie groups. He is HPCN consultant and projectleader at NLR, responsible for the ISNaS and NICE working environments.
Dr E.H Baalbergen's PhD thesis concerns distributed operating systems. He is projectleader at NLR for the SPINE development in interaction with applications such as mentioned above.

49

# Improving construction information communications: A development framework

*A.Grilo*
*PhD Candidate, University of Salford*
*Bridgewater Building, Salford, M5 4WT, UK, e-mail:*
*a.grilo@mail.telepac.pt*

*L.T. Almeida*
*Professor of Instituto Superior Técnico*
*Av. Rovisco Pais, 1000 Lisboa, Portugal*

**Abstract**

Electronic data exchange will be one of the key element for raising the low productivity levels of construction projects. This paper advocates the use Information and Communication Technologies (ICT) for improving construction communications, and describes the business and technical objectives of a framework which aims to create, implement, test and evaluate an EDI-based communication infrastructure between the various parties involved in the manufacturing process of construction. The infrastructure explores the potential of both STEP and EDIFACT, and is to automate the ordering, delivery, invoicing and payment process of construction systems, equipment and services in a supply chain whose members are on very different levels regarding ICT.

**Keywords**

Construction, virtual enterprises, EDI, EDIFACT, STEP, interorganisational information systems.

Computer Applications in Production and Engineering. F. Plonka and G. Olling (Eds.)

# 1. INTRODUCTION

The construction process is characterised by temporary networks of "co-operating" organisations also designated as virtual enterprises. The coordination and control within these virtual enterprises is far from efficient. Thus, construction industry productivity is lagging behind manufacturing and service industries. One of the developments that may improve productivity is the deployment of computerised interorganisational information systems between the various parties. Indeed, the establishment of effective communication and logistics processes involving designers, contractors, subcontractors and material suppliers, is perceived by many construction researchers and practitioners as an area which deserves further research and development.

ICT systems have long been used by firms on manufacturing and service industries, specially on banking, automotive and retailing industries. Research studies have shown that there is scarce use of ICT systems by firms involved on construction projects. Electronic Data Interchange, using EDIFACT standards for commercial information and product data exchange using STEP are two available technologies that are useful for building a ICT infrastructure for construction virtual enterprises.

This paper starts by describing the potentialities for the development of an ICT infrastructure for construction virtual enterprises and the technologies available for building the infrastructure. It follows by describing the business and technical objectives, as well as the predicted industrial impact of a development framework which aims to create, implement, test and evaluate an EDI-based communication infrastructure between the various parties involved in the construction process.

# 2. THE IMPORTANCE OF INFORMATION COMMUNICATIONS IN CONSTRUCTION

There is a well established consensus about the low productivity on the construction industry, specially when compared with other industries and even that the gap is increasing (Atkin and Pothecary, 1994; Latham, 1994). The construction industry is a mature industry and in the last few years, due economical recession and globalisation, there has been an increase of the competition within the industry. Moreover, products are becoming more complex and clients more demanding requiring cheaper, with lower lead times, and with higher quality products (Atkin and Pothecary, 1994)

The construction process is characterised by temporary networks of "co-operating " organisations (Cherns and Bryant, 1983). Indeed, for each project a virtual enterprise is assembled in which architects, engineers, specialist designers, contractors, subcontractors, suppliers, etc. organisations are brought together in order to build the product. In a traditional and simplistic way, construction projects are split into the design and construction phases. The architect is the project leader, developing a design and design management responsibility and devolving a role for specialist design and management functions to engineers, surveyors and the like. On the construction phase a main contractor is responsible for the completion of the entire project and procures the services of specialist firms. These specialist firms are subcontractors who carry out work on-site, and suppliers who manufacture products off-site and deliver them as needed.

In order to improve productivity, current developments in the sector are increasingly focusing on more effective management of the construction virtual enterprise, through developments such as design and build, multi-disciplinary design and project management, and inter-organisational information systems. Good project management must nowadays pay as much attention to the production as to the overall information flow. Increases of 15% to 20% in the performance of projects (cost, quality, speed, customers satisfaction) may be accomplished if the information flows within the virtual enterprise are carefully addressed and improved (Latham, 1994). However, the short-term duration of construction projects, the non-repetitive nature of the industry, and the geographical distance between headquarters of the companies and the construction sites which have a limited existence in time and space, makes it difficult to have timely, adequate, and accurate information for project coordination and control activities (Atkin and Pothecary, 1994). Moreover, little attention has been given to the establishment of effective communication and logistics processes involving designers, contractors, subcontractors and material suppliers.

Information and Communication Technologies (ICT) have been a major enabler and facilitator of the effective management of the interdependencies and information flows of the banking, manufacturing and retailing industries. Indeed, a contrasting difference between manufacturing/service virtual enterprises and construction virtual enterprises is that the former are enabled and supported by wide ICT infrastructures. Construction projects are characterised by the elaboration by the various parties of large amounts of computer generated information, that circulates and is exchanged on a paper format (Thorpe and Murray, 1996). Thus, there is wide scope for the development of an ICT infrastructure that allows closer working between the various parties involved on construction projects, i.e. between designers and contractors; contractors and subcontractors, material suppliers, builders merchants and/or plant hirers. An ICT infrastructure imply that information flows on construction projects would be partially automated and aiming at a paperless working place. Technical information, i.e. drawings, technical advice, etc.; management and control information, i.e. project planning, progress reports, delivery schedules, etc.; and commercial information like orders, BoQ, tenders, invoices, valuations, etc. could flow seamless through ICT infrastructure between the parties involved in the virtual enterprise (DOE, 1995).

# 3. ICT INFRASTRUCTURE AVAILABLE FOR CONSTRUCTION FIRMS

## 3.1. -Electronic Data Interchange (EDI)

EDI is the electronic transfer from computer to computer of commercial and administrative information using an agreed standard to structure the transaction or message (Emmelhainz, 1993). The essence of EDI is the structured data transfer, which allows information to flow from one computer to another without manual intervention.

The development of EDI is dependent on (Akintoye and McKellar, 1997): Transaction message standards; Translation software which interface between the application software and the message standards; Telecommunications to transmit the structured data from one computer to another.

The main benefits from the use of EDI by construction firms are envisaged to be (Baldwin et al, 1995):

- reductions in paper handling;
- shifting personnel work from no-added value tasks to more relevant work;
- elimination of data re-keying;
- dramatic reduction in data processing errors;
- savings in communication costs;
- increased production efficiency;
- reduction in supply and distribution costs (through a better supply chain management);
- more flexibility and responsiveness;
- shorter communication cycle time.

The international standards for commercial data is based on the EDIFACT (Electronic Data Interchange for Administration, Commerce and Transport, ISO 9735). This standard defines a significant number of messages for different applications (e.g. order, delivery, inquiry etc.) which reduces the communication overhead for the information exchange between companies. Today there exist more than 40 standard messages and more than 150 messages are under development.

Table 1 indicates some of the EDIFACT messages relevant for the construction industry. Two of them are related directly to the building invoice, the rest is without special emphasis to the industry in question. Subsets of the above listed EDIFACT messages which are dealing with building and construction industry are not available by now.

| | | | |
|---|---|---|---|
| Business transaction | | | |
| CONITT | Invitation to Tender Message | CONEST | Establishment of Contract Message |
| CONTEN | Tender Message | | |
| Materials management | | | |
| PRICAT | Price/Sales Catalogue Message | REQUOTE | Request for Quote Message |
| PARTIN | Party Information Message | QUOTE | Quote Message |
| PRODAT | Product Data Message | ORDERS | Purchase Order Message |
| QUALITY | Quality Data Message | ORDRSP | Purchase Order Response Message |
| ORDCHG | Purchase Order Change Message | DESADV | Despatch Advice Message |
| DELFOR | Delivery Schedule Message | RECADV | Receiving Advice Message |
| DELJIT | Delivery Just In Time Message | INVOICE | Invoice Message |
| building invoice | | | |
| CONWQD | Tender Message | CONPVA | Payment Valuation Message |
| finances/accountancies | | | |
| CREADV | Credit Advice Message | FINCAN | Financial Cancellation Message |
| PAYORD | Payment Order Message | FINSTA | Financial Statement |
| DEBADV | Debit Advice Message | | |
| Other fields | | | |
| PROTAP | Project Tasks Planning Message | CONDRO | Drawing Organisation |
| CONAPW | Advice on Pending Works | CONDRA | Drawing Administration |

**Table 1 - Relevant EDIFACT messages**

Several research studies have shown that there is scarce use of EDI by construction firms. In the UK, studies show that the only firms using EDI are builders merchants, which are electronically linked with some material suppliers and manufacturers (Baldwin et al, 1995; Akintoye and McKellar, 1997). The main reasons for the low dissemination of EDI on the construction industry are the industry's fragmentation; fragmented clients; unique nature of each project; sheer complexity of the construction information flows; and lack of IT (DOE, 1995).

### 3.2. - Product Data Exchange

EDIFACT has been developed in support of administration and commercial activities. In construction industry, we are not dealing with standard of-the-shelf products in the majority of cases. Ordering of "make-to-order" products such as dormer windows, conservatories, boilers, etc. accompanies significant level of engineering information and is normally accompanied by an intense data-exchange process on design refinement. The international standard which supports the exchange of product data for manufacturing is STEP (STandard for Exchange of Product model data).

Although there has been sporadic interest and involvement in STEP from within the construction sector reaching back to the mid 1980's, the current level of involvement began to take shape with an Application Protocol Planning Project for Building and Construction (APPP-BC) that was formally initiated in October 1993. The APPP identified nested families of models required to represent information from building construction industries. The AP's currently under development within the building construction group are as follows (Katranuschkov and Scherer, 1996):

- **AP225** - Building Elements Using Explicit Shape Representation (ISO 1995). AP225 is aimed at representing buildings as assemblies of elements — e.g., beams, columns, windows, etc. — along with the explicit (i.e., non-parametric) 3D geometry of each element and some additional information such as material properties, building element classification or element versions. The AP has been developed as a German nationally funded project headed by W. Haas, and it is the furthest along in the standards process of the building construction AP's, having reached Committee Draft stage in January 1996. Experimental implementations have been completed that exchange complex building CAD models between heterogeneous CAD systems.

  The major Units of Functionality (i.e., object groupings) defined in AP225 are listed as follows:
  - **building elements** are the discrete, large-scale pieces of or things in the building
  - **building components** correspond to individual shapes that make up an overall building element. For example, a column element may consist of

a main cylinder component along with other additive components to form base and capital sections and subtractive components to form blockouts.

- the **composition** Units of Functionality (UoF) identifies buildings which decompose into building sections and levels. the building elements, which can be arranged into element assemblies, are positioned within these sections and levels.
- the **design** administration Units of Functionality (UoF) identifies information such as approvals, modifications, or acceptance of building elements.
- the **properties and classification** Units of Functionality (UoF) represents non-geometric element information such as material properties and classifications.

In addition, there are several geometry UoF's to describe specific shape representations (Katranuschkov and Scherer, 1996):.

- **AP230** - Structural Frame: Steelwork. AP230 arose from a large European EUREKA project called CIMsteel. One of CIMsteel's goals was to advance information integration within the structural steel industry, a challenge met with the development of product models and integration prototypes. In 1994, the CIMsteel product model was promoted as a STEP AP project covering construction steelwork frame design, analysis and detailing, and fabrication. The development is lead by A. Watson and M. Ward of Leeds University.
- **AP228** - Building Services: HVAC. AP228 focuses on heating, ventilation, and air conditioning building services. The project has drawn heavily from two European projects, JOULE COMBINE and ESPRIT ATLAS. The project is lead by P. Poyet and J. Monceyron of CSTB, France.

# 4. A FRAMEWORK FOR DEVELOPING AN ICT INFRASTRUCTURE FOR CONSTRUCTION

## 4.1. - Generic description of the framework

Grounded on the context described by the two previous chapters, we have developed a high-level framework which the overall objectives are the development of a information and communication management infrastructure, including standards (STEP and EDIFACT), to provide transport and transparent presentation of product data and business information in the multi-supplier, multi-site environment of construction industry (Figure 1). The framework intents through the application on real cases to accelerate and enhance the ability of European construction industry to capitalise on the emergence of a powerful Information Infrastructure.

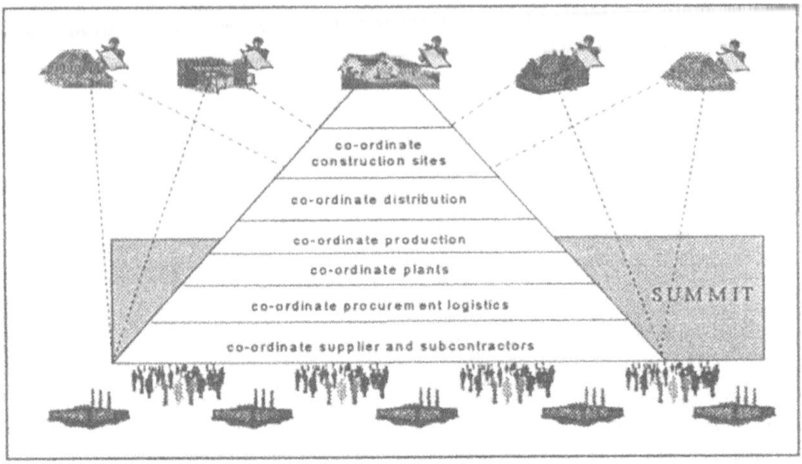


Figure 1: Multi-supplier, multi-site environment ICT infrastructure R&D framework

The goal is to achieve an "information logistics" infrastructure providing the required data at every step of the business processes, to underpin the logistics of the supply and distribution of buildings and equipment. The framework considers that the building of an ICT infrastructure must be tailored with respect to the heterogeneous supply chain typical for construction industry, which involves partners of all company sizes and ICT-skill levels.

The development framework applications will focus on the commercial and architectural refinement business chains and will be primarily targeted at supporting the production process. It will be targeting the complete integration of product, process and business data for the above chains. The development of EDI, standard interfaces and inter-organisational information flow system will lead to a complete electronic working environment.

### 4.2. - Technical objectives

The technical objectives of the development framework are as follows:

*Inter-organisational information flow system*

- Supporting the co-ordination of distributed business processes in temporary architectural and production networks.

*EDIFACT-message types for construction industry*

- Defining construction and building specific EDIFACT messages respectively subsets for selected commercial business processes and engineering processes.

*STEP product modelling*

- Contribute to the development of the Application Protocol for electronic exchange of Explicit Shape Representations.

*STEP and EDIFACT processor development*

- Developing an EDI environment to support the management of technical data and commercial data for the construction project business chains.

*Integrated EDI, STEP-EDIFACT processors, and information flow system and application*

- A prototype implementation of business chain scenarios for purchasing and architectural refinement.

*Implementation and demonstration*

- Implementing and demonstrating the applications developed, and resulting benefits through data exchange cases between firms based on real business scenarios.

*Dissemination and exploitation*

- Provide the applied R&D results to the public especially to SMEs by establishing Supplier/Subcontractor forums.

Recently a consortium of four industrial firms and a research institute have started to apply this research and development framework into real cases. The results will be described elsewhere.

### 4.3. - Business and industrial impact

The development of EDI and ICT on construction virtual enterprises is expected to lead to important changes in its structure and organisation. Some of the factors that are perceived by some construction researchers as hindering the development of electronic information exchange are expected to change (Grilo et al, 1996).

*Relationships.* The relationships on construction industry are usually adversarial, committed to the project duration, and with low co-operation and collaboration. Following trends in other industries, with the deployment of electronic communications, it is envisaged that construction parties develop more trustful, long-term committed and collaborative relationships. The current project partnering trend is expected to be extended to strategic partnering.

*Information Exchange.* Due its complexity and uncertainty the information requirements of the construction industry are very high. However, due the usual contractual arrangements and the type of relationships, information sharing is restricted to operational levels and the strictly necessary to the completion of the projects. Moreover, the quality of the information is low. It is envisaged that the

EDI/Email will facilitate more better information sharing and improve its timeliness, accuracy, adequacy, and transparency.

*Process Innovation.* Construction companies do not see procurement and logistics as core processes. There is a lack of believe that improvements on those processes may bring real project benefits. Moreover, it is stressed in the industry that benefits may only occur if radical changes are made.This applied research and development framework envisage to demonstrate that incremental changes on the procurement and logistics processes of the construction virtual enterprises enabled and supported by an IT infrastructure can provide real benefits to construction projects and firms.

*Technology.* There are very few ICT applications developed specifically to the construction virtual enterprises. As construction business processes have peculiarities when compared with manufacturing and service industries, it is important to develop not only tailored applications but also to construction specific ICT expertise.

## 5. CONCLUSIONS

Electronic exchange of information within construction virtual enterprises is seen as having a significant role in improving the productivity of construction processes. In order to achieve this we have presented a development framework which aims at exploiting the potentials of both the STEP and EDIFACT approaches to product and process data communication by a concept of combining the complementary nature (business versus engineering data) of both approaches. This, together with an EDI system based on a interorganisational information flow system, will facilitate the realisation of a virtual enterprise of smallest and largest companies. It is expected that an ICT infrastructure like the one described here will impact the relationhsips; information exchange; process innovation and technology of the construction industry.

## 6. REFERENCES

Akintoye, A. and McKellar, T. (1997), Electronic Data Interchange in the UK Construction Industry; *RICS Research paper series, Volume 2, Number 4*

Atkin, B. and Pothecary, E. (1994), Building Futures; University of Reading, Dept. of Construction Management and Engineering

Baldwin, A., Thorpe, A, and Carter, C. (1995), Data Exchange in Construction: EDI, MFE or IE? in *Developments in Computational Techniques For Civil Engineering*, pp 11-15, B.H.V Topping, Civil-Comp Press, Edinburgh, UK

Cherns, A. and Bryant, D. (1983), Studying the Client's Role in Construction Management; *Construction Management and Economics*, **2** , pp117

DOE, (1995), Construct IT - Bridging the Gap, HMSO

Emmelhainz, M.A. (1993), Electronic Data Interchange, A Total Management Guide; Van Nostrand Reinhold International, London

Grilo, A., Betts, M. and Mateus, M. (1996), Electronic Interaction in Construction: Why Is It Not a Reality?; *in CIB Proceedings of the Construction on The Information Highway*, Bled, Slovenia

Katranuschkov, P. and Scherer, R.J. (1996), Schema mapping an object matching: a STEP-based approach to engineering data management in open integrated environments; *in CIB Proceedings of the Construction on The Information Highway*, Bled, Slovenia

Latham, Sir M. (1994); Constructing the Team; HMSO

Thorpe, A. and Murray, J.J (1996), COMPOSITE - Site Communications Survey; *Loughborough University of Technology, unpublished report*

# 50

# Multi-agent and manufacturing-
## A multilevel point of view

*Patriti V., Schäfer K., Ramos M., Charpentier P., Martin P., Veron M.*
*Henri Poincaré University of Nancy.*
*Centre de Recherche en Automatique de Nancy B.P. 239, 54506 Vandoeuvre-lès-Nancy Cedex, France.*
*Tel.: 33 (0)3 83 91 20 00, Fax: 33 (0)3 83 91 23 90.*
*{patriti, schafer, charpentier, martin, veron}@cran.u-nancy.fr, mramos@pegasus.dci.ubiobio.cl*

**Abstract**

The increasing demand for flexibility has led to new manufacturing control paradigms based on the concept of self-organization and on the notion of agents. But there is a lack of methodologies in the design of agent oriented manufacturing systems. We explore the design of such systems at three different levels of the manufacturing process: workshop, cell and machine-tool level, emphasize the specificity of each level and outline possible solutions.

At the workshop level, the heterogeneity of the system leads to agent identification problems. We present a model of an autonomous agent that facilitates the identification. For an efficient man-machine integration, we propose a self-organizing protocol that benefits both from the initiative of the human spirit and the efficiency of the artificial machines.

The complete automation of the cell level allows for the use of scheduling techniques, but short term disturbances and the complexity of the problem led to a very fast but low efficient self-organizing protocols. We propose a variation of the contract-net that uses genetic algorithms.

Finally, long term changes in production is the specificity at the machine tool level. A formal method to describe both the machine and the control system in terms of reliability is outlined. It enables the designer to choose a composition of the agent system that reduces communication and optimizes the total reliability.

Computer Applications in Production and Engineering. F. Plonka and G. Olling (Eds.)

**Keywords**
Bionic, contract net, CIM, design, FMC, FMS, heterarchic, HMS, machine tool, multi-agent, reliability, self-organization, workshop.

## 1 INTRODUCTION

The first manufacturing control architectures were usually centralized or hierarchical. The poor performance of these structures in very dynamic environments (Duffie, 1987) and their difficulties with unforeseen modifications (Dilts, 1991) led to new control architectures. **Multi-agent** paradigms emerged like Multi-Agent (Ferber, 1995), Holonic Manufacturing (Christensen, 1994), Heterarchical (Hatvany, 1985) and Bionic (Okino, 1993) Systems. They all present a relevant interest to the manufacturing community because they bring a solution to the management of the uncertainty of the manufacturing environment.

The different Multi-agent paradigms have a common feature. They all propose **Self-Organized Systems** that change their internal organization on their own account. The aim of this paper not being to differentiate the various paradigms, we will use **Multi-agent** as a generic term for **self-organized**.

Therefore, a multi-agent manufacturing system is composed of self-organizing agents, that may be completely informational (i.e., order or scheduling agents) or representing subsystems of the physical world.

We propose a basic decomposition of the design of multi-agent oriented manufacturing systems :

1. Identification of the agents.
2. Design of the self-organizing protocol.

In these two steps of the design we propose to identify some specificity and guidelines tied to the three following levels of the manufacturing process:

- Workshop level that represents the usual factory workshop, with a mix of CNC and traditional machine tools, human operators, robots, etc. .
- Cell level that corresponds to a completely automated manufacturing system, that can act with a minimum interference of the operators.
- Machine tool level where the different components of the system are completely integrated in the same platform.

## 2 DESIGN OF A MULTI-AGENT WORKSHOP

Workshops are usually heterogeneous: Not only are the material resources different in function and nature but they belong to different organizations (human organization, automated control). This heterogeneity of the system makes the identification of the agents rather unclear.

Our agent identification method proposition (Schäfer, 1996) is based on the idea that an agent should be an **autonomous intelligent operator** (Morel, 1994) to improve the system fault tolerance capabilities (Duffie, 1994). We can thus deduce the agent basic capacities:

- to transform its environment in at least one of the dimensions shape, space and time.
- to control the result through observation
- to communicate to palliate its lack of observation capacity.

The resulting model for our manufacturing agent is shown in Figure 1, and an application for a specific workshop is given in Table 1.

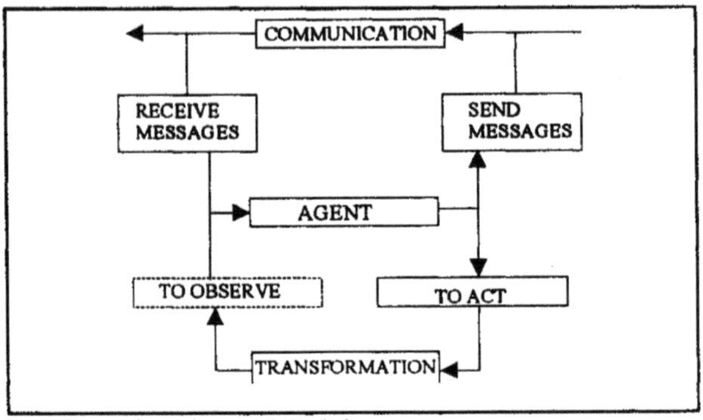


**Figure 1** The Manufacturing Agent Model.

**Table 1** Sample Workshop Composition

| | *Transformation* | *How to observe?* | *How to act?* |
|---|---|---|---|
| Resource Agent | Form | camera or human operator | to use machining or assembling tools |
| Part Agent | Time | electronic tag | to cause resource utilization |
| Storage Agent | Time | human operator | to store and distribute in the stockage area |
| Transport Agent | Space | camera, sensor or human operator | to effect delivery with AGV or human operators |

However, what distinguishes the workshop level from the cell level is the human operator. To integrate the operator in the automated system, a solution consists in interfacing an agent with him (Christensen, 1994). Inter-agent organization is then taken in charge by the artificial agents and the human being is simply considered as a resource.

We claim that the operators could participate directly in a self-organizing process at the same level with the artificial agents. This could be realized with reactive agents (Ferber, 1995), that have simple behaviors based on their perceptions. Although individually very simple, a reactive multi-agent system may exhibit very complex group behavior. An example for the transport of the parts mixing human and auto-guided vehicle could be made with a simple system of lamps:

When a workstation needs a transport agent it sends a red light that signals its need. Artificial agents controlling the AGV detect the signal, and if they have no task to do, they automatically approach the source. The human transport operator can also see the signals. He may participate in the transport process or not depending on his own judgment of the situation.

In this section we have shown the specific heterogeneity of the workshop, outlined a model for agent identification and presented a self-organization protocol adapted to human integration in such a system.

## 3 THE FLEXIBLE MANUFACTURING CELL

The specificity of the Flexible Manufacturing Cell (FMC) is to be completely automated. In that case there is no basic contrast to the agent identification in the workshop. Figure 2 presents the composition of our generic system with the OOA formalism (Coad, 1991). There are only two types of agents: the stations and the transfer system. Parts and storage area are not considered as agents because they have no resources enabling them to be autonomous (Ramos, 1997).

Complete automation allows the use of traditional scheduling methods. But in the case of job-shop manufacturing, the problem is both dynamic and NP-hard. The scheduling is then confronted with a combinatorial explosion of the number of solutions with a very limited search time. Multi-agent specific scheduling techniques have already been employed to solve job-shop problems. Among them the contract net protocol (Smith, 1981) was used in several manufacturing systems (Parunak, 1988), (Duffie, 1987). This self-organizing protocol was found to give low efficient scheduling (Nof, 1994). The challenge is now to increase the system performance. Dividing the problem in two and using a combination with a traditional scheduling method may bring a solution.

### *The internal problem of the Workstation*

The workstation has several Parts to machine and must find a schedule optimizing an internal criteria. For this problem the Genetic Algorithm (GA) approach was used (Aizana, 1994).

### *The problem of the allocation of Parts to the Workstation*

The contract net approach is applied here : The arrival of a part to the FMC is transmitted to the transfer agent that must find a workstation for it. An offer is broadcast to the stations with the message "location" which activates their own GA. The workstation then sends the message to the transfer agent "acceptpart" which contains the proposal of acceptance at a specific date. The transfer agent chooses the workstation and transports the part with a minimum processing date. This dynamic is shown in Figure 2.

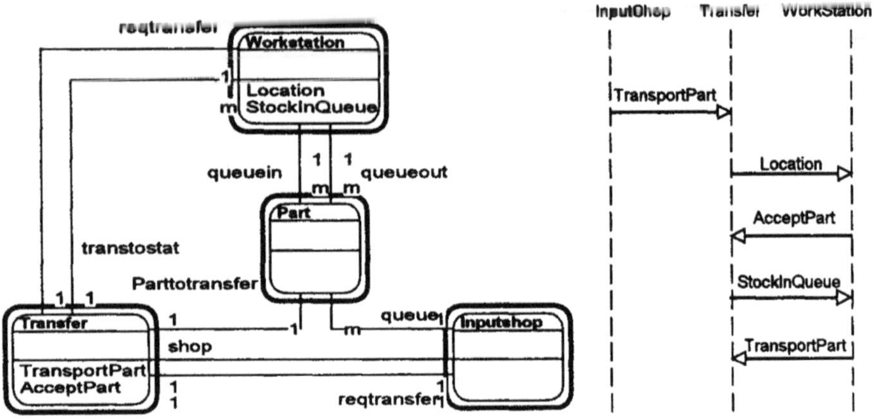


**Figure 2** Composition and dynamic of the cell

We have modeled a FMC with one transfer and five machine agents. The internal criterion of the workstation is the minimization of the staying time of the parts (Cmax) on the machine. The parts arrival ratio at the FMC is 0,3 1/min and processing times are random. Figure 3 shows a global criterion of FMC, the average number of jobs still to be completed by time t.

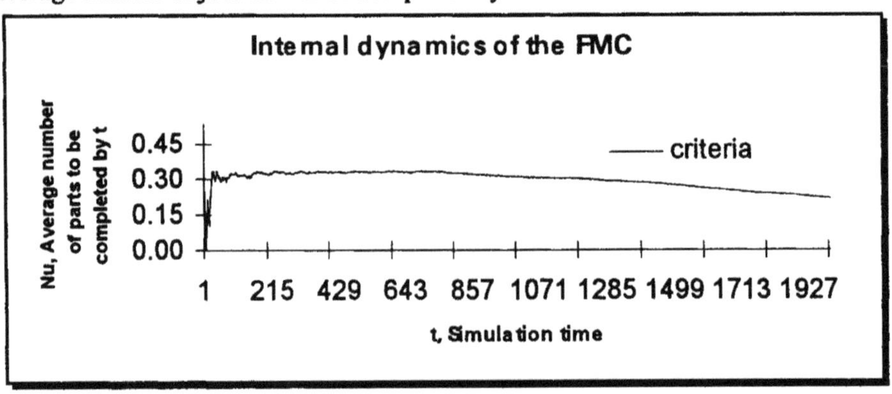


**Figure 3** Evolution of a the average number of jobs to be completed

In this section we have stressed the automation of the FMC and its dynamic job-shop scheduling problem, outlined a possible solution combining GA and the contract net.

## 4 MULTI-AGENT MACHINE TOOL

The specificity of multi-agent design for a machine tool lies in the adaptation to important changes in production rather than short term disturbances. A possible solution is to lower the size of the agents in the system and increase their number.

For example, a robot, composed of a gripper and two NC axis, can be controlled with one agent (the robot), or with three (the gripper and the two axis).

But increasing the number of agents led to a loss in communication bandwidth and in time (Ferber, 1995). For example in a system composed of N agents using the contract net self-organizing protocol, the number of the messages is going to be in $o(N^2)$. So a limitation in the agents number may be compulsory. And due to the non-autonomy of the machine tools agent, this is not obvious at all. We propose a method to value the different solutions, based on the reliability analysis of the system and on the dependencies between agents.

For a machine tool S composed of n agents Ai and m material components Cj, where the agent Ai controls the ki components $\{C_{(i-1)ki+1},\dots, C_{i.ki}\}$.
ci represents the state of the component Ci : $c_i=1$ if the component is functional and $c_i=0$ if the component is out of order.
$a_i$ represents the state of Ai : $a_i=1$ if the agent is alive and $a_i=0$ if the agent is dead. The mathematical formulation of $a_i$ is then,

$$a_i = \left(\prod_{j=(i-1).ki}^{j=i.ki} c_j\right).\Phi_i(a_1,\dots,a_n) = \left(\prod_{j=(i-1).ki}^{j=i.ki} c_j\right).\Phi_i(a)\,. \qquad (1)$$

Where the function $\Phi_i$ is the structural function that expresses the relationship between the agents of the system and agent $A_i$. If $\Phi_S$ is the structure function of the system, the global reliability R of the system is then,

$$R = P(\Phi_S(a_1,\dots,a_n)=1)\,. \qquad (2)$$

R has a maximum value when each agent controls only one component. We can now give our design principle concerning non-autonomous agents :

- The number of agents should be maximum to increase long term flexibility.
- The maximum number of agents is given by the limitation of the communication network and the self-organizing protocol used.
- In case of communication overhead, agents could control more than one material component.
- The ideal regrouping is a regrouping whose reliability tends to the maximum reliability that the machine components can give.

The reliability of the different agent composition is calculated with formula (1) and (2).

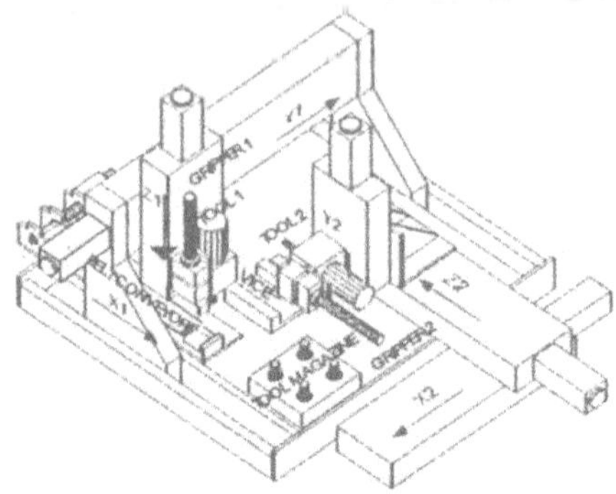

**Figure 4** Shiva

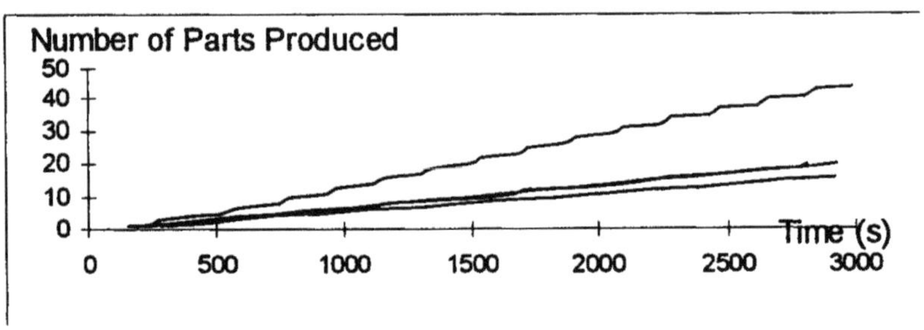


**Figure 5** Production for different machine configurations

An application of this design proposal was made with the machine tool Shiva. This double milling machine has redundant transport and machining capacities. Our agent design procedure showed that an agent controlling the three axis module, the spindle and gripper associated, implies a satisfactory minimum decrease from the maximum reliability.

This multi-agent control system was successfully tested on several simulated machine configurations (Figure 5). It showed that the control system could adapt itself easily to a new production.

## 5 CONCLUSION

We have outlined design identification methods for different levels of the manufacturing system and shown their specificity :

- man-machine integration and heterogeneity at the workshop level
- short term disturbances in an automated environment at the cell level
- long term changes in production at the machine tool level

Applications of these principles have been presented and all of them offer benefits in integration, efficiency, flexibility and reliability in partially unknown manufacturing situations.

## 6 REFERENCES


Aizana A.N., Wah B. (1994) Scheduling of Genetic Algorithms in a noise environment. *Evolutionary Computation*, **2**, N° 2, 97-122.

Christensen J.H. (1994) Holonic Manufacturing Systems : Initial Architecture And Standards Directions, 1st European Conference on Holonic Manufacturing Systems, Hannover, Germany.

Coad P., Yourdon E. (1991) Object-oriented Analysis (2nd edition), Prentice Hall.

Dilts D.M. (1991) The Evolution of Control Architecture for Automated Control Systems. *Journal of Manufacturing Systems*, **10**, No 1, 79-93.

Duffie N.A., Piper R.S. (1987) Non-Hierarchical Control of a Flexible Manufacturing Cell. *Robotics & Computer-Integrated Manufacturing*, **3**, No 2, 175-179

Duffie N.A., Prabhu V. (1994) Real-Time Distributed Scheduling of Heterarchical Manufacturing Systems. *Journal of Manufacturing Systems*, **13**, No 2, 94-104

Ferber J. (1995) les systèmes multi-agents : Vers une inteligence collective, InterEditions, Paris.

Hatvany J. (1985) Intelligence and Cooperation in Heterarchic Systems. *Robotics and Computer Integrated Manufacturing*, **2**, N° 2, 101-104.

Nof S.Y. (1994) Critiquing the potential of object orientation in manufacturing. *International Journal of Computer Integrated Manufacturing*, 7, No 1, 3-16

Morel, G., Lhoste, P., Iung, B. (1994) Towards Intelligent Actuation and Measurement System. Advanced Summer Institute '94 in *Computer Integrated Manufacturing & Industrial Automation* (CIMIA), 26th June-1st July, Rion Patras, Greece, 121-126.

Okino N. (1993) Bionic Manufacturing System, in *Flexible Manufacturing System : Past - Present - Future*, CIRP, Paris, 73-95.

Parunak H.V.D (1988) Manufacturing Experience with the Contract Net. In *Distributed Artificial Intelligence*, edited by M H Huns, Morgan Kaufmann, California, 285-310.

Ramos M., Charpentier P., Martin P. (1997) Reactive distributed and self-organized scheduling of FMS. 7th Mini Euro Conference, Bruges, 24-27 march 97.

Schäfer K., Patriti V., Charpentier P., Martin P., Spath D. (1996) The multi-agent approach in scheduling and control of manufacturing systems. *First International conference and exhibition on the Practical aplication of intelligent agents and multi-agent technology*, Westminster Central Hall, London, UK, 497-521.

Smith R G et Davis R. (1981) Frameworks for Cooperation in Distributed Problem Solving. *IEEE Transactions on System, Man and Cybernetics*, **11**, n°1, 61-70.

# 51

# The application of Integrated Intelligent Systems (IIS) to production scheduling

*Kesheng Wang and Wenfen Lin*
*Department of Production and Quality Engineering*
*NTNU,*
*N-7034 Trondheim, Norway*
*Tel. +47 73 597119*
*Fax. +47 73 597117*
*e-mail: kesheng.wang@protek.ntnu.no*

**Abstract**

One of the most important issues in the process of development and implemention of a manufacturing system is production scheduling. Different scheduling rules and algorithms have been widely developed and used for supporting decision-making in production scheduling. However, in practice, it is very difficult for a user to understand, build or select a suitable and efficient model for the system considered. Hence, an intelligent system is to be built for problem solving. This paper describes how the concept of Integrated Intelligent Systems (IIS), which is developed by Wang (1995) at NTNU in order to meet requirements for higher efficiency, great flexibility, better product quality, and low costs in manufacturing, should be applied to integrate different software packages to solve production scheduling problems. The prototype system developed may be used for daily production scheduling in a manufacturing environment.

**Keywords**

Intelligent Manufacturing Systems, Integrated Intelligent Systems, distributed AI, Expert System (ES), production scheduling.

Computer Applications in Production and Engineering. F. Plonka and G. Olling (Eds.)

# 1 INTRODUCTION

As a well known fact, the modern manufacturing industry does not only need high technology, but also the expertise in various different manufacturing domains in order to meet requirements for higher efficiency, great flexibility, better product quality, and lower costs. The core of this manufacturing technology is integration of domains of specific knowledge, that is, the integration of industry design, manufacturing, planning, managing and marketing activities as well as decision-making automation. The development and application of Integrated Intelligent Systems (IIS) will speed up the manufacturing process and improve the production efficiency, product quality, consequently, and it will enhance company's competition ability in the international market. For this purpose, Integrated Intelligent Systems (IIS) has been developed at Department of Production and Quality Engineering by Prof. Wang. [17] The concept and structure is well suitable for small and medium size companies to realize "balanced automation" in their manufacturing environment.

Production scheduling remains as an important aspect in manufacturing systems. In the international market, it is a very important that companies have to focus on delivering their products to customers within shortest time and higher quality. It becomes very critical to use company's resource effectively and flexibly. In production scheduling, different conditions, such as the importance and the availability of jobs, and different objectives, such as minimizing average lateness, makespan, average flowtime, etc., have to be considered. In the past, those working in the field of operations research have made an important contribution. (Barker 1974, French 1982, Gere 1966). Scheduling is seen primarily as combinatory optimization problem: the question of which is most effective sequence for orders as to due-date performance and utilization is addressed. In attempting to solve this problem, simplifications have to be made as regards to concrete constraints. This leads to low acceptance of the proposed solutions in actual practice in industry. In contrast, the contribution of production researchers is characterized by the endeavor to develop heuristics and dispatching rules under practical constraints leading to acceptable approximations in a reasonable computing time. (Alexander 1978, Balckstone 1982, Conway 1967, Kusiak 1992, , Panwallkar 1977, Pinedo 1995). Despite the above-mentioned attempts to simplify the production process, the production scheduling problem is still an important research in manufacturing environment.

Different scheduling models and algorithms have been widely developed and used to support decision-making in many industries including manufacturing, petroleum, steel, forestry, communications and banking. However, difficulties have been encountered with formulation of models, management of data, and interpretation of the results. Because the complexity of models, the use of these models has been limited to professionals who have enough domain knowledge in mathematics, optimization, and Operation Research (OR). In practice, a user may not know how to build or select a model required for the system considered. For example a manager who determines a production schedule may not know which kind of models is appropriate for solving the problem, or may not be aware of the best solution approaches. Hence, an intelligent system is needed to be built for problem solving.

Integrated Intelligent Systems provide new sight to production scheduling. The increasing complexity of selecting the right procedure, understanding the procedure, integrating the scheduling system with other applications and solving an instant, can be dramatically reduced by the use of the IIS conception. This paper describes how the concept of Integrated Intelligent Systems should be applied to integrate different software packages to solve production scheduling problems. The prototype system developed may be used to daily production scheduling in a manufacturing environment.

In this paper, Section 2 gives a brief survey of IIS and some advantages of using it in manufacturing environments. Section 3 illustrates the approach of solving production scheduling problems which is the theoretical base for developing the scheduling expert system. Section 4 focuses on the development of the subsystems of IIS. A case study is also demonstrated in section 5 and a conclusion is put in section 6.

## 2 INTEGRATED INTELLIGENT SYSTEMS (IIS) APPROACH

Integrated Intelligence Systems (IIS) have significant advantages over conventional structured computer programs in applications such as CIM. The structure of IIS is shown in Figure 1. IIS is a knowledge integration environment, which consists of several numerical computation packages, symbolic reasoning systems, database management systems, computer graphics packages, multimedia techniques, neural networks, domain expert systems, and a meta-system. The integrated software environment allows the running of programs written in different languages and communication among programs as well as the exchange of data between programs and database. These separated subsystems need not be intelligent, but the supervising system, the meta-system, should be intelligent. The meta-system manages the selection, co-ordination, operation and communication of these programs. The conception of IIS is perfectly suitable for manufacturing integration. The existing computer systems, such as CAD, CAE, CAPP, CAM, etc. in a manufacturing enterprise might be integrated together through an intelligent meta-system. One major advantage is that Integrated Intelligent Systems offer a modular architecture for building large programs. Knowledge in the form production rules may be added, deleted or modified in the knowledge base, without any change in the control structure. An Integrated Intelligent System's ability to perform symbol manipulation permits users to choose a variety of representation schemes for components.

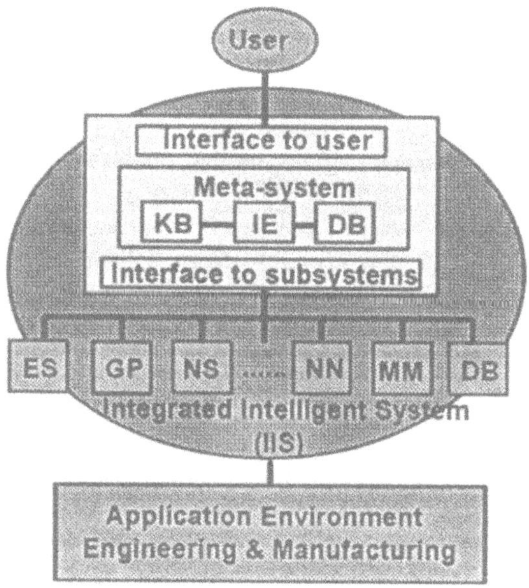


**KB**: Knowledge Base, **IE**: Inference Engine, **DB**: Data Base, **ES**: Expert Systems, **GP**: Graphics Packages, **NS**: Numerical Software, **NN**: Neural Networks, **MM**: Multi-Media systems.

**Figure 1** The structure of Integrated Intelligent System (IIS)

The meta-system was developed by the use of KnowledgePro - an intelligent system development tool. The details on the meta-system are presented in the following references (KnowledgePro, 1991).

# 3 PRODUCTION SCHEDULING

## 3.1 Classification of production scheduling problem

The pure sequencing problem is a specialized scheduling problem in which an ordering of the jobs completely determines a schedule. Moreover, the simplest pure sequencing problem is one in which there is a single resource or machine. The objective is to schedule n jobs on one machine such that one or more performance measures are satisfied. Some of the widely used performance measures are minimizing the number of tardy jobs, earliness, lateness, tardiness and some cost functions. The solution approaches very greatly depending on where the problem is static or dynamic; deterministic or probabilistic; A scheduling problem is defined static if the arrival times of all the jobs are known in advanced. otherwise, it is classified as dynamic scheduling problem. On the other hand, a scheduling problem is called deterministic if all of the parameter such as processing times, setup times, etc. are known with certainty. Otherwise it is classified as probabilistic. (See Figure 2.) The decision tree for classification of production scheduling problem is considered as following: (1) Single Machine Scheduling. Each job consists a single operation. This is the case of simplest of all possible machine environments and is a special case of all other more complicated machine environment. (2) Parallel Machines Scheduling. More than one machine to perform the processing. and (3) Flow Shop Scheduling. There is a nature ordering of the machines in a shop. All parts flow in one direction. (see Figure 2.)

## 3.2 Assumptions On Scheduling Problems

We know that the real world is not so neat as we have envisaged, so it is necessary to make some assumptions to make the model more feasible. Follows are the six general assumptions for the whole system and assumptions for each shop type, respectively.

3.2.1 Assumptions on General Case: (1) Static Scheduling Problem. (2) Deterministic Scheduling Problem. (3) Independent Jobs. (4) Sequence-Independent Setup Times. (5) No Cancellation Allowed. (6) No Breakdown Allowed (the machines have no other tasks and it will be continually available until all jobs are completed).

3.2.2 Assumptions on Individual Case:

- Single Machine Scheduling: (1) Single-Operation Jobs. (2) One Machine Always Available. (3) No Preemption Allowed.
- Parallel Machine Scheduling (1) Single-Operation Jobs. (2) m Identical Machines Continuously Available. (3) Preemption Allowed.
- Flow Shop Scheduling: (1) Multiple-Operation Jobs. (2) m Different Machines Continuously Available. (3) No Preemption Allowed.

Here, preemption means the processing is not interrupted and a job is not removed from a machine before an operation is completed, i.e., no job has any priority.

3.2.3 Objectives Handled

After the assumptions above, the system is ready to be modeled. But before we establish it, we must know which kind of objective is our interest since this is nature in the real workshop for a manager to know his/her objectives. Follows are some objectives that are common used in real case. Baker 1974, Gere 1966, Gursel 1995, Bellman 1982).

1. **Average Completion Time(C).** 2. **Average Lateness(L).** The *lateness* of job is defined as the difference between job's completion time $C_i$ and

job's due date $d_i$, i.e., $L_i=c_i-d_i$, which is positive when job is completed late and negative when it is completed early. 3. **Average Waiting Time(W).** 4. **Average Flow Time(F).** The sum of the completion time of n jobs is called *flow time*. It gives an indication of the total holding, or inventory, costs incurred by the schedule. 5. **Average Tardiness(T).** 6.**Maximum Lateness(ML).** 7. **Maximum Tardiness(MT).** 8. **Number of Tardy Jobs(nT).** 9. **Minimum Makespan(Ms).** The makespan is defined as max $(C_1,....C_n)$, is equivalent to the completion time of the last job to leave the system. 10. **Minimize Maximum Cost of Processing(MM).**

3.2.4 Conditions Considered

To make a decision in scheduling, we should also consider some shop conditions, these conditions are as follows,

1. Shop Configuration (Static and deterministic): a). Single Machine; b). Parallel Machines; c). Flow Shop.
2. Importance of Jobs: a). All jobs equally important; b). At least one job has different importance.
3. Availability of Jobs: a). All jobs available at time zero; b). At least one job is not available at time zero.
4. Preemption: a). Allowed; b). Not allowed.
5. Number of Machines/Processors: a). Single Machine; b).Multiple Machines

# 4 DEVELOPMENT OF SUBSYSTEMS

As described in section 2, IIS is configured with a meta-system as its core component and several subsystems connecting parallel to the meta-system. One of the advantages of such a kind of structure is to let system developers focus on the development of subsystems. The subsystems of production scheduling problem includes: (1) Scheduling expert system, (2) rules and algorithms packages.

## 4.1 Scheduling expert system

A rule-based knowledge representation scheme is selected to develop the prototype of production scheduling system. For convenience, the expert system is also written in KnowledgePro. When the consultation starts, the user is asked the following questions:

(1) Shop configuration; (2) Importance of jobs (equally importance or not); (3) Objective of the user (Minimize makespan); (4) Availability of jobs (ready time =0, ready time >0).

Depending on the responses specified by the user, the expert system selects the appropriate scheduling rule or algorithm to solve the problem. Having determined the procedure, an interface is provided between meta-system and user, thus enabling the user to solve instant of the problem by entering the necessary data in a user-friendly environment.

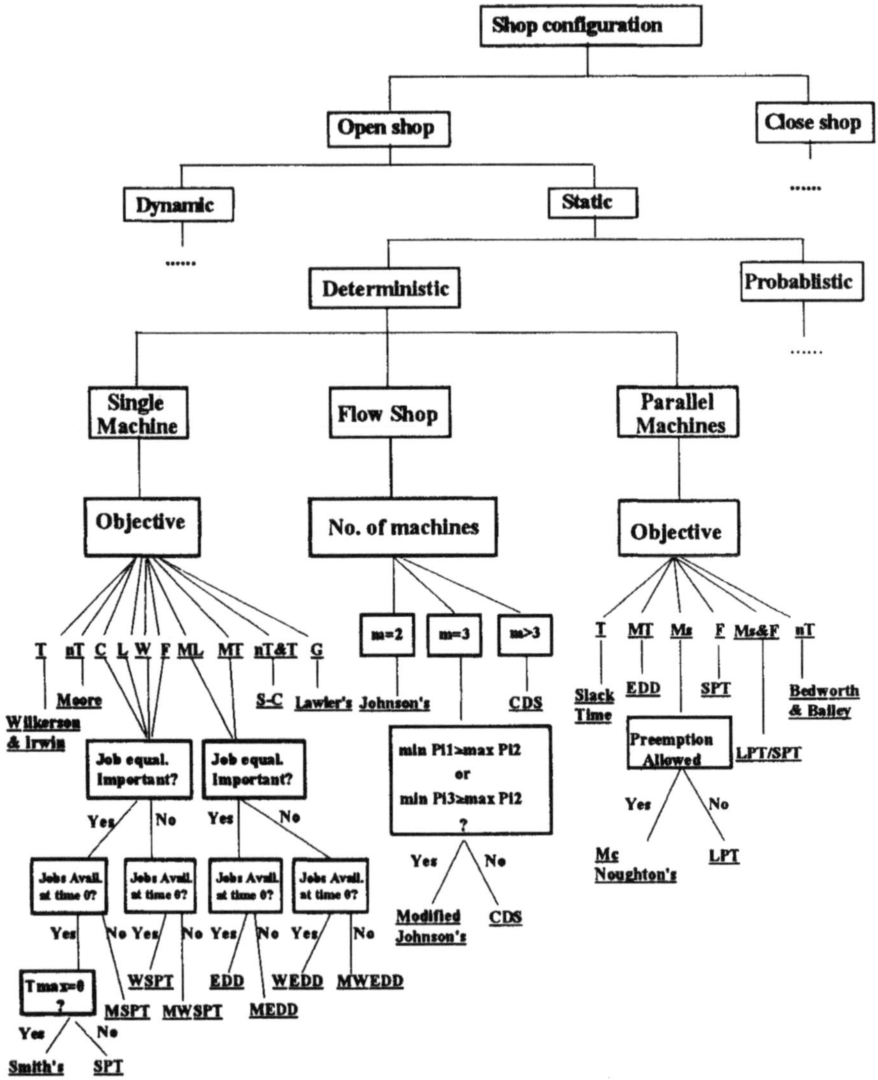


**Figure 2** The decision tree of production scheduling problems

## 4.2 Rules and Algorithms packages

The rules and the algorithms included in the production scheduling, and under what conditions they are chosen are shown in Figure 2 and listed as following:

> (1) Shortest Processing Time (SPT); (2) Weighted SPT (WSPT); (3) Earliest Due Data (EDD); (4) Modified SPT (MSPT); (5) Modified WSPT (MWSPT); (6) Modified EDD (MEDD); (7) Modified WEDD (MWEDD); (8) Moore's Algorithm; (9) Smith's Algorithm; (10) Lawler's Algorithm; (11) Wilkerson-Irwing Algorithm; (12) S-C Algorithm; (13) Largest Processing Time (LPT)-Parallel Machines; (14) SPT - Parallel machines; (15) LPT-SPT - Parallel machines; (16) Bedworth and Bailey Algorithm; (17) Slack Time Rule; (18) EDD - parallel machines; (19) Mc Noughton's algorithm; (20) Johneson's algorithm (flow shop, 2 machines); (21) Modified Johson's algorithm; (22) C_D_S algorithm /Flow shop, m machines), ......, etc.

The rules and algorithms were developed in high-level language C, spreadsheet Excel and Operation Research software Lindo, depending on the features and the complexity of rules and algorithms. The reason why we select these software may be:

> (1) Ease of use; (2) Common-used in Companies; (3) PC-based platform.

Excel was used for the developing of simple rules (e.g. SPT) and for input data, C for complex rules (e.g., Johnson's algorithm) and Lindo for OP algorithms (e.g., integer programming). All these software are easily and rapidly integrated with the meta-system.

# 5 SAMPLE CONSULTATION

Johnson's Algorithm Applied in Two-Machine Flow Shop is used for demonstrate how the system to function. Suppose the user's shop is a two- machine flow shop with parameters shown in the following:

**Table 1** Parameters of a two-machine flow shop

| *Operation number* | *Processing Time tij of operation I on machine* | |
|---|---|---|
| *i* | *j=1* | *j=2* |
| 1 | 6 | 3 |
| 2 | 2 | 9 |
| 3 | 4 | 3 |
| 4 | 1 | 8 |
| 5 | 7 | 1 |
| 6 | 4 | 5 |
| 7 | 7 | 6 |

In the "Shop Configuration" window, we select item "Flow Shop" among 'Single Machine', 'Parallel Machines' or 'Flow Shop' by double-clicking the item, as shown in Figure 3.

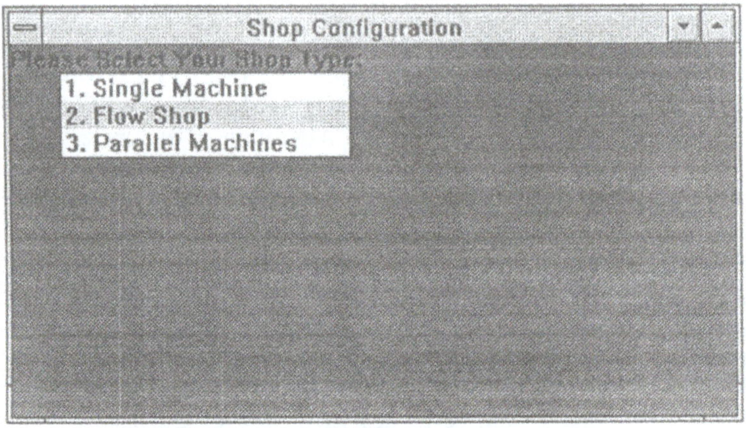


**Figure 3** Shop type selection (Flow Shop)

Another window (Figure 4) will appear and ask the user the number of machines in his shop. Here the selection is "m=2".

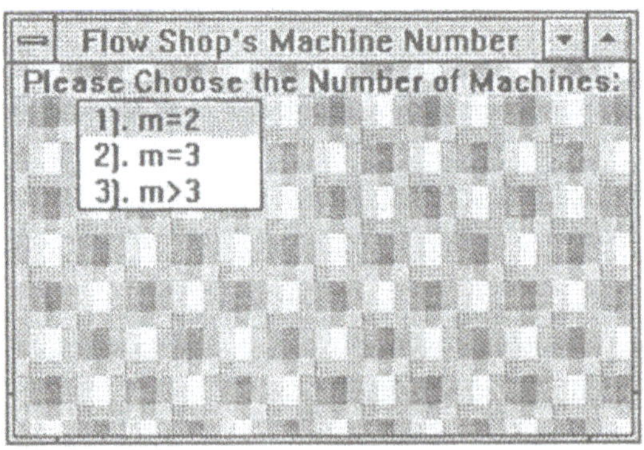


**Figure 4** Window of selecting number of machines

Now comes another window (Figure 5). The function of this window is to let the user to enter the corresponding data of the shop. Operation number, processing time of operations on machine 1 and processing time of operations on machine 2, respectively.

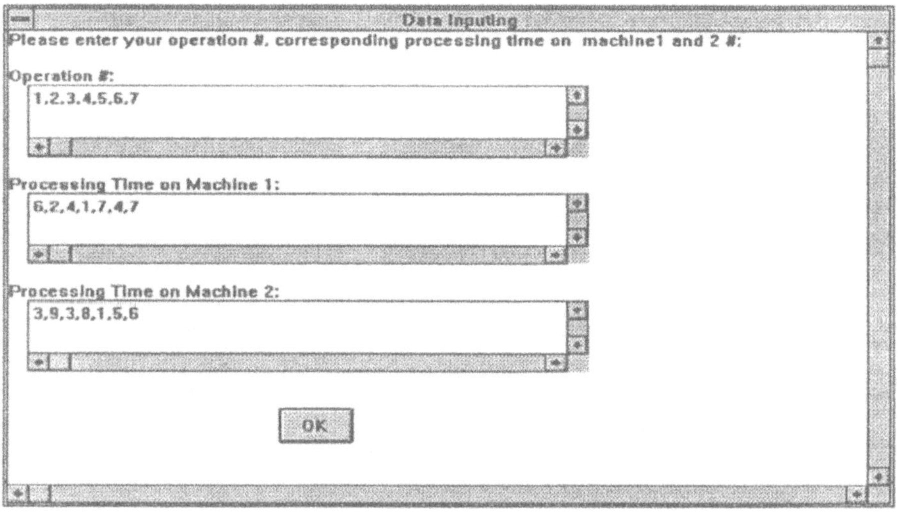


**Figure 5** Window of data input of work shop

After the data have been input, the window (Figure 6) will show up to let the user to confirm the data, if the user want to change some data, just click on the button 'Back', the window (Figure 5) of data input will show up again. If the user has nothing to change, just click on the button 'Confirm'.

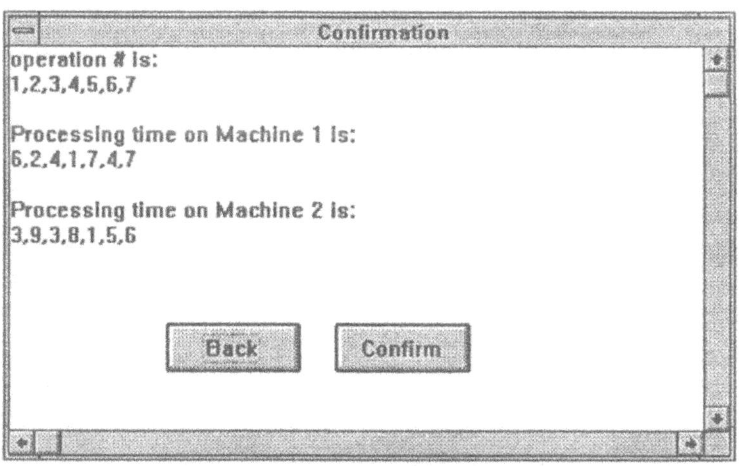


**Figure 6** Confirmation of data input

After confirmation, the scheduling system will run and process the data according to Johnson's algorithm. During this time, a prompt window (Figure 7) will pop up. First the data will be written into a file in Microsoft Excel for first-step processing.

Since Microsoft Excel has some functions on data sorting according to ascending or descending order of the data or according to some conditions, this function will save us lots of time in programming in C, so we make use of it and preprocess the data. Afterwards, the rearranged data is read by the meta-system, KnowledgePro. After reading, the meta-system will write and save the data into a text file and communicate the C program which will do the rest further processing of the data, at this time another window (Figure 8) will pop up to prompt user to wait for a few seconds.

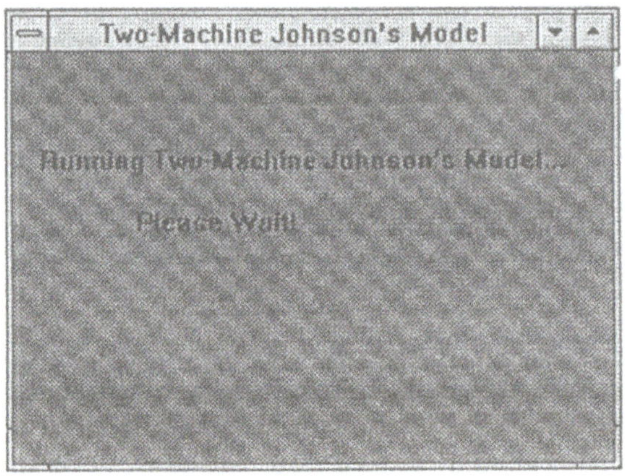


**Figure 7** The prompt window

Now the system is running corresponding C program to calculate the optimal operation sequence according to the Johnson's algorithm. The result will come out with a window (Figure 8).

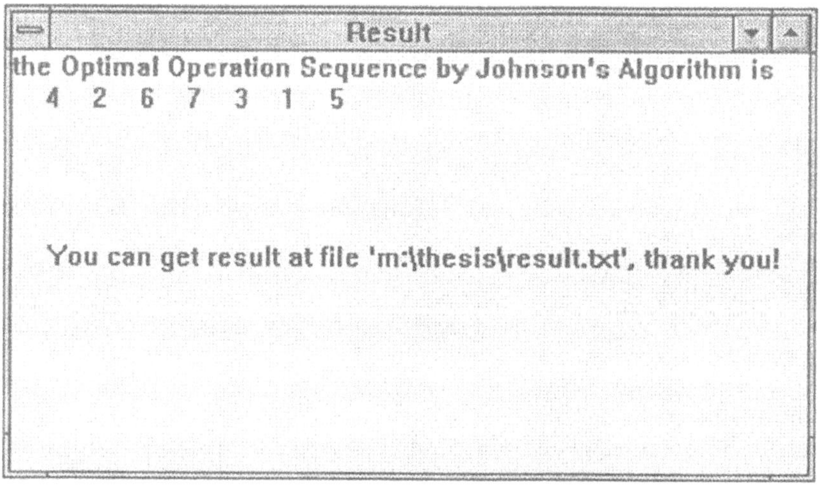


**Figure 8** Window with the final result of Johnson's algorithm

## 6 CONCLUSION

A prototype system for automatic scheduling, which mainly includes the Meta-system, the expert system for scheduling selection, and subsystems of rules and algorithms is established. At present, the prototype system is limited to the static and deterministic problems, but it is very easy to be extended to dynamic and probabilistic scheduling problems, because the structure of the system is based on the concept of IIS. The problem of scheduling two-machine flow shop, which should be solved by rule of Johnson's, has been used to demonstrate how the system functions. What the user need to do is just to specify, for example, the user's shop type, the user's objectives and shop's parameters, the intelligence-inside scheduling system will choose appropriate rules or algorithms to run the corresponding calculations and tell user the final results. The intelligent development environment, KnowledgePro, has been selected for building of the system. It shows that KnowledgePro is a high level language, which provides object oriented programming, expert systems and multimedia facilities.

## 7 REFERENCES

Alexander, S. M. (1978), An Expert system for the selection of scheduling Rules in a job shop, Computers and Industrial Engineering, Vol. 12, No. 3, pp. 167-171.

Baker, K. R. (1974), Introduction to Sequencing and scheduling, wiley, New York.
Bellman, R. E., Esogbue, A. O. (1982), and Nabeshima, I., Mathematical Aspect of Scheduling and Applications, Pergamon Press, Oxford.
Balckstone, J. H. Jr., Phillips D. T. and Hogg, G. L. (1982), A state-of-the-art survey of Dispatching Rules for Manufacturing Job Shop Operations, International Journal of Production Research, Vol. 20, No. 1, pp. 27-45.
Conway, R. W., Maxwell W. L., Miller L. W. (1967), *Theory of Scheduling*, Addison-Wesley.
Dorn J. and Froeschl K. A. (1993), Scheduling of Production Processes, Ellis Horwood Limited.
French, S. (1982), Sequencing and Scheduling: An Introduction to the mathematics of the job-shop, Wiley, New York,.
Gere, W. S. Jr. (1966), Heuristics in Job Shop Scheduling, Management Science, Vol. 13, No. 3, pp. 167-190.
Gursel A., Suer and Juan F. M. (1995), *A Prototype Knowledge-Based System for Production Scheduling Problems*, University of Puerto Rico., Proceedings of the first world congress on Intelligent manufacturing processes and systems, pp. 501-511.
*KnowledgePro Windows(1991), Reference Manual*, version 2.0, Knowledge Garden, October.
*KnowledgePro Windows(1991), User Manual*, version 2.0, Knowledge Garden, October.
Kusiak A. and Ahn J. (1992), Intelligent Scheduling of Automated Machining Systems, Intelligent Design and Manufacturing, (Ed. Kusiak A.) John Wiley & Sons, Inc., pp. 421-447.
Kusiak A. and Wang J. (1994), A knowledge-based system for building scheduling models, Artificial Intelligence in optimal Design and Manufacturing (Ed. Dong Z.), P T R Prentice Hall Inc. pp. 173-202.
Panwallkar, S. S. and Iskander, W. (1977), A survey of Scheduling Rules, Operation Research, Vol. 25, No. 1, pp 45-61.
Pinedo M. (1995), *Scheduling/theory, algorithms, and systems*, Prentice Hall.
Schultz, C. R. (1998), An expediting Heuristic for the Shortest Processing Time Dispatching Rule, International Journal of Production Research, Vol. 27, No. 1 pp. 41-51.
Wang, K. (1991), *Artificial Intelligence Applied to Mechanical Engineering*, NTH.
Wang, K. (1995), *SINTEF REPORT on Knowledge Integrated System in Manufacturing Engineering*, Guest Lecture at Beijing Institute of Petrol-Chemical Technology.
Zweben M. and Fox M. S. (1994), Intelligent Scheduling, Morgan Kaufmann Publishers.

## 8 BIOGRAPHY

**Kesheng Wang**, the professor of Department of Production and Quality Engineering, Norwegian University of Science and Technology (NTNU), He has received the B.S. (1968) and M.S.(1981) degree from The Shanghai University of Technology, Shanghai, China. and the Dr. Ing. (1988) from The Norwegian Institute of Technology (NTH), Trondheim, Norway. He has published two text books and over 60 technical papers in international journals and international conferences. He served as program committee member and session chairman in several international conferences, the chairman of Nordic and Baltic Summer School, and invited to given seminars at many universities and research institutes internationally. His research interests span structure design, kinematics and dynamics of robot manipulators, computer graphics simulation, manufacturing systems theory, mathematical modeling of mechanical systems, intelligent robotics, and expert systems and soft computing (ANN, FZ, Genetic Algorithms etc.) in production and engineering. Dr. Wang is the member of IFIP (International Federation of Information Process), TC5, WG. 5.3, the member of NAIA (Norwegian Artificial Intelligence Association) and The member of New York Academy of Science.

**Wengfen Lin** is a graduate student at the Department of Production and Quality Engineering, Norwegian University of Science and Technology (NTNU). He has received the B.S. (1992) from Tianjing University, China and M.S. (1997) from NTNU, Norway.

# 52

# Simulation of embedded decision processes in manufacturing systems

*S. Cem Karacal*
*Southern Illinois University*
*Mechanical and Industrial Engineering, Edwardsville, IL 62026*
*skaraca@siue.edu*

**Abstract**

This paper addresses a new unified framework for simulation that includes both physical and decision making processes of manufacturing systems. The developed methodology uses a state-space representation based simulation modeling formalism along with object oriented software design. The model developer perceives the manufacturing system in terms of several physical entities, augmented by a number of decision making elements, each capable of making rational decisions that affect system behavior and contribute to the collective state of the system. The modularity of the user's conceptual model in terms of physical and decision making entities with their programmed and non-programmed decisions and the capability of modeling these entities and processes at different hierarchical levels can vastly improve simulation's role as a decision making tool.

**Keywords**

Manufacturing system simulation, knowledge based simulation, object oriented modeling

## 1 INTRODUCTION

Computer simulation modeling is the only viable approach to the detailed analysis and design of complex manufacturing systems. Yet, current simulation languages permit only gross approximations to the actual systems being studied. The simulation methodology still suffers from its traditional deficiencies. During the model development process various system assumptions are hardwired into the

Computer Applications in Production and Engineering. F. Plonka and G. Olling (Eds.)

model code and there are no provisions to simulate the decision processes which are the actual driving forces of purposeful systems. The modification of modeling assumptions usually requires major model overhauls with extensive programming efforts, resulting in minimal ease of model development and code reusability.

The performance of a manufacturing system is highly influenced by control policies used in its operation. The decisions are based on available information, which is often incomplete, inaccurate, and delayed. A decision maker at each level uses heuristics, personal expertise, company rules and policies to arrive at a control decision. Traditional simulation tools do not provide convenient structures for specifying these interactions

This research addresses to the design and implementation of a fundamentally new and superior approach to the modeling of complex systems, based upon a new formalism, state-space representation, and the object oriented programming approach. Specifically, this new simulation modeling environment will permit the distinct and separate specification of physical elements, decision elements, and data/information elements of a manufacturing system. The developed system uses artificial intelligence techniques to imitate the non-programmed decision processes. Realistic models can be constructed at any level of detail desired, and can be retrieved and reused as needed. The ability to perform detailed analysis using this new simulation environment will dramatically reduce the time needed for planning/designing and analyzing complex manufacturing systems. The developed prototype software environment is also compared against conventional simulation approaches using the analytic hierarchy process technique to reach a scale of preference between the two.

## 2 SIMULATION FORMALISM AND METHODOLOGY

The Discrete Event Simulation of Manufacturing Systems (DEMS) formalism developed (Karacal and Mize, 1996a) is a set of conventions for the construction of simulation models. It gives a definite form to how and what can be expressed about a system to be modeled by using set theory and state-space representation for the abstraction. In the end, it generates a science base and a uniform convention of notation and communication. The DEMS formalism is based on five distinct levels for a system entity to be in and can be summarized as follow:

<u>*Level 0:*</u> At the bottom of the hierarchy lies the ***Source System*** represented with:

- Physical components set which contains
  - Set of physical inputs, $X$
  - Set of physical outputs, $Y$
  - Communication channels, $C$
  - Material ports, $M$
  - Set of manufacturing operations, $O$
- Observed facts set, $F$
- Set of real numbers for time, $T$

- Function *read*, $\rho$, that maps elements of physical inputs, outputs, or communication channels to the facts set
  *F*.

<u>*Level 1:*</u> Next level in the hierarchy is the ***Data System*** and expressed with:
- ***Source System*** from level 0
- Universe of discourse set, *U*, that represents the meanings for observed facts
- Data set *D* where each element is defined in terms of a fact from set *F* and a meaning from *U*
- Function *assign*, $\theta$, that maps an element of observed facts set and an element of universe of discourse set to data set *D*
- Function time that maps a real number for time to an element of data set to represent temporal data

<u>*Level 2:*</u> When the relationships and the operations between the elements of the data set are provided, the data system becomes an Information ***System*** that is defined through:
- ***Data System*** from level 1
- Relation definitions set, R
- Information (internal state) set, I
- *Information-generation* function $\gamma_I$ that maps elements of data set D and elements of operations set O and/or
  Relations set R to information set I
- *look* function $\lambda$ that is used to obtain information about the states of other system entities
- *action* function $\alpha$ for programmed decisions based on present internal and external states
- *update-internal* function $\nu_{int}$ to reflect the effects of actions selected on internal state
- *update-external* function $\nu_{ext}$ to reflect the effects of actions selected through $\alpha$ on external state

The dynamic behavior, moving in time from one state to another, of the information system during the simulation is handled by a set of pseudo functions. These functions first observe the internal and external states through functions $\gamma_I$ and $\lambda$ at time $t_{i-1}$. Next, they obtain a programmed decision through action function $\alpha$ at time $t_{i-1}$. Then, the internal and external states are updated using $\nu_{int}$ and $\nu_{ext}$ functions for next event time $t_i$. This process is repeated as next events take place in simulation.

<u>*Level 3:*</u> When the entity is transformed from a procedural format to a symbolic format, it is referred to as a ***Knowledge System*** and represented with:
- ***Information System*** from level 2
- Structured universe of discourse set, Us, that defines the relationships among the meanings

- *knowledge-generation* function $\gamma_k$ that generates knowledge from a given information set I and structured universe of discourse set $U_s$
- knowledge base set $K$

Level 4: A knowledge system becomes an ***Intelligent System*** when a reasoning mechanism is associated with the knowledge base. At this level the entity is abstracted through:

- ***Knowledge System*** from level 3
- External knowledge base $B$ that represents the knowledge about the total system
- Goals set $G$ that define the set of goals (production orders) defined for the entity
- Decision set $H$ that represents the set of decisions reached by searching through the knowledge base $K$
- *perceive* function $\pi$ to asses the knowledge about the total system
- *decision* function $\delta$ to determine the actions that need to be taken to satisfy the goals defined in set $G$
- *update-external-knowledge* function $\omega_{ext}$ to reflect the changes that occurred in the total system as a result of implementing the decision obtained through decision function $\delta$
- *update-internal-knowledge* function $\omega_{int}$ to reflect the changes that occurred in entities internal knowledge base $K$ as a result of implementing the decision obtained through decision function $\delta$.

The dynamic behavior of the intelligent system during the simulation is handled by a set of pseudo functions similar to those defined for the information system. These functions first observe the internal and external knowledge states through functions $\gamma_k$ and $\pi$ at time $t_{i-1}$. Next, they obtain a non-programmed decision through decision function $\delta$ at time $t_{i-1}$ by searching their knowledge bases. Then, the internal and external knowledge bases are updated using $\omega_{int}$ and $\omega_{ext}$ functions for time $t_i$. Although the dynamic behavior for information and intelligent system levels are similar on the surface, they are very different. The information system level uses information as opposed to knowledge used in intelligent system level. Furthermore, the representation schemes used (procedural format in information, symbolic format in intelligent) in two levels are very different.

## 2.1 System Entities

Two types of entities, decision making entities (DME) and information driven physical entities (IDPE) are defined based on the intelligent and information system levels of the formalism, respectively. The other three levels are mainly definition tools to assess the sets necessary in the operations of DMEs and IDPEs. The DMEs are the basic building blocks of the planning and control system. The IDPEs form the foundation of the manufacturing system. Their activities correspond to real physical activities that are taking place on the floor and are direct results of decisions made by DMEs. The interactions between DMEs and IDPEs as well as interactions among DMEs can be established through the use of control, communication and material flow relations. When individual entities are bound together with data, information and knowledge, structural and behavioral representation at the total system level can be easily achieved. Three different classes are defined for the DMEs of a manufacturing system.

i) Entities that deal with the planning and control activities at the system level. These entities utilize the current state of the system in a filtered form, the work load, and the requirements for product orders.

ii) Entities that plan and control the major activities that need to be carried out and synchronized in order to conform to the plans prepared by the entities of (i ). The type of knowledge utilized by these entities are the current collective state of each unit (shop/department) planned and controlled by each entity. These entities create their own individual plans and release job orders aimed at the satisfaction of product orders coming from above.

iii) Entities that perform planning and control at work-center or cell level. At this level, the orders are further broken down into task orders that need to be synchronized to conform the job orders received from above. This is the lowest level in which intelligent behavior takes place in the hierarchy. The task orders are further broken down into activity orders that are translated into a finite set of ordered physical activities. This is where the logical system connects to the physical system.

A major advantage of these three levels defined for DMEs is its ability to allow the natural analysis of information components. The information and knowledge elements are the main driving and binding forces of the physical and logical systems. Each intelligent entity monitors the orders released by its superior entity, performs its own decision making and planning processes, and releases proper orders to its own subordinates. Thus, each production planning and control problem is solved in its own local domain by the most knowledgeable entity about that area.

## 3 OBJECT ORIENTED SIMULATION TOOL

The Smalltalk object oriented programming language (OOP) is chosen for the implementation of the developed formalism and methodology. A hierarchy of object classes that represent system, department, work-center, machine physical entities along with a hierarchy of control and communication objects are defined (Karacal and Mize, 1997a). The following structure summarizes the hierarchy of defined Smalltalk object classes. The indentation represents the class subclass relationships.

```
Object
  Simulation
         Simulate
  SimulationObject
         SystemPhys
               DeptPhys
                 WorkCenterPhys
                   MachinePhys
         SystemCntrl
               DeptCntrl
                 WorkCenterCntrl
                   MachineCntrl
         SystemCommunication
               DeptCom
                 WCCom
                   MachCom
         MaterialPort
         ProductOrder
               CmptOrder
                 BtchOrder
```

Most of these class names are self explanatory and the instances of them are the basic building blocks of a simulation model. As the model builder defines the physical system configuration, the instances of above classes are automatically created and configured during model building process.

## 3.1 Software implementation

To take full advantage of the inheritance property of OOP, subclasses inheriting their basic behavior from super classes, the whole environment is designed around three abstract tree structures that are transparent to the user during simulation. The first tree, *SystemStructure*, represents the hierarchical configuration of the physical entities of the manufacturing system being modeled. These entities are defined through instances of physical objects of the above hierarchy and include machine tools, handling devices, etc. and correspond to ***SourceSystem*** of the formalism. The software automatically creates a default control entity, communication channel, and material port for each physical entity created and allows the model developer to customize them depending on the capabilities and functions of the physical entity created.

The second tree, *ProductDataBase*, maintains information on all the products produced and their product structure trees including all the relevant information on parts and components. In order to keep track of the dynamic information involved in the simulation, a highly dynamic third tree structure, *OrderDataBase*, is designed and frequently manipulated during the simulation. This tree holds all the information on product, component, and part orders involved during the simulation period. At the beginning of the simulation, this is a tree consisting of nothing but a root linked to a system control object. As the orders arrive, the branches and sub-branches representing customers, their individual orders, and a break down of those orders are created. The status of orders are updated as the operations and assemblies are performed. When the final operation of a product order is completed, the branch originating from that node is pruned and the related statistics are updated. This process prevents infinite growth of the *OrderDataBase.*

# 4 PRODUCTION CONTROL KNOWLEDGE BASES

After defining the physical configuration of the system, the next step is the definition of the knowledge bases for each control entity defined in the hierarchy. Three generic knowledge base objects and their inference rules are defined for system, department/shop, and work-center levels and are called *systemPlanning*, *shopPlanning*, and *workCenterPlanning*, respectively. The simulation model developer can express the operational policies and expertise for each intelligent entity during the knowledge base and inference rule definition process. An example class of knowledge bases are defined to implement the production planning and resource allocation policies of a typical make-to-order manufacturing facility. The instances of these knowledge bases are created and linked to the control objects of each intelligent entity in the hierarchy. The inference rules include a certainty value (1.0 complete certainty, 0.0 complete uncertainty) that represents how strongly system believes that the decision, the value of parameter action, is the correct one. This value is later used by the system to search for the most certain decision for a given goal. The system utilizes a grammar, based on concepts from formal language theory, to translate customer orders into component orders and then component orders to batch orders (Karacal, 1997b). The customer orders are broken into detailed shop, work-center, and batch orders in a hierarchical fashion as they are released by decision making entities to subordinate entities.

## 4.1 System level planning

The instances of the *systemPlanning* knowledge base first checks the timing of the product order through a series of rules upon receiving a consultation request from a system control object. If timing is critically close to due-date, it immediately translates the product order into component/sub-assembly orders that are released to the relevant shop control entities. Otherwise, it evaluates a set of rules using order size, product type and customer identification to derive the importance level for the order. The next step in knowledge processing is the determination of the timing priority for the order using order importance, lead and slack time information. Then, the *systemPlanning* object acquires the present shop and capacity knowledge from the model in real time while the simulation is running. The following is the basic structure and some example rules of the Smalltalk based example *systemPlanning* knowledge base.

*systemPlanning* knowledge base

```
    Parameters:
        action, customer, order, productionLeadTime        , product        ,
quantity, rangeOne, rangeTwo    shopCapacityStatus, shopLoadStatus, slack,
SlackMinusLeadTime, timing
     Rules:
        emergencyRelease
                if: (slack ≤ slackMinusLeadTime)
                  then: [action is:'release' withCertainty: 1.0]
        importantOrders
                if: (slackMinusLeadTime ≤ rangeOne & (order = 'important'))
                  then: [timing is: 'urgent' withCertainty: 0.95].
                if:     (slackMinusLeadTime     >     rangeOne     &
(slackMinusLeadTime ≤ rangeTwo) &
                        (order='Important'))
                  then: [timing is: 'normal' withCeratinty: 0.85].
        notImportantOrders
        notUrgentOrders
        orderRating
        rangeFirst
        rangeSecond
          veryImportantOrders
        urgentOrders
        normalOrders
                if: (timing ='normal' & shopCapacityStatus = 'High'))
                  then: [if: (shopLoadStatus = 'NotHeavy')
                          then: [action is: 'release' withCertainty: 0.85].
                        if: (shopLoadStatus = 'Medium')
                          then: [action is: 'putItInPlan' withCertainty: 0.75].
                        if: (shopLoadStatus = 'Heavy')
                          then: [action is: 'putItInPlan' withCertainty: 0.35].
                if: (timing ='normal' & shopCapacityStatus = 'Average'))
```

```
    then: [if: (shopLoadStatus = 'NotHeavy')
              then: [action is: 'release' withCertainty: 0.75].
          if: (shopLoadStatus = 'Medium')
              then: [action is:' putItInPlan' withCertainty: 0.65].
          if: (shopLoadStatus = 'Heavy')
              then: [action is: 'putItInPlan' withCertainty: 0.35].
if: (timing ='normal' & shopCapacityStatus = 'Low'))
    then: [if: (shopLoadStatus = 'NotHeavy')
              then: [action is: 'putItInPlan' withCertainty: 0.55].
          if: (shopLoadStatus = 'Medium')
              then: [action is:' putItInPlan' withCertainty: 0.45].
          if: (shopLoadStatus = 'Heavy')
              then: [action is: 'putItInPlan' withCertainty: 0.15]].
```

According to the timing of the order and the shop capacity at a given time, the normalOrders rule of the *systemPlanning* knowledge base given above evaluates all combinations with shop load status and finds an action and its certainty level. During this process, the quantitative information on shop loads and capacities are dynamically retrieved by the system control object from the shop control objects involved and converted into symbolic form in real simulation time. The conversion process takes place as follows:

1) The system controller looks at the shop load in terms of a moving monthly time bucket. As product orders are released, the bucket of the shop involved are loaded with orders using the lead time and quantity information.

As breakdowns/problems, changes in plan are encountered, the time buckets are updated in real time to reflect the changes. When a shop load status is requested for a particular shop, a quantitative expression that relates present shop load, unused time, and a flexibility factor is evaluated to find a numeric value at that instant of time. Depending on which predefined range this value falls into, one of the possible symbolic values such as high, low, etc. is returned to the knowledge base.

2) A symbolic value for the shop capacity status is determined using another expression that relates the number of operational machines, the type of orders being processed at that instant of time, shop reliability, and total number of available machines in the shop. Again, depending upon which range this value falls into, a symbolic value such as full-capacity, low-capacity, etc. is returned to the knowledge base.

Once the *systemPlanning* knowledge base finds a value to the parameter action, the value is passed back to the system controller object that implements the action by updating the internal and external states. The rules try to evenly spread the work load in terms of shop loads and order timing. The planning scheme uses a simple non-monotonic reasoning mechanism based on goal regression and is explained in detail in (Karacal, 1997b).

## 4.2 Shop level planning

The next layer of knowledge bases, an instance of the *shopPlanning* knowledge base for each shop, are defined for non-programmed shop planning decisions. They are customized from their default structure by the model developer through definition of new parameters and rules. These knowledge bases deal with component orders and their main design principles are similar to those in *systemPlanning*. When they are interrogated, these knowledge bases asses a symbolic value for component order timing using due-date and lead time information from the interrogating shop control object. A set of rules classify the component on hand according to its importance and position in the product structure tree. The symbolic knowledge regarding the load and capacity status of the work-centers involved in processing of the present component order are obtained in real simulation time. The methods used in deriving these symbolic values are very similar to the ones used in the *systemPlaning* knowledge base, with the main difference being the weekly time bucket used. These knowledge bases search through a set of rules representing various combinations of work-center load and capacity status values, order timing, and the present shop plan to find a value for parameter action. This value is passed back to the shop controller which in turn implements the action.

## 4.3 Work-center level planning

The last non-programmed decision level in the hierarchy is handled by a set of *workCenterPlaning* knowledge bases that deal with batch orders released to machine controllers. These are relatively simple structures that decide on what to do with each individual batch order using the real time symbolic values derived for order timing, machine status, machine reliability, and present work-center plan. The work-center control object in turn implements the action returned by its *workCenterPlaning* knowledge base.

When physical machines receive batch orders from work-center control objects, they translate them into a set of activity orders that are carried out sequentially based on a programmed control that may perform condition checks such as physical material being available at that particular location, etc. This is where non-programmed control links to programmed control and decision processes are connected to physical activities.

The other model relevant data such as product order arrival patterns, customer types, order sizes, requested due-dates, processing times, MTTB, and MTTR are all specified by the model developer during model definition using the standard probability distributions provided in the system.

## 5 EXPERIMENTATION

The developed Smalltalk based simulation environment is tested through a simple make-to-order production system. The example with its system, shop, and work-center planning entities is simulated for three months period (43,200 min. with 480 min./day). A one factor four levels experiment is designed to compare the performance of the system with or without different levels of knowledge based control. Considering the make-to-order nature of the manufacturing system, the following three statistics are analyzed.
1) *Throughput time*: Time between the release of a product order by the system controller and the completion of that order.
2) *Order lateness*: Time difference between the completion of an order and its due-date.
3) *Customer response time*: Time between the arrival of a customer to the system and the completion time for all the products requested by the customer in that order.

In addition, traditional simulation statistics such as machine utilizations and queue statistics are collected. Throughput time is selected as the main statistic of interest.

### 5.1 Experimental levels

The four experimental levels are defined as follow:

1) Manufacturing system without non-programmed control. The orders at all levels are translated into suborders and immediately released to the next level. The orders mostly accumulate at the machine control level where they are processed according to FIFO.

2) Only system level non-programmed control is employed using *systemPlanning* knowledge base. The lower level controls are programmed decisions and orders are processed using FIFO.

3) The system and shop control object both use their knowledge bases simultaneously.

4) The system, shop, and work-center control objects all use their knowledge bases simultaneously.

The main idea behind this experimental design is to perform a tighter timing and status control around product, component, and batch orders as they move downward in the control hierarchy. The frequency of consultations with the relevant knowledge bases during the simulation is different for each control level. The work-center knowledge bases are the most frequently queried ones, shop knowledge bases next, and the system knowledge base is the least. Five replications are made for each level. Common random number seeds are used to reduce variance during pair wise comparison of the difference between throughput times (in minutes) of levels. The random number seeds are changed between replications but kept the same across the levels. Furthermore, to better observe the effect of non-programmed control, the manufacturing system is slightly overloaded.

## 5.2 Output analysis

The simulation output is analyzed as follow: First, level 1 is compared with level 2 by taking the difference between mean throughput times of five replication pairs. Then, a 95% confidence interval is constructed for the true mean difference. The same procedure is applied for pair-wise comparison of other levels.

The pair-wise statistical analysis of the simulation output yielded the following conclusions.

*Levels 1 - 2*: The confidence interval for the true mean difference does not contain zero and completely lies in the positive region. Therefore, the difference is statistically significant and the system yields smaller mean throughput values when system level non-programmed control is employed.

*Levels 2 - 3*: The confidence interval for the true mean difference contains zero, implying that there is not enough statistical evidence to claim that one level is better than the other. The length of the interval suggests that more replications needed to reach a conclusion. Therefore, we can not claim that system performs better when shop and system level non-programmed control are employed simultaneously. Main reason for this conclusion is that the performance of the system heavily depends on the particular knowledge bases designed. Since this pair wise comparison did not yield a preference between the levels, levels 2 and 3 are pair-wise compared to level 4.

*Levels 2 - 4*: Although relatively wide, the confidence interval for the true mean difference does not contain zero and lies in the positive values region. Therefore, with the sample runs on hand we can claim that the throughput time is shorter when system, shop, and work-center levels use their knowledge bases simultaneously.

*Levels 3 - 4*: The confidence interval for the true mean throughput time difference lies in the right hand side of zero. Thus, the system yields shorter throughput times when all knowledge bases are employed simultaneously.

# 6 CONCLUSIONS

From the above statistical analysis, it is concluded that system performs best when non-programmed control is used at all control levels. This conclusion was somewhat expected and suggests that unless a sound non-programmed and programmed control scheme is applied at the shop floor level, the benefits that will be obtained from upper level non-programmed control will diminish and will not significantly impact the overall performance of the system. The other statistics collected such as customer response time and order lateness showed a similar trend. In general, throughput time can be improved by using shortest processing time (SPT) rule in programmed control, but since it does not take due-date information into account, it may severely deteriorate order lateness statistics. By using due-date, lead time, present state of the system together in the knowledge bases, we can define rules that make measured compromises among conflicting aspects of several system performance measures. Although not statistically analyzed, traditional measures such as utilization statistics and queue statistics showed that as layers of non-programmed hierarchical control are added, queue lengths were shorter and machine utilizations gave smaller values due to better batch timing.

The other possible set of experiments such as making replications with only shop or work-center knowledge base or other combinations to see combined and/or stand alone effects of the knowledge bases is left as a future investigation area. Also, other programmed control rules such as LIFO, STP, other control heuristics, and more refined knowledge bases and inference rules will be investigated in the future.

Another major advantage of this modeling framework developed is the flexibility it brings into the simulation and modeling process. The operations of both physical and logical aspects of a manufacturing system modeled not only closely represents reality but, are very modular and easy to change. This system can easily be used as a demonstration tool to show that various local optimization rules and procedures of different control levels (or even different modules of the same level), when put together, may deteriorate total system performance. It can also be a very useful tool to shown how conflicting multiple objectives of different control levels interact and affect global performance. The system will allow the design of operational policies and rules at each control level that will best fit overall system goals. The developed simulation tool is compared against traditional simulation approaches, where only physical entities with their implicit control structures are simulated, using Analytic Hierarchy Process (AHP) (Karacal et. al, 1996b). The results of the AHP study clearly indicate that this new approach is preferable to the traditional approach.

## 7 REFERENCES

Karacal, S. C., and J. Mize (1996a) A Formal Structure for Discrete Event Simulation, Part I: Modeling Multiple
Level Systems. IIE Transactions, **28**, 753-760, 1996.

Karacal, S. C., T. Beaumariage, Z. Karacal (1996b) Comparison of Simulation Environments Through Analytic Hierarchy Process. Proceedings of 1996 Winter Simulation Conference, San Diego, CA

Karacal, S. C., and J. Mize (1997a) A Formal Structure for Discrete Event Simulation, Part II: Object Oriented Software Implementation for Manufacturing Systems. will appear in IIE Transactions, 1997.

Karacal, S. C. (1997b) A goal Decomposition Language for Manufacturing System Simulation. Proceedings of IE Research Conference, 1997, Miami Beach, FL.

Karacal, S. C. (1997c) A Formal Structure for Discrete Event Simulation, Part III: Knowledge Processing During Simulation. Working technical paper, 97-2, SIUE, Industrial Engineering, Edwardsville, IL, working technical paper 97-2.

## 8 BIOGRAPHY

S. Cem Karacal is an assistant professor of Industrial Engineering at Southern Illinois University at Edwardsville. He received his B.S. degree in IE from Orta Dogu Teknik Universitesi, Turkey, in 1982, and M.S. and Ph.D. degrees in IE from Oklahoma State University in 1986 and 1991, respectively. He has tree years of experience in industry and consulting. His primary areas of interest are object oriented modeling methodologies, AI applications in simulation, and semiconductor manufacturing scheduling. He is a member of IIE, SME, Alpha Pi Mu, and Tau Beta Pi.

# 53

# An intelligent planning network for manufacturing systems management

*G. L. Kovács, I. Mezgár*
*Computer and Automation Research Institute, HAS*
*H-1111 Budapest, Kende u. 13-17.,*
*Hungary*
*Fax: 36-1-1667-503*
*e-mail: h673kov@ella.hu*

**Abstract**

The paper describes a planning network (PN) which is to assist the better harmonization and higher quality and production volume of Small and Medium Size Enterprises (SME), if they are joining their efforts by being active members of the PN. The PN means a real-time, on-line network with three basic functions. The local planning module (LPM), the co-ordination unit (CU) and the evaluation module (EM) are the three software units that cover the functions. This PN is a kind of virtual, or extended enterprise, however it is different because of the long-term co-operation of the partners, instead of working together only for 1-2 given orders. The intelligence of the PN is supported by expert systems in the CU and EM.

**Keywords**

Computer networks, enterprise modelling, expert systems, SME.

## 1 INTRODUCTION

In order to fulfil the market demands the flexible, effective manufacturing system architectures become more and more popular around the world. Manufacturing enterprises have a geographically distributed nature, so computer networks for production management are important feature of their operation.

There are different approaches, different names that basically cover the same idea: a flexible network of co-operating autonomous manufacturing units. The holonic manufacturing systems is an approach for a theoretical framework for

Computer Applications in Production and Engineering. F. Plonka and G. Olling (Eds.)

autonomous and decentralized manufacturing organizations e.g., agile manufacturing enterprise (AME). There are different projects and developments on AME (AIMS/Stanford & EIT, A-PRIMED/SNL, FFC/MIT, etc.) that use different names for the AME, e.g., "extended enterprise" or "virtual enterprise (VE)".

The structure of a virtual enterprise can be seen as a heirarchy, in that it is a temporary, goal-oriented aggregation of several individual enterprises. Each virtual enterprise is created to pursue a specific business objective, and remains in life for as long as this objective can be pursued. After that, the individual nodes resume their independence from each other. The resource of a node that was previously allocated to the expired business is re-directed toward the node's individual goals, or toward other virtual enterprises it may have joined.

The virtual enterprise model has been developed for decomposing large companies that have enough financial, human and organizational resources. The decomposition is based on functions that can result in replications across the network.

Many geographic regions can be characterised with special industrial organisational structures called Small and Medium Sized Enterprise (SME). These SMEs are well-known for their dynamic behaviour, but their prosperity, and sometimes their existence, is continuously exposed to risks of the limited investment capability, the difficulty of diverting skilled personnel from day-by-day activities, to undertake process re-engineering initiatives, the lack of advanced planning support tools specifically conceived for them. Because of these reasons it is even a harder problem for the SMEs to give proper answer for the market challenges. The co-ordination of the different SME's production in case of producing a product jointly generates similar problems as in the case of large firms, but the solution is different (Bonfatti 3, 1996).

In a distributed manufacturing environment the production planning has a key role. The co-ordination of the orders, the optimal assignment of the different resources in a co-operative production of several SMEs is a very difficult task. In an SME network there is a strong need of a network model that is based on the planning strategy (Bonfatti 1, 1994). Another important goal during the software development is the product independence, i.e. the network model has to be general enough, to be able to apply it in a wide range of different products, in different production environments.

Our SME network development work is done in the frame of the "PLENT"-ESPRIT Project No. 20723 with the participation of firms from Italy, Greece, Hungary and Spain. The main goal of the project is to support organizations that manufacture mechanical parts and products in SME-like production environments. The paper shortly describes a special application of the manufacturing network model for agriculture production (oil and seed production) to demonstrate the applicability of this management philosophy and network model in fully different fields.

# 2 THE PLENT PROJECT

## 2.1 Comparison of the holonic/virtual and the PLENT approach

In the PLENT project a practical approach of the virtual enterprise has been realized for SMEs. In order to give a better understanding the PLENT approach will be shortly introduced in comparison with the classical holonic theory as it was discussed by Koestler (1989).

The holonic manufacturing system is a system of co-operating holons that are organized to achieve a production goal. This system integrates the whole range of manufacturing activities from order booking through design, production and marketing to form an autonomous and decentralized manufacturing organization.

According to the holonic organization paradigm the manufacturing environment is going to transform itself into a holonic system as the openness, the flexibility and the similarity in building blocks are vital advantages. The virtual enterprise is a practical instantiation of the holonic paradigm in the form of a multilayer, open, flexible (through continuous, dynamic re-configuration) network.

As the PLENT project aims to coordinate the production of SMEs the holonic approach had to be modified. The SMEs have limited financial and human resources. Usually they have no advanced planning support tools that are essential for a fully open VE. There is also a historical background namely the traditional individualistic attitude of SMEs. This means the facing of marketing, design, engineering, technological innovation and purchasing problems alone. Handling the SME network as a limited number of independent nodes has the following advantages:

- More complex and technologically advanced products can be realised by putting together skills and design capabilities of the network nodes.
- Higher manufacturing volumes are obtained by cumulating node capacities, especially if two or more nodes concur in performing the same manufacturing phases.
- Fluctuations of market demand volumes are better borne by sharing workload peaks and shortages among the network nodes.
- The limited resources of each SME are better spent in technological innovation and process re-engineering rather than in hard competition with other SMEs.

In consideration of the requirements expressed by SMEs, it is possible to compare the PLENT idea of virtual enterprise with that currently derived from the holonic theory (Bonfatti 2, 1995). Indeed, a number of properties commonly attributed to the virtual enterprise are no longer valid when transferred to the PLENT organisation model. The most significant differences between the two approaches are listed:

- Functional specialization versus flexibility;
- System duplication versus identity preservation;
- Temporary versus stable aggregation;
- Local versus global network co-ordination.

In conclusion, the PLENT VE model project focuses on distributed production management in a stable network of co-operating SMEs. The initial phases of network design and creation, as well as the pre-existing relationships that made co-operation possible, are outside the project scope. A detailed description can be found in Deliverable D2 (1996).

## 2.2 PLENT manufacturing network model

In order to achieve the required network timeliness and co-ordination neutrality, the PLENT network organisation must be supported by expressly designed planning tools. In particular, three software modules are required: a co-ordination module, a local planning module and a performance evaluation module.

- Co-ordination module
  The co-ordination module realises the network planning policy. The co-ordination module is responsible for controlling the connection outside the network, for keeping the contact with the customers, for selecting the proper nodes (production units) and for distributing production tasks to them.
- Local planning module
  The local planning module supports the network-related activities in charge of each node, aimed at managing and communicating delivery plans and delivery conditions with the co-ordination unit and the supplier and client nodes. The local planning modules realise the network controlling tasks of the node, in order to fulfil the goals of the management and communication, and deliver the status information of the node for the other nodes.
- Performance evaluation module
  The performance evaluation module is used by the co-ordinating unit to calculate node reliability starting from measures of their past behaviours, and network reaction capability by simulating possible scenarios. The performance evaluation module supports the work of the co-ordination unit in selecting the best node for fulfilling a task. This node generates different measures, statistics; estimations based on the past behaviour of the nodes.

Based on the PLENT VE approach the four different national networks of the project participants are under development. The product profiles of the national networks are different, demonstrating by this fact that this type of virtual manufacturing approach can be applied under different circumstances. In the following chapter the main characteristics and the organization of the Hungarian Network will be presented.

# 3 DESCRIPTION OF THE HUNGARIAN NETWORK

The main activities in the Hungarian Network (HN) are connected to the co-ordination unit that is an investment Co. These are: financing oil seed growing on plantations, seed-oil production and trading with the products which are the seeds and the seed-oils. The products as physical objects are seeds, seed-oils and contracts for production with farms and factories, and contracts for trading with trading houses. The market of the products is in Hungary and abroad. The main functionality is contracting partners to produce and to sell and buy. There is a management and a staff to prepare contracts using advanced forecasting and trend analysis tools. The product delivery cycle is unique: no cycle for the contract, however there is a special cycle for the seeds and oils covered by the contracts, as financing starts very early, 3-12 months before harvesting. There are three different profiles of individual nodes in the network:

- Big farms and oil pressing factories. Their activities include market research, approval, contract preparation, contracting, growing the seeds on the plantations and delivery of seeds or pressed oils.
- Small farms and seed-producers. Their activities are basically the same as above, but they are organized in one big group.
- Trading houses. Their activities include the seed and oil purchasing, the selling of the purchased goods and the cashing of the money.

For detailed description and analysis of the HN please see in Deliverable D01 (1996). The evaluation module is an independent software node in the first pilot implementation.

# 4 PLANNING REQUIREMENTS FOR THE HN

The PN means a real-time, on-line network with three basic functions. The intelligence of the Hungarian PN is supported by expert systems in the CU and EM. The CU and the EM software may be included into any of the nodes, or they may be independently implemented, a LPM must belong to all participating nodes. The tasks of the expert systems are double; they solve the planning problems of the network and parallel handle/control the complex communication among the CU and the EMs.

Before starting the ES development the planning requirements for the ESs have to be investigated very carefully, in order to avoid critical problems later.

## 4.1 Planning requirements for the co-ordination unit

- Subcontracted seed and oil production orders monitoring.
  It is interesting for the co-ordination unit be able to consult in any moment the production order's list launched for a given order. In addition it shows all

the associated data with each order, like the following: start date, forecast delivery, progress state of the work, etc.

- Node workload monitoring
  The co-ordination unit could see in any moment the forecast workload for each node for a period of time. This information is very important for the workload distribution between the nodes. In order to get this, it is necessary to update periodically the information used by the co-ordination unit.
- Monitoring of the accepted and pending subcontracting offers
  The co-ordination unit requires having a list of the subcontracting offers for each special product and partner. So the co-ordination unit could control the state of each offer like accepted, pending of acceptance, to be sent to the node.
- Sending of the planning of the subcontracted groups to the nodes for their fulfilment.
  The node needs to receive the current information and the group planning. The co-ordination unit defines some milestones. The node would establish the milestone's date and this information would return to the co-ordination unit.
- Linking between the co-ordination unit planning and the node planning.
  The co-ordination unit divides the planning in some activities. These activities might be used in the node planning, so they could be controlled from the co-ordination unit that should know the manufacturing progress. This information exchange might be in an electronic environment or similar. So each time the co-ordination unit connects with a node it is getting the last information.

*Task distribution and task assignment criteria*

As it was mentioned above, in principle all nodes are capable of accomplishing any of the production tasks. Due to historical reasons and work sharing it is normal to have a distribution as not all partners have oil pressing facilities among producers, and the trading houses are different in relations and in their main lines (special seeds, or oils, or both).

*Workload distribution*

The workload distribution is accomplished when the needs calculations are performed. This is the moment when the seed growing, oil production and marketing launches for each group are assigned. The local planning task is made using different methods (not necessarily computerized) at different sites.

## 4.2 Planning requirements for the nodes

- Forecasting, trends and market analysis.
  The co-ordination unit and the node's computer systems are similar, so it is interesting to have a more automatic information exchange method.
  The first application for this automation might be the exchange of the forecasting and analysis data from the co-ordination unit to the nodes. With

this automation some actual steps could be avoided and some benefits, like: paper reduction, reduce the time required in the information entry, and less writing errors, etc. might be obtained like.

- Access to the co-ordination general planning in order to foresee the workload. After making the first planning from the co-ordination unit this information might be sent to each node telling them the potential production/trading needs and the estimated dates. With this information the node might foresee their necessary production/trading for a period of time. One benefit of this policy would be that the nodes would avoid or would reduce some bottlenecks in their production.
- Anticipated prevision of the potential orders and workload. This point would be a consequence of the previous point.
- Group design evolution in the co-ordination unit. If the node knows in advance his workload, the node might take some information from the co-ordination unit about the state of the design activities related with the product group it has to produce. So depending upon the design state the node might foresee potential delays in the preparation and re-planning its local planning.
- To dispose a local planning tool with a finite capacity. It might be interesting in order to optimize the workload.
- To define the verification cards between the co-ordination unit and the nodes. The co-ordination unit sends to the nodes all the required information about the production group. Besides the co-ordination unit sends to the nodes a verification card, where it defines the verification requirements. So the node might participate in the verification card definition in order to optimize the quality process.

In Table 1, a few rules/actions are introduced for re-planning the original production plan in case of special, unscheduled events (problems).

Table 1. Some selected rules/actions for re-planning the original production plan

| Problem | Action |
|---|---|
| The node refuses the appraised offer. | 1. Subcontract to another node.<br>2. Make new offer appraises.<br>3. Production subcontracting to other nodes, out of the network. |
| The node can not finish the work on time. | 1. To urge the node in order to finish the work on time.<br>2. Depending of the final evolution.<br>2.1. If it not suppose perturbation in the final business, the activity is re-planned.<br>2.2. If it suppose perturbation in the final business, the activity is re-planned and the customer is advised and explained the reasons and the future actions. |
| The node's supplier is out of the delivery time. | 1. Ask to the customer to urge the supplier in order to supply on time.<br>2. Ask to the co-ordination unit to urge the supplier in order to supply on time. |
| Customer modification. | 1. Re-negotiate with the customer.<br>2. To communicate to the nodes.<br>3. Project re-planning. |
| Disfunction on the production groups. | 1. If it is very expensive, advice to the node in order to re-organize it in the co-ordination unit.<br>2. If it is simple, it is re-organized by the co-ordination unit. |

### 4.3 Communication and information exchange

In case of a planning network the definition of the regular communication relations, routes in the design phase of the network are very important. Table 2 shows part of the communication and information exchange requirements with the following assumptions (Information exchange is really bi-directional in most cases, this is shown by multiple arrows):

- There is no communication between production and trade nodes. They communicate only with the co-ordination unit
- The customer has no direct contact to the production and trade nodes, only to the co-ordination unit
- The co-ordination unit is the investment Co. in our special case (as soon as an independent co-ordination unit will be established it would be changed to a more special local node)

Table 2. A part of the information exchange among the nodes and the CU

| DOCUMENT | CUSTO-MER | CO-ORDINATI-ON UNIT | PRODUC-TION NODE | TRADE NODE |
|---|---|---|---|---|
| Consult | ⇨ | | | |
| Standards | ⇨ | | | |
| Offer | | ⇦ | ⇦ | ⇦ |
| Order | ⇨ | ⇨ | | |
| Demand | ⇨ | ⇨ | | |
| Supply | | ⇦ | ⇦ | ⇦ |
| Planning | | ⇦ | ⇦ | ⇦ |
| Accepted offer | | ⇦ | ⇦ | ⇦ |
| Rejected offer | | ⇦ | ⇦ | ⇦ |
| Order | ⇨ | ⇨ | | |
| Product | | | ⇦ | ⇦ |
| Capacity | | | ⇦ | ⇦ |
| Forecast | | ⇨ | ⇦ | ⇦ |
| Contract | ⇨ | ⇦ ⇨ | ⇦ | ⇦ |

### 4.4 Expected benefits

The main advantage of using the described network is the more effective usage of each SMEs (farms, oil pressing factories) resources, faster reaction for market demands while keeping the individual characteristic of each node (farm). Through this coordination the production of a very unstable, unreliable (working with high risk) production field, the agricultural production can become more reliable, more safe both for the customer and the farmers that are members of the network. The reliability leads to more orders, stabilized and higher income, less costs i.e. more profit. The expected costs of the investment (network installation and software) are low, to learn the applied information technology needs only short time, so the PLENT manufacturing network has good chances for success in agricultural field as well.

## 5 CONCLUSIONS

In the PLENT approach, a production network is conceived as a set of operational nodes with equal rights, co-ordinated by a central unit that interacts with customers, distributes tasks to nodes on the basis of prefixed criteria and up-to-date information on node state and reliability, and informs each node on its position in the network with respect to the manufacturing process. These tasks are realized by an expert system, that deals both with the planning/re-planning and the control of communication among CU and the nodes.

This new approach for SME network coordination is very promisable, because it offers the advantages of the holonic manufacturing paradigm parallel giving the possibility of keeping the traditional individualism of SMEs. The realization of the method is going on in four countries involving SMEs from three different fields of production (in machine- and textile industry, in agriculture).

The results achieved so far prove that it is possible to develop network based co-ordination software for SMEs that is general enough to be applied in fully different production fields. The early experiments show that the ISDN-based Hungarian Network has a good perspective. The program development phase has already started using Visual C++ and SYBASE.

## 6 REFERENCES

Bonfatti 1, F., Monari, P. D. and Paganelli, P. (1994). Modeling manufacturing resources and activities: an ontology. In: *Proc. of ICCIM '95 Intern.Conf., Computer Integrated Manufacturing, Singapore, 1995*, Edited by J. Winsor, etc., p.p. 101-108. World Scientific, Singapore.

Bonfatti 2, F. and Monari, P. D. (1995) Planning small-medium enterprise networks. In: *Proc. of the IMPDE Internal. Conf., Edinburgh, 1995*, p.p. 13-22, Sponsored by European Commission DGIII, ESPRIT Consortium 9245.

Bonfatti 3, F., Monari, P. D. and Paganelli, P. (1996) Co-ordination Functions in a SME Network. In: *Proc. of BASYS '96 Intern. Conf., Balanced Automation Systems II, Lisbon, 1996*, Edited by L.M. Camarinha-Matos etc., p.p. 383-390. Chapman & Hall, London.

Koestler A. (1989) *The Ghost in The Machine*, Arkana Books.

PLENT ESPRIT project 20723, Deliverable D01 (1996). Requirement Specification and Analysis.

PLENT ESPRIT project 20723, Deliverable D02 (1996). Planning Policy Formalisation.

## 7 BIOGRAPHY

**George L. Kovács** graduated at the Technical University of Budapest, Faculty of Electrical Engineering, 1966. Dr. degree (Ph.D.) at the same university, 1976. Candidate of sciences degree at the Hungarian Academy of Sciences, 1978 (CAD/CAM in electronics). Research fellow in the Computer and Automation Institute of the Hungarian Academy of Sciences since 1966. He got his habilitation and Prof. degree at the Technical Univ. of Budapest in 1995. Recently head of CIM Research Laboratory since 1990. Visiting researcher in the USA (one year), Soviet Union (two years), West Germany (one year) and visiting professor in Mexico (six months). In 1994 he was visiting professor in Italy, University of Trento. More than 100 scientific publications. Deputy chairman of the Eastern European MAP/TOP Interest Group, member of several scientific organizations. Scientific interest: CIM, computer aided design and manufacturing, expert and hybrid systems, industrial networks.

**István Mezgár** [Diploma in m.e.: 1977, special Diploma in automation engineering: 1988, dr.Univ in m.e.: 1990, all from the *Technical University of Budapest (TU)*, C.Sc. in m.e.: 1995, from the *Hungarian Academy of Sciences*] is a senior researcher at the *CIM Research Laboratory at the Computer and Automation Research Institute, Hungarian Academy of Sciences.* Visiting researcher/professor at the *University of Trento*, at the *University of Genoa* (Italy, in 1989-90), at the *University of Waikato* (New Zealand, in 1995), and at the *CAD/CAM Research Laboratory, Korea Institute of Science and Technology* (South-Korea, in 1995-96). IPC member of several international *IFAC, IFIP* conferences. More than 60 scientific publications. His current interests focus on manufacturing automation, integration of product and enterprise models, agile manufacturing systems, design methodologies (e.g. concurrent engineering) and complex quality control.

# 54

# An enterprise integration framework for manufacturing environments

*F.B. Vernadat*
*LGIPM - Fac. des Sciences*
*University of Metz, Ile du Saulcy, F-57012 Metz cedex 1, France*
*Phone: +33 3 87 34 67 23 Fax: +33 3 87 34 69 35*
*E-mail: vernadat@agip.univ-metz.fr*

**Abstract**

Enterprise Integration (EI) deals with increasing interoperability among people, machines and applications to enhance synergy within an enterprise to better achieve business objectives. EI is both an organizational and a technological problem. An enterprise integration framework is presented in this paper for manufacturing environments based on works performed in projects of the European ESPRIT program (AMICE, AIT, OPAL). The framework relies on advanced technologies for systems and application integration (integration platforms, request brokers, electronic data and information interchange standards, workflow engines). It also includes an enterprise modeling framework to deal with business process and organizational aspects at the business integration level, with a special emphasis on human aspects.

**Keywords**

Enterprise Integration, Enterprise modeling, Manufacturing systems, CIM, Integration platforms, AIT, OPAL

## 1 INTRODUCTION

Enterprise Integration (EI) deals with increasing interoperability among people, machines and applications to enhance synergy within an enterprise to better achieve business objectives. This is a technological as well as an organizational problem. It can be limited to the scope of one enterprise or extended to several enterprises involved in a common supply chain (extended enterprise).

Computer Applications in Production and Engineering. F. Plonka and G. Olling (Eds.)

There is the need to develop frameworks for enterprise integration as well as technical solutions to achieve integration. Enterprise integration frameworks provide reference architectures and guidelines for business users to understand the purpose and scope of EI, position and compare potential solutions and explain relationships among these solutions. Examples of such frameworks are CIMOSA (AMICE, 1993), the European pre-norm CEN ENV 40 003 (CEN, 1990) or the GERAM framework of the IFAC/IFIP Task Force on Architectures for Enterprise Integration (Williams *et al.*, 1994; Williams, 1995). Technical solutions consist of methods, modeling tools, software packages, and standards as well as particular architectures. The bad news for business users is that they are characterized by their tremendous diversity and frequent incompatibility.

In this paper, EI is first defined with regards to the manufacturing context (including inter- and intra-enterprise integration). A global framework for enterprise integration is then presented as a result of a study conducted by AIT, a European initiative for advanced IT in design and manufacturing. The framework relies on advanced technologies for systems and application integration, including communication networks and protocols, distributed computing environments, shared databases, electronic data interchange and data exchange formats as well as hypertext. The business integration level addresses business process modeling at various stages of the enterprise life cycle (requirements, design, implementation) as recommended by reference architectures for EI (CIMOSA, ENV 40 003, GERAM). Emphasis is placed on the modeling of resource and organizational aspects of manufacturing enterprises, with a special emphasis on human aspects. The last section presents some conclusions.

## 2 ENTERPRISE INTEGRATION

Enterprise Integration (EI) is mostly concerned with breaking down organizational barriers and making the enterprise, or even a network of enterprises in the case of the extended enterprise, interoperable to improve enterprise efficiency and reactivity. It is essentially concerned with facilitating decision-making in distributed environments, simplifying business processes across the enterprise and providing the right information at the right place at the right time (Petrie, 1992; Vernadat, 1996).

**Organizational issues:** EI is first of all an organizational problem. If information and decisions are not properly transmitted, understood, managed or processed, then the enterprise will not operate correctly and its organizational structure has to be revisited before any technological change be made. Furthermore, the role of human resources remain central and essential in EI.

**Interoperability:** From a technological point of view, to make integration possible there is the need to facilitate communication exchange and sharing as well as inter-working throughout the company. This assumes the availability of an integrating infrastructure, i.e. a middleware facility with a set of computer services to support the exchange of messages, information or objects and to send requests to remote systems and receive responses.

Two types of enterprise integration problems can be distinguished: intra-enterprise integration versus inter-enterprise integration.

Intra-enterprise integration, or 'inside the four walls integration', typically refers to the CIM concept extended to the whole enterprise. Technologically, it could be achieved if company standards are imposed on the enterprise in terms of a limited number of compatible and interoperable pieces of equipment, standard interfaces and normalized procedures and data structures to be used. Although feasible, this would be a too rigid approach to meet the need for reactivity imposed nowadays by fluctuating market, business and technological conditions. The CIM concept must evolve towards EI to take into account agility, human factors as well as knowledge and decision-making distribution requirements.

Inter-enterprise integration concerns have emerged with the extended enterprise concept. The challenge is to face such realities as global markets, the rise of mass customization and the need to develop environmentally benign products and processes (Browne et al., 1995). The solution is to build networks of enterprises to look beyond 'the four walls of the manufacturing plants', i.e. control the whole value added chain to better serve the customer world-wide and have access to resources (human or technological) outside the enterprise. Inter-enterprise networking is the key. Again, this is first of all an organizational problem (e.g. choice of partners, business network, legal issues, intellectual rights, etc.) before being a technical problem (e.g. computer networks, distributed databases, EDI).

# 3 ENTERPRISE INTEGRATION FRAMEWORKS

## 3.1 General EI framework

Traditionally, three levels of integration are differentiated: physical or system integration, application integration and business integration (AMICE, 1993). Table 1 provides an indication of integration aspects covered by each level while Figure 1 provides an indication of technologies involved. Physical system integration is mostly concerned with system interconnection and message passing using computer communications networks. Integration services, distributed computing environments and object request brokers can then be implemented on top of these. Application integration builds on physical systems integration and is more concerned with application interoperability and distributed co-operative applications and requires data and information exchange using integration platforms (such as CORBA, AIT-IP or OPAL). Finally, business integration goes beyond application integration in terms of business process co-ordination and enterprise networking. It must take into account organizational issues and human factors and requires enterprise-wide knowledge sharing. This assumes a precise modeling of intimate enterprise details concerning enterprise procedures, organization, knowledge and know-how in the form of a shared enterprise model. Part of this model can be enacted using workflow engines and computer support for collaborative work (CSCW).

**Table 1** Integration levels and aspects

| Integration levels | Integration aspects | |
|---|---|---|
| Business | Business process coordination<br>Enterprise-wide knowledge sharing<br>Interworking; enterprise internetworking | Organisation and human issues |
| Application | Distributed cooperative applications<br>Data/information exchange<br>Application interoperability | Technological issues |
| Physical | Basic computer communication<br>Message passing<br>Interconnection | |

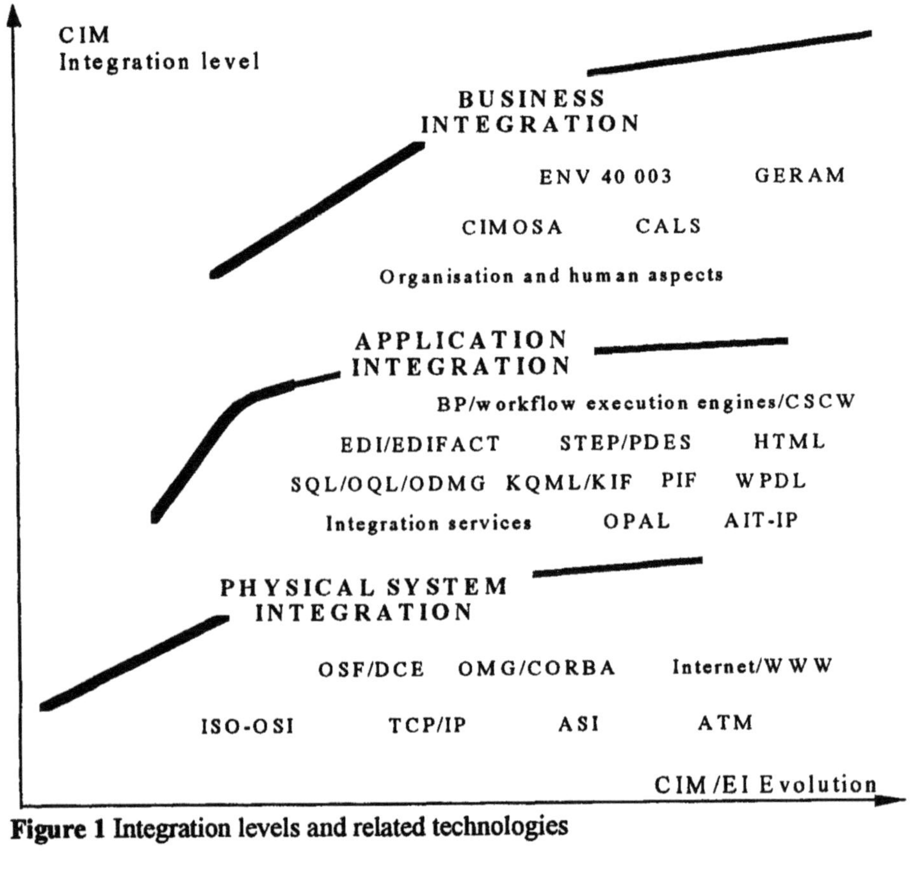


**Figure 1** Integration levels and related technologies

Figure 1 shows the diversity and complexity of technologies involved in EI. These are briefly discussed in subsequent sections. Historically, they have been tackled from the bottom level, i.e. from a technical point of view because of technology evolution reasons. However, from a methodological point of view and taking advantage of recent technology advances (concerning high speed networks, distributed computing environments, object-oriented technology, hypermedia technology, workflow management and CSCW), EI must be addressed first at the business level (concentrating on business process and organizational issues) and then at the technological levels (application and system levels).

To illustrate parts of the general framework, two examples (AIT-IP and OPAL) are discussed from our experience in integration platform development for integration in manufacturing, and especially from the ESPRIT program and its AIT initiative.

## 3.2 AIT-IP

AIT is a European initiative launched in 1993 for Advanced Information Technology in design and manufacturing activities. It is sponsored jointly by all major European manufacturers of the automotive and aerospace industries and by the ESPRIT Program of the Commission of the European Communities (CEC). Its aim is to identify industry requirements for future IT solutions and influence IT product development on the basis of a consensus built among IT users.

Among major requirements identified by AIT there is the need for an integration platform making the business support applications or BSAs (CAD/CAE, CAPP, MRP, CAM, SFC) independent from the IT basic infrastructure proposed by IT vendors, thus allowing their independent evolution (principle of application isolation). The integration platform must enable integration of business support applications using a 'plug and play' strategy to guarantee IT vendor independence and protection of previous investments (principles of modularity and interoperability).

To specify the requirements for such an integration platform, a reference model, called AIT ITRM for AIT IT Reference Model, has been defined (AIT, 1995). The AIT ITRM is an open, standard-based, non proprietary reference model defining middleware requirements for integration in large distributed manufacturing environments. The ITRM envisions integration as a set of interoperable integration platforms being installed at different user sites and providing a number of integration services. The ITRM is organized around a software bus (which could be CORBA-like object request broker) as depicted in Figure 2. Integration services include generic execution services (GESs), application front-ends (AFEs), machine front-ends (HFEs), human front-ends (MFEs), data server front-ends (DFEs) and communication front-ends (CFEs). In addition, system-wide actor directory management services record all functional entities (humans, machines or applications) used in the enterprise architecture and system-wide information management services access information models containing the enterprise model are mandatory.

These integration platforms with the necessary services can be installed on various sites of a company to integrate specified application systems. They can then be interconnected to one another to form an enterprise-wide network forming an integrating infrastructure for some part of an enterprise or for a group of enterprises (extended enterprise).

## 3.3 OPAL

OPAL is a software platform for integrated information and process management dedicated to design and manufacturing environments (OPAL, 1996). OPAL is developed as an ESPRIT project as part of the AIT initiative. OPAL takes advantage of modern technologies for information management and sharing including object request brokers, object-oriented database technology, neutral product and process data exchange formats such as STEP, workflow engines and hypermedia technology such as the HTML and the world-wide web (WWW).

The global system architecture of OPAL is presented by Figure 3. It consists of a data repository, an execution environment based on a workflow engine as well as a middleware layer (based on the CORBA object request broker) and central services for system-wide message and object exchange and interoperability.

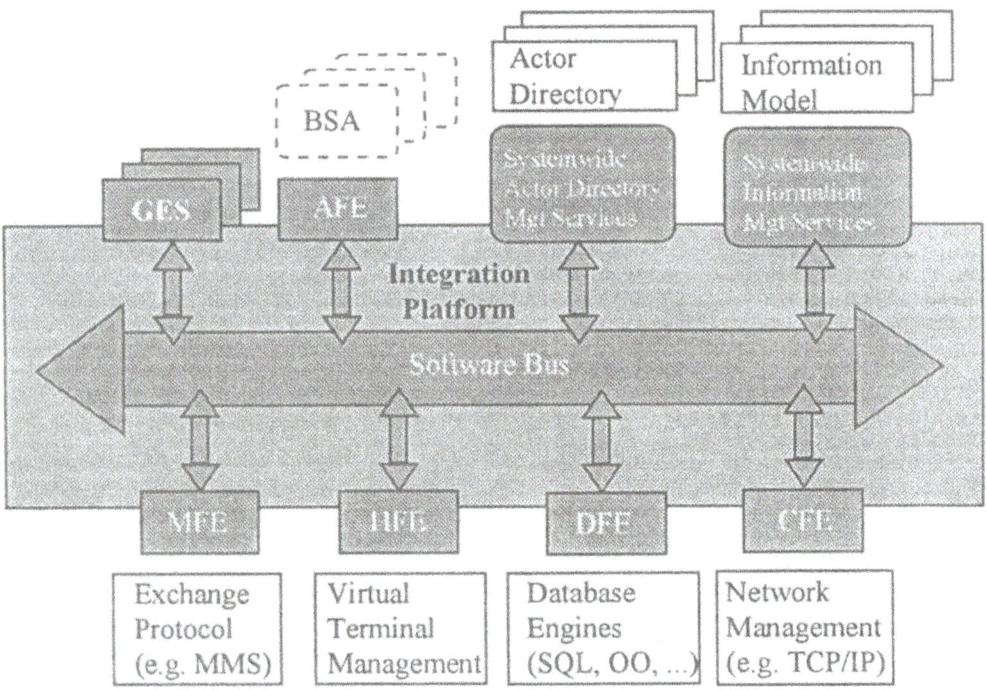


**Figure 2** The AIT integration platform

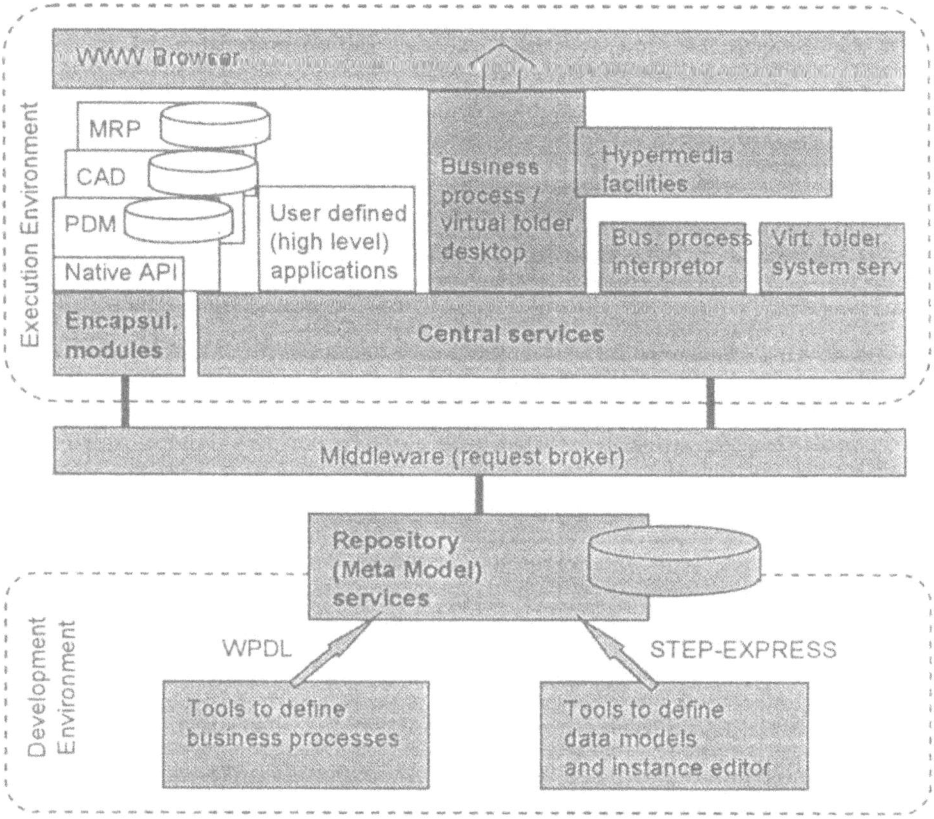


**Figure 3** OPAL general architecture

The enterprise repository containing business process, organization and data models to be used to control business support applications. Process models and data models are stored using a common object-oriented structure. Each application package (e.g. CAD, PDM or MRP system) must be encapsulated using its application program interface (API) to become an agent in the integrated system (encapsulation services). It can then be accessed by other modules via the middleware layer (based on CORBA) and the central services (naming services, time services, communication services and information services). Since this integrating infrastructure is dedicated to engineering and manufacturing data management, it also provides so-called virtual folder system services and WWW-browser facilities to deal with product data. The virtual folders are used to collect and transmit technical documents (e.g. CAD drawings, bills-of-materials, product documentation, simulation data, text files, etc.) put together as one document and to be exchanged by users or application systems across the system. Hypermedia web browsers facilities provide users with the ability to navigate through the product and process data to which they have access wherever they are located in the system.

The specification of OPAL took place in 1996 and a prototype is planned for the end of 1998. Two industrial pilot test cases are under development at PSA in France and Robert Bosch in Germany.

## 4 SYSTEMS INTEGRATION

The system integration layer has been the focus of tremendous research efforts over the last two decades both from the traditional EDP standpoint and the CIM standpoint. OSI (MAP/TOP) and non-OSI communications protocols (Ethernet, SNA) are now widely available both for local and wide area networks. The current trend is on one hand improving the performance of computer networks (bandwidth and speed) and on the other hand having simple, fast, low-cost communication at the equipment level.

The state of the art in manufacturing environments is to use field-buses (based on FIP or ASI protocols) at the equipment level, local area networks based on TCP/IP at the station, cell or plant levels and ATM technology at the cell, plant and enterprise levels.

Furthermore, Internet and web technology are rapidly penetrating the manufacturing area from design offices to shop floors. This is made possible by the emergence of the object-oriented technology and distributed computing environments such as OSF/DCE and OMG/CORBA.

## 5 APPLICATION INTEGRATION

For many companies it is important that their applications can inter-operate, i.e. work together and not in isolation whatever the operating systems, database systems or communication network regardless of the systems. Therefore, application integration concerns data/information exchange and sharing as well as application interoperability. Three complementary trends are currently under development in this area:

Data exchange formats and data and knowledge manipulation languages: Manufacturing and engineering data appear in various forms in an enterprise, including text, drawings, images and signals. Central to these are product and process data. Application integration thus relies on standards such as EDI for administrative data exchange, STEP for product and process data exchange and SGML for technical document exchange. In addition, access to data can be made via SQL to relational databases, OQL or ODMG for object-oriented databases and QKML/KIF can be used to exchange knowledge. PIF is a language developed as a process interchange format while WPDL is the workflow process description language of the Workflow Management Coalition (WfMC).

Integration services and integration platforms: The client/server architecture provides a basic model for the communication between two (remotely located) interacting or co-operative agents: the client and the server. The infrastructure linking agents in a client/server architecture is called an integration platform. AIT-IP and OPAL are examples of such platforms for the manufacturing industry. An integration platform is a set of computer services together with a middleware layer built on top of communication systems to facilitate message and request exchange among agents (or functional entities or actors) of a system. These services can deal with data transmission, data access security, transaction management, concurrency control, clock synchronization, binding a name to an object, tracing a request to a client, data presentation to an application, computer network access, to name a few.

Workflow management and enactment: Application packages are often used according to predefined business procedures called business processes and made up of a chain of activities to be executed in a given order to perform a business task. To control the execution of these processes, they can be modeled in the form of a workflow which can then be executed under the control of workflow execution engines.

To learn more about basic principles and techniques for application integration, the interested reader is referred to (Vernadat, 1996).

## 6 BUSINESS INTEGRATION AND ENTERPRISE MODELLING

So far the discussion has concentrated on the technological aspects of EI, essentially because this is the facet of EI which is best understood although still incompletely solved. In this section, we focus on logical aspects, and especially the organizational and human aspects, of EI. In practice, these are the concerns which must be addressed first.

From the experience gained on the development of CIMOSA (AMICE, 1993), it is the author's opinion that enterprise modeling (EM) plays a crucial role in EI. In fact, EM is a pre-requisite to EI (Vernadat, 1996).

Reference architectures for EI (CIMOSA, ENV 40 003, GERAM) suggest modeling business entities or enterprise domains according to four views (function, information, resources and organization views) and three modeling levels (requirements definition, design specification, implementation description).

Various methods have been recently published for enterprise modeling in manufacturing (IDEF suite of methods, GRAI/GIM, CIMOSA, IEM, ARIS, OMT). Users of the above modeling methods must make sure that in addition to modeling functional and information features other features such as resource and organization aspects, and especially human factors in terms of competencies and skills as well as decision-making abilities in terms of responsibilities and authorities, are correctly represented.

However, according to the PERA methodology (Williams, 1992), first it is fundamental that any integration project be preceded by a master planning activity to define the scope of the EI project, the mission to be achieved and the policies and strategies to be deployed. Second, during system development, it is essential to define the role and place of humans within the information and control architecture as well as in the manufacturing equipment architecture.

Therefore, enterprise modeling methods and tools must pay special attention to three fundamental aspects of industrial systems: business processes, agents and organizational aspects.

The modeling of business processes covers the modeling of the control, information and material flows within an enterprise. The control flow is represented by a workflow depicting the sequence of activities to be performed as an event-driven process chain. The information and material flows are defined by the inputs and outputs of activities involved in a business process. IDEF3 (Mayer et al. 1993) and the CIMOSA (Vernadat, 1993) process model are state-of-the-art methods in this field.

Agents represent the functional entities or actors of the system, i.e. any entity able to send, receive, process requests or even store information. They may represent autonomous devices, software applications or humans. Because of their dynamic nature and autonomy in terms of behavior, they need to be modeled separately from processes and be binded to processes only at run-time. Agents are usually characterized by their set of provided services (or interface), their set of offered capabilities, location, availability and sometimes capacity. In the case of human resources, important characteristics are skills and competencies. Once defined, these can be used to define a user's profile to fulfill a role as required by the execution of some activities of a process. Human skills are defined in terms of capabilities that a person can have or exhibit. Competencies are defined in terms of knowledge trees which describe domains of expertise and know-how possessed by users. The elaboration of knowledge trees requires the help of knowledge engineers.

Organizational aspects can be modeled in terms of organization units and organization cells. An organization unit is any functional entity or agent having some responsibility and authority. In other terms, it has some decision-making power on some part of the enterprise. Its area of responsibility and job profile must be known. Knowledge and know-how required for this duty can be modeled using knowledge trees and compared with knowledge trees of employees qualified for this job. Organization cells are aggregations of organization units or smaller organization cells to form a decision center within the enterprise. Each organization cell must be placed under the responsibility of an organization unit which must be a person. Decision centers can be organized into decision levels to construct the organization structure of the enterprise (be it hierarchical or decentralized).

While a lot of work has been done on the modeling of business processes and information systems of an enterprise, further work remains to be done on resource and organization aspects, and especially human factors, to build human-centered integrated manufacturing systems.

## 7 CONCLUSION

Enterprise Integration should be a target for any industrial company either struggling in a competitive environment or contributing to a network of partner companies. The benefits of EI should be increased efficiency and competitiveness by means of better communication, co-operation and co-ordination of the functional entities of the enterprise (in terms of co-ordination of business processes and enterprise-wide information sharing) and better reactivity to changing business conditions by a controlled management of change.

Nevertheless, business users must keep in mind that first EI is not a technology but a goal. It is first of all an organizational problem before being a technological problem. Moreover, EI is a never ending process. Even the best integrated manufacturing system can always be further integrated. New technologies and management principles can be constantly used to push integration boundaries forward. However, the real challenge with EI remains to be able to provide humans with the right tools, information, decision support or empowerment they need to perform their work more efficiently and in symbiosis with the rest of the enterprise.

## 8 REFERENCES

AIT (1995) The AIT IT Reference Model. AIT EP 7704, TWP7 Deliverable, December.

AMICE (1993). *CIMOSA: Open System Architecture for CIM, 2nd revised and extended version*. Springer-Verlag, Berlin.

Browne,J., Sackett, P. and Wortmann, H. (1995) Industry requirements and associated research issues in the extended enterprise, in *Integrated Manufacturing Systems Engineering* (P. Ladet and F. Vernadat, eds.), Chapman & Hall, London, 2-28.

CEN (1990) ENV 40 003: Computer-Integrated Manufacturing - Systems Architecture. - Framework for Enterprise Modeling. CEN/CENELEC, Brussels, January.

Mayer, R.J., Cullinane, T.P., deWitte, P.S., Knappenberger, W.B., Perakath, B., Wells, M.S. (1992) Information Integration for Concurrent Engineering (IICE) IDEF3 Process Description Capture Method Report. Air Force Systems Command, Wright-Patterson Air Force Base, Ohio 45433, AL-TR-1992-0057.

OPAL (1996) OPAL Architecture Definition. OPAL EP 20377, Deliverable 3.1.1, Dec.

Petrie, C. (ed.) (1992) *Enterprise Integration Modeling*, The MIT Press, Cambridge, MA.

Vernadat, F. (1993) CIMOSA: Enterprise modeling and enterprise integration using a process-based approach. In (H. Yoshikawa and J. Goossenaerts, eds.) *Information Infrastructure Systems for Manufacturing*, North-Holland, Amsterdam. pp. 65-84. (Invited paper).

Vernadat, F. (1996). *Enterprise Modeling and Integration: Principles and Application*. Chapman & Hall, London.

Williams, T.J. (1992) *The Purdue Enterprise Reference Architecture*, Instrument Society of America, Research Triangle Park, NC.

Williams, T.J. *et al.* (1994) Architectures for integrating manufacturing activities and enterprises, *Computers in Industry*, **24**(2-3), 111-139.

Williams, T.J. (1995) Development of GERAM, a generic enterprise reference architecture and enterprise integration methodology, in *Integrated Manufacturing Systems Engineering* (P. Ladet and F. Vernadat, eds.), Chapman & Hall, London, 279-288.

## 9 BIOGRAPHY

**François Vernadat** is a French and Canadian citizen. He holds a Master degree (1979) and the Ph.D. degree (1981) in Electronics and Automatic Control. He has been a research officer at the Division of Electrical Engineering, National Research Council of Canada, Ottawa (1981-1988) and then at INRIA, a French research institute in computer science and automatic control (1988-1995). He is currently a professor in automatic control and automation at University of Metz, France.

His research interests include CIM, database technology and information systems, enterprise modelling, enterprise integration, manufacturing systems specification, formal description techniques, Petri nets and workflow enactment. Beside his work on the M* methodology for CIM information systems, he has headed the development of a main-memory database system (DBS/R) and was one of the chief architects of CIMOSA, an Open Systems Architecture for CIM developed as a series of ESPRIT projects (AMICE). He is the author of over 120 scientific papers in journals, conferences and books. He is the author of "*Enterprise Modeling and Integration: Principles and Applications*", a co-author of the book "*Practice of Petri nets in Manufacturing*" and a co-editor of the book "*Integrated Manufacturing Systems Engineering*", all published by Chapman & Hall. He has been a co-chairman and invited speaker of several conferences on CIM. He is the European editor for the *International Journal of Computer-Integrated Manufacturing* and a member of the scientific committee of other journals and conferences.

Dr. Vernadat served several times as a technical expert for the CIM programme of the Commission of the European Communities (CEC). He is the vice-chairman of two IFAC Technical Committees (Manufacturing Modelling, Management and Control and Architectures for Enterprise Integration) and a member of the IFAC/IFIP Task Force on Architectures for Enterprise Integration. He is a member of the IEEE Computer Society, ACM and SME.

# 55

# IMAGIM+
# A knowledge-based system for enterprise modeling

*A. Moudden, E. Reategui, G. Doumeingts.*

*LAP/GRAI, University of Bordeaux I*
*351, Cours de la Libération, 33405 - Talence - France*
*Tel: (+33) (5) 56 84 64 30*
*Fax: (+33) (5) 56 84 66 44*
*{ moudden, reategui, doumeingts}@lap.u-bordeaux.fr*

**Abstract**

From the beginning of the 80s, several methods for enterprise modelling have been developed, among which the GRAI approach. The GRAI Integrated Methodology (GIM) is one methodology belonging to the GRAI approach, enabling the modelling of the enterprises' physical and informational systems, as well as their decisional system. *Imagim+* is the software support to GIM, providing assistance for the implementation of the approach. Imagim+ is composed of a set of integrated graphic editors for each formalism used in the GIM methodology (*grids, nets, Idef0 and E/R diagrams*). Besides its graphical capabilities, the software has an expert system to validate and diagnose malfunctions in the models built. This paper presents *Imagim+*, describing its main functionalities and use in enterprise modelling.

**Keywords**

Enterprise modelling, consistency check, diagnostic, knowledge-based systems, GRAI approach.

## 1. INTRODUCTION

GIM (GRAI Integrated Methodology) has been conceived with the main goal of providing techniques and flexible tools for enterprise modelling. Having been

Computer Applications in Production and Engineering. F. Plonka and G. Olling (Eds.)

inspired on the GRAI approach (Doumeingts 84), GIM has extended it in order to model the totality of the enterprise, instead of focusing only on the decisional subsystem.

The GIM approach is implemented in three main phases: *the modelling phase*, where the initial model of the enterprise is produced; *the inconsistency search*, whose main objective is to detect inconsistencies and weak points in the enterprise studied; *the design phase,* where the design of the new system is elaborated based on the results of the previous phases. The software *Imagim+* has been built in order to support the implementation of GIM through all three phases. The software is composed of four graphic tools for the edition of the graphical formalisms employed, namely: GRAI grids, nets, Idef0 and Entity/Relationship (E/R) diagrams. Besides its graphical capabilities, *Imagim+* incorporates an expert system that validates and diagnoses malfunctions in the models built.

This paper presents the software *Imagim+*, describing its architecture and main functionalities. This paper is organised as follows: Section 2 gives a brief introduction to the formalisms used in GIM: Section 3 presents the architecture of *Imagim+*, outlining the structure and operation of its main components. Section 4 presents a practical example of the use of Imagim+ in the modelling of an enterprise which manufactures products under demand, in small scale; Section 5 presents some conclusions and directions for future work.

## 2. THE GIM FORMALISMS

The GIM formalisms have been chosen through a comparative study of different existing methods (Roboam 88). The main criteria used in the selection of each method have been the exactitude of the representation and its ease in interpretation. The formalisms employed in GIM are:

- *Idef0 (ICAM Definition)* - used for the modelling of the enterprise's functions and physical system. This formalism has been developed in the American project ICAM (Integrated Computed Aided Manufacturing), with the goal of representing in a hierarchical fashion and from a static point of view the functionalities of an enterprise. We will focus mainly on the modelling of the physical system. The models highlight the use of physical and human resources, as well as the flow of products (e.g. in case of manufacturing systems). The description of the physical system is initially done from a global level, indicating top-activities and then subdividing each activity to the level of specificity desired.
- the GRAI formalisms (grids and nets): used in the modelling of the enterprise's decisional system. The main advantage of using the two representation mechanisms is that while the grids enable the representation of the global structure of the decisional system, the nets can be used in the representation of the details and internal operation of the components of the decisional system. The grid has a matrix form which determines temporal

and functional aspects of the decisional system. The nets provide a more refined view of the decisional system, detailing the activities defined in the decision centres of the grid.

- *Entity/Relationship*: used in the modelling of the informational system. In the context of a GIM study, this representation mechanism is used mainly for the description of the conceptual and structured information models.

Below, the GRAI grids are further explained, as they are used later to illustrate the modelling of the decisional system of an enterprise. The reader is referred to Zanettin (1994) for a more detailed description of all the formalisms used in GIM.

The GRAI grids have been conceived to describe the global structure of the decisional systems. The horizontal axis of the grid is decomposed in different functions (in the example of figure 1: to manage resources, to plan, etc.), while the vertical axis is divided into two temporal lines: horizon and period. The decisional system is then globally described in the grid by placing decision centres according to their function and to the scope of their decision.

Links between the different decision centres are also described in the grid, Two types of links exist: informational and decisional. The latter is called decision frame and comprises objectives to reach, constraints, decision variables and criteria. In the grid, the decision frame is represented by a framed arrow and the information flow by a simple arrow. The basic structure of a GRAI grid is presented in Figure 1.

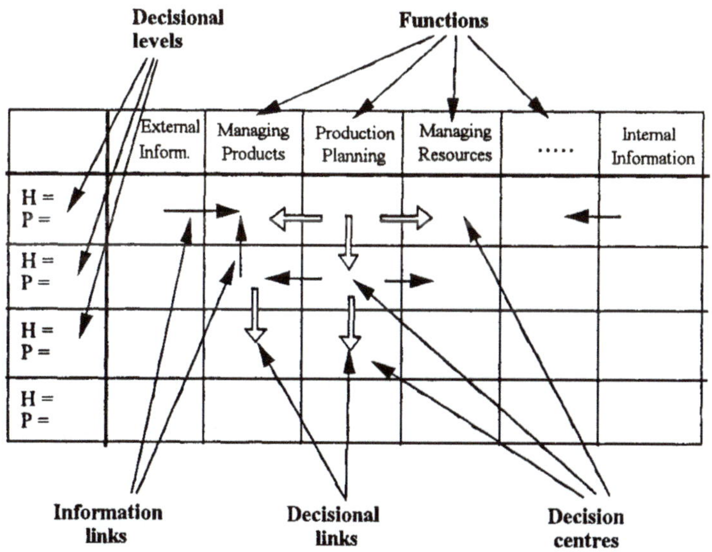


**Figure 1**: The GRAI grid.

## 3. THE ARCHITECTURE OF IMAGIM+

Figure 2 presents the architecture of Imagim+. The knowledge-based system has been divided into three portions: the editors, the database system and the rule-based system. The next subsections describe each of these components.

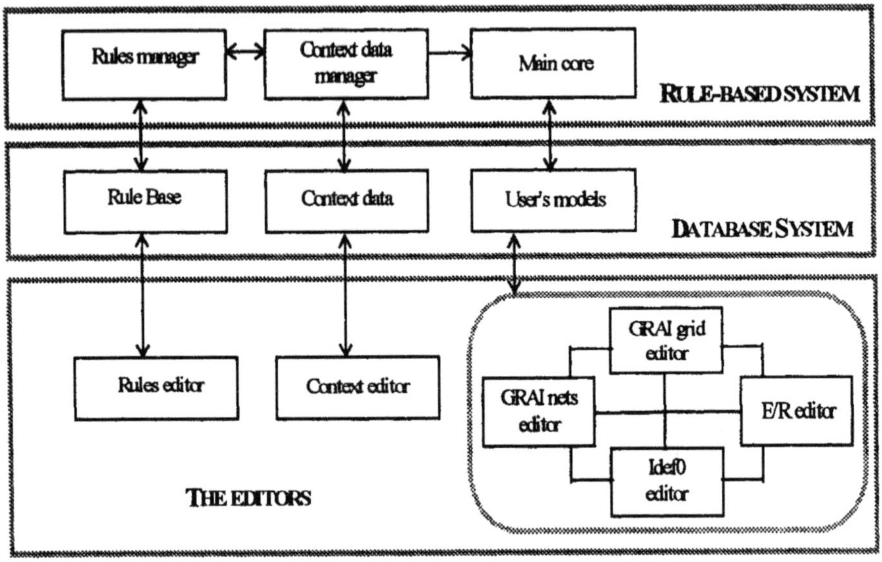


**Figure 2**: The basic architecture of *Imagim+*

### 3.1. The Editors

The editors of Imagim+ have been organised in three groups, as described below:

- The *Rules editor*, which enables the user to create new rules, to modify or delete them. This editor can also be used to select and mark a set of rules as the active set, which means that when the system activates the rules, these are the only rules of *Rule Base* to be verified.
- The *Context editor* enables the user to create, view and modify the context information. The term *context* is used here to classify the data describing an enterprise, as well as its environment (e.g. the company's type, size, position in the market, etc.). According to the company's type, several other attributes are defined. For instance, for a manufacturing company, the *context* will detail the types of products manufactured, the quality constraints, technology features, etc.
- *Graphic editors*: four graphic editors have been defined in Imagim+, for each of the formalisms of GIM: GRAI grids, GRAI nets, Idef0 and E/R diagrams. The editors enable the user to create new models

and eventually modify them. As the operation of all editors is fairly similar, we present below the main functionalities of the GRAI grid editor.

The *GRAI grid* editor provides flexible tools for the construction of a grid. Figure 3 shows an initial empty grid created by the editor.

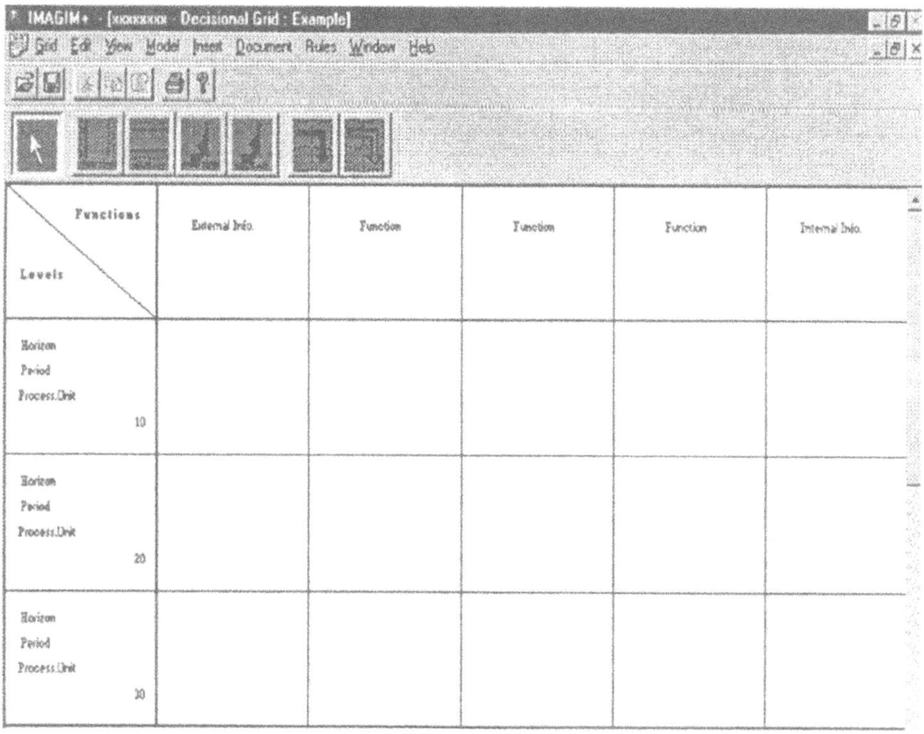


**Figure 3**: The GRAI grid editor.

When creating a new grid, the editor provides a grid skeleton which is filled-out by the user with the appropriate information. By using the buttons shown in the tool-bar, he may select elements of the grid, add functions, add levels, delete functions or levels, add informational or decisional flows. By clicking on the elements displayed on the grid, the user may also change the information shown. For example, if the user wants to change the first couple horizon/period of the grid, by clicking on the corresponding square, a dialogue box is displayed where the user enters the new information (figure 4).

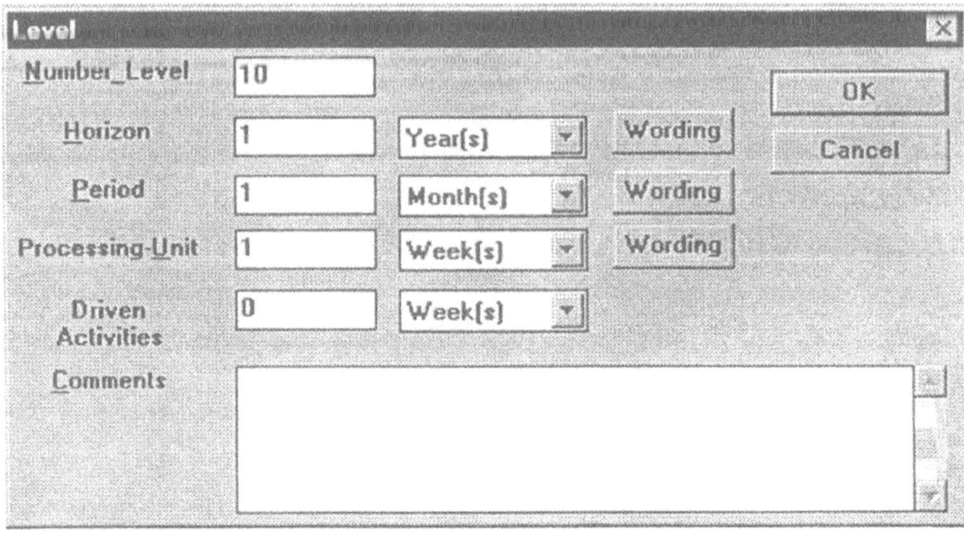


**Figure 4**: Changing the information of a decision center.

### 3.2. The Database system

The database system is responsible for the storage of the "environment of a GIM study", ie. the models built, as well as the rules and the context data. Each study has thus a particular database where all this information is stored.

The part of the database concerning the rules contains some essential knowledge that is always delivered with the system. This knowledge can be later adjusted by the user according to his needs, through the addition of new rules, the activation and switching-off of certain rule-sets. The structure of the Rule-Based system is presented next.

### 3.3. The Rule-Based system

The Rule-Based System has the goal of identifying inconsistencies and malfunctions in the models built by the user, according to the models themselves and some further information about the enterprises (the context). Figure 5 shows the four main components of the Rule-based system.

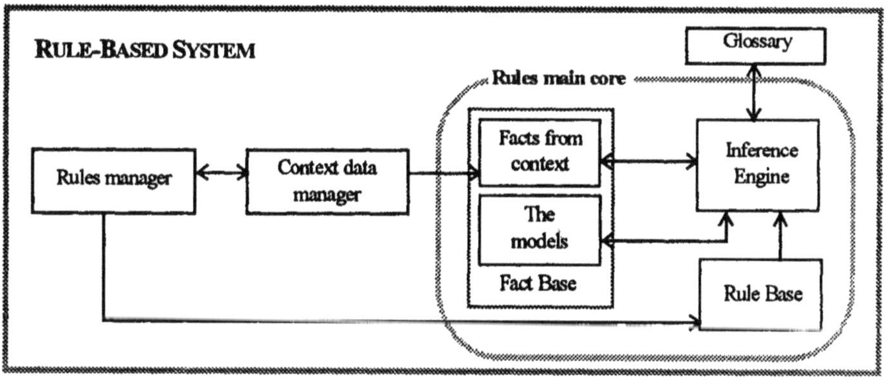


**Figure 5**: The detailed architecture of the Rule-based system

- The *Rules manager* makes sure new rules entered in the system will not conflict with already existing rules. The rules consistency is managed by the *Rules manager* in two aspects: static and dynamic. The former deals with the consistency of rules taking into account only the rules described in the *Rule base,* without considering the facts contained in the *Fact base* (systems such as COVADIS (Rousset 88) and INDE (Pipard 88) are based on this approach too). The inconsistencies that may be found at this level concern redundancy, contradiction and cycles. The redundancy of rules happens when two or more rules are identical (same conditions and conclusions); the contradiction, when the rules have the same conditions but different conclusions; and the cycles when there is a chain of rules in the *Rule base* where the first rule has a condition A and the last has a conclusion A, thus forming an endless loop. The consistency in the dynamic level concerns both the facts stored in the *Fact base*, and the rules themselves (systems such as TMS (Doyle 79) and ATMS (De Kleer 86) are based on this approach as well). At this level, the consistency is verified at all times. When the conditions which have conducted to the deduction of a fact are no longer valid, this fact is removed from the *Fact base*. Therefore, there is no risk that another rule takes into account this inconsistent fact.
- The *Context data manager* makes available to the *Rule-based system* all sorts of information about the enterprise studied (the context).
- The *Main Core* is further divided into three components.
  - ⇒ The *Rule Base* is composed by the rule sets which have been selected by the user.
  - ⇒ The *Fact Base* stores the facts used to test the condition parts of the rules. Two types of data are kept in the base: *facts from the user's models* (grids, nets, Idef0 and E/R diagrams), and from the enterprise *context*.
  - ⇒ The *Inference Engine* accesses the Rule Base to obtain the rules selected for the current study. The *Fact Base* (*context data* and *user's models*) are

also checked in order to identify true statements in the condition part of the existing rules.

- The *Glossary* is the component of the system that enables the user to use the vocabulary of his choice when describing the models created. The glossary translates the expressions commonly used into standard terms which have a particular "meaning" to the system.

The rules stored in the *Rule Base* have been organised in a hierarchical structure as shown below:

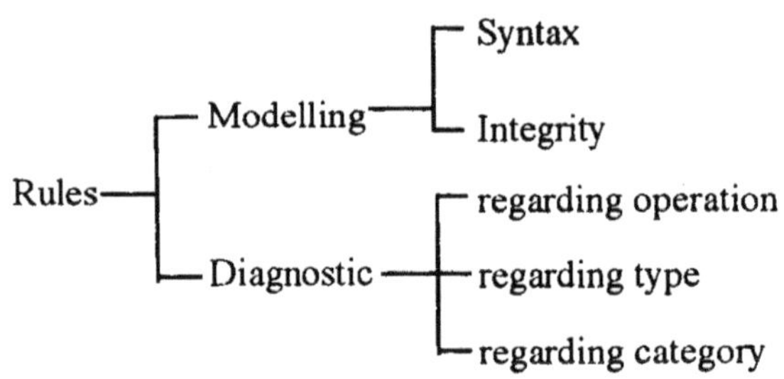


**Figure 6**: The hierarchy of rules

- *Modelling rules*: ensure that the models built do not present inconsistencies. They have been divided into:
  - GRAI syntax rules: concern the detection of inconsistencies related to the syntax defined for each formalism. Eg.: *"for a given level, the horizon of decision-making must have at least five periods for reviewing the decisions"*
  - Integrity rules: detect inconsistencies in the models of a given system. The aim of these rules is to ensure a global coherence among the models. Eg.:*"all the information contained in a GRAI grid must appear explicitly in the GRAI net"*

    Dividing the modelling rules into two distinct sub-sets, helps the user to understand the inconsistencies detected. Furthermore, it gives the user the opportunity to enable or disable a whole set of rules, which may be wanted in some circumstances (e.g. enabling only the syntax, or only the integrity rules).

- *Diagnostic rules*: have as a main goal to identify inconsistencies in the studied enterprise at the semantic level. The inconsistencies are observed both in the models built, taking into account the context of the company. The diagnostic rules have been divided into three sub-sets:
  - Rules regarding the operating of the enterprise (GRAI rules): they are characterised by being independent of the context;
  - Rules which are inherent to the type of enterprise studied (one-of-a-kind, discrete production or continous production.);

- Rules linked to a specific domain (Chemicals, Weapons, Spaceship components.)

The different classes of rules are applied in a specific order, according to their type and the GIM phase in which their are used. The *syntax rules* have to be taken into consideration in the modelling and design phases. In fact, these rules are used in real-time during the construction of the model. The *integrity rules* are triggered after the completion of each model, their goal being to check the models' consistency. Regarding the inter-model *consistency rules*, they are applied after the *integrity rules*, when all the models of the different views are produced. Concerning the diagnosis rules, they are verified, beginning with the GRAI rules and then applying the rules inherent to the type of enterprise, followed by the domain specific rules. This progressive approach allow the users to analyse with efficiency their models, avoiding, for instance, to check the GRAI rules on inconsistent models.

## 4 A PRACTICAL EXAMPLE: MODELLING A MANUFACTURING COMPANY WITH IMAGIM+

IMAGIM+ gives support to the users in all phases of the GIM approach. Figure 7 shows the list of all models constructed during the *modelling phase* of a particular enterprise.

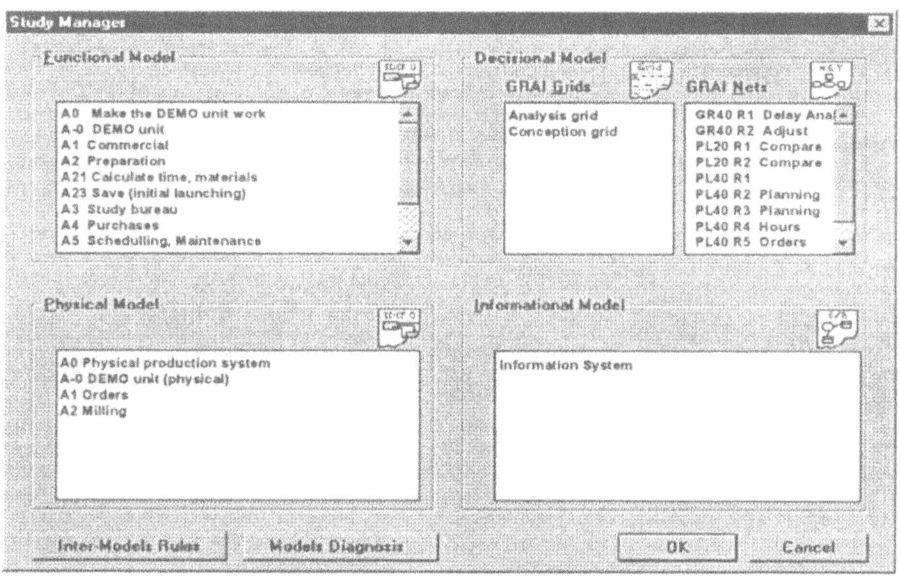


**Figure 7**: The models of a particular GIM study

The view of the functional and physical models is composed of *Idef0* diagrams, all being organised in a hierarchy. The decisional model has one or more *GRAI grids*, as well as a set of *GRAI nets* which represent in detail the decision centres of the grids. The view of the information model is composed of one or more *E/R* diagrams, each detailing the information kept and dealt with by the system.

Figure 8 presents the analysis grid describing the decisional system of the company.

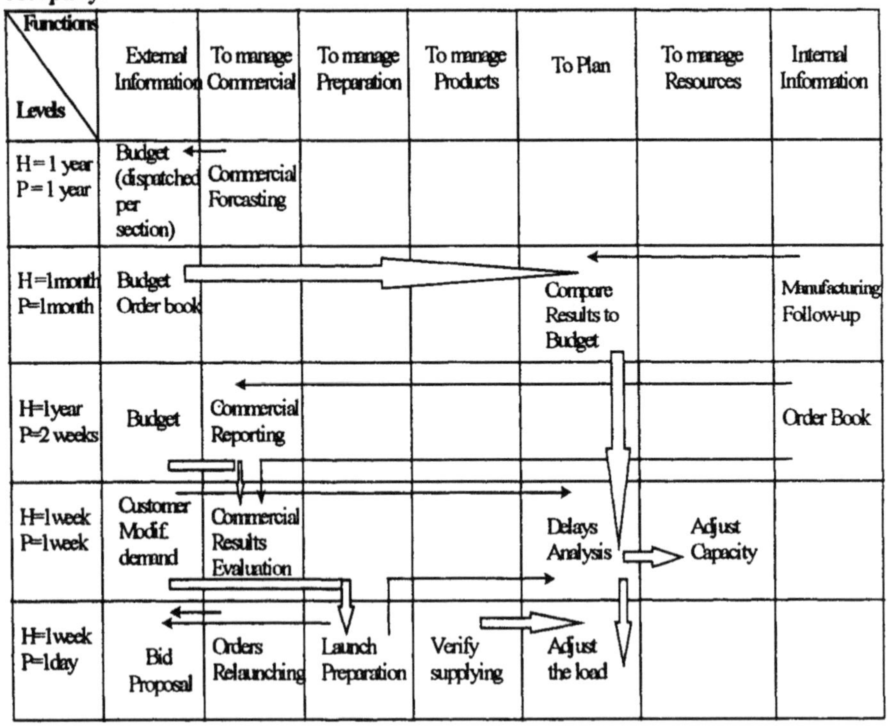


**Figure 8**: Example of analysis grid

In this grid we can point out the concentration of the activity in the middle and the short term level, denoting, a possible lack in terms of long term decisions. The inconsistencies identified in the grid are signaled by the *rule-based system*, as shown in figure 9.

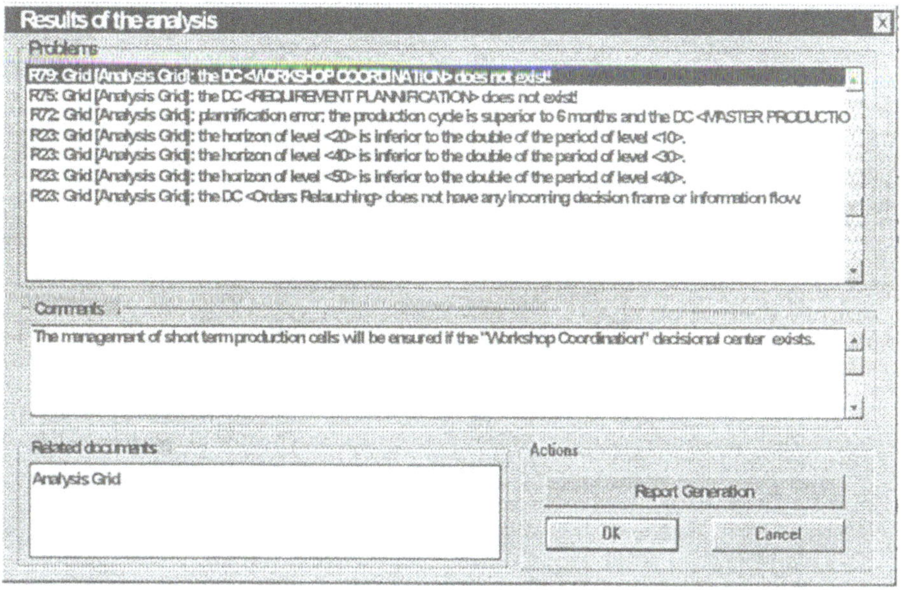


**Figure 9**: The problems identified in the grid

The problems identified guide the analysts in the improvement of the models. The final conception grid designed for the manufacturing system studied, according to goals established and eliminating the inconsistencies detected is presented in figure 10.

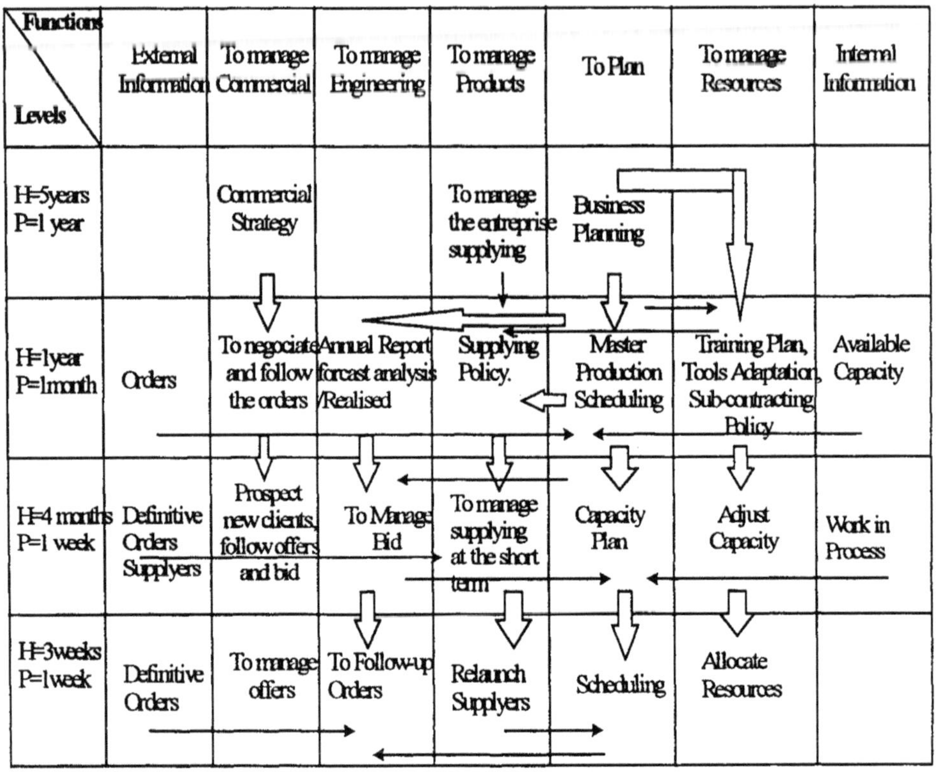


**Figure 10**: The conception grid

This grid gives priority to the production planning aspects that were lacking in the existing decision system. In fact, the number of decisions levels has been reduced (from 5 to 4) and the values associated to the couples Horizon/Period have been recalculated to allow an efficient synchronisation according to the GRAI rules. Concerning the other components of the grid, decision centres have been added for the function *To plan*: Strategic (Business Plan), *Tactical* (Master Production Scheduling and Capacity Plan) and *Operational* (Scheduling).

## 5. CONCLUSIONS AND FUTURE WORK

At present, IMAGIM+ is in the beta-test stage and is being used by several consulting companies in Europe, for manufacturing systems design and diagnosis of problems.

We are starting to work on the development of a complementary tool which uses Case-Based Reasoning (CBR) techniques to enable the re-use of design solutions created with *Imagim+*. The new system will be capable of finding previous cases that may help the user to model the enterprise analysed, and to identify weak points in the solution proposed. The idea of using CBR in enterprise

modelling is innovative and can be justified for several reasons. Firstly, modifying a solution that has been successfully used in the past is certainly less complicated than building a solution from scratch (Kolodner 93). Secondly, users are usually more willing to accept solutions provided by concrete cases than solutions that are ready-made (Georgin et al. 94). Such a tool should provide further assistance in the modelling of enterprises with GIM.
IMAGIM+ gives now a real support to the use of GIM. It was the computerized tool we were waiting for giving a strong development to the GRAI Approach.

# 6. REFERENCES

De Kleer, J. (1986). An Assumption-based TMS. *Artificial Intelligence, Elsiever Science Publishers*, **28**, 127-2.

Doumeingts, G. (1984). *Méthode GRAI, méthode de conception des systèmes en productique*. Thèse de doctorat d'état, University of Bordeaux 1.

Doyle, J. (1979). A truth maintenance system. *Artificial Intelligence*, Elsiever Science Publishers, **12**,. 231-5.

Georgin, E., McDonald, J., Ricard, B. and Jacquot, J-P (1994). "The use of cases in diagnostic explanations", *Proceedings IEE Colloquium on Case-based reasoning: prospects for applications* - digest 055, pp. 2V1-2V3.

J. Kolodner (1993). *Case-Based Reasoning*, San Mateo, CA: Morgan Kaufmann.

E. Pipard (1988). Détection d'incohérences et d'incomplétudes dans les bases de règles : le système INDE-Un système interactif pour le maintien de la cohérence d'une base de règles, in Proceedings of *Avignon'88, EC2*, session 29, Avignon, France.

Roboam, M. (1988). *Modèles de référence et Integration des méthodes d'analyse pour la conception des systèmes de production.* Doctoral thesis, University of Bordeaux I.

Rousset, M. C. (1988). *Sur la cohérence et la validation des bases de connaissances : le système COVADIS.* Doctoral thesis (doctorat d'état), University of Paris-Sud, Centre d'ORSAY.

Zanettin, M. (1994). *Contribution à une méthode de conception de systèmes de production.* Doctoral thesis, University of Bordeaux I.

# 7. BIOGRAPHY

**Adnane Moudden** is a research Engineer at the GRAI research group belonging to the LAP (Laboratoire d'Automatique et de Productique). He obtained his PhD degree from the University of Bordeaux I in 1997. His research interests include case-based reasoning, neural-fuzzy systems, machine learning and the application of these fields to production systems modelling and design

**Eliseo Reategui** is a research Engineer at AUGRAI. He has worked for his PhD degree at the Computer Science Department of University College London. Prior to that, he has obtained his MSc from the Federal University of Rio Grande do Sul - Brazil, where he participated of different research projects in the application of Artificial Intelligence in domains such as cardiology and petrography. His main research interests are case-based reasoning, machine learning, neural networks and knowledge representation.

**Guy Doumeingts** is Professor at the University of Bordeaux I. He obtained his PhD degree in 1967, from this same institution. He participated in the setting-up of the GRAI research group from the LAP, of which he is the Director since 1989. He has held many research contracts, published two books, and over 200 papers on CIM. He is expert for the Commission of the European Communities (ESPRIT Project), French representative to IFIP, Chairman of the Technical Commite #5 (Computer Application in Technology), and member of the editorial board of several international journals.

# 56
# Modeling dynamic management features of virtual enterprises

*Peter Bernus[a], Peter Bertok[b], Laszlo Nemes[c]*
*[a]Griffith University Nathan (Brisbane) QLD 4111, Australia*
*email: bernus@cit.gu.edu.au*

*[b]Royal Melbourne Institute of Technology P.O.Box 71, Bundoora Vic 3083, Australia, email: pbertok@rmit.edu.au*

*[c]CSIRO Division of Manuf. Technology, Locked Bag 9, Preston Vic 3072, Australia email: lnm@mlb.dmt.csiro.au*

**Abstract**

We investigate essential properties of virtual enterprises and the consequent modeling requirements. Agent autonomy is defined. Virtual enterprises are treated as autonomous entities built out of autonomous entities. Requirements are derived from two types of virtual enterprises, a repetitive and a one-of-a-kind production or service enterprise. Properties that need to be represented in virtual enterprise models include the dynamics of decision making, the negotiations among participants for the delineation of domains of autonomy, authority, beliefs and responsibilities, the mapping of organizational entities to decisional roles, the ability to identify and analyze a variety of conflict types and the existence of conflict resolution paths. These properties have to be analyzed by matching enterprise engineering tools. An ontological theory is also needed to systematize the concepts that must be supported by the protocol languages for parallel distributed planning, scheduling and control algorithms in the virtual enterprise.

**Keywords**

Virtual enterprise, enterprise modeling, co-ordination

Computer Applications in Production and Engineering. F. Plonka and G. Olling (Eds.)

# 1 INTRODUCTION

A virtual enterprise is a temporary alliance of companies for the lifetime of a common project, solution for a problem, or joint production of service or product. The rapid development of communication and networking infrastructures gave new impetus to the development of virtual enterprises, because new ways of interactions between participants have eliminated the time and space gap between partners.

Virtual enterprises are such entities which, from the point of view of their service to the customer, appear to be one entity, but in fact are formed from several autonomous entities, or partners. The property that differentiates a virtual enterprise from an ordinary value chain is the fact that there is a single locus which takes full responsibility for the entire value chain of its product or products, even though the task is carried out by many participants.

Several disciplines have treated the problem of how to build a larger autonomous system out of autonomous components. The artificial intelligence literature developed blackboard systems and co-operative dialogues to externalize mental states and beliefs (Erman et al 1980, Minsky 1996, Winograd-Flores, 1990), the planning and scheduling area developed co-operative planning (Balasubramanian 1997) and holonic manufacturing cells (Deen 1993, Mathews 1995, Tamura 1995) similar techniques were used for computer supported co-operative work (Schmidt 1996 ), management science developed dynamic forms of organization, e.g., matrix organizations (Lawson 1986, Wall 1984). Co-ordination science attempts to develop methodologies and paradigmatic models for the same purpose (Malone, 1993). All have an application of the basic approach: building agents out of agents.

There is a new interest in how virtual companies can be created easier than using traditional methods. Enterprise modeling holds a promise because it takes out some of the trial and error component from creating a new, better managed value chain. Enterprise modeling languages have been developed and used to describe and simulate business processes, but the development of viable structures, good quality reusable models for virtual enterprises is far from trivial. We investigate some of the properties that virtual enterprises need to have. These properties must then be predictable from the models which we use to design such enterprises.

Typical virtual enterprise formations are:

- One of a kind engineering endeavors such as designing and building large petrochemical plant, roads, major facilities, organized as major projects - often on an international scale
- Consortia for production, service or for research, with an alliance of partners limited to a common mission.
- The creation of virtual enterprises is mainly done by business executives, or highly paid (and stressed) project managers who have little more help then their experience as to how, under time pressures, successful virtual

and methods, once a design is in place the change of such a virtual organization is often lagging behind the needs.

Our goal is twofold:

- We want to analyze, and identify what are the desired *types* of properties that management should be able to design and verify at the initial creation of a virtual enterprise, and to continuously assess and control during its operation;
- We want to derive needs, or requirements, based on this analysis, as to what types of modeling tools and languages are, or would be especially suitable for the support of the virtual-enterprise engineering process. Hopefully an appropriate combination of existing tools, or some extension to such combination, will be able to answer to the so identified needs.

## 2 RESEARCH METHOD

We draw conclusions from previous case study experience, in the Globeman 21 consortium (on project enterprise); and use GERAM (Generalized Enterprise Reference Architecture and Methodology) as the theoretical framework for the analysis (Bernus, Nemes, 1996). The method is selected because GERAM is an open, very wide scope life-cycle architecture with enterprise creation and change being its main focus. We also use the theory of GRAI Grids which are the foundation for the decisional modeling capability of GRAI-GIM (Doumeingts, 1994) (a GERAM compliant enterprise reference architecture and methodology). Further, the division between the management architecture and the mission fulfillment architecture corresponds to PERA (Williams, 1994).

We identify typical virtual enterprise types, and essential types of properties that should be accounted for in the Enterprise Models (EMs) describing them. Enterprise modeling languages (EMLs) and appropriate enterprise engineering tools (EETs) can be selected for the support of virtual-enterprise engineering based on their competency to support the description and analysis of the above properties.

We hope that through the use of suitable modeling tools business executives will get help to better design multi-company ventures, e.g., to be able to analyze and optimize, through explicit models, the global behavior of their virtual enterprise.

Because the management system of virtual enterprises needs to be different from incorporated ones (due to looser connection between partners) it has to be studied and understood what special needs virtual enterprise designers face, and only after that attempt to select the modeling methods and languages to model them. Although the types of views through which to model virtual enterprises can be predicted (based on CIMOSA (Vernadat, purpose of representing these views needs to be gauged to the problem domain.

## 2.1 Available methods for enterprise modeling

Business process modeling has been extensively used to improve the material and information flow in a company, ameliorating the process from some respect or another (cost, quality of product, time to market etc.). Similar modeling exercises are expected to be applicable (with like expected results) in the context of virtual enterprises improving the information and material exchange among the parts of the process as implemented by the participating partners. In other words such models help integrate the supply chain. Special care must be taken with virtual enterprises in the information exchange and management of the chain (or product life-cycle), to avoid misinterpretation and rework. The specification of the interfaces using semantically rich schema languages (such as Express) is used in the extensive efforts to define STEP protocols for product data exchange (Kahn 1995)

CIMOSA advocates the modeling of the enterprise's control system such that the resulting models, when mapped to the implementation and operational levels, can be used to control business processes. The resulting paradigm is called model-based control and is an important technique of supply chain integration, because of its ability to integrate the operational control level. In virtual enterprises the same operational control integration is applicable, only the integration infrastructure must be distributed over a wider area.

Traditional enterprise modeling (applied extensively in many industries in the design of flexible manufacturing cells, job shops, banking business processes, or integrated circuit development processes) separates the design of the business process from the management and operation of the process. i.e., first design (or re-design) the processes of the enterprise, institutionalise them and then operate them.

Virtual enterprises are dynamic in nature (eg a project enterprise starts operating its project management component before the actual project gets fully designed) and enterprise design and change is a function of the operation itself (more specifically it is part of its management component).

Virtual-enterprise design needs various level interactions with partners who take part of the virtual enterprise's business functions. Thus the design process involves various interactions between partners. But because this interaction is also part of the enterprise operation, enterprise modeling must extend to the determination of protocols among partners which are suitable for negotiating about enterprise design.

# 3 CHARACTERISATION OF VIRTUAL ENTERPRISES

## 3.1 Virtual enterprise

A virtual enterprise, as any enterprise, must have a clear goal and a clear mission. It also should demonstrate a goal seeking behavior in its autonomous decision making, act upon its set of beliefs, and interact with its environment (O'Leary 1997). In general it is expected that a virtual enterprise makes plans, and its activities follow those plans to achieve the objectives. The term 'agent' is used to describe this type of behavior, in the traditional AI meaning of planning agent. From the point of view of the applicability of this model it is immaterial if planning indeed takes place or not, and if missions and goals are made explicit; what matters is that an external observer can describe the enterprise as (if it were) a planning agent.

Since the partners that make up the virtual enterprise are also agent-like, in the followings we make an attempt to treat a virtual enterprise as an agent, or collection of agents, which contribute to the virtual enterprise's mission but 'keep their autonomy'. Since what this autonomy is not defined yet, we placed the statement between inverted commas – autonomy being defined later in this paper.

Modeling an enterprise has to consider the *function* of the enterprise, from its mission down to operational level procedures. The level of modeling detail should correspond to the level for which there are suitable human organizational, hardware or software entities that can perform each elementary activity modeled. The description not only needs to give a static picture, the dynamics (e.g. the expected life history) is also to be accounted for.

The model must also reflect the actual *structure* of the enterprise, including its resources (such as human and machine), so that the behavior, reactions and operation (i.e. the functions) can be understood in relation to the structure. This latter type of relationship becomes an important issue when autonomy is considered.

In the following we concentrate on the modeling of the management and control of the virtual enterprise.

Functionally, enterprise management can be described as carrying out three main types of functions (a) managing the products, (b) managing its resources, and (c) co-ordinating (a) and (b) (Doumeingts, 1994). Product management covers all product-related activities from product planning to production planning and related services. Resource management includes human, machine, financial and other resources that are needed to perform the operations that fulfill the enterprise's mission, and is responsible for operational level control. Co-ordination is resolving the conflicts between the objectives of (a) and (b) as well as gives them direction or mission. These functions make up the decisional system of the enterprise.

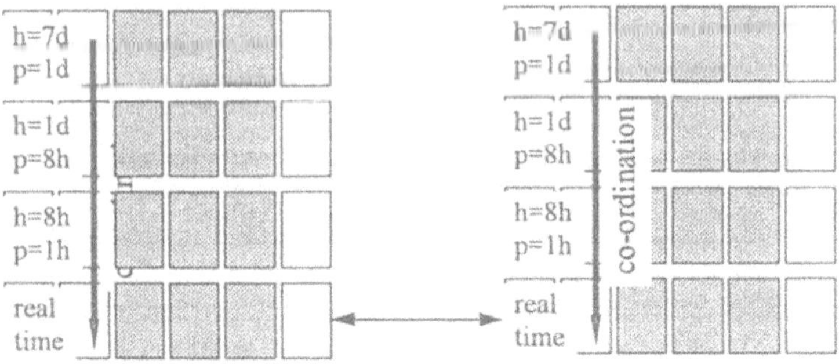


**Figure 1** Interaction in a Traditional Value Chain

Structurally, enterprise management can be described as a management organization, consisting of the agents[1] (people and groups of people) who take the decisions. The above mentioned relationships among these individuals and groups are determined by a) the decisional roles they take and the dynamics of this system (b) intangible social relationships. It is expected that at least the tangible relationships are brought to light in the form of a model, such that organizational conflicts be apparent and can be designed-out of the system.

In traditional value chains one problem is that links between participating agents are limited to the operational or executional levels. This is represented in Fig. 1.

## 3.2 Service level agreements / outsourcing

One approach that has been adopted by many large organizations is to decompose what was once one organization into several autonomous parts. This is done through giving increased autonomy for the individual components, and choosing a co-operation method (e.g. from 1-3 above). The technique is commonly known in today's management as service level agreements and outsourcing (depending on the level of autonomy of the components).

The method is trying to avoid conflicts by setting out the rules in the enterprise design phase and requiring clarification or explicit agreement on these rules before any decision is taken. The co-ordination among the organizational partners is implemented in a hierarchical manner (method 3), and upper level decisions in the domain of non-autonomous functions are observed at lower levels ('level' refers here to strategic, tactical and operational). This is not to say that information exchange and feedback is not preceding such hierarchical decisions.

The strategic level interactions define the rules, (or redesign them) and the component agents have high autonomy in the design dialogue. The strategic level dialogue ends with the definition of autonomy domains and non-autonomy domains. The co-ordination starts on the strategic level, where the domains of autonomous actions are determined for each participant and the interfaces for communication and co-operation get defined. This sets then the environment for co-operation at all other levels. The tactical and operational levels will interact obeying those rules.

The planning and operational levels are working within this framework, the interfaces between participants comply with the settings defined on the strategic level. Mechanisms are provided for feedback to the level above, so the efficiency of the system can be continuously monitored. Policies (i.e. the rules) are set at the strategic level, and they can be modified if the system's behavior deviates from normal significantly. The feedback mechanisms can be used to modify the structure of the whole framework, adjust interfaces or domains of autonomous actions, etc., in order to improve the system's overall performance.

The system is organized in a hierarchical manner, meaning that at any one time when a decision is taken the co-ordinating agent (via method 3) can determine the contents of the decisional objectives passed down to the lower level agent. However, the co-ordinating agent's tactical level does not have authority to change the decisional structure, so this hierarchical relationship (and loss of autonomy) is limited in scope.

The more the tactical decision frameworks encroach on the lower level's autonomy the more the amount of communication between the levels. This additional load put on the communication system will eventually impact on overall system performance. The functional responsiveness of the system may be slowed down, as the agreements take time to evolve and the upper, decision making level receives the information through a preliminary filtering of the lower ones.

> Designers of virtual enterprises must be able to model the dynamics of decision making and the efficiency of responsiveness of the different design variants.

Evaluating this architecture from the enterprise modeling aspect the system has the advantage of having a clear, well-organized and easily traceable structure. Functions at all levels are distinctly defined, the interfaces are handled without ambiguity. As we stated earlier, agents are providing solutions that satisfy certain criteria, but are not expected to provide strictly optimal solutions. This can lead to performance deficiencies. Each level has certain autonomy, but its degree varies at different levels. The higher level entity does not have in fact full autonomy, because it has responsibility for the lower level, e.g. it must observe constraints that are legitimately (according to the rules) submitted as information by the lower level agents.

> The lesson from this analysis is that the protocols which must be set up as a part of the design of the enterprise must be suitable for the definition of authority and obligation, and responsibility, in a formal enough manner, so that the resulting set of beliefs, responsibilities,

For example, the decision framework set by the higher level restricts the lower levels' autonomy. At the same time, if the coupling between the higher and lower levels is not close enough, then the limited autonomy of the lower levels can result in conflicts, or lack of harmony, between the higher and the lower levels' objectives. This distance between the decisional centers can be a serious issue, and indicates the need for tighter coupling, albeit curtailing lower level's autonomy. In fact, a reasonable balance between tight coupling and local autonomy can be easier to establish than trying to maintain local autonomy at all costs and going through several steps of iteration to achieve an acceptable outcome.

### 3.3 Project enterprise

Project enterprises are typical forms of virtual enterprise, used in one-of-a-kind production or other one-of-a trend human endeavors. Project enterprises are built on the basis of the knowledge of the life-cycle of the product the design and, or building of which is the mission of the enterprise.

A particular property of project enterprises is that the management structure is designed and operated before the rest of the enterprise is set up. Therefore the project enterprise is self-building in nature. It is not necessarily adaptive (the project enterprise is usually built after the pattern of earlier projects used as blueprints), because adaptivity assumes that the pattern itself is capable of being changed by the enterprise itself in response to changes in the environment.

> However, the dynamics of the organization and its adaptability is a system property which would be of interest to investigate by designers of project enterprise.

Unlike in virtual enterprises, which are created by breaking up large organizations into autonomous parts to form a better quality value chain, virtual project enterprises are assembled according to a unique business process tailored to the particular product or service in question. The individual entities (partners, or agents) can usually be selected on the basis of competencies, geographic location, and other characteristics, including price of service or product, strategic alliance possibilities etc. In project enterprises often hundreds of participants must be co-ordinated, but the selection of potential partners may be quite limited for any particular service and product to be made available at the time, in the desired quality and at the desired location. In addition, the time pressure on enterprise design decisions is usually great, either because it is part of a tendering process with short deadlines, or because it is part of the project itself. Structurally, this type of brokerage is simple to represent, but *protocols should be defined (definable) and an ability to create a system of management of resource types is needed.*

For large projects to run smoothly it is necessary to have a clearly delineated responsibility structure and protocols are needed to set up and follow these.

design standard interfaces between the respective levels of participants to ease the burden of negotiations by project management and make it more automated.

On the strategic level, commitments are sought and obtained with the precision of usual planning negotiations. It is necessary to be able to prove of any virtual enterprise model that the types of information necessary for parallel distributed planning will be available through the decisional frameworks passed among the partners. For this to be a viable analysis possibility *an ontology of distributed parallel planning should be defined and be made available for the enterprise modeller.*

Similarly the ability of the virtual enterprise to carry out parallel distributed scheduling necessitates the definition of information requirements (and interfaces through which to supply them).

Finally, operational level interfaces could be analyzed as for their ability to support an enterprise-wide monitoring of state.

> The ontology (i.e. the formal definition) of concepts which must be supported by the protocol languages could be derived from studying various parallel distributed planning, scheduling and control algorithms.

# 4. MODELLING NEEDS

## 4.1 Conflicts in the decisional model

The decisional subsystem of an enterprise implements the goal seeking behavior. It is navigating the enterprise within the constraints of the environment while trying to pursue an enterprise level goal, and adjust and react to any changes in this set-up. An ideal decision making structure would work in this framework for the sole benefit of the organization, and would do all to find the optimum solution in any situation. In practice, however, finding or even defining the optimum can be a too time consuming or sometimes impossible task. Therefore, the participating agents are usually not required to produce optimum decisions: if the outcome satisfies a set of criteria, it is accepted.

Another, even more important limitation is the possible conflict of interest between the decision making system and its components. These factors indicate that any decision structure needs to be examined for efficacy and conflict of interests. As decision making is performed by a system of individuals, the objectives and striving of the human as an individual can not be neglected. Decisional roles taken by an individual may be in conflict with a) the individual's role in another part of the system, b) with the individual's personal aspirations, or c) with the interests of another individual in the same organization. The same is true of group interests and aspirations.

> This can be done in a formal manner, once appropriate tools or frameworks are set up for verification of the decisional structure.

When two or more enterprises are combining their efforts for a common project, a new type of conflict emerges: that between the organizational structures. The common goal is supposed to be the main driving force for the participants (with regards to the joint action), but the interests of individual companies may interfere with that of another participant.

> It is necessary to be able to demonstrate that no conflict is present between the interest of the virtual enterprise as a whole and that of its components, and if conflicts arise, as they eventually do, that there is suitable conflict resolution path provided for the virtual enterprise to resolve them.

The harmonization of the mental models and beliefs of the individuals (e.g. the assumptions on trust, or what is the 'way things are done here') makes up a company culture and precisely by developing and explicitly displaying such mental models and beliefs can a company culture be ingrained. When a virtual enterprise is set up, partners will have slightly (or extremely) different cultures, so the harmonization of the mental models and beliefs to create a culture of the virtual enterprise needs special attention.

In virtual enterprises where participants change and structure is never constant, it is necessary to be able to explicitly represent agreements and common beliefs that will govern interaction on the lower levels. This is an important part of the 'enterprise engineering process'.

It is expected that autonomy, responsibilities, obligations and beliefs should be able to be analyzed from a structural point of view to reveal conflicts among decisional roles and conflicts that arise from the way they are assigned to organizational entities.

Figure 2 shows an example how the decisional roles can be represented using a GRAI Grid, while Figure 3 shows a mapping of organizational entities to decisional roles.

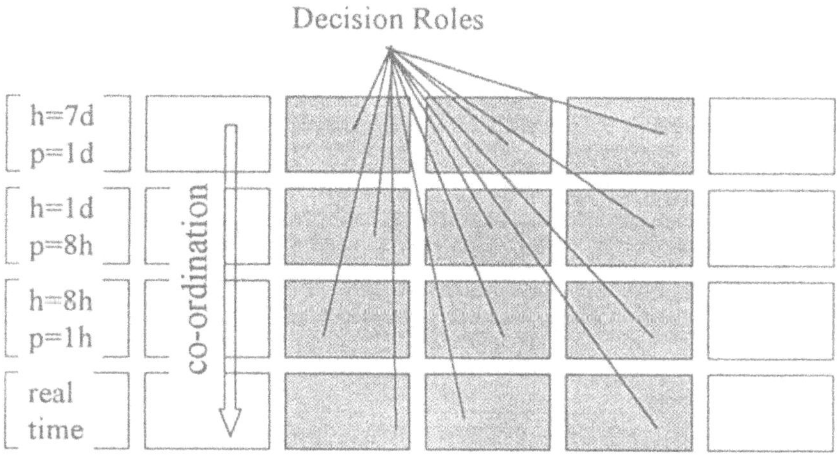


**Figure 2** Decision Roles Represented in GRAI Grid

## 4.2 Autonomy

A virtual enterprise is intended to work for the benefit of its participants, while endeavoring to harmonize the individual interests. This requires the co-operation of autonomous systems in a conflict-prone environment. Considering each participant in the virtual enterprise to be an agent, there is a need to co-ordinate the autonomous behavior of these agents. Various approaches to this problem are:

1. Agents make decisions in their own environment, detect and try to resolve conflicts locally when implementing those decisions;
2. Agents interact with one another and make decisions in co-operation with the others;
3. A dedicated agent is assigned to representing the interests of the whole (virtual) enterprise and co-ordinates the activities and decisions of the others.

Co-operation of autonomous entities always requires careful consideration. In optimistic control where only individual goals are pursued in the hope that there will be no conflict in most of the cases, the conflicts can become unresolvable when they do occur. It is very important to define the domain where autonomous decisions should take place, and clearly identify the points where harmonization of individual interests must occur. In other words:

> Autonomy is assumed only in a well-defined domain of functions (decisional or operational), and it is limited both in space and in time. The models of virtual enterprise thus must take into account the need for explicit conflict resolution, as a type of co-ordination activity.

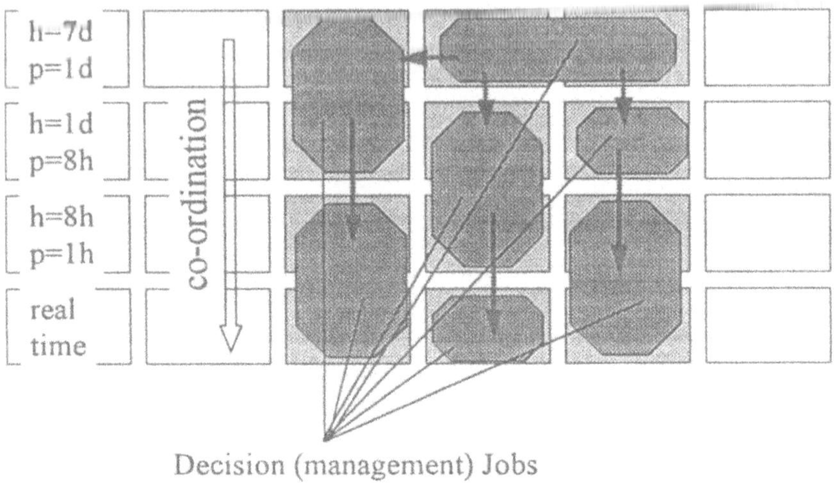


**Figure 3** Organizational Entities and Decisional Roles

## 5 CONCLUSION

Virtual enterprises are becoming increasingly popular for addressing and solving special problems, for organizing common projects or for joint production. To understand their operation and suggest efficiency improvements, the methods of modeling virtual enterprises were examined in the paper. We identified a number of requirements that virtual enterprise models need to satisfy. The requirements were based on real-life problem cases encountered in the Globeman consortium. In particular, we identified

- autonomy at all levels
- comprehensive conflict handling and resolution and
- agent-like behavior of components

as key issues. In future, these requirements will have to be translated into technical terms, so that the expressive power of the proposed enterprise modeling languages can be evaluated, and necessary adjustments can be made.

## 6 REFERENCES

Balasubramanian, S.; Maturana, F.P.; Norrie, D.H. (1997), Multi-agent planning and co-ordination for distributed concurrent *engineering Int.J. of Coop. Inf. Sys.*, 5 (2-3) pp. 153-79

Bernus, P.; Nemes, L. (1996) A framework to define a generic enterprise reference architecture and methodology, *Computer-Integrated Manuf. Systems*, vol.9, no.3, pp. 179-91

Deen, S.M.(1993) Co-operation issues in holonic manufacturing systems, *IFIP Tr.B (Appl.inTechn.),*B-14, pp.401-12

Doumeingts, G.; Fenie, P.; Chen, D. (1994), GIM (Grai Integrated Methodology): a methodology to specify and to design advanced manufacturing systems, Proc. ILCE '94. Integr. Logistics and Conc. Engineering, pp. 346, 271-80

Erman, L.D.; Hayes-Roth, F.; Lesser, V.R.; Raj Reddy, D. (1980) The Hearsay-II speech-understanding system: integrating knowledge to resolve uncertainty *Computing Surveys*, 12 (2) pp. 213-55

Kahn, H.J. (1995) STEP methodology – an overview, *Object Technology and its Appl. in Engng.*,p. v+178, 66-75

Lawson, J.W. (1986) A quick look at matrix organization from the perspective of the practicing manager *Engineering Management International*, 4(1) pp.61-70

Malone, T.W.; Crowston, K.; Jintae Lee; Pentland, B. (1993) Tools for inventing organizations: toward a handbook of organizational processes, Proc. 2nd Worksh. on Enabling Technologies Infrastructure for Collab. Enterp.pp.72-82

Mathews, J. (1995) foundations of intelligent manufacturing systems: the holonic viewpoint *Comp. Integ. Manuf. Syst.* 8 (4) pp. 237-43

Minsky, Marvin Lee (1996), First person : the society of mind, Voyager Company.

O'Leary, D.; Kuokka, D.; Plant, R. (1997) Artificial Intelligence and Virtual Organizations, *Communications of the ACM* vol.40 /1 pp.52-59

Schmidt, K.; Simone, C. (1996) Co-ordination mechanisms: towards a conceptual foundation of CSCW systems design, *J CSCW* 5(2-3) pp. 155-200

Tamura, S.; Luh, P.B.; Oblak, J.M.; Watanabe, S., (1995) A planning and scheduling architecture for holonic manufacturing systems, Proc 1st World Congr. on Intell. Manuf. Processes and Sys., vol.2 pp790-801.

Vernadat, F.B. (1994) Business process and enterprise activity modeling: CIMOSA contribution to a general enterprise reference architecture and methodology (GERAM), ICARCV '94 vol.1 pp. 378-82

Vernadat, F.; Drira, K.; Azema, (1996) P. An integrated description technique for distributed co-operative applications. CESA'96 IMACS. *Comp. Eng. in Sys. Applications,* pp. 794, 608-12

Wall, W.C., Jr. (1984) Integrated management in matrix *organization IEEE Trans. on Eng. Mgmt*, 31 (1) pp. 30-6

Williams, T.J. (1994) The Purdue Enterprise Reference Architecture *Computers in Industry*, 24, (2-3) pp. 141-58

Winograd, T; Flores, (1990) Understanding computers and cognition: a new foundation for design, Addison-Wesley

# 57

# Enterprise modeling and integration in Mexican manufacturing and service companies

*Arturo Molina and Angel Arriaga*
*CSIM - ITESM*
*Ave. Eugenio Garza Sada 2501 Sur*
*Monterrey, N.L. 64849 MEXICO*
*e-mail: armolina@campus.mty.itesm.mx*

**Abstract**

This paper describes the result of an assessment study carried out to analyse the use of enterprise modelling in Mexican micro, small, medium, and large companies to achieve Enterprise Integration. An assessment tool was developed based on a questionnaire on how Strategic Planning, Technology Planning and Technology Integration is performed and what models and methodologies are used in Mexican companies. The study has been undertaken in 32 manufacturing/services companies. The results of the exploratory exercise where: medium companies, on average, are the more integrated enterprises, large companies do a lot of strategic planning but they have problems in implementing and integrating technology, finally micro-companies are not aware of the need for enterprise integration.

**Keywords**

Assessment Tool, Enterprise Integration, Strategic Planning, Technology Planning, Technology Integration

## 1 INTRODUCTION

New concepts such as enterprise integration and modeling have been recognized to be key for the successful alignment of strategies and technologies within a company. However, not all the stages of a complete master plan for the integration

Computer Applications in Production and Engineering. F. Plonka and G. Olling (Eds.)

of enterprise are carried out by all companies, because master plans take a lot of effort to be developed and long time to be implemented. The objective of this research carried out in micro, small and medium, large Mexican manufacturing and service companies was to identify how companies are integrating technologies accordingly to the company's strategic plans. The study was carried out in 32 companies belonging to the service and manufacturing sectors. A key issue of the research was to analyze what companies are doing to define technological strategic plans and what actions are being undertaken to design and implement integrated information systems to achieve the defined strategies. Based on these results it was possible to recognize the areas of opportunity for the introduction of enterprise integration and modeling concepts to formalize the process of implementing technological strategies. A program has been defined to support the application of enterprise integration concepts in small and medium enterprises (SMEs).

## 2. SCOPE OF THE RESEARCH STUDY

The study was carried out in two neighbouring states in the north part of Mexico (Nuevo Leon and Coahuila) in the cities of Monterrey and Saltillo. The study included a total of 32 micro, small & medium, and large manufacturing and services companies, subdivided accordingly to the number of employees (Table 1). The service companies which participated in the study were software, insurance, and finance companies. Manufacturing companies were from the plastic, metal-mechanic and automotive sectors. These type of companies were selected because they represent sectors of major importance in this region.

Companies were selected randomly. The subjects interviewed were CIO's and Planning Managers in large and medium companies, where this position exists. In small and micro companies the subjects interviewed were General Managers, Directors or Owners.

**Table 1** Number of Services and Manufacturing Companies interviewed

| | *Micro companies* *1-15 employees* | *SMEs* *16-250 employees* | *Large companies* *more than 250 employees* |
|---|---|---|---|
| Services | 7 | 5 | 4 |
| Manufacturing | 5 | 5 | 6 |
| TOTAL | 12 | 10 | 10 |

## 3 ASSESSMENT TOOL FOR ENTERPRISE INTEGRATION

The assessment tools was designed as an interview of 55 questions based on what PERA (Williams 1991) and GERAM methodology (Bernus and Nemes 1994) have defined as the underlying methodology for enterprise integration.

Major challenge in the design of the questionnaire was to map the concepts defined in the Life Cycle of an Enterprise (Identification, Concept, Requirements, Design, Operation, Decommission) to concepts used by industry such as strategic planning, system design, system implementation and operation, etc. Therefore the questionnaire was divided in three parts: **Strategic Planning, Technology Planning, and Technology Integration and Implementation**.

The section related to **Strategic Planning** aimed to identify general questions regarding the identification phase for the preparation of Enterprise Integration Plans (e.g. establishment of the initial program, champion identification, getting management support, and steering committee definition); it also has questions regarding the identification of the enterprise business entity (EBE); and definition and documentation of the enterprise strategic plans (e.g. mission, vision and company values, objectives, strategies, goals, business plans, critical success factors and policies).

The second part, defined as **Technology Planning**, was concerned with the requirements phase, the identification and building of the enterprise integration planning team; general EBE process description; identification of initiatives and opportunities; As-Is definition of the human and organisational architecture, information systems architecture, and manufacturing and service equipment architecture; To-Be definition of the three architectures; development of a transition plan; identification of the required standards selection process; identification of logical transition path from As-Is to To-Be; development of training and education plan; identification of feasible solutions in the form of a set of enterprise integration projects; and the analysis of costs, benefits and risks for the proposed integration program.

The last part of the questionnaire, defined as **Technology Integration and Implementation**, was related to the design phase which contains the identification and analysis of the requirements of the human and organisational architecture, information systems architecture, and of the customer product or service equipment architecture to attain the To-Be model proposed; the detailed design of solutions about the personnel skills development, organisational planning, and training programs development in the human and organisational architecture; the detailed design of solutions about the equipment selection and systems layout in the information systems architecture; and the detailed design of the required equipment in the customer product or service equipment architecture. The final questions were regarding to the implemented vs. planned programmes; final evaluation, dissemination and feedback of the master plan; and the creation of continuous education and training plan. There were no questions regarding the operation or decommission of technology.

The questionnaire also included three open questions about methodologies used to:

- Analyse and describe the business process.
- Manage and control the integration program.
- Manage and integrate information systems.

These open questions were included to find out if there were already in use modelling methodologies for Enterprise Integration.

# 4 RESULTS OF THE RESEARCH STUDY

The analysis of the data collected was carried out in three ways:

1. Obtain percentages to see the tendency of how Enterprise Integration concepts are being achieved.
2. Create polar graphics to determine the areas of opportunity to introduce Enterprise Integration and Modelling.
3. Determine different methodologies used to manage, design and implement Enterprise Integration Programmes.

In the next subsections discussions of the findings are presented.

## 4.1 Enterprise Integration Concepts Realization

Strategic planning is not a common practice in micro companies, as only half of them have a certain form of strategic planning. However micro manufacturers are more aware of the importance of strategic planning than the services companies. In Table 2 the percentage of use of enterprise concepts in manufacturing micro companies is larger than in service companies. Small, Medium and Large service companies are practising more strategic planning than manufacturing enterprises, the reason of this is the strong competition that services companies are facing nowadays in Mexico. Manufacturing companies are more concentrated in every day operation activities. Nevertheless not all SMEs have formalised the use of strategic planning, and even if they do have it, due to changes in the competitive environment they usually ignored it in practice.

**Table 2** Enterprise Integration Concepts Realisation

| | *Strategic Planning* | *Technology Planning* | *Technology Integration and Implementation* |
|---|---|---|---|
| Micro-services companies | 49% | 48% | 29% |
| Micro-manufacturing companies | 55% | 59% | 52% |
| Middle-services companies | 92% | 92% | 83% |
| Middle-manufacturing companies | 88% | 77% | 82% |
| Large-services companies | 97% | 92% | 87% |
| Large-manufacturing companies | 89% | 87% | 87% |

Related to technology planning, service micro companies are not interested in technology planning. Nevertheless, micro manufacturing firms are worried about what technology to use to improve their production and therefore technology planning is part of their vocabulary, as it represents a major investment. Services SMEs are concentrating their efforts to plan what technology is needed to improve their services. For Manufacturing, SMEs technology planning is important but production realisation is key factor for survival. Usually technology is not planned, if there is a need, companies will find the technological resources to fulfil orders. In large companies, either services or manufacturing, technology planning is part of their activities, however this does not mean that they are actually following a formal procedure to perform such a task.

The situation found for the technology integration and implementation, in micro companies, especially in the service sector, is not important because no special technology is needed. However in manufacturing, technology is key to the success of the company therefore a lot of effort is spent in integrating technologies and creating added value with specialised technologies (e.g. CAD/CAM/CNC, laser cutting). SMEs are focusing their technologies to create added value for customers therefore they are better integrated than large companies. A lot of effort in large companies is spend in strategic and technology planning. Nevertheless, a lot of the plans for the integration and implementation of technology never are realised because the organisation structure is too complex, and usually there is a lack of leadership. Large companies usually start integration programmes supported by consulting firms in order to foresee possibilities for integration, hence technology based re-engineering is a common practice.

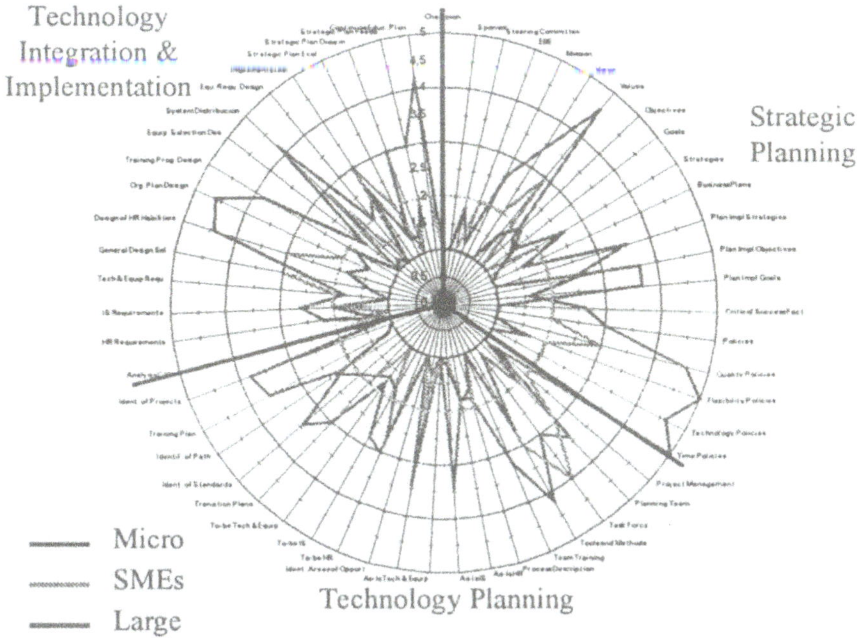


**Figure 1** Opportunities in Manufacturing Companies.

## 4.2 Opportunities for the Introduction of Enterprise Integration and Modeling

Areas of opportunity were analysed using polar graphics (figures 1 and 2). The polar graphs describes major phases in the development of Enterprise Integration Programmes, for example in Strategic Planning, definitions of mission, vision, values, etc.; in Technology Planning, definition of As-Is situation or To-Be Situation; and Technology Integration, design and implementation of IT architectures, etc.

The polar graphs represent pikes where major opportunities are identified. The more concentrated to the centre of the graph the more companies are complying with ideal Enterprise Integration Programs. Important opportunities can be found in micro companies, as there is a need for strategic planning due to the absence of a formal definition of what the enterprise or business is. There is also the necessity for technology planning, as the concepts of enterprise integration are unknown. Consequently, there is no technology integration due to the lack of planning and skills to implement basic technologies. However, in micro companies there is more integration in manufacturing companies than services

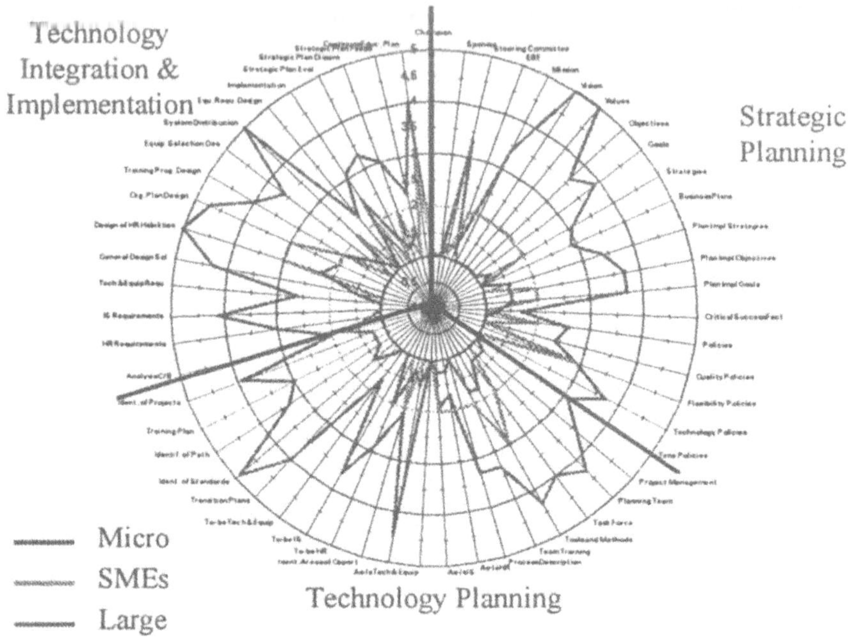


**Figure 2** Opportunities for Service Companies.

companies due to the fact that there is a need to produce end-products within certain quality specification, due dates and costs.

In SMEs, there are some opportunity areas: in the strategic planning section there is a need to reinforce the business definition and its strategic plans, i.e. focus the company. Regarding technology planning, there are no formal Enterprise

Integration teams, nor formal techniques to perform technological plans. Therefore, programmes for training middle managers to develop skills for organisational planning, and EI programmes is a major issue. SMEs related to the service industry are more focused than manufacturing SMEs.

In Large companies the situation is better. Large companies usually uses the services of international consulting firms to initiate Enterprise Integration programmes. Nevertheless the problems faced by these projects and the lack of continuity. Therefore in large companies there is strategic and technology planning but there is no technology integration. Due to the high percentage of failures in these programs, large companies are looking for new IT tool (e.g. ERP systems) to achieve enterprise integration.

## 3.3 Methodologies to manage Enterprise Integration Programs

The following sections describe different methodologies used to model business process, manage enterprise integration programmes, and manage and integrate information systems.

In micro companies the methodologies to analyse and describe the business process are:

- Flow charts
- Job instructions
- Direct observation
- Process charts
- Costs analysis
- Procedure description

There is no methodology to manage and control integration programs, the programs are carried out by engineers who have acquired expertise on the job training. In a similar way there is no use of formal methods for managing and integrating of information systems.

In addition to the methodologies, already mentioned used in micro companies, in SMEs the methodologies to analyse and describe the business process are:

- Competitive Oriented Business Plan
- Pragmatic Hermeneutics
- Elements creation and patterns generation

The methodologies used to manage and control the integration program are the creation of Task Forces with the more experienced personal using company specific methods.
The methodologies found to manage and integrate information systems are:

- Object oriented
- Out sourcing
- One Page Management

Methodologies used in large companies to analyse and describe the business process are (in addition to the one mentioned previously) :

- SADT
- Relations diagrams
- Anderson Consulting Group
- One Page System
- Boston Consulting Group
- Solution Development Design

The methodologies used by Task Forces to manage and control the integration program are:

- Pilot Studies
- Priority Based Programs
- Anderson Consulting Group
- MicroSoft Framework
- Boston Consulting Group
- One Page System

The methodologies to manage and integrate information systems are:

- MicroSoft Framework
- Solution Development Design
- SAP
- Client-servers Architectures
- J D Edwards

From these results, we can conclude that there are no formal methods in micro companies to analyze process. Even more, our research revealed that in micro companies there are no written procedures or standards. Common methods among all companies are the ones used to analyze processes such as: flow charts, job instructions and process charts. The practice of using Task Forces in SMEs and Large companies for tackling integration problems is widely used. Companies who can afford integrated solutions are buying them from vendors for example SAP and JDEdwards.

# 5 CONCLUSIONS

There are a lot of opportunities to formalize the use of Enterprise Integration concepts in Mexican Companies, especially in Micro, Small and Medium Enterprises. These companies are an interesting target for programs in this field. Nowadays the issue of global markets and Mexican economic grown is pushing these firms to accept new concepts to improve their competitiveness. A program named IMMPAC (Acronym in Spanish for Integration and Modernization of Micro, Small and Medium Enterprises to Achieve Competitiveness) has been created to introduce the concept of Enterprise Modeling and Integration in Micro and SMEs. This project integrates training and consultancy programs to support enterprise engineering projects.

# 6 REFERENCES

Bernus P., and Nemes L., 1994, “A Framework to Define a Generic Enterprise Reference Architecture and Methodology”, Task Force Meeting 9, Ottawa, Canada, August 25-26.

Williams T.J., 1991, The Purdue Enterprise Reference Architecture, Report Number 154, Purdue Laboratory for Applied Industrial Control, December.

Arraiga A., 1996, "Análisis Situacional de la Planeación e Integración Tecnológica de Empresas a través de una Herramienta de Diagnóstico", Master Degree Thesis, ITESM, December, in Spanish

## 7 BIOGRAPHY

Dr. Arturo Molina is an Associate Professor in the Integrated Manufacturing System Center at Monterrey Institute of Technology (ITESM), Campus Monterrey, Mexico. He received his M.Sc. degree in Computer Science from ITESM, Campus Monterrey in December 1990, his University Doctor degree in Mechanical Engineering at the Technical University of Budapest in November 1992, and Phd in Manufacturing Engineering from Loughborough University of Technology in 1995 His current research interests include information systems support for concurrent engineering, information modeling, enterprise modeling and integration.

Angel Arraiga is an independent consultant in the area of Information Systems development. He received his M.Sc. degree in Information Technology Management from ITESM, Campus Monterrey in December 1996.

58

# VIRSIM: a methodology supported by an integrated software for the Re-engineering of the factories

*J BORDA ELJABARRIETA,*
*A. POLO*
*DA TALDE SISTEPLANT, S.A. and Deusto University*
*Parque Tecnologico Edificio 105 48170 ZAMUDIO SPAIN*
*Phone.- (34) 4 452 06 11 Fax: (34) 4 452 12 66*
*E-mail.- datalde@redestb. es*

*R. JOCHEM,*
*Fraunhofer Institute of production Systems and Design Technology (IPK) Berlin*
*Pascaslstrasse 8-9, D- 1 058 7 BERLIN GER@NY*
*Phone.- (49) 30 39006 195 Fax.- (49) 30 39 32 503*
*E-mail.- rolandjochem@ipkjhg.de*

*G. DOUMEINGTS, A. MOUDDEN*
*LAPIGRAI, Universiti Bordeaux 1*
*351 Cours de la Libiration, 33405 TALENCE France*
*Phone (33) 5 56 84 65 30 Fax.- (33) 5 56 84 66 44*
*E-mail.- doum@lap.u-bordeauxft*

Computer Applications in Production and Engineering. F. Plonka and G. Olling (Eds.)

**Abstract**

Frequent plant lay-out and process automation changes is becoming more and more critical for production efficiency and reliability in companies with self developed or induced product design changes.

The paper presents VIRSIM (VIrtual reality and SIMulation), a methodology supporting the complete reengineering process based on GIM (GRAI Integrated Methodology) and IEM (Integrated Enterprise Modeling), and the associated software tool consisting of five subsystems, some of them commercial available low cost software packages. Potential interested industries are automotive components-makers and those with large production engineering departments in general.

**Keywords**

Virtual reality simulation, layout optimization, GIM, IEM.

## 1. INTRODUCTION

A yearly layout change? The continuous evolution of business oblige the manufacturing companies to re-engineer processes and to move machines to optimize the flow of products through the workshops: these tasks oblige to re-design, to implement solutions to train people. These changes are performed generally in a very short time, using some periods in which the company decreases its business (usually summer in Europe).

A methodology for re-engineering factories and an integrated software system supporting the enterprise modeling and design for both the physical process and the organizational aspects at the conceptual level, that represents in virtual reality physical systems and that simulates correspondent management processes (order processing, planning, scheduling, dispatching, etc.), giving also practical output design issues such detailed drawings, MTM data, specifications, for automation etc. is going to be decisive in interactive design and Virtual Reality trial and error and training, thus saving more than 70% of the lead-time needed in the complete process from idea to implementation. Another critical point is that will appear a remaining time immediately useful in two critical aspects: concentrating in preventive actions to avoid delicate adjustments in the machines with the move, and also in designing very well fitted man/machine interfaces strategy.

# 2. THE VIRSIM METHODOLOGY

The VIRSIM Methodology combines the strengths of the GRAI approach (Doumeingts 84, Zanettin 94) and IEM (Mertins, 92). It uses the GRAI approach for the modeling and design of the decisional part of manufacturing systems and IEM for the modeling and design of the physical system. Before giving the main principles of the VIRSIM methodology, we describe briefly the key concepts of the GRAT approach and IEM.

## 2.1. The GRAI Approach

Four different formalisms are used in the modeling of manufacturing systems with the GRAI approach: (GRAI grids and nets, IDEFO and Entity/Relationship diagrams). However, in order to simplify the presentation, we will focus solely on the decisional system and its representation through the *GRAI grid*. The grid has a matrix form which is used to detail temporal and functional aspects of the decisional system, as shown in Figure 1.

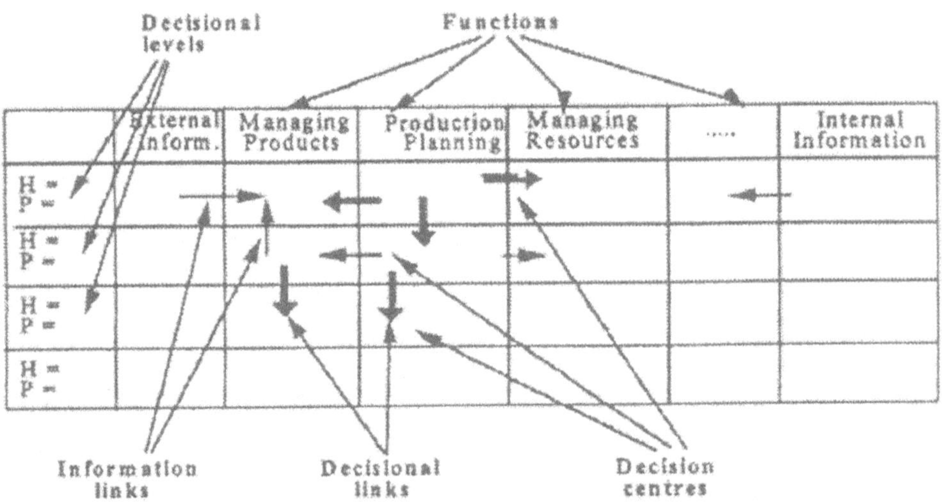


**Figure 1: GRAI grids formalism.**

The following components can be identified in the grid:

- *the functions,* describing the set of decision activities that are performed in order to achieve a particular goal. In Figure I we show the three basic functions of manufacturing systems: *Managing Products, Production Planning and Managing Resources.*
- *the decisional levels,* defined in terms of Horizon/Period pairs. The Horizon corresponds to an interval, on which a decision is valid, while the Period corresponds to a time interval when the decisions established in the Horizon are reconsidered.
- *the decision centers,* represented in the slots of the grid, group together all the activities belonging to the same function and the same *decision level.*
- *the information links,* determining the information flow from one *decision center* to another.
- *the decisional links,* determining the information items which is necessary for a decision to be taken.
- *the external information,* representing external data which serves as an interface between the system studied and its environment. The *internal information,* in contrast, represents the data that is created within the manufacturing system.

The grid, as well as the other GRAI formalisms, are used in the first phase of the GRAI approach (the *modeling phase)* to model the existing manufacturing system, giving an emphasis on the decisional subsystem. The two subsequent phases of the approach are: *the inconsistency search phase,* whose main objective is to detect weak points in the system studied; and *the design phase,* where the design of the new manufacturing system is elaborated based on the results of the previous phase.

Throughout a *GRAI study',* several groups of people are formed. Among them, two have a very important role:

- *the synthesis group,* composed of managers and other members of staff who are responsible for the manufacturing functions considered. The synthesis group is in charge of validating the results obtained in the different phases of a GRAI study.
- *the analysis group,* composed of one or more analysts (according to the work load), and one GRAI specialist. The role of the analysis group is to collect the relevant information for the study, to analyze it and to propose solutions for the problems detected.

## 2.2. The IEM methodology

In order to provide a comprehensive and extendible enterprise model, the IEM method uses the object-oriented modeling approach, thus allowing the integration of different views on an enterprise in one consistent model as well as the easy adaptation of the model to changes within the enterprise.

*Generic classes of objects*

The generic classes 'Product', 'Resource' and 'Order' are the basis of Integrated Enterprise Modeling for developing models from a user's point of view. They will be specified according to the specifications of an individual enterprise. Each generic class prescribes a specific generic attribute structure, thus defining a frame for describing the structure and behavior of objects of its subclasses. Real enterprise objects will be modeled as objects of these subclasses.

Required enterprise data and the business processes, i.e. the tasks referring to objects, be structured in accordance with the object classes. Furthermore, the relations between objects are determined. The result is a complete description of tasks, business processes, enterprise data, production equipment and information systems of the enterprise at any level of detail.

The model core comprises two main views. The tasks, which are to be executed on objects, and the business processes are the focal point of the Process Model View, whereas the Information Model View primarily regards the objects describing data. Therefore, the core of the enterprise model consists of the data and process representation of classes of objects. The views are interlinked by referring to the same objects and activities, although they represent them in different ways, levels of detail and context. Any view on the model can be derived from this standardized model core. Additional features may be attaches to the core if necessary.

*Business Processes as Interactions of Objects*

Everything that happens in a manufacturing enterprise as part of the manufacturing process can be described by activities. In general, activities process and modify objects which were classified above as 'Products', 'Orders' and 'Resources'. The execution of any activity requires direct or indirect planning and scheduling. It is executed by resources which posses the required capacities. The IEM method suggests three levels when describing the essentials of an activity.

- The **Action** is an object-independent description of any task or business, a verbal description of some task, process step or procedure.
- The **Function** describes the processing of objects as a transformation from one determined (beginning) state to another determined (ending) state.
- The **Activity** specifies the order, which controls the execution of the function, and the resource(s), which is (are) in charge of executing the function.

Figure 2 graphically represents the Generic Activity Model. The beginning and ending states are connected with the action rectangle by arrows from left to right. The controlling of the activity is represented by an order state description and a dashed vertical arrow from the top; the required or actually assigned capability for executing the function is represented by a resource state description and a dashed vertical arrow from the bottom.

[1]*A GRAI study* is the term used to refer to a complete enterprise modeling case using the GRAI approach.

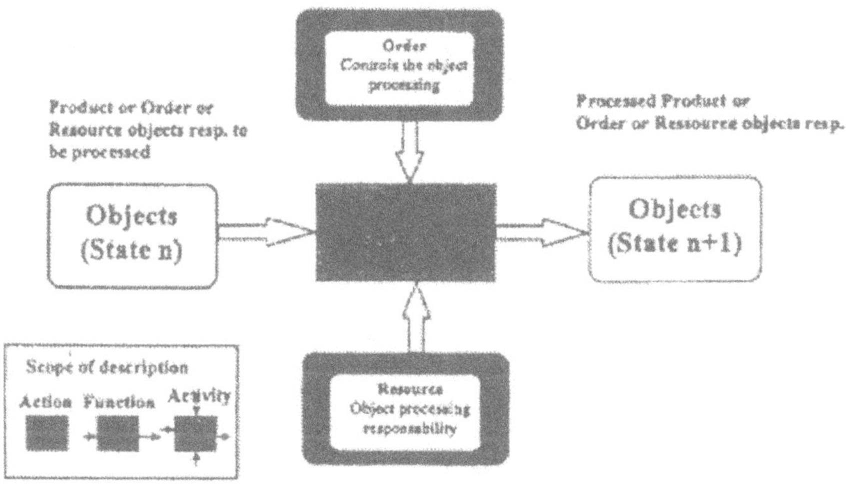


**Figure 2:** Interactions of Objects Described by the Generic Activity Model.

The Generic Activity Model represents the processing of objects of the product, order or resource class respectively indicating the interactions of objects while processing. The related organizational structure is described by specific resource classes along with their interrelations.

Using special linking constructs, actions, functions and activities are combined to represent business processes. The decomposition and aggregation of processes is also supported.

*VIRSIM main principles*

Unlike the GRAI approach and IEM, the VIRSIM methodology intends to support the process of plants reengineering beginning from enterprise modeling and finishing with the implementation of the new optimized plant.

For enterprise modeling, VIRSIM uses the formalisms of IEM (the Process Model using the Generic Activity Model) for representing the physical system and the formalisms of the GRAI approach (GRAI grids and nets) to model the decisional system. IEM and the GRAI approach are integrated trough the concepts of 'Product' and 'Resource'. As we can see in the grid in Figure 1, the two functions 'Managing Products' and 'Managing Resources' use as subject the objects derived or instanciated from the IEM generic classes 'Product' and 'Resources'.

The different steps of the VIRSIM methodology approach are given below:

1. Model the existing physical system using IEM formalisms (Process Model)
2. Model the existing decisional system (driving the physical system) using the GRAI formalisms (GRAI grids and nets)
3. Evaluate and optimize the models by determining the weak points and by correcting them
4. Use the optimized physical system model to generate a rough layout of the future plant and transmit it to a CAD system
5. Enhance the rough layout using the CAD system and transmit it to a simulator
6. Simulate global logistics and get the logistic optimum model and the transfer lot
7. Automatically adjust the CAD layout
8. Design and simulate cell and work-place systems by means of Virtual Reality and obtain MTM optimum processes
9. Perform the 6 and 8 steps until proper results are obtained
10. Automation and man/machine interfacing
11. Perform step 7
12. Adapt the initial models if necessary

To do this last issue, it is necessary to characterize the physical layout, and this is done in tens of two items extracted from the logistic simulator (see Figure 3, system 5):

- Production strategy: MTS (Manufacturing to stock), ATO (assemble to order), MTO (manufacturing to order)
- Related main and auxiliary lines:

The main line is synchronized, time buffered inventory, contains the process technology, and sets the manufacturing lead-times. Main line ( differentiation on product inventory, quality, flexibility and service, auxiliary lines (machines and subcontractors) are just opposite decoupled systems.

## 3. THE VIRSIM TOOL

In order to support the VIRSIM methodology, a software tool is being developed. The architecture of this tool is given in Figure 3. It is composed of five subsystems and six interfaces between these subsystems.

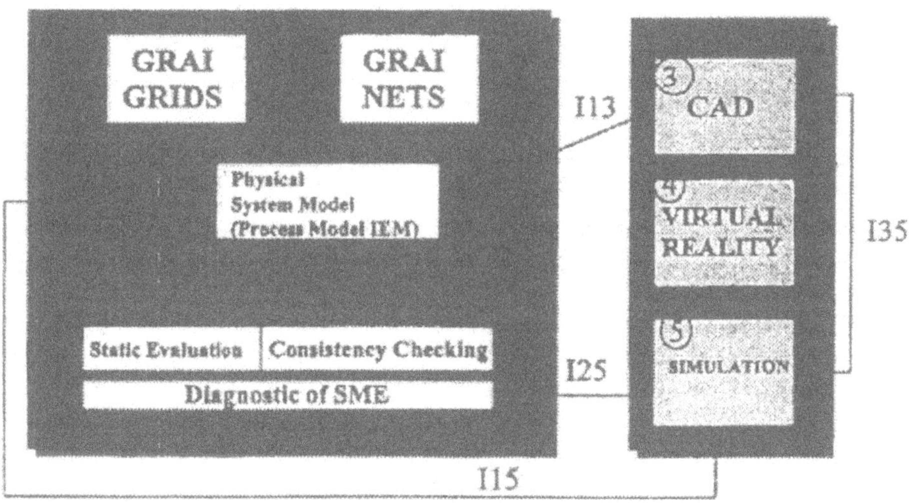


**Figure 3:** The architecture of the VIRSIM tool.

| | |
|---|---|
| *System 1:* | Integrated VIRSIM graphical editors. |
| *Function:* | Enterprise Modeling |
| *System 2:* | Static Evaluation, Consistency Checking and Diagnostic of the SME system |
| *Function:* | Static evaluation of the physical system model against selected criteria (rough costs and lead-time). Consistency Checking of the models (at the syntactical level). Rule-based diagnostic of the SME system (semantic check). |
| *System 3:* | 2D/3D low cost standard CAD. |

| | |
|---|---|
| *Function:* | I/O layout dimensions |
| *System 4:* | Low cost Virtual Reality (VR) software. |
| *Function:* | Solid representation of Icons . |
| | Workplace ergonomics and interference's. |
| *System 5.-* | Simulation software. |
| *Function:* | Material handling optimization, queuing and line balancing. |

The interfaces description is given below:

a) Interface 134
Use of the layout obtained through CAD as the background of the simulator.
The figures (dimensions) drawn in CAD are integrated in the mathematics of the simulator.

b) Interface $I_{35}$

Double clicking on a particular area or system either of the CAD drawing or the simulator will allow zooming a 3D solid representation in the VR system.
The 2D dimensions displayed in the CAD system or the ones optimized by the simulator (i.e.: buffer sizing) can be used as restrictions to build the 3D solid model of the VR system.
3D dimensions from the VR are imported to automatically build up a CAD 3D drawing.

c) Interface $I_{45}$
Double clicking on the simulator allows zooming a 3D solid representation in the VR system.
2D dimensions of the layout displayed on the simulator can be used as restrictions to build the 3D solid model of the VR system.
Coherence between cycle times deduced from the simulator and the workplace MTM analysis obtained by the VR system.

d) Interface $I_{13}$
The model of the physical system obtained using the editors (System 1) and the VIRSIM methodology is used as input by the CAD system (system 3). Using the data contained in this model, the interface generates automatically a rough drawing.

e) Interface $I_{25}$
Through this interface, the rule-based diagnostic system will analyze the results of the simulation and will present the results to the user. In addition, the simulation

tools will receive **specific** constraints from the diagnostic module (to focus the simulation on a particular area, for instance, to point out bottlenecks).

f) Interface $I_{15}$
The results of the simulation will lead, if they are not satisfactory, to the modification of the physical model, the whole process will have to be repeated.

## 4. CONCLUSIONS

We have presented in this paper the main principles of a new methodology dedicated to complete frequent factory re-engineering. In addition, we described the associated software tool, giving the details of its different modules and interfaces.
The VIRSIM methodology and its supporting tool are presently under development by the R&D Department of DATALDE SISTEPLANT, S.A. in consortium with the LAP/GRAI, the division of Systems Planning of the Fraunhofer IPK Berlin, INTEGRAI and several leading car components-makers in Spain.

## 5. REFERENCES

Doumeingts, G., (I *984). Methode GRAI, methods de conception des syst@mes en productique.* Doctoral Thesis, Universitd Bordeaux 1.

Zanettin, M., (1994). *ContributionLi une mgthode de conception de systems de production.* PhD Thesis,Universit6 Bordeaux 1.
Mertins, K., Jochem, R (1992) An Object Oriented Method for Integrated Enterprise modeling as a basis for Enterprise Coordination. *International Conference on Enterprise Integration Modeling Technolo8y (ICEIMT).* Hilton Head (South Carolina), US Air Force-Integration Technology Division.

## 6. BIOGRAPHIES

**ProL Dr. Javier Borda Elejabarietta** has been working as plant Engineer and Production Manager staff for 7 years, and from 1984 he is the managing director and C.E.O. of DATALDE, S.A., a Spanish 35 people industrial engineering company, sited in the Basque Country. He read in 1989 the Doctoral Mechanical Engineering dissertation on "CIM for plastic injection workshops". He is also Professor of Production and Engineerincr Management in the University of

Deusto, Bilbao, and the author of several international papers and a book titled: "Advanced Maintenance Techniques" (1990). He has become recently an IFIP WG 5.7 member.

Alvaro Polo is a Mechanical Engineer at DATALDE SISTEPLANT, S.A. Bilbao Spain.

**Dipi.-Ing. Roland Jochem** has obtained his MS in 1987 in Mechanical Engineering at the Technical University of Berlin. He has been working as Mechanical engineer at a company for special machines in Berlin from 1987 to 1988. Since 1989, he is a Scientist at the Fraunhofer-Institute for Production System and Design Technology (IPK) and since 1992 he is the responsible for the research group Business Process Modeling. His is an expert on business planning, specialized on production integration strategies, business process modeling, and information modeling and modeling methods. Roland Jochem is a member of ISO TC 184 SC5/WGI (Modeling and Architecture) and CEN/CENELEC/WG-ARC (Architecture and Enterprise Modeling).

**Guy Doumeingts** is Professor at the University Bordeaux 1. He obtained his PhD degree in 1967, from this same institution. He participated in the setting-up of the GRAI research group from the LAP, of which he is the Director since 1989. He has held many research contracts, published two books, and over 200 papers on CIM. He is expert for the Commission of the European Communities (ESPRIT Project), French representative to IFIP,

Chairman of the Technical Committee 45 (Computer Application in Technology), and member of the editorial board of several international journals.

**Adnane Moudden** is a research Engineer at the GRAI research group belonging to the LAP (Laboratoire d'Automatique et de Productique). He obtained his PhD degree from the University Bordeaux I in 1997. His research interests include case-based reasoning, neural-fuzzy systems, machine learning and the application of these fields to enterprise modeling and design.

59

# Teaching Engineering Technology with the World Wide Web

*Derral R. Linder*
*Orangeburg-Calhoun Technical College*
*3250 St. Matthews Road*
*Orangeburg, SC 29118-8299*
*Phone: (803) 535-1294*
*Fax: (803) 535-1388*
*E-mail: linderd@org.tec.sc.us*

**Abstract**

The Mechanical Engineering Department at Orangeburg-Calhoun Technical College has begun using the World Wide Web as an information source to supplement information presented to students. This instruction is currently being done in three ways. First, students are required to use at least three documents from the web when writing research papers for Mechanical Engineering Technology courses. Second, instructors research the web for examples that may be more current than examples given in the text. The URL's of these examples are then given to the students and homework assignments based on these examples are assigned. Third, students are expected to use the Internet to prepare parts lists and to find information about manufacturing companies. At the end of the first year of exposure to the World Wide Web, graduates are experiencing unusual rewards for their work.

**Keywords**

World Wide Web, Internet, URL

## 1. INTRODUCTION

With today's ever tightening educational budgets from local, state and federal governments, it is essential that colleges and universities reduce their operating expenses. One area where costs are skyrocketing is resource materials that must

Computer Applications in Production and Engineering. F. Plonka and G. Olling (Eds.)

keep pace with ever changing technology. In many cases, students are forced to use material that may be as much as twenty to thirty years out of date as colleges can no longer afford to replenish resource materials. There is one very practical way that is used here at Orangeburg-Calhoun Technical College (OCTC) to combat the high cost of resource materials - the Internet. OCTC has had access for nearly two years and is the only two year college in the state that presently offers more than one accredited course in the use of the Internet. For students in the Mechanical Engineering Technology (MET) department a workshop on the use of the Internet is mandatory.

## 2. CLASSROOM PROCEDURES

### *Student Indoctrination*

Many students who come to OCTC do not have any prior experience with using the Internet so they may not be able to use the net immediately. This presents no problems to any student entering the college, as OCTC is the first and presently the only two year institution in South Carolina offering more than one course for credit to teach the student how to function on the web. These courses are IST 225, IST 226, IST 227 and IST 228. IST 225 is the introductory course and offers topics associated with the Internet and Internet communications such as techniques on how to access various types of information, how to find resources and how to navigate the Internet. The course also introduces the students to E-mail and how they may set up their own web page. Presently, there is no account available for either student E-mail or web sites. Due to resource limitations, the college is unable to provide accounts for students. IST 225 is offered as an elective to all students and the response is so great that it is usually filled by the end of the first week of pre-registration (Hulsey, 1996). Also, students who take all four courses are finding employment as Web Masters earning as much as forty dollars per hour in the Orangeburg area. Students in the MET department are offered IST 225 as an elective but they are also required to attend a three hour workshop taught by the department head on using the Internet. This workshop is mandatory for MET seniors, but students from other curriculums are welcome to attend. It is offered several times a semester for student convenience. It teaches students how to access the web, open files if the URL is known and to use search engines, primarily, *Excite, Savvy Search, Yahoo and HotBot.* Once the students have attended the workshop, they are then given assignments to complete using the web.

### *Student Assignments*

Student assignments are usually broken down into three broad categories. The first category involves the professor finding a suitable web page or article beforehand and giving the URL to the students and requiring that a report be written on the article. The next category is the old fashion research paper, and the final is for students to research the net for information concerning manufacturers. These assignments are usually given in the order listed to facilitate the students development as they learn to navigate the web.

An example of the first category is that during the first week of MET 222, (Thermodynamics), one class discussion centers on temperature, the different temperature scales used, history of temperature measurement, absolute temperature and the effects of temperature on some environment. The students are given the following URL:

**http://www.unidata.ucar.edu/staff/blynds/tmp.html**

This address opens an excellent article about temperature and the students write a five hundred word summary on the article complete with keywords and abstract. The purpose of this assignment is three fold. It gives the students an opportunity to open a website using a known URL, refresh skills learned in the English and Technical Writing courses and to learn something about temperature.

As everyone knows, students everywhere love writing research papers. MET students are given a topic, length the paper must be in number of words or number of page., the number of resources to be cited and are asked to write a paper. Presently, at least half of the required number of resources must come from the Internet. The students use a search engine(s) to find materials related to the topic and are allowed to print one copy for their personal use in completing the paper. This is permitted along the same grounds that a student is allowed to make one copy of reference material for their personal use when using material that is closely guarded in the campus library. MET 231, (Machine Design), students are given the topic 'Engineering Ethics' and are expected to complete a fifteen hundred word research paper with a minimum of four references. Students usually find more than the required four references for this topic on the net and often use only these without going to the campus library for additional resources which gives rise to an issue that may need future discussion: Should students be allowed to find all the required resources on the web or should they be required to find some from traditional places such as the campus library? The MET department head has no problem with students using the web exclusively. The belief is that students will benefit more from using the Internet because the Internet is being used more often in places of employment. In addition, it is a concentrated source of information and does not require travel time to other facilities for research purposes. Although, not every instructor agrees with this view point, the MET department believes it is a valid one.

Finally students are required to use the Internet to find information about different manufacturing companies that have sites on the web. In MET 224 (Hydraulics and Pneumatics), the students are required to develop a list of vendors for a particular hydraulic or pneumatic equipment. This is not a new assignment as students have always been required to develop a vendor list from materials in the campus library such as the *Thomas Registry*. One particular aspect of this assignment is that there can be no repeat vendors in the class, which not only forces the students to use the web but also forces them to communicate with each other. In another assignment used in PHY 201 (Physics), students are given an engine's RPM, transmission gear ratio, differential gear ratio and tire specifications, i.e., LT265/75R16. The students then go to the Internet, search for a tire company page and find the tire diameter based on the specification. With this information, the student should be able to calculate the speed of the automobile in miles per hour. A future enhancement of this assignment may be to give the student the make of a particular vehicle, i.e., Ford Mustang GT along with the engine RPM and have them find all the information about the vehicle including gear ratios and tire specifications before calculating the speed of the automobile.

This final category of assignment is probably the most beneficial to the student. Once students leave OCTC and begin working, they often find themselves in positions where they must purchase supplies, equipment or gather information about a customer or even a competitor. If the students already have a background in using the Internet to search for such materials, this portion of their job will be easier.

## 3. INSTRUCTOR PREPARATION

Professors and instructors typically spend more time preparing for classes than they do actually teaching the class. This is true even if they teach the same course more than once per semester. The internet offers a distinct advantage for instructors that may considerably reduce preparation time. Many colleges and universities have home pages on the web and many departments within those institutions have a web page. Orangeburg-Calhoun Technical College may be visited at: **http://www.octech.org**. The URL of most colleges can be found at: **http://www.mit.edu:8001/people/cdemello/univ.html**.

Information posted on these pages may contain courses required for completion of the program and many times contain course outlines and syllabi as well. This readily accessible information allows an instructor to review many different ways of administering any given course and possibly select methods that may be better than the method previously used.

Also, laboratory experiments can be very expensive and often require extensive equipment which many colleges can no longer afford. Therefore, instructors at OCTC are currently searching the net to find alternative methods of providing labs. For example, early in MET 222 the perfect gas laws are taught. The instructor found very inexpensive methods of providing laboratory experiments to prove both Charles and Boyle's laws at: http:**//www.gp.k12.mi.us:80/main/schools/high/gpn/science/exp/exp.htm**. These experiments were adopted for the laboratory sections of the class.

## 4. DOCUMENTATION OF RESOURCES

The faculty and administration at OCTC consider all material on the web to be copyrighted unless the material states otherwise. Therefore, all material taken from the Internet, either by student or professor,

must be properly documented. The MET department at OCTC currently uses the following method (Perrin):

Author's name (if known), the full title of the article in quotations, the title of the complete work, if applicable, in italics, the date of the visit, and the complete URL.

EXAMPLE: Beverly T. Lynds, "About Temperature," Oct. 10, 1996, http://www.unidata.ucar.edu/staff/blynds/tmp.html.

## 5. CONCLUSIONS

The MET department has been requiring students to learn to use the Internet for two years and has had some very positive results. Students enjoy 'surfing the net' much more so than going to the campus library and have even used the web as a resource in classes where using the web is not required. One non-engineering class MET students are required to take is (HSS 101), Introduction to Humanities. Students in this course are required to write several papers based on cultural events and have started using the net to find information. Students have also found that the web can be used as a source to search for prospective employers in other areas of the country or world. The MET department considers the students' enthusiasm and quickly acquired expertise as a success in the program of using the web as a learning resource. Also, two very unique successes of the program have arisen. First, one graduating senior was selected over several four year graduates because the student could assemble parts and vendor list rather easily from the web. The other graduate is now managing a farm and is using the Internet to monitor the commodity market and weather in order to make more informed decisions on what and when to plant, when to harvest crops and when to buy and sell livestock.

The MET department is planning to expand the use of the Internet in the classroom. The MET home page is expected to be on-line by the 1997 fall semester and will be used as an aid in recruitment of students. Another plan for next year is to post tests on the MET page and have students complete them co-operatively. The students would then E-mail the results back to the professor for grading which will allow more time for class room and lab instruction..

## 6. REFERENCES

Hulsey, D. (1996), IST 225 Internet, OCTC Course Outline.

Perrin, R. (1997), *The Beacon Handbook,* 4th. Edition, Houghton Mifflin, New York.

## 7. BIOGRAPHY

Derral R. Linder holds a master's degree in Industrial Engineering and a bachelor's degree in Mechanical Engineering Technology from Clemson University as well as an associate's degree in MET from OCTC. He is the MET department head at OCTC having held that position for three years. During this time he has been instrumental in pioneering student use of the Internet at the college. Prior to this position, Mr. Linder worked in industry in various engineering functions including designer, process and quality engineering and engineering supervisor.

# 60
# Workforce Implications for the Virtual Manufacturing Environment

Dr. James R, Gray, CMfgE, CQA
Professor of Technology
gray$j@nku.edu
Northern Kentucky University, Highland Heights, KY, 4107

**Abstract**

There is a new reality in manufacturing today which calls for a global focus. This focus is upon what may be identified as a virtual manufacturing environment. The driving forces behind the virtual manufacturing environment are: a global economic system, a need for products with the most modern features, a lean and agile delivery system, and the highest quality. This new reality has placed great pressure upon the existing workforce. The need for new or innovative approaches to retrain workers that are in place must be identified. The methodology behind training for the virtual manufacturing environment must be developed.

We must examine the need for training in team work within the quality organization and training-the-trainer efforts to support and sustain organizational change. This paper is concerned with how training content can be structured and how Distance Learning technology can be used to establish a Learning Organization. The paper deals with the creation of a Learning Organization, whose purpose is to promote and sustain continuous learning through the use of computer based technology.

## 1. UPDATING THE WORK FORCE

Over the past three decades, U.S. workers with above average education and skills generally have adjusted better to changes in the economy then the less skilled and educated individual in the workforce. The country has had to confront chronic problems with economically and educationally disadvantaged workers. The structure

Computer Applications in Production and Engineering. F. Plonka and G. Olling (Eds.)

of the modern manufacturing economy, based upon rapid technological change, adds new urgency to identifying effective workforce development training and educational approaches.

Perhaps the greatest challenge confronting the workforce today is the declining demand for low skilled workers. More than half of the new employment in the past few years has been in higher paying occupations; only about one fourth of new jobs have been in the low wage category. Most new jobs are concentrated in the managerial, professional, and technical fields, which now comprise over 30 percent of all jobs in the United States. Rapid technological developments, especially in communications and information processing, define many of the skills in demand. In this job market, educated workers with high skills are seeing their earnings increase, but those with less education and fewer skills are experiencing stagnant and even declining real wages.

With the advent of the new reality of a global manufacturing environment, one which puts the U.S. worker in direct skill competition with the workforce of other nations, we must look to new approaches for the education and training of our workers. In particular the low skilled or educationally deficient worker. Methodologies that will deliver quality training programs in the most timely way are needed. Educational technology that allows for the delivery of efficient and effective instruction is necessary if we are to serve our existing workforce.

## 2. THE LEARNING ORGANIZATION

What is needed today is a total and comprehensive orientation to training and education, both on and off the job, in order to capitalize upon the human resource potential available to the labor market. One such approach is what James DeVito calls the "Learning Organization." DeVito has stated that "the learning organization is a relatively new concept that has had a profound effect on how we think about organizational life." He further indicates that "the learning organization concept challenges a company to use knowledge as a basis for its competitive strategy and to see organizational learning as the bedrock for its ability to be truly global."[1]

Dave Gravin defines the learning organization as:

> an organization skilled at creating, acquiring, and transferring knowledge,

and

> at modifying its behavior to reflect new knowledge and insights.

---

[1] DeVito, J.D. "The Learning Organization", The ASTD Training & Development Handbook, 1996.

The learning organizations are skilled at five main activities: systematic problem solving, experimentation with new approaches, learning from the experiences and best practices of others, and transferring knowledge quickly and efficiently throughout the organization. By creating systems and processes that support these activities and integrate them into the fabric of daily operations, companies can manage their learning more effectively.[2]

One of the main challenges to the establishment of such an organization within any company is to invision the structure of the educational system which is needed to delivery such an environment. Both DeVito and Gravin advocate the total integration of the education/training activity with the business function of the organization. Naturally, the basis of such an undertaking becomes "knowledge". Knowledge becomes the product and process of our attention. How to structure and deliver knowledge upon demand, instantaneously throughout an organization, is key to the establishment of a Learning Organization. Such a paradigm is offered in figure 1.

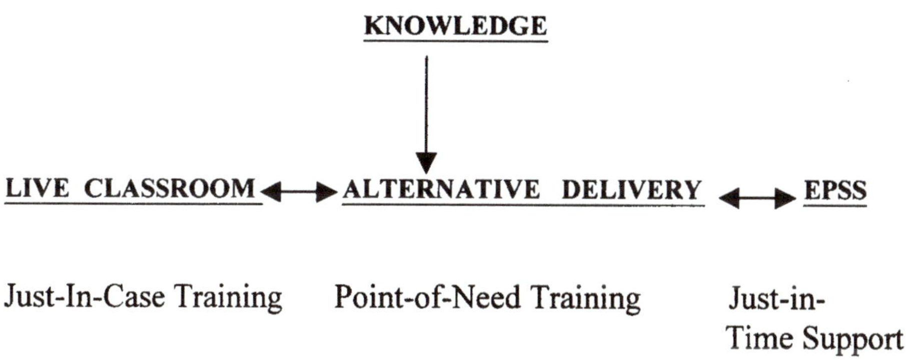


**Figure 1** Education Support System

As figure 1 suggests, a learning organization requires parallel educational processes that can support and react to delivering knowledge at the time a learner needs information. The more traditional Just-in-Case training occurs through the traditional institutional channels, courses and educational degree programs, based upon the anticipation of knowledge and upon our past experience of need. The Point-of- Need training has been recognized as accessing satellite broadcast, playing video discs, or other self directed learning, delivered closer to the time of need by the learner. In-plant workshops, seminars, and conferences or common training methods are utilized

[2] Garvin, D., "Building a Learning Organization", Harvard Business Review, July-August, 1993.

for this type of education. Electronic Performance Support Systems (EPSS) provides just enough knowledge, Just-In-Time, for the immediate need of the learner. EPSS is a set of tools that aids the learner in accessing the knowledge and supporting its application in an immediate task. Our need is to integrate these three very different types of educational processes into a total approach. This approach must complement all three processes without interfering with the delivery of any one.

## 3. AN INSTRUCTIONAL APPROACH: INTERACTIVE MULTIMEDIA

The task to deliver knowledge "on demand" in an effective and efficiently way has been greatly aided by the advent of computer aide instruction (CAI). CAI has been in existence for some time within the public educational system, but has not been fully explored by industry as a means of training. What is unique about Interactive Multimedia (IM) is its marriage of computer based training (CBT) and audiovisual (AV) technology, which results in a powerful and flexible delivery method. IM is designed to integrate text, graphics, animation, audio, motion video, and computers so that content can be delivered to the learner in any of the three educational processes above described. Because the knowledge is computer based, learners can interact with it and go through content in a sequence and depth that meets their particular needs. And because IM systems are designed for the micro or personal computers, IM training programs can be used at any point and any time within the organization.

The advantages of IM technology is sighted by Howell and Silvey[3] as:

1. Meets the individual needs of many learners, accommodating users at all levels of expertise.

2. Lets each user work at the pace that best suits him or her.

3. Offers the best presentation for different subjects.

4. Reverses the traditional student-teacher ratio, bringing many teachers or experts to the individual student.

5. Provides "creative" learning experiences that give each student a continuing functional reason to learn.

---

[3] Howell, J.J., Silvey, L.O., "Interactive Multimedia Training Systems", The ASTD Training & Development Handbook, 1996.

6. Can be designed to encourage learners to explore a topic rather than simply seek a single right answer.

7. Allows learners at different levels to bring their own expertise and creative capabilities into the learning process.

8. Can create a "virtual classroom" wherever a microcomputer or workstation can be placed.

9. Permits small groups of two or three learners to engage in team problem solving activities.

10. Can function as an in class electronic performance support system, containing the information, guidance, and tools needed to complete complex activities.

IM educational technology can be imbedded within the firm's computer network, thereby integrating the training activity into the job itself at the point of need. Small units can be delivered the moment the content is needed on the job and at the workstation. In this way, training and job function are considered one in the same by the trainee. IM can move the training activity beyond teaching and into the realm of direct work performance. This is particularly important given that the global economy is moving from an orientation on production towards emphasizing the converting of information to knowledge.

The traditional approaches to training, with its dependence on classroom presentation, becomes too restrictive in the learning organization. The manufacturing organization today presents workers with a challenge to continuously be innovative in the process of solving problems. There are few "right" answers that the worker can depend upon to be so stable that they would never change. This calls for a continuous learning process, with a continuous training process in place for support, to be the goal of training methodology. Within this training system the worker/learner must be in control of the learning process directly, able to analyze the problems at hand, and arrive at reasonable solutions in a systematic way. This, then, becomes the training goal of the learning organization. The learning organization must put in place processes and systems that make it essentially a teaching concern. IM technology delivers the "means" of accomplishing this goal.

## 4. INSTRUCTIONAL INFORMATION AND RESOURCES

The need for firms to obtain the most current information on how to establish a learning organization is crucial. Such information is available in many sources.

Possibly the most up to date information on training and the learning organization would come from the research journals. Several are listed below.

*Adult Education Quarterly*, American Association for Adult and Continuing Education
*Educational Technology*, Educational Technology, Inc.
*Group & Organizational Management*, Sage Periodicals Press
*Human Resource Development Quarterly*, American Society for Training and Development
*Performance and Instruction*, International Society for Performance Improvement

Several more specific IM directed journals are listed below.

*Microcomputer Trainer*, System Literacy, Inc.
*Training*, Lakewood Publications
*Training and Development*, American Society for Training and Development
*Workforce Training News: The Newsmagazine for Employee Learning and Development*,
Enterprise Communication, Inc.

Additionally, professional associations are vital in obtaining the necessary information and direction when implementing the learning organization through IM. Several helpful associations are:

American Society for Training and Development
1640 King Street, Box 1443
Alexandria, VA 22323

American Vocational Association
1410 King Street
Alexandria, VA 22314

Association for Business Simulations and Experiential Learning
Center for Business Simulations
Georgia Southern College
Statesboror, GA 30460-8127

Association for Supervision and Curriculum Development
1250 North Pitt Street
Alexandria, VA 22314

Instructional Systems Association
P.O. Box 1196
Sunset Beach, CA 90742-1196

Organization Development Institute
11234 Walnut Ridge Road
Chesterland, OH 44026

Organization Development Network
P.O. Box 69329
Portland, OR 97201

Society for Applied Learning Technology
50 Culpepper Street
Warrenton, VA 22186

The Internet, with over 22,000 computer and computer networks, represents the prime source for help in establishing a IM based learning organization. The many *listservs* available on the Internet would be a logical starting point for information. A few would be:

| | |
|---|---|
| AEE-LIST@PUCC.PRINCETON.EDU | (Experiential education list) |
| ALTLEARN@SJUVM.STJOHNS.EDU | (Alternative approaches to learning) |
| ASAT-EVA@UNLVM.UNL.EDU | (Distance education evaluation group) |
| DISRES-L@RYERSON.BITNET | (Distance education research list) |
| HRD-L@MIZZOU1.MISSOURI.EDU | (Human resource development group) |
| TRDEV-L@PSUVM.PSU.EDU | (Training and development discussions list) |

Another source on the NET would be news groups. The following news groups would have vital information, helpful in the establishment of a training program.

| | |
|---|---|
| ALT.EDUCATION.DISTANCE | (Learning over networks) |
| BIT.LISTSERV.ERL-L | (Educational technology list) |
| BIT.LISTSERV.QUALITY | (Total Quality Management in |

Manufacturing and Service)
MISC.EDUCATION.MULTIMEDIA (Multimedia discussions)
COMP.GROUPWARE.LOTUS-NOTES.MISC (Improving group work processes)

## 5. CONCLUSION

If we are to develop educational methodologies that are focused upon today's training needs, than we must look at the environment within which training occurs. We must realize that the manufacturing environment must be seen as a learning environment. This learning environment must be supported by a learning organization, whose purpose is to promote and advance the individual's educational efforts at understanding and using knowledge on an "as needed" basis. The Interactive Multimedia technology systems available today are both efficient and effective at providing the means to delivering this type of learning organization. There is sufficient information, resources, and technology available to us to accomplish this goal.

## 6. BIOGRAPHY

**Dr. James R. Gray**

Dr. Gray teaches Manufacturing Engineering and Industrial Technology in the Department of Technology at Northern Kentucky University. He has served the institution for nineteen years. Dr. Gray received his doctorate from West Virginia University and his masters from Western Kentucky University. His undergraduate work was completed at Western Kentucky University in 1971. He is a Certified Manufacturing Engineer, through the Society of Manufacturing Engineers, and is certified as a Quality Auditor by the American Society for Quality Control. He is a qualified Lead Auditor for ISO 9000.

Dr. Gray has over 25 years of experience in education and training in industrial manufacturing subjects. He has specialized in the field of quality control and automated manufacturing processes. Dr. Gray teaches classes such as Quality Control, Manufacturing Processes, Automated Systems, Robotics, etc. He has trained with companies such as Mazak Corporation, Sachs Corporation, Graphic Resources, Esco, F & N Sheppard, Clarion Corporation, ITT, Rockwell, etc.

61

# The relationship between competencies learned in Manufacturing Engineering programs and competencies represented in the CASA/SME Enterprise Wheel Model

*B. Lahidji, Ph.D., CMfgT*
*College of Technology*
*Eastern Michigan University*
*Ypsilanti, MI, 48197*
*313-487-2040*
*313-487-8755*
*bob.lahidji@emich.edu*

*T. Tillman, Ph.D., CMfgE, CEI*
*College of Technology*
*Eastern Michigan University*
*Ypsilanti, MI, 48197*
*313-487-2040*
*313-487-8755*
*tracy.tillman@emich.edu*

**Abstract**

This paper presents a comparison of what manufacturing engineering programs are teaching and what industry expects manufacturing engineers to know, as presented by the CASA/SME Manufacturing Enterprise Wheel. This comparison suggests that manufacturing engineering programs should encompass a broader scope of

Computer Applications in Production and Engineering. F. Plonka and G. Olling (Eds.)

engineering, technology, and management, and work to integrate content and projects across the curriculum.

**Keywords**
Manufacturing engineering, manufacturing education, manufacturing curriculum, and manufacturing enterprise wheel.

## 1 INTRODUCTION

The emergence of new technology during the past decade has revolutionized the manufacturing industry. However, in order to be more competitive in the global market a knowledgeable and technically competent workforce is also needed. Engineering education programs should reflect the needs and changes of today's industry and prepare young engineers to meet the challenges of the competitive world of manufacturing. Industry needs engineers who have the understanding of basic manufacturing engineering theory and the ability to apply knowledge that is relevant to the real world of manufacturing. Moreover, companies need individuals who have expertise in their field of specialty and who have knowledge and understanding of the integrated manufacturing environment. As such, there is a need for a comparison between the competencies required by industry today and the competencies learned in manufacturing engineering programs.

## 2 PURPOSE

The purpose of this paper is to report on the relationship between the competencies represented by the new Computer and Automated Systems Association of the Society of Manufacturing Engineers (CASA/SME) enterprise integration wheel model and the competencies learned in manufacturing engineering programs. There have been major changes in manufacturing in the United States and globally, and these changes have been reflected in the new CASA/SME enterprise model. Furthermore, these changes should be accommodated in existing manufacturing engineering programs.

## 3 DEFINITION OF ENGINEERING

According to the American Society for Engineering Education (1993b) and the Engineering Technology Council (1991), engineering involves the knowledge of advanced mathematical and natural sciences, and is devoted to the creation of new technology for the benefit of humanity. In addition, engineering is defined by the Accreditation Board for Engineering and Technology (ABET) as:

> "A profession in which knowledge of the mathematical and natural sciences gained by study, experience, and practice is applied with judgment to develop ways to utilize, economically, the materials

and forces of nature for the benefit of mankind" (Accreditation Board for Engineering and Technology, 1993b, p. 5).

Walker (1961) stated that "engineering is fundamentally committed to the translation of scientific facts and information to create machines, structures, materials, processes, [systems] and the like that can be used . . ." Furthermore, The engineer creates new products, devices, structures, materials, processes, and systems through the use of science, mathematics, and engineering science (Duderstadt, Knoll, and Springer, 1982).

## 4 GOALS OF ENGINEERING EDUCATION

The goals of undergraduate engineering education is to provide a base and a means for life-long learning rather than only to prepare a person as a specialist to perform a particular function in a particular industry. The following objectives were identified for undergraduate engineering curricula:

"1. To provide an understanding of fundamental scientific principles and a command of basic knowledge underlying the student's field.

2. To convey an understanding of engineering methods such as analysis and computation, modeling, design and experimental verification, as well as experience in applying these methods to realistic engineering problems and processes.

3. To provide the student with the following:

    a. An understanding of social and economic forces and their relationship with engineering systems, including the idea that the best technical solution may not be feasible when viewed in its social, political, or legal context;
    b. A sense of professional responsibility developed through consideration of moral, ethical, and philosophical concepts; and
    c. Mastering of the ability to organize and express ideas logically and persuasively in both written and oral communication." (Engineering Undergraduate Education, 1986, pp. 9-10)

## 5 ENGINEERING PROGRAMS

A review of the literature reveals that programs offered under engineering are very diverse in scope and emphasis. According to the Directory of Engineering and Engineering Technology published by ASEE in 1994, a total of 1442 engineering baccalaureate programs were accredited by the EAC/ABET. Moreover, 13 of those programs are in the area of manufacturing engineering.

The basic engineering education curricular components are mathematics, basic sciences, humanities, social sciences, engineering sciences, engineering design methods, and an engineering specialty. Thus, the content of engineering programs must be integrated in such a way that it will enable a graduate to function as an engineer (Accreditation Board for Engineering and Technology, 1993a).

## 6 CAREERS IN ENGINEERING

The graduates of engineering programs hold many different industrial positions with many of them being related to their undergraduate area of specialization, such as: automotive engineer, civil engineer, computer engineer, construction engineer, electrical engineer, industrial engineer, mechanical engineer, nuclear engineer, plant engineer, structural engineer, systems engineer, etc. In addition, research and development units are usually supervised and managed by engineers. According to Israel (1995) "engineers may also manage different divisions or units of a company and they hold management positions in such areas as computer-aided design, computer aided manufacturing, inventory control, manufacturing, production, process design, product design, quality control, systems, and technical sales."

Figure 1 represents the historical interfacing of the engineers in the occupational and educational spectrum (Lahidji, 1996).

**Theory** **Practice**

**Pre 1940s**

| Scientist | Engineer | Technician | Craftsman |
|---|---|---|---|

**Today**

| Scientist | Engineer | Engineering Technologist | Industrial Technologist | Technician | Craftsman |
|---|---|---|---|---|---|

**Figure 1** The placement of engineers in the occupational and educational spectrum.

## 7 MANUFACTURING ENGINEERING

Based on the ABET Accreditation Yearbook (1996), there are 13 manufacturing engineering programs at the baccalaureate degree level which are accredited by ABET. In addition, according to SME's Directory of Manufacturing Education (1993) there are approximately 70 engineering programs that offer manufacturing engineering as an option. In the Directory of Manufacturing Education (1990, p.3) SME defined manufacturing engineering as:

> "that specialty of professional engineering which requires such education and experience as is necessary to understand, apply and control engineering procedures in manufacturing processes and methods of production of industrial commodities and products and requires the ability to plan the practices of manufacturing, to research and develop the tools, processes, machines and equipment, and to integrate the facilities and systems for producing quality products with optimal expenditures."

Furthermore, SME (1997) suggested that the graduates of manufacturing engineering curriculum must be proficient in the following areas:

> "1. Materials and manufacturing processes: understanding the behavior and
> properties of materials as they are altered and influenced by processing in manufacturing.
>
> 2. Process, assembly, and product engineering: understanding the design of products and the equipment, tooling, and environment necessary for their manufacturing.
>
> 3. Manufacturing competitiveness: understanding the creation of competitive
> advantage through manufacturing planning, strategy and control.
>
> 4. Manufacturing systems design: understanding the analysis, synthesis, and control of
> manufacturing operations using statistical and calculus-based methods.
>
> 5. Graduates must be able to measure manufacturing process variables in a
> manufacturing laboratory and make technical inferences about the process."

The traditional role of a manufacturing engineer is changing from functioning in a segregated fashion to a more integrated one. They are more and more involved in the coordination of people, information, and technology within an organization. SME's Profile 21 (1988) study brought to light the more integrative role of today's manufacturing engineers.

## 8 MANUFACTURING ENTERPRISE WHEEL

The Computer and Automated Systems Association (CASA) of the Society of Manufacturing Engineers (SME) developed the CIM Wheel in 1985, which was received enthusiastically by both the membership of SME and industry (CASA,1993). The CIM Wheel represented a new manufacturing environment and focused on a computer information system architecture for the integration of manufacturing automation. The 1985 CIM Wheel included the following five major components:

1. General business management,
2. Product and process definition,
3. Manufacturing planning and control,
4. Factory automation, and
5. Information resources management.

At the same time that U.S. manufacturing companies were implementing CIM into their operations, they were out-performed by a number of manufacturers who were adapting a new and very different approach, called lean/agile production (Womack, Jones, and Roos, 1991). They identified the superiority of the lean production system over conventional mass production systems in the following areas:

1. Higher productivity (both in space and per employee),
2. Higher profitability,
3. Higher product quality,
4. Cooperative industrial relations,
5. Cross-training,
6. Multi-skilled employee development,
7. Job rotation, and
8. Greater worker satisfaction.

In addition, Rehder (1990) in the article entitled "Japanese Transplant: After the Honeymoon" identified the following elements as being unique to a lean production system:

1. Employee empowerment,
2. Greater responsibility,
3. Teamwork,
4. Lateral communication,

5. Continuous improvement,
6. Multi-skilled employees,
7. Commitment to training (on-going training),
8. Job security,
9. Reduction of job classifications, and
10. Workers involvement in the specification of work methods.

Recently, the Boeing Company (ASEE PRISM, 1996, p.11) identified a list of desired attributes of engineering graduates. The list included the following factors.

1. A good understanding of the engineering fundamentals, including:
   Mathematics(including statistics),
   Physical and life sciences, and
   Information technology.
2. A good grasp of the design and manufacturing process.
3. A basic understanding of the context in which engineering is practiced, including:
   Economics and business practice,
   History,
   The environment, and
   Customer and societal needs.
4. A multidisciplinary systems perspective.
5. Good communication skills:
   Written,
   Verbal,
   Graphic, and
   Listening.
6. High ethical standards.
7. An ability to think critically and creatively as well as independently and cooperatively.
8. Flexibility-an ability and the self-confidence to adapt to rapid/major change.
9. Lifelong desire and commitment to learn.
10. A profound understanding of the importance of teamwork.

To reflect the new manufacturing environment, CASA redeveloped the CIM Wheel into the new Manufacturing Enterprise Wheel (Figure 2). According to Tillman (1994) the Manufacturing Enterprise Wheel provides an overview of today's best practices in a manufacturing integrated enterprise. In justifying this new approach, CASA (1993) stated that:

> "In the mid-1980s we understood the need to break down the walls between design and manufacturing . We did not articulate other issues so well, such as the importance of simplifying processes before automation and the enterprise with its customers and suppliers. New insight brings us to the new

Manufacturing Enterprise Wheel. This wheel is a graphical index to the knowledge and organizational approach required in today's manufacturing world."

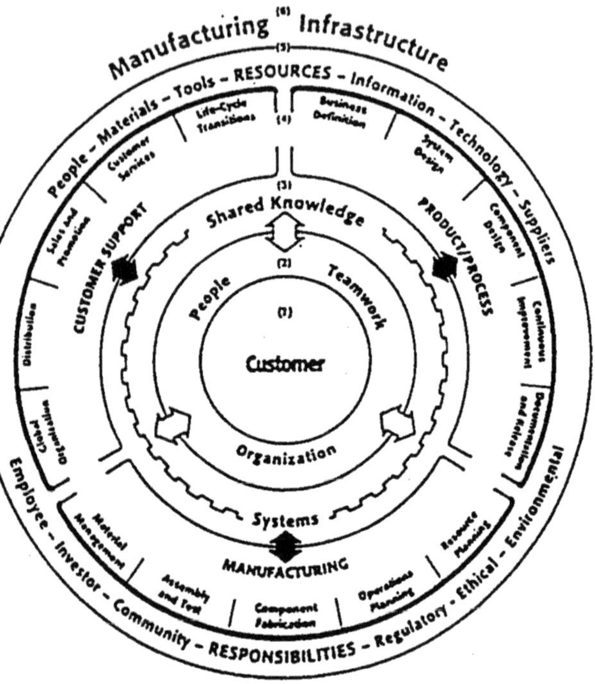


**Figure 2** The New Manufacturing Enterprise Wheel.

According to CASA (1993) the new wheel enhances the understanding of six key areas which are critical to success in today's competitive manufacturing environment. They are as follows:

1. The customer becomes the central focus of the organization.
2. The importance of teams and human networking.
3. The interface between knowledge and the system for the purpose of sharing information.
4. A focus on key processes from marketing through design, manufacturing, and customer support.
5. A leaner and more agile organization, and less bureaucratic structure.
6. Recognition and integration of external environmental factors such as customers, competitors, suppliers, and the global manufacturing infrastructure.

Considering this, one can conclude that in order for professionals entering or working in today's manufacturing environment to be successful, they must have the following competencies (Tillman, 1993):

1. Interface successfully with the customer, form teams, and work with a multi-cultural workforce.
2. Gather and process data, and formulate accurate concepts.
3. Determine system and software architecture requirements.
4. Implement and supervise system tests.
5. Manage and control projects.

## 9 THE COMPARISON OF COMPETENCIES

The new wheel represents an integrated manufacturing environment which requires a workforce with strong technical and people skills. Therefore, the graduates of manufacturing engineering programs must have the knowledge and skills to direct, organize, motivate, and be able to work with today's multi-cultural workforce. SME/CASA (cited in Tillman, 1993) defined a successful enterprise integrator as:

> "An individual who can facilitate the implementation of complex business changes using enterprise information technology to enhance products and services. He/She understands the computer and information side of design through manufacturing and can lead companies in the implementation of programs."

A comparison between the competencies which are presented in the Manufacturing Enterprise Wheel and the competencies taught in engineering programs suggests that there is a need for a greater emphasis and/or improvement in the following curricular areas:

1. People and managerial skills.
2. Written and oral communications skills.
3. Greater emphasis on educating students to work with a multi-cultural workforce.
4. Study of the global market place.
5. More emphasis on resources management.
6. Ethical and environmental responsibilities.
7. Capstone projects emphasizing team work.
8. Greater emphasis on hands-on projects that simulate the real working environment.
9. Cooperative educational experiences.

## 10 CONCLUSION

Today's engineer is becoming that of an integrator, and more of a coordinator of information, technology, and people. Thus, team work and people skills will play an important role in the work of engineers. Industry needs individuals who are experts in their special area of interest and who have a working knowledge and understanding of the integrated manufacturing environment (Lahidji,1996). Moreover, the graduates of engineering programs should have the skills, knowledge, and abilities to form and work in teams, collect data, formulate concepts, determine system needs, administer system tests, and determine software architecture. Engineering programs should be based on a broader perspective of engineering, technology, and management and work to integrate content and processes across the curriculum.

## 11 REFERENCES

Accreditation Bard for Engineering Technology (1992). *Criteria for accrediting programs in engineering technology.* New York- Author.

Accreditation Board for Engineering and Technology. (1993b). *Definitions of engineering and engineering Technology* . Unpublished Document.

Accreditation Board for Engineering and Technology. (1996). *1996 ABET accreditation yearbook.* New York: Author.

American Society for Engineering Education. (1993a). *ASEE organizational chart.* Unpublished document.

American Society for Engineering Education. (1993b). *Directory of engineering and engineering technology undergraduate programs.* Washington, DC: Author.

American Society for Engineering Education. (1994). *Directory of Engineering and Engineering Technology Undergraduate Programs.* Washington DC: Author.

America Society for Engineering Education (1996, December). Briefings: Employers checklist. Prism **6** 4, 11.

Computer and Automated Systems Association. (1993). *The new manufacturing enterprise wheel.* Dearborn, MI: Society of Manufacturing Engineers.

Directory of Engineering & Engineering Technology-Undergraduates programs (1994). America Society for Engineering Education.

Duderstadt, J. J., Konoll, G. F., & Springer, G. S. (1982). *Principles of engineering.* New York: John Wiley & Sons.

Engineering Technology Council. (1991). *Educational issues of importance to the engineering technology council (ETC) of the ASEE.* Unpublished manuscript.

Engineering Technology Council. (1991). *Educational issues of importance to the engineering council (ETC) of the ASEE.* Unpublished manuscript.

*Engineering Undergraduate education.* (1986). Washington, DC: National Academy Press.

Israel, E. N. (1995). *Technology education and other technically related programs.* Foundations of technology education. In G.E. Martin (Ed.), 44th Yearbook. New York: Glencoe, McGraw-Hill.

Lahidji, B. (1996). *The state of manufacturing education.* America Society for Engineering Education, North Central Section Spring Conference.

Rehder, R. R. (1990, January-February) Japanese transplants: After the honeymoon. *BusinessHorizons*, pp.87-98.

Society of Manufacturing Engineers (1988). Countdown to the future: The Manufacturing Engineering in the 21[st] Century. Society of Manufacturing Engineers: Dearborn, MI.

Society of Manufacturing Engineers (1997). Program criteria for manufacturing and similarly named engineering programs. Society of Manufacturing Engineers: Dearborn, MI.

Tillman, T. (1989). A Delphi study to identify fundamental competency areas for certification testing of manufacturing technologists and entry-level manufacturing engineers. (Doctoral Dissertation, Purdue University, 1989). *Dissertation Abstracts International*, 50, 3501A

Tillman, T. (1993, November). *The Manufacturing Enterprise Integrator certification program*. Presentation at Autofact 93. Chicago, IL.

Tillman, T. (1994) *A new model of manufacturing enterprise integration: the CASA/SME manufacturing enterprise wheel*. Eastern Michigan University, USA 94LM032

Walker, R. A. (1961). Engineers and/or scientists. *Journal of Engineering Education*. 51:419-21 (February).

Womack, J. P., Jones, D. T., & Roos, D. (1991).*The machine that changed the world: The story of lean production*. Harper Perennial

**Major Points:**

- Explain the new CASA/SME Enterprise model.
- Discuss the competencies learned in Manufacturing Engineering programs.
- Discuss the relationship between competencies represented by the CASA/SME model and the competencies learned in Manufacturing Engineering programs.
- Discussion and suggestion for updating the competencies of Manufacturing Engineering programs.

**Summary:**
This presentation will help instructors to assess the competencies learned in their Manufacturing Engineering programs by comparing them to competencies needed by industry, and for possible improvement of their programs.

The competitive edge in manufacturing is no longer based upon the utilization of high tech equipment. The advantages associated with possessing high tech equipment has been diminished due to the availability and downward pricing of equipment. For example, in the automobile industry obtaining high tech equipment does not provide a competitive edge over the competitors. Today the emphasis is on continuous improvement, simplifying in manufacturing processes, and optimizing of human resources.

# 62

# THE EUROPEAN VIEW ON GLOBAL ENTERPRISE COMPUTER APPLICATION IN PRODUCTION AND ENGINEERING

*G. DOUMEINGTS*
LAP/GRAI, University Bordeaux 1
351, Cours de la Libération, 33405 TALENCE France
Phone (33) 5 56 84 65 30 Fax (33) 5 56 84 66 44
E.mail : doum@lap.u-bordeaux

*P. KOROHONEN, K. HUTTUNEN*
Nokia Mobil Phone
Bo Box 86, 24101 SALO, Finland
Phone (358) 10 5051 Fax (358) 10 505 5370
E.mail : pertti.korhonen@nmp.nokia.com

These two papers will give an overview on the European situation in the domain of Computer Application in Production and Engineering.

We will present hereafter the summary of the Guy DOUMEINGTS paper. It is written with the support of well known European researchers : Prof. Jim BROWNE (CIMRU - National University of IRELAND - GALWAY and UMIST), Prof. Hans GRABOWSKI (RPK, University of Karlsruhe), Prof. Frank-Lothar KRAUSS (IPK - Berlin), Dr Kei MERTINS (IPK - Berlin).

Today's manufacturing enterprises face a completely changed economic environment. The market has moved from a local market to a world wide global economy, the competitors become more and more agressif due to the emergence of open markets, reductions in trade barriers and improvement in transportation and communications links. Europeans manufacturing enterprises have adopted the same strategy than the enterprises belonging to the other continents : improvement of the competitiveness in all functions, reactivity to the market change by integrating all functions, adopting a Business Processes Structures and finally working more closely with their suppliers and customers by building Extended Enterprises in order to improve the whole Value Chain.

We will use the model of Manufacturing Business proposed by [Browne 96] to structure our presentation :

Computer Applications in Production and Engineering. F. Plonka and G. Olling (Eds.)

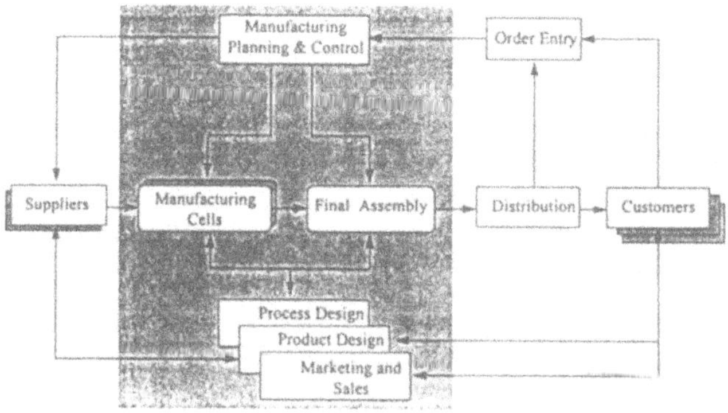


Integration in Manufacturing

The first paragraph describes the evolution of the concepts of the Extented Enterprise which can concern all the parts of the model.

The second part presents the use of EDI (Electronic Data Interchange) in the Product and Process Design : CDI (CAD/CAM Data Interchange). CDI is developed today in Europe through European Consortium (as AIRBUS Industry). Its development is facilitated by the development of product data modelling (PDM) and the standardization through STEP.

The third part describes the evolution of Production Management from MRP II to ERP (Enterprise Ressources Planning), evolving also from MTS (Make to Stock) to MTO (Make to Order). The Supply Chain Management and the Demand Chain Management are described in details by the joint paper.

The fourth part will discuss the need of technics in order to elaborate the various model of the Integrated Manufacturing System. The Computer Aided Technics, today available, cannot be used efficiently if the company is not able to design, at a conceptual level, the optimised model in terms of Business Processes. Enterprise Modelling Technics will be more and more used in order to facilitate the implementation of New Technology.

The European View on Global Enterprise in the domain of Computer Application in Production and Engineering is certainly very closed than the views in other continents due to the globalization of the economy. Anyway through the various Research and Development supported by European Commission (ESPRIT, BRITE/EURAM,...) and also by the European States (EUREKA) it exists a European way to introduce the Advanced Technology in the Enterprises.

## REFERENCES

Browne, J., Jagdev, H.S. (1996) The Extended Enterprise : a Context for Product Development and Production. *Internal Publication* (CIMRU - National University of IRELAND - GALWAY and UMIST).

Krause, F.L., Doblies M. (1997) A Communication Environment for Global Automotive Engineering. *Proceeding International Symposium on Global Engineering Networking* - Antwerpen 1997 - Eds J. GAUSEMEIER.

Krause, F.L., Doblies M. (1995) Product Development using IBC. Proceeding of the First International SMC *Workshop Integrated Broadband Communications and Collaborative Work in the Automotive Industry (CWIBC)* - May 10-11/1995 - University of Trento - Italy.

Grabowski, H., Pocsai Z.S. (1997) Electronic Market Place : Beyond the Vision.
*Proceeding of the International Symposium on Global Engineering Networking* - April 97 - Antwerpen.

Kurz, A., Pusch R. (1997) BKKN : Berliner Kreis Kompetenz Netzwerk : Know How Transfer from Campus to Industry via Internet.
*Proceeding of the International Symposium on Global Engineering Networking* - April 97 - Antwerpen.

Faux, J., Kestelet, P., Langtoz, G., Pocsai, Zs., Radeke, E., Stewing, F.J. (1997) Exploitation of Product Data Technology by the Global Engineering Networking Initiative.
*Proceeding of the European Conference Product Data Technology Days* - April 97 - Sophia Antipolis - France.

Elovaino, K., Kunz J. (1997) DOCSTEP : Technical Documentation Creation and Management using STEP.
*SGML Europe 97 Conference* - May 97 - Barcelona - Spain.

Grabowski, H., Rude, S., Pocsai, Zs. (1997) Ontology Technology : the KEY for Intelligent migration and retrieval of Information in Engineering Networks.
*International Conference on Engineering Design ICED 97* - August 97 - Tampere - Finland.

Mertins, K., Edeler, H., Jochem, R., Hofmann J. (1995) Object-Oriented Modelling and Analysis of Business *Processes in Integrated Manufacturing Systems Engineering* - Chapman & Hall.

Doumeingts, G., Ducq, Y.(1996) Production Management : which Future.
*Advances in Production Management Systems Conference* - Kyoto - Japan.

Doumeingts, G., Vallespir, B., Marcotte, F. (1995) A Proposal for an Integrated Model of Manufacturing System : Application to the re-engineering of an Assembly Shop.
*Control Engineering, Special Section on Models for Management and Control, Vol.3 n°1, Oxford, Pergamon Press Ltd*, pp 59-67.

Doumeingts, G., Vallespir, B., Chen, D. (1995) Methodologies for Designing CIM systems.
*A survey - Computers in Industry, Special Issue on CIM in the Extended Enterprise, Vol. 25 n°3*, Amsterdam, Elsevier, pp 263-280.

Doumeingts, G., Vallespir (1995) A Methodology Supporting Design and Implementation of CIM Systems including Economic Evaluation.
*in Book "Optimization Models and Concepts in Production Management" Ed. P. Brandimarte & A. Villa - Gordon and Breach Science Publishers*, pp. 307-331.

63

# Information Management in Demand Chain Management - A Global Enterprise View

Mr. Pertti Korhonen, M. Sc.
Vice President, Global Logistics
Nokia Mobile Phones
Finland

Ms. Kati Huttunen, M. Sc.
Supply Chain Analyst
Nokia Mobile Phones
Finland

**Abstract**

Information Management has a critical role as an enabler and contributor to successful business strategy implementation. At Nokia Mobile Phones this has been highlighted especially in the context of Global Demand Chain Management. In this paper basic principles and differences of Supply Chain Management and Demand Chain Management are explained. The role of Information Management and Technology in Demand Chain Management is discussed. Finally, key drivers and criteria for Information Management system design are outlined.

## 1 Introduction

Current Information Management (IM) systems in many companies have been developed following the needs arising from administration, control, reporting and transaction management. The systems are often a result of evolution and serving of discrete needs of different parts of the organization rather than a result of a holistic plan and implementation derived from the strategy and the business needs of the company. In many cases, the solutions have been built following the needs of functional line organizations rather than key business processes and thus, at worse, information management solutions further reinforce the walls and gaps between the different functional islands within a business process.

Information technology capital spending per white collar worker has tripled since 1980 and overall IT spending is projected to increase by 60% per year.[1] Still too few companies are getting true business benefits from these investments in form of improved customer satisfaction, increased market share and improved profitability.

Creation of IM strategy and investment decisions need to be guided by business strategy and needs. Companies need to analyze on which areas they are spending their IM budget: is most of the money spent on administrational areas or are the investments focused so that they support and enable key business processes and strategic imperatives of the company?

---

[1] The McKinsey Quarterly, 1996 number 3

Computer Applications in Production and Engineering. F. Plonka and G. Olling (Eds.)

## 2 The Strategic Role of Information Management in Supply Chain Management

Supply Chain Management is, to large extent, about the management of information flows. Information Technology has had a key role in the transformation of the logistics function at leading-edge companies. Unfortunately, lack of sophistication in information systems is still one of the biggest roadblocks to supply chain integration today. The 'single solution' pipeline management system is still a dream for most companies who have to manage combinations of technologies and transactional systems that manage order processing, inventories, shop floor production, materials and other discrete business functions.

Information Management focus must be shifted from general management and control to a development of the means and solutions to enable integration of cross functional teams, key business processes, performance management, information and knowledge - all this with a market and customer driven focus targeting to increased profitable market share. Thus, the strategic questions and drivers for Information Management in Supply Chain Management are:

- How to improve customer satisfaction through
  - product availability
  - delivery accuracy
  - responsiveness and flexibility
  - value-adding services offering
  - learning and improvement through effective feedback
- How to increase profitable sales revenue
- How to improve efficiency of operations through eliminating unnecessary activities, reducing inventory and improving utilization of assets.
- How to improve and support the understanding of logical links and causalities in the Supply Chain
- How to manage performance in real time, process based mode instead of traditional functional performance management
- How to improve relevance, quality, timeliness and visibility of information

It is of elementary importance that transparency and visibility to market and customer driven needs is achieved and that most effective and efficient way to respond to these needs is created through information management and supply chain structure (speed and flexibility) rather than through spending more to assets.

Effectiveness and efficiency of any supply chain is dependent upon the visibility that can be gained from materials flows, inventories, and demand throughout the pipeline. As Christopher states, without the ability to see down the pipeline into end-user markets, to read actual demand and subsequently to manage replenishment in virtual real time, the system is doomed to depend upon inventory[2]. Time lapses in information flows are directly translated into inventory.

By utilizing enabling information technologies a lot of the complexity of Supply Chain Management can also be eliminated. Today we see a lot of people spending a lot of time creating, communicating and executing inaccurate forecasts and constantly

---

[2] Christopher, 1992, p.122

chancing plans leading to self-induced turbulence in the chain. By utilizing advanced, integrated information systems we can create more accurate forecasting and planning systems and communicate the plans as well as their exceptions more effectively up and down the supply chain. The aim is to achieve speed and simplicity by eliminating unnecessary activities and tasks.

The logistics information systems must incorporate several principles to meet Supply Chain Management needs and adequately support operations. In order to keep the focus of the whole supply chain on to the customer, an integrative framework for the whole information system is needed. The idea of *Demand Chain Management* is based on the principle of using demand instead of supply as the factor integrating the information needs in the supply chain.[3]

## 3 Demand Chain Management as a Driver for Information Technology and Management Strategy

Traditionally, the key focus and scope in Supply Chain Management has been in managing the flow of materials and goods from suppliers through manufacturing and distribution chain to the customer. Important considerations are materials requirements planning, capacity management, production planning and scheduling, inventory levels and supply allocation. In many cases the information flow from customer to the chain including suppliers is narrow. This information is often presented in form of periodical forecasts and internal (often bundled) stock orders - the entire chain too rarely is driven by and has the visibility to true market demand information and customer orders in real time. This traditional view of Supply Chain Management is illustrated in Figure 1.

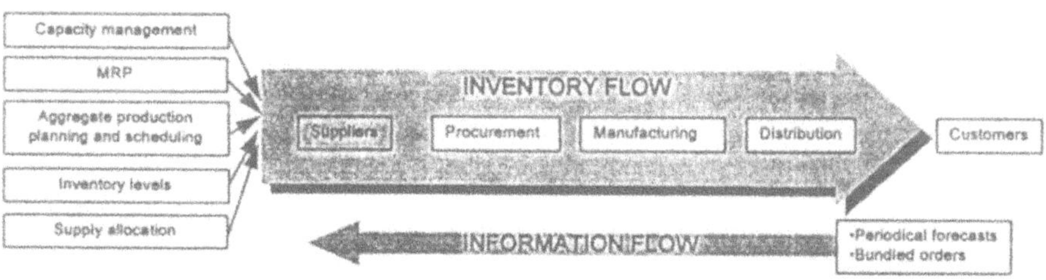


**Figure 1: Scope of Supply Chain Management**

In Demand Chain Management the key focus is *the continuous flow of the demand information* from customers and end users through distribution and manufacturing to suppliers. The shared objective of the chain is fulfilling customer demand. The most important controlling inputs are rolling forecasts and plans, point-of-sales data, daily orders, management decisions and performance feedback. The controlling trigger of the chain is the customer order (or replenishment signal) and the order penetration point is varying dependent on what is the optimum way to provide required level of service in a most efficient way.

[3] Vollman, 1996

The focus in Demand Chain Management is in information management. The information flow can be described as "thick", timely, meaningful and transparent. The material flow from the suppliers through manufacturing to customers is thin and as much as possible controlled by daily consumption in order to guarantee the availability of goods in demand and at the same time minimize the inventories. This view of Demand Chain Management is illustrated in Figure 2.

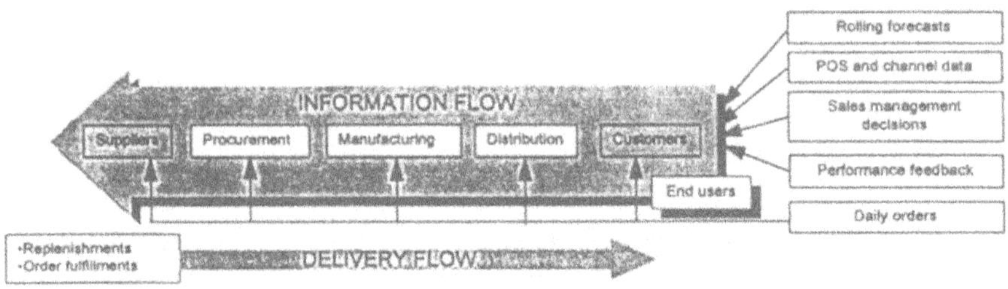


**Figure 2: Scope of Demand Chain Management**

The main difference between Supply and Demand Chain Management is the focus and starting point of planning and controlling: in Supply Chain Management it is the material supply push, in Demand Chain Management it is the end user demand pull. Real pull control can only be achieved by using timely end-user demand information as a pull trigger from end users to suppliers as a primary planning and execution source. This is the way to integrate supply chain in an effective and efficient manner.

The role of Information Management and Technology is to be a key enabler for Demand Chain Management. It means capturing the market and end user demand information in accurate, timely (real time) and relevant manner: capturing at all times the Point-of-Sales, sell-through and channel inventory information. It also necessitates the ability of being able to, in a proactive manner, search for alternative supply scenarios, carry out risk and profitability analysis in almost real time manner and prepare the needed capability and capacity to serve the foreseen customer demand when the triggering order arrives.

## 4 Global Enterprise View to Demand Chain Information Management

Nokia Mobile Phones is present on market of more than 120 countries in the world and has a global manufacturing and logistics infrastructure enabling the combination of local responsiveness and global synergy in form of flexibility, optimum use of resources and lowest total cost. Nokia Mobile Phones manufacturers cellular phones for all major systems in the world.

The main information flows at Nokia Mobile Phones Demand Chain consist of *Planning process information* and *Execution process information* flows. Planning process captures the best possible view of market and customer demand in order to plan and implement required capacity and capability to meet the demand. Execution process is customer order pull driven focusing on fulfillment of customer orders rather than executing to plan. The objective of logistics Information Management is to establish information systems support for these integrated business processes by providing seamless information capturing, integration, visibility and transparency enabling demand based steering of the supply chain.

In the process of searching the maximum exploitation of market and business opportunities and global economies of scale, the main objective is to achieve *responsiveness* through regional supply and *flexibility* through reallocation of global resources in line with market and customers demand at any given time. In order to do this it is of vital importance that a company has global business processes and respective information systems so that customers can be served by reconfiguring the supply chains to meet the emerging and changing customer demand. This approach also allows a flexible combination and reconfiguration of focused factories and regional factories as part of the supply chain.

Other special challenges and requirements in Global Demand Chain Information Management are in seamless process and product quality management and in product data management including configuration control and change management. Seamless integration of product management information is vital for the integrated development and management of global product families and regional and local product variants.

## 5 Key Requirements for the Information Management Solution

Based on the theoretical framework of Demand Chain Management as well as on practical needs of a global enterprise, the key requirements for a state-of-the art Demand Chain Information Management solution can be summarized as follows:

Strategic direction and focus

The creation and implementation of Information Management strategy need to be derived from and guided by business strategy and key business process requirements rather than by technology, functional or internal adminstration and control demands.

Integration

Key aspects of integration that need to be covered are business process integration including customers and suppliers, end-to-end demand and availability information integration and integration of process wise performance management. Also, seamless integration of product management information is needed in order to manage global and regional/local product families and products.

Information coverage and availability

The foundation for successful Demand Chain Management is access to real time Point-of-Sale and channel inventory information and sharing the demand information between all parties in the chain end-to-end including customers and suppliers.

Information quality

As Demand Chain Management is to great extent about information management the quality of the end result is of course dependent on the quality of the information. Information quality can be described by following characteristics:

- relevance
- timeliness
- continuous flow
- validity
- accuracy
- intelligibility
- accessibility
- visibility

Decision making support

Information system should be capable of identifying exception situations in order to guide management attention and decision making to these critical areas. This is particularly important when the number of transactions, customers and products is large and therefore due to massive amount of information it becomes difficult to spot the areas requiring focused attention. Handling of these exceptions must be supported by proper tools that enable the identification and almost real-time simulation of alternative supply solutions and their risk and profitability analysis.

Flexibility and Adaptability

Flexibility and adaptability are of strategic importance: market and industry changes are today faster than ever and being able to change and adapt IT solutions to new requirements rapidly is very important. Unfortunately, there is too often major inertia and slow-down factor in implementing improved or re-engineered business processes due to rigidity and inflexibility of information management tools. This is a major challenge especially in case of enterprise systems.

Cutting down the cost of complexity

The best way to reduce the development and running costs of the Information Management solution is to narrow down different standards and systems used in the company. This reduces complexity, number of interfaces and development and maintenance cost. Normally this also improves the integration of key business processes as interfaces and boundaries between different systems gets minimized.

## 6 Summary

The role of Information Management as an enabler and contributor to successful business strategy implementation has been discussed. Creation and implementation of IM strategy and investment decisions need to be guided by business strategy and needs rather than by technology, functional or internal administration and control demands. The key in Demand Chain Management is the continuous flow and sharing of the demand information from customers and end users through distribution and manufacturing to suppliers. The role of Information Management and Technology is to be a key enabler by providing means of capturing the market and end user demand information in accurate, timely (real time) and relevant manner and sharing this information across the whole chain. The paper concludes that the key requirements for the Demand Chain Information Management system are strategic direction and focus, integration, information coverage and availability, information quality, decision making support, flexibility and adaptability as well as cutting down the cost of complexity.

## REFERENCES

1. Christopher, M. (1992) Logistics and Supply Chain Management - Strategies for Reducing Costs and Improving Services. Pitman Publishing, London.

2. The McKinsey Quarterly (1996), Number 3. McKinsey & Company, NY.

3. Vollmann, T. (1996) Supply Chain Management. Manufacturing 2000, Business Briefing 8/96. International Institute for Management Development (IMD), Lausanne.

## BIOGRAPHIES

Pertti J. Korhonen (born 1961 in Tampere, Finland) is Vice President, Global Logistics and Member of the Management Board at Nokia Mobile Phones. He has held several positions in different locations at Nokia Mobile Phones since 1987: Integrated Circuit Design Engineer, Design Manager, Product Development Manager, Vice President, Product Development (R&D, Oulu, Finland); Project Executive (R&D, Camberley, England); Vice President, Manufacturing Europe (Finland). Mr Korhonen received his M. Sc. (EE) in Microelectronics and Telecommunications at University of Oulu 1987.

Kati A. M. Huttunen (born 1970 in Espoo, Finland) is Supply Chain Analyst at Nokia Mobile Phones. Prior joining Nokia Mobile Phones she has worked as a communications consultant at BNL Information, Ltd. and as a researcher with the IIA-Research Center at the Helsinki University of Technology. Ms Huttunen received her M. Sc. (Soc. Sc.) in Communications and Economics at University of Helsinki 1994 and M. Sc. (Eng.) in Industrial Management and Telecommunications at Helsinki University of Technology 1997.

# A Real-Time distributed Multimedia virtual environment for Collaborative Engineering

*J.J. LaViola, R.J. Barton, G. Newton, and R. Cross*
*Fraunhofer Center for Research in Computer Graphics, Inc.*
*321 S. Main St., Suite 2*
*Providence, RI 02903 USA*
*(401) 863-6363*
*{jlaviola, rbarton, gnewton, rcross}@crcg.edu*

**Abstract**

In this paper we present the concept of Telepresence to describe an emerging and enabling communication medium. We define a Virtual Collaborative Environment (VCE) to exist when virtual reality and multimedia are combined to create a shared environment for human interaction and cooperation. We describe the fundamental problem with current attempts to evolve today's CAD software into a practical, shared, collaborative environment. We then present a new approach to the design of a shared virtual environment that addresses issues of scalability, networking, and synchronization, and discuss its applicability to collaborative engineering.

**Keywords**

Virtual collaborative environments, virtual reality, BARCO table, CAD

## 1 INTRODUCTION

### 1.1 Background

The rapidly developing information technology infrastructure is radically changing the methods and media by which people communicate and interact. As this evolution unfolds, human interactions will no longer be limited by the constraints of physical location, cultural and political barriers, or disabilities. Advanced computer graphics and high speed networking form the basis for what is now commonly called **Telepresence**. Telepresence describes a communications medium that enables a person to feel as if he or she is actually present in a different place or time. **Virtual reality** is an enabling technology that is described as

Computer Applications in Production and Engineering. F. Plonka and G. Olling (Eds.)

immersive, interactive, and perceptively believable to the users' experience. The creation, delivery and reception of audio, video, text, and imagery data is defined as **multimedia**. Combining these technologies, we define a **Virtual Collaborative Environment** (VCE) to exist when multiple physically separated users share a distributed multimedia virtual environment for the purpose of sharing information or accomplishing a common objective. (Barton, Newton, 1997)

## 1.2 Problems with existing CAD systems

Existing industry standard CAD systems are inadequate and incomplete for a collaborative engineering environment because of three key areas, namely, point-to-point communication issues, network latency, and user interface technology.

*Point-to-Point*

Most implementations today are unicast in nature, not supporting many-to-many distributed users. Off -the-Shelf collaborative CAD today most often takes the form of shared data bases, shared x-windows, and comprehensive client server applications. A good example of this is the current release of AutoCAD v13c4, which uses the infrastructure of the World Wide Web and native browser software to share designs amongst distributed engineers. This model works well for distributed users, but is certainly **not real-time** collaboration.

*Latency*

There are several commercial off-the-shelf shared X-Windows type applications readily available on the market today. These systems are moderately successful on local high-speed networks, or LANs, i.e., 10 or 100 BaseT only, due to the high bandwidth required for acceptable performance. In order to realize a geographically distributed engineering environment, a practical solution must function in a high-latency environment. Currently, such a system does not exist. TCP/IP is not an adequate transport mechanism for a real-time or near real-time multi-point environment.

*User interfaces*

The current state of user interface design is centered around the theme of one-machine, one-person interactions. This is inadequate for a collaborative engineering environment. New interfaces must be designed that are focused on groups of users, working together, sharing ideas on a single model or prototype in this environment. These new interfaces could be radical in nature, such as, immersion of the users and model in a shared Virtual Environment (VE) or using a projective display system such as the BARCO table, see Figure 1. Gesture recognition and visual coherency techniques such as motion blurring and ghosting can be integrated into an interface which mitigates problems associated with latency, as well as promotes collaboration amongst users.

Figure 1 BARCO Table at CRCG.

### 1.3 Previous work

Industry is currently evaluating various ways to capture the talent of their design and engineering personnel, without the need for physical co-location, in order to reduce cost, speed the design process, and remain competitive in the global economy. The design and review process must be collaborative, real-time, and distributed, often traversing great geographical distances and cultural boundaries.

The Shared 3D Viewer (Kress and Anderson, 1996), see Figure 2, is an application enabling a cooperative, distributed discussion of the three-dimensional geometry and product structure of CAD data. This tool is designed to support communication during the product development process particularly in the design phase. The innovative 3D functionality offers designers and project planners the proper format for the discussion of CAD data. Shared camera views, three-dimensional cursors and annotations allow the participants to discuss specific details of a product. An immersive experience is provided by stereo projection on either the desktop or BARCO table.

A set of 3D cursors can be used to direct interest at specific locations on the model. Cursors can be used to mark a point, length or area of the product, and are color coded according to the user that is controlling the cursor. Additional tools allow the measuring of lengths and angles within the three-dimensional window. Text messages can also be placed in the 3D scene, expanding the communication possibilities. In addition to the synchronous communication offered by the 3D cursors, the Shared 3D Viewer allows the creation of 3D annotations for asynchronous communication. Text, audio, and video messages can be created and attached to the CAD model so that users in later sessions can view the annotations. Three-dimensional icons represent the location and type of the annotation data. Through the use of MIME types, additional formats of annotation data can also be supported.

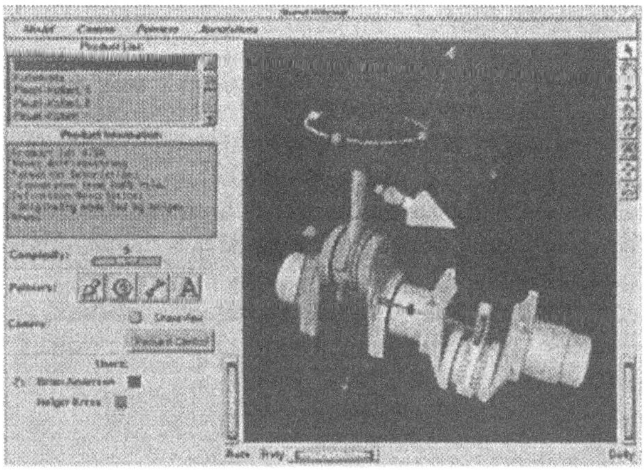

**Figure 2: HP 3D Shared Viewer.**

## 1.4 Use of VCEs to support collaboration

Effective communication is vital to nearly all aspects of business, yet the tendency towards global enterprise is making in-person communication harder. Face to face meetings are often prohibitively expensive, not only because of the cost of travel but also because of the valuable time lost while traveling. Face to face meetings involve multiple modes of communication which can not be duplicated by any ubiquitous communication device. The attendees can not only hear each other, they can also see each other and can interact with other objects together (e.g. a blueprint, a design prototype). Telephone conference calls allow people to speak to each other but do not permit any non-verbal communication. Video conferencing goes one step further and restores some of the missing non-verbal communication by allowing the participants to see live video of each other's faces, yet they are still unable to interact in any other way. Virtual teleconferencing provides participants with a VCE in which they can hold a virtual meeting. The multimedia aspects of the VCE allow the insertion of audio and video streams into the virtual environment, providing the participants with the same audio/video exchange capabilities found in video conferencing. However, the media streams are not limited to audio and video capture of the participants. Text, images, sound clips and video clips can also be embedded in the environment.

Virtual objects of interest (e.g. a 3D model of a design prototype) can be placed in the environment for the participants to view, interact with and discuss. A further advantage of virtual reality is that the virtual space can be divided into "rooms" as a way of organizing information that humans find intuitive (Card, 1991).

# 2 A SYSTEM ARCHITECTURE FOR VCE'S

## 2.1 Multiple network model

The architecture outlined here is based on the observation that different VCE components have very different networking and synchronization requirements. Past attempts at mapping these disparate requirements to a single networking protocol have failed to produce solutions scalable to wide area general purpose networks. However, protocols currently exist to implement most, if not all, of these components individually. We have identified five classes of networked data which must be supported in order to provide a general purpose VCE architecture. These classes are shown in Table 1.

| Class | Example Data | Requirements |
|---|---|---|
| **Renderer** | Synchronization between renderers | Lowest latency |
| **Agent** | Communication between agents | Guaranteed delivery, flexibility |
| **Simulation** | Distributed shared world state updates | Low latency, variable QOS |
| **Device** | Input/Output device events | Low latency, LAN use only |
| **Live Media** | Video textures, live audio | Like Internet conferencing |

**Table 1 Classes of Data**

The architecture is based on assigning each class of data its own network. Potentially, several of these virtual networks can be implemented using the same network transport protocol. However, at this time, we anticipate using a different protocol for each class.

## 2.2 Component model

Each component of a VCE is allowed to participate in any set of these networks. The networks do not form a protocol stack, but rather parallel communication channels with different characteristics. Figure 3 shows an example set of components connected by the five networks. In the figure, each vertical cylinder represents a component. These components can be implemented as separate processes running on a set of networked computers. Components become clients of the various networks through a protocol-independent API represented by the five clouds in Figure 3. Because this interface is independent of the network protocol choices, this architecture will allow our research groups to research and develop better solutions for each class separately. The implementation section below expands on these protocol choices and possibilities.

*Inter-Component communication*

The different "Networks" present a shared data abstraction to the components, which is accessed through a well defined API. Communication between components is permitted only in so far as multiple components can access the same objects in the shared data. Component developers therefore do not need to be aware of communication implementation details. The use of an API for inter-component communication allows local communication as well as remote communication in a transparent manner. When multiple components are operating on the same node in the physical network, then their communication can be via shared memory rather than network packets. In the trivial case, a monolithic high-performance VE application running on a single machine can be assembled from reusable, networkable components. In this case, only shared memory communication would take place, providing a clean separation between components without generating network traffic. The API presented by each network is based on asynchronous sampling of the states of the objects that occupy the given network. Since components sample the various networks asynchronously, they can operate in a decoupled manner. Decoupled operation implies that components can operate independently of other components. This is an important characteristic of any VE design, because it allows rendering components to operate at a constant frame rate, independently of the current update rate of simulation components. The well-defined inter-component communication mechanism also allows different components to run on different processors, when available. In such a case, parallelization and pipelining of rendering, simulation, agent operation and device handling is possible.

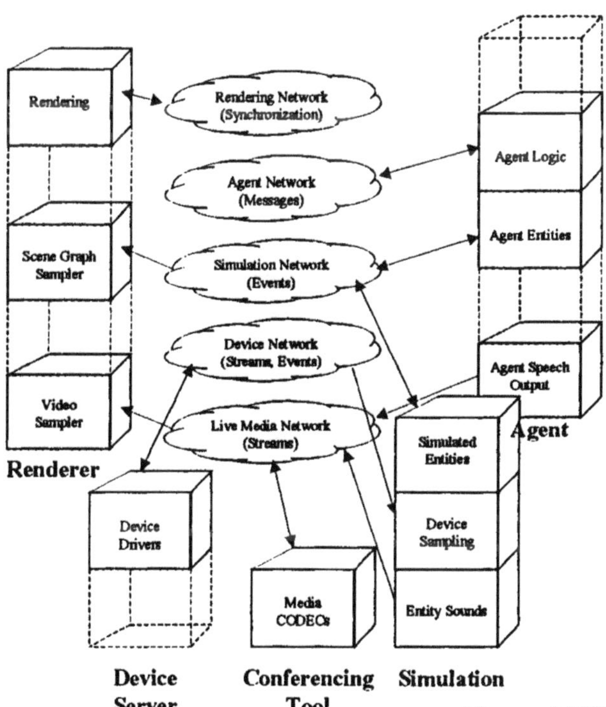


**Figure 3 VCE Architecture Overview**

## 2.3 Simulation component

Note that some components, for example a simulation server, need to participate in only one type of network. The Simulation Network represents a shared world which is consistent even in the absence of the other networks. Simulations can join the network, explore the shared world and affect entities within it. However, they need not be concerned with issues of rendering or video conferencing. This will allow developers of simulation modules to remain unaffected by development concentrating on other areas of VCE. It also allows simulation-intensive virtual worlds to make use of computational resources which do not have graphics capabilities, such as server machines. We envision a typical virtual world utilizing multiple servers which provide the simulation for automated entities, while the computers used to display the various participants' views would run only very limited amounts of simulation, such as the individual user's avatar simulation.

## 2.4 Rendering component

*Live media rendering*

In order to provide spatial audio and video texture mapping, renderers for both graphical views and audio must have access to the Live Media Network. Stored audio effects as well as live network streams from remote dynamic sound sources, such as the voices of participants, have to be processed by a spatial audio renderer locally. The positions of the sound sources are known to the renderer since they are entities in the simulated world, which is being sampled by the renderer. The rendering of texture mapped video can be supported in the same way. Live video streams from the Live Media Network, as well as locally stored video clips, can be accessed by the renderer. The video streams are then sampled into texture memory and used as texture maps during rendering of the views. Fraunhofer CRCG's virtual teleconferencing application shown at ACM '97 demonstrated this capability.

*Sampling of the simulation network*

To allow the renderer to sustain a near-constant frame rate, it must operate independent of the simulation components. Such a decoupling is vital to the interactive experience (Pausch, 1994). We define the interface to the Simulation Network in such a way, that the renderer or other clients can easily sample the states of entities at specific points in simulated time. The client can construct a consistent snapshot of the world, which is then used to update the scene graph and rendered.

## 2.5 Live media components

The purpose of the Live Media network is to carry low-latency traffic such as audio and video streams. This type of traffic usually enjoys no quality of service assurances. Algorithms from Internet Telephony can be used on top of a multicast network infrastructure to implement the transport of these data types independently of the other types of information in the CVE system. Consequently, conferencing components could choose to participate just in the Live Media network. This could allow participants using non-VE systems, such as videophones, to join the collaborative world via only live media. Conforming to standards for video and audio encoding, such as G.728 and H.261, will ensure such interoperability. CRCG has demonstrated this capability with the VETAF system (Barton, 1997).

### 2.6 Device components

The purpose of the device network is to allow very high frequency and low latency connections between Virtual Reality hardware devices and the simulations that use these devices. In general, this network conists of devices connected locally or on the LAN. Connections on this network are usually only the polling or event processing of an input device to control a parameter in a simulation. However, combinations of input and output devices, such as haptic feedback devices coupled with trackers, may require direct connections between devices at the device frequency, potentially much higher than the simulation frequency. In order to support the highest possible fidelity, such direct inter-device connections will be implemented at the Device Network level and will not involve the simulation components.

## 3 INTERFACE ISSUES

### 3.1 Motivation

The use of the BARCO Table as our display device has numerous advantages in the collaborative engineering environment. The table is large enough to provide room for several participants to work together on the same physical display. Also, a group of networked tables allows collaboration locally as well as across intercontinental networks. The use of the table does present some human-computer interaction problems such as:

- Single machine, several users – who grabbed the object first?
- Who has priority in a conflict situation?
- How do we minimize the effects of latency?
- How do we let users know that objects are in the control of another user?
- How do we provide a natural interface for creating and manipulating objects?

All of these issues will be addressed in the following sections.

### 3.2 Locking and control

In order to have a stable collaborative engineering environment, users must be able to create and manipulate objects easily and in an orderly fashion. The idea of object manipulation and ownership in a VCE is known as *floor control*. A distributed collaborative environment requires a strong mechanism to provide concurrency and floor control for its included objects. Model movements, attribute alterations, and other object property manipulation must be tightly controlled, without being centralized. Centralization reduces scalability and performance. The VCE developed for this project includes a distributed signal-locking device for object data in this environment. A site will make a request to the group for a specific key, which would then be granted in the event that it was not already in use. In the event that a key is in use, the requester would receive the key in turn, as it is released from other members of the group. In reference to the discussion of signaling protocols earlier, this type of data would not necessarily require near real time delivery to the group, but would require a guarantee of delivery. (Bukowski, 1995)

### 3.3 Latency issues

In order to realize a geographically distributed collaborative environment, a practical solution system must function in a *high-latency environment*. (Macedonia, 1994) High latency performance results in "popping" or "jerking" motions of graphical objects within the environment. One method for minimizing the negative impact of latency on the user interface is to apply what is known as *visual coherency techniques*. Our system includes advanced rendering techniques that address the latency problem, to include motion blurring and transparency, "ghosting".

Currently, known blurring algorithms are far too slow for the 3D interactive environment. A novel approach to blurring for 3D objects gives real time performance and demonstrates smooth and visually consistent motion. Besides looking more natural, motion blur establishes visual coherence between temporarily disparate renderings of the same object. This visual coherency is often disregarded in rendering, replaced instead with "popping" or "iconifying" of the object. Loss of coherency degrades the user's ability to synthesize meaningful actions occurring in the environment. Motion blur also assists interaction with moving objects in the virtual world. Blurring fast-moving objects simplifies the user's task of **intercepting** the object. By minimizing the strobing effect of motion and adding trails to the object, the user is better able to predict its motion path and velocity changes. Thus, the incorporation of motion blur enhances the natural rendition of the 3D environment to its participants, 3D interfaces become less confusing, and interaction with fast moving objects becomes easier. (Zeleznik, 1995, 1996a)

Similarly, transparency is useful in a shared CAD environment. Ghost locking makes the user aware of many aspects of manipulating a shared object in a networked environment. The user has an immediate response to his or her actions, affording a feeling of control over the environment. The user also sees immediately that lag is occurring, because of the appearance of a "partial" or transparent object. Finally, fading out the copy that lost the lock gives the user time to understand the changed state of the manipulated object. (Conner, 1997)

This effect can be customized by varying levels of opacity in either the grabbed object or the original object, depending on outside knowledge about the state of the lock or the likelihood that the lock will be taken successfully. For example, a lock is more likely to fail for a highly contended object. In this case, the grabbed object can be more transparent, while the remaining object is more opaque, showing the user the likely results of trying to grab a highly contended object. (Conner, 1997)

## 3.4 Gesture recognition

Gesture-based interfaces offer an alternative to traditional keyboard, menu, and direct manipulation interfaces. The ability to specify objects, an operation, and additional parameters with a single intuitive gesture appeals to both novice and experienced users. Gesture-based interfaces for platforms such as the BARCO table are desirable, as they permit far more natural interaction than traditional mouse and keyboard interfaces. Our system includes gesture recognition techniques developed for SKETCH, a rapid virtual prototyping environment, developed at Brown University (Zeleznik, 1996b). In the early stages of a design, often what is required is a rapid conceptual model of the desired product. SKETCH is designed to bridge the gap between hand sketches and computer-based modeling programs, combining some of the features of pencil-and-paper sketching and some of the features of CAD systems to provide a lightweight, **gesture-based interface** to ``approximate'' 3D polyhedral modeling. SKETCH uses a gestural mode of input in which all operations are available directly in the 3D scene through a three-button mouse or three-button stylus.

**Figure 4: Annotation of a Supertool**

**Figure 5: Annotation of a van design**

The problem with the SKETCH interface is that it does not handle placing free-formed gestures at arbitrary locations in 3 space. It is useful if users can make free-formed gestures for annotation purposes so a particular piece of geometry can be referenced. This feature is good for design reviews or brainstorming. These free-formed gestures are placed on a 2D plane close to the film plane. They then must be transformed to point to an object in the 3D world. This is a very difficult task because a lot of guesswork is involved in determining where the user actually wants the gesture to be placed. Figures 4 and 5 show some snap shots of free-formed gestures used to annotate a model. If the user was to rotate the objects using a trackball, the annotations would stay in place in relationship to the 3D location that the annotation is pointing to. Using these annotations, managers can let engineers know what they think of designs, and make comments so communication can be enhanced.

Static hand posture recognition is currently the most common and widely used method for interaction involving glove based input devices. In order improve the naturalness of interaction, and thereby decrease the user-interface learning time, there is a need to be able to recognize dynamic gestures. Fraunhofer IGD has recently demonstrated a **camera based tracking technique**. This research will be integrated into a later version of our VCE.

## 4 HAPTICS

Performing detailed manipulative tasks in a collaborative virtual environment is a significant challenge. Virtual environments tend to address only the human visual system, ignoring the other senses. Since many interactions in virtual environments tend to involve direct manipulation (i.e., grabbing an object), the lack of tactile perception is particularly noticed. The addition of haptic feedback systems has proven to enhance understanding and performance in virtual environments. (Brooks, 1990) Our system will address the issues involved in adding haptic feedback to non-spatially immersive environments with the BARCO table.

Furthermore, it will explore techniques and user interface design for tactile vision substitution in the form of spatial, interactive haptic, tactile force, and static tactile displays. (Kaczmarek, 1995)

## 5 CONCLUSION

In this paper, we have presented the concept of the virtual collaborative environment (VCE). A VCE exists when virtual reality and multimedia are combined to create a shared environment or collaborative engineering. We have discussed the problems with such a system such as latency, interface issues and networking issues, and we have presented an architecture for creating such a system which addresses these issues. We have also discussed ways of interacting with the VCE so that users can perform tasks naturally and intuitively. A VCE is an excellent paradigm for collaborative engineering because it allows design and product teams to meet and discuss projects with tools necessary for enhanced communication especially when teams are separated by large geographic regions.

## 6 FUTURE WORK

We will continue to develop and experiment with more visual-coherency techniques such as bending and stretching of objects. We are incorporating camera-based tracking and haptic interfaces into our VCE discussed in section 4. Finally, we plan to perform some user studies to determine if the system could be implemented as a commercial product.

## 7 REFERENCES

Barton, R.J., Newton, G.P., Cross, R.A., and Goettsch, A. (1997) An Architecture for Virtual Collaborative
Environments, submitted for review, 1997 SIGMM.

Brooks, F.P., Ouh-Young, M., Batter, J. and Kilpatrick, P.J. (1990) Project GROPEHaptic Displays for
Scientific Visualization, ACM SIGGRAPH '90, 177-186.

Bukowski, R. and Séquin C. (1995) Object associations: A simple and practical approach to virtual 3D
manipulation, Computer Graphics (1995 Symposium on Interactive 3D Graphics), Apr. 1995.
131-138.

Conner, B. (1997) Providing A Low Latency User Experience In A High Latency Application, Proceedings
of the 3D Symposium on Interactive Graphics, 45-48.

Kaczmarek, K A., Bach y Rita, P. (1995) Tactile Displays, in *Virtual Environments and Advanced Interface Design*, (Eds. W. Barfield, T. A. Furness) Oxford University Press, London.

Kress, H. and Anderson, B. (1996) HP Shared 3D Viewer - Ein verteiltes 3D Visualisierungssystem für Produktdaten,unix/mail, Carl Hanser Verlag München, 329-334.

Pausch, R. (1994) Alice: A Rapid Prototyping System for Virtual Reality. ACM SIGGRAPH Course Notes 15.1-15.6.

Macedonia, M. (1994) Networking and Communications, in, *Virtual Reality Scientific and Technological Challenges*, (Eds. N. Durlach and A. Mavor) National Academy Press, Ch 10.

Zeleznik, R.C. and Wloka, M. (1994) Interactive Real-Time Motion Blur, Proceedings of CGI'94: Insight Through Computer Graphics. 74-85.

Zeleznik, R.C., Herndon, K., Hughes, J. (1996a) Sketch: An Interface for Sketching 3D Scenes, Proceedings of SIGGRAPH'96, 163-170.

Zeleznik, R.C. and Wloka, M. (1996b) *Interactive Real-Time Motion Blur ,Visual Computer*, Springer Verlag, 1996.

## 8 BIOGRAPHY

Joseph J LaViola Jr.

Joseph J LaViola Jr. is a research intern at Fraunhofer, CRCG. He received his B.S.C.S from Florida Atlantic University in 1996. He is also a Master's student at Brown University studying computer science. His research interests include virtual environments, augmented reality, and human-computer interaction.
He has received numerous awards for scholastic achievement including the Microsoft Senior Achievement award. He is a member of Phi Eta Sigma and Phi Kappa Phi honor societies. He is also a member of ACM SIGGRAPH.

Robert J Barton III, Engineer, Project Leader

Robert J Barton III received a BS in Mechanical Engineering and an active duty commission from the US Naval Academy, Annapolis, MD. in 1985. Follow on assignments included engineering billets on US Naval Surface ships, instructor duty at the Naval Academy, and systems engineering branch head for the Trident Missile Program of Strategic Systems Programs Office, Sunnyvale, CA. In 1995, Lt Barton completed Masters of Science degrees in Electrical Engineering and Computer Science from Naval Postgraduate School, Monterey, CA. and was awarded the Armed Forces Communications and Electronics Award for academic achievement. Areas of research and interest include VLSI High-radix arithmetic circuits, computing the average number of nodes of Ordered Binary Decision Diagrams (OBDDs), and the modeling and analysis of multicast network protocols. Mr. Barton has recently joined the staff of Fraunhofer CRCG, in Providence,RI as an Engineer and Project Leader for the Transatlantic Research and Development Environment (TRADE). Member of IEEE Computer Society and Eta Kappa Nu.

Gregory P. Newton

Greg Newton is a Researcher and Assistant Project Leader at CRCG. He holds a M.S. in Computer Science from the Georgia Institute of Technology, where he performed a Master's Project on "A Collaborative Environment for the Responsive Workbench". He held a Graduate Research Assistantship at the Georgia Tech Graphics, Visualization & Usability Center (GVU), where his work supported research in scientific visualization, Distributed Interactive Simulation, terrain visualization, and Simulation-Based Design. He performed several internships at the Naval Research Laboratory, where his work supported research in Simulation-Based Design and Command & Control for the Responsive Workbench.

His current work is in the areas of real-time computer graphics, Distributed Interactive Simulation (DIS) and collaborative virtual reality. His research has been published in the Proceedings of the SPIE Aerospace/Defense Sensing & Controls Symposium and in IEEE Computer Graphics & Applications.
He is a member of the Association of Computer Machinery and the IEEE Computer Society.

Dr. Robert Cross, Scientist and Project Leader

Dr. Cross is a Scientist and Project Leader at CRCG. He holds a Ph.D. in Computer Science, with a dissertation on "Interactive Visual Realism Using Distributed Rendering." He held an ASEE Post-doctoral fellowship at the Advanced Information Technology Branch of the Naval Research Laboratory, and an Associate Instructorship of Computer Science and a College of Arts and Sciences Fellowship at Indiana University. His research into the problems inherent in real-time volume rendering was published in "Interactive Visualization Methods for Four Dimensions" and "Virtual Reality Performance for Virtual Geometry" in the Proceedings of IEEE Visualization '93 & '94. In his current work, he seeks solutions to the computationally complex problems of real-time modeling & simulation and virtual reality, with particular focus on the use of distributed computing to support real-time, high fidelity computer graphics. His work has been published in the Computer Graphik Topics, the Proceedings of IEEE Visualization '93 -- '95 and in a book chapter in Graphics Gems V. He has also presented his work at invited seminars at Brown University and the Naval Research Laboratory as well as at the Virtual Reality Room at ACM SIGGRAPH

'94. He has also been the recipient of grants from the Franklin Institute, the Office of Naval Research, the American Society for Engineering Education, and the Indiana University College of Arts and Sciences. He is a member of the Association of Computer Machinery, the IEEE Computer Society, the Mine Warfare Association and the United States Naval Institute.

65

# Collaborative work using our Virtual Reality Network System (VLNET)

*Nadia Magnenat Thalmann, Igor Pandzic*
*MIRALab - CUI, University of Geneva*
*24 rue du Général-Dufour*
*CH1211 Geneva 4, Switzerland*
*tel. +41-22-705 77 69 ; fax +41-22-705 77 80*
*{Nadia.Thalmann, Igor.Pandzic}@cui.unige.ch*
*http://miralabwww.unige.ch/*

**Abstract**

Networked Collaborative Virtual Environments (NCVE) are systems that allow several geographically distant users to collaborate within the common 3D virtual environment. The users become part of the environment represented by graphical embodiments and they can interact with the environment and with each other. We analyze the importance of good graphical representation of each user for communication and collaboration. The Virtual Life Network (VLNET) system is an NCVE using sophisticated Virtual Humans as user embodiments to improve collaboration. We describe the system and some experimental applications.

**Keywords**

Networked Collaborative Virtual Environments, Collaboration, Virtual Humans

## 1 INTRODUCTION

Networked Collaborative Virtual Environments (NCVEs) are systems that allow multiple geographically distant users to evolve in a common virtual environment, interact with it and with each other. Each workstation has a copy of the virtual environment. All events that have an impact on the environment are transmitted to other sites so that all environments can be updated and kept consistent, giving the impression for the users of being in the same, unique environment. The users

Computer Applications in Production and Engineering. F. Plonka and G. Olling (Eds.)

become a part of the environment, embodied by a graphical representation that should ideally be human-like.
Networked Collaborative Virtual Environment (NCVE) systems are suitable for numerous collaborative applications ranging from games to medicine (Doenges, 1997), for example:

- Virtual teleconferencing with multimedia object exchange
- All sorts of collaborative work involving 3D design
- Multi-user game environments
- Teleshopping involving 3D models, images, sound (e.g. real estate, furniture, cars)
- Medical applications (distance diagnostics, virtual surgery for training)
- Distance learning/training
- Virtual Studio/Set with Networked Media Integration
- Virtual travel agency.

The NCVE systems are often described as systems that permit to the users to feel as if they were together in a shared Virtual Environment. Indeed, the feeling of "being together" is extremely important for collaboration, as well as for the sense of presence felt by the subjects. A very important factor for the feeling of being together in a virtual world is the way users perceive each other: their embodiment. In a broader sense, this includes not just the graphical appearance but also the way movements, actions and emotions are represented.
In the following section we discuss the importance of the user representation in NCVEs. After that we describe the Virtual Life Network (VLNET), a NCVE system using Virtual Humans for user representation. In the results section we describe several experimental applications of our system.

## 2 THE IMPORTANCE OF VIRTUAL HUMANS IN NCVE

The participant representation in a networked VE system has several functions:
- perception (to see if anyone is around)
- localization (to see where the person is)
- identification (to recognize the person)
- visualization of interest focus (to see where the person's attention is directed)
- visualization of actions (to see what the person is doing)
- communication (lip movement in synchronization with speech, facial expressions, gestures).

Virtual Humans can fulfill all these functions in an intuitive, natural way resembling the way we achieve these tasks in real life. Even with limited sensor information, a virtual human frame can be constructed in the virtual world, reflecting the activities of the real user. Slater and Usoh (Slater, 1994) indicate that such a body, even if crude, already increases the sense of presence that the participants feel. The participants visualize the environment through the eyes of their virtual actor, and move their virtual body by different means of body control. In addition, introducing the human-like autonomous actors for various tasks increases the level of interaction within the virtual environment.

## 3 VIRTUAL LIFE NETWORK

Based on the considerations from the previous section we have developed the Virtual Life Network (VLNET) system (Capin 1997). From the networking point of view, VLNET is based on a fairly simple client/server architecture. Next subsections discuss in more detail the server and the client architecture.

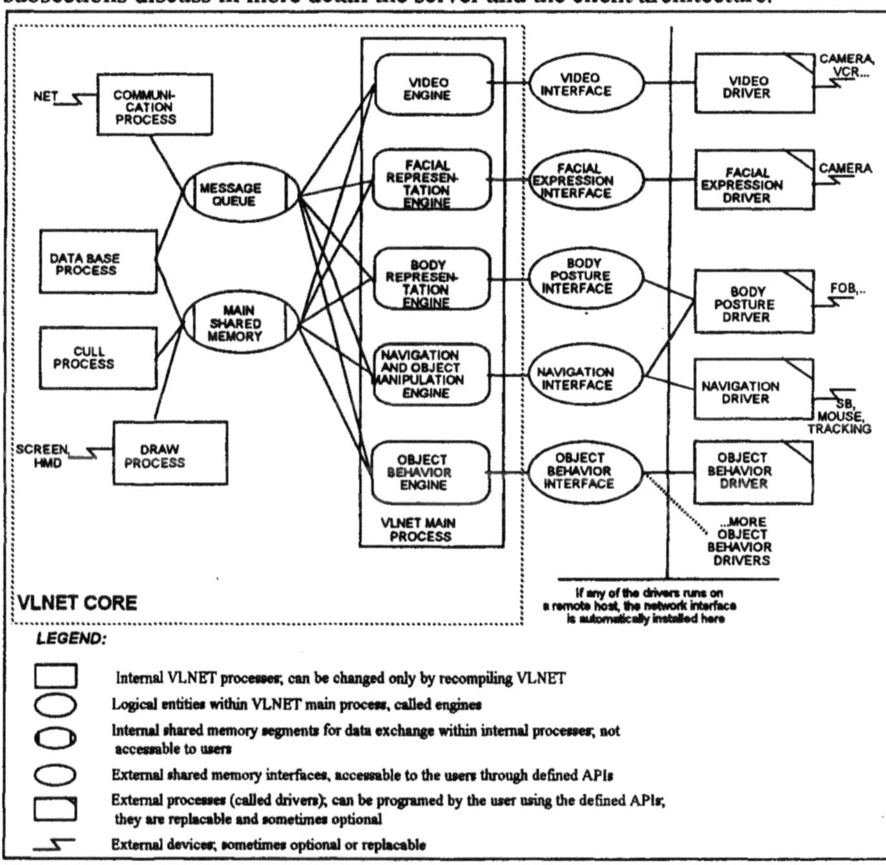


**Figure 1** Virtual Life Network system overview.

## 3.1 VLNET Server

A VLNET server site consists of a HTTP server and a VLNET Connection Server. They can serve several worlds, which can be either VLNET files or VRML 1.0 files. For each world, a World Server is spawned as necessary, i.e. when a client requests a connection to that particular world. The life of a World Server ends when all clients are disconnected.
A VLNET session is initiated by a Client connecting to a particular world designated by a URL. The Client first fetches the world database from the HTTP server using the URL. After that it extracts the host name from the URL and connects to the VLNET Connection Server on the same host. The Connection Server spawns the World Server for the requested world if one is not already running and sends to the Client the port address of the World Server. Once the connection is established, all communication between the clients in a particular world passes through the World Server.

## 3.2 VLNET Client

The design of the VLNET Client is highly modular, with functionalities split into a number of processes. Figure 1 presents an overview of the modules and their connections. VLNET has an open architecture, with a set of interfaces allowing a user with some programming knowledge to access the system core and change or extend the system by plugging custom-made modules, called drivers, into the VLNET interfaces. In the next subsections we explain in some detail the VLNET Core with its various processes, as well as the drivers and the possibilities for system extension they offer.

### *3.2.1 VLNET Core*

The VLNET core is a set of processes, interconnected through shared memory that perform basic VLNET functions. The Main Process performs higher level tasks, like object manipulation, navigation, body representation, while the other processes provide services for networking (Communication Process), database loading and maintenance (Database Process) and rendering (Cull Process and Draw Process).
**The Main Process** consists of five logical entities, called engines, covering different aspects of VLNET. It also initializes the session and spawns all other processes and drivers. Each engine is equipped with an interface for the connection of external drivers.
The *Object Behavior Engine* takes care of the predefined object behaviors, like rotation or falling. The *Navigation and Object Manipulation Engine* takes care of the basic user input: navigation, picking and displacement of objects. The *Body Representation Engine* is responsible for the deformation of the body. In any given body posture (defined by a set of joint angles) this engine will provide a deformed body ready to be rendered. The body representation is based on the Humanoid body model (Boulic, 1995). This engine provides the interface for changing the

body posture. A standard Body Posture Driver is provided, that connects also to the navigation interface to get the navigation information, then uses the Walking Motor and the Arm Motor (Boulic, 1990, Pandzic, 1996) to generate the natural body movement based on the navigation. The *Facial Representation Engine* provides the synthetic faces with a possibility to change expressions or the facial texture. The facial representation is a polygon mesh model with Free Form Deformations simulating muscle actions (Kalra, 1992). The *Video Engine* manages the streaming of dynamic textures to the objects in the environment and their correct mapping.

All the engines in the VLNET core process arc coupled to the main shared memory and to the message queue.

**Cull and Draw Processes** access the main shared memory and perform the functions of culling and drawing as their names suggest. These processes are standard SGI Performer (Rohlf, 1994) processes.

**The Communication Process** handles all network connections and communication in VLNET. All other processes and engines are connected with it through the Message Queue. They fill the queue with outgoing messages for the Communication Process to send. The messages are sent to the server, distributed and received by Communication Processes of other clients. The Communication Process puts these incoming messages into the Message Queue from where the other processes and engines can read them and react.

All messages in VLNET use the standard message packet. The packet has a standard header determining the sender and the message type, and the message body. The message body content depends on the message type but is always of the same size (80 bytes), satisfying all message types in VLNET. The video data from the Video Engine is a special case and is handled using a separate communication channel. It is given lower priority than the other data. By isolating the communications in this separate process, and by keeping the VLNET Server relatively simple, we leave the possibility to switch relatively easily to a completely different network topology, e.g. multicasting instead of client/server.

**The Data Base Process** takes care of the off-line fetching and loading of objects and user representations. By keeping these time consuming operations in the separate process non-blocking operation of the system is assured.

### *3.2.2 VLNET Drivers*

The drivers provide the simple and flexible means to access and control all the complex functionalities of VLNET. Simple, because each driver is programmed using a very small API that basically consists of exchanging crucial data with VLNET through shared memory. Flexible, because using various combinations of drivers it is possible to support all sorts of input devices ranging from the mouse to the camera with complex gesture recognition software, to control all the movements of the body and face using those devices, to control objects in the environment and stream video textures to them, to build any amount of artificial intelligence in order to produce autonomous or semi-autonomous virtual humans in the networked virtual environment.

The Drivers are directly tied to the Engines in the VLNET Main Process. Each engine provides a shared memory interface to which a driver can connect. Most drivers are optional and the system will provide minimal functionality (plain navigation and manipulation of objects) without any drivers.

**Figure 2** Snapshots from applications.

# 4 RESULTS

Several experimental applications were developed using the VLNET system. Some snapshots are presented in Figure 2.

## 4.1 Entertainment

NCVE systems lend themselves to development of all sorts of multi user games. We had successful demonstrations of chess and other games played between Switzerland and Singapore, as well as between Switzerland and several European countries.

A virtual tennis game has been developed (Noser, 1996) where the user plays against an opponent who is an autonomous virtual human. The referee is also an autonomous virtual human capable of refereeing the game and communicating the points, faults etc. by voice.Currently a multi user adventure game is under development.

## 4.2 Teleshopping

In collaboration with Chopard, a watch company in Geneva, a teleshopping application was successfully demonstrated between Geneva and Singapore. The users were able to communicate with each other within a rich virtual environment representing a watch gallery with several watches exposed. They could examine the watches together, exchange bracelets, and finally choose a watch.

## 4.3 Medical education

In collaboration with our colleagues working on a medical project we have used the 3D data of human organs, muscles and skeleton reconstructed from MRI images (Beylot, 1996) to build a small application in the field of medical education. The goal is to teach a student the position, properties and function of a particular muscle. In the virtual classroom several tools are at the disposition of the professor. MRI, CT and anatomical slice images are on the walls showing the slices where the muscle is visible. A 3D reconstruction of the skeleton is available together with the muscle, allowing to examine the shape of the muscle and the points of attachment to the skeleton. Finally, an autonomous virtual human with a simple behavior is there to demonstrate the movements resulting from a contraction of the discussed muscle.

## 4.4 Stock exchange

Currently an application is being developed to visualize in 3D the real time updates of stock exchange data and allow interactions of users with the data and with each other.

# 5 CONCLUSIONS

We have discussed problems involved with introducing high level human representations in the Networked Collaborative Virtual Environments and presented one solution to this problem - the Virtual Life Network. The system's modular architecture, the function of each component and their interconnections were described in detail. Various experimental applications highlighted in the results section show that this kind of system lends itself to a wide variety of collaborative applications.

## 6 ACKNOWLEDGMENTS

This research is financed by "Le Programme Prioritaire en Telecommunications de Fonds National Suisse de la Recherche Scientifique" and the TEN-IBC project VISINET.

## 7 REFERENCES

Beylot P., Gingins P., Kalra P., Magnenat-Thalmann N., Maurel W., Thalmann D., Fasel J. (1996) 3D Interactive Topological Modeling using Visible Human Dataset, *Proceedings of EUROGRAPHICS 96*, Poitiers, France

Boulic R., Magnenat-Thalmann N. M.,Thalmann D. (1990) A Global Human Walking Model with Real Time Kinematic Personification, *The Visual Computer*, Vol.6(6)

Boulic R., Capin T., Huang Z., Kalra P., Lintermann B., Magnenat-Thalmann N., Moccozet L., Molet T., Pandzic I., Saar K., Schmitt A., Shen J., Thalmann D. (1995) The Humanoid Environment for Interactive Animation of Multiple Deformable Human Characters, *Proceedings of Eurographics '95*

Capin T.K., Pandzic I.S., Noser H., Magnenat Thalmann N., Thalmann D. (1997) Virtual Human Representation and Communication in VLNET Networked Virtual Environments, *IEEE Computer Graphics and Applications*, Special Issue on Multimedia Highways

Doenges P.K., Capin T.K., Lavagetto F., Ostermann J., Pandzic I.S., Petajan E.D. (1997) MPEG-4: Audio/Video & Synthetic Graphics/Audio for Mixed Media, *Image Communication Journal, Special issue on MPEG-4*

Kalra P., Mangili A., Magnenat Thalmann N., Thalmann D. (1992) Simulation of Facial Muscle Actions Based on Rational Free Form Deformations, Proc. Eurographics '92, pp.59-69.

Noser H., Pandzic I.S., Capin T.K., Magnenat Thalmann N., Thalmann D. (1996) Playing Games through the Virtual Life Network, *Proceedings of Artificial Life V*, Nara, Japan

Pandzic I.S., Capin T.K., Magnenat Thalmann N., Thalmann D. (1996) Motor functions in the VLNET Body-Centered Networked Virtual Environment, *Proc. of 3rd Eurographics Workshop on Virtual Environments*, Monte Carlo

Rohlf J., Helman J., (1994) IRIS Performer: A High Performance Multiprocessing Toolkit for Real-Time 3D Graphics", *Proc. SIGGRAPH'94*

Slater M., Usoh M. (1994) Body Centered Interaction in Immersive Virtual Environments", in *Artificial Life and Virtual Reality*, N. Magnenat Thalmann, D. Thalmann, eds., John Wiley, pp 1-10

## 8 BIOGRAPHIES

**Nadia Magnenat Thalmann** founded Miralab, a Research Lab at the University of Geneva, in 1989. She is a pioneering researcher in the field of virtual humans and has authored or co-authored more then 200 scientific papers. She has received several awards, including the 1985 Communications Award from the Government of Quebec, the 1992 Moebius Award from the European Community, and the British Computer Science Award in 1993. She received a PhD in quantum physics and computer graphics from the University of Geneva.

**Igor S. Pandzic** is a PhD student at Miralab, University of Geneva. His research interests include collaborative virtual environments, parallel computing, computer-generated film production and real time facial expression analysis and synthesis. He finished his undergraduate studies at the University of Zagreb in 1993. and obtained a Masters degree in computer graphics from the Swiss Federal Institute of Technology in Lausanne in 1994.

# INDEX OF CONTRIBUTORS

# KEYWORD INDEX

www.ingramcontent.com/pod-product-compliance
Ingram Content Group UK Ltd.
Pitfield, Milton Keynes, MK11 3LW, UK
UKHW020129290926
15471UKWH00003B/373

*9781475748321*